READINGS IN THE
PHILOSOPHY
OF LANGUAGE

READINGS IN THE PHILOSOPHY OF LANGUAGE

Edited by

JAY F. ROSENBERG / *University of North Carolina*

and

CHARLES TRAVIS / *University of Calgary*

PRENTICE-HALL, INC., Englewood Cliffs, New Jersey

© 1971 by
PRENTICE-HALL, INC.
Englewood Cliffs, New Jersey

13–759332–5

Library of Congress Catalog Card Number: 70–132170

Current printing (last digit):
10 9 8 7 6 5 4 3 2 1

Printed in the United States of America

PRENTICE-HALL INTERNATIONAL, INC., *London*
PRENTICE-HALL OF AUSTRALIA, PTY. LTD., *Sydney*
PRENTICE-HALL OF CANADA, LTD., *Toronto*
PRENTICE-HALL OF INDIA PRIVATE LIMITED, *New Delhi*
PRENTICE-HALL OF JAPAN, INC., *Tokyo*

CONTENTS

6 SEMANTICS 467

7 SPEECH ACTS 557

READINGS IN THE PHILOSOPHY OF LANGUAGE

INTRODUCTION

Generally, the purpose of an introduction is to explain what a book is to be about. So this introduction might be expected to include a definition, or at least a detailed explanation, of philosophy of language. In fact, it will not include anything of the sort. The contents of the book *show* what philosophy of language is, but nothing in the book *says* what it is. The main reason for this is that neither we nor, to our knowledge, anyone else, know how to give such an account. In what follows, we shall say why this is so. We shall also provide a guide to the contents of the book, describing the structure it is intended to have.

Our inability to say what philosophy of language is does not by itself show philosophy of language to be in any worse shape than philosophy in general. It might well be, however, that philosophy of language is one of the areas principally responsible for the difficulty in saying what philosophy is. At least it is one of the areas where it is at best difficult and not clearly useful to distinguish between empirical and nonempirical questions.

The question "What is a philosophical problem?" is itself a traditional philosophical problem. Though it is a question many philosophers have discussed from time to time, there seems to be nothing like a consensus on the answer. Despite this apparent handicap of not being able to say exactly what it is they are doing, in practice philosophers seem to have little difficulty in recognizing a philosophical problem when one comes along. In this respect, at least, a philosopher's ability to recognize a philosophical problem is similar to an English speaker's ability to recognize an English sentence[1] (though in other respects there are vast differences).

---

[1] *Cf.* Noam Chomsky, "Methodological Preliminaries," Section 4.

1

At this point, we can invoke an argument leading from recognition behavior of the right sort to the existence of a recognition competence, and hence of something to be recognized. It is an argument used both by Grice and Strawson[2] with regard to a technical philosophical distinction and, in a modified form, by Chomsky with regard to English sentences. For any expression (and in particular, for the expression "philosophical problem"), if those who appear to use it competently generally agree on an indefinitely large class of cases to which it applies, and an indefinitely large class of cases to which it does not, we may conclude that the expression does pick out things with certain discoverable distinguishing characteristics, and that the people who are in such general agreement have a competence to (more or less accurately) recognize things with such characteristics. So, presumably, there is a distinction to be drawn between philosophical and other problems.

Perhaps the least charitable view of a philosophical problem is that a philosophical problem is simply one which interests a substantial number of philosophers. Even so, an indefinite number of problems seems to satisfy that condition, at least in a given state of the problem, and an indefinite number fail to do so. We may conclude that there are some underlying principles determining what sort of problem interests philosophers, and hence what a philosophical problem is.

There seems to be every reason to treat philosophy of language like philosophy in general. We may assume that there are some principles which determine what it is. But these principles need not be such that anyone is now conscious of them, or even such that they are likely to be discovered in the foreseeable future. They are not even guaranteed to be interesting when discovered. So we shall not take up space trying to discover what these principles are. We present the book as a specimen of the best of what contemporary philosophers of language do. We hope that, in some cases at least, this will be sufficient to impart the competence to do it.

Philosophy of language is frequently contrasted with, among other things, linguistics, philosophy of linguistics, and linguistic philosophy. We do not doubt that it is possible to give distinct abstract characterizations of each of these enterprises. Sorting out work under one heading or another is quite another matter. It is characteristic of these fields that most of the problems that are central to one also have considerable bearing on problems in other fields, or can only be studied by studying problems in other fields. Nevertheless, it is worth considering what these distinctions are supposed to be.

Trivially, philosophy of language is concerned with philosophical questions about language. Traditionally, it includes, but is far from exhausted by, the following questions: What, if anything, is meaning? Are there meanings? What is it for something to be meaningful? What is it for something to mean such and such? What sort of attribute is the ability to speak a language? How does one learn or acquire it? What is conventionality? What is the relation

---

[2] "In Defence of a Dogma," Section 1.

between meaning and reference? How does one manage to use words with preestablished meanings to refer to or talk about particular things?

These problems have come to be part of philosophy of language by a variety of routes. Tracing a few of them makes it initially implausible that one can divide off philosophy of language from the other areas mentioned above. For example, questions about language acquisition are clearly part of philosophy of language for historical reasons, if nothing else. Both Locke and Leibniz provided lengthy and detailed treatments of language acquisition as an integral part of their treatments of other general philosophical problems. Since then, theories of language acquisition of more or less substance have been important parts of the works of many philosophers down to and including Russell and Quine.

As one would expect, linguists and psychologists have also been quite interested in questions about how we come to speak a language. Given the *a priori* nature of philosophical work, one might expect that the sorts of questions philosophers ask about language acquisition are radically different from those posed by the linguists and psychologists. As one soon discovers in contrasting Quine and Chomsky, this is just not true. As it turns out, answers to questions in linguistics can have a profound effect on this area of philosophy of language, and, through that, on a variety of other philosophical problems that philosophers have connected with it. The converse may also be true.

In contrast, the question, "Are there meanings, and if so, what are they?" would seem a prime candidate for purely philosophical treatment if anything is. It is surely a part of philosophy of language for more than historical reasons. But it has become clear that even this is a question which cannot be answered without studying the technical apparatus available to linguists who study semantics and without studying the relation between that apparatus and what may be said in natural language. One way to show that something exists is to exhibit it. Those who work in technical semantics frequently exhibit things which at least look like they might be meanings. Further, at least some of the objections to talk about meanings do not hold for these things. One could perhaps produce *a priori* arguments to show that what semantic theorists talk about couldn't be meanings, but in view of the recent history of philosophy, one might be better advised to study semantics.

Linguistics, in contrast to philosophy of language, is generally explained as the scientific study of language and languages. It is traditionally concerned with writing grammars and dictionaries for natural languages, and with describing phonetic and phonemic systems. Less traditionally, it is concerned with universal theories of grammar and semantics, that is, with describing the principles of grammar and meaning that underlie all possible natural languages.

Since the contrast between linguistics and philosophy of language turns largely on the contrast between "philosophic" and "scientific," it is worth noting that linguistics is one of the branches of science that has forced changes in what we are prepared to regard as scientific. Regardless of what scientific practice may have always been, it is traditional to regard a discipline as scientific just in case it provides rigorous experimental procedures for establishing some class of facts, known as data, and perhaps some further class of claims made by the discipline. Such a view of what is scientific has led linguists for some time to direct their attentions to formulating rigorous procedures for discovering and testing facts about the basic technical concepts they employ. This involved, for example, devising procedures for establishing phonemic systems for languages, for differentiating between morphemes, and for determining whether something was or was not a sentence. In roughly the last dozen years, however, many linguists have come to the view that work in linguistics can be directed toward more realistic goals, and hence be more fruitful, if they concern themselves with the immense technical problems of organizing data already in hand, rather than seeking procedures for developing new data. Their interest in discovery procedures for grammars has sharply waned. It has become more and more common for linguists to discuss facts about languages, which they already know as speakers of the languages. This does not mean that linguistics is not scientific or that it is properly a part of philosophy. It does, however, make what linguists do more difficult to distinguish from the traditional *a priori* activities of philosophers.

Philosophy of linguistics is generally viewed as a branch of philosophy of science, concerned, like philosophy of psychology or philosophy of physics, with a particular branch of science, linguistics. As such, it might ask questions such as: What sorts of facts are to be included in a linguistic theory? How can these facts be established? What is the relation between facts about particular languages and facts about language in general? When can one sort of fact be used to establish the other? In what sense are grammars and dictionaries 'real'? What is the relation between linguistics and psychology?

On occasion, philosophy of linguistics has been identified with philosophy of language. This may seem strange at first. However, at least to the extent that problems in linguistics and philosophy of language overlap, and to the extent to which philosophy of science in general overlaps with the sciences it studies, philosophy of linguistics and philosophy of language will be treating common problems. Nevertheless, at present such an identification seems at best bad heuristics. It encourages philosophers of language to direct their attention toward certain kinds of general problems about theories before it is clear that that is where the problems in philosophy of language lie.

All of the above fields are generally contrasted with linguistic philosophy. Linguistic philosophy might be characterized as the application of facts and techniques learned through the study of language to standard philosophical problems. For example, one might attempt to approach the problem of free will and determinism through a study of words like 'voluntary', 'accidentally', 'inadvertently', and 'compelled'. This might be done, as it has been by Ryle, Austin, and many others, by making a direct attempt to collect facts about the ways in which these words are used. Given sufficiently developed grammatical and semantic theories, one might also be able to obtain further significant data from the forms these theories have. Even given a quite undeveloped state of linguistics, one might still be able to rank the importance of facts about the use of a word by considering what role such facts would play in grammar and semantics. Similarly, one might attempt to study the relation between knowledge and belief by studying the formal properties of the grammatical objects of "know" and "believe."[3] In philosophy of mind, it has become quite common to study the relation between thinking and events (either conscious or neural) by investigating the semantic properties of expressions for thinking.

At least one difficulty with the distinction between linguistic philosophy and philosophy of language is that, at this point, it is far from clear which questions are genuinely about language, and which are not. Formally, most if not all questions in philosophy can be viewed as questions about language. For example, suppose we want to know whether, generally speaking, someone who sees a tomato sitting on a table knows that there is a tomato sitting on that table. We can proceed by describing some cases where someone sees a tomato on a table, and ask whether in those cases it is correct to apply the expression "He knows that there is a tomato on the table." In doing so, we are asking a question formally very similar to the following question, "In cases where someone realizes that the bank robber was John's uncle, is it generally correct to say that that person realizes that the bank robber was the person who is the brother of John's mother or father or the husband of the sister of John's mother or father?" The latter question arises in Chomsky's treatment[4] of the verb 'realize', and via that, of a theory of semantic interpretation in general.

It doesn't follow from the formal properties of our question about knowledge that it is in any way a linguistic question. The answer may depend on what generally happens when one sees a tomato, or thinks he does. Or it may depend on general facts about sound epistemic strategies, that is, questions about when one ought to claim to know something. None of these facts need play any role in a linguistic theory. Nor need they play any role in a definition of 'know', even if, as in the case of epistemic strategies, the facts involved may be in some sense necessary. For example, it may be that what follows from the correct definition of 'know' is that X knows that Y if, according to the *best* available strategy, X ought under the circumstances to *take* Y as known. At this point, we don't know exactly what type of information it is that determines the status of someone who sees a tomato. Neither work on the problem nor work on linguistic theory is that advanced. Deciding how to classify the missing information is equally a part of philosophy of language, linguistics, and linguistic philosophy.

Another difficulty with the distinction between linguistic philosophy and philosophy of language is that there are a number of traditional areas of philosophy of language which can only be treated satisfactorily by considering other areas of philosophy. When working in these areas it is difficult to say whether one is working on problems about language or not. Frequently, the problems

---

[3] For a justification of this approach, *cf.* Vendler, *Linguistics in Philosophy* (Ithaca, N.Y., 1967), Chapter 1.

[4] "Deep Structure, Surface Structure and Semantic Interpretation."

are about language and other things as well. The study of propositions is a good example of such an area. There are actually a number of philosophical problems about propositions. The selections in this book concentrate on the problem of characterizing them adequately, that is, specifying their distinguishing features, telling one from another, and telling one from a sentence or statement. To a lesser extent, the selections are concerned with the problem of whether propositions exist at all, and if so, what their existence comes to. In dealing with either of these problems it is important to remember that propositions are part of long traditions both in logic and in philosophical psychology. In logic, propositions are traditionally characterized as having a certain role in inferences. This role is usually described by saying that propositions are the things (or at least some things) which are true or false. They are thus the objects which enter into truth-functional and inferential relations. On one view of logic, they are what logic is ultimately about.

One reason, at least, that propositions play such a large role in philosophical psychology is that according to one tradition (a tradition that influenced, among others, Cook Wilson) logic is simply a branch of philosophical psychology. The usual argument for this view goes something as follows. Logic is the science of inference. Inferences are a particular sort of mental activity performed by human beings. Therefore, logic is concerned with that sort of mental activity. Put in modern terms, logic is the study of human (and nonhuman, if necessary) inference recognition competences.

We need not discuss here the adequacy of this view as a theory of logic. In any case, it leads naturally enough to what is by now another traditional view of propositions. On this view, propositions (or sometimes what propositions express) are thoughts, or sometimes, complete thoughts. They are what people are thinking when they are thinking that such-and-such.

We shall say more about the connection between these traditions and the role of propositions in language in Section 3. But whatever that connection may be, a description of propositions which made it impossible for them to play anything like their traditional roles in inferences and in thinking would be at best highly suspect. Since propositions have so many roles to fill, it is entirely possible that they cannot consistently fill all of them. An adequate description of propositions need not solve all the problems for which they are traditionally called into service. But if it fails to solve significant ones, we shall want to know why—whether it is because the problems have been misconceived or because a number of different things have been confused under the heading of propositions. For example, it might turn out that for propositions to serve their proper role in language they cannot be things which are true or false in the way traditionally required by logicians. If so, we should want to know whether they must be true or false in this way to play their traditional role in inferences, whether anything could be true or false in the traditional logicians' sense, and if so, which sort of thing, if either, has the best claim to the title 'proposition'. Given their role in philosophical psychology, it also seems reasonable to hope that, if we understand what propositions are, we will better understand the relation between language and thought and the extent to which thought is grounded in language or vice versa. Again, if a treatment of propositions fails to make this clear, we should not be satisfied until we see why it must fail to do so. Most studies of propositions fall into a number of areas of philosophy at once. So it is quite natural, when studying propositions, to be doing linguistic philosophy and philosophy of language simultaneously.

An even better example of the overlap of purely philosophical questions with questions about language is provided by necessity and analyticity. There are a number of standard ways of explicating both concepts. For the moment we shall not try to define 'necessity'. Analyticity may be taken as a property that something has if it is either true or false in virtue of the words which either express it or make it up. Whether they express it or make it up depends on just what sorts of things are true or false. For example, if sentences or statements are true or false, we can take words as components, in some sense, of what is true and false. If thoughts are the sorts of things which are true, or primarily true, then truths are the sorts of things that words may combine to express. For greater generality, analyticity is sometimes explicated as a property of things which are true or false in virtue of the rules of language. For a further explanation of both these notions see Section 1. At present, the subtle differences between various accounts of analyticity and necessity will not matter. We shall be discussing some general facts about the relation between the two.

Of the two notions, necessity is both the older and the more intuitive. 'Analyticity' is a more or less technical term in philosophy. It found its way into philosophy in large measure as part of an attempt to account for necessity. This makes it comparatively easy to define 'analyticity'. The difficulty in defining 'necessity' is that there is some prior notion of necessity which any definition must more or less successfully capture. We could define 'necessity' any way we liked. For example, we could define it as synonymous with 'analyticity'. But if we did so, there would be no guarantee that our definition would capture the notion of necessity. In fact, it now seems likely that that particular definition includes both too much and too little.

Traditionally, necessity has been held to carry with it a set of metaphysical properties. These properties may be conveyed roughly by saying that if something is necessary then it couldn't be otherwise. There are, of course, many ways of interpreting that last phrase. An attempt to account for necessity is an attempt to show how truths and falsehoods with some further property would, in virtue of that, have some large set of these metaphysical properties. For example, in seventeenth- and eighteenth-century writers such as Descartes and Leibniz it is common to find accounts of at least some kinds of necessary truths in terms of the nature of God. Given that God exists necessarily, any fact about the world which follows from God's nature should also be necessary. Thus, given that traditional claims about God are coherent and correct, God seems a plausible candidate for an account of at least some necessary truths.

It is more usual nowadays to attempt to account for necessity in terms of language. This attempt is part of a tradition that goes back at least to Hobbes, though it reached ascendancy only in the late eighteenth and nineteenth centuries. A variant of it grounds necessity in the nature of some set of concepts which somehow underlie language. This variant fits in nicely with much recent work on language, especially that concerned with universal theories of language.

As with God, there is a plausible case to be made for language. If something is true, and its truth follows from the meanings of the words involved, then it is difficult to see how one could construct circumstances under which it would be false. Of course, the meanings of the words might change. But then, what the words expressed would change, too, so that we would no longer be talking about the same thing that we previously held to be true.

One *prima facie* requirement in an account of analyticity, then, is that it provide at least a partial account of necessity. At a minimum, one would think, if something is analytic then it ought to be necessary. If an account fails to have that consequence, then we shall need a pretty good idea why this is so before we can find the account acceptable. But an account of analyticity has other commitments as well. It must ultimately be grounded in an adequate descriptive theory of language. Whatever it says about the meanings of words must be sayable in terms of the machinery of such a theory. Where it says two words have the same or different meanings, whether the two words actually mean the same or not will be determined, ultimately, by what such a descriptive theory would say.

It is at least possible that no account of analyticity can meet both these *prima facie* responsibilities. For example, we might discover when we have an adequate dictionary and interpretation rules for English sentences that some sentence is true in virtue of the meanings of the words, yet we can conceive of its being false. In that case, there are a number of paths open. We might decide that some of our accounts of the meanings of the words were wrong. We might decide that certain conceivable situations just don't count against necessity. Finally, we might decide that analyticity fails to account for necessity. This might be because the machinery connecting meaning and truth is such that what the meanings of words determine about truth and falsity may change while the meanings remain the same. Given adequate semantic machinery, for example, there may be more than one way of representing the same meaning.

In our present state of ignorance both about necessity and about semantics, there are many particular cases where all three of the above possibilities must be taken seriously. In such cases, any discovery about either meaning or necessity will, in a fairly straightforward way, be a discovery about both. Again, one finds oneself applying philosophical facts to language and facts about language to philosophy at the same time.

In this collection we try to present some of the best of *contemporary* philosophy of language. Thus we have limited ourselves to selections appearing later then 1900, although we have attempted to provide historical guidelines in the suggestions for further reading following each section introduction. We have divided the collection into seven sections, but the reader is advised to view these divisions as demarcating rough "communities of interest" rather than sharply distinguished subject matters. The textual divisions are as *inter*connected as philosophy of language itself is connected with allied and kindred disciplines. Again, both in the separate introductions to the various sections and in the suggestions for futher reading which follow them, we have attempted to provide some guidelines for tracing these interconnections.

The first three sections grow out of traditional philosophy and share a general concern which might be put as the question of relations between words and the world. In Section 1, *Analyticity*, we explore in detail the possibility of purely linguistic truth. As we have already remarked, philosophy traditionally accepts the possibility of truth insulated, epistemologically or ontologically, from the experiential world. In the section on Analyticity, we examine the thesis that some or all of these truths result solely from the contribution of language. The selections here treat mainly of two questions. The first we have already adumbrated. It is the question of the extent to which an account of analyticity can meet the various demands placed on it by traditional philosophy. The second examines the critical presupposition of the first enterprise, that there is a well-defined class of analytic truths which can be effectively demarcated from truths in general.

Section 2, *Reference*, is, in a way, the obverse of Section 1. There we asked whether language could generate truths autonomously. Here we explore one classical account, dating at least to Plato's *Theatetus*, of how language achieves extra-linguistic import. The *Theatetus* account of language holds that words are *names* standing for entities, and that the essence of language consists of the combining of these names. In this section, the selections are concerned specifically with the putative relation of *reference* whereby a word comes to stand for or name an object. The selections explore the meanings and functioning of two sorts of referential terms—definite descriptions and proper names. Here, too, we find adumbrated some consideration of the *pragmatics* of language use which will develop into the study of Speech Acts constituting Section 7.

Section 3, *Propositions*, canvasses an intricate subject matter that lies simultaneously on the boundaries between, on the one hand, philosophy of language and logic and, on the other, philosophy of language and philosophy of mind. Traditional philosophy has offered accounts of propositions as entities constituting the bearers of truth, the meanings of sentences, and the objects or contents of thoughts. The selections of Section 3 examine the question of the existence and nature of a domain of entities which can fulfill some or all of these demands.

Section 4, *Methodology*, is nominally concerned with philosophy of language as philosophy of linguistics. The selections explore the scope and limits of the scientific study of language. Specifically, the selections examine in detail, first, whether empirical linguistics is inherently limited by the in-principle inaccessibility of crucial data (a suggestion already advanced in the critique of the analyticity concept found in Section 1) and, second, whether the outcome of linguistic theorizing has or can have significant consequences for empirical psychology. At a deeper level, these methodological disputes can be seen as grounded in variant conceptions of the content and adequacy of empiricism as a general philosophical stance, a contemporary development of the classical dialectic between empiricism and rationalism.

The next two sections approach the traditional philosophical problem of *meaning* from distinct perspectives that reflect, in part, the differing methodological orientations examined in Section 4. Section 5, *Theories of Meaning*, surveys attempts to develop accounts of meaning, meaningfulness, and synonymy in the style of classical philosophy—responsive either to *a priori* considerations or to traditional conceptions of empirical method. The theories of meaning canvassed here are alike in aiming at a reductive set of necessary and sufficient conditions for meaning, meaningfulness, or sameness of meaning.

In Section 6, *Semantics*, by contrast, a theory of meaning is not viewed as a reductive specification of criteria, but rather is envisioned as a descriptively and explanatorily adequate account of human semantic recognition competences. The selections in this section are generally responsive to a richer set of semantic concepts than those of Section 5—anomaly and ambiguity, for example, as well as significance and synonymy. Sharing a methodological orientation emerging from the critique of classical empiricism developed in Section 4, these selections see an account of the semantic categories not as autonomous, but rather as embodied in the semantic component of a general empirical theory of language.

Finally, in Section 7, *Speech Acts*, the scope of philosophy of language is broadened in yet another direction, making contact with general theories of human action. The selections here depart from the observation (already implicit in Section 2) that in speaking a language one is carrying out a variety of complex public performances which may encompass or eventuate in actions which are not in any clearly circumscribed sense *linguistic* and which significantly outstrip the consequences traditionally envisioned for linguistic performances. The selections in Section 7 aim at a description, a typology, and, ultimately, a theory of some of these ramifications of the act of speech.

ANALYTICITY 1

INTRODUCTION

Whether what we say is or expresses a truth or falsehood generally depends both upon what is to be found in the world and upon what our words mean. An inventory of biological species reveals "There are unicorns" to be a falsehood. If the world were different from what it is—if horses grew horns—the same words might express a truth. But, equally, if by 'unicorn' we meant not 'single-horned equine quadruped' but simply 'single-horned *animal*', the claim then expressed by "There are unicorns" would be rendered true by narwhales and by certain rhinoceroses.

Insofar as any truth or falsehood must be couched in or expressed by language, a nonzero contribution of word-meaning to truth or falsity seems unavoidable. There is at least a *prima facie* possibility, however, that there are truths and falsehoods whose truth or falsity depends *only* on the meanings of the words in which they are framed or expressed, truths or falsehoods which are, in this way, insulated from the world. Such, according to one traditional characterization, would be *analytic* truths and falsehoods—truths and falsehoods true or false *ex vi terminorum*, "by virtue of the terms."

What kind of thing is analytic will depend, of course, upon what kind of thing is true or false. Three candidates of long standing are sentences, statements, and propositions. The job of sorting out these categories is an intricate one, but we may make a beginning here by noting at least three "principles of counting" which may be applied to linguistic acts. Sentences are *uttered;* statements *made;* and propositions *expressed.* If two persons use the same words in the same order on distinct occasions, they have uttered (two tokens of) the same sentence (type). Thus, if I say of Tom "He is in pain" and you say of Jim "He is in pain," we have uttered the same sentence. On the account which has

11

become standard, however, we have made different statements. *Stating* has been analyzed as consisting of reference plus description, picking something out and saying something about it. Necessary conditions, then, of sameness of statement will be sameness of reference and sameness of predication. Hence, since I referred to Tom and you to Jim, our statements are distinct. Conversely, it is possible to use different sentences to make the same statement, if, e.g. , I say *of* Tom "He is in pain" and you say *to* Tom "You are in pain."

Propositions, on the other hand, are more complicated to sort out, for they lead a sort of philosophical double life. Our interest here is in propositions, not as objects of the so-called "propositional attitudes" (knowledge, belief, desire, etc.), but as truth-vehicles. To serve as such, propositions have traditionally been assigned one crucial feature, they are not to be "context-bound." The truth-value of a proposition is not to change with changing circumstances. One way of attempting to meet this requirement has been to hold that two sentences express the same proposition if and only if the sentences are *synonymous*. On this proposal, for example, "The fifteenth U. S. president was a bachelor" and "The fifteenth U. S. president was an unmarried man" will express the same proposition. By contrast, "James Buchanan was a bachelor" will express a different proposition (although the sentence can be used to make the same statement), for, although James Buchanan was the fifteenth U. S. president, the phrase "James Buchanan" is not *synonymous* with the phrase "the fifteenth U. S. president." This proposal for interpreting talk about propositions is, of course, neither unique nor unproblematic. The competing analyses of propositions constitute a complex set of issues in their own right that are explored in Section 3. It is sufficient here simply to note that, on any of the various proposals examined there, the principles for counting propositions will differ from those for counting sentences or statements.

We have expressed ourselves cautiously in terms of truths and falsehoods *couched in* or *expressed by* language. By so doing, we have avoided committing ourselves to a choice of truth-vehicles. A second traditional characterization of analyticity also strives for this neutrality. On this account, a truth or falsehood is *analytically* true or false if it is true or false by virtue of the *rules of language*. Rules of language, of course, will be different sorts of things given different choices of truth-vehicle. If sentences are true or false, rules of language will specify the conditions under which a sentence *is* true or false. If statements are the vehicles of truth or falsity, rules of language will be needed to specify in addition *which* statement, if any, is made by a particular use of a particular sentence. And, similarly, if propositions are the bearers of truth-values, rules of language are required to specify *which* propositions are expressed by which sentences. On any choice of truth-vehicle and on either characterization of analyticity, the intended import is clear. Analytic truths and falsehoods are to derive their truth or falsity from *language alone*.

Philosophy traditionally recognizes three classes of truths (and falsehoods, but let us confine ourselves henceforth to truths) that are *insulated* from the world. Their home grounds are philosophy of language, metaphysics, and epistemology. Philosophy of language, we have already seen, gives us the notion of *analytic* truth—truth by virtue of meaning. The analogous metaphysical notion is that of a *necessary* truth, insulated from the world in that, whatever the state of the world, it could not be otherwise. Finally, from epistemology we take the notion of an *a priori* truth, insulated in that it is knowable independently of ("prior to") experience. Whether the analytic exhausts and explains the necessary and the *a priori* is a central philosophical issue of long standing.

To hold that all necessary truths are analytic, and necessary *because* analytic, is to espouse the thesis of *conventionalism*. On this account, the necessity of necessary truths derives from *linguistic conventions*. A necessary truth is necessary not because of how the world is (or could be) but rather because of how we choose to speak of how the world is (or could be).

A truth which is not analytic is *synthetic*. To ask whether all necessary truths are analytic, then, is to ask whether the class of *synthetic necessary* truths is empty. The historically more discussed problem, dating to Kant, asks the same question of the class of *synthetic a priori* truths. To hold that all *a priori* truths are analytic, and a priori *because* analytic, is to espouse the *linguistic theory of the a priori*. On this account, an *a priori* truth is knowable independently of particular experience, not because, as a Kantian would have it, it articulates the structural preconditions of any experience, but rather simply because, since its truth derives solely from language, it is knowable (and known) when the language is known. We find a version of the linguistic theory of the *a priori* espoused by LEWIS:

> There are no synthetic statements which can be known true *a priori*: what may appear to be such, must be regarded as representing some failure to elicit by analysis the criteria operative in the actual, or ideally consistent, application of the terms in questions. . . .

The stance adopted by Lewis rests on two central presuppositions. First, his account presupposes that terms have criteria of application which are *fixed* and *univocal*. Second, and more deeply, the Lewis account presupposes the ability to distinguish situations in which an empirical discovery results in a change of *belief* from situations in which we find a change of *meaning*. The centrality of these presuppositions is argued, and their cogency challenged, in the succeeding selections by DONNELLAN and PUTNAM.

The criticisms of DONNELLAN and PUTNAM are criticisms *in detail* or what we might call *internal* criticisms. They accept the cogency of the notion of analyticity in general, and question the explication offered that notion by Lewis in particular. In QUINE, on the other hand, we find a criticism *in principle* or what we might call an *external* criticism. The attack here is on the notion of analyticity in general and on its cousins—synonymy, necessity, and semantic rules. This *family* of concepts, argues Quine, is devoid of empirical grounding and, hence, of empirical significance. Analyticity is a mere dogma, a metaphysical article of faith. (For the detailed epistemological underpinnings of Quine's position, see Selection 4.1.)

The substantive criticisms of Quine and others (notably White and Goodman) stimulated a variety of replies. GRICE and STRAWSON approach Quine's argument directly. In an important anticipation of the technical notion of a *linguistic competence*, they argue that where there is general agreement regarding the application of a classification to an open reference class, there must necessarily be a genuine distinction grounding the classification. And they suggest that a proposal of Quine's, which he himself rejects, for explicating the notion of statement-synonymy and, hence, indirectly that of analyticity can be amended to yield a viable empirical synonymy concept:

> All we have to say now is that two statements are synonymous if and only if any experiences which, *on certain assumptions about the truth-values of other statements,* confirm or disconfirm one of the pair, also, *on the same assumptions,* confirm or disconfirm the other to the same degree.

PUTNAM, too, finds Quine's rejection of the analytic/synthetic dichotomy radically misguided. "I do not understand," he writes, "what it would mean to say that a distinction between two things *that* different does not exist." But Putnam views the division between analytic and synthetic truths as one of limited scope and interest. His key distinction is between what he terms "law-cluster concepts," the identity of which is determined by a bundle of general laws, and "one-criterion concepts," terms applied on the basis of only a single generally accepted criterion. In terms of this distinction, Putnam offers a set of criteria for analyticity which yields a class of analytic truths roughly coincident with the tradition.

Like Lewis's original explication, Putnam's characterization turns on the notion of criteria of application for a term. To discover whether a characteristic is criterial for a term, say *A*, it is necessary not merely to know whether people *do* apply *A* on the basis of that characteristic, but also whether they *would* continue to apply the term *A* to a thing were it to *lack* the relevant characteristic. Thus the centrality to the analyticity concept of questions beginning "What would we say if. . . ?" FODOR distinguishes two sorts of what-would-we-say questions and argues that there is no reason to suppose that a speaker's knowledge of his language equips him to *answer* questions of that sort deemed crucial for attributions of analyticity.

Finally, in KATZ the technical machinery of transformational linguistics is used to develop precise definitions of 'analytic', 'synthetic', and 'contradictory' as adjuncts of a general semantic theory, intended, among other things, to satisfy Quine's critical demands. The philosophically most striking outcome of Katz's analysis is its rejection of the conventionalist thesis, for the class of necessary truths is not, on his account, exhausted by the class of analytic sentences.

Suggestions for Further Reading

Carnap, Rudolf. "Meaning Postulates," *Philosophical Studies*, III (1952), 65–73.

Feigl, H. and W. Sellars. *Readings in Philosophical Analysis*. New York: Appleton-Century-Crofts, 1949. (For the articles by Lewis, Quine, and Schlick cited below.)

Goodman, Nelson. "On Likeness of Meaning." *Analysis* (1949). Reprinted in Linsky, cited below. This essay, together with White (cited below), supplements and completes Quine's attack on the analytic/synthetic dichotomy.

Hall, Roland. "Bibliography on Analytic-Synthetic." *Philosophical Quarterly*, XVI (1966), 178–81.

Kant, I. *Critique of Pure Reason*. Translated by Norman Kemp Smith. New York: St. Martin's Press, 1958. Introduction, pp. A1–A16, B1–B30.

Lewis, C. I. "The Pragmatic Conception of the *A Priori*." Reprinted as pp. 286–96 of Feigl and Sellars, cited above.

Linsky, Leonard, ed. *Semantics and the Philosophy of Language*. Urbana, Ill.: University of Illinois Press, 1952. Chapters 4 and 14.

Mates, Benson. "Analytic Sentences." *Philosophical Review*, LX (1951), 525–34. An important early reply to Quine.

Pap, Arthur. *Semantics and Necessary Truth*. New Haven: Yale University Press, 1958. Contains both historical materials and a thorough investigation of the conventionalist thesis.

Quine, W. V. O. "Truth by Convention." Reprinted as pp. 250–76 of Feigl and Sellars, cited above.

———. See also selection 4.1 in this volume, pp. 290–324.

Schlick, M. "Is There a Factual *A Priori*?" Reprinted as pp. 277–85 of Feigl and Sellars, cited above.

White, Morton. "The Analytic and the Synthetic: An Untenable Dualism." Chapter 14, pp. 272–86 of Linsky, cited above.

C. I. LEWIS

1.1 *The Modes of Meaning*

1. Every statement we know to be true is so known either by reason of experience or by reason of what the statement itself means. There are no other sources of knowledge than on the one hand data of sense and on the other hand

Reprinted from C. I. Lewis, *An Analysis of Knowledge and Valuation* (LaSalle, Illinois: The Open Court Publishing Co., 1946), Chapter III, pp. 35–70, by permission of the publisher.

our own intended meanings. Empirical knowledge constitutes the one class; all that is knowable independently of sense experience—the *a priori* and the analytic—constitutes the other, and is determinable as true by reference to our meanings.

Traditionally a statement which can be certified by reference exclusively to defined or definable meanings is called *analytic;* what is non-analytic being called *synthetic.* And traditionally that knowledge whose correctness can be assured without reference to any particular experience of sense is called *a priori;* that which requires to be determined by sense experience being called *a posteriori.*

All analytic statements are, obviously, true *a priori;* whatever is determinable as true by reference exclusively to the meaning of expressions used, is independent of any empirical fact. That the converse relation also holds; that whatever is knowable *a priori*, including the principles of logic and all that logic can certify, is also analytic, is not so obvious. It has, of course, frequently been denied; most notably in the Kantian doctrine which makes *synthetic a priori* truth fundamental for mathematics and for principles of the knowledge of nature.

The thesis here put forward, that the *a priori* and the analytic coincide, has come to be a matter of fairly wide agreement amongst logicians in the last half-century. It is, however, by no means universal; and so far as it obtains, it is in part verbal only, since it has not been accompanied by any corresponding agreement concerning the nature of analytic truth, the nature of logic, and the ground on which, and sense in which, what logic assures is certifiable. The original and traditional conception of the analytic as that which may be known by reference to meanings (definable or connotational or intensional meanings) has in some part been lost sight of and displaced by conceptions more complex. In particular, there has appeared a tendency to regard the distinction between analytic and non-analytic as one which is relative—e.g., relative to vocabulary or to 'language system'—and as linguistic or logico-procedural rather than epistemological in significance. If the implications of conceptions of this sort should be well worked out, it must appear that they are fatal to the thesis that what is *a priori* coincides with what is analytic; since the notion that what may be known true without recourse to sense experience, is relative to vocabulary or dependent on conventions of procedure, is not credible.[1]

---

[1] In spite of what is said above, I believe that there is more agreement on essentials, which is implicit in current conceptions, than appears on the surface. Logical theory is today in a chaotic condition, rendered almost inevitable by the rapid and extensive advances of recent and current investigations. The results of this research have not as yet undergone that sorting and sifting process by which, eventually, the durable elements will be elicited, and the clearer and more adequate conceptions in which these may be grasped will be separated from the partly incorrect, the inadequate, and those which by being unnecessarily complicated are ill-chosen instruments for consolidating and formulating what has been learned. At the moment, not only are there almost innumerable issues, large and small, which have come to light and have not yet been decided, but also there is much diversity in the modes of approach which are chosen, as well as in the classifications made use of and the terminology which is favored.

2. In order to approach such questions of the *a priori* and the analytic, it will be necessary to examine this traditional conception of analytic truth as that which is determinable by reference to meanings alone; and to isolate and clarify, if possible, the meaning of 'meaning' which is here in question.

For this it will be required first to make some excursion into logical theory. . . . Consideration will be restricted to main points, and discussion of these will be limited to what is required in order that the analysis presented may be understood. Further issues, many of which are matters of present controversy, will be omitted, as well as consideration of points of view alternative to the one here outline. . . .

Even with these attempted abbreviations, the presentation to be given may run beyond the interest of those whose concern is more narrowly epistemological. . . . The main conclusions concerning meaning and the analytic which will be reached . . . may be set down [for their benefit] summarily as follows. (They will not, however, appear in just the order here indicated):

(1) In general, the traditional conception of analytic truth as truth which is determined, explicitly or implicitly, by meanings alone, is justified and can be made adequate, and does not need to be displaced by any which is more complex.

(2) The requisite meaning of 'meaning' can be arrived at by more precise specification of what is traditionally intended by 'connotation' or 'intension' and by developing the conception—traditionally omitted or inadequately treated—of the intension of propositions.

(3) Such intensional meaning can still be specified in alternative ways: as *linguistic meaning*, constituted by the pattern of definitive and other analytic relationships holding between linguistic expressions; or as *sense meaning*, constituted by the criterion in mind by which what is meant is to be recognized. It is sense meaning which is epistemologically the more important signification of 'intension.' Linguistic *expression* of what is meant and what is apprehended, is the dependent and derivative phenomenon: it is meaning and apprehension themselves which are the fundamental cognitive phenomena, and these are independent of any formulation in language.

(4) The principles of logic are analytic in this sense: their truth is certifiable by reference to intensional meanings involved in the statement of them.

In consequence, what now appear as rival theories represent only in part divergences with respect to material and important points of logic: and although present controversies undoubtedly include basic issues which will eventually become sharply delimited, if not decided, these are, at the moment, quite thoroughly entangled with others which are less important and may even be recognized later on as having been mainly verbal. Real agreement in fundamentals, while by no means complete, is somewhat more extensive than it might seem.

In any case, it may be salutary, in confronting present-day complications, to remember that general logic formulates what everybody knows upon reflection. *Information* in logic can be only verbal or concern the logician's conventions of classification and formulation. What runs into intricacies too far beyond the ordinary grasp may, with some assurance, be set aside as perhaps not logic but logomachy. Occasionally we should go wrong by following this precept. But even so, the eventual effect of it might still be salutary, by inducing logicians with something to say to strive for clarity in exposition.

(5) There is, however, no way of distinguishing fundamentally between principles of logic and other analytic truths. Such distinction is conventional, in the sense that it turns upon relative importance for the critique of inference, and upon comparative generality. There are, thus, alternative ways in which what is taken as belonging to logic may be marked off.

(6) There are no synthetic statements which can be known true *a priori*: what may appear to be such, must be regarded as representing some failure to elicit by analysis the criteria operative in the actual, or the ideally consistent, application of terms in question, or some failure to recognize implications which validly obtain.

3. The task of eliciting that sense of 'intensional meaning' for which it can be said that whatever is analytic is certifiable by reference to such meaning, is most easily approached through consideration of the various modes of meaning. And though it is propositions and propositional functions whose intensional meanings it will be most important to consider, it will be best to begin with terms, since the meaning of terms is more frequently discussed and will be, in consequence, initially clearer.

A *term* is a linguistic expression which names or applies to a thing or things, of some kind, actual or thought of.

It is sometimes said that what is not actual cannot be named. But such assertion is either an arbitrary and question-begging restriction upon use of the verb 'to name'—since plainly whatever is thought of can be spoken of—or it is merely silly. One does not easily imagine what those who make this assertion would say to persons who have given a name to a hoped-for child, or named a projected building which in fact is never erected. Apparently those who commit this absurdity have in mind some such analogical consideration as that you cannot name what does not exist just as you cannot kick what does not exist. But kicking is a physical operation while naming is an operation of thought. And if we could not think of what did not exist, or at least of things whose existence is undetermined, it is doubtful if thinking would be possible at all, and whether, if it should be possible, it would be of any use. However, there are difficulties connected with this point which are genuine—in particular that if the non-existent can be named, then naming is not denoting; and it will be the intention so to write here as to minimize dependence upon it. In line with that intention, the above definition of a term may be rephrased: A *term* is an expression capable of naming or applying to a thing or things, of some kind.

All terms have meaning in the sense or mode of denotation or extension; and all have meaning in the mode of connotation or intension. These two modes of the meaning of terms are traditional and familiar (though not always specified in the same way). For reasons of clarity it is desirable to recognize two further modes also, which will here be called, respectively, comprehension and signification. Briefly put, these four modes of meaning are as follows:

(1) The *denotation* of a term is the class of all actual things to which the term applies.

(2) The *comprehension* of a term is the classification of all possible or consistently thinkable things to which the term would be correctly applicable.

(3) The *signification* of a term is that property in things the presence of which indicates that the term correctly applies, and the absence of which indicates that it does not apply.

(4) Formally considered, the *intension* of a term is to be identified with the conjunction of all other terms each of which must be applicable to anything to which the given term would be correctly applicable.

The *denotation* or *extension* of a term is, as above, the class of all actual or existent things which the term correctly applies to or names. The qualification 'actual or existent' here is limiting and not merely explicative: things which are, or would be, nameable by a term but which do not in fact exist, are not included in the denotation.

In common speech, a term is said to denote the existent or existents to which it is applied on any given occasion of its use. For example, in the statement, "Those three objects are books," 'book' is said to denote the three objects indicated, or any one of them. This usage has the slightly awkward consequence that what a term is said to denote, though always *included in* the denotation of it, does not coincide with this denotation. (Even if a term correctly applies to one existent only, as is the case for all singular terms, it is still doubtful to identify this one object denoted with the class of which it is the only member; and it is the class which is the denotation of the term.) But in spite of this awkwardness, we shall continue to use both 'denote' and 'denotation' with their commonplace significances.[2]

A class may have no members, in which case it is said to be empty or null. A term whose denotation is such an empty class (e.g., 'unicorn') denotes no object; but it is unprecise to say that it has no denotation; especially since that manner of speaking would suggest that it has no meaning in the correlative mode of meaning. We shall say that a term which applies to no existent has *zero denotation;* indicating that its denotation is a zero or null class. Such terms still possess the potentiality or function of denoting; and are in this respect different from nonsense-locutions like 'zukor', which denote nothing because they do not denote.

Membership in any class and denotation of any term are, thus, restricted to what exists. When it is desirable to refer to whatever a term would correctly apply to, whether existent or not, we shall speak of a *classification* instead of a class, and of the comprehension of the term. The *comprehension* of a term is, thus, the classification of all consistently thinkable things to which the term would correctly apply—where anything is consistently thinkable if the assertion of its existence would not, explicitly or implicitly, involve a contradiction. For example, the comprehension of 'square' includes all imaginable as well as all actual squares, but does not include round squares.

The confusion of denotation with comprehension has in the past been fre-

---

[2] Some avoid the awkward consequence mentioned by saying that a term *designates* a thing that it names. This terminology is apt, but is not adopted here.

quent, and it continues to be a source of errors in logic. For instance, the failure to make this distinction allows confusion between the relation asserted by "All existents to which the term '*A*' correctly applies are existents to which the term '*B*' also applies" or "The class of *A*'s is contained in the class of *B*'s" and the different relation asserted by "The applicability of the term '*A*' to a thing entails or strictly implies the applicability of the term '*B*' to that thing." The former statement asserts that the denotation of '*A*' is contained in the denotation of '*B*'. The latter statement requires that all consistently thinkable things to which '*A*' would correctly apply should be things to which '*B*' would apply; that the comprehension of '*A*' be contained in the comprehension of '*B*'. It will be important here to mark clearly this distinction between denotation and comprehension.

The denotation of a term is, obviously, included in its comprehension; but the converse relation does not hold.

The connotation or intension of a term is delimited by any correct definition of it. In traditional language, one says that if nothing would be correctly nameable by a term '*T*' unless it possess the attribute *A*, then '*T*' connotes *A*; and the totality or conjunction of attributes so connoted constitutes the connotation of '*T*'. But on account of ambiguity in the notion of attribute—and for other reasons as well—this is not entirely clear. And even traditionally, connotation is in fact more characteristically taken as a relation of the term in question to other *terms*. We shall wish to reserve 'connotation' for such usage, and shall call this relation of the term to essential properties of what is denoted, by another name. Let us therefore postpone discussion of connotation for the moment, and take up first these related matters which may help to clarify it.

Traditionally any attribute required for application of a term is said to be *of the essence* of the thing named. It is, of course, meaningless to speak of the essence of a thing except relative to its being named by a particular term. But it is desirable or even necessary to have some manner of marking this distinction between characters or properties of a thing which are essential to its being named by a term in question and other characters of the thing which are not thus essential. For example, in order to be correctly named by 'square', a thing must be a plane figure, must have equal sides, and must have all its angles right angles; but it is not required that it be of a particular size or of a particular color. We shall say that a term *signifies* the comprehensive character such that anything which should have this character would be correctly nameable by the term, and whatever should lack this character, or anything included in it, would not be so nameable. And we shall call this comprehensive essential character the *signification* of the term.

Abstract terms are those which name what some other term signifies; e.g., 'roundness' names that character or property which is essential in order that the term 'round thing' should apply. Non-abstract terms are *concrete*.

For every concrete term, '*C*', there is a cognate abstract term—let us call it '*C*-ness'—which denotes the signification of '*C*'. "The character which a thing must have in order to be nameable by '*C*'," would in any case be such an abstract term, cognate with '*C*', even if there be no linguistically simpler expression which would be synonymous with this phrase. Also for every abstract term, '*C*-ness', there is a cognate term, '*C*', whose signification is named by '*C*-ness'—if no other, then the term 'thing having the property *C*-ness'.

Things which incorporate or are characterized by what an abstract term, '*C*-ness', names, are *instances* of *C*-ness. Anything named by the cognate term, '*C*', will be such an instance, but will not be named by '*C*-ness': any round object, for example, is an instance of roundness but is not nameable or denoted by 'roundness'.

Question arises whether abstract terms signify as well as denote; and if so, what the signification of an abstract term will be. Is there some property whose presence is essential in order that 'roundness' or 'redness' should apply? Plainly, there is; and this property is simply roundness or redness itself. When roundness is presented, both 'round' and 'roundness' apply correctly: the difference is that 'round' applies to the individual object characterized by roundness, whereas 'roundness' names this property itself and has no other application. Otherwise put; what 'round' applies to is something to which also either 'red' or 'not-red' must apply, and either 'hot' or 'not-hot', and so on. But in calling anything by the name 'roundness', we do *not* imply that it is either red or not-red; in fact, we imply the opposite, that it is neither red nor not-red, as well as that it is neither redness nor (not-red)-ness.

Thus we might have defined abstract terms, alternatively, as the class of those which name their significations.[3]

By the idiom of language, there are certain words and phrases—e.g. , predicate-adjectives like 'red'—which when they occur as grammatical subject are abstract in sense, but which may occur as concrete terms in the predicate. Thus "This rose is red" is equivalent to "This rose is a red thing"; and 'red' is here a concrete term, naming the object to which it applies as a whole. But "Red is a color" is equivalent to "Redness is a specific color-property"; and 'red' is here the name of the specific color-property in question. Such words and phrases are sometimes called attributive terms. We shall refer to them simply as *attributives*, because they are not strictly terms but only ambiguous symbolizations or locutions having now one, now another meaning.[4] This classification 'attributive' is worth remarking mainly in order that we may avoid certain confusions about abstract and concrete terms which might otherwise be possible.

We may now return to the consideration of connotation or intension. Though these designations are in common use, they have frequently been left ambigu-

---

[3] It should be noted that although 'round' and 'roundness' have the same signification, they do not have the same comprehension or same denotation. And as the examples used above will indicate, they also have different intension: if we assert "*A* is round," we imply "*A* is red-or-not-red"; but the assertion "*A* is roundness" does not have this implication.

[4] Sometimes the designation 'attributive term' is used more narrowly, being confined to the concrete sense; and in that case the definition may be given. "An attributive term is one which denotes a thing and connotes an attribute of it." But such a definition fails to define: *every* concrete term denotes things and connotes (or in our usage, *signifies*) an attribute of them.

and different comprehension. And this leads us to observe that the comprehension of a singular term is not confined to the single existent thing it denotes (if it denotes any). Although the term connotes singularity of the existent denoted, within the classification of thinkable things comprehended, still the connotation is never sufficient—without recourse to other and logically adventitious facts—to select this individual from amongst all thinkable things which otherwise satisfy the connotation of the term. Thus the denotation of a singular term is a class which is either a class of one or is empty. But its comprehension is the classification of *all* the things consistently thinkable as being the one and only member of that class. For example, 'the red object on my desk' comprehends all the red objects which imaginably might be the only one on my desk; and differs from the comprehension of the general term 'red object on my desk' only by excluding any actual or imaginable red objects which are members of inseparable pairs or triads, etc.

It will be noted that, for any term, its connotation determines its comprehension; and conversely, any determination of its comprehension would determine its connotation; by determining what characters alone are common to all the things comprehended. In point of fact, however, there is no way in which the comprehension can be precisely specified except by reference to the connotation, since exhaustive enumeration of all the thinkable things comprehended is never possible.

The connotation of a term and its denotation do not, however, mutually determine one another. The connotation being given, the denotation is thereby limited but not fixed. Things which lack any essential attribute, specified or implied in the connotation, are *excluded from* the denotation; but what is *included in* the denotation, and what not, depends also on what happens to exist; since the class of things denoted—as distinguished from what the term comprehends—is confined to existents.

Also; the denotation of a term being determined, the connotation is thereby limited but not fixed. The connotation cannot include any attribute absent from one or more of the things named; but it may or may not include an attribute which is common to all existents named by the term; since such an attribute may or may not be essential to their being so named. 'Featherless biped', for example, does not connote 'rational being', even if the class denoted contains only rational beings.

As has been remarked, a term may have zero comprehension. For example, 'round square' has zero comprehension; the classification of consistently-thinkable things so named is empty. But many terms—e.g. , 'unicorn' and 'non-rational animal that laughs'—have zero denotation without having zero comprehension: things which would be correctly so named are consistently thinkable.

The classic dictum that denotation varies inversely as connotation, is false; e.g. , 'rational featherless biped' has the same denotation as 'featherless biped'. But this relation does hold between connotation and comprehension. Any qualification added to a connotation (and not already implied) further restricts the comprehension: and with any omission of a qualification from a connotation, the classification comprehended is enlarged to include thinkable things which retention of that qualification would exclude.

This relation of connotation and comprehension is worth remarking for the sake of one consequence of it: a term of zero comprehension has *universal* connotation. This may at first strike the reader as a paradox. But the correctness of it may be observed from two considerations. Only terms naming nothing which is consistently thinkable have zero comprehension. And "*A* is both round and square", for example, entails "*A* is *y*", for any value of '*y*'. That is, the attribution of 'both round and square' entails *every* attribute; and the connotation of 'round square', since it includes every mentionable attribution, is universal.[6]

This fact clarifies one matter which might otherwise be puzzling. Plainly, it is incorrect to say that terms like 'round square' have no connotation, or that they are meaningless. This term is distinguished from a nonsense-locution by definitely implying the properties of roundness and squareness. And it is only by reason of this meaning—this connotation—which it has, that one determines its inapplicability to anything consistently thinkable.

Thus what is (presumably) intended by the inaccurate statement that such terms are meaningless, can be stated precisely by saying that they have zero comprehension, or that their connotation is universal.

The diametrically opposite kind of term—those having universal comprehension and zero connotation—are also often said to be meaningless. 'Being' and 'entity'—supposing everything one could mention is a being or entity—are such terms. Also any which is of the form 'either *A* or not *A*'. The accurate manner of indicating the lack of significance which characterizes these terms, is to observe that attribution of them implies no attribute that could be absent from anything; that their connotation is zero and their comprehension unlimited. But if they genuinely lacked any meaning—any connotation—this character of them could not be determined.

4. So far we have been concerned with conceptions which are at least provisionally clear by their connection with familiar matters of traditional logic. The properties of propositions and propositional functions which are parallel to the modes of meaning remarked in the case of terms, are not thus familiar: discussion of the intension and extension of propositions has usually been meager or lacking; and no distinction of propositional functions from propositions is traditionally recognized. But it is by reference to these properties

---

[6] "*A* is both *x* and not-*x*" entails "*A* is *x*."

And "*A* is *x*" entails "Either *A* is both *x* and *y* or *A* is *x* but not *y*."

Hence "*A* is both *x* and not-*x*" entails "Either *A* is both *x* and *y* or *A* is *x* but not *y*."

But also "*A* is both *x* and not-*x*" entails "*A* is not *x*."

Hence "*A* is both *x* and not-*x*" entails "It is false that *A* is *x* but not *y*."

But "Either *A* is both *x* and *y* or *A* is *x* but not *y*" and "It is false that *A* is *x* but not *y*" together entail "*A* is both *x* and *y*."

And "*A* is both *x* and *y*" entails "*A* is *y*."

Hence "*A* is both *x* and not-*x*" entails "*A* is *y*."

of propositions and functions that the connections between meaning and analytic truth can most easily be made clear. We can establish the parallel in question if we think of propositions as a certain kind of terms, and of propositional functions as another kind of terms; and such interpretation not only is entirely valid but is almost compelled by logical facts which are of first importance.

A proposition is a term capable of signifying a state of affairs. To define a proposition as an expression which is true or false, is correct enough but inauspicious, because it easily leads to identification of the proposition with the statement or assertion of it; whereas the element of assertion in a statement is extraneous to the proposition asserted. The proposition is something assert*able*; the *content* of the assertion; and this same content, signifying the same state of affairs, can also be questioned, denied, or merely supposed, and can be entertained in other moods as well.[7]

For example the statement, "Mary is making pies," asserts the state of affairs, Mary making pies now, as actual. "Is Mary making pies?" questions it; "Oh that Mary may be making pies," expresses it in the optative mood; and "Suppose that Mary is making pies," puts it forward as a postulate. When we say "If Mary is making pies, then pies are being made by Mary," we consider it and affirm that it has a certain logical consequence. And if we state, "Either Mary is making pies or we shall have no dessert," we likewise entertain it without assertion but affirm its being one of two alternatives.

If we wish to disengage this common content from any particular mood of its entertainment, we might do so—in a manner more precise than ordinary language commonly affords—if we should have symbolic devices indicating these various moods of entertainment; e.g. , "$\vdash p$" for assertion of 'p,' "$H\ p$" for the postulation of it, "$!\ p$" for the mere greeting of it as a presentation of sense or imagination, "$?\ p$" for putting it in question, "$M\ p$" for entertainment of it as consistently thinkable or possible, and so on.[8] And the common content, here represented by 'p', would be something expressible in the manner of indirect discourse, e.g., '*that* Mary is making pies now', or by a participial phrase, 'Mary making pies (now)', which can be asserted, questioned, and entertained in all these different ways, and which signifies the state of affairs which they all concern.

Giving the name 'proposition' to such a clause or participial phrase, instead of to the corresponding statement, is of course, a conventional decision. What justifies it is the fact that it provides a basis for explanation of important facts

---

[7] This conception is first due to Professor H. M. Sheffer . . . . Professor C. W. Morris has also advanced a similar conception.

[8] Exact logic has not as yet much concerned itself with these various moods of entertaining propositions. Assertion is recognized, and postulation—though postulation is usually dealt with inconsistently and confused with assertion. Also it begins to be understood that the imperative or hortatory mood has its own logical principles, and that the so-called modal statements, of possibility and necessity, demand separate consideration. If these matters were to be adequately treated, we should, of course, expect some attempt at economy; the reduction of some moods to expression in terms of others.

which logicians have been compelled to recognize. In particular, it has come to be a matter of general agreement that the extension of any true proposition is universal, and the extension of any false proposition is zero or null; hence that all true propositions have the same extension, and that all false propositions have the same extension, and the important extensional property of a proposition is thus its truth-value (truth or falsity). But logicians have arrived at these conclusions by following analogies which are impressive, somewhat as mathematicians before Dedekind learned to deal correctly with $\sqrt{2}$, and just what it is which is responsible for the facts observed, has remained obscure.

Also, it begins to be understood that propositions have important *intensional* properties, quite distinct and different from those extensional ones which can be expressed in terms of truth and falsity. For example, it is such intensional properties which are in question when we ask what is deducible from a proposition, or what is consistent with it, and whether a proposition is logically necessary or logically contingent. This last point especially concerns us since, as will appear, the logically necessary coincides with that the statement of which is analytic.

However, if this adopted procedure is to succeed in its explanatory purpose, there are several small difficulties, mainly due to language, which must be cleared away. First, it may not readily appear that expressions of the type 'that Mary is making pies' are terms, and that they are replaceable by participial phrases like 'Mary making pies (now)'. Second, we shall have to note the participial phrases which correspond precisely to statements of certain forms. Third, we must remark two senses of such participial phrases, and the important relation of these to the state of affairs or matter of fact which is concerned. And fourth, we must clarify somewhat the notion of the state of affairs itself.

The first point need not detain us long. It will be sufficient to assure the fact that expressions such as 'that Mary is making pies' are really terms if we observe that they can stand as subject in sentences or as predicate. E.g., "That Mary is making pies is what I doubt"; "That Mary is making pies calls for three cheers"; "The gratifying fact is that Mary is making pies"; "We believe that Mary is making pies." Also, with some violence to customary idiom, the participial phrase, 'Mary making pies (now)' is always substitutable for this other manner of indicating a state of affairs: e.g., "The gratifying fact is Mary making pies now"; "Mary now making pies is what I doubt"; and so on.

Second, if a participial phrase is to convey accurately the content of an assertion, a little verbal ingenuity may on occasion be called for in the interest of precision. For one thing, verbs have tense, and this temporal reference of a statement must be preserved; as 'Mary making pies (now)' or '(in past)' or '(in future)'. Some states of affairs, however, are essentially timeless, like the international dateline being the 180th meridian; or that signified by any law of nature. Indeed *all* actual states of affairs are timelessly ingredient in the factual—once a fact, always a fact: it is the content of them which may be temporal.

Again; if the statement in question is compound or complex, the corresponding participial term may be similarly compound or complex: to "*A* is *B* and *C* is *D*" would correspond '*A* being *B* and *C* being *D*'; and to "*A* is *B* or *C* is *D*," '*A* being *B* or *C* being *D*'. However, for any statement, '*p*,' regardless of its form, there is always the corresponding participial term 'It being the case that *p*.'

Negative statements call for caution, because oftentimes '*A* not being *B*' would fail to correspond precisely to the asserted content of "It is false that *A* is *B*." The safe general procedure is indicated by the awkward phrase, 'It being not the case that *A* is *B*'.

(In confining our paradigms to simple statements having the form "*A* is *B*," no implication that all simply indicative statements are reducible to this form is intended.)

Hypothetical statements also require circumspection, because expressions of the form "If *A* is *B* then *C* is *D*" are ambiguous. For one meaning, '*C* being *D* or it being not the case that *A* is *B*' would correspond; for the other, a corresponding term would be " '*C* is *D*' being deducible from '*A* is *B*'."

The third point is somewhat more difficult but also more important. It will be noted that the state of affairs referred to is the *signification* of the proposition: not its denotation. "Mary is making pies" asserts that the state of affairs, Mary making pies now, has a certain status; namely, that it is actual; that it is incorporated in the real world. And if this statement is true, then the denotation or extension of the propositional term, 'Mary making pies now', is not the limited state of affairs which it indicates but is the actual world which incorporates that state of affairs and is characterized by it.

For a combination of reasons, this may not at first be clear. But we can disentangle the matters which are likely to cause confusion. First, let us observe that when a term denotes a thing that thing must likewise be denoted by one or other of every pair of mutually negative terms which could meaningfully be applied to it. That is what is required by the Law of the Excluded Middle. If, then, what 'Mary making pies now' denotes should be the limited state of affairs, Mary making pies now, this same state of affairs should likewise be denoted by 'It being hot' or by 'It being not hot'; and by 'Nero fiddling while Rome burned' or by 'No fiddling by Nero in burning Rome'; and so on, for every pair of contradictory propositions. But that fails to be the case. Mary making pies now, neither includes its being hot nor its being not hot. Either of these alternatives is simply outside the state of affairs in question and irrelevant to it. What could be so denoted by 'Mary making pies now', and likewise denoted by one or other of every pair of contradictory propositions, is the kind of entity we call a world. Nothing short of the whole of reality could determine simultaneously, for *every* proposition, the truth or falsity of it. Thus the denotation or extension of a proposition, in case it is true, is the actual world. The statement asserting the proposition *attributes* it to the actual world; affirms that this actual world incorporates it and is characterized by it. The limited state of affairs, like Mary making pies now, is merely the essential attribute which any world must possess in order that the proposition in question should hold of, apply to, or denote it.

Thus the extension of any proposition is the actual world, in case it is true. And since denotation or extension is in all cases confined to the existent or actual, the extension of any false proposition is null or zero; it applies to nothing actual.

A final point to be remarked here, is the fact that any participial phrase like 'Mary making pies now' can have either of two senses. In one of these it is a predicable expression, like the adjective 'hot' or 'sweet': in the other it is abstract and pronomial, like 'hotness' or 'sweetness.' It is the former of these in which it is equivalent to 'that Mary is making pies' and is to be identified with the proposition. It is in this sense that it is predicable of a world. In the other—the abstract sense—it *names* the attribute predicated; that is, *names* the state of affairs attributed to the actual world by asserting "Mary is making pies."

If this is puzzling, let us observe the parallel for such a predicable term as 'sweet'. If we say something is sweet, the predicate which is applied to and denotes the thing in question, is the term 'sweet', but the *name* of the property or attribute thus asserted to characterize this thing is the cognate abstract term 'sweetness'. And we should note that 'sweetness' cannot apply to or denote any sweet *thing*, but only the property itself. The assertion "Mary is making pies" attributes the state of affairs, Mary making pies now, to the actual world. But it is the predicable sense of the expression, 'Mary making pies now' which may apply to and denote the actual world; and it is the abstract sense of it (in which it is the cognate abstract term) in which it *names* the state of affairs attributed.

To sum up: Every statement asserts a proposition and attributes a state of affairs to the actual world. The proposition so asserted is a predicable term, which can apply to and denote what one or other of every pair of contradictory propositions can also apply to and denote. Every *true* proposition denotes, or has as its extension, the actual world. And every false proposition has, likewise, the same extension as every other which is false; namely, zero extension. Thus all true propositions are equivalent in extension, and all false propositions are equivalent in extension; and the important extensional property of any proposition is simply its truth-value.

The fact that the *name* of any state of affairs is an abstract term, may serve to sharpen and clarify the meaning of this slightly vague expression 'state of affairs' (or the even vaguer and less appropriate expression, 'matter of fact', which we have sometimes used as a synonym). Such a state of affairs is *not* a concrete entity; a space-time slab of reality with all that it contains, but is a property or attribute. It includes nothing beyond what the *abstract* participial expression naming it entails or requires. It is confined to precisely what must be the case in order that the correlative predicable term, which is the proposition, should be applicable to reality.

For example, while Mary is making pies in the kitchen, either she burns her fingers or she does not. The space-time slab, or Whiteheadian event, which comprises Mary making pies now, either includes Mary burning her fingers or it definitely excludes this and is characterized throughout by Mary's fingers being unburned. But the state of affairs, Mary making pies now, which is asserted as actual by the statement "Mary is making pies," neither includes what is asserted by "Mary burns her fingers," nor what is asserted by "Mary does not burn her fingers." It includes only what Mary now making pies requires in order to be the fact.

One state of affairs or matter of fact may include another; as Mary now making pies includes pies being made, and includes Mary working. And one state of affairs may definitely exclude another; as Mary now making pies excludes Mary remaining motionless. But in the sense which is here requisite, what the state of affairs, Mary now making pies, includes is only what is deducible from "Mary is making pies." And what this state of affairs definitely excludes is only that whose non-factuality is deducible from "Mary is making pies."

Thus a state of affairs is not the kind of entity for which the doctrine of internal relations would hold. That doctrine arises from confusing states of affairs with space-time slabs of reality.

The flower growing in the crannied wall, as absolute idealism conceives it, is not what is signified by "There is a flower growing in the crannied wall," but is such a space-time slab, including every cell of this flower and every atom, and every last fact of the relationships of these. If one maintain that any two such space-time slabs of reality, S_1 and S_2, are related that the whole truth about S_1 involves the truth about S_2, this would be difficult to disprove. As the doctrine of internal relations asserts, S_1 must have some relation to S_2 in order to be just what it is and just as it is: it would not be precisely this space-time slab unless it had exactly that relation to every other, and to the content of every other, which in fact it has. The whole truth about the flower in the crannied wall requires the whole truth about the universe. But all that anyone can *know* about the flower in the crannied wall—and could express in a statement or a set of statements connected by 'and'—is a state of affairs. And what one could thus know does *not* entail or implicitly require the truth about everything else and about the universe. It requires nothing beyond what old-fashioned logic recognizes as validly deducible from the statement of what is thus known. The epistemological and metaphysical consequences which absolute idealism draws from the doctrine of internal relations rest on nothing more impressive than (1) the infinite specificity, logically, of any individual object—which is required by the Law of the Excluded Middle—and (2) the ambiguity of the verb 'to know'; which may refer to, as its object, an individual thing or may refer to an apprehended fact. An individual object is a space-time slab; and is something which we can no more know, in all its infinite specificity, than we can similarly know the whole of reality: on that point, the doctrine is on firm ground. But what we know in the sense of apprehending as fact or believing with assurance, is merely some limited state of affairs, which exhausts neither reality nor the object to which cognition is addressed, but comprises only those factualities about the object which our knowledge of it would enable us to state. It will be important, therefore, to observe the abstract and adjectival character of what is appropriately called a state of affairs, as something knowable and statable: it includes all that the assertion of this state of affairs as actual implies, but it includes nothing which is not thus deducible from such statement. It is the signification of some formulated or formulatable proposition; not a 'chunk' of reality.

5. We have spoken of a proposition (propositional term) as true when statement or assertion of it is true, and as false when the corresponding statement is false. So also, two propositions are contradictory if the statements of them are contradictory; and are consistent if the statements of them are consistent. And if one statement implies or entails another, then the one proposition implies or entails the other.[9]

The *intension* of a proposition comprises whatever the proposition entails: and it includes nothing else.

This would in fact follow from our explanation of the intension of terms. If application of the given term, 'A', to anything requires that another term, 'B,' should also be applicable to that thing, then 'A' connotes 'B', and 'B' is contained in the intension of 'A'. The only thing to which any propositional term would meaningfully apply would be the kind of entity called a world. And if any world to which the proposition 'p' would apply is required to be one to which also 'q' would apply, then 'p' entails 'q.'

All the deducible consequences of a proposition, taken together, exhibit the intension of it discursively. It would not, of course, be possible to recite all these consequences, for any proposition. But it is entirely correct to say that whatever deducible a proposition is contained in the intension of it, and that anything so contained can be exhibited by some consequence deducible from it. In that sense at least, the intension of a proposition may be said to coincide with its deductive significance. Also will be the case that any two propositions have the same intension if and only if each is deducible from the other. Intension is that mode of meaning which is the same for two propositions if and only if whatever is deducible from one is deducible from the other also.

Alternatively, we might say that the intension of a proposition comprises whatever must be true of any possible world in order that this proposition should be true of or apply to it.

The conception of a possible or conceivable or consistently thinkable world,

---

[9] It would be more logical to regard truth and falsity, and the relations of consistency, implication, etc., as pertaining in the original sense to propositions, and as attributable to statements because the logical properties of statements are derivative from those of the corresponding propositions. But we are accustomed to think of these properties and relations in connection with statements.

thus introduced, is not jejune. Anything which could appropriately be called a world, must be such that one or other of every pair of contradictory propositions would apply to or be true of it; and such that all the propositions thus holding of it will be mutually consistent. And any set of consistent propositions which includes one or other of every contradictory pair, may be said to determine a possible world. Such a possible world is thinkable, in whatever sense the actual world or whole of reality is thinkable. The actual world, so far as anyone knows it or could know it, is merely one of many such which are thus possible. For example, I do not know at the moment how much money I have in my pocket, but let us say it is thirty cents. The world which is just like this one except that I should have thirty-five cents in my pocket now, is a consistently thinkable world—consistent even with all the facts I know. When I reflect upon the number of facts of which I am presently uncertain, the plethora of possible worlds any one of which might, so far as my knowledge goes, be the one which is actual, becomes a little appalling.

The propositions deducible from a given proposition, 'p', together constitute the intension of 'p'. And any proposition 'q' contained in the intension of 'p' is such that 'q' must apply to any possible world to which 'p' would apply.

A proposition *comprehends* any consistently thinkable world which would incorporate the state of affairs it signifies; and the classification of such possible worlds to which the proposition would apply, constitutes the comprehension of that proposition.

The extension of a proposition is, as we have seen, a class of one—the actual world—in case it is true, and is an empty class in case it is false. But the comprehension of a proposition is always a classification of many, if the proposition is self-consistent, and is zero or null only if the proposition is self-contradictory. And while all propositions which are true have the same extension, they do not in general have the same comprehension: they will coincide in comprehension only in case they have the same intension. False propositions also, though they all have the same zero extension, will be different in what they comprehend unless their intension is the same.

An *analytic* proposition is one which would apply to or hold of every possible world; one, therefore, whose comprehension is universal, and correlatively, one which has zero intension. At this point, the distinction previously remarked between terms of zero intension and nonsense-locutions which literally have no meaning, becomes important. An analytic proposition does not fail to have implications—though all entailments of it are likewise analytic or logically necessary propositions which would hold of any possible world. That an analytic proposition has zero intension is correlative with the fact that in being true of reality it does not distinguish this actual world from any other which is consistently thinkable; that it does not impose any restriction or limitation on the actual which could conceivably be absent.

As has been said, a *self-contradictory* or self-inconsistent proposition is one which has zero comprehension, and could apply to or hold of no world which is consistently thinkable. Correlatively, such a proposition has universal intension; it entails all propositions, both true and false.[10] If the self-contradictory should be true, then anything and everything would follow, including all the absurdities one could think of. It would, however, be a mistake to say that self-contradictory propositions are meaningless. A locution which genuinely had no meaning, like "Didmash etmas gint," could not possibly contradict itself, because it says nothing. By contrast, that today is Monday but tomorrow is not Tuesday, is known *a priori* not to be the case *because of the meaning which the statement has*. The sense in which what is self-contradictory lacks significance, is in fact most precisely expressed by saying that the intension of it is unlimited, or that it has zero comprehension.

All synthetic propositions, excepting the self-contradictory, have an intension which is neither zero nor universal, and a comprehension which is neither universal nor zero. They entail some other propositions but not all other propositions. And they are deducible from some other propositions but not from all. Consonantly, what they assert is compatible with some consistently thinkable states of affairs and not with other consistently thinkable states of affairs. The state of affairs signified by any synthetic proposition would characterize some possible worlds but would fail to characterize other possible worlds.

6. The subject of propositional functions is one which is of first importance for logic; but also one of great complexity. We shall not attempt any full discussion of it, but shall confine attention to what is required for clarity, and to those topics which bear directly upon questions about analytic truth.

A *statement function* is an expression containing one or more blank or variable constituents which becomes a statement when each such variable is replaced by certain constant (non-variable) expressions. Thus "x is a man," "$x < \sqrt{2}$," "x precedes y," "All A is B," "If p then q," "y is between x and z," are statement functions. We shall symbolize expression of this general kind in the usual manner, by 'φx', '$\psi(x, y)$', '$f(p, q)$', '$\theta(x, y, z)$', etc.

In the statement function "x precedes y," substitution of the constant term 'Sunday' for the variable constituent 'x', and of 'Monday' for 'y', turns it into a statement—as it happens, one which is true. And substitution of '9' for 'x' and '7' for 'y' also turns it into a statement—one which is false. 'Sunday' and '9' are called *values* of 'x' in "x precedes y," and 'Monday' and '7', values of 'y.' In any statement function, '$\theta(x, y, z, \ldots)$', if substitution of the constant expression 'a' for 'x', 'b' for 'y', 'c' for 'z', and so on transforms '$\theta(x, y, z, \ldots)$' into a statement '$\theta(a, b, c, \ldots)$', then 'a', 'b', 'c', etc. are called values, respectively, of 'x', 'y', 'z', etc. in this function.

In "x precedes y," it happens that any constant which is a value of 'x' is likewise a value of 'y', and *vice versa*. But in "x is a property of y," for example,

---

[10] Every self-contradictory statement is equivalent, for some choice of p and q, to a statement of the form, "p is true and p is false and q is true." This last entails "r is true," for any choice of r. The manner of the deduction would be analogous to that of the paradigm given in the footnote, p. 25, for expressions of the form "A is both x and not-x."

'yellowness' is a value of 'x', and 'gold' is a value of 'y', whereas "Gold is a property of yellowness" is neither true nor false but is nonsense: that is, no value of 'x' in this function is a value of 'y', or *vice versa*.[11]

It should be noticed that what is here called a value of, for example, 'x' in "x is a man" is the *term* or *expression* 'Socrates' or 'Apollo' or 'the speaker for tonight', and not the *thing named* by such a term. This is merely a conventional decision as to what will be meant by speaking of values of a variable. But it seems an appropriate one: it is the name 'Socrates,' not Socrates the man, which can be a constituent in discourse. Also this decision is important, for reasons which will appear when we come, later, to discuss what will be called formal statements.

Oftener than not what we here call statement functions are called also propositional functions. But we shall have to distinguish between propositional functions and statement functions, just as we have distinguished between propositions and the statements or assertions of them. "Socrates is a man" is a statement, and 'that Socrates is a man' or 'Socrates being a man' is the corresponding proposition. So also "x is a man" is a statement function; and it is the corresponding predication or participial expression, 'x being a man' or 'x characterized by humanity' which is to be identified with the propositional function. However, a statement function is *not* the assertion of the corresponding propositional function: what are sometimes called asserted propositional functions do not coincide with the class of statement functions, but are propositions of a particular type which will be considered later.

When we speak of functions without qualification, what is said may be applied to statement functions or to propositional functions, either one.

We can avoid several kinds of difficulties, at one and the same time, if we recognize that, speaking most judiciously, there is only *one* variable in any function. In what are called functions of two variables, 'x' and 'y', this one variable is the ordered couple '(x, y)'; in what are called functions of three variables, it is an ordered triad, '$(x, y, z,)$', and so on.[12] But it is necessary to insist here on the consideration of *order*—order of occurrence in the function. This is the case both because what is a value of one variable constituent in a function may not be a value of another variable constituent in the same function, and because order or position of variable constituents is of the essence of

---

[11] By some logicians it is held that entities in general are divisible into 'types'; individuals, classes of individuals, classes of such classes, etc.; and also held that if a be a value of 'x' in any function 'φx', or in '$\Psi(x, y)$', etc., then anything which is of the same type as a is also a value of 'x' in that same function. It would appear that this division into types is not exhaustive of entities which can be spoken of; and at least doubtful that restriction to some one type is in all cases essential, as well as that it is the only restriction ever required upon constants meaningfully substitutable for variables in a given function. We shall, however, omit these questions.

[12] We may still, by convention, speak of a value of 'x' in "x precedes y" or in any function of more than one variable constituent. If for some substitution of a constant, 'b', for 'y' in '$\Psi(x, y)$', substitution of the constant 'a' for 'x' transforms '$\Psi(x, y)$' into a statement '$\Psi(a, b)$', then 'a' may be called a value of 'x' in '$\Psi(x, y)$.'

what any function expresses: '$\psi(a, b)$' is always a different statement from '$\psi(b, a)$', and one of these might be true when the other is false.

To put this same matter in another way: a variable constituent in discourse is one which has no meaning except one which is conferred by and relative to its context. But it would be a serious oversight if we should overlook the fact that *in* its context a variable constituent has a kind of meaning determined by its place (or places) in the expression and by the syntax of that expression. Thus in "x precedes y," 'x' is grammatical subject of the verb 'precedes' and 'y' is grammatical object. And in "x is a property of y" it is the syntax of the expression, together with the meaning of the noun 'property', which determines that what is a value of 'x' cannot be a value of 'y'. Also, in such an expression as "If x precedes y, then y is preceded by x," it is, of course, required that any constant substituted for 'x', or for 'y', in one place, should be substituted for that same variable constituent in its other occurrence also. Variable constituents may also have what might be called *notational* meaning, which is a species of syntactic meaning arising from conventions of notation. Thus if we write "When xRy, it may or may not hold also that yRx," it will be understood that 'R' takes only relation-words as its values; and hence the component expressions 'xRy' and 'yRx', though as written they contain no constant constituent, nevertheless do have an element of constant meaning. They have such meaning both by reason of this understanding about the symbol 'R' and on account of the syntactic relation between 'x' and 'R' and 'y' which is conveyed by this manner of writing.[13]

With this understanding about variables, namely, that strictly speaking there is only one variable in any function, we may observe that any statement function can be so formulated that this one variable becomes the grammatical subject of the predication. Sometimes, as in "x is a man," this is already the case, but in another function with one variable constituent it might not be— e.g., "Either x is not red or x is colored." But there is one general procedure by which this suggested manner of formulation can always be effected; which is to express what is said as *characterization* of the variable: "x is characterized by being not red or else colored," "x is characterized by being a man," etc. The same procedure can be carried out where there is more than one variable constituent. Thus "x precedes y" can be expressed, "The ordered couple (x, y) is characterized by being in the relation of predecessor to preceded." And "All x is y" can be phrased, "(x, y) is characterized by being in the relation of included class to including class."

It is the predicate or characterization here—'characterized by being a man' or merely 'being a man'; 'characterized by being in the relation of predecessor

---

[13] We use 'syntax' and 'syntactic' here in their usual English significance; that is, as signifying what belongs to the linguistic structure of an expression and is conveyed by the order of its constituents; not in the wider meaning which would include under 'syntax' all that could be covered by formation-rules and transformation-rules of language. (*Cf.*, e.g., Carnap, *Logical Syntax of Language*, pp. 1, 2.)

to preceded', or merely 'being in the relation of predecessor to preceded'—
which is that part of the expression which has a determined meaning. And
this fact is important.

Statement functions never occur in discourse except as subordinate constituents. By themselves, they are never true or false; and when they occur it is
because something is said *of* them. And in every such case, what is thus stated
depends for its truth or falsity, and for its meaning, upon the predicate or
predication in the function which thus occurs. The point of using a statement
function 'φx' is not that it enables us to say something about what 'x' stands
for; because 'x' stands for nothing in particular; but that it enables us to speak
of something or of anything which has the characteristic or predicate represented by 'φ'; e.g., the character of being a man or the character of being
either not red or else colored. And the statement function involving two variable constituents, 'x' and 'y', is used not for the purpose of saying anything
about what the symbolism '(x, y)' stands for—because it stands for any
ordered couple—but in order to speak of something, or of anything, characterized by standing in a certain relation, such as the relation of predecessor to
preceded, or that of an included class to one which includes it.

As has been observed, the variable constituents in a function have no meaning save the syntactic meaning which is conferred by their context. They are
in fact merely a notational device by which the syntax of the predication may
be preserved—and in some cases, syntactically related in the intended way to
other such predications in the same context—without the necessity of saying
what in particular this predication is predicated of, or whether in fact it is
predicated of anything.

For reasons thus suggested, the *propositional function*, corresponding to any
statement function 'φx', is to be identified with 'x characterized by φ'; and it
is the characterization 'φ' which is here important; 'x' is superfluous except
for some convenience of syntactic reference. Thus the propositional function
corresponding to "$x < \sqrt{2}$" is 'x characterized by being less than $\sqrt{2}$'; and
'x' is here redundant, except for some purpose of syntactic reference to further
context: the participial phrase 'characterized by being less than $\sqrt{2}$' has the
same meaning and applies to exactly the same things. And the propositional function corresponding to "x precedes y" is '(x, y) characterized by
being in the relation of predecessor to preceded', or merely 'characterized
by the former preceding the latter', which could apply to nothing except some
ordered pair.

This characterization or predication which is the propositional function, is
always a participial term (or may be given that form); but it is not, like a
proposition, the kind of participial phrase which could be predicated of reality
or a world. Instead it is predicable of the kind of entities (or pairs or triads,
etc.) names of which are values of the one variable in the corresponding statement function.

Such a participial phrase as 'being a man', 'being less than $\sqrt{2}$', 'being in
the relation of predecessor to preceded', is an attributive phrase; and ambiguous in the general manner of attributives. But the prefixed phrase 'character-

ized by' in 'characterized by being a man', 'characterized by being so and so', restricts the expression to its concrete sense; or more accurately—since the values of the variable may in some cases be names of properties and not of concrete entities—this prefix restricts 'being so and so' to its *predicable* sense. And the abstract sense of such a phrase—the cognate abstract term—is the name of the *characteristic* which predication of this phrase to anything attributes. Thus in the case of 'x characterized by being a man' this attribute is the property of being human; and in the case of '(x, y) characterized by being in the relation of predecessor to preceded', this attribute is the property common to all ordered pairs which stand in that relationship.

The logical properties of a statement function are those which it has by virtue of the predication it expresses—since the variable in it has no meaning except one conferred by this context. Thus the extension, intension, etc., of any statement function is the extension or intension of the predicable term which is the corresponding propositional function. The various modes of the meaning of any propositional function are determinable from what has been said above about the modes of meaning of terms in general; and these modes of meaning are ascribable also to the corresponding statement function.

The denotation or *extension* of a function is the class of existents (individuals or ordered couples or triads, etc.) of which this predication is truly predicable; the class of existents to which the term which is the propositional function truly applies. Thus the extension of 'x characterized by being a man' or of "x is a man" is the class of existent men; the extension of 'characterized by being in the relation of predecessor to preceded' or of "x precedes y" is the class of existent couples such that the former member of this pair precedes the latter. More briefly—though less clearly—we may say that the extension of any function 'φx' or 'x characterized by φ' is the class of existent x's for which 'φx' is true.

The *comprehension* of a function, 'φx', or 'x characterized by φ', is the classification of things consistently thinkable as being characterized by this predicate. Otherwise put: if for a constant expression 'a', "a exists" is not self-contradictory, and 'φa' is not self-contradictory, then 'φx' or 'x characterized by φ' comprehends a. And the totality of what is thus comprehended constitutes the comprehension of the function.

The connotation or *intension* of a function comprises all that attribution of this predicate to anything entails as also predicable to that thing. It will be appropriate to restrict the intension of any statement function, 'φx' to expressions in the form of statement functions; and to restrict the intension of any propositional function, 'x characterized by φ', to other expressions having this same form.

Thus we shall say that the intension of 'φx' contains or includes 'ψx' if and only if, for all values of 'x', 'φx' entails 'ψx'. And that the intension of 'x characterized by φ' contains or includes 'x characterized by ψ' if and only if every consistently thinkable thing characterized by φ must also be characterized by ψ. And the totality of what a function connotes or thus entails constitutes the intension of it.

The *signification* of a function 'φx', or 'x characterized by φ', is the essential property which anything must have in order that the predicate 'φ' should apply to it. Thus the signification of "x is a man" or 'x characterized by being a man', is the property of being human; and the signification of "x precedes y," or '(x, y) characterized by being in the relation of predecessor to preceded' is the property of standing in this relationship. As has been noted, the term which is the propositional function does not *name* this property; it is the cognate abstract term which is this name of the property signified by the function.

As is the case for terms of other kinds, a function may have zero comprehension. For example, "x is a cube with seventeen edges," and, for any constant 'A', "x is both A and not-A," are functions of zero comprehension.

Also a function may have zero extension but not zero comprehension: "x is the fiftieth state admitted to the Union" and "x is a sea-serpent which climbs aboard vessels in the Red Sea" are such functions.

There are also functions of universal comprehension; e.g., "x is not human or x is an animal," and, for any constant 'A', "x is A or x is not-A."

Also, there are functions having universal extension but not universal comprehension, such as "Either x pays no Massachusetts poll tax or x is over twenty-one."

Unlike propositions, functions may have an extension which is neither universal nor zero: "x is a man" and "x precedes y" are such functions.

7. The logical properties of statements are correlative with and derivative from those of the corresponding propositions, since statements merely assert propositions and attribute the states of affairs they signify to the actual. Likewise the logical properties of statement functions follow from those of the corresponding propositional functions. Since propositions are a kind of terms, and propositional functions also are a kind of terms, all expressions whose logical properties need come in question have the same four modes of meaning, extension, intension, signification and comprehension.

Of these four, the last three belong together in a certain sense in which they stand in contrast to extension. Any two expressions which have the same intension or the same comprehension, are the same in all three of these modes of meaning. (We cannot say that two expressions having the same signification will in all cases have the same intension and the same comprehension, because of abstract terms. 'Round' and 'roundness' have the same signification but not the same intension or same comprehension.) Whoever understands the intensional meaning of an expression, or the comprehension of it, can always determine for himself the other two of these three modes of meaning, merely by thinking about it consistently and without any recourse to experiences he has not yet had or to facts of existence as yet unknown to him. (Also one who understands the signification of an expression may so determine its intension and comprehension, provided only he observes whether the given expression is abstract or not). We might thus call all three of these, intensional modes of meaning. They all of them have to do with meaning as something which we have in mind when so and so is meant, or with something which should be in mind and may be brought to mind by thinking, or is logically determined by what we have in mind when we entertain a meaning.

It is also true that if two expressions have the same intension or the same comprehension, then—since the facts of existence are always fixed, even when we do not know just what these facts of existence are—these two expressions will also have the same extension. But two expressions having the same extension may not, and in many cases do not, have the same extension or signification or comprehension. Thus 'man' and 'animal that laughs' have the same extension, since they truly apply to the same class of existents; but these terms do not have the same intensional meaning. Application of one of them to a thing does not logically require applicability of the other. Also "x is a large mammal which habitually walks erect" and "x is a man" have the same extension: the characterizations 'being a large mammal which habitually walks erect' and 'being a man' are predicable of the same class of existents. But they do not comprehend the same classification of consistently thinkable things. Again, the statements "January 1, 1944, is a Saturday" and "Potatoes are edible" have the same extension, being both true; but they do not signify the same states of affairs as characteristic of reality. Nor do they have the same logical consequences or follow logically from the same premises.

One main point here is that no one can *know* the extension of any expression he uses except through knowing facts of existence. In exceptional cases, we may know such facts of existence by knowing that they have no consistently thinkable alternatives, i.e., through knowing that they are logicallynece ssary facts; as for example, we know that every man which exists is an animal without making any empirical investigation. But apart from what is thus logically necessary, we know facts of existence only by experience and through induction. One may well say, in a particular instance, "I do not know whether so and so exists or not, or is the fact or not, but still I know what I *mean*." We should understand this statement; and whoever would make it could *not* be meaning whatever he meant in the sense of extension. Whoever means anything in this sense in which meaning may be completely determined within the mind itself and by taking thought, must be entertaining whatever he means in some one of the intensional modes.

One bearing of this simple and obvious point is that it should indicate to us that all logical truth and all truths that logic can warrant must turn upon meaning in the sense of intension. Because logic and the logically certifiable comprise only such facts as are independent of all particular experience and are capable of being known with certainty merely through clear and cogent thinking. The same must hold of any analytic truth: if it is capable of being known by taking thought about it, then it must be independent of meaning in the sense of extension and turn upon meanings only in the sense of intension. And we have already discovered that this is indeed the case; an analytic proposition is one having universal comprehension and hence zero intension, and an analytic statement asserts what such a proposition signifies as characteristic of reality. However, we have yet to develop the full significance of this fact.

Many logicians have supposed that logic should be, or at least could be, developed in terms of extensional meaning exclusively. Especially in the last fifty years, many extended and complex developments have been built up on the basis of that assumption. But that supposition is about as wrong as anything could be: nothing that logic asserts depends upon experience or requires anything not determinable by taking thought upon it. No statement is a statement belonging to logic unless it is analytic and hence certifiable from facts of intensional meaning.

This assumption that extensional meaning is fundamental for logic has usually been connected with and supported by one or both of two further suppositions. First, that the basic sense of meaning, in which an expression stands for or represents something, is the sense of denoting. Second, that all other facts which can be known and all other statements which can be assured are finally derivative, logically or epistemologically, from facts about individuals and singular statements which express these; and that no statement which, when properly construed, is a statement about an individual, can be true if the individual meant does not exist.

The first of these suppositions concerns a matter which troubled us at the outset of this discussion. We observed that there are those who would deny that a non-existent thing can be named or any term correctly applied to it. Although this contention seems *prima facie* absurd, we could not at that point clarify the matter; but in terms which the discussion has made available, this difficulty can now be simply resolved. A term names or correctly applies to anything which that term *comprehends;* any consistently thinkable thing which, as thought of, has the characteristics essential to application of that term. (On a particular occasion of its use, this comprehension of a term—what it names— may be limited by context; either a linguistic context of qualifying adjectives or a context provided by the use of the term, such as is indicated by a limiting word like 'this' or 'my'.) What a term names is always something thought of; but to name is not *ipso facto* to denote: a term denotes what it names or applies to just in case the thing or things referred to happen to exist.

As regards the second supposition mentioned: it is indeed a fact that we could hardly say anything precise if we are not privileged to say "*A* is so and so" in a sense in which our statement will be false if there *isn't* any *A* (if *A* does not exist) to be so and so. This sense of singular predication may well be felt to be fundamental; and the difficulty which thus arises concerning a truth about merely thought-of individuals is one which becomes more impressive, and not less so, the further we probe the logic of it. But omitting all intervening considerations, the solution is in the end simple. The most frequently intended meaning of a singular statement, "*A* is so and so" is "*A* characterized by so and so *exists*," or even "One and only one *A* characterized by so and so exists." In either of these senses, "*A* is so and so" is obviously false when '*A*' has zero extension. Truth of such a statement about an individual thus depends upon the extension of the term '*A*' as well as upon the relation of this extension to that of 'so and so'. But by no means all statements in which singular terms occur are so intended; and if (*per impossibile*) they were to be so restricted by linguistic convention, there would still be something true of, and important to say about, things which are merely thought of without existing, or thought of without knowing whether they exist or not. For such a thought-of individual named by '*A*', "*A* is so and so" may mean "What '*A*' denotes is contained in what 'so and so' denotes." As when one says, "The book you will study in this course is one of the philosophical classics." With that meaning, "*A* is so and so" will be *true* without regard to any further question, if what '*A*' names does not exist. Any class which is empty is contained in every class: if the student addressed studies no book in the course, then any he so studies will be anything you please.[14] Or a statement of this form, "A is so and so," may mean, "The comprehension of '*A*' is contained in the comprehension of 'so and so'," as when one says, "The area of the triangle with vertices at these three points can be expressed in terms of their distances from one another." This will be true, provided nothing properly called '*A*' could lack the character signified by 'so and so', whether '*A*' names an actual individual or only—as is the case with us in the present example—something imaginary.

Thus both the assumptions mentioned above are in error. Things merely thought of can be named; and concerning anything thought of, and required by our manner of thinking of it to have certain essential characters, there is a truth which can be told—as well as any number of statements about it which would be false. If this were not so, then nobody could make a plan concerning the execution of which there could be doubt, or entertain any expectation in which he could conceivably be disappointed. And if that should be the case, then thinking would be a pointless and perhaps impossible procedure. Since many things can be correctly thought of though they do not exist, and many more the existence of which is uncertain, it is meaning and naming in the sense of comprehending and not in the sense of denoting which is fundamental.

As has been mentioned, any expression whose intension is determined has a meaning which is thereby fixed in all the modes of meaning—though as regards the extension of it, one may still not *know* just *how* it is fixed. That being so, intensional meaning meets a basic requirement, laid down long ago by Leibnitz; the requirement, namely, that if the expressions '*A*' and '*B*' have the same meaning, then the substitution of '*A*' for '*B*' or '*B*' for '*A*' in any statement will not alter the truth of that statement.[15]

Meaning in the sense of extension does not meet this test. For example, the statement, "That the creature described is a large mammal which habitually walks erect, is consistent with its being something other than human," is a true statement. But if we substitute for 'large mammal which habitually walks erect' the term 'human' which has the same extension, this statement becomes false. Or again, "That some fish are edible follows logically from the fact that

---

[14] Strictly speaking there is only one empty class: every term which names no existent has the same denotation, namely zero denotation.

[15] Leibnitz lays down this requirement for terms only, and calls those which meet it '*eadem*' or '*coincidentia*.' See Gerhardt, *Die Philosophischen Schriften von G. W. Leibniz*, Vol. VII, p. 232.

some fish are food," is a true statement. But "That some fish are edible follows logically from the fact that many leaves are green" is false; though "Some fish are food" and "Many leaves are green" are expressions having the same extension, both being true.

Nevertheless it would be a mistake to conclude that expressions having the same intension will in all cases have the same meaning in every called-for sense of the word 'meaning'. In particular, this conclusion would lead to the anomolous result that all expressions having universal intension have the same meaning, and all which have zero intension have the same meaning. Thus we should have to recognize that 'round square' means the same as 'triangular circle' and 'Tuesday that falls on Monday'; and that 'man or not man' means the same as 'cat or not cat'. These results would not accord with common sense, and would impose serious difficulties for our understanding of analytic truth. . . .

KEITH S. DONNELLAN

1.2   *Necessity and Criteria*

I

In *An Analysis of Knowledge and Valuation*,[1] C. I. Lewis makes a connection between criteria of application and our knowledge of necessary truths. He introduces first his notion of sense meaning. To know the sense meaning of an expression is to know what *features* in a situation would be necessary and sufficient for the expression to apply correctly to it.

> . . . attribution of meaning in this sense requires only two things; (1) that determination of applicability or non-applicability of a term, or truth or falsity of a statement, be possible by way of sense-presentable characters, and (2) that *what* such characters will, if presented, evidence applicability or truth should be fixed in advance of the particular experience, in the determination of the meaning in question (135).

How we use this knowledge to determine necessary truths is brought out in the following passage:

> We know that "All squares are rectangles" because in envisaging the test which a thing must satisfy if 'square' is to apply to it, we observe that the test it must satisfy if 'rectangle' is to apply is already included. This experiment in the

Reprinted from *The Journal of Philosophy*, LIX, No. 22 (1962), 647–58, by permission of the author and of *The Journal of Philosophy*.

[1] La Salle, Indiana: The Open Court Publishing Co., 1946. [See selection 1.1 above, pp. 15–42.]

imagination—which we must be able to make if we know what we mean and can recognize squares and rectangles when we find them—is sufficient to assure that the intentional meaning of 'square' has to that of 'rectangle' the relation prescribed by 'all-are' (152).

Seeing that the features a thing must have to be a square include those which are sufficient for calling it a "rectangle," we know that all squares are rectangles. The features here are found as the result of applying tests. Thus, a figure is a square only if we would find four sides upon counting, ninety-degree angles upon measurement, and equality of the sides upon measuring. But the first two features are sufficient for calling any figure a "rectangle."

In this paper I do not propose to discuss the specific details of Lewis's view. Instead, I wish to take up some more general questions that his position seems to me to raise about the relationship between necessity and what might be called "criteria of application."

It is important to stress that Lewis is interested in the epistemological question: How do we know necessary truths? And this question, as he intends it, presupposes, I believe, that apprehension of necessity is apprehension of a pre-existing state of affairs. A proposition *is* necessarily true, and we may then become aware of this fact.

On his view there must be for every descriptive term a set of criteria in virtue of which it is correctly applied to things, situations, etc. Necessity arises when there is a relationship holding among the criteria for two or more terms and, in the simplest case, as we have seen, the relationship is that of inclusion. Seeing the necessity of a proposition consists in apprehending this relationship. For Lewis this is possible because, if we are to know what we mean by a term, we must be able to envisage in advance our criteria for applying it. About his views on the process of envisagement, which are illustrated in the passage quoted above, I shall not have anything to say.

My question is rather about the idea that there is between terms a pre-existing relationship among their criteria which can be said to determine the necessity of certain propositions into which they enter and which, by whatever means, might allow us a basis for the awareness of necessity.

The concept of *criteria* itself is none too clear. Lewis seems to me often to use it in such a way that it is not clearly distinguishable from logically necessary and sufficient conditions. If that is how it is intended it seems hardly to supply the *ultimate* or "original" determination of necessity. In what follows I shall use it more broadly, to mean (still vaguely) that in virtue of which we apply a term to a situation. I think that what I want to say can be said without clarifying the notion further.

Using the intuitive notion of "inclusion of criteria" I want to examine two cases in which it seems to me dubious whether we can speak of this relationship holding prior to our acceptance of a statement as necessarily true. In one the inclusion seems to arise as the result of learning the necessary truth; in a second, knowledge of the necessary truth seems to be a prerequisite for understanding the terms involved, and thus there seems no room for a pre-existing connection.

II

The first example is often used in the literature. We find, upon consulting a dictionary, that whales are mammals. Zoologists classify whales as mammals, and the more sophisticated layman knows this. For the zoologist and the sophisticated layman, that whales are mammals may seem to have the status of a necessary truth. One may wonder whether this *is* genuinely a necessary truth. I share this apprehension, and more will be said about it. Here I shall assume that it is.

The things I shall say about this truth will go also for such statements as: Under standard conditions of pressure, water boils at 100°C; Hearts pump blood; Clouds are composed of vapor. I do not go into the interesting question of whether, as these examples suggest, truths of this type are all connected with a rather advanced body of scientific knowledge.

Although for many of us, it seems, the criteria that something must satisfy if it is to be properly called a "mammal" must be present if we are properly to call an animal a "whale," we do not usually demand an investigation of their presence. Normally 'whale' is applied simply on the basis of the general look a of thing—its shape, size, and, perhaps, color. There seem to be two distinct sets of criteria in use: one, roughly speaking, the *gestalt* of the creature, which we usually find sufficient, and two, the presence of mammary glands. The second we assume to be satisfied, though we rarely make any investigation. We often have no doubts about our identification even though we have no opportunity to examine the animal with the care needed to find the characteristics that indicate a mammal.

Not only do we often neglect the second set of criteria, those for applying the word 'mammal', but many of us are ignorant of any necessity for them in the correct application of the word 'whale'. As children we learn the meaning of 'whale' through pictures, through being told they are large creatures living in the sea, etc.

In these first stages, we are often not told they are mammals. For some of us the connection never gets established. A sailor may have the ability to spot whales with great accuracy; he may know their habits and migrations; yet, for all of this, he can be ignorant of the fact that they are members of the same family as the cow. Moreover, this is perfectly possible though he knows what mammals are.

For the sailor no relationship of inclusion exists among the criteria for applying the terms 'whale' and 'mammal'. He could not come to see a necessary truth here in the way Lewis suggests we discover that all squares are rectangles. The sailor does not use the criteria attaching to the word 'mammal' in his application of the word 'whale'. And, for him, this is not a matter of taking anything for granted; being a mammal is not a requirement at all. So he cannot learn the necessary truth by discovering an inclusion among his criteria.

III

However, one may think this an unfair example—not a genuine counter-instance. He might reply by arguing that the zoologist and the sailor attach two distinct meanings to the word 'whale'. Only with the meaning the zoologist has in mind is it a necessary truth that whales are mammals. Hence, the reason Lewis's view will not work is that *as the sailor uses the word 'whale'* there is no necessary truth to discover. And in support of this contention, there is a very plausible argument. If two people attach the same meaning to an expression, one would think they must be prepared to apply it in the same way. If a new kind of marine animal were discovered, one looking like a whale in all respects except that it is not a mammal, the zoologist and other sophisticated people might refuse to call this a "whale" just on the grounds that it is not a mammal. Possibly they would speak of "pseudo-whales." But in our example, the sailor has no reason for hesitation. Since he picks out whales by their shape, size, and color, these new animals satisfy his criteria. So, one might argue, we can see that two distinct concepts are involved.

In a moment I should like to question this conclusion, for it does not seem so simple as all that. But suppose we accept it for now. 'Whales are mammals', we shall grant, simply does not express a necessary truth as the sailor uses the word 'whale'. Hence he cannot be expected to discover the necessary truth by an examination of his criteria of application. And there is no reason to suppose that there is a pre-existing connection among the criteria.

Still, if this is true, there *is* a sentence that expresses a necessary truth: the sentence 'Whales are mammals' *as used by a zoologist*. How then does the sailor come to know the necessary truth expressed by it? First, evidently, he must learn to use the word 'whale' as the zoologist does. Now the crucial question is this: Can the sailor first learn the zoologist's use of the word 'whale' and then, by discovering that the criteria for 'mammal' are included, come to see the necessary truth? I should think the answer is "No." The way he learns the zoologist's use, if it *is* a different use, is through being taught the necessary truth. He may be told that whales *must* be mammals—in a tone of voice which shows that a defining condition is being indicated. Or he may discover a definition of the word in a dictionary. Or he may be told that zoologists classify the whale as a mammal—the word 'classify' possibly indicating that he is being told a defining condition.

Once the sailor has learned and accepted the fact that whales are classified as mammals it becomes plausible to say that he includes among his criteria for applying the word 'whale' the criteria for the word 'mammal'. But this state of affairs was brought about by teaching him the truth that whales are mammals. He now may regard this as "true by definition." And on the assumption that this is a necessary truth, were he to think that zoologists considered it a contingent truth, subject to refutation by observation of these animals, then he would not have grasped the point of the teaching; he would not yet understand how zoologists use the word 'whale'. So, it does not appear to be a matter of discovering something about one's own criteria. Nor can we speak of a pre-existing connection. Rather, if anything, the sailor discovers that other people include the criteria for applying one word among those for applying another—a discovery brought about by being taught to accept something as a necessary truth.

IV

A child may not know the facts of life and yet be said to understand the word 'father'. So too, I think, we would say that our sailor knew what the word 'whale' meant even though he was ignorant of the fact that whales are mammals. I do not believe that we ordinarily distinguish two concepts in such circumstances. Still, I am not sure what this comes to. One may say that we ought to even though we do not.

But there is one set of circumstances in which I think it would be wrong and misleading to say that the sailor had a *different* concept of a whale. Most of us who understand what mammals are know that animals are classified as being mammals or not and that this classification enters into the dictionary definitions of words designating kinds of animals. Given that in these cases 'X's are mammals' will express a necessary truth, one is often in the position of knowing that a sentence of this form expresses either a necessary truth or a necessary falsehood without knowing which. For example, I know that it is either necessarily true or necessarily false that the duckbill platypus is a mammal, but I may not know which. I know that every sentence of the form 'Dodecahedrons have n edges' expresses either a necessary truth or a necessary falsehood, but I may be ignorant of what number to substitute for 'n' to obtain the necessary truth.

Now it seems to me misleading to say in such cases that I have a *different* concept just because I do not include among my criteria for, e.g., the word 'platypus' the criteria for the word 'mammal'. For I am prepared to do so *if* an acceptable dictionary tells me that the platypus is a mammal. Hence my use is intimately connected with what zoologists say.

Our sailor uses as his only criteria for applying the word 'whale' such things as a certain size, color, and shape of marine animals. If we think that these criteria exhaust the meaning of the word for him, then we shall conclude that for him the sentence 'Whales are mammals' expresses a contingent statement. But in the sort of circumstances I have been describing this would be a mistake. He may know that this sentence expresses a necessary statement, either true or false, without knowing which. He knows that a dictionary is quite relevant if he wants to find out which. He does not utilize the criteria attaching to the word 'mammal', but he is quite prepared to if this is the way zoologists classify these animals. There *is* an indisputably contingent truth lurking in the background, but it is contingent for the zoologist as well as for the sailor. It is merely contingent that large marine animals with a certain characteristic size and shape (which we might specify through a picture) also have mammary glands and suckle their young. But while both the sailor and the zoologist would regard this as contingent, neither may regard it as contingent that whales are mammals.

In these circumstances, then, our sailor cannot discover that whales are mammals by inspecting his own criteria, but neither can we explain this away by saying 'Whales are mammals' means something different for the sailor, that it is merely a contingent statement.

V

In our first example, new criteria seemed to be included as the result of learning a necessary truth. In some cases, however, knowledge that two expressions are logically connected seems to be a pre-requisite for understanding both. This appears true of one of Lewis's favorite examples. The truth that all cats are animals is unlike the truth that all whales are mammals. One may know what whales are and what mammals are without being aware of the connection. But if one knows what cats are and what animals are, I believe he must see that cats are animals.

If a child seriously asks us whether cats are animals, I think he automatically raises doubt about his understanding of the two words 'cat' and 'animal'. If he has a pet cat and if he correctly identifies other cats, then probably we suspect his grasp of the concept of animality. Even if he seems to know that cows and various other beasts are animals—at least *says* they are—his doubt about cats does not sit easy with us.

Another truth in the same category is: Blue is a color. Can a child know what the word 'color' means, realize that yellow and red are colors, but maintain a doubt about blue? I think not. The one case is sufficient to cast a shadow over our confidence.

These considerations might lead us to say that the criteria for applying the word 'animal' (whatever they may be) are *always* included among the criteria for applying the word 'cat'. This is merely a way of expressing the difference between our second case and the first. A man may know what whales are without knowing they are mammals, even while understanding the word 'mammal'.

The reasons that lead one to say this, however, show that the doctrine of pre-existing connections is again inadequate. For no one can come to see that cats are animals or that blue is a color by discovering something about his criteria for applying the words involved. He cannot because he does not yet understand those words if doubts about these truths remain.

We decide that something is a cat by seeing what it looks like, how it behaves, etc. Having decided in this way that we are looking at a cat, and if we do not know that cats are mammals, we might investigate to see if this is a *mammal*.

But we cannot, it seems, in the same way investigate to see if it is an *animal*. For what has the *gestalt* of a cat has thereby the *gestalt* of an animal. Some have a more sophisticated understanding of the word 'whale'; they have added to their criteria the requirement of being a mammal. But there is not a more sophisticated understanding of the word 'cat' in which animality is made a requirement.

VI

The notion of inclusion of criteria seems to work best if we think of a term as having attached to it distinct sets of criteria in an additive fashion. The criteria we utilize in determining whether something is a whale are a certain shape, color, etc., *plus* the characteristics of a mammal. It seems very plausible to think of the attachment of criteria in this way for a term such as 'whale'. For we can easily imagine detaching from the concept any requirements having to do with mammalian characteristics, and this in fact seems to be the case concerning the less sophisticated use of the word. The same sort of idea is much less tempting in regard to the relationship between the words 'cat' and 'animal'. What would be left over if we subtract the requirement of animality?

But for a reason I have not so far mentioned it is with just such terms as 'whale', where the additive scheme seems most plausible, that the notion of inclusion of criteria appears to be weak as a basis for necessity. Just because the mammalian requirements are so easily detachable, it becomes dubious whether we can say with confidence that they are, even for the sophisticated, necessary to the correct application of the term, and hence, whether they are or are not included in the relevant sense.

Consider once more the discoveries that might convince us that some of those creatures we otherwise would have unhesitatingly called "whales" do not have mammalian characteristics. These creatures look like whales, and any mariner who had not learned that whales were mammals would call them whales. What is the zoologist or sophisticated layman to say?

It is not really clear that he would say unhesitatingly, "Those creatures are not whales because they are not mammals." Nor, on the other hand, is it clear that he would say that some whales are not mammals. So, apparently, it is simply not now possible to say either that mammalian characteristics are essential to whales or not. Or, in another terminology, that mammalian characteristics are or are not included among the criteria we use.

What is disturbing about this is that the sentence 'Whales are mammals' does not seem definitely to express either a necessary truth or a contingent truth. For if it did, then the question about what is correct to say about the hypothetical possibility of discovering that many of the creatures we have called "whales" lack mammalian characteristics ought to have a definite answer one way or the other.

Such cases are often handled by making a distinction between circumstances that call for a change in belief and circumstances that call for a change in meaning. Thus, if one wishes to hold on to the position that 'All whales are mammals' does express a necessary truth, he might say that the discovery of nonmammalian creatures looking just like whales may lead us to change the meaning of 'whale'. So if we then said that some whales are not mammals we would not contradict our present assertion that whales are all mammals. For 'whale' would mean two different things in the two cases. At present mammalian characteristics are a necessary condition, but in the changed situation, they might be dropped and a whale would be a large marine creature of certain characteristic shape, etc., which may or may not be a mammal.

An analogy with games may seem to help us in drawing the distinction. We can distinguish in a game moves that are either dictated or prohibited by rules from those which are made or not made because of tactical or strategical considerations. Thus in the opening position of chess, because it is not good tactics, P-R4 is not a move we make. But P-K5 is not made because it violates the rules. Now we can imagine that P-R4 comes to be made by good players: despite appearances it is discovered that it is not a bad move after all. We can also imagine that P-K5 comes to be made. But here the considerations that might prompt this change in the regularities of the game are going to be different. It is not, as things stand, an acceptable reason for making the initial move P-K5 that it puts us in a favorable position to win the game, as it would be if it could be shown to hold for P-R4. Rather the sorts of reasons we would give, reasons, we would say, for changing the rules, will have to lie in part outside the body of theory about tactics and strategy. For example, if, for the normal openings of white, a strategy has been developed for black that almost always leads to a dull but drawn game and if allowing P-K5 seems to eliminate this while still allowing black a fair chance to draw or win, then we might have a reason for changing the rules.

In the case of a game we seem to be able to draw a distinction between the sorts of reasons that might be given for the fact that a move which has heretofore not been played is now being adopted. In the one case the reasons will have to do solely with considerations of tactics and strategy, in the other they will have to do, roughly speaking, with the point of the game. Our question, then, is whether such a distinction can be drawn in the cases of the debatable counterexample to the necessity of 'All whales are mammals'.

Speaking in terms of the analogy, the reasons that are alleged to be reasons for adopting a new terminology rather than a new belief seem, unfortunately, to be strategy and tactics considerations rather than considerations about the point of the game. Supposedly there are two possible meanings for the word 'whale', in regard to one of which the connection between being a whale and being a mammal is necessary, while in regard to the other it is contingent. If we designate the first as 'whale$_1$' and the second as 'whale$_2$', then the view is that what we now hold to be true is that all whales$_1$ are mammals, and this is supposedly a necessary truth. Against the objection that if we were to discover that many of those creatures we have been calling "whales" do not have mammalian characteristics our response might well be to say that some whales are not mammals, it is alleged that this discovery might be a reason for shifting the meaning of 'whale' to that of 'whale₂'. But the supposed reason for shifting the meaning of 'whale' is not different in kind from reasons for shifting a belief. For it, the discovery about what we have been calling "whales" is on the hypothesis just the sort of reason which ought to lead to the belief that some whales₂ are not mammals. Hence it is the sort of reason which would lead us to change our belief, if we have it, in the truth of 'All whales₂ are mammals'. Without begging the question, we cannot support the position that we now mean one thing 'whale' but something different by it in the hypothetical situation through an attempt at distinguishing reasons for changing meaning from reasons for changing belief.

But, on the other hand, we cannot with assurance go to the other side and hold that after all 'Whales are mammals', as we now mean it, expresses a contingent statement. For it is not clear that the *correct* response to the hypothetical situation, according to our present usage, is to say that some whales are not mammals.

VII

The difficulty brought up in the last section may look as if it were a challenge to the distinction between questions about meaning and questions about facts. But that would be, I think, the wrong conclusion. Rather, what is shown is that there is a difficulty in holding that, e.g., 'All whales are mammals' *now* expresses a necessary truth, since in the face of a certain kind of counterexample the reply, "That would be to change the meaning of 'whale'," cannot be clearly supported. It is the distinction, in particular cases, between "*change* in meaning" and "*change* in belief" that seems to be in question. But if we were faced with the circumstances envisaged in the counterexample, e.g., the discovery that many things now called whales do not possess the characteristics of mammals, the alternative before us: to refuse to call those creatures whales, and to say that some whales are not mammals, may still call for a decision about meaning. Schematically, the situation is this: The decision we are faced with in certain circumstances, to opt for alternative *A* or alternative *B*, is a decision about meaning, but there is a question whether we can characterize either of these options as on the one hand preserving the meaning or on the other changing the meaning.

But it might be questioned whether we even have the right to mark the decision as one concerned with what we shall mean by, e.g., 'whale'. The argument I have in mind is the one which relies on the position that in the face of any experience we can hold on to any statement by appropriate denials and affirmations of others. Thus, if I hold that all cats drink milk and you produce a cat that turns up its nose at a bowl of milk, I might continue to affirm my statement by, for example, holding that the cat drinks milk surreptitiously while no one is looking. Here, on the basis of the same experiences, you are inclined to say one thing and I am inclined to say another. How are we to distinguish the choice in this example between your position and mine and the choice represented by the whale example? Is one a choice between opposing beliefs and the other a choice between ways of speaking?

The governing word, it seems to me, is 'choice'. We have a choice, in the whale example, between saying that whales are mammals and these creatures we have discovered are not whales and saying that some whales are not mammals. If, in these circumstances, I am inclined to say that these creatures simply are not whales while you want to represent the situation as the discovery that not all whales are mammals, we can easily come to see that our apparent disagreement is to be resolved by a decision to talk one way or the other. As soon as you see that I refuse to call these whales simply on the grounds that they are not mammals the apparent disagreement about the facts will vanish. You can state what has happened in my language and I in yours. (For example, "Some whales have been discovered not to be mammals" *versus* "Some creatures which in all other respects are just like whales have been discovered not to be mammals and hence not to be whales.")

But in the example about cats there is not, as yet at least, a place for this sort of accommodation. It may be true that I can hold on to the statement that all cats drink milk by explaining away every apparently falsifying experience. Eventually I may have to describe some as hallucinations or illusions. But the two of us are not faced with a *choice* as to whose way of describing the situation is to be used.

VIII

The only way we have of deciding what our present usage prescribes concerning hypothetical situations is now to pass a judgment on them. In doing this we are not, of course, predicting what in fact we would say. Rather we now say something about the situation. But where we cannot at present pass a judgment one way or the other there is nothing else we can appeal to as showing what is correct. There is no reason, a priori, why our present usage should legislate for all hypothetical cases. Given present circumstances, the correct thing to say is that all whales are mammals. But whether this is, as we intend it, a necessary truth or contingent is indeterminate. It is indeterminate because the decision as to which it is would depend upon our being able to say now what we should say about certain hypothetical cases. And evidently we are not prepared to do that.

If this is so, Lewis's idea that what criteria are attached to a given term as part of its meaning must be "fixed" in advance of experience seems to be false. And the corollary, that it would always be clear upon investigation whether or not the criteria attaching to one term are or are not included in those attaching to another is likewise false.

This is not to say that the concept of necessity is useless here. It might be thought of as an ideal rigidity in our judgments about what to say concerning hypothetical cases. I have dealt here only with the first of the two examples used in the first part of the paper. Whether a similar indeterminacy can be found concerning, say, the statement that all cats are animals I have not dealt with. If it can, then a more sweeping reinterpretation of the notion of necessity might be called for.

HILARY PUTNAM

1.3   *It Ain't Necessarily So*

The two statements that Donnellan considered in his paper [see above] are both more or less analytic in character. By that I mean that they are the sort of statement that most people would consider to be true by definition, if they considered them to be necessary truths at all. One might quarrel about whether 'all whales are mammals' is a necessary truth at all. But if one considers it to be a necessary truth, then one would consider it to be true by definition. And, similarly, most people would say that 'all cats are animals' is true by definition, notwithstanding the fact that they would be hard put to answer the question, "true by *what* definition?"

I like what Donnellan had to say about these statements, and I liked especially the remark that occurs toward the end of his paper, that there are situations in which we are confronted by a question about how to talk, but in which it is not possible to describe one of the available decisions as deciding to retain our old way of talking (or "not to change the meaning") and the other as deciding to adopt a "new" way of talking (or to "change the meaning").

In this paper I want to concentrate mostly on statements that look necessary, but that are not analytic; on "synthetic necessary truths," so to speak. This is not to say that there are not serious problems connected with analyticity. On the contrary, there certainly are. The general area of necessary truths might be broken up, at least for the sake of preliminary exploration (and we philosophers are still in the stage of preliminary exploration even after thousands of years) into three main subareas: the area of analytic truths, the area of logical and mathematical truths, and the area of "synthetic a priori" truths. I don't mean to beg any questions by this division. Thus, separating logical and mathematical truths from analytic truths is not meant to prejudge the question whether they are or are not ultimately analytic.

Reprinted from *The Journal of Philosophy*, LIX, No. 22 (1962), 658–71, by permission of the author and of *The Journal of Philosophy*.

I. ANALYTIC TRUTHS

The "analyticity" of 'all cats are animals' or, what is closely related, the redundancy of the expression 'a cat which is an animal' seems to depend on the fact that the word 'animal' is the name of a semantic category[1] and the word 'cat' is a member of that category.

In an earlier paper[2] I called words that have an analytic definition "one-criterion words." Many words that are not one-criterion words fall into semantic categories—in fact, all nouns fall into semantic categories. 'House', for example, falls into the semantic category *material object*, 'red' falls into the semantic category *color*, and so on. Thus, for any noun one can find an analytic or quasi-analytic truth of the sort 'a cat is an animal', 'a house is a material object', 'red is a color', and so forth. But it hardly follows that all nouns are one-criterion words—in fact, there are only a few hundred one-criterion words in English.

It is important to distinguish "analytic" truths of the sort 'all cats are animals' from analytic truths of the sort 'all bachelors are unmarried', in part because the former tend to be *less* necessary than the latter. It might not be the case that all cats are animals; they might be automata!

There are, in fact, several possibilities. If *some* cats are animals in every sense of the word, while others are automata, then there is no problem. I think we would all agree that these others were neither animals nor cats but only fake cats—very realistic and very clever fakes to be sure, but fakes nonetheless. Suppose, however, that all cats on earth are automata. In that case the situation is more complex. We should ask the question, "Were there *ever* living cats?" If, let us say, up to fifty years ago there were living cats and the Martians killed all of them and replaced them all overnight with robots that look exactly like cats and can't be told from cats by present-day biologists (although, let us say, biologists will be able to detect the fake in fifty years more), then I think we should again say that the animals we all call cats are not in fact cats, and also not in fact animals, but robots. It is clear how we should talk in this case: "there were cats up to fifty years ago; there aren't any any longer. Because of a very exceptional combination of circumstances we did not discover this fact until this time."

Suppose, however, that there never have been cats, i.e., genuine non-fake cats. Suppose evolution has produced many things that come close to the cat but that it never actually produced the cat, and that the cat as we know it is and always was an artifact. Every movement of a cat, every twitch of a muscle, every meow, every flicker of an eyelid is thought out by a man in a control

---

[1] The notion of a "semantic category" is taken from J. A. Fodor and Jerrold Katz, "The Structure of a Semantic Theory." [See selection 6.1 below, pp. 472–514.]

[2] "The Analytic and the Synthetic," in Herbert Feigl and Grover Maxwell, eds., *Minnesota Studies in the Philosophy of Science*, Vol. III. [See selection 1.6 below, pp. 94–126.]

center on Mars and is then executed by the cat's body as the result of signals that emanate not from the cat's "brain" but from a highly miniaturized radio receiver located, let us say, in the cat's pineal gland. It seems to me that in this last case, once we discovered the fake, we should continue to call these robots that we have mistaken for animals and that we have employed as house pets "cats," but not "animals."

This is the sort of problem that Donnellan discussed in connection with the "all whales are mammals" case. Once we find out that cats were created from the beginning by Martians, that they are not self-directed, that they are automata, and so on, then it is clear that we have a problem of how to speak. What is not clear is which of the available decisions should be described as the decision to keep the meaning of either word ('cat' or 'animal') unchanged, and which decision should be described as the decision to change the meaning. I agree with Donnellan that this question has no clear sense. My own feeling is that to say that cats turned out not to be animals is to keep the meaning of both words unchanged. Someone else may feel that the correct thing to say is, "It's turned out that there aren't and never were any cats." Someone else may feel that the correct thing to say is, "It's turned out that some animals are robots." Today it doesn't seem to make much difference what we say; while in the context of a developed linguistic theory it may make a difference whether we say that talking in one of these ways is changing the meaning and talking in another of these ways is keeping the meaning unchanged. But that is hardly relevant here and now; when linguistic theory becomes *that* developed, then 'meaning' will itself have become a technical term, and presumably our question now is not which decision is changing the meaning in some future technical sense of 'meaning', but what we can say in our present language.

II. SYNTHETIC NECESSARY STATEMENTS

Later I shall make a few remarks about the truths of logic and mathematics. For the moment, let me turn to statements of quite a different kind, for example, the statement that *if one did X and then Y, X must have been done at an earlier time than Y*, or the statement that *space has three dimensions*, or the statement that *the relation earlier than is transitive*. All of these statements are still classified as necessary by philosophers today. Those who feel that the first statement is "conceptually necessary" reject time travel as a "conceptual impossibility."

Once again I will beg your pardon for engaging in philosophical science fiction. I want to imagine that something has happened (which is in fact a possibility) namely, that modern physics has *definitely* come to the conclusion that space is Riemannian. Now, with this assumption in force, let us discuss the status of the statement that *one cannot reach the place from which one came by traveling away from it in a straight line and continuing to move in a constant sense*. This is a geometrical statement. I want to understand it, however, not as a statement of pure geometry, not as a statement about space "in the abstract," but as a statement about physical space, about the space in which we live and move and have our being. It may be claimed that in that space, in the space of actual physical experience, the notion of a "straight line" has no application, because straight lines are supposed to have no thickness at all and not the slightest variation in curvature, and we cannot identify by any physical means paths in space with these properties (although we can approximate them as closely as we desire). However, this is not relevant in the present context. Approximate straight lines will do. In fact, it is possible to state one of the differences between a Riemannian and a Euclidean world *without using* the notion of "straightness" at all. Suppose that by a "place" we agree to mean, for the nonce, a cubical spatial region whose volume is one thousand cubic feet. Then, in a Riemannian world, there are only a finite number of disjoint "places." There is no path, curved *or* straight, on which one can "go sight-seeing" in a Riemannian world and hope to see more than a certain number N of disjoint "places." Thus, the statement that *one can see as many distinct disjoint places as one likes if one travels far enough along a suitable path* is one which is true in any Euclidean world, and not in any Riemannian world.

Now, I think it is intuitively clear that the two propositions just mentioned: that one cannot return to one's starting point by traveling on a straight line unless one reverses the sense of one's motion at some point, and that one can visit an arbitrary number of distinct and disjoint "places" by continuing far enough on a suitable path—that is, that there is no finite upper bound on the total number of "places"—had the *status of* necessary truths before the nineteenth century.

Let me say, of a statement that enjoys the status with respect to a body of knowledge that these statements enjoyed before the nineteenth century and that the other statements alluded to enjoy today, that it is "necessary *relative to* the appropriate body of knowledge." This notion of *necessity relative to a body of knowledge* is a technical notion being introduced here for special purposes and to which we give special properties. In particular, when we say that a statement is necessary relative to a body of knowledge, we imply that it is included in that body of knowledge and that it enjoys a special role in that body of knowledge. For example, one is not expected to give much of a reason for that kind of statement. But we do not imply that the statement is necessarily *true*, although, of course, it is thought to be true by someone whose knowledge that body of knowledge is.

We are now confronted with this problem: a statement that was necessary relative to a body of knowledge later came to be declared false in science. What can we say about this?

Many philosophers have found it tempting to say that nothing significant happened, that we simply changed the meaning of words. This is to assimilate the case to Donnellan's first case, the whales-mammals case. Just as 'whale' may, perhaps, have two meanings—one for laymen and one for scientists—so 'straight line' may have two meanings, one for laymen and one for scientists. Paths that are straight in the layman's sense may not be straight in the scientist's sense, and paths that are straight in the scientist's sense may not be straight in the layman's sense. One cannot come back to one's starting point by proceeding indefinitely on a path that is straight in the old Euclidean sense; when the scientist says that one can come back to one's starting point by continuing long enough on a straight line, there is no paradox and no contradiction with common sense. What he means by a straight line may be a curved line in the layman's sense, and we all *know* you can come back to your starting point by continuing long enough on a closed curve.

This account is not tenable, however. To see that it isn't, let us shift to the second statement. Here we are in immediate difficulties because there seems to be *no* difference, even today, between the layman's sense of 'path' and the scientist's sense of 'path'. Anything that the layman could trace out if we gave him but world enough and time, the scientists would accept as a "path," and anything that the scientist would trace out as a "path," the layman would accept as a "path." (Here I do not count microscopic "paths" as paths.) Similarly with 'place'. To put it another way: if Euclidean geometry is only apparently false owing to a change in the meaning of words, then if we keep the meanings of the words *unchanged*, if we use the words in the old way, Euclidean geometry must *still* be true. In that case, in addition to the N "places" to which one can get by following the various paths in our Riemannian space, there must be infinitely many additional "places" to which one can get by following other paths that somehow the scientist has overlooked. Where are these places? Where are these other paths? In fact, they don't exist. If someone believes that they exist, then he must invent special physical laws to explain why, try as we may, we never succeed in seeing one of these other places or in sticking to one of these other paths. If someone did accept such laws and insisted on holding on to Euclidean geometry in the face of all present scientific experience, it is clear that he would not have simply "made a decision to keep the meanings of words unchanged"; he would have adopted a metaphysical theory.

The statement that *there are only finitely many disjoint "places" to get to, travel as you may* expresses a downright "conceptual impossibility" within the framework of Euclidean geometry. And one cannot say that *all* that has happened is that we have changed the meaning of the word 'path', because in that case one would be committed to the metaphysical hypothesis that, in addition to the "paths" that are *still* so called, there exist others which are somehow physically inaccessible and additional "places" which are somehow physically inaccessible and which, together with what the physicists presently recognize as places and paths, fill out a Euclidean space.

Insofar as the terms 'place', 'path', and 'straight line' have any application at all in physical space, they still have the application they always had; something that was literally inconceivable has turned out to be true.

Incidentally, although modern physics does not *yet* say that space is Riemannian, it does say that our space has variable curvature. This means that if two light rays stay a constant distance apart for a long time and then come closer together after passing the sun, we do *not* say that these two light rays are following curved paths through space, but we say rather that they follow straight paths and that two straight paths may have a constant distance from each other for a long time and then later have a decreasing distance from each other. Once again, if anyone wishes to say, "Well, those paths aren't straight in the old sense of 'straight'," then I invite him to tell me *which* paths in the space near the sun are "really straight." And I guarantee that, first, no matter which paths no chooses as the straight ones, I will be able to embarrass him acutely. I will be able to show, for example, not only that light rays refuse to travel along the paths he claims to be really straight, but that they are not the shortest paths by any method of measurement he may elect; one cannot even travel along those paths in a rocket ship without accelerations, decelerations, twists, turns, etc. In short, the paths he claims are "really straight" will look crooked, act crooked, and feel crooked. Moreover, if anyone does say that certain non-geodesics are the really straight paths in the space near the sun, then his decision will have to be a quite arbitrary one; and the theory that more or less *arbitrarily* selected curved paths near the sun are "really straight" (because they obey the laws of Euclidean geometry and the geodesics do not) would again be a metaphysical theory, and the decision to accept it would certainly *not* be a mere decision to "keep the meaning of words unchanged."

III. THE CLUSTER CHARACTER OF GEOMETRIC NOTIONS

Distance cannot be "operationally defined" as distance according to an aluminum ruler, nor as distance according to a wooden ruler, nor as distance according to an iron ruler, nor as distance according to an optical measuring instrument, nor in terms of any other *one* operational criterion. The criteria we have for distance define the notion collectively, not individually, and the connection between any one criterion and the rest of the bundle may be viewed as completely synthetic. For example, there is no contradiction involved in supposing that light sometimes travels in curved lines. It is because of the cluster character of geometrical concepts that the methods usually suggested by operationists for demonstrating the falsity of Euclidean geometry by isolated experiments would not have succeeded before the development of non-Euclidean geometry. If someone had been able to construct a very large light-ray triangle and had shown that the sum of the angles exceeded 180°, even allowing for measuring errors, he would not have shown the ancient Greek that Euclidean geometry was false, but only that light did not travel in straight lines.

What accounted for the necessity of the principles of Euclidean geometry relative to pre-nineteenth-century knowledge? An answer would be difficult to give in detail, but I believe that the general outlines of an answer are not hard to see. Spatial locations play an obviously fundamental role in all of our scientific knowledge and in many of the operations of daily life. The use of spatial locations requires, however, the acceptance of some systematic body of geometrical theory. To abandon Euclidean geometry before non-Euclidean geometry was invented would be to "let our concepts crumble."

IV. TIME TRAVEL

I believe that an attempt to describe in ordinary language what time travel would be like can easily lead to absurdities and even downright contradictions. But if one has a mathematical technique of representing all the phenomena subsumed under some particular notion of "time travel," then it is easy to work out a way of speaking, and even a way of thinking, corresponding to the mathematical technique. A mathematical technique for representing at least one set of occurrences that might be meant by the term 'time travel' already exists. This is the technique of *world lines* and Minkowski space-time diagrams. Thus, suppose, for example, that a time traveler—we'll call him Oscar Smith—and his apparatus have world lines as shown in the diagram.

From the diagram we can at once read off what an observer sees at various times. At t_0, for example, he sees Oscar Smith not yet a time traveler. At time t_1 he still sees Oscar Smith at place A, but also he sees something else at place B. At place B he sees, namely, an event of "creation"—not "particle-antiparticle creation," but the creation of two macro-objects which separate. One of these macro-objects is easily described. It is simply an older Oscar Smith, or an

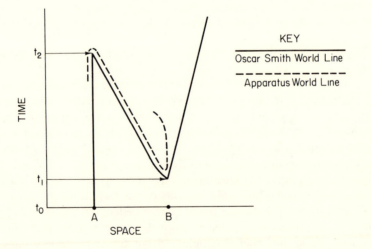

individual resembling in all possible ways an older version of Oscar Smith, together with the apparatus of a time machine. The world-line diagram shows that the older Oscar—let's call him Oscar$_3$—leaves his time machine. The other object that was created in the same event is a somewhat peculiar object. It is a system consisting of a third Oscar Smith, or, more precisely, of a body like that of Oscar Smith, seated in a time machine. But this system consisting of the Oscar Smith body and the time machine is a very exceptional physical system. If we take a moving picture of this physical system during its entire period of existence, we will find that if that movie is played backward then the events in it are all normal. In short, this is a system running backward in time—entropy in the system is decreasing instead of increasing, cigarette butts are growing into whole cigarettes, the Oscar Smith body is emitting noises that resemble speech sounds played backward, and so forth. This system that is running backward in time continues to exist until the time t_2, when it merges with Oscar Smith, and we see annihilation—not "particle-antiparticle annihilation," but the annihilation of the real Oscar Smith and the running-backward system. During a certain period of time, there are three Oscar Smiths: Oscar Smith$_1$, Oscar Smith$_3$, and the Oscar Smith who is living backward in time (Oscar Smith$_2$, we shall call him). We can even predict subjective phenomena from the word-line diagram. We can say, for example, what sort of memories Oscar Smith$_3$ has at the moment of his "creation." He has, namely, all the memories that someone would have if he had all the experiences of Oscar$_1$ up to the moment of his annihilation and then all the experiences shown as occurring to the living-backward Oscar, Oscar$_2$, on a movie film, provided the movie film is reversed so that these experiences are shown as happening in the normal order. I have no doubt whatsoever as to how any reasonable scientist would describe these events, if they actually transpired. He would interpret them in terms of the world-line diagram; i.e., he would say: "There are not really three Oscar Smiths; there is only one Oscar Smith. The Oscar Smith you call Oscar Smith$_1$ lives forward in time until the time t_2; at t_2 his world line for some reason bends backward in time, and he lives backward in time from t_2 back to the time t_1. At t_1 he starts living forward in time again and continues living forward in time for the rest of his life."

I remember having a discussion concerning time travel with a philosopher friend a number of years ago. I told him the story I have just told you. My friend's view, in a nutshell, was that time travel was a conceptual impossibility. The phenomena I described can, of course, be imagined; but they are correctly described in the way I first described them; i.e., Oscar Smith$_1$ lives until t_2, at which time he collides with the strange system. When the two systems merge, they are both annihilated. At the time t_1 this strange physical system was created, as was also another individual very much resembling Oscar Smith$_1$, but with an entirely fictitious set of memories including, incidentally, memories of Oscar Smith$_1$'s existence up to the time t_2.

Let us ask ourselves what makes us so sure that there is here a consistently imaginable set of circumstances to be described. The answer is that it is the mathematical representation, i.e., the world-line diagram itself, that gives us this assurance. Similarly, in the case of space with variable curvature, near the sun, the only thing that makes us sure that there is a consistently imaginable set of phenomena to be described is their representation in terms of the mathematics of non-Euclidean geometry.

The present case also exhibits *dis*analogies to the geometric case. In the geometric case we could not go on using language in the old way—if to preserve Euclidean geometry is to go on using language in the old way—without finding ourselves committed to ghost places and ghost paths. In the present case, we can go on using language in the old way—if my friend's way of describing the situation *is* the one which corresponds to "using language in the old way"— without having to countenance any ghost entities. But there are a host of difficulties which make us doubt whether to speak in this way is to go on using language without any change of usage or meaning. First of all, consider the sort of system that a physicist would describe as a "human being living backward in time." The same system would be described by my friend not as a *person* at all, but as a human *body* going through a rather nauseating succession of physical states. Thus, on my friend's account, $Oscar_2$ is not a person at all, and $Oscar_1$ and $Oscar_3$ are two quite different persons. $Oscar_1$ is a person who had a normal life up to the time t_2 when something very abnormal happened to him, *namely, he vanished*, and $Oscar_3$ is a person who had a normal life from the time t_1 on, but who came into existence in a very abnormal way: *he appeared out of thin air*. Consider now the legal problems that might arise and whose resolution might depend on whether we accepted the physicist's account or the account of my friend. Suppose $Oscar_1$ murders someone but is not apprehended before the time at which he vanishes. Can we or can we not punish $Oscar_3$ for $Oscar_1$'s crime? On the physicist's account, $Oscar_3$ *is* $Oscar_1$, only grown older, and can hence be held responsible for all the actions of $Oscar_1$. On my friend's account, $Oscar_3$ is only a person under the unfortunate delusion that he is $Oscar_1$ grown older, and should be treated with appropriate kindness rather than punishment. And, of course, no one is responsible for $Oscar_2$'s actions on this view, since they are not really *actions* at all. And if $Oscar_1$'s wife lives with $Oscar_3$ after t_2, she is guilty of unlawful cohabitation, while if she lives with $Oscar_3$ prior to t_2, the lady is guilty of adultery. In this kind of case, to go into court and tell the story as my friend would tell it would be to use language in a most *extraordinary* way.

This case differs importantly from Donnellan's cases in that, although our problem can be described as a problem of how to speak, it is not merely a problem of how to speak, since moral and social questions depend on how we decide to speak.

V. CONCLUSIONS

In the last few years I have been amused and irritated by the spate of articles proving that time travel is a "conceptual impossibility." All these articles make the same mistake. They take it to be enough to show that, if we start talking about time travel, things go wrong with ordinary language in countless places and in countless ways. For example, it makes no sense to *prevent an occurrence that is in the past*, yet a time traveler about to visit the Ice Age in his time machine may well take an overcoat to keep from freezing to death several million years *ago.* Exactly similar objections could have been raised against the notion of there being only finitely many "places" prior to the development of Riemannian geometry. It is precisely the existence of the world-line language that makes us sure that all these apparently insurmountable difficulties about "preventing," "expecting," etc., can be met. For example, the proper way to reformulate the principle that it makes no sense to prevent an occurrence in the past is to introduce the relativistic notion of *proper time*, i.e., time along the world line, and to say that it makes no sense to prevent an occurrence not in one's proper future. Also, even if an event is in one's proper future, but one already knows its outcome, say, because it is in the objective past and has been recorded, then it cannot be prevented (although one can try). For example, if reliable records show that an older self of you is going to freeze to death two million years ago, then, try as you may, you will not succeed in preventing this event. But this actually introduces nothing new into human life; it is the analogue of the principle that, if you know with certainty that something is going to happen to you in the future, then, try as you may, you won't succeed in forestalling it. It is just that there is a new way of knowing with certainty that something is going to happen to you in your proper future—namely, if your proper future happens to be also your present past, then you may be able to know with certainty what will happen to you *by using records.*

The principle of the transitivity of the relation *earlier than* involves similar considerations. If the world line of the universe as a whole happened to be a closed curve, then we should have to abandon that principle altogether. As Gödel has pointed out,[3] there is no contradiction with General Relativity in the supposition that the universe may have a closed world line.

The history of the causal principle is yet another case in point. Before quantum mechanics, if we found that an event *A* was sometimes succeeded by an event *B* and sometimes by a different event *B'*, this was taken as *conclusive* proof that there were factors, say *C* and *C'*, differing in the two situations. Physicists abandoned the principle that in such cases one should *always* postulate such unknown factors only because a worked-out mathematical language of an acausal character appeared on the scene, the mathematical language of unitary transformation and projections that is used in quantum mechanics. This is a mathematical way of representing phenomena, but it is not *just* a mathematical way of representing phenomena. Once again, it influences the way in which ordinary men decide questions. When cases arise of the sort Donnellan foresaw in his paper, then ordinary men may choose one way of speaking over another precisely because one way of speaking links up with a scientific way of talking and thinking whereas the other way of speaking does not link up with *any* coherent conceptual system.

The causality case is analogous to the geometry case in that the decision to preserve the older way of speaking—that is, to say, whenever an event *A* appears to produce either of two different events *B* and *B'*, that there must

---

[3] Kurt Gödel, "A Remark about the Relationship between Relativity Theory and Idealistic Philosophy," in Paul Arthur Schilpp, ed., *Albert Einstein: Philosopher-Scientist.*

be some hidden difference in the attendant circumstances—involves postulating ghost entities. The ghost entities in question are called "hidden variables" in the literature of quantum mechanics.

I am inclined to think that the situation is not substantially different in logic and mathematics. I believe that if I had the time I could describe for you a case in which we would have a choice between accepting a physical theory based upon a nonstandard logic, on the one hand, and retaining standard logic and postulating hidden variables on the other. In this case, too, the decision to retain the old logic is not merely the decision to keep the meaning of certain words unchanged, for it has physical and perhaps metaphysical consequences. In quantum mechanics, for example, the customary interpretation says that an electron does not have a definite position prior to a position measurement; the position measurement causes the electron to take on suddenly the property that we call its "position" (this is the so-called "quantum jump"). Attempts to work out a theory of quantum jumps and of measurement in quantum mechanics have been notoriousy unsuccessful to date. Recently it has been pointed out[4] that it is entirely unnecessary to postulate the absence of sharp values prior to measurement and the occurrence of quantum jumps, if we are willing to regard quantum mechanics as a theory formalized within a certain nonstandard logic, the modular logic proposed in 1935 by Birkhoff and von Neumann, for precisely the purpose of formalizing quantum mechanics.

There seems to be only one conclusion to come to, and I herewith come to it. The distinction between statements necessary relative to a body of knowledge and statements contingent relative to that body of knowledge is an important methodological distinction and should not be jettisoned. But the traditional philosophical distinction between statements necessary in some eternal sense and statements contingent in some eternal sense is not workable. The rescuing move which consists in saying that if a statement which appears to be necessary relative to a body of knowledge at one time is not necessary relative to the body of knowledge at a later time, then it is not really the same statement that is involved, that words have changed their meaning, and that the old statement would still be a necessary truth if the meanings of the words had been kept unchanged, is unsuccessful. The rescuing move which consists in saying that such statements were only mistaken to be necessary truths, that they were contingent statements all along, and that their "necessity" was "merely psychological" is just the other side of the same blunder. For the difference between statements that can be overthrown by merely conceiving of suitable experiments and statements that can be overthrown only by conceiving of whole new theoretical structures—sometimes structures, like Relativity and Quantum Mechanics, that change our whole way of reasoning about nature—is of logical and methodological significance, and not just of psychological interest.

---

[4] This was pointed out by David Finkelstein in his lecture to the informal subgroup on Measurement in Quantum Mechanics at the Boulder Symposium on Mathematical Physics, sponsored by the American Mathematical Society in the summer of 1960.

WILLARD VAN ORMAN QUINE

1.4   *Two Dogmas of Empiricism*

Modern empiricism has been conditioned in large part by two dogmas. One is a belief in some fundamental cleavage between truths which are *analytic*, or grounded in meanings independently of matters of fact, and truths which are *synthetic*, or grounded in fact. The other dogma is *reductionism*: the belief that each meaningful statement is equivalent to some logical construct upon terms which refer to immediate experience. Both dogmas, I shall argue, are ill-founded. One effect of abandoning them is, as we shall see, a blurring of the supposed boundary between speculative metaphysics and natural science. Another effect is a shift toward pragmatism.

1. BACKGROUND FOR ANALYTICITY

Kant's cleavage between analytic and synthetic truths was foreshadowed in Hume's distinction between relations of ideas and matters of fact, and in Leibniz's distinction between truths of reason and truths of fact. Leibniz spoke of the truths of reason as true in all possible worlds. Picturesqueness aside, this is to say that the truths of reason are those which could not possibly be false. In the same vein we hear analytic statements defined as statements whose denials are self-contradictory. But this definition has small explanatory value; for the notion of self-contradictoriness, in the quite broad sense needed for this definition of analyticity, stands in exactly the same need of clarification as does the notion of analyticity itself. The two notions are the two sides of a single dubious coin.

Kant conceived of an analytic statement as one that attributes to its subject no more than is already conceptually contained in the subject. This formulation has two shortcomings: it limits itself to statements of subject-predicate form, and it appeals to a notion of containment which is left at a metaphorical level. But Kant's intent, evident more from the use he makes of the notion of analyticity than from his definition of it, can be restated thus: a statement is analytic when it is true by virtue of meanings and independently of fact. Pursuing this line, let us examine the concept of *meaning* which is presupposed.

Meaning, let us remember, is not to be identified with naming. Frege's example of 'Evening Star' and 'Morning Star', and Russell's of 'Scott' and

Reprinted by permission of the author and of the publishers from W. V. O. Quine, *From A Logical Point of View* (Cambridge, Mass.: Harvard University Press, Copyright 1953, 1961, by the President and Fellows of Harvard College), pp. 20–46.

'the author of *Waverley*', illustrate that terms can name the same thing but differ in meaning. The distinction between meaning and naming is no less important at the level of abstract terms. The terms '9' and 'the number of the planets' name one and the same abstract entity but presumably must be regarded as unlike in meaning; for astronomical observation was needed, and not mere reflection on meanings, to determine the sameness of the entity in question.

The above examples consist of singular terms, concrete and abstract. With general terms, or predicates, the situation is somewhat different but parallel. Whereas a singular term purports to name an entity, abstract or concrete, a general term does not; but a general term is *true of* an entity, or of each of many, or of none. The class of all entities of which a general term is true is called the *extension* of the term. Now paralleling the contrast between the meaning of a singular term and the entity named, we must distinguish equally between the meaning of a general term and its extension. The general terms 'creature with a heart' and 'creature with kidneys', for example, are perhaps alike in extension but unlike in meaning.

Confusion of meaning with extension, in the case of general terms, is less common than confusion of meaning with naming in the case of singular terms. It is indeed a commonplace in philosophy to oppose intension (or meaning) to extension, or, in a variant vocabulary, connotation to denotation.

The Aristotelian notion of essence was the forerunner, no doubt, of the modern notion of intension or meaning. For Aristotle it was essential in men to be rational, accidental to be two-legged. But there is an important difference between this attitude and the doctrine of meaning. From the latter point of view it may indeed be conceded (if only for the sake of argument) that rationality is involved in the meaning of the word 'man' while two-leggedness is not; but two-leggedness may at the same time be viewed as involved in the meaning of 'biped' while rationality is not. Thus from the point of view of the doctrine of meaning it makes no sense to say of the actual individual, who is at once a man and a biped, that his rationality is essential and his two-leggedness accidental or vice versa. Things had essences for Aristotle, but only linguistic forms have meanings. Meaning is what essence becomes when it is divorced from the object of reference and wedded to the word.

For the theory of meaning a conspicuous question is the nature of its objects: what sort of things are meanings? A felt need for meant entities may derive from an earlier failure to appreciate that meaning and reference are distinct. Once the theory of meaning is sharply separated from the theory of reference, it is a short step to recognizing as the primary business of the theory of meaning simply the synonymy of linguistic forms and the analyticity of statements; meanings themselves, as obscure intermediary entities, may well be abandoned.

The problem of analyticity then confronts us anew. Statements which are analytic by general philosophical acclaim are not, indeed, far to seek. They fall into two classes. Those of the first class, which may be called *logically true*, are typified by:

(1) No unmarried man is married.

The relevant feature of this example is that it not merely is true as it stands, but remains true under any and all reinterpretations of 'man' and 'married'. If we suppose a prior inventory of *logical* particles, comprising 'no', 'un-', 'not', 'if', 'then', 'and', etc., then in general a logical truth is a statement which is true and remains true under all reinterpretations of its components other than the logical particles.

But there is also a second class of analytic statements, typified by:

(2) No bachelor is married.

The characteristic of such a statement is that it can be turned into a logical truth by putting synonyms for synonyms; thus (2) can be turned into (1) by putting 'unmarried man' for its synonym 'bachelor'. We still lack a proper characterization of this second class of analytic statements, and therewith of analyticity generally, inasmuch as we have had in the above description to lean on a notion of "synonymy" which is no less in need of clarification than analyticity itself.

In recent years Carnap has tended to explain analyticity by appeal to what he calls state-descriptions.[1] A state-description is any exhaustive assignment of truth values to the atomic, or noncompound, statements of the language. All other statements of the language are, Carnap assumes, built up of their component clauses by means of the familiar logical devices, in such a way that the truth value of any complex statement is fixed for each state-description by specifiable logical laws. A statement is then explained as analytic when it comes out true under every state description. This account is an adaptation of Leibniz's "true in all possible worlds." But note that this version of analyticity serves its purpose only if the atomic statements of the language are, unlike 'John is a bachelor' and 'John is married', mutually independent. Otherwise there would be a state-description which assigned truth to 'John is a bachelor' and to 'John is married', and consequently 'No bachelors are married' would turn out synthetic rather than analytic under the proposed criterion. Thus the criterion of analyticity in terms of state-descriptions serves only for languages devoid of extralogical synonym-pairs, such as 'bachelor' and 'unmarried man'—synonym-pairs of the type which give rise to the "second class" of analytic statements. The criterion in terms of state-descriptions is a reconstruction at best of logical truth, not of analyticity.

I do not mean to suggest that Carnap is under any illusions on this point. His simplified model language with its state-descriptions is aimed primarily not at the general problem of analyticity but at another purpose, the clarification of probability and induction. Our problem, however, is analyticity; and here the major difficulty lies not in the first class of analytic statements, the logical truths, but rather in the second class, which depends on the notion of synonymy.

---

[1] Carnap [1], pp. 9ff; [2], pp. 70ff.

2. DEFINITION

There are those who find it soothing to say that the analytic statements of the second class reduce to those of the first class, the logical truths, by *definition;* 'bachelor', for example, is *defined* as 'unmarried man'. But how do we find that 'bachelor' is defined as 'unmarried man'? Who defined it thus, and when? Are we to appeal to the nearest dictionary, and accept the lexicographer's formulation as law? Clearly this would be to put the cart before the horse. The lexicographer is an empirical scientist, whose business is the recording of antecedent facts; and if he glosses 'bachelor' as 'unmarried man' it is because of his belief that there is a relation of synonymy between those forms, implicit in general or preferred usage prior to his own work. The notion of synonymy presupposed here has still to be clarified, presumably in terms relating to linguistic behavior. Certainly the "definition" which is the lexicographer's report of an observed synonymy cannot be taken as the ground of the synonymy.

Definition is not, indeed, an activity exclusively of philologists. Philosophers and scientists frequently have occasion to "define" a recondite term by paraphrasing it into terms of a more familiar vocabulary. But ordinarily such a definition, like the philologist's, is pure lexicography, affirming a relation of synonymy antecedent to the exposition in hand.

Just what it means to affirm synonymy, just what the interconnections may be which are necessary and sufficient in order that two linguistic forms be properly describable as synonymous, is far from clear; but, whatever these interconnections may be, ordinarily they are grounded in usage. Definitions reporting selected instances of synonymy come then as reports upon usage.

There is also, however, a variant type of definitional activity which does not limit itself to the reporting of preëxisting synonymies. I have in mind what Carnap calls *explication*—an activity to which philosophers are given, and scientists also in their more philosophical moments. In explication the purpose is not merely to paraphrase the definiendum into an outright synonym, but actually to improve upon the definiendum by refining or supplementing its meaning. But even explication, though not merely reporting a preëxisting synonymy between definiendum and definiens, does rest nevertheless on *other* preexisting synonymies. The matter may be viewed as follows. Any word worth explicating has some contexts which, as wholes, are clear and precise enough to be useful; and the purpose of explication is to preserve the usage of these favored contexts while sharpening the usage of other contexts. In order that a given definition be suitably for purposes of explication, therefore, what is required is not that the definiendum in its antecedent usage be synonymous with the definiens, but just that each of these favored contexts of the definiendum, taken as a whole in its antecedent usage, be synonymous with the corresponding context of the definiens.

Two alternative definientia may be equally appropriate for the purposes of a given task of explication and yet not be synonymous with each other; for they may serve interchangeably within the favored contexts but diverge elsewhere. By cleaving to one of these definientia rather than the other, a definition of explicative kind generates, by fiat, a relation of synonymy between definiendum and definiens which did not hold before. But such a definition still owes its explicative function, as seen, to preëxisting synonymies.

There does, however, remain still an extreme sort of definition which does not hark back to prior synonymies at all: namely, the explicitly conventional introduction of novel notations for purposes of sheer abbreviation. Here the definiendum becomes synonymous with the definiens simply because it has been created expressly for the purpose of being synonymous with the definiens. Here we have a really transparent case of synonymy created by definition; would that all species of synonymy were as intelligible. For the rest, definition rests on synonymy rather than explaining it.

The word 'definition' has come to have a dangerously reassuring sound, owing no doubt to its frequent occurrence in logical and mathematical writings. We shall do well to digress now into a brief appraisal of the role of definition in formal work.

In logical and mathematical systems either of two mutually antagonistic types of economy may be striven for, and each has its peculiar practical utility. On the one hand we may seek economy of practical expression—ease and brevity in the statement of multifarious relations. This sort of economy calls usually for distinctive concise notations for a wealth of concepts. Second, however, and oppositely, we may seek economy in grammar and vocabulary; we may try to find a minimum of basic concepts such that, once a distinctive notation has been appropriated to each of them, it becomes possible to express any desired further concept by mere combination and iteration of our basic notations. This second sort of economy is impractical in one way, since a poverty in basic idioms tends to a necessary lengthening of discourse. But it is practical in another way: it greatly simplifies theoretical discourse *about* the language, through minimizing the terms and the forms of construction wherein the language consists.

Both sorts of economy, though prima facie incompatible, are valuable in their separate ways. The custom has consequently arisen of combining both sorts of economy by forging in effect two languages, the one a part of the other. The inclusive language, though redundant in grammar and vocabulary, is economical in message lengths, while the part, called primitive notation, is economical in grammar and vocabulary. Whole and part are correlated by rules of translation whereby each idiom not in primitive notation is equated to some complex built up of primitive notation. These rules of translation are the so-called *definitions* which appear in formalized systems. They are best viewed not as adjuncts to one language but as correlations between two languages, the one a part of the other.

But these correlations are not arbitrary. They are supposed to show how the primitive notations can accomplish all purposes, save brevity and convenience, of the redundant language. Hence the definiendum and its definiens may be expected, in each case, to be related in one or another of the three ways lately noted. The definiens may be a faithful paraphrase of the definiendum into the narrower notation, preserving a direct synonymy[2] as of antecedent usage; or the definiens may, in the spirit of explication, improve upon the antecedent usage of the definiendum; or finally, the definiendum may be a newly created notation, newly endowed with meaning here and now.

In formal and informal work alike, thus, we find that definition—except in the extreme case of the explicitly conventional introduction of new notations— hinges on prior relations of synonymy. Recognizing then that the notion of definition does not hold the key to synonymy and analyticity, let us look further into synonymy and say no more of definition.

3. INTERCHANGEABILITY

A natural suggestion, deserving close examination, is that the synonymy of two linguistic forms consists simply in their interchangeability in all contexts without change of truth value—interchangeability, in Leibniz's phrase, *salva veritate*.[3] Note that synonyms so conceived need not even be free from vagueness, as long as the vaguenesses match.

But it is not quite true that the synonyms 'bachelor' and 'unmarried man' are everyhere interchangeable *salva veritate*. Truths which become false under substitution of 'unmarried man' for 'bachelor' are easily constructed with the help of 'bachelor of arts' or 'bachelor's buttons'; also with the help of quotation, thus:

'Bachelor' has less than ten letters.

Such counterinstances can, however, perhaps be set aside by treating the phrases 'bachelor of arts' and 'bachelor's buttons' and the quotation "bachelor" each as a single indivisible word and then stipulating that the interchangeability *salva veritate* which is to be the touchstone of synonymy is not supposed to apply to fragmentary occurrences inside of a word. This account of synonymy, supposing it acceptable on other counts, has indeed the drawback of appealing to a prior conception of "word" which can be counted on to present difficulties of formulation in its turn. Nevertheless some progress might be claimed in having reduced the problem of synonymy to a problem of wordhood. Let us pursue this line a bit, taking "word" for granted.

The question remains whether interchangeability *salva veritate* (apart from occurrences within words) is a strong enough condition for synonymy, or whether, on the contrary, some heteronymous expressions might be thus interchangeable. Now let us be clear that we are not concerned here with synonymy in the sense of complete identity in psychological associations or poetic quality; indeed no two expressions are synonymous in such a sense. We are concerned only with what may be called *cognitive* synonymy. Just what this is cannot be

---

[2] According to an important variant sense of 'definition', the relation preserved may be the weaker relation of mere agreement in reference. But definition in this sense is better ignored in the present connection, being irrelevant to the question of synonymy.

[3] Cf. Lewis [1], p. 373.

said without successfully finishing the present study; but we know something about it from the need which arose for it in connection with analyticity in §1. The sort of synonymy needed there was merely such that any analytic statement could be turned into a logical truth by putting synonyms for synonyms. Turning the tables and assuming analyticity, indeed, we could explain cognitive synonymy of terms as follows (keeping to the familiar example): to say that 'bachelor' and 'unmarried man' are cognitively synonymous is to say no more nor less than that the statement:

(3) All and only bachelors are unmarried men

is analytic.[4]

What we need is an account of cognitive synonymy not presupposing analyticity—if we are to explain analyticity conversely with help of cognitive synonymy as undertaken in §1. And indeed such an independent account of cognitive synonymy is at present up for consideration, namely, interchangeability *salva veritate* everywhere except within words. The question before us, to resume the thread at last, is whether such interchangeability is a sufficient condition for cognitive synonymy. We can quickly assure ourselves that it is, by examples of the following sort. The statement:

(4) Necessarily all and only bachelors are bachelors

is evidently true, even supposing 'necessarily' so narrowly construed as to be truly applicable only to analytic statements. Then, if 'bachelor' and 'unmarried man' are interchangeable *salva veritate*, the result:

(5) Necessarily all and only bachelors are unmarried men

of putting 'unmarried man' for an occurrence of 'bachelor' in (4) must, like (4), be true. But to say that (5) is true is to say that (3) is analytic, and hence that 'bachelor' and 'unmarried man' are cognitively synonymous.

Let us see what there is about the above argument that gives it its air of hocus-pocus. The condition of interchangeability *salva veritate* varies in its force with variations in the richness of the language at hand. The above argument supposes we are working with a language rich enough to contain the adverb 'necessarily', this adverb being so construed as to yield truth when and only when applied to an analytic statement. But can we condone a language which contains such an adverb? Does the adverb really make sense? To suppose that it does is to suppose that we have already made satisfactory sense of 'analytic'. Then what are we so hard at work on right now?

Our argument is not flatly circular, but something like it. It has the form, figuratively speaking, of a closed curve in space.

Interchangeability *salva veritate* is meaningless until relativized to a language whose extent is specified in relevant respects. Suppose now we consider a

---

[4] This is cognitive synonymy in a primary, broad sense. Carnap ([1], pp. 56ff.) and Lewis ([2], pp. 83ff.) have suggested how, once this notion is at hand, a narrower sense of cognitive synonymy which is preferable for some purposes can in turn be derived. But this special ramification of concept-building lies aside from the present purposes and must not be confused with the broad sort of cognitive synonymy here concerned.

language containing just the following materials. There is an indefinitely large stock of one-place predicates (for example, '*F*' where '*Fx*' means that *x* is a man) and many-place predicates (for example, '*G*' where '*Gxy*' means that *x* loves *y*), mostly having to do with extralogical subject matter. The rest of the language is logical. The atomic sentences consist each of a predicate followed by one or more variables '*x*', '*y*', etc.; and the complex sentences are built up of the atomic ones by truth functions ('not', 'and', 'or', etc.) and quantification. In effect such a language enjoys the benefits also of descriptions and indeed singular terms generally, these being contextually definable in known ways. Even abstract singular terms naming classes, classes of classes, etc., are contextually definable in case the assumed stock of predicates includes the two-place predicate of class membership. Such a language can be adequate to classical mathematics and indeed to scientific discourse generally, except in so far as the latter involves debatable devices such as contrary-to-fact conditionals or modal adverbs like 'necessarily'. Now a language of this type is extensional, in this sense: any two predicates which agree extensionally (that is, are true of the same objects) are interchangeable *salva veritate*.[5]

In an extensional language, therefore, interchangeability *salva veritate* is no assurance of cognitive synonymy of the desired type. That 'bachelor' and 'unmarried man' are interchangeable *salva veritate* in an extensional language assures us of no more that that (3) is true. There is no assurance here that the extensional agreement of 'bachelor' and 'unmarried man' rests on meaning rather than merely on accidental matters of fact, as does the extensional agreement of 'creature with a heart' and 'creature with kidneys'.

For most purposes extensional agreement is the nearest approximation to synonymy we need care about. But the fact remains that extensional agreement falls far short of cognitive synonymy of the type required for explaining analyticity in the manner of §1. The type of cognitive synonymy required there is such as to equate the synonymy of 'bachelor' and 'unmarried man' with the analyticity of (3), not merely with the truth of (3).

So we must recognize that interchangeability *salva veritate*, if construed in relation to an extensional language, is not a sufficient condition of cognitive synonymy in the sense needed for deriving analyticity in the manner of §1. If a language contains an intensional adverb 'necessarily' in the sense lately noted, or other particles to the same effect, then interchangeability *salva veritate* in such a language does afford a sufficient condition of cognitive synonymy; but such a language is intelligible only in so far as the notion of analyticity is already understood in advance.

The effort to explain cognitive synonymy first, for the sake of deriving analyticity from it afterward as in §1, is perhaps the wrong approach. Instead we might try explaining analyticity somehow without appeal to cognitive synonymy. Afterward we could doubtless derive cognitive synonymy from analyticity satisfactorily enough if desired. We have seen that cognitive synonymy

---

[5] This is the substance of Quine, *121.

of 'bachelor' and 'unmarried man' can be explained as analyticity of (3). The same explanation works for any pair of one-place predicates, of course, and it can be extended in obvious fashion to many-place predicates. Other syntactical categories can also be accommodated in fairly parallel fashion. Singular terms may be said to be cognitively synonymous when the statement of identity formed by putting '=' between them is analytic. Statements may be said simply to be cognitively synonymous when their biconditional (the result of joining them by 'if and only if') is analytic.[6] If we care to lump all categories into a single formulation, at the expense of assuming again the notion of "word" which was appealed to early in this section, we can describe any two linguistic forms as cognitively synonymous when the two forms are interchangeable (apart from occurrences within "words") *salva* (no longer *veritate* but) *analyticitate*. Certain technical questions arise, indeed, over cases of ambiguity or homonymy; let us not pause for them, however, for we are already digressing. Let us rather turn our backs on the problem of synonymy and address ourselves anew to that of analyticity.

4. SEMANTICAL RULES

Analyticity at first seemed most naturally definable by appeal to a realm of meanings. On refinement, the appeal to meanings gave way to an appeal to synonymy or definition. But definition turned out to be a will-o'-the-wisp, and synonymy turned out to be best understood only by dint of a prior appeal to analyticity itself. So we are back at the problem of analyticity.

I do not know whether the statement 'Everything green is extended' is analytic. Now does my indecision over this example really betray an incomplete understanding, an incomplete grasp of the "meanings," of 'green' and 'extended'? I think not. The trouble is not with 'green' or 'extended', but with 'analytic'.

It is often hinted that the difficulty in separating analytic statements from synthetic ones in ordinary language is due to the vagueness of ordinary language and that the distinction is clear when we have a precise artificial language with explicit "semantical rules." This, however, as I shall now attempt to show, is a confusion.

The notion of analyticity about which we are worrying is a purported relation between statements and languages: a statement S is said to be *analytic for* a language L, and the problem is to make sense of this relation generally, that is, for variable 'S' and 'L'. The gravity of this problem is not perceptibly less for artificial languages than for natural ones. The problem of making sense of the idiom 'S is analytic for L', with variable 'S' and 'L', retains its stubbornness even if we limit the range of the variable 'L' to artificial languages. Let me now try to make this point evident.

For artificial languages and semantical rules we look naturally to the writings of Carnap. His semantical rules take various forms, and to make my point I

---

[6] The 'if and only if' itself is intended in the truth functional sense. See Carnap [1], p. 14.

shall have to distinguish certain of the forms. Let us suppose, to begin with, an artificial language L_0 whose semantical rules have the form explicitly of a specification, by recursion or otherwise, of all the analytic statements of L_0. The rules tell us that such and such statements, and only those, are the analytic statements of L_0. Now here the difficulty is simply that the rules contain the word 'analytic', which we do not understand! We understand what expressions the rules attribute analyticity to, but we do not understand what the rules attribute to those expressions. In short, before we can understand a rule which begins 'A statement S is analytic for language L_0 if and only if . . . ', we must understand the general relative term 'analytic for'; we must understand 'S is analytic for L' where 'S' and 'L' are variables.

Alternatively we may, indeed, view the so-called rule as a conventional definition of a new simple symbol 'analytic-for-L_0', which might better be written untendentiously as 'K' so as not to seem to throw light on the interesting word 'analytic'. Obviously any number of classes K, M, N, etc., of statements of L_0 can be specified for various purposes or for no purpose; what does it mean to say that K, as against M, N, etc., is the class of the "analytic" statements of L_0?

By saying what statements are analytic for L_0 we explain 'analytic-for-L_0' but not 'analytic', not 'analytic for'. We do not begin to explain the idiom 'S is analytic for L' with variable 'S' and 'L', even if we are content to limit the range of 'L' to the realm of artificial languages.

Actually we do know enough about the intended significance of 'analytic' to know that analytic statements are supposed to be true. Let us then turn to a second form of semantical rule, which says not that such and such statements are analytic but simply that such and such statements are included among the truths. Such a rule is not subject to the criticism of containing the un-understood word 'analytic'; and we may grant for the sake of argument that there is no difficulty over the broader term 'true'. A semantical rule of this second type, a rule of truth, is not supposed to specify all the truths of the language; it merely stipulates, recursively or otherwise, a certain multitude of statements which, along with others unspecified, are to count as true. Such a rule may be conceded to be quite clear. Derivatively, afterward, analyticity can be demarcated thus: a statement is analytic if it is (not merely true but) true according to the semantical rule.

Still there is really no progress. Instead of appealing to an unexplained word 'analytic', we are now appealing to an unexplained phrase 'semantical rule'. Not every true statement which says that the statements of some class are true can count as a semantical rule—otherwise *all* truths would be "analytic" in the sense of being true according to semantical rules. Semantical rules are distinguishable, apparently, only by the fact of appearing on a page under the heading 'Semantical Rules'; and this heading is itself then meaningless.

We can say indeed that a statement is *analytic-for-L_0* if and only if it is true according to such and such specifically appended "semantical rules," but then we find ourselves back at essentially the same case which was originally discussed: '*S* is analytic-for-L_0 if and only if. . . . ' Once we seek to explain '*S* is analytic for *L*' generally for variable '*L*' (even allowing limitation of '*L*' to artificial languages), the explanation 'true according to the semantical rules of *L*' is unavailing; for the relative term 'semantical rule of' is as much in need of clarification, at least, as 'analytic for'.

It may be instructive to compare the notion of semantical rule with that of postulate. Relative to a given set of postulates, it is easy to say what a postulate is: it is a member of the set. Relative to a given set of semantical rules, it is equally easy to say what a semantical rule is. But given simply a notation, mathematical or otherwise, and indeed as thoroughly understood a notation as you please in point of the translations or truth conditions of its statements, who can say which of its true statements rank as postulates? Obviously the question is meaningless—as meaningless as asking which points in Ohio are starting points. Any finite (or effectively specifiable infinite) selection of statements (preferably true ones, perhaps) is as much *a* set of postulates as any other. The word 'postulate' is significant only relative to an act of inquiry; we apply the word to a set of statements just in so far as we happen, for the year or the moment, to be thinking of those statements in relation to the statements which can be reached from them by some set of transformations to which we have seen fit to direct our attention. Now the notion of semantical rule is as sensible and meaningful as that of postulate, if conceived in a similarly relative spirit—relative, this time, to one or another particular enterprise of schooling unconversant persons in sufficient conditions for truth of statements of some natural or artificial language *L*. But from this point of view no one signalization of a subclass of the truths of *L* is intrinsically more a semantical rule than another; and, if 'analytic' means 'true by semantical rules', no one truth of *L* is analytic to the exclusion of another.[7]

It might conceivably be protested that an artificial language *L* (unlike a natural one) is a language in the ordinary sense *plus* a set of explicit semantical rules—the whole constituting, let us say, an ordered pair; and that the semantical rules of *L* then are specifiable simply as the second component of the pair *L*. But, by the same token and more simply, we might construe an artificial language *L* outright as an ordered pair whose second component is the class of its analytic statements; and then the analytic statements of *L* become specifiable simply as the statements in the second component of *L*. Or better still, we might just stop tugging at our bootstraps altogether.

Not all the explanations of analyticity known to Carnap and his readers have been covered explicitly in the above considerations, but the extension to other forms is not hard to see. Just one additional factor should be mentioned which sometimes enters: sometimes the semantical rules are in effect rules of translation into ordinary language, in which case the analytic statements of the

---

[7] The foregoing paragraph was not part of the present essay as originally published. It was prompted by Martin (see Bibliography).

artificial language are in effect recognized as such from the analyticity of their specified translations in ordinary language. Here certainly there can be no thought of an illumination of the problem of analyticity from the side of the artificial language.

From the point of view of the problem of analyticity the notion of an artificial language with semantial rules is a *feu follet par excellence*. Semantical rules determining the analytic statements of an artificial language are of interest only in so far as we already understand the notion of analyticity; they are of no help in gaining this understanding.

Appeal to hypothetical languages of an artificially simple kind could conceivably be useful in clarifying analyticity, if the mental or behavioral or cultural factors relevant to analyticity—whatever they may be—were somehow sketched into the simplified model. But a model which takes analyticity merely as an irreducible character is unlikely to throw light on the problem of explicating analyticity.

It is obvious that truth in general depends on both language and extra-linguistic fact. The statement 'Brutus killed Caesar' would be false if the world had been different in certain ways, but it would also be false if the word 'killed' happened rather to have the sense of 'begat'. Thus one is tempted to suppose in general that the truth of a statement is somehow analyzable into a linguistic component and a factual component. Given this supposition, it next seems reasonable that in some statements the factual component should be null; and these are the analytic statements. But, for all its a priori reasonableness, a boundary between analytic and synthetic statements simply has not been drawn. That there is such a distinction to be drawn at all is an unempirical dogma of empiricists, a metaphysical article of faith.

5. THE VERIFICATION THEORY AND REDUCTIONISM

In the course of these somber reflections we have taken a dim view first of the notion of meaning, then of the notion of cognitive synonymy, and finally of the notion of analyticity. But what, it may be asked, of the verification theory of meaning? This phrase has established itself so firmly as a catchword of empiricism that we should be very unscientific indeed not to look beneath it for a possible key to the problem of meaning and the associated problems.

The verification theory of meaning, which has been conspicuous in the literature from Peirce onward, is that the meaning of a statement is the method of empirically confirming or infirming it. An analytic statement is that limiting case which is confirmed no matter what.

As urged in §1, we can as well pass over the question of meanings as entities and move straight to sameness of meaning, or synonymy. Then what the verification theory says is that statements are synonymous if and only if they are alike in point of method of empirical confirmation or infirmation.

This is an account of cognitive synonymy not of linguistic forms generally, but of statements.[8] However, from the concept of synonymy of statements we could derive the concept of synonymy for other linguistic forms, by considerations somewhat similar to those at the end of §3. Assuming the notion of "word," indeed, we could explain any two forms as synonymous when the putting of the one form for an occurrence of the other in any statement (apart from occurrences within "words") yields a synonymous statement. Finally, given the concept of synonymy thus for linguistic forms generally, we could define analyticity in terms of synonymy and logical truth as in §1. For that matter, we could define analyticity more simply in terms of just synonymy of statements together with logical truth; it is not necessary to appeal to synonymy of linguistic forms other than statements. For a statement may be described as analytic simply when it is synonymous with a logically true statement.

So, if the verification theory can be accepted as an adequate account of statement synonymy, the notion of analyticity is saved after all. However, let us reflect. Statement synonymy is said to be likeness of method of empirical confirmation or infirmation. Just what are these methods which are to be compared for likeness? What, in other words, is the nature of the relation between a statement and the experiences which contribute to or detract from its confirmation?

The most naïve view of the relation is that it is one of direct report. This is *radical reductionism*. Every meaningful statement is held to be translatable into a statement (true or false) about immediate experience. Radical reductionism, in one form or another, well antedates the verification theory of meaning explicitly so called. Thus Locke and Hume held that every idea must either originate directly in sense experience or else be compounded of ideas thus originating; and taking a hint from Tooke we might rephrase this doctrine in semantical jargon by saying that a term, to be significant at all, must be either a name of a sense datum or a compound of such names or an abbreviation of such a compound. So stated, the doctrine remains ambiguous as between sense data as sensory events and sense data as sensory qualities; and it remains vague as to the admissible ways of compounding. Moreover, the doctrine is unnecessarily and intolerably restrictive in the term-by-term critique which it imposes. More reasonably, and without yet exceeding the limits of what I have called radical reductionism, we may take full statements as our significant units—thus demanding that our statements as wholes be translatable into sense-datum language, but not that they be translatable term by term.

This emendation would unquestionably have been welcome to Locke and Hume and Tooke, but historically it had to await an important reorientation

---

[8] The doctrine can indeed be formulated with terms rather than statements as the units. Thus Lewis describes the meaning of a term as "*a criterion in mind,* by reference to which one is able to apply or refuse to apply the expression in question in the case of presented, or imagined, things or situations" ([2], p. 133).—For an instructive account of the vicissitudes of the verification theory of meaning, centered however on the question of meaning*fulness* rather than synonymy and analyticity, see Hempel.

in semantics—the reorientation whereby the primary vehicle of meaning came to be seen no longer in the term but in the statement. This reorientation, explicit in Frege (§60), underlies Russell's concept of incomplete symbols defined in use; also it is implicit in the verification theory of meaning, since the objects of verification are statements.

Radical reductionism, conceived now with statements as units, set itself the task of specifying a sense-datum language and showing how to translate the rest of significant discourse, statement by statement, into it. Carnap embarked on this project in the *Aufbau*.

The language which Carnap adopted as his starting point was not a sense-datum language in the narrowest conceivable sense, for it included also the notations of logic, up through higher set theory. In effect it included the whole language of pure mathematics. The ontology implicit in it (that is, the range of values of its variables) embraced not only sensory events but classes, classes of classes, and so on. Empiricists there are who would boggle at such prodigality. Carnap's starting point is very parsimonious, however, in its extralogical or sensory part. In a series of constructions in which he exploits the resources of modern logic with much ingenuity, Carnap succeeds in defining a wide array of important additional sensory concepts which, but for his constructions, one would not have dreamed were definable on so slender a basis. He was the first empiricist who, not content with asserting the reducibility of science to terms of immediate experience, took serious steps toward carrying out the reduction.

If Carnap's starting point is satisfactory, still his constructions were, as he himself stressed, only a fragment of the full program. The construction of even the simplest statements about the physical world was left in a sketchy state. Carnap's suggestions on this subject were, despite their sketchiness, very suggestive. He explained spatio-temporal point-instants as quadruples of real numbers and envisaged assignment of sense qualities to point-instants according to certain canons. Roughly summarized, the plan was that qualities should be assigned to point-instants in such a way as to achieve the laziest world compatible with our experience. The principle of least action was to be our guide in constructing a world from experience.

Carnap did not seem to recognize, however, that his treatment of physical objects fell short of reduction not merely through sketchiness, but in principle. Statements of the form 'Quality q is at point-instant $x;y;z;t$' were, according to his canons, to be apportioned truth values in such a way as to maximize and minimize certain over-all features, and with growth of experience the truth values were to be progressively revised in the same spirit. I think this is a good schematization (deliberately oversimplified, to be sure) of what science really does; but it provides no indication, not even the sketchiest, of how a statement of the form 'Quality q is at $x;y;z;t$' could ever be translated into Carnap's initial language of sense data and logic. The connective 'is at' remains an added undefined connective; the canons counsel us in its use but not in its elimination.

Carnap seems to have appreciated this point afterward; for in his later writings he abandoned all notion of the translatability of statements about the physical world into statements about immediate experience. Reductionism in its radical form has long since ceased to figure in Carnap's philosophy.

But the dogma of reductionism has, in a subtler and more tenuous form, continued to influence the thought of empiricists. The notion lingers that to each statement, or each synthetic statement, there is associated a unique range of possible sensory events such that the occurrence of any of them would add to the likelihood of truth of the statement, and that there is associated also another unique range of possible sensory events whose occurrence would detract from that likelihood. This notion is of course implicit in the verification theory of meaning.

The dogma of reductionism survives in the supposition that each statement, taken in isolation from its fellows, can admit of confirmation or infirmation at all. My countersuggestion, issuing essentially from Carnap's doctrine of the physical world in the *Aufbau*, is that our statements about the external world face the tribunal of sense experience not individually but only as a corporate body.[9]

The dogma of reductionism, even in its attenuated form, is intimately connected with the other dogma—that there is a cleavage between the analytic and the synthetic. We have found ourselves led, indeed, from the latter problem to the former through the verification theory of meaning. More directly, the one dogma clearly supports the other in this way: as long as it is taken to be significant in general to speak of the confirmation and infirmation of a statement, it seems significant to speak also of a limiting kind of statement which is vacuously confirmed, *ipso facto*, come what may; and such a statement is analytic.

The two dogmas are, indeed, at root identical. We lately reflected that in general the truth of statements does obviously depend both upon language and upon extralinguistic fact; and we noted that this obvious circumstance carries in its train, not logically but all too naturally, a feeling that the truth of a statement is somehow analyzable into a linguistic component and a factual component. The factual component must, if we are empiricists, boil down to a range of confirmatory experiences. In the extreme case where the linguistic component is all that matters, a true statement is analytic. But I hope we are now impressed with how stubbornly the distinction between analytic and synthetic has resisted any straightforward drawing. I am impressed also, from prefabricated examples of black and white balls in an urn, with how baffling the problem has always been of arriving at any explicit theory of the empirical confirmation of a synthetic statement. My present suggestion is that it is nonsense, and the root of much nonsense, to speak of a linguistic component and a factual component in the truth of any individual statement. Taken collectively, science has its double dependence upon language and experience; but

---

[9] This doctrine was well argued by Duhem, pp. 303–328. Or see Lowinger, pp. 132–40.

this duality is not significantly traceable into the statements of science taken one by one.

The idea of defining a symbol in use was, as remarked, an advance over the impossible term-by-term empiricism of Locke and Hume. The statement, rather than the term, came with Frege to be recognized as the unit accountable to an empiricist critique. But what I am now urging is that even in taking the statement as unit we have drawn our grid too finely. The unit of empirical significance is the whole of science.

6. EMPIRICISM WITHOUT THE DOGMAS

The totality of our so-called knowledge or beliefs, from the most casual matters of geography and history to the profoundest laws of atomic physics or even of pure mathematics and logic, is a man-made fabric which impinges on experience only along the edges. Or, to change the figure, total science is like a field of force whose boundary conditions are experience. A conflict with experience at the periphery occasions readjustments in the interior of the field. Truth values have to be redistributed over some of our statements. Reëvaluation of some statements entails reëvaluation of others, because of their logical interconnections—the logical laws being in turn simply certain further statements of the system, certain further elements of the field. Having reëvaluated one statement we must reëvaluate some others, which may be statements logically connected with the first or may be the statements of logical connections themselves. But the total field is so underdetermined by its boundary conditions, experience, that there is much latitude of choice as to what statements to reëvaluate in the light of any single contrary experience. No particular experiences are linked with any particular statements in the interior of the field, except indirectly through considerations of equilibrium affecting the field as a whole.

If this view is right, it is misleading to speak of the empirical content of an individual statement—especially if it is a statement at all remote from the experiential periphery of the field. Furthermore it becomes folly to seek a boundary between synthetic statements, which hold contingently on experience, and analytic statements, which hold come what may. Any statement can be held true come what may, if we make drastic enough adjustments elsewhere in the system. Even a statement very close to the periphery can be held true in the face of recalcitrant experience by pleading hallucination or by amending certain statements of the kind called logical laws. Conversely, by the same token, no statement is immune to revision. Revision even of the logical law of the excluded middle has been proposed as a means of simplifying quantum mechanics; and what difference is there in principle between such a shift and the shift whereby Kepler superseded Ptolemy, or Einstein Newton, or Darwin Aristotle?

For vividness I have been speaking in terms of varying distances from a sensory periphery. Let me try now to clarify this notion without metaphor. Certain statements, though *about* physical objects and not sense experience, seem peculiarly germane to sense experience—and in a selective way: some statements to some experiences, others to others. Such statements, especially germane to particular experiences, I picture as near the periphery. But in this relation of "germaneness" I envisage nothing more than a loose association reflecting the relative likelihood, in practice, of our choosing one statement rather than another for revision in the event of recalcitrant experience. For example, we can imagine recalcitrant experiences to which we would surely be inclined to accommodate our system by reëvaluating just the statement that there are brick houses on Elm Street, together with related statements on the same topic. We can imagine other recalcitrant experiences to which we would be inclined to accommodate our system by reëvaluating just the statement that there are no centaurs, along with kindred statements. A recalcitrant experience can, I have urged, be accommodated by any of various alternative reëvaluations in various alternative quarters of the total system; but, in the cases which we are now imagining, our natural tendency to disturb the total system as little as possible would lead us to focus our revisions upon these specific statements concerning brick houses or centaurs. These statements are felt, therefore, to have a sharper empirical reference than highly theoretical statements of physics or logic or ontology. The latter statements may be thought of as relatively centrally located within the total network, meaning merely that little preferential connection with any particular sense data obtrudes itself.

As an empiricist I continue to think of the conceptual scheme of science as a tool, ultimately, for predicting future experience in the light of past experience. Physical objects are conceptually imported into the situation as convenient intermediaries—not by definition in terms of experience, but simply as irreducible posits comparable, epistemologically, to the gods of Homer. For my part I do, qua lay physicist, believe in physical objects and not in Homer's gods; and I consider it a scientific error to believe otherwise. But in point of epistemological footing the physical objects and the gods differ only in degree and not in kind. Both sorts of entities enter our conception only as cultural posits. The myth of physical objects is epistemologically superior to most in that it has proved more efficacious than other myths as a device for working a manageable structure into the flux of experience.

Positing does not stop with macroscopic physical objects. Objects at the atomic level are posited to make the laws of macroscopic objects, and ultimately the laws of experience, simpler and more manageable; and we need not expect or demand full definition of atomic and subatomic entities in terms of macroscopic ones, any more than definition of macroscopic things in terms of sense data. Science is a continuation of common sense, and it continues the common-sense expedient of swelling ontology to simplify theory.

Physical objects, small and large, are not the only posits. Forces are another example; and indeed we are told nowadays that the boundary between energy and matter is obsolete. Moreover, the abstract entities which are the substance of mathematics—ultimately classes and classes of classes and so on up—are another posit in the same spirit. Epistemologically these are myths on the same footing with physical objects and gods, neither better nor worse except for differences in the degree to which they expedite our dealings with sense experiences.

The over-all algebra of rational and irrational numbers is underdetermined by the algebra of rational numbers, but is smoother and more convenient; and it includes the algebra of rational numbers as a jagged or gerrymandered part. Total science, mathematical and natural and human, is similarly but more extremely underdetermined by experience. The edge of the system must be kept squared with experience; the rest, with all its elaborate myths or fictions, has as its objective the simplicity of laws.

Ontological questions, under this view, are on a par with questions of natural science.[10] Consider the question whether to countenance classes as entities. This, as I have argued elsewhere, is the question whether to quantify with respect to variables which take classes as values. Now Carnap [3] has maintained that this is a question not of matters of fact but of choosing a convenient language form, a convenient conceptual scheme or framework for science. With this I agree, but only on the proviso that the same be conceded regarding scientific hypotheses generally. Carnap ([3], p. 32n) has recognized that he is able to preserve a double standard for ontological questions and scientific hypotheses only by assuming an absolute distinction between the analytic and the synthetic; and I need not say again that this is a distinction which I reject.[11]

The issue over there being classes seems more a question of convenient conceptual scheme; the issue over there being centaurs, or brick houses on Elm Street, seems more a question of fact. But I have been urging that this difference is only one of degree, and that it turns upon our vaguely pragmatic inclination to adjust one strand of the fabric of science rather than another in accommodating some particular recalcitrant experience. Conservatism figures in such choices, and so does the quest for simplicity.

Carnap, Lewis, and others take a pragmatic stand on the question of choosing between language forms, scientific frameworks; but their pragmatism leaves off at the imagined boundary between the analytic and the synthetic. In repudiating such a boundary I espouse a more thorough pragmatism. Each man is given a scientific heritage plus a continuing barrage of sensory stimulation; and the considerations which guide him in warping his scientific heritage to fit his continuing sensory promptings are, where rational, pragmatic.

---

[10] "L'ontologie fait corps avec la science elle-même et ne peut en être separée." Meyerson, p. 439.

[11] For an effective expression of further misgivings over this distinction, see White.

Bibliographic References

Carnap, Rudolf. [1]. *Meaning and Necessity*. Chicago: University of Chicago Press, 1947.

———. [2]. *Logical Foundations of Probability*. Chicago: University of Chicago Press, 1950.

———. [3]. "Empiricism, semantics, and ontology," *Revue internationale de philosophie*, IV (1950), 20–40.

Duhem, Pierre. *La Théorie physique: son objet et sa structure*. Paris: 1906.

Frege, Gottlob. *Foundations of Arithmetic*. New York: Philosophical Library, 1950.

Hempel, C. G. "Problems and Changes in the Empiricist Criterion of Meaning." *Revue Internationale de Philosophie, IV* (1950), 41–63.

Lewis, C. I. [1]. *A Survey of Symbolic Logic*. Berkeley: 1918.

———. [2]. *An Analysis of Knowledge and Valuation*. La Salle, Ill.: Open Court Publishing Co., 1946.

Lowinger, Armand. *The Methodology of Pierre Duhem*. New York: Columbia University Press, 1941.

Martin, R. M., "On 'Analytic'." *Philosophical Studies*, III (1952), 42–47.

Meyerson, Émile. *Identité et réalité*. Paris: 1908; 4th ed., 1932.

Quine, W. V. *Mathematical Logic*. New York: W. W. Norton & Company, Inc., 1940; Cambridge: Harvard University Press, 1947; rev. ed., 1951.

White, Morton. "The Analytic and the Synthetic: An Untenable Dualism." In Sidney Hook, ed., *John Dewey: Philosopher of Science and Freedom*. New York: The Dial Press, Inc., 1950, pp. 316–30.

H. P. GRICE / P. F. STRAWSON

1.5 *In Defense of a Dogma*

In his article "Two Dogmas of Empiricism,"[1] Professor Quine advances a number of criticisms of the supposed distinction between analytic and synthetic statements, and of other associated notions. It is, he says, a distinction which he rejects.[2] We wish to show that his criticisms of the distinction do not justify his rejection of it.

Reprinted from *The Philosophical Review*, LXV, No. 2 (1956), 141–58, by permission of the authors and of *The Philosophical Review*.

[1] W. V. O. Quine, *From a Logical Point of View* (Cambridge, Mass., 1953), pp. 20–46. All references are to page numbers in this book. [See above, pp. 63–80.]

[2] Page 80.

There are many ways in which a distinction can be criticized, and more than one in which it can be rejected. It can be criticized for not being a sharp distinction (for admitting of cases which do not fall clearly on either side of it); or on the ground that the terms in which it is customarily drawn are ambiguous (have more than one meaning); or on the ground that it is confused (the different meanings being habitually conflated). Such criticisms alone would scarcely amount to a rejection of the distinction. They would, rather, be a prelude to clarification. It is not this sort of criticism which Quine makes.

Again, a distinction can be criticized on the ground that it is not useful. It can be said to be useless for certain purposes, or useless altogether, and, perhaps, pedantic. One who criticizes in this way may indeed be said to reject a distinction, but in a sense which also requires him to acknowledge its existence. He simply declares he can get on without it. But Quine's rejection of the analytic-synthetic distinction appears to be more radical than this. He would certainly say he could get on without the distinction, but in a sense which would commit him to acknowledging its existence.

Or again, one could criticize the way or ways in which a distinction is customarily expounded or explained on the ground that these explanations did not make it really clear. And Quine certainly makes such criticisms in the case of the analytic-synthetic distinction.

But he does, or seems to do, a great deal more. He declares, or seems to declare, not merely that the distinction is useless or inadequately clarified, but also that it is altogether illusory, that the belief in its existence is a philosophical mistake. "That there is such a distinction to be drawn at all," he says, "is an unempirical dogma of empiricists, a metaphysical article of faith."[3] It is the existence of the distinction that he here calls in question; so his rejection of it would seem to amount to a denial of its existence.

Evidently such a position of extreme skepticism about a distinction is not in general justified merely by criticisms, however just in themselves, of philosophical attempts to clarify it. There are doubtless plenty of distinctions, drawn in philosophy and outside it, which still await adequate philosophical elucidation, but which few would want on this account to declare illusory. Quine's article, however, does not consist wholly, though it does consist largely, in criticizing attempts at elucidation. He does try also to diagnose the causes of the belief in the distinction, and he offers some positive doctrine, acceptance of which he represents as incompatible with this belief. If there is any general prior presumption in favor of the existence of the distinction, it seems that Quine's radical rejection of it must rest quite heavily on this part of his article, since the force of any such presumption is not even impaired by philosophical failures to clarify a distinction so supported.

Is there such a presumption in favor of the distinction's existence? Prima facie, it must be admitted that there is. An appeal to philosophical tradition

---

[3] Page 74.

is perhaps unimpressive and is certainly unnecessary. But it is worth pointing out that Quine's objection is not simply to the words "analytic" and "synthetic," but to a distinction which they are supposed to express, and which at different times philosophers have supposed themselves to be expressing by means of such pairs of words or phrases as "necessary" and "contingent," "a priori" and "empirical," "truth of reason" and "truth of fact"; so Quine is certainly at odds with a philosophical tradition which is long and not wholly disreputable. But there is no need to appeal only to tradition; for there is also present practice. We can appeal, that is, to the fact that those who use the terms "analytic" and "synthetic" do to a very considerable extent agree in the applications they make of them. They apply the term "analytic" to more or less the same cases, withhold it from more or less the same cases, and hesitate over more or less the same cases. This agreement extends not only to cases which they have been *taught* so to characterize, but to new cases. In short, "analytic" and "synthetic" have a more or less established philosophical *use*; and this seems to suggest that it is absurd, even senseless, to say that there is no such distinction. For, in general, if a pair of contrasting expressions are habitually and generally used in application to the same cases, *where these cases do not form a closed list*, this is a sufficient condition for saying that there are *kinds* of cases to which the expressions apply; and nothing more is needed for them to mark a distinction.

In view of the possibility of this kind of argument, one may begin to doubt whether Quine really holds the extreme thesis which his words encourage one to attribute to him. It is for this reason that we made the attribution tentative. For on at least one natural interpretation of this extreme thesis, when we say of something true that it is analytic and of another true thing that it is synthetic, it simply never is the case that we thereby mark a distinction between them. And this view seems terribly difficult to reconcile with the fact of an established philosophical usage (i.e., of general agreement in application in an open class). For this reason, Quine's thesis might be better represented not as the thesis that there is *no difference at all* marked by the use of these expressions, but as the thesis that the nature of, and reasons for, the difference or differences are totally misunderstood by those who use the expressions, that the stories they tell themselves *about* the difference are full of illusion.

We think Quine might be prepared to accept this amendment. If so, it could, in the following way, be made the basis of something like an answer to the argument which prompted it. Philosophers are notoriously subject to illusion, and to mistaken theories. Suppose there were a particular mistaken theory about language or knowledge, such that, seen in the light of this theory, some statements (or propositions or sentences) appeared to have a characteristic which no statements really have, or even, perhaps, which it does not make sense to suppose that any statement has, and which no one who was not consciously or subconsciously influenced by this theory would ascribe to any statement. And suppose that there were other statements which, seen in this light, did not appear to have this characteristic, and others again which presented an uncertain appearance. Then philosophers who were under the influence of this theory would tend to mark the supposed presence or absence of this characteristic by a pair of contrasting expressions, say "analytic" and "synthetic." Now in these circumstances it still could not be said that there was no distinction at all being marked by the use of these expressions, for there would be at least the distinction we have just described (the distinction, namely, between those statements which appeared to have and those which appeared to lack a certain characteristic), and there might well be other assignable differences too, which would account for the difference in appearance; but it certainly could be said that *the* difference these philosophers supposed themselves to be marking by the use of the expressions simply did not exist, and perhaps also (supposing the characteristic in question to be one which it was absurd to ascribe to any statement) that these expressions, as so used, were senseless or without meaning. We should only have to suppose that such a mistaken theory was very plausible and attractive, in order to reconcile the fact of an established philosophical usage for a pair of contrasting terms with the claim that *the* distinction which the terms purported to mark did not exist at all, though not with the claim that there simply did not exist a difference of any kind between the classes of statements so characterized. We think that the former claim would probably be sufficient for Quine's purposes. But to establish such a claim on the sort of grounds we have indicated evidently requires a great deal more argument than is involved in showing that certain explanations of a term do not measure up to certain requirements of adequacy in philosophical clarification—and not only more argument, but argument of a very different kind. For it would surely be too harsh to maintain that the *general* presumption is that philosophical distinctions embody the kind of illusion we have described. On the whole, it seems that philosophers are prone to make too few distinctions rather than too many. It is their assimilations, rather than their distinctions, which tend to be spurious.

So far we have argued as if the prior presumption in favor of the existence of the distinction which Quine questions rested solely on the fact of an agreed *philosophical* usage for the terms "analytic" and "synthetic." A presumption with only this basis could no doubt be countered by a strategy such as we have just outlined. But, in fact, if we are to accept Quine's account of the matter, the presumption in question is not only so based. For among the notions which belong to the analyticity-group is one which Quine calls "cognitive synonymy," and in terms of which he allows that the notion of analyticity could at any rate be formally explained. Unfortunately, he adds, the notion of cognitive synonymy is just as unclarified as that of analyticity. To say that two expressions *x* and *y* are cognitively synonymous seems to correspond, at any rate roughly, to what we should ordinarily express by saying that *x* and *y* have the same meaning or that *x* means the same as *y*. If Quine is to be consistent in his adherence to the extreme thesis, then it appears that he must maintain not only that the distinction we suppose ourselves to be marking by the use of the terms "analytic" and "synthetic" does not exist, but also that the distinction we suppose ourselves to be marking by the use of the expressions "means the same as," "does not mean the same as" does not exist either. At least, he must maintain this insofar as the notion of *meaning the same as*, in its application to predicate-expressions, is supposed to differ from and go beyond the notion of *being true of just the same objects as*. (This latter notion—which we might call that of "coextensionality"—he is prepared to allow to be intelligible, though, as he rightly says, it is not sufficient for the explanation of analyticity.) Now since he cannot claim this time that the pair of expressions in question (viz., "means the same," "does not mean the same") is the special property of philosophers, the strategy outlined above of countering the presumption in favor of their marking a genuine distinction is not available here (or is at least enormously less plausible). Yet the denial that the distinction (taken as different from the distinction between the coextensional and the noncoextensional) really exists, is extremely paradoxical. It involves saying, for example, that anyone who seriously remarks that "bachelor" means the same as "unmarried man" but that "creature with kidneys" does not mean the same as "creature with a heart"—supposing the last two expressions to be coextensional—*either* is not in fact drawing attention to any distinction at all between the relations between the members of each pair of expressions *or* is making a philosophical mistake about the nature of the distinction between them. In either case, what he says, taken as he intends it to be taken, is senseless or absurd. More generally, it involves saying that it is always senseless or absurd to make a statement of the form "Predicates x and y in fact apply to the same objects, but do not have the same meaning." But the paradox is more violent than this. For we frequently talk of the presence or absence of relations of synonymy between kinds of expressions—e.g., conjunctions, particles of many kinds, whole sentences— where there does not appear to be any obvious substitute for the ordinary notion of synonymy, in the way in which coextensionality is said to be a substitute for synonymy of predicates. Is all such talk meaningless? Is all talk of correct or incorrect *translation* of sentences of one language into sentences of another meaningless? It is hard to believe that it is. But if we do successfully make the effort to believe it, we have still harder renunciations before us. If talk of sentence-synonymy is meaningless, then it seems that talk of sentences having a meaning at all must be meaningless too. For if it made sense to talk of a sentence having a meaning, or meaning something, then presumably it would make sense to ask "What does it mean?" And if it made sense to ask "What does it mean?" of a sentence, then sentence-synonymy could be roughly defined as follows: Two sentences are synonymous if and only if any true answer to the question "What does it mean?" asked of one of them, is a true answer to the same question, asked of the other. We do not, of course, claim any clarifying power for this definition. We want only to point out that if we are to give up the notion of sentence-synonymy as senseless, we must give up the notion of sentence-significance (of a sentence having meaning) as senseless too. But then perhaps we might as well give up the notion of sense.—It seems clear that we have here a typical example of a philosopher's paradox. Instead of examining the actual use that we make of the notion of *meaning the same,* the philosopher measures it by some perhaps inappropriate standard (in this case some standard of clarifiability), and because it falls short of this standard, or seems to do so, denies its reality, declares it illusory.

We have argued so far that there is a strong presumption in favor of the existence of the distinction, or distinctions, which Quine challenges—a presumption resting both on philosophical and on ordinary usage—and that this presumption is not in the least shaken by the fact, if it is a fact, that the distinctions in question have not been, in some sense, adequately clarified. It is perhaps time to look at what Quine's notion of adequate clarification is.

The main theme of his article can be roughly summarized as follows. There is a certain circle or family of expressions, of which "analytic" is one, such that if any one member of the circle could be taken to be satisfactorily understood or explained, then other members of the circle could be verbally, and hence satisfactorily, explained in terms of it. Other members of the family are: "self-contradictory" (in a broad sense), "necessary," "synonymous," "semantical rule," and perhaps (but again in a broad sense) "definition." The list could be added to. Unfortunately each member of the family is in as great need of explanation as any other. We give some sample quotations: "The notion of self-contradictoriness (in the required broad sense of inconsistency) stands in exactly the same need of clarification as does the notion of analyticity itself."[4] Again, Quine speaks of "a notion of synonymy which is in no less need of clarification than analyticity itself."[5] Again, of the adverb "necessarily," as a candidate for use in the explanation of synonymy, he says, "Does the adverb *really make sense?* To suppose that it does is to suppose that we have already *made satisfactory sense* of 'analytic'."[6] To make "satisfactory sense" of one of these expressions would seem to involve two things. (1) It would seem to involve providing an explanation which does not incorporate any expression belonging to the family-circle. (2) It would seem that the explanation provided must be of the same general character as those rejected explanations which do incorporate members of the family-circle (i.e., it must specify some feature common and peculiar to all cases to which, for example, the word "analytic" is to be applied; it must have the same general form as an explanation beginning, "a statement is analytic if and only if . . ."). It is true that Quine does not explicitly state the second requirement; but since he does not even consider the question whether any other kind of explanation would be relevant, it seems reasonable to attribute it to him. If we take these two conditions together, and generalize the result, it would seem that Quine requires of a satisfactory explanation of an expression that it should take the form of a pretty strict definition but should not make use of any member of a group of interdefinable terms to which the expression belongs. We may well begin to feel that a satisfactory explanation is hard to come by. The other element in Quine's position

---

[4] Page 63.
[5] Page 65.
[6] Page 69, our italics.

is one we have already commented on in general, before enquiring what (according to him) is to count as a satisfactory explanation. It is the step from "We have not made satisfactory sense (provided a satisfactory explanation) of *x*" to "*x* does not make sense."

It would seem fairly clearly unreasonable to insist *in general* that the availability of a satisfactory explanation in the sense sketched above is a necessary condition of an expression's making sense. It is perhaps dubious whether *any* such explanations can *ever* be given. (The hope that they can be is, or was, the hope of reductive analysis in general.) Even if such explanations can be given in some cases, it would be pretty generally agreed that there are other cases in which they cannot. One might think, for example, of the group of expressions which includes "morally wrong," "blameworthy," "breach of moral rules," etc.; or of the group which includes the propositional connectives and the words "true" and "false," "statement," "fact," "denial," "assertion." Few people would want to say that the expressions belonging to either of these groups were senseless on the ground that they have not been formally defined (or even on the ground that it was impossible formally to define them) except in terms of members of the same group. It might, however, be said that while the unavailability of a satisfactory explanation in the special sense described was not a *generally* sufficient reason for declaring that a given expression was senseless, it was a sufficient reason in the case of the expressions of the analyticity group. But anyone who said this would have to advance a reason for discriminating in this way against the expressions of this group. The only plausible reason for being harder on these expressions than on others is a refinement on a consideration which we have already had before us. It starts from the point that "analytic" and "synthetic" themselves are technical philosophical expressions. To the rejoinder that other expressions of the family concerned, such as "means the same as" or "is inconsistent with," or "self-contradictory," are not at all technical expressions, but are common property, the reply would doubtless be that, to qualify for inclusion in the family circle, these expressions have to be used in specially adjusted and precise senses (or pseudo-senses) which they do not ordinarily possess. It is the fact, then, that all the terms belonging to the circle are *either* technical terms *or* ordinary terms used in specially adjusted senses, that might be held to justify us in being particularly suspicious of the claims of members of the circle to have any sense at all, and hence to justify us in requiring them to pass a test for significance which would admittedly be too stringent if generally applied. This point has some force, though we doubt if the special adjustments spoken of are in every case as considerable as it suggests. (This seems particularly doubtful in the case of the word "inconsistent"— a perfectly good member of the nontechnician's meta-logical vocabulary.) But though the point has some force, it does not have whatever force would be required to justify us in insisting that the expressions concerned should pass exactly that test for significance which is in question. The fact, if it is a fact, that the expressions cannot be explained in precisely the way which Quine seems to require, does not mean that they cannot be explained at all. There is no need to try to pass them off as expressing innate ideas. They can be and are explained, though in other and less formal ways than that which Quine considers. (And the fact that they are so explained fits with the facts, first, that there is a generally agreed philosophical use for them, and second, that this use is technical or specially adjusted.) To illustrate the point briefly for one member of the analyticity family. Let us suppose we are trying to explain to someone the notion of *logical impossibility* (a member of the family which Quine presumably regards as no clearer than any of the others) and we decide to do it by bringing out the contrast between logical and natural (or causal) impossibility. We might take as our examples the logical impossibility of a child of three's understanding Russell's Theory of Types. We might instruct our pupil to imagine two conversations one of which begins by someone (X) making the claim:

(1) "My neighbor's three-year-old child understands Russell's Theory of Types,"

and the other of which begins by someone (Y) making the claim:

(1′) "My neighbor's three-year-old child is an adult."

It would not be inappropriate to reply to X, taking the remark as a hyperbole:

(2) "You mean the child is a particularly bright lad."

If X were to say:

(3) "No, I mean what I say—he really does understand it,"

one might be inclined to reply:

(4) "I don't believe you—the thing's impossible."

But if the child were then produced, and did (as one knows he would not) expound the theory correctly, answer questions on it, criticize it, and so on, one would in the end be forced to acknowledge that the claim was literally true and that the child was a prodigy. Now consider one's reaction to Y's claim. To begin with, it might be somewhat similar to the previous case. One might say:

(2′) "You mean he's uncommonly sensible or very advanced for his age."

If Y replies:

(3′) "No, I mean what I say,"

we might reply:

(4′) "Perhaps you mean that he won't grow any more, or that he's a sort of freak, that he's already fully developed."

Y replies:

(5′) "No, he's not a freak, he's just an adult."

At this stage—or possibly if we are patient, a little later—we shall be inclined to say that we just don't understand what Y is saying, and to suspect that he just does not know the meaning of some of the words he is using. For unless he is prepared to admit that he is using words in a figurative or unusual sense, we shall say, not that we don't believe him, but that his words have *no* sense. And whatever kind of creature is ultimately produced for our inspection, it will not lead us to say that what Y said was literally true, but at most to say that we now see what he meant. As a summary of the difference between the two imaginary conversations, we might say that in both cases we would tend to begin by supposing that the other speaker was using words in a figurative or unusual or restricted way; but in the face of his repeated claim to be speaking literally, it would be appropriate in the first case to say that we did not believe him and in the second case to say that we did not understand him. If, like Pascal, we thought it prudent to prepare against very long chances, we should in the first case know what to prepare for; in the second, we should have no idea.

We give this as an example of just one type of informal explanation which we might have recourse to in the case of one notion of the analyticity group. (We do not wish to suggest it is the only type.) Further examples, with different though connected types of treatment, might be necessary to teach our pupil the use of the notion of logical impossibility in its application to more complicated cases—if indeed he did not pick it up from the one case. Now of course this type of explanation does not yield a formal statement of necessary and sufficient conditions for the application of the notion concerned. So it does not fulfill one of the conditions which Quine seems to require of a satisfactory explanation. On the other hand, it does appear to fulfill the other. It breaks out of the family circle. The distinction in which we ultimately come to rest is that between not believing something and not understanding something; or between incredulity yielding to conviction, and incomprehension yielding to comprehension. It would be rash to maintain that *this* distinction does not need clarification; but it would be absurd to maintain that it does not exist. In the face of the availability of this informal type of explanation for the notions of the analyticity group, the fact that they have not received another type of explanation (which it is dubious whether *any* expressions *ever* receive) seems a wholly inadequate ground for the conclusion that the notions are pseudo-notions, that the expressions which purport to express them have no sense. To say this is not to deny that it would be philosophically desirable, and a proper object of philosophical endeavor, to find a more illuminating general characterization of the notions of this group than any that has been so far given. But the question of how, if at all, this can be done is quite irrelevant to the question of whether or not the expressions which belong to the circle have an intelligible use and mark genuine distinctions.

So far we have tried to show that sections 1 to 4 of Quine's article—the burden of which is that the notions of the analyticity group have not been satisfactorily explained—do not establish the extreme thesis for which he appears to be arguing. It remains to be seen whether sections 5 and 6, in which diagnosis and positive theory are offered, are any more successful. But before we turn to them, there are two further points worth making which arise out of the first two sections.

(1) One concerns what Quine says about *definition* and *synonymy*. He remarks that definition does not, as some have supposed, "hold the key to synonymy and analyticity," since "definition—except in the extreme case of the explicitly conventional introduction of new notations—hinges on prior relations of synonymy."[7] But now consider what he says of these extreme cases. He says: "Here the definiendum becomes synonymous with the definiens simply because it has been expressly created for the purpose of being synonymous with the definiens. Here we have a really transparent case of synonymy created by definition; would that all species of synonymy were as intelligible." Now if we are to take these words of Quine seriously, then his position *as a whole* is incoherent. It is like the position of a man to whom we are trying to explain, say, the idea of one thing fitting into another thing, or two things fitting together, and who says: "I can understand what it means to say that one thing fits into another, or that two things fit together, in the case where one was specially made to fit the other; but I cannot understand what it means to say this in any other case." Perhaps we should not take Quine's words here too seriously. But if not, then we have the right to ask him exactly what state of affairs he thinks *is* brought about by explicit definition, what relation between expressions *is* established by this procedure, and why he thinks it unintelligible to suggest that the same (or a closely analogous) state of affairs, or relation, should exist in the absence of this procedure. For our part, we should be inclined to take Quine's words (or some of them) seriously, and reverse his conclusions; and maintain that the notion of synonymy by explicit convention would be unintelligible if the notion of synonymy by usage were not presupposed. There cannot be law where there is no custom, or rules where there are not practices (though perhaps we can understand better what a practice is by looking at a rule).

(2) The second point arises out of a paragraph on page 71 . . . . We quote:

> I do not know whether the statement "Everything green is extended" is analytic. Now does my indecision over this example really betray an incomplete understanding, an incomplete grasp, of the "meanings" of "green" and "extended"? I think not. The trouble is not with "green" or "extended," but with "analytic."

If, as Quine says, the trouble is with "analytic," then the trouble should doubtless disappear when "analytic" is removed. So let us remove it, and replace it with a word which Quine himself has contrasted favorably with "analytic" in respect of perspicuity—the word "true." Does the indecision at once disappear? We think not. The indecision over "analytic" (and equally, in this case, the indecision over "true") arises, of course, from a further indecision: viz., that which we feel when confronted with such questions as "Should we count a *point* of green light as *extended* or not?" As is frequent enough in such cases, the hesitation arises from the fact that the boundaries of application of words are not determined by usage in all possible directions. But the example

---

[7] Page 68.

Quine has chosen is particularly unfortunate for his thesis, in that it is only too evident that our hesitations are not *here* attributable to obscurities in "analytic." It would be possible to choose other examples in which we should hesitate between "analytic" and "synthetic" and have few qualms about "true." But no more in these cases than in the sample case does the hesitation necessarily imply any obscurity in the notion of analyticity; since the hesitation would be sufficiently accounted for by the same or a similar kind of indeterminacy in the relations between the words occurring within the statement about which the question, whether it is analytic or synthetic, is raised.

Let us now consider briefly Quine's positive theory of the relations between the statements we accept as true or reject as false on the one hand and the "experiences" in the light of which we do this accepting and rejecting on the other. This theory is boldly sketched rather than precisely stated.[8] We shall merely extract from it two assertions, one of which Quine clearly takes to be incompatible with acceptance of the distinction between analytic and synthetic statements, and the other of which he regards as barring one way to an explanation of that distinction. We shall seek to show that the first assertion is not incompatible with acceptance of the distinction, but is, on the contrary, most intelligibly interpreted in a way quite consistent with it, and that the second assertion leaves the way open to just the kind of explanation which Quine thinks it precludes. The two assertions are the following:

(1) It is an illusion to suppose that there is any class of accepted statements the members of which are in principle "immune from revision" in the light of experience, i.e., any that we accept as true and must continue to accept as true whatever happens.

(2) It is an illusion to suppose that an individual statement, taken in isolation from its fellows, can admit of confirmation or disconfirmation at all. There is no particular statement such that a particular experience or set of experiences decides once for all whether that statement is true or false, independently of our attitudes to all other statements.

The apparent connection between these two doctrines may be summed up follows. Whatever our experience may be, it is in principle to hold on to, or reject, any particular statement we like, so long as we are prepared to make extensive enough revisions elsewhere in our system of beliefs. In practice our choices are governed largely by considerations of convenience: we wish our system to be as simple as possible, but we also wish disturbances to it, as it exists, to be as small as possible.

The apparent relevance of these doctrines to the analytic-synthetic distinction is obvious in the first case, less so in the second.

(1) Since it is an illusion to suppose that the characteristic of immunity in principle from revision, come what may, belongs, or could belong, to any statement, it is an illusion to suppose that there is a distinction to be drawn between statements which possess this characteristic and statements which lack it. Yet,

---

[8] Cf. pages 74–80.

Quine suggests, this is precisely the distinction which those who use the terms "analytic" and "synthetic" suppose themselves to be drawing. Quine's view would perhaps also be (though he does not explicitly say this in the article under consideration) that those who believe in the distinction are inclined at least sometimes to mistake the characteristic of strongly resisting revision (which belongs to beliefs very centrally situated in the system) for the mythical characteristic of total immunity from revision.

(2) The connection between the second doctrine and the analytic-synthetic distinction runs, according to Quine, through the verification theory of meaning. He says: "If the verification theory can be accepted as an adequate account of statement synonymy, the notion of analyticity is saved after all."[9] For, in the first place, two statements might be said to be synonymous if and only if any experiences which contribute to, or detract from, the confirmation of one contribute to, or detract from, the confirmation of the other, to the same degree; and, in the second place, synonymy could be used to explain analyticity. But, Quine seems to argue, acceptance of any such account of synonymy can only rest on the mistaken belief that individual statements, taken in isolation from their fellows, can admit of confirmation or disconfirmation at all. As soon as we give up the idea of a set of experiential truth-conditions for each statement taken separately, we must give up the idea of explaining synonymy in terms of identity of such sets.

Now to show that the relations between these doctrines and the analytic-synthetic distinction are not as Quine supposes. Let us take the second doctrine first. It is easy to see that acceptance of the second doctrine would not compel one to abandon, but only to revise, the suggested explanation of synonymy. Quine does not deny that individual statements are regarded as confirmed or disconfirmed, are in fact rejected or accepted, in the light of experience. He denies only that these relations between single statements and experience hold independently of our attitudes to *other* statements. He means that experience can confirm or disconfirm an individual statement, only given certain assumptions about the truth or falsity of other statements. When we are faced with a "recalcitrant experience," he says, we always have a choice of what statements to amend. What we have to renounce is determined by what we are anxious to keep. This view, however, requires only a slight modification of the definition of statement-synonymy in terms of confirmation and disconfirmation. All we have to say now is that two statements are synonymous if and only if any experiences which, *on certain assumptions about the truth-values of other statements*, confirm or disconfirm one of the pair, also, *on the same assumptions*, confirm or disconfirm the other to the same degree. More generally, Quine wishes to substitute for what he conceives to be an oversimple picture of the confirmation-relations between particular statements and particular experiences, the idea of a looser relation which he calls "germaneness" (p. 79). But however loosely "germaneness" is to be understood, it would apparently continue to make

---

[9] Page 75.

sense to speak of two statements as standing in the same germaneness-relation to the same particular experiences. So Quine's views are not only consistent with, but even suggest, an amended account of statement-synonymy along these lines. We are not, of course, concerned to defend such an account, or even to state it with any precision. We are only concerned to show that acceptance of Quine's doctrine of empirical confirmation does not, as he says it does, entail giving up the attempt to define statement-synonymy in terms of confirmation.

Now for the doctrine that there is no statement which is in principle immune from revision, no statement which might not be given up in the face of experience. Acceptance of this doctrine is quite consistent with adherence to the distinction between analytic and synthetic statements. Only, the adherent of *this* distinction must also insist on another; on the distinction between that kind of giving up which consists in merely admitting falsity, and that kind of giving up which involves changing or dropping a concept or set of concepts. Any form of words at one time held to express something true may, no doubt, at another time, come to be held to express something false. But it is not only philosophers who would distinguish between the case where this happens as the case where this happens at least partly as a result of a shift in the sense of the words. Where such a shift in the sense of the words is a necessary condition of the change in truth-value, then the adherent of the distinction will say that the form of words in question changes from expressing an analytic statement to expressing a synthetic statement. We are not now concerned, or called upon, to elaborate an adequate theory of conceptual revision, any more than we were called upon, just now, to elaborate an adequate theory of synonymy. If we can make sense of the idea that the same form of words, taken in one way (or bearing one sense), may express something true, and taken in another way (or bearing another sense), may express something false, then we can make sense of the idea of conceptual revision. And if we can make sense of this idea, then we can perfectly well preserve the distinction between the analytic and the synthetic, while conceding to Quine the revisability-in-principle of everything we say. As for the idea that the same form of words, taken in different ways, may bear different senses and perhaps be used to say things with different truth-values, the onus of showing that this is somehow a mistaken or confused idea rests squarely on Quine. The point of substance (or one of them) that Quine is making, by this emphasis on revisability, is that there is no absolute necessity about the adoption or use of any conceptual scheme whatever, or, more narrowly and in terms that he would reject, that there is no analytic proposition such that we *must* have linguistic forms bearing just the sense required to express that proposition. But it is one thing to admit this, and quite another thing to say that there are no necessities within any conceptual scheme we adopt or use, or, more narrowly again, that there are no linguistic forms which do express analytic propositions.

The adherent of the analytic-synthetic distinction may go further and admit that there may be cases (particularly perhaps in the field of science) where it would be pointless to press the question whether a change in the attributed truth-value of a statement represented a conceptual revision or not, and correspondingly pointless to press the analytic-synthetic distinction. We cannot quote such cases, but this inability may well be the result of ignorance of the sciences. In any case, the existence, if they do exist, of statements about which it is pointless to press the question whether they are analytic or synthetic, does not entail the nonexistence of statements which are clearly classifiable in one or other of these ways and of statements our hesitation over which has different sources, such as the possibility of alternative interpretations of the linguistic forms in which they are expressed.

This concludes our examination of Quine's article. It will be evident that our purpose has been wholly negative. We have aimed to show merely that Quine's case against the existence of the analytic-synthetic distinction is not made out. His article has two parts. In one of them, the notions of the analyticity group are criticized on the ground that they have not been adequately explained. In the other, a positive theory of truth is outlined, purporting to be incompatible with views to which believers in the analytic-synthetic distinction either must be, or are likely to be, committed. In fact, we have contended, no single point is established which those who accept the notions of the analyticity group would feel any strain in accommodating in their own system of beliefs. This is not to deny that many of the points raised are of the first importance in connection with the problem of giving a satisfactory general account of analyticity and related concepts. We are here only criticizing the contention that these points justify the rejection, as illusory, of the analytic-synthetic distinction and the notions which belong to the same family.

HILARY PUTNAM

1.6   *The Analytic and the Synthetic*

The techniques employed by philosophers of physics are usually the very ones being employed by philosophers of a less specialized kind (especially empiricist philosophers) at the time. Thus Mill's philosophy of science largely reflects Hume's associationism; Reichenbach's philosophy of science reflects Viennese positivism with its conventionalism, its tendency to identify (or confuse) meaning and evidence, and its sharp dichotomy between "the empirical facts" and "the rules of the language"; and (coming up to the present time) Toulmin's philosophy of science is an attempt to give an account of what scientists do

Reprinted from *Minnesota Studies in the Philosophy of Science*, Vol. III, H. Feigl and G. Maxwell, eds. (Minneapolis: University of Minnesota Press, 1966), by permission of the publisher. © Copyright 1962, University of Minnesota.

which is consonant with the linguistic philosophy of Wittgenstein. For this reason, errors in general philosophy can have a far-reaching effect on the philosophy of science. The confusion of meaning with evidence is one such error whose effects are well known: it is the contention of the present paper that overworking of the analytic-synthetic distinction is another root of what is most distorted in the writings of conventional philosophers of science.

The present paper is an attempt to give an account of the analytic-synthetic distinction both inside and outside of physical theory. It is hoped that the paper is sufficiently nontechnical to be followed by a reader whose background in science is not extensive; but it *has* been necessary to consider problems connected with physical science (particularly the definition of 'kinetic energy', and the conceptual problems connected with geometry) in order to bring out the features of the analytic-synthetic distinction that seem to me to be the most important.

In addition to the danger of overworking the analytic-synthetic distinction, there is the somewhat newer danger of denying its existence altogether. Although, as I shall argue below, this is a less serious error (from the point of view of the scientist or the philosopher interested in the conceptual problems presented by physical theory) than the customary overworking of the distinction, it is, nevertheless, an error. Thus the present paper fights on two fronts: it tries to "defend" the distinction, while attacking its extensive abuse by philosophers. Fortunately, the two fronts are not too distant from each other; one reason that the analytic-synthetic distinction has seemed so difficult to defend recently is that it has become so bloated!

Replies to Quine. In the spring of 1951 Professor W. V. Quine published a paper entitled "Two Dogmas of Empiricism."[1] This paper provoked a spate of replies, but most of the replies did not match the paper which stimulated them in originality or philosophic significance. Quine denied the existence of the analytic-synthetic distinction altogether. He challenged doctrines which had been dear to the hearts of a great many philosophers and (in spite of the title of his paper) not only philosophers in the empiricist camp. The replies to Quine have played mostly on a relatively small number of stereotyped themes. The tendency has been to "refute" Quine by citing examples. Of course, the analytic-synthetic distinction rests on a certain number of classical examples. We would not have been tempted to draw it or to keep on drawing it for so long if we did not have a stock of familiar examples on which to fall back. But it is clear that the challenge raised by Quine cannot be met either by pointing to the traditional examples or by simply waving one's hand and saying how implausible it is that there should be no distinction at all when there seems to be such a clear one in at least some cases. I do not agree with Quine, as will be clear in the sequel. I am convinced that there is an analytic-synthetic distinction that we can correctly (if not very importantly) draw, and I am

---

[1] Reprinted in *From a Logical Point of View* (Cambridge, Mass.: Harvard University Press, 1953), pp. 20–46. [See selection 1.4 above, pp. 63–80.]

inclined to sympathize with those who cite the examples and who stress the implausibility, the tremendous implausibility, of Quine's thesis—the thesis that the distinction which certainly seems to exist does not in fact exist at all.

But to say that Quine is wrong is not in itself very fruitful or very interesting. The important question is How is he wrong? Faced with the battery of Quine's arguments, how can we defend the existence of any genuine analytic-synthetic distinction at all? Philosophers have the right to have intuitions and to believe things on faith; scientists often have no better warrant for many of their beliefs, at least not for a time. But if a philosopher really feels that Quine is wrong and has no statement to make other than the statement that Quine is wrong and that he feels this in his bones, then this is material to be included in that philosopher's autobiography; it does not belong in a technical journal under the pretense of being a reply to Quine. From this criticism I specifically exempt the article by P. F. Strawson and H. P. Grice,[2] who offer *theoretical* reasons for supposing that the analytic-synthetic distinction does in fact exist, even if they do not very satisfactorily delineate that distinction or shed much real light on its nature. Indeed, the argument used by them to the effect that *where there is agreement on the use of the expressions involved with respect to an open class, there must necessarily be some kind of distinction present*, seems to me correct and important. Perhaps this argument is the only one of any novelty to have appeared since Quine published his paper.

But important as it is to have a theoretical argument supporting the existence of the distinction in question (so that we do not have to appeal simply to "intuition" and "faith"), still the argument offered by Strawson and Grice does not go far toward clarifying the distinction, and this, after all, is Quine's challenge. In other words, we are in the position of *knowing* that there *is* an analytic-synthetic distinction but of not being able to make it very clear just what the nature of this distinction is.

Of course, in some cases it is not very important that we cannot make clear what the nature of a distinction is, but in the case of the analytic-synthetic distinction it seems that the nature of the distinction is far more imporant than the few trivial examples that are commonly cited, e.g., 'All bachelors are unmarried' (for the analytic side of the dichotomy) and 'There is a book on this table' (for the synthetic side). To repeat: philosophers who do not agree with Quine have found themselves in the last few years in this position: they *know* that there *is* an analytic-synthetic distinction but they are unable to give a satisfactory account of its nature.

It is, in the first place, no good to draw the distinction by saying that a man who rejects an analytic sentence is *said* not to understand the language or the relevant part of the language. For this is a comment on the use of the word 'understand' and, as such, not very helpful. There could be an analytic-synthetic distinction even in a language which did not use such words as 'analytic', 'synthetic', 'meaning', and 'understanding'. We do not want, after all, to draw

---

[2] In Defense of a Dogma," *Philosophical Review*, LXV (1956), 141–58. [See above, pp. 81–94.]

the analytic-synthetic distinction in terms of dispositions to use the words 'analytic' and 'synthetic' themselves, nor dispositions to use related expressions, e.g., 'have the same meaning' and 'does not understand what he is saying'. What is needed is something quite different: We should be able to indicate the nature and rationale of the analytic-synthetic distinction. What happens to a statement when it is analytic? What do people do with it? Or if one wishes to talk in terms of artificial languages: What point is there to having a separate class of statements called analytic statements? Why mark these off from all the others? What do you do with the statements so marked? It is only in this sort of terms that I think we can go beyond the level of saying, "Of course there are analytic statements. I can give you examples. If someone rejects one of these, we say he doesn't understand the language, etc." The real problem is not to describe the language game we play with words like 'meaning' and 'understanding' but to answer the deeper question, "What is the point of the game?"

The analytic-synthetic distinction in philosophy. It should not be supposed that the axe I have to grind here is that Quine is wrong. That Quine is wrong I have no doubt. This is not a matter of philosophical argument: it seems to me there is as gross a distinction between 'All bachelors are unmarried' and 'There is a book on this table' as between any two things in the world, or, at any rate, between any two linguistic expressions in the world; and no matter how long I might fail in trying to clarify the distinction, I should not be persuaded that it does not exist. In fact, I do not understand what it would mean to say that a distinction between two things *that* different does not exist.

Thus I think that Quine is wrong. There are analytic statements: 'All bachelors are unmarried' is one of them. But in a deeper sense I think that Quine is right; far more right than his critics. I think that there is an analytic-synthetic distinction, but a rather trivial one. And I think that the analytic-synthetic distinction has been so radically overworked that it is less of a philosophic error, although it is an error, to maintain that there is no distinction at all than it is to employ the distinction in the way that it has been employed by some of the leading analytic philosophers of our generation. I think, in other words, that if one proceeds, as Quine does, on the assumption that there is no analytic-synthetic distinction at all, one would be right on far more philosophic issues and one will be led to far more philosophic insights than one will be if one accepts that heady concoction of ideas with which we are all too familiar: the idea that every statement is either analytic or synthetic; the idea that all logical truths are analytic; the idea that all analytic truth derives its necessity from "linguistic convention." I would even put the thesis to be defended here more strongly: ignore the analytic-synthetic distinction, and you will not be wrong in connection with any philosophic issues not having to do specifically with the distinction. Attempt to use it as a weapon in philosophical discussion, and you will consistently be wrong.

It is not, of course, an accident that one will consistently be wrong if one attempts to employ the analytic-synthetic distinction in philosophy. 'Bachelor' may be synonymous with 'unmarried man' but that cuts no philosophic ice.

'Chair' may be synonymous with 'movable seat for one with a back' but that bakes no philosophic bread and washes no philosophic windows. It is the belief that there are synonymies and analyticities of a deeper nature—synonymies and analyticities that cannot be discovered by the lexicographer or the linguist but only by the philosopher—that is incorrect.[3]

I don't happen to believe that there are such objects as "sense data"; so I do not find "sense-datum language" much more interesting than phlogiston language or leprechaun language. But even if sense data did exist and we granted the possibility of constructing sense-datum language, I do not think that the expression 'chair', although it is synonymous with 'movable seat for one with a back', is in the same way synonymous with any expression that one could in principle construct in the sense-datum language. This is an example of the type of "hidden" synonymy or "philosophic" synonymy that some philosophers have claimed to discover and that does not exist.

However, misuse of the analytic-synthetic distinction is not confined to translationists. I have seen it argued by a philosopher of a more contemporary strain that the hypothesis that the earth came into existence five minutes ago (complete with "memory traces," "causal remains," etc.) is a *logically* absurd hypothesis. The argument was that the whole use of time words presupposes the existence of the past. If we grant the meaningfulness of this hypothesis, then, it is contended, we must grant the possibility that there is no past at all (the world might have come into existence at this instant). Thus, we have an example of a statement which uses time words, but which, if true, destroys the possibility of their use. This somewhat fuzzily described situation is alleged to be tantamount to the meaninglessness or self-contradictoriness of the hypothesis I described.

Now I agree that the hypothesis in question is more than empirically false. It *is* empirically false, if by empirically false one means simply that it is false about the world—the world did not come into existence at this instant nor did it come into existence five minutes ago. It is not empirically false if one means by 'empirically false statement' a statement which can be confuted by *isolated* experiments. But while it is important to recognize that this is not the sort of hypothesis that can be confuted by isolated experiment, it is not, I think, happy to maintain that the existence of a past is analytic, if one's paradigm for analyticity is the 'All bachelors are unmarried' kind of statement.[4] And I think that, while few philosophers would explicitly make the kind of mistake I have described, a great many philosophers tend to make it implicitly. The idea that every truth which is not empirical in the second of the senses I mentioned must be a "rule of language" or that all necessity must be traced down to the obligation not to "violate the rules of language" is a pernicious one, and Quine is

---

[3] I do not wish to suggest that linguistic regularities, properly so called, are never of importance in philosophy, but only that analytic statements, properly so called, are not.

[4] To accept the hypothesis that the world came into existence five minutes ago does not make it necessary to give up any *particular* prediction. But I deny (a) that it "makes no difference to prediction," and (b) that "it therefore (*sic!*) amounts to a change in our use of language."

profoundly right in rejecting it; the reasons he gives are, moreover, the right reasons. What I maintain is that there are no further rules of language beyond the garden variety of rules which a lexicographer or a grammarian might discover, and which only the philosopher can discover.

This is not to say that there are not some things which are very much *like* "rules of language." There is after all a place for *stipulation* in cognitive inquiry, and truth by stipulation has seemed to some the very model of analyticity. There is also the question of linguistic misuse. Under certain circumstances a man is said not merely to be in error but to be making linguistic mistakes—not to know the meaning of the very words he is employing. Philosophers have thought that by looking at such situations we could reconstruct a codex which might constitute the "implicit rules" of natural language. For instance, they hold that, in many circumstances, to say of a man that he knows that p implies that he has, or had at some time, or can produce, or could produce at some time, evidence that p—and that such an implication is very much like the implication between being a bachelor and being unmarried. But, as I shall argue below, there are differences which it is absolutely vital to recognize. It is not that the statements I have mentioned fall into a third category. They fall into many different categories. Over and beyond the clear-cut rules of language, on the one side, and the clear-cut descriptive statements, on the other, are just an enormous number of statements which are not happily classified as either analytic or synthetic.

The case of stipulation is one in point. One must consider the role of the stipulation and whether the truth introduced by stipulation retains its conventional character or whether it later figures in inquiry on a par with other truths, without reference to the way in which it was introduced. We have to consider the question of the arbitrariness versus systematic import of our stipulations. There is one kind of wholly arbitrary stipulation which does indeed produce analytic statements, but we should not be led to infer that, therefore, every stipulation produces analytic statements. The Einstein stipulation that the constancy of the light velocity should be used to "define" simultaneity in a reference system does not, Reichenbach to the contrary, generate an analytic truth of the same order as 'All bachelors are unmarried'. And even the case of *knowing* and *having or having had evidence* requires much treatment and involves special difficulties. I shall in the body of this paper try to draw some of the distinctions that I think need to be drawn. For the moment let me only say this: if one wants to have a model of language, it is far better to proceed on the idea that statements fall into three kinds—analytic, synthetic, and lots-of-other-things—than to proceed on the idea that, except for borderline fuzziness, every statement is either analytic or synthetic.

Of course many philosophers are aware that there are statements which are not happily classified as either analytic or synthetic. My point is not that there exist exceptional examples, but that there is a far larger class of such statements than is usually supposed. For example, to ask whether or not the principles of logic are analytic is to ask a bad question. Virtually all the *laws* of natural science are statements with respect to which it is not *happy* to ask the question "Analytic or synthetic? It must be one or the other, mustn't it?" And with respect to the framework principles that are often discussed by philosophers, the existence of the past or the implication that some time exists between knowing and having had evidence, it is especially a mistake to classify these statements as "rules of language" or "true because of the logic of the concepts involved" or "analytic" or "L-true" or . . . This is not to say that all these principles have the same nature or that they form a compact new class, e.g., framework principles (as if one were to take seriously the label I have been using). 'There is a past' is recognizably closer to the law of conservation of energy than 'If Jones knows that p, then he must have or have had evidence that p' (in the cases where the latter inference seems a necessary one); and 'If Jones knows that p, then he must have or have had evidence that p' is more like 'All bachelors are unmarried' than is 'There is a past'. But neither statement is of exactly the same kind as the law of conservation of energy, although that law too is a statement with respect to which it is not happy to say, "Is it analytic or synthetic?" and neither statement is of exactly the same kind as 'All bachelors are unmarried'. What these statements reveal are different degrees of something like convention, and different kinds of systematic import. In the case of 'All bachelors are unmarried', we have the highest degree of linguistic convention and the minimum degree of systematic import. In the case of the statement 'There is a past', we have an overwhelming amount of systematic import—so much that we can barely conceive of a conceptual system which did not include the idea of a past. That is to say, such a conceptual system differs so greatly from our present conceptual system that the idea of ever making a transition from one to the other seems fantastic.[5] In the case of knowing without ever having any reason to believe, still other considerations are involved. We have to ask what we would say if people appeared to be able to answer questions truthfully about a certain subject matter although they had never had any acquaintance with that subject matter as far as we could detect. *Knowing* is something that we do not have much of a theory about. It makes little difference at *present* whether we say that such people would be correctly described as "knowing" the answers to the various questions in the area in which they are able to act as an oracle, or whether we say that they have an "uncanny facility at guessing the correct answer"; although, in the light of a more advanced theory, it might very well make a good deal of difference what we say. The concept of the past, on the other hand, and the concept of time, are deeply integrated into our physical theory, and any tampering with these concepts would involve a host of revisions if simple consistency is to be maintained. In the sequel I shall try to describe in somewhat more

---

[5] For example, we *could* accept the hypothesis that the world came into existence January 1, 1957, without changing the *meaning* of any word; but to do so would have a crippling effect on many sciences, and on much of ordinary life. (Think of the *ad hoc* hypotheses that would have to be invented to account for the "creation." And consider the role played by data concerning the past in, say, astronomy—not to mention ordinary human relations!)

detail the diverse natures of the statements in that vast class with respect to which it is not happy to say "analytic or synthetic." But on the whole my story will resemble Quine's. That is to say, I believe that we have a conceptual system with centralities and priorities. I think the statements in that conceptual system—except for the *trivial* examples of analyticity, e.g., 'All bachelors are unmarried', 'All vixens are foxes'—fall on a continuum, a multidimensional continuum. More or less stipulation enters; more or less systematic import. But any one of these principles might be given up, farfetched though it may seem, and perhaps without altering the meaning of the constituent words. Of course, if we give up a principle that is analytic in the trivial sense ('All bachelors are unmarried'), then we have clearly changed the meaning of a word. But the revision of a sufficient number of principles, no one of which is by itself analytic in quite the way in which 'All bachelors are unmarried' is analytic, may also add up to what we should describe as a change in the meaning of a word. With Quine, I should like to stress the monolithic character of our conceptual system, the idea of our conceptual system as a massive alliance of beliefs which face the tribunal of experience collectively and not independently, the idea that "when trouble strikes" revisions can, with a very few exceptions, come anywhere. I should like, with Quine, to stress the extent to which the meaning of an individual word is a function of its place in the network, and the impossibility of separating, in the actual use of a word, that part of the use which reflects the "meaning" of the word and that part of the use which reflects deeply embedded collateral information.

Linguistic conventionalism. One more point will terminate this rather interminable set of preliminary remarks. The focus of this paper is the analytic-synthetic distinction, not because I think that distinction is of itself of overwhelming importance. In fact, I think it is of overwhelming unimportance. But I believe that the issues raised by Quine go to the very center of philosophy. I think that appreciating the diverse natures of logical truths, of physically necessary truths in the natural sciences, and of what I have for the moment lumped together under the title of framework principles—that clarifying the nature of these diverse kinds of statements is the most important work that a philosopher can do. Not because philosophy is necessarily about language, but because we must become clear about the roles played in our conceptual systems by these diverse kinds of truths before we can get an adequate global view of the world, of thought, of language, or of anything. In particular, I think we might begin to appreciate the real problems in the domain of formal science once we rid ourselves of the easy answer that formal truth is in some sense "linguistic in origin"; and in any case I think that one's whole view of the world is deeply affected, if one is a philosopher, by one's view of what it is to have a view about the world. Someone who identifies conceptualization with linguistic activity and who identifies linguistic activity with response to observable situations in accordance with rules of language which are themselves no more than implicit conventions or implicit stipulations (in the ordinary unphilosophic sense of 'stipulation' and 'convention') will, it seems to me, have a deeply distorted conception of human knowledge and, indirectly, of some or all objects of human knowledge. We must not fall into the error of supposing that to master the total use of an expression is to master a repertoire of individual uses, that the individual uses are the product of something like implicit stipulation or implicit convention, and that the conventions and stipulations are arbitrary. (The notion of a nonarbitrary *convention* is of course an absurdity—conventions are used precisely to settle questions that are arbitrary.) For someone who uses language in the way that I have just described, there are observable phenomena at the macrolevel and there are conventional responses to these, and this is all of knowledge; one can, of course, say that "there are atoms" and that "science is able to tell us a great deal about atoms," but *this* turns out to be no more than making noises in response to macrostimuli *in accordance with arbitrary conventions.* I do not think that any philosopher explicitly maintains such a view of knowledge; and if he did it is clear that he would be a sort of mitigated phenomenalist. But I do think that a good many philosophers implicitly hold such a view, or fall into writing as if they held such a view, simply because they tend to think of use as a sum of individual uses and of linguistic use on the model suggested by the phrase 'rules of language'.

To sum up: I do not agree with Quine, that there is no analytic-synthetic distinction to be drawn at all. But I do believe that his emphasis on the monolithic character of our conceptual system and his negative emphasis on the *silliness* of regarding mathematics as consisting in some sense of rules of language," represent exceedingly important theoretical insights in philosophy. I think that what we have to do now is to settle the relatively trivial question concerning analytic statements properly so called ('All bachelors are unmarried'). We have to take a fresh look at the framework principles so much discussed by philosophers, disabusing ourselves of the idea that they are "rules of language" in any literal or lexicographic sense; and above all, we have to take a fresh look at the nature of logical and mathematical truths. With Quine's contribution, we have to face two choices: We can ignore it and go on talking about the "logic" of individual words. In that direction lies sterility and more, much more, of what we have already read. The other alternative is to face and explore the insight achieved by Quine, trying to reconcile the fact that Quine is overwhelmingly right in his critique of what other philosophers have *done* with the analytic-synthetic distinction with the fact that Quine is wrong in his literal thesis, namely, that the distinction itself does not exist *at all.* In the latter direction lies philosophic progress. For philosophic progress is nothing if it is not the discovery of new areas for dialectical exploration.

ANALYTIC AND NONANALYTIC STATEMENTS

The "kinetic energy definition." As a step toward clarification of the analytic-synthetic distinction, I should like to contrast a paradigm case of analyticity— 'All bachelors are unmarried'—with an example which superficially resembles it: the statement that kinetic energy is equal to one half the product of mass and velocity squared, 'e $= \frac{1}{2}$mv^2'. I think that if we can see the respect in which these two examples differ, we will have made important progress toward such a clarification.

Let us take the second statement first, 'e $= \frac{1}{2}$mv^2'; this is the sort of statement that before relativistic physics one might well have called a "definition of 'kinetic energy'." Yet, its history is unusual. Certainly, before Einstein, any physicist might have said, " 'e $= \frac{1}{2}$mv^2'; that is just the definition of 'kinetic energy'. There is no more to it than that. The expression 'kinetic energy' is, as it were, a sort of abbreviation for the longer expression 'one-half the mass times the velocity squared'."

If this were true, then the expression 'kinetic energy' would, of course, be in principle dispensable. One could simply use '$\frac{1}{2}$mv^2' wherever one had used 'kinetic energy'.

In the early years of the twentieth century, however, Albert Einstein developed a theory, a physical theory—but of an unusual sort. It is unusual because it contains words of a rather high degree of vagueness, at least in terms of what we usually suppose the laws of physics to be like. All this notwithstanding, the theory is, as we all well know, a precise and useful theory.

What I have in mind is Einstein's principle that all physical laws must be Lorentz-invariant. This is a rather vague principle, since it involves the general notion of physical law. Yet in spite of its vagueness, or perhaps because of its vagueness, scientists have found it an extremely useful leading principle. Of course, Einstein contributed more than a leading principle. He actually proceeded to find Lorentz-invariant laws of nature; and the search for a Lorentz-invariant law of gravitation, in particular, produced the general theory of relativity.[6]

But it would be a mistake to think of the special theory of relativity as the sum of the special laws that Einstein produced. The general principle that all physical laws are Lorentz-invariant is certainly a legitimate part of the special theory of relativity, notwithstanding the fact that it is stated in what some purists might call "the metalanguage." And it is no good to say that 'a physical law' means 'any true physical statement': for so interpreted Einstein's principle would be empty. Any equation whatsoever can be made Lorentz-invariant by writing it in terms of suitable magnitudes. The principle that the laws of nature must be Lorentz-invariant is without content unless we suppose that the magnitudes to be contained in laws of nature must be in some sense real magnitudes —e.g., electricity, gravitation, magnetism—and that the equations expressing the laws must have certain characteristics of simplicity and plausibility. In practice, Einstein's principle is quite precise, in the only sense relevant to physical inquiry, notwithstanding the fact that it contains a vague term. The point is that the vagueness of the term 'physical law' does not affect the applica-

---

[6] Of course, the general theory of relativity itself *replaces* the requirement of Lorentz-invariance with the requirement of covariance.

tions which the physicist makes of the principle. In practice, the physicist has no difficulty in recognizing laws or putative laws: any "reasonable" equation proposed by a physicist in his right mind constitutes at least a putative law. Thus, the Einstein principle, although it might bother those logicians who are worried, and rightly worried, about the right distinction between a natural law and any true statement whatsoever, is one whose role in physical inquiry is clear-cut. It means simply that those equations considered by physicists as expressing possible laws of nature must, if they are to remain candidates for that role in the age of relativity, be Lorentz-invariant. Of course, the principle does not play only the purely negative role of ruling out what might otherwise be admissible scientific theories: the fact that laws of nature must be Lorentz-invariant has often been a valuable clue to fundamental new discoveries. The Einstein gravitation theory has already been mentioned; another famous example is Dirac's "hole" theory, which led to the discovery of the positron.

Returning now to our account of the history of the "energy definition": the principle just described led Einstein to change a great many physical laws. Some of the older laws, of course, survived: the Maxwell equations, for instance, turned out to be Lorentz-invariant as they stood. Some of the principles that Einstein revised would ordinarily be regarded as being of an empirical nature. The statements 'Moving clocks slow down' and 'One cannot exceed the velocity of light' are certainly statements which we should regard as synthetic. The interesting thing is that Einstein was to revise, and in an *exactly similar fashion*, principles that had traditionally been regarded as definitional in character. In particular, Einstein, as we all know, changed the definition of 'kinetic energy'. That is to say, he replaced the law 'e $= \frac{1}{2}mv^2$' by a more complicated law. If we expand the Einstein definition of energy as a power series, the first two terms are 'e $= mc^2 + \frac{1}{2}mv^2 + \ldots$' We might, of course, reply that classically speaking '$\frac{1}{2}mv^2$' defines not 'energy' in general (e.g., 'potential energy') but only 'kinetic energy'; we might try to say that the energy that a body has because of its rest mass (this is represented by the term 'mc^2') should not be counted as part of its kinetic energy, as Einstein does. The point is that even the magnitude in the thoery of relativity that corresponds to the classical kinetic energy of a particle, that is, its total kinetic energy minus the energy due to its rest mass, is not equal to $\frac{1}{2}mv^2$ except as a first approximation. If you take the total relativistic kinetic energy of a particle and subtract the energy due to its rest mass, you will obtain not only the leading term '$\frac{1}{2}mv^2$' but also terms in 'mv^4' etc.

It would clearly be a distortion of the situation to say that 'kinetic energy $= \frac{1}{2}mv^2$' was a definition, and that Einstein merely changed the definition. The paradigm that this account suggests is somewhat as follows: 'kinetic energy', before Einstein, was *arbitrarily* used to stand for '$\frac{1}{2}mv^2$'. After Einstein, 'kinetic energy' was arbitrarily used to stand for '$m + \frac{1}{2}mv^2 + \frac{3}{8}mv^4 + \ldots$'[7] This account is, of course, incorrect.

---

[7] This formula assumes that the unit of time is chosen so that the speed of light $= 1$.

What is striking is this: whatever the status of the "energy definition" may have been before Einstein, in revising it, Einstein treated it as just another natural law. There was a whole set of pre-existing physical and mechanical laws which had to be tested for compatibility with the new body of theory. Some stood the test unchanged—others only with some revision. Among the equations that had to be revised (and formal considerations indicated a rather natural way of making the revision, one which was, moreover, borne out richly by experiments) was the equation 'e $= \frac{1}{2}mv^2$'.

The moral of all this is not difficult to find. The "energy definition" may have had a special status when it came into the body of accepted physical theory, although this is a question for the historian of science to answer. It may even, let us suppose, have originally been accepted on the basis of explicit stipulation to the effect that the phrase 'kinetic energy' was to be used in the sense of '$\frac{1}{2}mv^2$'. Indeed, there was some discussion between Newton and Leibniz on the question whether the term 'energy' should be applied to what we now do call 'energy' or what we call 'momentum'. Suppose, however, that a congress of scientists had been convened in, say, 1780 and had settled this controversy by legislating that the term 'kinetic energy' was to be used for $\frac{1}{2}mv^2$ and not for mv. Would this have made the principle 'e $= \frac{1}{2}mv^2$' analytic? It would be true by stipulation, wouldn't it? It would be true by stipulation, yes, *but only in a context which is defined by the fact that the only alternative principle is* 'e $=$ mv'.

Quine has suggested that the distinction between truths by stipulation and truths by experiment is one which can be drawn only at the moving frontier of science. Conventionality is not "a lingering trait" of the statements introduced as truths by stipulation. The principle 'e $= \frac{1}{2}mv^2$' may have been introduced, at least in our fable, by stipulation; the Newtonian law of gravity may have been introduced on the basis of induction from the behavior of the known satellite systems and the solar system (as Newton claimed); but in subsequent developments these two famous formulas were to figure on a par. Both were used in innumerable physical experiments until they were challenged by Einstein, without ever being regarded as themselves subject to test in the particular experiment. If a physicist makes a calculation and gets an empirically wrong answer, he does not suspect that the mathematical principles used in the calculation may have been wrong (assuming that those principles are themselves theorems of mathematics) nor does he suspect that the law 'f $=$ ma' may be wrong. Similarly, he did not frequently suspect before Einstein that the law 'e $= \frac{1}{2}mv^2$' might be wrong or that the Newtonian gravitational law might be wrong (Newton himself did, however, suspect the latter). These statements, then, have a kind of preferred status. They can be overthrown, but not by an isolated experiment. They can be overthrown only if someone incorporates principles incompatible with those statements in a successful conceptual system.

Principles of geometry. An analogy may be drawn with the case of geometry. No experiments—no experiments with light rays or tape measures or with anything else—could have overthrown the laws of Euclidean geometry before someone had worked out *non*-Euclidean geometry. That is to say, it is inconceivable that a scientist living in the time of Hume might[8] have come to the conclusion that the laws of Euclidean geometry are false: "I do not know what geometrical laws are true, but I know the laws of Euclidean geometry are false." Principles as central to the conceptual system of science as laws of geometry are simply not abandoned in the face of experiment *alone*. They are abandoned because a rival *theory* is available.

On the other hand, before the development of non-Euclidean geometry by Riemann and Lobachevski, the best philosophic minds regarded the principles of geometry as virtually analytic. The human mind could not conceive their falsity. Hume would certainly not have been impressed by the claim that 'straight line' means 'path of a light ray', and that the meeting of two light rays mutually perpendicular to a third light ray could show, if it ever occurred, that Euclidean geometry is false. It would have been self-evident to Hume that such an experimental situation, if it ever occurred, would be correctly explained by supposing that the light rays traveled in a curved path in Euclidean space, and *not* by supposing that the light rays traveled in two straight lines which were indeed mutually perpendicular to a third straight line but which nevertheless met. Hume, had he employed the vocabulary of contemporary analytic philosophy, might even had said that this follows from the "logic" of the words 'straight line'. It is a "criterion," to use another popular word, for lines being straight that if two of them are perpendicular to a third the two do not meet. It may be another criterion that light travels in *approximately* straight lines; but only where this criterion does not conflict with the deeply seated meaning of the words 'straight line'. In short, the meaning of the words 'straight line' is such that light rays may sometimes be said not to travel in straight lines; but straight lines cannot be said to behave in such a way as to form a triangle the sum of whose angles is more than 180°. If he had used the jargon of another fashionable contemporary school of philosophy, Hume might have said that straight lines are "theoretical constructs." And that light ray paths constitute a "partial interpretation" of geometrical theory but one that is only admissible on condition that it does not render false any of the "meaning postulates" of the geometrical theory.

Of course Hume did not employ this jargon. But he employed what was for him an equivalent jargon: the jargon of conceiving, visualizing, mental imagery. One cannot form any image of straight lines that do not conform to the laws of Euclidean geometry. This, of course, was to be true because any image of lines not conforming to the axioms of Euclidean geometry is an image which is not *properly* called an image of *straight* lines at all. Hume did not put it that way, however. Rather he explained the alleged "impossibility of imagining"

---

[8] This is not a historical remark. I mean that no scientist *ought* to have come to this conclusion at that time, no matter what experimental evidence might have been presented.

straight lines not conformant to the laws of Euclidean geometry in terms of a theory of relations between our ideas.

Was Hume wrong? Reichenbach[9] suggested that 'straight line', properly analyzed, means 'path of a light ray'; and with this "analysis" accepted, it is clear that the principles of geometry always are and always were synthetic. They are and always were subject to experiment. Hume simply overlooked something which could *in principle*[10] have been seen even by the ancient Greeks. I think Reichenbach is almost totally wrong. If the paradigm for an analytic sentence is 'All bachelors are unmarried'—and it is—then it is of course absurd to say that the principles of geometry are analytic. Indeed, we cannot any longer say that the principles of Euclidean geometry are analytic; because analytic sentences are true, and we no longer say that the principles of Euclidean geometry are true. But I want to suggest that before the work of nineteenth-century mathematicians, the principles of Euclidean geometry were as *close* to analytic as any nonanalytic statement ever gets. That is to say, they had the following status: no experiment that one could describe could possibly overthrow them, by itself.[11] Just plain experimental results, without any new theory to integrate them, would not have been accepted as sufficient grounds for rejecting Euclidean geometry by any rational scientist.[12] After the development of non-Euclidean geometry, the position was rather different, as physicists soon realized: give us a rival conceptual system, and some reason for accepting it, and we will consider abandoning the laws of Euclidean geometry.

When I say that the laws of Euclidean geometry were, before the development of non-Euclidean geometry, as analytic as any nonanalytic statements ever get, I mean to group them, in this respect, with many other principles: the 'f = ma' (force equals mass times acceleration), the principle that the world did not come into existence five minutes ago, the principle that one cannot know certain kinds of facts, e.g., facts about objects at a distance from one,

---

[9] Reichenbach actually claimed that there were various possible alternative "coordinative definitions" of 'straight line'. However he contended that this one (and the ones physically equivalent to it) "have the advantage of logical simplicity and require the least change in the results of science." Moreover: "The sciences have implicitly employed such a coordinative definition all the time, though not always consciously"—i.e., it renders the customary meaning of the term 'straight line'. *Space and Time* (New York: Dover Publications, 1956), p. 19.

[10] Reichenbach does not assert that the Greeks could (as a matter of psychological or historical possibility) have understood the "true" character of geometric statements prior to the invention of non-Euclidean geometry: in fact, he denies this. But there is nothing in Reichenbach's analysis in Ch. I of *Space and Time* which *logically* presupposes a knowledge of non-Euclidean geometry. Thus, if Reichenbach is right, then the Greeks could *in principle* have "realized" (a) that the question whether Euclidean geometry is correct for physical space presupposes the choice of a "coordinative definition," and (b) that once the customary definition has been chosen, the question is an "empirical" one.

[11] As Mill very clearly states; see *System of Logic*, Ch. V, Secs. 4, 5, 6. As Mill foresaw, "There is probably no one proposition enunciated in this work for which a more unfavorable opinion is to be expected" (than, that is, his denial of the a priori character of geometrical propositions, notwithstanding the "inconceivability" of their negations).

[12] This is not a historical remark.

unless one has or has had evidence. These principles play several different roles; but in one respect they are alike. They share the characteristic that no isolated experiment (I cannot think of a better phrase than 'isolated experiment' to contrast with 'rival theory') can overthrow them. On the other hand, most of these principles can be overthrown if there is good reason for overthrowing them, and such good reason would have to consist in the presentation of a whole rival theory embodying the denials of these principles, plus evidence of the success of such a rival theory. Any principle in our knowledge can be revised for theoretical reasons; although many principles resist refutation by isolated experimentation. There are indeed some principles (some philosophers of science call them "low-level generalizations") which can be overthrown by isolated experiments, provided the experiments are repeated often enough and produce substantially the same results. But there are many, many principles—we might broadly classify them as "framework principles"—which have the characteristic of being so central that they are employed as auxiliaries to make predictions in an overwhelming number of experiments, without themselves being jeopardized by any possible experimental results. This is the classical role of the laws of logic; but it is equally the role of certain physical principles, e.g., 'f = ma', and the principles we have been discussing: the laws of Euclidean geometry, and the law 'e = $^1/_2$mv^2', at the time when those laws were still accepted.

I said that any principle in our knowledge can be revised for theoretical reasons. But this is not strictly correct. Any principle in our knowledge can be revised or abandoned for theoretical reasons unless it is really an analytic principle in the trivial sense in which 'All bachelors are unmarried' is an analytic principle. There are indeed analytic statements in science; and these are immune from revision, except the trivial kind of revision which arises from unintended and unexplained historical changes in the use of language. The point of the preceding discussion is that many principles which have been mistaken for analytic ones have actually a somewhat different role. There is all the difference in the world between a principle that can never be given up by a rational scientist and a principle which cannot be given up by rational scientists merely because of experiments, no matter how numerous or how consistent.

To summarize this discussion of geometry: I think that Hume was perfectly right in assigning to the principles of geometry the same status that he assigned to the principles of arithmetic. I think that in his time the principles of geometry *had* the same status as the principles of arithmetic. It is not that there is something—"an operational definition" of 'straight line'—which Hume failed to apprehend. The idea that, had he been aware of the "operational definition of straight line" on the one hand and of the "reduction of mathematics to logic" on the other hand, Hume would have seen that geometry is not really so much like arithmetic after all, that geometry is synthetic and arithmetic analytic, seems a crude error. The principle that light travels in straight lines is not a definition of 'straight line': as such, it is hopeless since it contains the geometrical term 'travels'. The same objection arises if we say a "straight line is defined as the path of a light ray." In this case the definition of 'straight line' uses the topological term 'path'. The principle that light travels in a straight line is simply a law of optics, nothing more or less serious than that. What is often called "interpreting mathematical geometry" is more aptly described as testing the conjunction of geometric theory and optical theory. The implicit standpoint of Hume was that if the conjunction should lead to false predictions, then the optical theories would have to be revised; the geometric theory was analytic. The Reichenbachian criticism is that the geometry was synthetic and the optical theory was analytic. Both were wrong. We test the conjunction of geometry and optics indeed, and if we get into trouble, then we can alter either the geometry or the optics, depending on the nature of the trouble. Before Einstein, geometrical principles had exactly the same status as analytic principles, or rather, they had exactly the same status as all the principles that philosophers mistakenly cite as analytic. After Einstein, especially after the general theory of relativity, they have exactly the same status as cosmological laws: this is because general relativity establishes a complex interdependence between the cosmology and the geometry of our universe.

Thus, we should not say that 'straight line' has changed its meaning: that Hume was talking about one thing and that Einstein was talking about a different thing when the term 'straight line' was employed. Rather, we should say that Hume (and Euclid) had certain beliefs about straight lines—not just about mental images of straight lines, but about straight lines in the space in which we live and move and have our being—which were, in fact, unknown to them, false. But we can say all this, and also say that the principles of geometry had, at the time Hume was writing, the same status as the laws of mathematics.

Law-cluster concepts. At this point, a case has been developed for the view that statements expressing the laws of mathematics and geometry and our earlier example 'e = $^1/_2$mv^2' are not analytic, if by 'an analytic statement' one means a statement that a rational scientist can never give up. It remains to show that 'All bachelors are unmarried' *is* an analytic statement in that sense. This is not a trivial undertaking: for the "shocking" part of Quine's thesis is that there are no analytic statements in this sense—that all of the statements in our conceptual system have the character that I have attributed variously to the laws of logic, the laws of the older geometry at the time when they were accepted, and certain physical principles. But before considering this question, there are certain possible objections against the account just given which must be faced. The objections I have in mind are two. (1) It may be argued, especially in connection with logical principles, that revision of these principles merely amounts to a change in the meaning of the constituent words. Thus, logical principles are not *really* given up; one merely changes one's language. (2) It may be held that the case of the principle 'e = $^1/_2$mv^2' merely shows that we were able to "change our definition of 'kinetic energy'," and *not* that a principle which was at one time definitional or stipulative could be later abandoned for reasons not substantially different from the reasons given for abandoning certain principles which philosophers would classify as synthetic.

The first objection I have discussed elsewhere.[13] The main point to be made is this: the logical words 'or', 'and', 'not' have a certain core meaning which is easily specifiable and which is *independent* of the principle of the excluded middle. Thus, in a certain sense the meaning does not change if we go over to three-valued logic or to intuitionist logic. Of course, if by saying that a change in the accepted logical principles is tantamount to a change in the meaning of the logical connective, what one has in mind is the fact that changing the accepted logical principles will affect the global use of the logical connectives, then the thesis is tautological and hardly arguable. But if the claim is that a change in the accepted logical principles would amount *merely* to redefining the logical connectives, then, in the case of intuitionist logic, this is demonstrably false. What is involved is the acceptance of a whole new network of inferences with profound systematic consequences; and it is a philosophical sin to say, even indirectly by one's choice of terminology, that this amounts to no more than stipulating new definitions for the logical connectives. A change in terminology never makes it impossible to draw inferences that could be validly drawn before; or, if it does, it is only because certain words are missing, which can easily be supplied. But the adoption of intuitionist logic as opposed to "classical" logic amounts to systematically forswearing certain classically valid inferences. Some of these inferences can be brought in again by redefinition. But others, inferences involving certain kinds of nonconstructive mathematical entities, are really forsworn in any form. To assimilate the change from one system of logic to another to the change that would be made if we were to use the noise 'bachelor' to stand for 'unmarried woman' instead of 'unmarried man' is assimilating a mountain to a molehill. There is a use of the term 'meaning' according to which any change in important beliefs may be said to change the "meaning" of some of the constituent concepts. Only in this fuzzy sense may it be said that to change our accepted logical principles would be to change the "meaning" of the logical connectives. And the claim that to change our logical system would be merely to change the meaning of the logical connectives is just false. With respect to the second objection, there are some similar remarks to be made. Once again, to speak of Einstein's contribution as a "redefinition" of 'kinetic energy' is to assimilate what actually happened to a wholly false model.

Leibniz worried about the fact that statements containing a proper name as subject term seem never to be analytic. This seemed to be absurd, so he concluded that all such statements must be analytic—that is, that they must all follow from the nature of what they speak about. Mill took the different tack of denying that proper names connote; but this leaves it puzzling that they mean anything at all. Similarly, philosophers have wondered whether any statement containing the subject term 'man' is really analytic. Is it analytic

---

[13] "Three-Valued Logic," *Philosophical Studies*, VIII (1957), 73–80.

that all men are rational? (We are no longer so happy with the Aristotelian idea that a necessary truth can have exceptions.) Is it analytic that all men are featherless? Aristotle thought not, thus displaying a commendable willingness to include our feathered friends, the Martians (if they exist), under the name 'man'. Suppose one makes a list of the attributes P_1, P_2 . . . that go to make up a normal man. One can raise successively the questions "Could there be a man without P_1?" "Could there be a man without P_2?" and so on. The answer in each case might be "Yes," and yet it seems absurd that the word 'man' has no meaning at all. In order to resolve this sort of difficulty, philosophers have introduced the idea of what may be called a *cluster concept*. (Wittgenstein uses instead of the metaphor of a "cluster," the metaphor of a rope with a great many strands, no one of which runs the length of the rope.) That is, we say that the meaning in such a case is given by a cluster of properties. To abandon a large number of these properties, or what is tantamount to the same thing, to radically change the extension of the term 'man', would be left as an arbitrary change in its meaning. On the other hand, if most of the properties in the cluster are present in any single case, then under suitable circumstances we should be inclined to say that what we had to deal with was a man.

In analogy with the notion of a cluster concept, I should like to introduce the notion of a *law-cluster concept*. Law-cluster concepts are constituted not by a bundle of properties as are the typical general names like 'man' and 'crow', but by a cluster of laws which, as it were, determine the identity of the concept. The concept 'energy' is an excellent example of a law-cluster concept. It enters into a great many laws. It plays a great many roles, and these laws and inference roles constitute its meaning collectively, not individually. I want to suggest that most of the terms in highly developed science are law-cluster concepts, and that one should always be suspicious of the claim that a principle whose subject term is a law-cluster concept is analytic. The reason that it is difficult to have an analytic relationship between law-cluster concepts is that such a relationship would be one more law. But, in general, any one law can be abandoned without destroying the identity of the law-cluster concept involved, just as a man can be irrational from birth, or can have a growth of feathers all over his body, without ceasing to be a man.

Applying this to our example—'kinetic energy' = 'kinetic' + 'energy'— the kinetic energy of a particle is literally the energy due to its motion. The extension of the term 'kinetic energy' has not changed. If it had, the extension of the term 'energy' would have to have changed.[14] But the extension of the term 'energy' has not changed. The forms of energy and their behavior are the same as they always were, and they are what physicists talked about before and after Einstein. On the other hand, I want to suggest that the term 'energy' is

---

[14] Kinetic energy is only one of several kinds of energy, and can be transformed into other kinds (and vice versa). Thus an adequate physical theory cannot change the meaning of the term "kinetic energy" without changing the meaning of the term "energy," without giving up the idea that "kinetic energy" is literally a kind of energy.

not one of which it is *happy* to ask, What is its intension? The term 'intension' suggests the idea of a single defining character or a single defining law, and this is not the model on which concepts like energy are to be construed. In the case of a law-cluster term such as 'energy', any one law, even a law that was felt to be definitional or stipulative in character, can be abandoned, and we feel that the identity of the concept has, in a certain respect, remained.[15] Thus, the conclusions of the present section still stand: A principle involving the term 'energy', a principle which was regarded as definitional, or as analytic, if you please, has been abandoned. And its abandonment cannot be explained away as mere "redefinition" or as change in the meaning of 'kinetic energy', although one might say that the change in the status of the principle has *brought about* a change in the meaning of the term 'kinetic energy' in one rather fuzzy sense of 'meaning'.[16] It is important to see that the principle '$e = \frac{1}{2}mv^2$' might have been mistaken to have exactly the same nature as 'All bachelors are unmarried'. But 'All bachelors are unmarried' cannot be rejected unless we change the meaning of the word 'bachelor' and not even then unless we change it so radically as to change the *extension* of the term 'bachelor'. In the case of the terms 'energy' and 'kinetic energy', we want to say, or at any rate I want to say, that the meaning has not changed enough to affect "what we are talking about"; yet a principle superficially very much like 'All bachelors are unmarried' has been abandoned. What makes the resemblance only superficial is the fact that if we are asked what the meaning of the term 'bachelor' is, we can *only* say that 'bachelor' means 'unmarried man', whereas if we are asked for the meaning of the term 'energy', we can do much more than give a definition. We can in fact show the way in which the use of the term 'energy' facilitates an enormous number of scientific explanations, and how it enters into an enormous bundle of laws.

The statement '$e = \frac{1}{2}mv^2$' is the sort of statement in physical theory that is currently called a "definition." That is to say, it can be taken as a definition, and many good authors did take it as a definition. Analyticity is often defined as "truth by definition," yet we have just seen that '$e = \frac{1}{2}mv^2$' is not and was not analytic, if by an analytic statement one means a statement that no one can reject without forfeiting his claim to reasonableness.

At this point one may feel tempted to agree with Quine. If even "definitions" turn out to be revisable in principle—and not in the trivial sense that arbitrary revision of our use of *noises* is always possible—then one might feel inclined to say that there is *no* statement which a rational man must hold immune from revision. I shall proceed to argue that this is wrong, but those who agree with

---

[15] Even the conservation law has sometimes been considered to be in doubt (in the development of quantum mechanics)! Yet it was the desire to preserve this law which led to the changes we have been discussing. In one context the law of the conservation of energy can thus serve to "identify" energy, whereas in another it can be the Hamiltonian equations of particular systems that do this.

[16] The "fuzziness" is evidenced by the fact that although one can say that 'kinetic energy' has a new meaning, one cannot say that 'kinetic' has a new meaning, or that 'energy' has a new meaning, or that 'kinetic energy' is an idiom.

me that this is wrong have often overlooked the fact that Quine can be wrong in his most "shocking" thesis and still right about very important and very pervasive epistemological issues. To give a single example, I agree with Quine that in that context of argument which is defined by questions of necessity, factuality, of linguistic or nonlinguistic character, there is no significant distinction to be drawn between, say, the principle of the excluded middle and the principle that $f = ma$; and this is not to say that the law '$f = ma$' is analytic. (Of course we can imagine a physics based on $f = m^2a$, if we retain the identity of gravitational and inertial mass!) Nor is it to say that the laws of logic are "synthetic," if the paradigm for a synthetic sentence is 'There is a book on this table'. But still there are truths that it could never be rational to give up, and 'All bachelors are unmarried' is one of them. This thesis will be elaborated in the following section.

THE RATIONALE OF THE ANALYTIC-SYNTHETIC DISTINCTION

The problem of justification. Let us consider first the question, How could one draw the analytic-synthetic distinction as a formal distinction in connection with at least some hypothetical formalized languages? If the inventor of a formalized language singles out from all his postulates and rules a certain subset (e.g., "L-Postulates," "Meaning Postulates," and "logical axioms") and says that the designated statements, statements in the subset, are not to be given up, then these statements may be reasonably called "analytic" in that language. In the context of formal reconstruction, then, this is the first model of analyticity that comes to mind. We draw an analytic-synthetic distinction formally only in connection with formalized languages whose inventors list some statements and rules as "Meaning Postulates." That is, it is stipulated that to qualify as correctly using the language one must accept *those* statements and rules. There is nothing mysterious about this. A formal language has, after all, an inventor, and like any human being, he can give commands. Among the commands he can issue are ones to the effect that "If you want to speak my language, then do thus and so." If his commands have an escape clause, if he says, "Accept these statements unless you get into trouble, and then make such-and-such revisions," then his language is hardly one with respect to which we can draw a formal analytic-synthetic distinction. But if he says that certain statements are "to be accepted no matter what," then those statements in that language are true by stipulation, true by *his* stipulation, and that is all we mean when we say that they are "analytic" (in this model).

Hempel has proposed an answer to this sort of move. His answer is this: if by an analytic statement one means one which is not to be given up, then in science there are no such statements. Of course, an individual might invent a language and rule that in that language certain statements are not to be given up; but this is of no philosophic interest whatsoever, unless the language constructed by this individual can plausibly be regarded as reconstructing some feature which actually exists in ordinary unreconstructed scientific activity.

This brings us to our second question: If an artificial language in which a formalized analytic-synthetic distinction can be drawn is one in which there are rules of the form "Do not give up S under any circumstances," then what justification could there be for adopting such a language?

Certain philosophers have seen that the notion of a rule, in the sense of an *explicit* rule or explicit stipulation, is sufficiently clear to be worked with (Quine does not at all deny this), and they propose to define analytic statements as statements which are true by stipulation. Against this, there is Quine's remark that in the history of science a statement is often "true by stipulation" at one moment, but later plays a role which is in no way different from the role played by statements which enter the body of accepted truths through more direct experimental inquiry. Stipulation, Quine says, is a trait of historical events, not a "lingering trait" of the statements involved.

Philosophers who regard "true by stipulation" as explicating analyticity, and who take "true by stipulation" in its literal sense, that is to say, who mean by "stipulations" explicit stipulations, miss several points. In the first place, analytic statements in a natural language are not usually true by stipulation in anything but a metaphorical sense. "True by stipulation" is the nature of analytic statements only in the model. And even if we confine ourselves to the model and ignore the existence of natural languages, there is still the question What is the point of the model? But this is the question: *Why* should we hold certain truths immune from revision?

Suppose we can show that if we were to adopt an "official formalized language," it would be perfectly rational to incorporate into its construction certain conventions of the type described? Then I think we would have resolved the problem raised by Quine. Quine does not deny that some people *may* in fact hold some statements immune from revision; what he denies is that science does this, and his denial is not merely a descriptive denial: he doesn't think that science ought to do this. Thus the problem *really* raised by Quine is this: Once we have managed to make our own Quine's insight into the monolithic character of our conceptual system, how can we see why there should be any exceptions to this monolithic character? If science is characterized by interdependence of its principles and by the fact that "revision may strike anywhere," then why should any principles be held immune from revision? The question at the moment is not, What is the nature of the analytic-synthetic distinction? but rather, Why ought there to be an analytic-synthetic distinction?

Rationale. The reply that I have to offer to the question of the rationale of the analytic-synthetic distinction, and of strict synonymy within a language, is this: First of all, the answer to the question, Why should we have analytic statements (or strict synonymies[17]) in our language? is, in essence, Why not? or more precisely, It can't hurt. And, second, the answer to the derivative

---

[17] The close connection between synonymy and analyticity is pointed out by Quine in "Two Dogmas."

question, How do you know it can't hurt? is, I use what I know. But it is obvious that both of these answers will need a little elaborating.

The first answer should, I think, be clear. There are obvious advantages to having strict synonyms in a language. Most important, there is the advantage of *brevity*. Also, there is the question of *intelligibility*. If some of the statements in a language are immune from revision and if some of the rules of a language are immune from revision, then linguistic usage with respect to the language as a whole is to a certain extent frozen. Now, whatever disadvantages this freezing may have, there is one respect in which a frozen language is very attractive. Different speakers of the same language can to a large extent understand each other better because they can predict in advance at least some of the uses of the other speaker.

Thus, I think we can see that if we are constructing a language, then there are some prima-facie advantages to having "fixed points" in that language. Hence the only real question is, Why *not* have them? Quine, I believe, thinks that there is a reason why we should not have them. No matter what advantages in intelligibility and uniformity of usage might accrue, Quine is convinced that it would block the scientific enterprise to declare any statement immune from revision. And it may seem that I have provided Quine with more than sufficient ammunition. For instance, someone might have proposed, "Let's make the statement 'kinetic energy = $^{1}/_{2}mv^{2}$' analytic. It will help to stabilize scientific usage." And accepting this proposal, which might have seemed innocuous enough, would not have been very happy. On my own account, we would have been mistaken had we decided to hold the statement 'kinetic energy = $^{1}/_{2}mv^{2}$' immune from revision. How can we be sure that we will not be similarly mistaken if we decide to hold any statement immune from revision?

In terms of the conceptual machinery developed above, the reason that we can safely decide to hold 'All bachelors are unmarried' immune from revision, while we could not have safely decided to hold 'kinetic energy = $^{1}/_{2}mv^{2}$' immune from revision, is that 'energy' is a law-cluster term, and 'bachelor' is not. This is not to say that there are no laws underlying our use of the term 'bachelor'; there are laws underlying our use of any words whatsoever. But it is to say that there are no exceptionless laws of the form 'All bachelors are . . .' except 'All bachelors are unmarried', 'All bachelors are male', and consequences thereof. Thus, preserving the interchangeability of 'bachelor' and 'unmarried man' in all extensional contexts can never conflict with our desire to retain some other natural law of the form 'all bachelors are . . .'

This cannot happen because bachelors are a kind of synthetic "class." They are not a "natural kind" in Mill's sense. They are rather grouped together by ignoring all aspects except a single legal one. One is simply not going to find any laws, except complex statistical laws depending on sociological conditions, about such a class. Thus, it cannot "hurt" if we decide always to preserve the law 'All bachelors are unmarried'. And that it cannot hurt is all the justification we need; the positive advantages are obvious.

As remarked, there may be *statistical* laws, dependent on sociological conditions, concerning bachelors. But these cannot be incompatible with 'All bachelors are unmarried men'. For the truth of a statistical law, unlike that of a deterministic law, is not affected by slight modifications in the extension of a concept. The law '99 per cent of all A's are B's', if true, remains true if we change the extension of the concept A by including a few more objects or excluding a few objects. Thus, making *slight* changes in the extension of the term 'bachelor' would not affect any statistical law about bachelors; but by exactly the same token, neither would *refusing* to make such changes. And if the statistical law held true only provided we were willing to make a large change in the extension or putative extension of the term 'bachelor', then we would certainly reject the statistical law.

Let us consider one objection. I have maintained that there are no exceptionless laws containing the term 'bachelor'. But this statement is surely a guess on my part. Let us suppose that my "guess" is wrong, and that there are exceptionless laws about bachelors. Let us suppose for instance that all bachelors share a special kind of neurosis universal among bachelors and unique to bachelors. Not to be too farfetched, let us call it "sexual frustration." Then the statement 'All bachelors suffer from sexual frustration, and only bachelors suffer from sexual frustration' would express a genuine law. This law could still not provide us with a *criterion* for distinguishing bachelors from nonbachelors, unless we were good at detecting this particular species of neurosis. It is alleged that some primitive peoples can in fact do this by smell; but let us make a somewhat more plausible assumption, in terms of contemporary mores. Let us suppose that we all mastered some form of super psychoanalysis; and let us suppose that we all became so "insightful" that we should be able to tell in a moment's conversation whether someone suffered from the neurosis of "sexual frustration" or not. Then this law would indeed constitute a criterion for bachelorhood, and a far more convenient criterion than the usual one. For one cannot employ the usual criterion without asking a man a somewhat personal question concerning his legal status; whereas, in our hypothetical situation, one would be able to determine by a quick examination of the man's conversation whether he was a bachelor or not, no matter what one conversed about. Under such circumstances, possession of the neurosis might well become the dominant criterion governing the use of the word. Then what should we say, if it turned out that a few people had the neurosis without being bachelors? Our previous stipulation that 'bachelor' is to be synonymous with 'unmarried man' might well appear inconvenient!

The point of this fable is as follows: Even if we grant that 'bachelor' is not *now* a law-cluster term, how can we be *sure* that it will never become such a term? This leads to my second answer, and to a further remark, "I use what I know." It is logically possible that all bachelors should have a certain neurosis and that nobody else should have it; it is even possible that we should be able to detect this neurosis at sight. But, of course, there is no such neurosis. This I *know* in the way that I know most negative propositions. It is not that I have a criterion for as yet undiscovered neuroses, but simply that I have no good reason to suppose that there might be such a neurosis. And in many cases of this kind, *lack* of any good reason for supposing existence is itself the very best reason for supposing nonexistence.

In short, I regard my "guess" that there are no exceptionless laws about bachelors as more than a guess. I think that in a reasonable sense we may say that this is something that we *know*. I shall not press this point. But *bachelor* is not now a law-cluster concept; I think we can say that, although it is *logically* possible that it might become a law-cluster concept, in fact it will not.

Let us summarize the position at this point: I have suggested that the statement 'All bachelors are unmarried' is a statement which we might render true by stipulation, in a hypothetical formalized language. I have argued that this stipulation is convenient, both because it provides us with one more "fixed point" to help stabilize the use of our hypothetical language, and because it provides us with an expression which can be used instead of the somewhat cumbersome expression 'male adult human being who has never in his life been married'; and I have argued that we need not be afraid to accept these advantages, and to make these stipulations, because it can do no harm. It can do no harm because *bachelor* is not a law-cluster concept. Also it is not independently "defined" by standard examples, which might only contingently be unmarried men. I have admitted that my knowledge (or "state of pretty-sureness") that 'bachelor' will not become a law-cluster term is based upon what we might call, in a very broad sense, empirical argumentation. That *there are no exceptionless laws containing the term 'bachelor'* is empirical in the sense of being a fact about the world; although it is not empirical in the sense of being subject to confrontation with isolated experiments. More precisely: it occupies the anomalous position of being falsifiable by isolated experiments (since isolated experiments could verify an empirical generalization which *would* constitute a "law about all bachelors"); but it could not be verified by isolated experiments. One cannot examine a random sample of *laws*, and verify that they are all not-about-bachelors. But the statement is empirical, at least in the first sense, and it is "synthetic" to the extent that it is revisable in principle. So my position is this: a "synthetic" statement, a statement which could be revised in principle, may serve as a warrant for the decision that another statement should not be revised, no matter what. One may safely hold certain statements immune from revision; but *this* statement is itself subject to certain risks.

But there is no real paradox here at all. To say that an intention is to do something permanently is not the same as saying that the intention is permanent. To marry a woman is to legally declare an intention to remain wedded to her for life; although the bride and groom know perfectly well that there exists such an institution as divorce, and that they may avail themselves of it. The existence of divorce does not change the fact that the legal and declared intention of the persons getting married is to be wedded for life. And this is the further remark that I wish to make in connection with my second answer.

It is perfectly rational to make stipulations to the effect that certain statements are never to be given up, and those stipulations remain stipulations to that effect, notwithstanding the fact that under certain circumstances the stipulations *themselves* might be given up.

All of this may sound like a bit of sophistry, if one forgets that we are still in the context of formalized languages. Thus, if one has in mind "implicit stipulations" and natural language, one might feel tempted to say: "What is the difference between having a stipulation to the effect that every statement can be revised, and having a stipulation to the effect that certain statements are never to be revised, if the latter stipulations are themselves always subject to revision?" But in connection with formalized languages, there is all the difference in the world. The rule "Let every statement be subject to revision" is not sufficiently precise to be a formal rule. It would have to be supplemented by further rules determining what revisions to make, and in what order. And there is all the difference in the world between making a decision in accordance with a pre-established plan, and making the decision by "getting together" and doing whatever seems most cogent in the light of the circumstances at the moment and the standards or codes we see accepted at the moment. The first case would arise in connection with a language in which Quine's ideas concerning priorities and centralities had been formalized—a language in which any statement may be given up and in which there are rules telling one which statements to give up first and under what circumstances. Such a language could in principle be constructed. But compare the case of a scientist who is in difficulties, and who resolves his difficulties by using a predetermined rule, with the following case: we imagine that we have a formalized language in which 'All bachelors are unmarried' is a "meaning postulate." We further imagine, as in our "fable," that all bachelors suffer from a neurosis and that only bachelors suffer from that particular neurosis. Also we suppose that the neurosis is detectable at sight and that it is used as the dominant criterion. Then it is discovered that one person or a very few people have the neurosis although they are married. The question might then arise as to which would be more convenient: to preserve 'All bachelors are unmarried' or to get together and modify the rules of the language. Contrast the procedure which would be employed if the latter alternative were the one adopted, with the procedure of settling the question in accordance with a predetermined plan. There would be, let us say, a convention at which some would argue that it is better to preserve the rules that were agreed upon for the language, and to give up the psychological law that had been thought to hold without exception; there might be others who would argue that the new use of the term 'bachelor' was so standard that it would be simpler to grace the new use with the hallmark of legality and to change the rules of the language. In short, the question would be settled by informal argument.

Thus, at the level of formalized languages, there *is* a difference, and a rather radical difference between these different systems: a formal language which can described as having rules to the effect that every statement may be revised, and a formal language having rules to the effect that certain statements are never to be revised—notwithstanding the fact that, even if one employs a formal language of the second kind, one retains the option of later altering or abandoning it. And even if one uses a system of the first kind, a "holistic" system of the sort Quine seems to envisage, there is still the possibility that one might find it desirable to revise the rules determining the nature and order of revisions, when they are to be made—the centralities and priorities of this system. And the same difference mirrors itself in the difference between those questions which one settles in accordance with the antecedently established rules and those questions which one settles by informal argument when they arise.

In short: if we think in terms of people using formalized languages, then we have to distinguish between the things that are done inside the language in accordance with whatever rules and regulations may have been previously decided upon and published, and the informal argumentation and discussion that takes place outside of the language, and which perhaps leads to a decision, in its turn to be duly formalized, to alter the language. This distinction is not the same as the analytic-synthetic distinction, but it is deeply relevant to it. If we use the model of people employing formalized languages, then we have to imagine those people as deciding upon and declaring certain rules. And it is perfectly rational in human life to make a rule that something is always to be done; and the rule is no less a rule that something is always to be done on account of the fact that the rule itself may someday be abandoned.

There are a host of examples: for instance, it is a rule of etiquette that one is not to address a person to whom one has never been introduced by his first name (with a few exceptions). The rule may someday be changed. But that does not change the fact that the present rule is to the effect that this is to be done under *all* circumstances. In the same way, a rational man may perfectly well adopt a rule that certain statements are *never* to be given up: he does not forfeit his right to be called reasonable on account of what he does, and he can give plenty of good reasons in support of his action.

THE ANALYTIC-SYNTHETIC DISTINCTION IN NATURAL LANGUAGE

The formal language model. The foregoing discussion is characterized by an air of fictionality. But this does not obliterate its relevance to Quine's difficulties. Quine does not deny that there may be some statements which some individuals will never give up. His real contention is that there are no statements which *science* holds immune from revision. And this is not a descriptive judgment; judgments by philosophers containing the word 'science' almost never are. What Quine really means is that he cannot see why science ought to hold any statements immune from revision. And this is the sort of difficulty that one may well resolve by telling an appropriate fable.

Still we are left with the problem of drawing an analytic-synthetic distinction in natural language; and this is a difficult problem. Part of the answer is clear.

We commonly use formalized objects to serve as models for unformalized objects. We talk about a game whose rules have never been written down in terms of a model of a game whose rules have been agreed upon and codified, and we talk about natural languages in terms of models of formal languages; and, if a formal language means a "language whose rules are written down," then we have been doing this for a long time, and not just since the invention of symbolic logic. The concept of a rule of language is commonly used by linguists in describing even the unwritten languages of primitive peoples, just as the concept of a rule of social behavior is used by anthropologists. Such reference is sometimes heavily disguised by current jargon, but is nevertheless present. For instance, if a linguist says: "The pluralizing morphophoneme —*s* has the zero allophone after the morpheme *sheep*," what he is saying is that it is a rule of English that the plural of 'sheep' is 'sheep' and not 'sheeps'. And his way of saying this is not so cumbersome either: he would not really write the sentence I just quoted, but would embed the information it contains in an extremely compact morphophoneme table.

Thus I think that we may say that the concept *rule of language*, as applied to natural language, is an "almost full-grown" theoretical concept. Linguists, sent out to describe a jungle language, describe the language on the model of a formal language. The elements of the *model* are the expressions and rules of a formal language, that is, a language whose rules are explicitly written down. The corresponding elements in the real world are the expressions of a natural language and certain of the dispositions of the users of that language. The model is not only a useful descriptive device, but has genuinely explanatory power. The distinction, at present very loosely specified, between a rule of language and a *mere* habit of the speakers of the language is an essential one. Speakers of English (except very small speakers of English) rarely use the word 'sheeps'. Speakers of English rarely use the word 'otiose'. But someone who uses the word 'sheeps' is said to be speaking incorrectly; whereas someone who uses the word 'otiose' is only using a rare word. That we behave differently in the two cases is explained, and it is a genuine explanation, by saying that it is a rule of English that one is to use 'sheep' as the plural of 'sheep', and it is not a rule of English that one is not to use the word 'otiose'; it is just that most people do not know *what* the rule for using the word 'otiose' is at all, and hence do not employ it.

But all this will not suffice. True, we have a model of natural language according to which a natural language has "rules," and a model with some explanatory and predictive value, but what we badly need to know are the respects in which the model is exact, and the respects in which the model is misleading. For example, in many circumstances it is extremely convenient to talk about electron currents on the model of water flowing through a pipe; but physical scientists know very well in which respects this model holds exactly and in which respects it is extremely misleading. The same can hardly be said in the case just described—the case wherein we employ a formal language as a model for a natural language. The difficulty I have in mind is not the difficulty of determining what the rules of a natural language are. The art of describing a natural language in terms of this kind of model is one that is relatively well developed; and linguists are aware that the correspondence between this kind of model and a given natural language is not unique: there are alternative "equally valid descriptions." The dispositions of speakers of a natural language are *not* rules of a formal language, the latter are only used to represent them in a certain technique of representation; and the difficulty lies in being sure that other elements of the model, e.g., the sharp analytic-synthetic distinction, correspond to anything at all in reality.

To give only one example: I argued above, and it was a central part of the argument, that there is a clear-cut difference between solving a problem by relying on a pre-established rule, and solving it by methods construed on the spot. But one might wonder whether the distinction is so sharp if the pre-established rule is only an *implicit* rule to begin with. It is clear that there is a difference between stipulations allowing for revisions and stipulations prohibiting revisions, but themselves always subject to informal revision. But is it so clear that there is such a distinction if the stipulations are themselves informal and "implicit"? In view of this difficulty, and other related difficulties, it seems to me that we must look at natural language directly, and try to draw the analytic-synthetic distinction without relying on the formal language model, if we are to be sure that it exists at all.

The nature of the distinction in natural language. The statements which satisfy the criteria presented below are a *fundamental subset* of the totality of analytic statements in the natural language. They are the so-called "analytic definitions," e.g., 'Someone is a bachelor if and only if he is an unmarried man'. Other statements may be classified as "analytic," although they do *not* satisfy the criteria, because they are consequences of statements which *do* satisfy the criteria. The older philosophers recognized a related though different distinction by referring to "intuitive" and "demonstrative" truths. The distinction had a point: there is a difference, even in our formal model, between those statements whose truth follows from *direct* stipulation and statements whose truth follows from the fact that they are *consequences* of statements true by direct stipulation. The latter statements involve not only arbitrary stipulation but also logic.

Nevertheless, the term 'intuitive' has bad connotations. And because of these bad connotations, philosophers have been led not to reformulate the distinction between intuitive and demonstrative truths but to abandon it. So today the fashion is to lump together the analytic statements which would traditionally have been classified as intuitive with all their consequences, and to use the word 'analytic' for the whole class. *The criteria to be presented do not, however, apply equally well to the whole class, or even to all the "intuitive" analytic truths, but to a fundamental subset. This fundamental subset is, roughly speaking, the set of analytic definitions; or less roughly, it is the set of analytic definitions which are also "intuitive" and not "demonstrative."*

In short, I shall present criteria which are intended to show what is unique or different about certain analytic statements. Such criteria do not constitute a definition but one might obtain a definition, of a rough and ready sort, from them: an analytic statement is a statement which satisfies the criteria to be presented, or a consequence of such statements, or a statement which comes pretty close to satisfying the criteria, or a consequence of such statements. The last clause in this "definition" is designed to allow for the fact that there are some "borderline" cases of analyticity, e.g., 'Red is a color'. However, it is not a very important point that the analytic-synthetic distinction is afflicted with "borderline fuzziness." The trouble with the analytic-synthetic distinction *construed as a dichotomy* is far more radical than mere "borderline fuzziness." Yet, there are borderline cases; and the reason for their existence is that the analytic-synthetic distinction is tied to a certain model of natural language and correspondence between the model and the natural language is not unique. To say that it is not unique is not, however, to say that it is arbitrary. Some statements in natural language really are analytic; others may be *construed* as analytic; still others really are synthetic; others *may be construed* as synthetic; still other statements belong to still other categories or may be construed as belonging to still other categories.

The following are the criteria in question:

(1) The statement has the form: "Something (Someone) is an A if and only if it (he, she) is a B," where A is a single word.[18]
(2) The statement holds without exception, and provides us with a *criterion* for something's being the sort of thing to which the term A applies.
(3) The criterion is the only one that is generally accepted and employed in connection with the term.
(4) The term A is not a "law-cluster" word.

Criteria (1) by itself is surely insufficient to separate analytic definitions from natural laws in all cases. Thus let us examine criteria (2), (3), and (4). A statement of the form "Something is an A if and only if it is a B" provides a criterion for something's being a thing to which the term A applies if people can and do determine whether or not something is an A by *first* finding out whether or not it is a B. For instance, the only generally accepted method for determining whether or not someone is a bachelor, other than putting the question itself, is to find out whether or not the person is married and whether or not he is an adult male. There are of course independent tests for both marital status (consult suitable records) and masculinity.

---

[18] The requirement that A be a single word reflects the principle that the meaning of a whole utterance is a function of the meanings of the individual words and grammatical forms that make it up. This requirement should actually be more complicated to take care of words which consist of more than one morpheme and of idioms, but these complications will not be considered here. We can now give another reason why 'Kinetic energy $= \frac{1}{2} mv^2$' was never an analytic statement: its truth did not follow from the meanings of the words 'kinetic' and 'energy'. On the other hand, it would be absurd to maintain that, during its tenure of office, it was an "empirical statement" in the usual sense (subject to experimental test, etc.).

One objection must be faced at the outset: it might be argued that these criteria are circular in a vicious way, since knowing that the two statements, (a) "Someone is a bachelor if and only if he is an unmarried man," and (b) "Someone is a bachelor if and only if he is an unwed man," provide the same criterion for the application of the term "bachelor" is the same thing as knowing that "unmarried" and "unwed" are *synonyms*. For the present purposes, however, identity of criteria can be construed behavioristically: criteria (say, X and Y) correspond to the same way of ascertaining that a term A applies if subjects who are instructed to use criterion X do the same thing[19] as subjects who are instructed to use criterion Y. Thus, if I were instructed to ascertain whether or not Jones is unmarried, I would probably go up to Jones and ask "Are you married?"—and answer "No" to the original question if Jones' answer was "Yes," and vice versa. On any such occasion, I could truthfully say that I "would have done the same thing" if I had been instructed to ascertain whether Jones was "unwed" instead of whether Jones was "unmarried." Thus, in my idiolect,[20] "being an unmarried man" and "being an unwed man" are not two criteria for someone's being a bachelor, but one.

But let us consider a somewhat different type of objection. On what basis are we to rule out the statement "Someone is a bachelor if and only if he is either an unmarried man or a unicorn" as nonanalytic?[21] Here three grounds are relevant: (a) the statement is a linguistically "odd"[22] one, and is not clearly true; (b) the statement would not be generally accepted; (c) people do not ascertain that someone is a bachelor by first finding out that he is either an unmarried man or a unicorn. To take these in turn: (a) The English "or" and "if and only if" are not synonymous with the truth functions "v" and "≡" of formal logic. Thus it is not even clear that the quoted statement is an intelligible English statement, let alone true. (b) Even if we grant truth, it would not be generally accepted. Many persons would reject it, and others, who might not actually reject it, might decline to accept it (e.g., they might query its intelligibility or express puzzlement). (c) People (other than formal logicians) would certainly deny that they ascertain that someone is a bachelor by first

---

[19] The use of the expression "do the same things" here will undoubtedly raise questions in the minds of certain readers. It should be noted that what is meant is not total identity of behavior (whatever that might be) but the absence of relevant and statistically significant regularities running through the behavior of the one group of subjects and not of the other. Separation of "relevant" from "irrelevant" regularities does not seem difficult in practice, however difficult it might be to "mechanize" our "institutions" in these matters.

[20] An "idiolect" is the speech of a single speaker.

[21] The difficulty here is that the class of bachelors = the sum of the class of bachelors and the class of unicorns (the latter being the null class). What has to be shown is that the so-called "intensional" difference between the two terms 'unmarried man' and 'unmarried man or unicorn' is reflected by our criteria, at least in connection with the definition of 'bachelor'.

[22] The quoted sentence is even *ungrammatical*, using the term in the sense of Noam Chomsky's *Syntactic Structures* (The Hague: Mouton and Co., 1957); for its transformational history involves the ungrammatical sentence "Someone is a unicorn." To change the example: "Someone is a bachelor if and only if he is either an unmarried man or eleven feet tall" is grammatical, but pretty clearly *false*, given the counterfactual force of the ordinary "if and only if."

finding out that he is *either* unmarried or a unicorn. In fine, the quoted statement does not provide a criterion for someone's being a bachelor, in the sense in which 'criterion' is being used here; and it is not a generally accepted criterion for someone's being a bachelor.

Since a good deal of the present discussion depends upon the way in which the word 'criterion' is being used, I should like to emphasize two points. Although sufficient conditions, necessary conditions, etc., are sometimes called "criteria" (e.g., the above "criteria" for analyticity), the sense of 'criterion' in which an analytic definition provides a criterion for something's being the sort of thing to which a term applies is a very strong one: (a) the "criteria" I am speaking of are necessary *and* sufficient conditions for something's being A; and (b) by means of them people *can and do determine* that something is an A. For instance, there are various things that we might call *indications* of bachelorhood: being young, high spirited, living alone. Using these, one can often *tell* that someone is a bachelor without falling back on the criterion; but the only *criterion* (satisfying (a) and (b)) by means of which one can *determine* that someone is a bachelor is the one which is provided by the analytic definition.

Returning now to our main concern, what is the relevance of the four criteria for analyticity? Someone imbued with the view that an analytic statement is *simply* one which is true by the rules of the language, i.e., one who insists on stating the distinction in terms of a model, instead of discussing the relevance of the model to that vast disorderly mass of human behavior that makes up a natural language, may be wholly dissatisfied with what has been said. I can imagine someone objecting: "What you are saying is that the difference between an analytic principle and a natural law consists in the accidental fact that no laws happen to be known containing the subject term of the analytic principle." That is almost what I am saying. But the emphasis is wrong; and in any case the thing is not so implausible once one has grasped the *rationale* of analyticity.

In the first place it is not just that there do not *happen* to be any *known* principles concerning bachelors other than the principle that someone is a bachelor if and only if he is an unmarried man: it is reasonable to suppose that there do not exist any exceptionless (as opposed to statistical) scientific laws to be discovered about bachelors.[23] And even if there were an exceptionless law about bachelors, it is extremely unlikely that it would have the form

---

[23] It has occurred to me that someone might argue that "all bachelors have mass" is an example of an exceptionless "law about bachelors." Even if this were granted, the objection is not serious. In the first place, in deciding whether or not a word is a "law-cluster" word, what we have to consider are not all the laws (including the unknown ones) containing the word, but only those statements which are accepted as laws and which contain the word. It does not even matter if some of these are false: if a word appears in a large number of statements (of sufficient importance, interconnectedness, and systematic import) which are accepted as laws, then in the language of that time it is a "law-cluster" word. And second, if a statement would be accepted as true, but is regarded as so unimportant that it is not stated as a law in a single scientific paper or text, then it can certainly be disregarded in determining whether or not a word is a "law-cluster" word.

"Someone is a bachelor if and only if . . ."—i.e., that it would provide a *criterion* for someone's being a bachelor.

But still we have to face the questions (1) Why is the exceptionless principle that provides the criterion governing a *one-criterion* concept analytic? (2) What happens if, contrary to our well-founded beliefs and expectations, a large number of exceptionless laws of high systematic import containing the subject term are someday discovered? The second question has already been discussed. If 'bachelor' ever becomes a "law-cluster" word, then we shall simply have to admit that the linguistic character of the word has changed. The word 'atom' is an example of a word which was once a "one-criterion" word and which has become a "law-cluster" word (so that the sentence 'Atoms are indivisible', which was once used to make an analytic statement, would today express a false proposition).

But to consider the first question: Why is a statement which satisfies the criteria analytic? Well, in the first place, *such a statement is certainly not a synthetic statement in the usual sense*; it cannot be confuted by isolated experiments, or, what amounts to the same thing, it cannot be verified by "induction" in the sense of induction by simple enumeration. To verify or confute a statement of the form 'Something is an A if and only if it is a B' in this way requires that we have *independent* criteria for being an A and for being a B. Moreover, since the subject concept is not a law-cluster concept, the statement has little or no systematic import. In short, there could hardly be *theoretical* grounds for accepting or rejecting it. It is for these reasons that such statements might plausibly be regarded as constituting the arbitrary fixed points in our natural language.

There they are, the analytic statements: unverifiable in any practical sense, unrefutable in any practical sense, yet we do seem to have them. This must always seem a mystery to one who does not realize the significance of the fact that in any rational way of life there must be certain arbitrary elements. They are "true by virtue of the rules of the language"; they are "true by stipulation"; they are "true by implicit convention." Yet all these expressions are after all nothing but metaphors: true statements, but couched in metaphor nonetheless. What is the reality behind the metaphor? The reality is that they are true because they are accepted as true, and because this acceptance is quite arbitrary in the sense that the acceptance of the statements has no systematic consequences beyond those described in the previous section, e.g., that of allowing us to use pairs of expression interchangeably.

Finally, the question as to whether it is rational to accept as true statements satisfying the four criteria is easily answered in the affirmative. This is the question as to whether all these statements may reasonably be taken as true in a "sensible" rational reconstruction of our actual language. To discuss this point in detail would involve repeating the argument of the preceding section, since this is just the problem which was treated in that section.

Does the fact that everyone accepts a statement make it rational to go on believing it? The answer is that it *does*, if it can be *shown* that it would be reasonable to render the statement immune from revision by stipulation, *if* we were to formalize our language.

In short, analytic statements are statements which we all accept and for which we do not give reasons. This is what we mean when we say that they are true by "implicit convention." The problem is then to distinguish them from other statements that we accept, and do not give reasons for, in particular from the statements that we *unreasonably* accept. To resolve this difficulty, we have to point out some of the crucial distinguishing features of analytic statements (e.g., the fact that the subject concept is not a law-cluster concept), and we have to connect these features with what, in the preceding section, was called the "rationale" of the analytic-synthetic distinction. Having done this, we can see that the acceptance of analytic statements is *rational*, even though there are no reasons (in the sense of "evidence") in connection with them.

JERRY A. FODOR

1.7 *On Knowing What We Would Say*

Philosophers, philosophizing, sometimes ask themselves or their colleagues questions of the form "What would we say if . . . ?" where the blank is filled by a description, more or less circumstantial, of a state of affairs in which some philosophically interesting word might get used, and where "we" are supposed to be fluent and judicious speakers of English with no philosophical axes to grind. I want to distinguish two quite different kinds of case in which philosophers seek answers to questions about what we would say and to argue that in one of them there is no reason to suppose the answers they get are trustworthy.

To describe a language is to formulate the rules which are internalized by speakers when they learn the language and applied in speaking and understanding it. The data for such a description derive from observation of particular speech episodes: incidents of talking in which the speaker's knowledge of the rules of his language is exercised. Very often philosophers ask what we would say as a means of obtaining such data. That is, they describe situations in which they think the word *might* be used (that is, situations in which a putative linguistic rule predicts that the word *could* be used without oddity) and then ask themselves or their informants what they would say about such situations. It would be equally effective, though less practical, actually to bring

Reprinted from *The Philosophical Review*, LXXIII, No. 2 (1964), 198–212, by permission of the author and of *The Philosophical Review*.

about the situations in question and see what the informant *does* say. In indefinitely many cases, either or both of these techniques might be employed.

For example, a philosopher interested in the use(s) of the word "responsible" might ask such questions as these: "My brakes fail and I go through a red light and hit a child. Am I responsible for the death of the child? What if I had known my brakes to be bad and had not bothered to have them fixed? What if at the moment my brakes failed, the car skidded on ice, so that I would have hit the child even if the brakes had worked? . . ." and so on through a series of questions designed to elicit the relation between responsibility, forethought, control over the events, and so forth. Notice that the hypothetical air of these questions is inessential and perhaps misleading, for the informant's answer is useful only in so far as it is a reliable index of what he would say if the situation described were actualized. The posing of the question is an indirect way of determining in which situations speakers willingly invoke notions of responsibility and in which ones they do not. Generalization is accomplished and insight into the structure of the language gained when we can formulate a rule which correctly extrapolates common features of observed situations in which the word "responsible" is used, thus permitting us to predict how "responsible" would be used in indefinitely many situations not yet observed.[1]

It is perfectly reasonable to ask: how good are speakers at answering the kind of questions instanced in the last paragraph? An answer would be forthcoming were we to check what speakers say they would say about problematic situations against what they in fact *do* say when such situations arise. The wise philosopher tests his own and his informant's intuitions against discourses produced in circumstances less academic than the philosophy seminar and the philosophy journal. We do not always say what we say that we would say.[2]

That we are at best imperfect observers of our own behavior is a commonplace. But this is only to say that the degree of reliability of the informant is as much a subject for empirical investigation as the rules of the language the informant speaks. It is not to say that there is any *general* reason to distrust the speaker's intuitions in the sorts of cases we have been considering. On the contrary, it seems reasonable to suppose that the speaker's knowledge of his language provides him with some basis for claims about what he would say in novel situations. In any event, we run no serious risk in making this supposition since if it is false we can find out that it is by comparing the speaker's claims with the linguistic facts.

There are, however, cases in which the intuitions of speakers about what

---

[1] There is a variety of ways of being naive about the notion of having something in common (what aspirin and codeine have in common is not something you will discover just by inspection). But there are also various ways of being naive about stating a rule. To say "the situations must resemble one another" is not to state a rule. Not even if you add "in a family way."

[2] *Cf.* J. A. Fodor and J. J. Katz, "The Availability of What We Say," *Philosophical Review*, LXXII (1963). The arguments in the present paper presuppose the conclusions in that one, since one can sensibly raise the question "In what circumstances is the informant right?" only if it is accepted that there are circumstances in which the informant is wrong.

they would say are to be distrusted on *a priori* grounds; cases in which it is unreasonable to suppose that a knowledge of what he would say is implicit in the speaker's mastery of his language. It is such cases that I wish to explore in this paper.

In one or another form, the following doctrine has considerable currency among philosophers. Of the features which regularly characterize the occasions upon which a word is used, some must be attributable to the meaning of that word. Such features are definitive or "criterial" in that their presence is a necessary condition of the proper use of the word. If F is such a feature relative to the word w, then "If w is properly used, then F" is held to be an analytic, or quasi-logical, or necessary truth.

"Occasion" and "feature" must not be taken too seriously, and "analytic," "necessary," "quasi-logical," and so forth are notoriously little more than the names of problems. (I do not wish even to suggest that they are names of the same problem.) In the sense of these terms intended here, it is a feature of occasions on which I correctly refer to someone as "the brother of x" that I am referring to a male, and *that* statement is analytic, necessary, or quasi-logical. When a feature is related to occurrences of a word in this way, I shall say that that feature is "logically characteristic" of the occurrence of the word. This is, of course, just another name.

Associated with the logically characteristic features of occurrences of a word there will often be features which we may call "empirically characteristic." A feature F' is empirically characteristic of the occurrences of w if:

1. There is some feature F which is logically characteristic of the occurrences of w; and
2. "If F' then generally F" expresses a true empirical generalization or a law of nature.

Put briefly, it is supposed that there often exist empirical correlates of logically characteristic features of words. I shall say that such correlates are empirically characteristic of the occurrences of words.

Empirically characteristic features of occurrences of words are sometimes considered to be symptomatic of logically characteristic features. "I cannot see what sort of animal it is, but I can see that it is clothed." It is, then, a good bet that it is human since humans are clothed much of the time and other sorts of animals hardly ever. The features which are logically characteristic of occurrences of "human" are correlated with the empirically characteristic feature "being clothed." Being clothed is not criterial for being human, but it is a reasonably reliable correlate of the features which *are* criterial. One way of formulating the difference between logically and empirically characteristic features of the occurrences of a word is this: questions of reliability can be raised in the latter case but not in the former. (This is, however, a point of no more than verbal interest since the "can" in the preceding sentence is the "can" of logic. Hence this formulation presupposes the distinction it is intended to explicate.)

Given that one accepts some version of this view, the following philosophical problem arises: how to distinguish between features which are logically characteristic of occurrences of w and features which are (only) empirically characteristic but perfectly reliable—that is, between "criteria" on the one hand and, on the other, "symptoms" which obtain when and only when the relevant criteria do.

That it is likely to be difficult to discover a *general* solution for this problem follows from this: it is clear that no observational datum can by itself suffice to distinguish between perfect reliability and logical characteristicness since, by definition, an empirically characteristic feature of the occurrences of a word is not perfectly reliable unless it obtains on each occasion upon which the word is properly used—that is, on each occasion on which the logically characteristic features of the occurrences of the word obtain. If a feature is perfectly reliable, then *ex hypothesi* we shall never observe a case in which the word is properly used where that feature does not obtain. But since this is also true of criterial features of the use of a word, it follows that we cannot distinguish between perfectly reliable empirical correlates and criteria on the basis of observation alone.

Faced with this difficulty, philosophers have often adopted the following strategy: if F is a feature that you know to be perfectly correlated with regular occurrences of w but which you suspect may not be logically characteristic of occurrences of w, ask your informant *whether he would be willing to use* w *even in the absence of* F. If so, then F must be only empirically characteristic of w, since something could count as a regular occurrence of w from which F is absent. If not, then F must be logically characteristic of w, since nothing could count as a regular occurrence of w from which F is absent.

It is very important to much recent philosophizing that this strategy should prove capable of vindication. Since no philosopher has ever proposed a tenable theory of the distinction between logical characteristicness and perfect reliability, the appeal to the informant's intuitions about what he would say must carry the whole burden of that distinction. Moreover, in this sort of case the appeal to the intuition of the informant is not subject to direct empirical check since, as we have seen, no observation can reveal a situation in which a word is properly used and a perfectly reliable empirically characteristic feature fails to obtain. Hence, there is in principle no way of directly verifying what an informant says about what he would say in such a situation. That is, there is no way of comparing what the informant says he would say with what he in fact says since, *ex hypothesi*, the situations under discussion never in fact arise.[3]

---

[3] Although this argument affords grounds for extreme caution in appealing to speakers' intuitions to distinguish symptoms from criteria, it cannot be considered conclusive since we might conceivably have *indirect* evidence in favor of the speaker's claims. For example, in certain simple cases we might be able so to deceive the speaker that he believes he has encountered a situation which is normal except that the relevant feature fails to obtain. We might then observe what a speaker so deceived is willing to say and what he is not. Somewhat more important is the consideration that we might have as a reason for accepting the speaker's claims about what he would say in situations we cannot observe cross-inductions based on the accuracy of the speaker's claims about what he would say in situations we can observe. Neither of these arguments would appear to supply very strong reasons for trusting the speaker's intuitions, but they suffice to block the claim that there could exist no reasons whatever for doing so.

To put the matter briefly: had we a theory of the distinction between empirical reliability and logical characteristicness, the fact that we cannot observationally verify the speaker's claims about what he would say should a certain feature fail to obtain would be relatively unimportant. For the speaker's claims about what he would say could be viewed as confirmed or disconfirmed depending upon their degree of consonance with the predictions of the theory, just as, in grammar, the speaker's claims about well-formedness are accepted, in part, on the grounds that they conform fairly well with syntactic theories which we have independent reasons for accepting. Conversely, had we a way of observationally checking the speaker's claims, we should not feel the lack of a theory so deeply, since we could assess the reliability of the speaker's claims about what he would say by the usual observational methods. These claims, in so far as they *were* reliable, would in turn support a distinction between empirical and logical characteristicness. In the present case, however, we do not have a theory, and the terms of the problem preclude observational verification of the speaker's claims since, *ex hypothesi*, they are claims about what he would say in situations which never arise. Hence, if there is any reason whatever to suppose that the speaker's intuitions are not to be trusted in this sort of case, that an ability to answer this sort of what-would-we-say question is not implicit in a speaker's mastery of his native language, then the philosopher's claim that a certain feature of the occurrence of a word is logically characteristic, rather than merely empirically reliable, would appear to have no evidential support whatever.

Let us consider a few examples of how the appeal to intuition is supposed to operate to distinguish criteria from symptoms; then we shall be ready to summarize the differences between the two types of what-would-we-say question which we have been attempting to distinguish and to argue for the claim that the intuitions of speakers are not to be trusted in the second sort of case, however trustworthy they may prove in the first.

A philosopher interested in determining the logically characteristic features of occurrences of "know" might require the following of his informant: "Suppose a man were capable of correctly answering any problem in elementary number theory but claimed neither to be able to state how he arrived at his solutions nor ever to have been taught any mathematics. Would you say that he knows number theory?" If the informant's answer is negative, then it would appear that explicit access to the rules employed in computation is a logically necessary condition upon knowledge of such things as number theory. If the informant's answer is affirmative, then it is only a psychological fact that people who know number theory are able to articulate their knowledge.

Or a philosopher interested in dreams might ask the following sort of question: "Suppose we observe a sleeper to have passed a restless night; we have seen him toss and turn and heard him mutter and cry out in his sleep. Upon awakening (and thereafter) he firmly and sincerely claims not to have dreamed. Would you say that he has dreamed and forgotten his dream or that he has not dreamed at all?" Or, conversely: "A man passes what, to casual observation, appears to be a quiet night. Moreover, EEG readings show no alteration of slow waves, his eye movements during sleep are not patterned, and he exhibits no change in GSR, perspiration, and so forth. Nevertheless, upon awakening, the subject reports terrible nightmares and anxiety dreams. Assuming that you know the subject's report to be sincere, would you say that the subject did, in fact, dream?" According to the strategy currently under investigation, if speakers claim that they would say in the second case that the subject had dreamed and in the first case that he had not, then it must follow that what is logically characteristic of occasions upon which we say of someone that he dreamed is a positive dream report. That is, the relation between "*S* dreamed" and "Upon awakening *S* feels inclined to say that he dreamed" is a logical relation, while the relation between "*S* dreamed" and "*S* exhibited alteration of slow wave during sleep" is at best a symptomatic relation, though the symptom is, *ex hypothesi*, perfectly reliable in this case.

It must be clear that the essential point about these examples is their counterfactuality. It is our belief that the situations they envisage do not normally occur—and hence are not typical of the situations in which the words involved are used—which makes them examples of the second sort of what-would-we-say question. We may, then, put the difference between the two sorts of situations about which such questions get asked in the following way. In the first kind of case, we are concerned with what speakers would say about quite normal, though perhaps hypothetical, situations. Although we may not know whether any speaker has ever actually encountered the state of affairs described, we know of no reason why such states of affairs should not occur. The situations described are normal ones in the sense that no feature known to be regularly correlated with occurrences of the word is supposed to fail to obtain. In the second kind of case, however, the situation we ask our informant to characterize is one which has been chosen precisely because it is the sort that we know either does not arise or arises only atypically. This is essential to our reason for asking the second sort of what-would-we-say question: namely, to test whether a feature which we know obtains in all *normal* cases of occurrences of a word does so by virtue of the meaning of the word. We hope to eliminate from our list of logically characteristic features any upon which an informant's willingness to use a word does not depend. The employment of essentially counterfactual questions purports to make it possible to do so even in the case of features which, in fact, always obtain when a word is used correctly.

What distinguishes the second sort of what-would-we-say question from the first is that in the former we are interested in what the informant would say in situations which we believe to be anomalous. Such situations are contrived so that all the merely empirical features of the use of a word are stripped away, revealing, so it is supposed, those features which are determined by the meaning of the word alone. It is essential to an understanding of the argument in the rest of this paper to see that the anomalous character of the situations described in the second sort of what-would-we-say question is no accident.

Rather, it is essential if the answer to such questions is to provide the basis for a distinction between logically and empirically characteristic features of occurrences of words.

I hold that there is no reason to suppose that what-would-we-say questions of the second sort are answerable on the basis of our knowledge of our language. Put slightly differently, there is no reason to trust our intuitions about what we would say in situations in which some of our relatively secure beliefs have proved false; the ability to answer questions about what we would say in such circumstances is not implicit in our mastery of the rules of our language. The question put is: "What would you say if you turned out to be mistaken in believing that a certain set of features (namely, the ones which obtain when w can be used correctly) are invariably correlated?" I shall argue that there is no reason to suppose that a knowledge of, say, English equips us to answer such questions.[4]

Before stating the argument, let me block two possible misunderstandings. First, I am not claiming that English speakers are unreliable in their answers to the second sort of what-would-we-say questions in the sense that they would disagree among themselves about what answers to give. The question of how much consensus obtains among English speakers about what they would say in anomalous situations is simply an empirical question which could be answered by simply empirical techniques. I am arguing not that the speaker's answer must be unreliable, but rather that it must be irresponsible; his knowledge of his language does not provide grounds for an answer and thus his answer could not be a source of information about his language. (I do not wish to deny that some sort of nonlinguistic information may be available to speakers which serves as a basis for answers to the second sort of what-would-we-say question and hence accounts for whatever consensus exists as to the answers such questions should receive. But the existence of such nonlinguistic information could not justify the philosophic appeal to the intuitions of the speaker *qua* speaker as a technique for distinguishing criteria from symptoms.)

Second, I am not arguing that the speaker is incapable of imagining or conceiving a situation in which some of his beliefs about the correlations among features regularly associated with occurrences of words prove false. "Imagine" and "conceive" are, so far as I can tell, technical terms in philosophy such that any situation which can be described consistently is *ipso facto* imaginable or conceivable. In this sense of these terms it follows immediately (though not helpfully) that any feature of the occurrences of a word which is not logically characteristic of such occurrences can be imagined not to obtain. Whether

---

[4] I assume throughout that the speaker's claims about what he would say should be understood as *predictions* as to what his verbal behavior would be under the conditions enumerated. It is clear, however, that sometimes such claims are best understood as *decisions* as to what the best thing to say in such circumstances would be. This fact need not influence the present arguments since the reasons for maintaining that the speaker's knowledge of his language does not supply adequate grounds for predicting what he would say in the critical cases are precisely the reasons for maintaining that the speaker's knowledge of his language does not supply adequate basis for a reasoned decision as to what he *ought* to say in those cases.

this would also be true in some less technical sense of "imagine" or "conceive" I do not care to inquire. I do not *think* that I can imagine, say, a world in which nothing exists but sounds, but I am not sure that I cannot and I would not wish to have an important argument rest upon this point.

I hold that there is no reason to trust the intuitions of speakers about what they would say should their current beliefs prove seriously false. That is, I hold that there is no reason to believe such intuitions to be *linguistic* intuitions and hence that there is no basis for an appeal to the speaker *qua* speaker. The reason is this: to ask what we would say should certain of our current beliefs prove false involves asking what new beliefs we would then adopt. But to answer this question we would now have to be able to predict what theories would be devised and accepted were our current theories to prove untenable.[5] Clearly, however, it is unreasonable to attempt to predict what theories would be accepted if our current theories were abandoned and, *a fortiori*, it is unreasonable to attempt to make such predictions on the basis of an appeal to our current linguistic intuitions. Hence, if it is right to claim that to ask the second sort of what-would-we-say question is tantamount to asking what beliefs we would adopt should our current beliefs prove false, then it must follow that the strategy of employing such questions to distinguish between logically and empirically characteristic features of words is an unreasonable strategy and one which ought to be abandoned.

That we cannot in general answer the second sort of what-would-we-say question without knowing what beliefs we would adopt should our current beliefs prove false follows from this: to suppose that a perfectly reliable feature fails to obtain is, by definition, to suppose that a proposition which we now believe to express a law of nature or a true empirical generalization is false. However, the discovery that such a proposition is false may, in turn, require the abandonment of other beliefs and, in the extreme case, of whole theories. Since there is no general way to determine how many of our beliefs may need to be altered as the result of such a discovery (since, that is, the set of beliefs that it would be reasonable to abandon should the belief that P prove false need not be coextensive with the set of beliefs formally incompatible with not P) there can be no general way to determine how much of our way of talking such a discovery may require us to revise.

Against this the following might be argued. "It is true that we cannot now say what beliefs we should adopt if our current beliefs proved false. We cannot, for example, predict what we would say should dream reports prove not to be correlated with the results of observations of EEG, GSR, eye movements, muscle tone, gross movements during sleep, and so forth, or should these prove not to be correlated with one another. What we should doubtless do in such

---

[5] I use "theory" very broadly to mean "system of beliefs." I would not use it at all except that it sounds odd to speak of "devising and accepting a belief" and I wish to emphasize that, should our current beliefs break down in some important way, it would require serious inquiry to determine which new beliefs we ought to adopt. In particular, the results of such inquiry cannot be predicted on the basis of our current linguistic habits.

a case is cast about for a new theory of the relation between central and molar events, and what such a theoretical revision of the foundations of psychology might require us to say about dreams cannot now be known. This is, however, all thoroughly beside the point. For, though we cannot now predict what ways of talking we would adopt if our current beliefs broke down, we *can* now say that if we were to adopt *certain* ways of talking (that is, those which involve the abandonment of logically characteristic features of the word in question) then that would constitute a change of meaning. But the fact that we cannot now assert with certainty that no changes in our beliefs could lead us to change the meanings of words cannot be a reason for doubting the reliability of speakers' intuitions about when they would use a word, given its present meaning."

There is another way of stating the argument. Suppose English speakers claim they would never say of S that he had dreamed unless upon awakening he felt inclined to report a dream. This claim may be understood in either of two ways. In the first place, it may be understood to show that no experimental or theoretical considerations could ever lead a rational individual to hold both that S had dreamed and that S had not felt inclined upon awakening to say he had dreamed. So understood, the claim would appear to involve a prediction as to what sort of view of dreams we would take were certain correlations to fail which are currently believed to obtain. And it seems reasonable to ask how the speaker's knowledge of his *language* could conceivably afford a basis for such a prediction. The claim could, however, also be understood in another way. It could be understood to show that no experimental or theoretical considerations could ever lead a rational individual to hold both that S had dreamed and that S had not felt inclined to say he had dreamed *unless the meaning of the word "dream" had been changed.* And it does not seem implausible that *this* claim should be one to which the speaker is entitled just on the basis of his knowledge of his language.

This argument in effect poses a dilemma. It admits that the intuitions of speakers could not afford grounds for predictions about what beliefs we would adopt should our current beliefs prove false. In so doing, it tacitly admits that the intuitions of speakers might sometimes themselves prove false in the literal sense that it might be the case that features which are intuitively logically characteristic of the use of a word (that is, features whose failure to obtain would, according to speakers, provide sufficient grounds for not using the word) could be abandoned without abandoning the word in question. But, according to this argument, such cases would be cases in which changes in our beliefs have led us to change the meaning of a word. Hence they do not provide arguments against the reliability of intuition; what they show instead is that what seems to be unreliable intuition is really unacknowledged equivocation. It appears, then, that the speaker's intuitions *could not be fallible*; for either the speaker is literally right about what we would say or, if he is literally wrong, this shows only that the meaning of some word has been changed. That the argument should arrive at so curious a conclusion is itself grounds for supposing that something has gone wrong.

What is wrong with the argument is that it presupposed some technique for determining change of meaning that is independent of an appeal to speakers' intuitions about what we would say. Given such a technique, we could define a logically characteristic feature as one the alteration of which would involve a change of meaning, and we could add that the intuitions of speakers are trustworthy whenever the features which are intuitively unalterable are in fact the logically characteristic ones. Lacking such a technique, however, we must go the other way around and say that a change of meaning occurs just in case a logically characteristic feature is abandoned, where a logically characteristic feature is simply one the abandonment of which is not intuitively acceptable to speakers. This, however, makes the isolation of change of meaning rest upon precisely the same appeal to intuition which provides support for the distinction between criterial and symptomatic features. Hence, it would be circular to attempt to defend the soundness of such intuitions by claiming that a change of meaning is the inevitable consequence of their violation.

In short, it is perhaps true that though the intuitions of speakers are inadequate to determine what beliefs we should adopt were our current beliefs to prove false, they are adequate to determine when a change in our beliefs would involve a change in the meaning of some word. But to *show* this one must have some way of demonstrating change of meaning which does not itself rely for its support solely upon the intuitions of speakers. And though there is no logical or methodological implausibility in the assumption that there could be a theory of change of meaning which we have reason to believe true, independent of appeal to intuition, it seems clear that no such theory is currently available.

Once we abandon the notion that the speaker's claims about his linguistic behavior have some special freedom from disconfirmation, methodological probity requires that we attempt to discover in which cases such claims are likely to prove trustworthy and in which cases they are not. I have argued that there can be no general objection to reliance upon the speaker's intuitions in cases where such intuitions are, at least in principle, capable of theoretical or observational confirmation. Philosophers, however, often want to know what we would say if certain propositions widely believed to be true should prove false. In these cases, observational confirmation of the speaker's claims is precluded by the terms of the question, and theoretical confirmation would presuppose a characterization of the distinction between logical and empirical relations which does not rely solely upon an appeal to the intuitions of speaker. Such a characterization has not been forthcoming.

The speaker's intuitions are to be trusted when, and only when, we have good reason to believe that they derive from his mastery of his language. It would, however, seem implausible to maintain that the speaker's supposed knowledge of what he would say, were certain of his beliefs to prove false, could be ascribable to his linguistic competence. Indeed, it seems implausible to maintain that the speaker *has* such knowledge. It is notorious that the disconfirmation of any of our more firmly entrenched beliefs may be an occasion for considerable conceptual revision and that neither the direction of such revision nor its impact upon our ways of talking is likely to be predictable ahead of time.

It may still be claimed that the speaker's intuitions suffice to determine when a revision in our ways of talking is tantamount to a change in the meaning of some word. I do not deny that this is so, but I deny that it is a claim to which we are entitled without argument. (And it is worth noticing that the cases in which we are hard put to make an intuitively correct decision between criteria and symptoms are invariably precisely the cases in which our intuitions about change of meaning are uncertain.) A demonstration that speakers' intuitions are adequate to determine change of meaning would involve the construction of a criterion for meaning change which is not itself wholly dependent upon appeals to the speaker's intuitions. I do not know of any philosopher who has ever proposed such a criterion.

JERROLD J. KATZ

1.8   *Analyticity and Contradiction in Natural Language*

The primary significance of this paper lies in its solution to the problem of distinguishing analytic and synthetic truths raised by W. V. Quine in his "Two Dogmas of Empiricism."[1] This solution is based on the conviction that Quine's skepticism can be overcome within the framework of a conception of the nature of a semantic theory of a natural language while, in the absence of such a framework, techniques such as those R. Carnap[2] and other empiricists have proposed cannot hope to surmount Quine's fastidious skepticism. Accordingly, this paper first presents a conception of the nature of a semantic theory to serve as a framework and then proceeds within this framework to draw the analytic-synthetic distinction by introducing definitions of the terms *analytic*

Reprinted from *The Structure of Language: Readings in the Philosophy of Language*, Jerry A. Fodor and Jerrold J. Katz, eds., © 1964, by permission of Prentice-Hall, Inc., Englewood Cliffs, New Jersey.
[1] W. V. Quine, "Two Dogmas of Empiricism," in *From a Logical Point of View* (Cambridge, Mass.: Harvard University Press, 1953), pp. 20–46. [See selection 1.4 above, pp. 63–80.]
[2] R. Carnap, "Meaning and Synonymy in Natural Language," *Philosophical Studies*, VI, No. 3, (April 1955), 33–47.

sentence, synthetic sentence, and *contradictory sentence* which beg no questions of empirical justification and which formally specify the set of analytic sentences, the set of synthetic sentences, and the set of contradictory sentences.

THE NATURE OF A SEMANTIC THEORY

A semantic theory of a natural language[3] has as its goal the construction of a system of rules which represents what a fluent speaker knows[4] about the semantic structure of his language that permits him to understand its sentences. The idea behind this conception of a semantic theory is that such knowledge takes the form of recursive rules that enable the speaker to compose, albeit implicitly, the meaning of any sentence of his language out of the familiar meanings of its elementary components.

This idea has the following two-part rationale. First, the most impressive fact about linguistic competence is that a fluent speaker can understand a sentence even though he has never previously encountered it. In principle,[5] he can understand any of the infinitely many sentences of his language. But since, at any time in his life, the speaker can have encountered only a finite subset of the infinite set of sentences of his language, we can conclude that his knowledge of the semantic structure takes the form of recursive rules which fix a meaning for each of the infinitely many sentences. Second, since a speaker's ability to understand sentences also depends on his knowing the meanings of their elementary components, the lexical items in the vocabulary of the language, we can conclude that the meaning the rules fix for a sentence must be a compositional function of the antecedently known meanings of the lexical items appearing in it. Hence, a semantic theory must contain rules that represent the speaker's knowledge of the semantic structure of his language. Such rules must explicate the compositional function which deter-

---

[3] J. J. Katz and J. A. Fodor, "The Structure of a Semantic Theory," *Language,* XL (1963), reprinted in this volume, pp. 472–514. I shall henceforth use the initials "SST" to refer to this paper.

[4] Here I anticipate such an objection as the following: "How can you say a fluent speaker *knows* something if he cannot say what it is you claim he knows?" I do not think anything hangs on my *having* the word *know.* I intend to convey the idea that the fluent speaker has acquired the means necessary for performing a task whose character compels us to admit that its performance results from the application of rules. Among the reasons which compel us to make this admission is that cited by Miller, Pribram, and Galanter, viz., that the task of understanding any twenty word sentence is one a fluent speaker can perform, yet the number of twenty word sentences is 10^{30} while the number of seconds in a century is only 3.15 times 10^9—G. A. Miller, K. Pribram, and E. Galanter, *Plans and the Structure of Behavior* (New York: Holt, Rinehart & Winston, Inc. 1960), pp. 146–47.

[5] I say "in principle" because in practice limitations of perception, memory, mortality, and so on, prevent the speaker from applying his knowledge of the rules of the language to provide himself with the meaning of certain sentences. This situation is exactly analogous to the case of a person's knowledge of the rules of arithmetic computation. Knowing how to perform any computation, knowing the rules of arithmetic computation, is not sufficient to enable someone to actually perform any (specific) computation; for, again, limitations of perception, memory, mortality, and the like stand in the way.

mines how he utilizes the meanings of the lexical items in a sentence to understand what that sentence means.

A semantic theory consists of two components. First, a dictionary which provides a meaning for each lexical item of the language. Second, a finite set of "projection rules." These use information supplied by the dictionary for the lexical items in a sentence and information about the sentence's syntactic structure supplied by the grammar of the language in order to assign the sentence a semantic interpretation.

Since information about a sentence's syntactic structure is needed to assign it a semantic interpretation, it is convenient to let the output of a grammar be the input to a semantic theory. In this way, each sentence considered by a semantic theory is represented as a concatenation of morphemes whose constituent structure is given in the form of a hierarchical categorization of the syntactical parts of the concatenation.[6] The sentence "The boys like candy" is represented by the concatenation of morphemes *the + boy + s + like + candy* which is hierarchically categorized as follows: the whole string is categorized as a sentence at the highest level of the hierarchy; *the + boy + s* is categorized as a noun phrase, and *like + candy* is categorized as a verb phrase at the next level of the hierarchy; *the* is categorized as an article; *boy + s* is categorized as a noun, *like* as a verb, and *candy* as a noun; and so forth on the next and lower levels of the hierarchy. We can represent such a categorization in the form of a labeled tree diagram in which the notion *the sequence of morphemes m belongs to the category c* is formalized by the notion *m is traceable back to a node labeled c*.[7] We call such a representation a *constituent structure characterization* of a sentence. The constituent structure characterization of "The boys like candy" is roughly [shown in Fig. 1].[8] The input to a semantic theory are sentences represented as terminal elements within their constituent structure characterizations, together with any further grammatical information that an optimal grammar supplies about them.[9]

A semantic theory takes, one after another, the discrete outputs of the grammar and operates on them. This operation reconstructs the manner in which a speaker employs the syntactic structure of a sentence to determine its meaning as a function of the meanings of its lexical items. The result of this operation is a semantic interpretation of the sentence. Hence, we must first consider just what a semantic interpretation ought to tell us about a sentence.

---

[6] Such information will be needed to provide the difference upon which rests the distinction in meaning between sentences composed of exactly the same morphemes, e.g., "Gourmets do approve of people eating," "Gourmets do approve of eating people," "Do gourmets approve of people eating?" and so on.

[7] N. Chomsky, *Syntactic Structures*, Second Printing (Mouton and Co., 's Gravenhage, 1962), Chapter 4. In general, we shall follow Chomsky's conception of syntax.

[8] I will use the notational abbreviations: *S* for a sentence, *NP* for a noun phrase, *VP* for a verb phrase, *N* for a noun, *V* for a verb, *T* for an article, *A* for an adjective, *C* for a co-ordinating conjunction, and the subscript symbols *sing*, *pl*, and *tr* for the syntatic properties of nominal singularness, nominal pluralness, and verbal transitivity, respectively.

[9] In particular, an optimal grammar will include a specification of the transformational history for each sentence. Cf. N. Chomsky, *op. cit.*

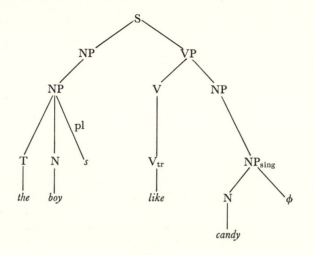

Figure 1

The semantic interpretations produced by a semantic theory constitute the theory's description of the semantic structure of a language. Since a speaker's knowledge of semantic structure manifests itself in his verbal performance, the fundamental question about this performance is "what manifests the speaker's knowledge of the semantic structure of his language?" Some of the ways in which the speaker manifests his knowledge are as follows: he differentiates semantically acceptable from semantically anomalous sentences; he recognizes ambiguities stemming from semantic relations; he detects semantic relations between expressions and sentences of different syntactic type and morpheme constitution; and so forth. Hence, semantic interpretations must formally mark as semantically acceptable and anomalous those sentences that the speaker differentiates as acceptable and anomalous, mark as semantically ambiguous those sentences that the speaker regards as such, mark as semantically related in such-and-such a fashion just those expressions and just those sentences that the speaker detects as so related, and so forth. Otherwise, the semantic theory cannot claim to represent the speaker's semantic knowledge. For example, a semantic theory of English would have to produce a semantic interpretation for "The bank is the scene of the crime" that marks it as semantically ambiguous, semantic interpretations for the sentences "He paints with silent paint" and "Two pints of the academic liquid!"[10] that mark them as semantically anomalous, semantic interpretations for "he paints silently" and "Two pints of the muddy liquid!" that mark them as semantically acceptable, and semantic interpretations which mark the sentences "Eye doctors eye blonds," "Oculists eye blonds," "Blonds are eyed by eye doctors," and so on, as paraphrases of each other but mark "Eye doctors eye what gentlemen prefer" as *not* a paraphrase of any of these sentences.

---

[10] For the first of these two examples, I am indebted to Professor Uriel Weinreich, and for the second to Professor George A. Miller.

Now, to finish describing the form of a semantic theory of a natural language, we need only characterize the notions *dictionary entry, semantic interpretation,* and *projection rule.*

Within a semantic theory, the dictionary entries provide the basis from which the projection rules of the theory derive the semantic interpretations they assign sentences. The notion *dictionary entry* must be such that in it we have a normal form for the dictionary entries in a semantic theory. This normal form must enable us to represent lexical information in a formal manner. Also, it must be sufficient in conceptual machinery to provide a representation of everything which the projection rules require to assign correct semantic interpretations.

In the majority of cases,[11] a dictionary entry consists of a finite number of sequences of symbols, each sequence consisting of an initial subsequence of syntactic markers, followed by a subsequence of "semantic markers," then, optionally, one "distinguisher," and finally a "selection restriction." Dictionary entries can be represented in the form of tree diagrams, such as in Fig. 2, where each sequence in the entry for a lexical item appears as a distinct path rooted at that lexical item.[12] Semantic markers are represented enclosed within parentheses, the distinguishers are represented enclosed within brackets, and the selection restrictions are represented within angles. Each complete path, each sequence, represents a distinct sense of the lexical item in whose entry it appears. Thus, in Fig. 2 the lexical item *bachelor* is represented as having four distinct senses.

Semantic markers are the formal elements a semantic theory employs to express semantic relations of a general nature. For example, the appearance of the semantic marker (Male) in the dictionary entries for senses of *bachelor, uncle, man, lion, priest, father,* etc., but not in the dictionary entries for senses of *spinster, stone, adult, philosopher, virtue, pea,* etc., represents the fact that the former items have a common semantic component in their meanings which the latter items lack, and, thus, the fact that these former items are semantically similar in a way that the latter ones are not. In contrast, distinguishers are the formal elements employed to represent what is idiosyncratic about the meaning of a lexical item. A distinguisher serves to distinguish a lexical item from those that are closest to it in meaning. Thus, a semantic marker found in the path of a certain lexical item will also be found in the paths of many other lexical items throughout the dictionary, whereas a distinguisher found in the path of a certain lexical item will not be found anywhere else in the dictionary. This

---

[11] In the small minority of cases, dictionary entries consist of instructions, e.g., the rules for *not* that are given in the third section of this paper. For a further discussion of the type of entry found in the vast majority of cases see Sect. 6 of SST.

[12] Two comments on Fig. 2. First, the word *bachelor,* although a noun, can select and exclude other nouns in various types of constructions, e.g., in noun-noun cases as "He is my bachelor friend," or in noun-in-apposition cases such as "Mr. Smith, the neighborhood bachelor, is here." Thus, we must represent *bachelor* having a selection restriction for each sense; thus, the terminal elements for each path in Fig. 2 is a selection restriction enclosed in angles. Second, the particular selections restrictions are omitted because their inclusion would only complicate matters unnecessarily at this point.

difference can be more fully appreciated if one compares the consequences of eliminating a semantic marker from a dictionary with the consequences of eliminating a distinguisher. In the former case, indefinitely many semantic relations between the expressions of the language which were marked by the eliminated semantic marker would no longer be marked, whereas in the latter case, only the distinction in sense which was marked by the eliminated distinguisher would no longer be marked.[13] Therefore, semantic markers and distinguishers represent the semantic properties from which the meaning of a lexical item is constructed. They may be regarded as expressing the most elementary components of the semantic content of lexical items, i.e., those components down into which the whole meaning of lexical items can be analyzed.

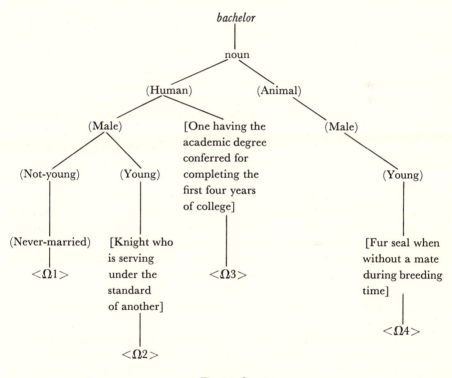

Figure 2

A lexical item is ambiguous if, and only if, its entry contains at least two distinct paths. Ambiguity at the lexical level is the source of semantic ambiguity at the sentence level. Thus, a necessary, although not sufficient, condition for a syntactically unambiguous sentence to be semantically ambiguous is that it contains an ambiguous lexical item. For example, the source of the semantic ambiguity of "He likes to wear a light suit in the summer" is the lexical ambi-

---

[13] For a further examination of the distinction between the notions *semantic marker* and *distinguisher* see Sect. 6 of SST.

guity of the word *light*. Since an adequate dictionary entry for a lexical item must mark every one of its ambiguities, the dictionary entry for *light* must represent this lexical item as branching into one path containing the semantic marker *Color* but not *Weight* and another containing the semantic marker *Weight* but not *Color*.

However, an ambiguous lexical item in a syntactically unambiguous sentence is not sufficient for that sentence to be semantically ambiguous. For example, the sentence "The stuff is light enough to carry," although it contains the ambiguous word *light*, is not understood in the sense in which *light enough to carry* means light enough in color to be carried. Thus, when there is an ambiguous lexical item in a semantically unambiguous sentence, the grammatical relations and the meanings of the other constituents can prevent this item from bearing more than one of its senses. The selection of some senses and exclusion of others occurs as a result of the other constituents of the sentence. Such selection is of fundamental importance because, together with lexical ambiguity, it partly determines whether a sentence is anomalous, whether a sentence is semantically unambiguous, whether two sentences are paraphrases of each other, and other semantic properties of sentences that a semantic theory marks.

Thus, a path for a lexical item must contain a selection restriction that determines the combinations into which the item can enter and the sense(s) it bears in those combinations. The formal representation of selection restrictions can be regarded as a device for indicating such information as *The Shorter Oxford English Dictionary's* qualification that the word *honest* when applied to persons means "of good moral character, virtuous, upright" and applied to women is ambiguous between this sense and the sense of *chaste*. We shall use left and right angles enclosing a Boolean function of syntactic or semantic markers to formally represent such selection restrictions. Such configurations of symbols will be affixed as the terminal element of a path and will be construed as providing a necessary and sufficient condition for a semantically acceptable combination of that path with another. Thus, for example, the selection restriction affixed to the path of a modifier determines the applicability of that path of the modifier to a sense of a head. Instances of modifier-head relations are: adjective-noun modification, adverb-verb modification, adverb-adjective modification. In particular, a path in the dictionary entry for *honest* will be: *honest* → adjective → (*Evaluative*) → (*Moral*) → [*Innocent of illicit sexual intercourse*] < (*Human*) and (*Female*) > . This is to be construed as saying that an adjectival occurrence of *honest* receives the interpretation, (*Evaluative*) → (*Moral*) → [*Innocent of illicit sexual intercourse*], just in case the head it modifies has a path containing both the semantic marker (*Human*) and the path semantic marker (*Female*).

In sum, a path contains syntactic markers that determine the syntactic classification of a lexical item, semantic markers that represent the semantic properties that the item has in common with many other lexical items, (optionally) a distinguisher that represents its idiosyncratic features, and finally a selection restriction.

The next notion to explain is *projection rule*. Let us suppose that an English grammar provides a semantic theory with the input sentence "The boys like candy" together with the constituent structure characterization as given in Fig. 1. The first step the theory performs in assigning a semantic interpretation to this sentence is to correlate each of its lexical items, i.e., *the*, *boy*, *s*, *like*, and *candy*, with all, and only, the paths from their dictionary entries that are compatible with the syntactic categorization the lexical items are given in the constituent structure characterization.

The correlation works as follows: if a path from the dictionary entry for the lexical item m_j contains syntactic markers which attribute to m_j the same syntactic categorization that it has in the constituent structure characterization d_i, then this path is assigned to the set of paths P_j^i which is correlated with the occurrence m_j in d_i. Thus, the lexical item m_1 is associated with the set of paths P_1^i, m_2 is associated with P_2^i, and so on.[14] Referring to Fig. 1, the result of this step may be pictured as converting the diagram into one in which *the* is associated with the set of paths P_1^i, *boy* is associated with P_2^i, *s* is associated with P_3^i, *like* is associated with P_4^i, and *candy* is associated with P_5^i (although no other change is made). Thus, for example, P_5^i contains paths representing each of the senses that *candy* has as a noun but none of the paths representing its senses as a verb (e.g. "The fruits candy easily"). This rule which associates senses with the occurrences of lexical items in constituent structure characterizations is the first projection rule.

There are type one projection rules and type two projection rules. Type one projection rules utilize the information about the meanings of the lexical items contained in the paths belonging to the sets of paths assigned in the above manner in order to provide a characterization of the meaning of every constituent of a sentence, including the whole sentence. For example, in "The boys like candy," besides the characterizations of the meaning of *the*, *boy*, *s*, *like*, and *candy* obtained from their dictionary entries, type one projection rules must provide characterizations of the meaning of *The boys*, *like candy*, and "The boys like candy." This type one projection rules do by combining the characterizations of the meaning of lower constituents to form a characterization of the meaning of the higher constituents. Thus, type one projection rules effect a series of amalgamations of paths, proceeding from the bottom to the top of a constituent structure characterization, by embedding paths into each other to form a new path, the amalgam. The amalgam is assigned to the set of paths associated with the node (i.e., the point at which an *n*-ary branching occurs) that immediately dominates the sets of paths from which the paths amalgamated were drawn. The amalgam provides one of the meanings for the sequence of

---

[14] For a full discussion of this step see the treatment of rule (I) in SST, Sect. 7.

lexical items that the node dominates. In this manner, a set of alternative meanings given in the form of derived paths is provided for every sequence of lexical items dominated by a syntactic marker in the constituent structure characterization, until the highest syntactic marker S is reached and associated with a set of derived paths giving the meanings for the whole sentence.

Amalgamation is the operation of forming a composite path made up of one path from each of the n-different sets of paths dominated by a syntactic marker. This composite path is then a member of the set of paths associated with the node that that syntactic marker labels. The joining of a pair of paths occurs just in case one of the paths satisfies the selection restrictions in the other. If the syntactic marker dominates just the sets of paths P_1^i, P_2^i, $\ldots$, P_n^i and P_1^i contains k_1 paths, P_2^i contains k_2 paths, $\ldots$, P_n^i contains k_m paths, then the set of paths that is associated with the dominating marker contains at most $(k_1 \cdot k_2 \cdot \ldots \cdot k_m)$ members and possibly zero members if selection restrictions prevent every possible amalgamation from forming. Each path which is in the set assigned to the dominating node marker is called *a reading for the lexical string that this marker dominates in the constituent structure characterization d_i*. The number of readings that is thus allotted to a string of lexical items determines its degree of semantic ambiguity. A string with no readings is anomalous, a string with exactly one reading is unambiguous, and a string with two or more readings is semantically ambiguous two or more ways.

An example of a projection rule of type one is:

(R1)   Given two paths associated with nodes branching from the same node labeled *SM*, one of the form
Lexical String$_1 \to$ syntactic markers of head $\to (a_1) \to (a_2) \to \cdots \to (a_n)$ $\to [1] \langle \Omega 1 \rangle$
and the other of the form
Lexical String$_2 \to$ syntactic markers of the modifier of the head $\to (b_1)$ $\to (b_2) \to \cdots \to (b_m) \to [2] \langle \Omega 2 \rangle$
such that the string of syntactic or semantic markers of the head has a substring σ which satisfies $\langle \Omega 2 \rangle$, then there is an amalgam of the form
Lexical String$_2$ + Lexical String$_1 \to$ dominating node marker $SM \to (a_1)$ $\to (a_2) \to \cdots \to (a_n) \to (b_1) \to (b_2) \to \cdots \to (b_m) \to [[2] [1]] \langle \Omega_1 \rangle$,
where any b_i is null just in case there is an a_j such that $b_i = a_j$, and $[[2] [1]]$ is simply $[1]$ just in case $[2] = [1]$. This amalgam is assigned to the set of paths associated with the node labeled *SM* that dominates Lexical String$_2$ + Lexical String$_1$.[15]

(R1) explicates the process of attribution, i.e., the process of creating a new semantic unit compounded from a modifier and head whose semantic properties are those of the head, except that the meaning of the compound is more determinate than the head's by virtue of the semantic information contributed by the modifier. The modifier-head relations which must be known for (R1) to

---

15 This erasure clause is included to avoid pointlessly duplicating semantic markers and distinguishers in the path for a compound expression. Thus, for example, it makes no sense to include the semantic markers (*Human*) and (*Female*) twice in the path associated with the compound *spinster aunt* because both of the constituent paths contain occurrences of both. The second occurrence of (*Human*) or (*Female*) would provide no semantic information whatever.

apply will be specified by the grammar of the language. An example of an amalgamation produced by $(R1)$ is the joining of the path, *colorful* → *adjective* → (*color*) → [*Abounding in contrast or variety of bright colors*] < (*Physical object*) v (*Social activity*) >, and the path, *ball* → noun → (*Physical object*) → [*Of globular shape*], to produce the new compound path, *colorful* + *ball* → noun → (*Physical object*) → (*color*) → [[*Abounding in contrast or variety of bright colors*] [*Of globular shape*]]. An example of an amalgamation that is prevented by a selection restriction is that of the path, *colorful* → adjective → (*Evaluative*) → [*Of distinctive character, vividness, or picturesqueness*] < (*Aesthetic Object*) v (*Social Activity*) >, with the path for *ball* just given above. This possible amalgamation is precluded because the selection restriction in the path of the modifier requires that this path be joined only with paths of heads that contain either the semantic marker (*Aesthetic object*) or the semantic marker (*Social activity*) whereas this path of *ball* contains neither one of these semantic markers.

Other type one projection rules are formulated in a similar manner, utilizing other grammatical relations to produce similar types of amalgamations. Type two rules work differently and are best explained after we explain the concept of a semantic interpretation of a sentence.

A semantic theory receives more than one constituent structure characterization for a sentence if that sentence is syntactically ambiguous. Figures 3 and 4 [see next page] show the two constituent structure characterizations for the syntactically ambiguous sentence "I like little boys and girls."

Let $d_1, d_2, \ldots, d_n$ be the constituent structure characterizations that the grammar provides for the n-ways syntactically ambiguous sentence S. We will define the "semantic interpretation of S" to be (1) the conjunction ψd_1 & ψd_2 & $\ldots$ & ψd_n of the semantic interpretations of the n-constituent structure characterizations of S, and (2) the statements about S that follow from the definition schema:

(D) S is *fully* X if and only if S is X on every d_i

The semantic interpretation ψd_i of the constituent structure characterization d_i of S is (1) the constituent structure characterization d_i, each node of which is associated with its full set of readings, (i.e., every reading that can belong to the set on the basis of the dictionary entries and the projection rules does belong to it), and (2) the statements about S that follow from (1) together with the definitions:

(D1) S is *semantically anomalous on* d_i if, and only if, the set of paths associated with the node labeled S in d_i contains no members.

(D2) S is *semantically unambiguous on* d_i if, and only if, the set paths associated with the node labeled S in d_i contains exactly one member.

(D3) S is *n-ways semantically ambiguous on* d_i if, and only if, the set of paths associated with the node labeled S in d_i contains exactly n-members ($n \geqslant 2$).

(D4) S_1 and S_2 are *paraphrases on a reading with respect to their characterizations* d_i and d_j if, and only if, the set of paths associated with the node labeled S in d_i and the set of paths associated with the node labeled S in d_j have a reading in common.

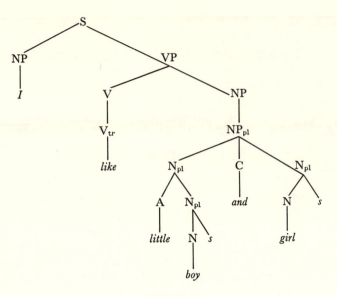

Figure 3

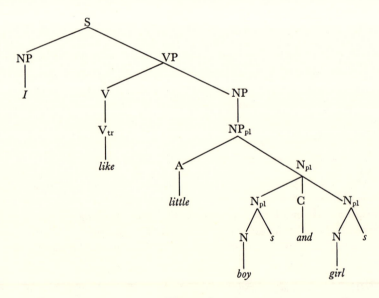

Figure 4

(D5) S_1 and S_2 are *full paraphrases with respect to their characterizations d_i and d_j* if, and only if, the set of paths associated with the node labeled S in d_i and the set of paths associated with the node labeled S in d_j have exactly the same membership.

as well as other definitions for other semantic properties of sentences and corresponding definitions for constituents of sentences, e.g., (D1.1). *NP is semantically* *anomalous on d_i* if, and only if, the set of paths associated with the node labeled *NP* in d_i contains no members.

Since these definitions are self-explanatory, we can now return to our account of the projection rules and explain the concept of a type two projection rule.

A grammar employs two types of syntactic rules to achieve its aim of assigning the correct constituent structure characterization to each sentence of the language.[16] The first type are rules which rewrite single symbols on the basis of information which comes from the linear context of the symbol. Such rules construct constituent structure characterizations such as those in Figs. 1, 3, and 4 in somewhat the following manner: the first rule rewrites the initial symbol *S* (standing for "*sentence*") as *NP* + *VP* (which categorizes a noun-phrase + verb-phrase sequence as a sentence), then a rule can be used to rewrite *NP* as either NP_{sing} or NP_{pl}, then other rules can be used to rewrite *VP* as either *V* + *NP* or V_{intr} or *be* + *Pred*, still other rules to rewrite VP_{sing} as *T* + *N*, *T* as *the*, *N* as *boy* (or *man, coat, mouse*, etc.) and so forth.[17]

It has been shown that a grammar can assign constituent structure characterizations correctly only if some of its rules use information about the derivational history of sentences.[18] Thus, in addition to the previous type of rules, grammars contain "transformational rules." Such rules operate on entire constituent structure characterizations, or any of their parts, and map labeled trees onto labeled trees. In this way, simpler sentences are transformed into more complex ones, and the transformed sentences are assigned a constituent structure characterization.

Type two projection rules are intended to explicate the manner in which transformational rules preserve or change meaning. Linguists have observed that, in general, the sentence resulting from the application of a transformational rule to a set of source sentences is related in meaning to these source sentences in a definite, systematic way.[19] The employment of type two rules is intended to reveal the facts of language that underly this observation.

Type two projection rules produce a semantic interpretation ψd_i for the constituent structure characterization d_i constructed by the operation of the transformation *T* out of the set of constituent structure characterizations d_1, $d_2, \ldots, d_n$. Such projection rules operate on a set of semantic interpretations

---

[16] Although this is not the only aim of a grammar. Cf. N. Chomsky, "On the Notion 'Rule of Grammar'," *Proceedings of the Twelfth Symposium in Applied Mathematics, The Structure of Language and its Mathematical Aspects*, ed. by Roman Jakobson, American Mathematical Society, (1961), pp. 6–24.

[17] *Cf.* N. Chomsky, "A Transformational Approach to Syntax" in A. A. Hill (ed.), *Proceedings of the Third Texas Conference on Problems of Linguistic Analysis in English*, 1958 (Austin, Texas: The University of Texas, 1962), pp. 124–58.

[18] *Cf.* Chomsky's *Syntactic Structures*, "On the Notion 'Rule of Grammar'," and *The Logical Structure of Linguistic Theory*, (1955), microfilm at M.I.T. Library. Also, *cf.* P. Postal, "Limitations of Phrase-Structure Grammars."

[19] This point has been discussed outside the context of the conception of a semantic theory adopted in the present paper in two recent articles: J. A. Fodor, "Projection and Paraphrase in Semantics," *Analysis*, XXI, No. 4 (March 1961), 73–77; and J. J. Katz, "A Reply to 'Projection and Paraphrase in Semantics'," *Analysis*, XXII, No. 2 (December 1961), 36–41.

$\sqrt{rd_1}$, $\sqrt{rd_2}$, ..., $\sqrt{rd_n}$. and the transformation T to produce the semantic interpretation $\sqrt{rd_i}$. They assign semantic interpretations in such a way as to reconstruct the manner in which the meaning of the sentence that was constructed
by T is a function of the meanings of each of the sentences that were used by
T in its construction.

THE SOLUTION TO QUINE'S PROBLEM

The present paper is an essay in semantic metatheory.[20] A metatheory of
semantic theories is needed to inform the field linguist of what types of facts to
look for and what is the most revealing form to arrange them in. Given that
he has acquired the relevant linguistic facts and has suitably arranged them,
definitions such as (D), $(D1)$, $(D2)$, $(D3)$, $(D4)$, and $(D5)$ are the basis on which
the field linguist can make illuminating statements about the sentences of the
language he is studying. However, these definitions are not by themselves
enough to enable the field linguist to say everything he should say about the
semantic properties of sentences. On the basis of $(D1)$ to $(D5)$, the linguist can
say what formal relations determine whether a sentence is acceptable or anomalous, what relations determine whether a sentence is unambiguous or ambiguous, and what relations determine whether a sentence is a paraphrase of another
or not. But the linguist requires a notion of semantic interpretation that, by
virtue of further definitions, will enable him to tell also when a sentence is
analytic, contradictory, or synthetic, when two sentences are inconsistent with
each other, and so on. Accordingly, the present paper extends the concept of
a semantic interpretation by adding definitions of the notions *analytic sentence,
contradictory sentence, synthetic sentence, inconsistent sentences,* among others. Thus, this
paper not only offers a reply to Quine's challenge to the empiricists to show
that the analytic-synthetic distinction is more than mere dogma but continues
the metatheoretic study into the nature of a semantic theory begun in previous
publications.[21]

In SST, the basic idea behind the present paper's treatment of the concept
of an analytic sentence was expressed as follows:

> The limiting case [of modification], where the addition to the compound of
> semantic material from the modifier is zero, is of considerable theoretical interest.
> The compound *unmarried bachelor* is a case in point. The erasure clause in $(R1)$,
> i.e., "any b_i is null when there is an a_j such that $b_i = a_j$, and $[[2]\,[1]] = [1]$ just
> in case $[2] = [1]$," tells us to delete from the path of the modifier any semantic
> material already represented in the path of the head. Thus, in forming the
> compound *unmarried bachelor* all the semantic information in the path of the
> modifier *unmarried* will be deleted so that the derived path for *unmarried bachelor*
> will contain no more than the semantic material which comes from the path for
> *bachelor*. The failure of the modifier to add semantic information would appear to
> account for the intuition that such expressions as *unmarried bachelor* are redundant

---

[20] A full discussion of the nature of a semantic metatheory will be found in SST, Sect 8.
[21] *Cf.* SST and J. J. Katz and P. Postal, *An Integrated Theory of Linguistic Descriptions,* M.I.T.
Press, 1964.

and that, correspondingly, such statements as "bachelors are unmarried" are "empty," "tautological," "vacuous," "uninformative." Thus, we have a new explanation of the analyticity of a classical type of analytic truth.[22]

The explanation of analyticity suggested in this passage, although it is developed only for sentences of the $NP + is + A$ type, can be extended to explain the analyticity of all copula sentences. The analyticity of noncopula sentences will be taken up after we conclude our whole discussion of the copula type.

To obtain a general, formal definition of *analytic sentence* for present tense copula sentences, we will require some auxiliary notions. We will use the symbol p_1 for a path from the set of paths associated with the node labeled NP that is immediately dominated by the node labeled S (i.e., the node that dominates the string of lexical items that is the subject of the sentence). We will use the symbol p_2 for a path from the set of paths associated with the node labeled VP that is immediately dominated by the node labeled S (i.e., the node that dominates the string of lexical items that consists of the verb *is* followed by its nominal or adjectival predicate). That is, p_1 and p_2 are paths that are amalgamated to produce a reading, which we shall represent by $r_{1,2}$, for the sentence as a whole. We will use the term *semantic element* to refer either to a semantic marker or to a distinguisher.

Given these auxiliary notions, we add to $(D1)$ to $(D5)$ the definition:

> $(D6)$ The copula sentence S is *analytic on the reading* $r_{1,2}$ if, and only if, every semantic element e_i in p_2 is also in p_1 and for any complex semantic element $\{e_1 \cup e_2 \cup \ldots \cup e_n\}$ in the path p_2, there is a semantic element e_j such that $1 \leqslant j \leqslant n$ and e_j is in the path p_1.[23]

$(D6)$ formalizes the idea that analyticity is the predicative vacuity that results from the failure of the path associated with the predicate to contribute semantic elements to the path associated with the subject when these paths are amalgamated to produce a reading for the sentence.

Checking $(D6)$ for its applicability to analytic sentences of each of the copula types, the $NP + is + A$ cases and the $NP + is + NP$ cases, we find that both types come under $(D6)$ as is indicated by the examples: "Bachelors are unmarried," "The happy child is happy," "The man who is cheerful is cheerful," and so on and "The pediatrician who loves her is a doctor who loves her," "The man who stole the cake is the man by whom the cake was stolen," "Stones are physical objects," "Spinsters are adult women who have never married," and so on. In each of these examples, the sentence is analytic because every semantic element in the path from the set of paths associated with the verb phrase is also found in the path from the set associated with the noun-phrase subject.

---

[22] SST, Sect. 7.

[23] The notation $\{e_1 \cup e_2 \cup \ldots \cup e_n\}$ will be explained below in connection with the discussion of the rules for *not*. In $(D7)$ and $(D8)$ we will take S to be a variable for copula sentences.

The concept of "analytic sentence" just characterized is that of "analytic on a reading," but there is another concept of sentential analyticity, *viz.*

> (D6′) S is *fully analytic on* d_i if, and only if, the set of readings assigned to the node labeled S in d_i is non-null and, for every reading $r_{1,2}$ in this set, S is analytic on $r_{1,2}$

Sentences that are merely analytic on a reading are as plentiful as natural numbers (e.g., the sentences usually encountered in philosophical discussions of analyticity, "Bachelors are unmarried," "Vixens are foxes.") On the other hand, sentences that are fully analytic are not found in natural language, except in areas where a highly technical nomenclature is in use. Some philosophers claim that, for example, "Bachelors are unmarried" is not analytic because *bachelor* can refer to married men or women who possess a bachelor's degree. Other philosophers regard such criticism as beside the point. Disagreement of this kind can be resolved using the above distinction.

In terms of (D6), analyticity is the counterpart, on the sentence level, of the relations of synonymy and meaning inclusion, found on the level of lexical items and expressions.[24] Intuitively, this is a desirable feature since it brings out the formal structure underlying the often made observation that analyticity is somehow connected with these relations. The question arises whether we can so construct our definition of "contradictory sentence" that it reconstructs contradictoriness as the counterpart, on the sentence level, of the relation of antonymy on the level of lexical items and expressions. It will become quite clear that an adequate definition of "contradictory sentence" must be constructed in such a way that this relationship between contradictoriness and antonymy is a feature of its definiens.

There are many special antonymy relations between words and expressions. One example, is the relation of "sex-antonymy."[25] A pair of lexical items is *sex-antonymous* just in case they have identical paths except that where one has the semantic marker (*Male*) the other has the semantic marker (*Female*). Some instances are: *woman and man; bride and groom; aunt and uncle; cow and bull.* The majority of antonymous lexical items are not sets of pairs but sets of *n*-tuples. For example, there are the species-antonymous lexical items, one example of a species-antonymous *n*-tuple being: *child, cub, puppy, kitten, cygnet,* and so on. Then, there are the age-antonymous *n*-tuples: *infant, child, adolescent,* and *adult; puppy and dog; cub and lion; cub and bear; cygnet and swan;* and so on. Moreover, there are *n*-tuples of lexical items that are distinguisher-wise antonymous, e.g., the *n*-tuple of simple color adjectives (*blue, yellow, green, red, orange*). These form an antonymous *n*-tuple because the path associated with each is identical

---

[24] We can say that a pair of lexical items are *synonymous on a sense* if, and only if, their dictionary entries have one path in common, and we can say a pair of lexical items are *fully synonymous* if, and only if, their dictionary entries are exactly the same. Two expressions are *synonymous on a pair of readings* if, and only if, they have a reading in common, and expressions are *fully synonymous* if, and only if, they have every reading in common.

[25] SST, Sect. 6.

except for the distinguisher which differentiates that color adjective from the others.

The definition of "sex-antonymy" cannot restrict the set of sex-antonymous pairs to a membership consisting only of lexical items. By definition, this set includes infinitely many cases of pairs of constructible expressions. For example, *the happy man and the happy woman; my mother's friend's father's aunt* and *my mother's friend's father's uncle; the cow that the farmer's son raised* and *the bull that the farmer's son raised;* and so on *ad infinitum.*[26] Moreover, the situation is the same for every other type of antonymy. Since every set of antonymous *n*-tuples contains infinitely many members, we will have to construct a definition of each type of antonymy and a definition of the general notion *antonymous n-tuple* that formally represents the relevant infinite set.

The most natural way to construct such definitions is the following. Let us suppose that the semantic markers and the distinguishers of a semantic theory are grouped into antonymous *n*-tuples. This will mean that the antonymous *n*-tuples of semantic elements are so represented by the notation of the theory that the membership of any *n*-tuple can be uniquely determined from the symbols that represent the semantic elements. Then, we can define the general notion of antonymy as follows:

(1) Two lexical items or constructible expressions m_i and m_j are *antonymous on their paths* p_{m_i} *and* p_{m_j} if and only if p_{m_i} and p_{m_j} contain different semantic elements from the same antonymous *n*-tuple of semantic elements.

(2) $m_1, m_2, \ldots, m_n$ are *an X-antonymous n-tuple of constructible expressions* if, and only if, the paths $p_{m_1}, p_{m_2}, \ldots, p_{m_n}$ associated with them respectively each contains a different semantic element from the *X*-antonymous *n*-tuple of semantic elements.

We can now define the notion *contradictory sentence*:

(D7) *S* is *contradictory on the reading* $r_{1,2}$ *of* d_i if, and only if, p_1 and p_2 contain different semantic elements from the same antonymous *n*-tuple of semantic elements.

Thus, what is asserted a sentence when its semantic interpretation marks it as contradictory is that the amalgamation that provides a reading for the sentence combines antonymous elements. Examples of contradictory sentences are: "A bride is a groom," "My round table is square," "Red is green," "Those who play badly are those who play well," "The loser of the game we are playing is the winner of the game we are playing," and so on.

Synthetic sentence can now be defined in terms of (D6) and (D7):

(D8) *S* is *synthetic on the reading* $r_{1,2}$ *of* d_i if, and only if, *S* is neither analytic on $r_{1,2}$ nor contradictory

---

[26] For the rules of grammar that explain why this set is infinite *cf.* R. B. Lees, "The Grammar of English Nominalizations," *International Journal of American Linguistics*, XXVI, No. 3 (July 1960).

Examples of synthetic sentences are: "That woman is a spinster," "The loser of the game we are playing is a bachelor," "The groom is reluctant," "Red is the color of my house."[27]

In order for definitions (D6) to (D8) to apply generally, certain other concepts need to be explicated. One such explication is the rules for determining the semantic effect of sentential negation.

The negation of a sentence can be formed in a number of ways. We can put the word *not* after the verb *be*, as in "The table is not an antique." We can put expressions such as "It is not the case that" in front of full sentences, as in the sentence "It is not the case that the table is an antique." We can prefix the sentence by *that* and add *is false* to the end, as in "That it is so is false."[28] We shall consider only the type of negativization in which the negation of a sentence is formed by adding *not*. Negations formed in other ways, by virtue of being actual sentence negations, are synonymous with the negations of the same sentences that are formed by adding *not*. Thus, restricting consideration to negations formed by adding *not* does not impose a limitation on our treatment because, by (D4) and (D5) which require that synonymous sentences receive the same readings at the sentence level, whatever semantic properties a semantic interpretation assigns to the negation of a sentence formed in this way will also be assigned to the negation of that sentence which is formed in another manner. Moreover, we shall make the reasonable assumption that the scope of a negative in a sentence is determined by the grammatical analysis of the sentence.[29] Then, we can formally characterize a range of application for the *not*-rules by allowing them to operate on any path in the set of paths that provides the readings for the constituent in the scope of *not*. This constituent will be the main verb phrase of the sentence so that the *not*-rules operate on p_2's. For example, in the case of the sentence "The table is not an antique," the *not*-rules apply to any path that provides a reading for the constituent *an antique*. What we have to determine now is the effect of the operation of the *not*-rules on the paths which fall in their range of application.

---

[27] Thus, set of synthetic sentences in English includes "There are no more integers than even integers" and other semi-sophisticated mathematical truths, as well as the sophisticated ones. We shall draw the moral at the very end of this paper.

[28] The use of a negative prefix does not convert a sentence into its negation. Thus, the sentence "John is unlucky" is not the negation of "John is lucky," whereas the sentence "John is not lucky" is the negation of "John is lucky." To appreciate this, one must observe that the sentences "John is unlucky" and "John is not lucky" are not synonymous. The former means that John has bad things happening to him regularly by chance, while the latter means that John has very few good things happening to him by chance. Thus, "John is not unlucky" means that John does not have bad things happening to him regularly, not that he has any good thing happening to him. On the other hand, "John is not not lucky" means that he has good things happening to him regularly.

[29] The question of whether a negative somewhere in a sentence makes that sentence the negation of the sentence without that negative is a matter for the grammar to decide. *Cf.* E. Klima "Negation in English," Ch. 8, pp. 246–323 of J. A. Fodor & J. J. Katz, eds., *The Structure of Language* (Englewood Cliffs, N. J.: Prentice Hall, Inc., 1964).

Preliminary to stating the *not*-rules, let us define an operator which we shall call the *antonymy operator* and symbolize by $A/$:

> (3) If the semantic elements $e_1, e_2, \ldots, e_n$ are an antonymous *n*-tuple, then
>   (a) $A/e_i \ (1 \leqslant i \leqslant n) = \{e_1 \cup e_2 \cup \ldots \cup e_{i-1} \cup e_{i+1} \cup \ldots \cup e_n\}$
>   (b) $A/A/e_i = e_i$

We will call a function of semantic elements a "complex semantic element" and will treat complex semantic elements exactly like semantic elements for the purpose of amalgamation.

Suppose we hear the English sentence "That adult is not a spinster." As fluent speakers, we know that this sentence says that the person referred to by its subject is not a spinster, but we do not know from this sentence alone whether this is because that person is male or because that person is married or both. On the other hand, we do know that that person's being human has nothing whatsoever to do with the fact that he or she is not a spinster. These considerations suggest the first of our *not*-rules.

> (*NR*) Let $e_1, e_2, \ldots, e_k$ be all the semantic elements in a path in the range of *not* such that no $e_i (1 \leqslant i \leqslant k)$ occurs in p_1 and no A/e_i occurs in p_1. Then $e_1, e_2, \ldots, e_k$ are replaced by the complex semantic element $\{A/e_1 \cup A/e_2 \cup \ldots \cup A/e_k\}$.

Each set in the union of sets $\{A/e_1 \cup A/e_2 \cup \ldots \cup A/e_k\}$ is a union of semantic elements, i.e., each $A/e_i \ (1 \leqslant i \leqslant k)$ is, according to (3) above, the union of all the members of the antonymous *n*-tuple to which e_i belongs except e_i itself; e.g., if e_i belongs to an antonymous pair, then A/e_i is simply the semantic marker distinguisher that is antonymous with e_i.

Using (*NR*) to obtain a reading for the sentence "That adult is not a spinster," we achieve, with respect to what factors are and what are not in the meaning of this sentence, a result which is fully in accord with our linguistic intuition as speakers of English. The amalgamation of a path for *that adult* and a path for *is not a spinster* which is required to provide a reading for the whole sentence is preceded by an operation of (*N/R*) which replaces the semantic markers (*Female*) and (*Unmarried*) in the path for *a spinster* by the complex semantic marker $\{A/(Female) \ A/(Unmarried)\}$, i.e., $\{(Male) \cup (Married)\}$. Thus, when the path for *is not a spinster* is amalgamated with the path for *that adult* by (*R*1)[30] the complex marker from the path of *a spinster*, $\{(Male) \cup (Married)\}$, will become an element of the reading for the whole sentence. This, then, is to say formally what we agreed on above, namely, that adult is either a male or married or both. We also agreed that the person's being human has nothing to do with he or she not being a *spinster*. Formally, the semantic marker (*Human*) which is in the path for *a spinster* already appears in the path for *that adult*, and therefore (*NR*) leaves it intact. But (*R*1)'s erasure clause deletes it so that it does not enter the path for *that adult*. Finally, (*D*8) enables us to mark "That adult is not a spinster" as a synthetic sentence.

---

[30] By (*R*1) because this is a modifier-head relation.

We now introduce the two further *not*-rules, (NR') and (NR''), which complete our account of the operation of negation.

(NR') (1) For all those e_i in a path in the range of *not* such that there is a semantic element antonymous to e_i in p_1, e_i is replaced by A/e_i.

(2) If (NR) did not apply and if (NR') (1) does not apply, then any e_i in a path in the range of *not* that also occurs in p_1 is replaced by A/e_i.

(NR'') If (NR') applies to a path, then any semantic element in that path that does not also occur in p_1 and that has not entered that path by the application of (NR') that permits this application of (NR'') is nullified.

With these rules, we can show that, in accordance with the dicta of logic, a semantic theory built on the model given in the previous section and supplemented with the definitions from the present section will mark the negation of a contradictory sentence as analytic and will mark the negation of an analytic sentence as contradictory. Now we want to explain why there is such a relation between contradictory and analytic sentences, and in so doing explain also the workings of (NR') and (NR'').

First, let us show that the negation of a contradictory sentence will be marked analytic. Assume we are given a sentence that is contradictory in the sense of $(D7)$. When the conversion of this contradictory sentence into its negation brings *not* in, there will then be semantic elements $e_1, e_2, \ldots, e_n \, (n \geqslant 1)$ in the path which will be in the range of *not* such that each element has an antonymous element in the path p_1. For example, if the contradictory sentence were "A bride is a groom," then $n = 1$, $e_1 = (Male)$, and e_1's antonymous element in $p_1 = (Female)$. The negation of the contradictory sentence has *not* located so that its range includes any path assigned as a reading to the verb phrase in the contradictory sentence. Thus, if p_3 is a path in the range of *not*, then by (NR') (1), each semantic element $e_i \, (1 \leqslant i \leqslant n)$ in p_3 will be replaced by A/e_i prior to the amalgamation of p_1 and p_2. Hence, in the amalgamation of p_1 and p_2, any semantic elements in p_2 that have an antonym in p_1 will be converted into their antonym so that the erasure clause of the projection rule amalgamating p_1 and p_2 deletes them as a duplication. For example, in the sentence "A bride is not a groom," the semantic marker $(Male)$ is replaced by $A/(Male)$, i.e., $(Female)$, so that in the amalgamation of the path for *is not a groom* and the path for *a bride* the former path does not contribute $A/(Male)$ because the presence of $(Female)$ in the latter path causes it to be deleted prior to amalgamation. Such deletion will also be the fate of any semantic elements in p_2 that are in p_1 as well; e.g., the semantic marker $(Human)$ in the path assigned as a reading to *is a groom* will not be added to a path for *a bride* when such a path is amalgamated with a path for *is not a groom* because $(Human)$ appears in the path for *a bride*. If there are any semantic elements in p_3 such that neither they nor their antonym is in p_1 (as there are not in "A bride is a groom" but are in "A bride is a reluctant groom"), then, by (NR''), each is nullified. Consequently, in the amalgamation of p_1 and p_2, p_2 will be vacuous, and so by $(D6)$, the sentence will be analytic. Therefore, we conclude that the negation of a contradictory sentence is analytic.

Next we must show that the negation of an analytic sentence is contradictory. Assume we are given a sentence that is analytic in the sense of $(D6)$. It follows that there are semantic elements $e_1, e_2, \ldots, e_n$ $(n \geqslant 1)$ in the path p_2 for this analytic sentence such that each e_i $(1 \leqslant i \leqslant n)$ is also in p_1. Thus, in the negation of the sentence, (NR') (2) replaces e_1 by A/e_1, e_2 by A/e_2, $\ldots$, and e_n by A/e_n. Consequently, p_1 and p_2 will each contain a different semantic element from the same n-tuple of antonymous semantic elements, and the negation of the analytic sentence will be contradictory by $(D7)$. For example, suppose we began with the analytic sentence "That spinster is a female who never married." Then, $n = 2$ and $e_1 = $ *(Female)* and $e_2 = $ *(never-married)*. Then, (NR') (2) converts *(Female)* into $A/$*(Female)*, i.e., *(Male)*, and *(never-married)* into $A/$*(never-married)*, i.e., *(at least once married)*. But since *that spinster* is assigned a path containing both *(never-married)* and *(Female)*, the sentence "that spinster is not a female who never married" is contradictory by virtue of the fact that its semantic interpretation now satisfies $(D7)$.

The negation of a synthetic sentence comes out, as it should, to be synthetic. By $(D8)$, a synthetic sentence will have a path p_2 which contains semantic elements $e_1, e_2, \ldots, e_n$ $(n \geqslant 1)$ that do not also occur in p_1. Moreover, by $(D8)$, $A/e_1, A/e_2, \ldots, A/e_n$ do not occur in p_1 either. The *not*-rules only replace e_1 by A/e_1, e_2 by A/e_2, $\ldots$, e_n by A/e_n in the path p_2 of the negation of the synthetic sentence. Since *ex hypothesi* $A/e_1, A/e_2, \ldots, A/e_n$ are not in p_1, the negation of a synthetic sentence does not satisfy $(D6)$. Since *ex hypothesi* $e_1, e_2, \ldots, e_n$ are not in p_1, it does not satisfy $(D7)$ either. Since the negation of a synthetic sentence is neither analytic nor contradictory, by $(D8)$, it is synthetic. For example, the paths p_2 for the sentences "That adult is not a spinster," "The apple is not red," and so on will add new semantic information that is consistent with what is in the corresponding paths p_1 when the p_1 and p_2 amalgamation takes place, and so each of these sentences will be marked synthetic.

The motivation for (NR'') deserves further comment. Consider the sentence "An uncle is a spinster." This sentence is contradictory because the path for *An uncle* and the path for *is a spinster* contain different semantic markers from the same n-tuple of antonymous semantic elements; i.e., the former contains *(Male)* and the latter *(Female)*. Thus, we require that the negation of this sentence be analytic. But, without (NR''), the negation of "An uncle is a spinster" would not be analytic, since there is a semantic element, viz., *(Unmarried)*, in the path p_2 which is not in p_1. Hence, the need for (NR'') stems from the need to cancel such semantic elements in order that we maintain the consequence that the negation of any contradictory sentence is analytic and that we preserve the generality of $(D6)$.

Before concluding this section, let us briefly look at some further consequences of our definitions. The definitions together with the *not*-rules provide a formal means of sharply distinguishing contradictory and analytic sentences, on the one hand, from anomalous sentences, on the other. The practice of regarding contradictory and analytic sentences as *odd* and *ipso facto* grouping them together with semantically anomalous sentences is not harmful when it is made fully clear that the term *odd* refers to sentence-uses in specific situations and means only that in those situations that use is somehow inappropriate. In this sense, synthetic sentences can be *odd*, e.g., "I just swallowed my nose," and anomalous sentences can, in some situations, i.e., giving an example, telling a joke, be *non-odd*.[31] However, often this sense of *odd* is not distinguished from the sense in which it means "violates the semantic restrictions necessary to meet the standard of semantic well-formedness," i.e., semantically anomalous. This is unfortunate because it has led some philosophers to believe that analytic, contradictory, and anomalous sentences are all odd, pure and simple, and this classifies together such dissimilar cases as "An uncle is a spinster" and "A bachelor is unmarried," on the one hand, and "the paint is silent" and "Two pints of the academic liquid," on the other. With the conceptual apparatus of selection restrictions on amalgamation (formulated in terms of functions of semantic elements enclosed within angles) and (*D*1) as the basis for marking anomaly and with (*D*6) and (*D*7) and the *not*-rules as the basis for marking analyticity and contradiction, we obtain the intuitively desirable result that semantic interpretations mark semantically anomalous sentences differently from the way they mark contradictory and analytic sentences. That is, sentences that are anomalous receive no reading at the sentence level while sentences that are either contradictory or analytic receive a reading having properties which enable them to be appropriately marked.

Another matter worth noticing is the following. Consider a sequence of sentences such as "The flower is red," "The flower is not red," "the flower is not not red," and so on.[32] The third sentence in this sequence is grammatically constructed from the second by the negation-transformation,[33] the fourth is so constructed from the third, the fifth from the fourth, and so on. We may thus regard the third sentence as having the syntactic bracketing (*The flower*) (*is not (not (red*))). Employing (*NR*) for the operation of the *not* whose range is the path that is associated with just the word *red*, we replace this path's distinguisher e_i by A/e_i. Again applying (*NR*), but this time for the *not* whose range is the path that is associated with the expression *not red*, i.e., the path resulting from the former operation of (*NR*), we replace the semantic element A/e_i by $A/A/e_i$, which is simply e_i by (3). Thus, the reading assigned to the third sentence is the same as that assigned to the first. But this means that

---

[31] *Cf.* J. J. Katz and J. A. Fodor, "What's Wrong with the Philosophy of Language?" *Inquiry*, V (1962), 215–18.

[32] The reader may object that at some point there are too many occurrences of the word *not* in the succeeding sentences for them to be acceptable English. This is perhaps so. But if there is such a point, then none of the sentences beyond it will be grammatical, and consequently none will be generated by the grammar and provided as input to the semantic theory. Thus, the semantic theory will interpret only those sentences in such sequences that are grammatical, since a semantic theory operates only on sentences it receives from the grammar. Hence, the projection rules are stated generally in order not to decide at what point sentences in such a sequence stop and ungrammatical strings begin.

[33] *Cf.* E. Klima, *op. cit.*

from the *not*-rules follows a version of the law of double negation: $X + not + not + Y = X + Y$.[34]

Furthermore, given the fact that the subject of both every odd numbered sentence in the above sequence of sentences and every even numbered sentence in this sequence is the same, it follows that every odd numbered sentence is synonymous with every other odd numbered sentence and that every even numbered sentence is synonymous with every other even numbered sentence. This is the intuitively correct result. Moreover, if we lay down the definition

> (D9) S_1 and S_2 are *inconsistent on a pair of readings* if the reading of one is the same as a reading of the negation of the other, i.e., if one sentence is synonymous with (or a paraphrase of) the other's negation

we can show that in the sequence of sentences we are considering (and, of course, in other similar sequences) the odd numbered sentences are inconsistent with the even numbered sentences, since every sentence in this sequence is inconsistent with its immediate successor.

Finally, a matter that needs to be mentioned for the sake of a complete treatment of contradiction, viz., the case of contradictory sentences that involve a conjunction of two incompatible predications, e.g., "The line is straight and not straight," "The creature is a cub and a pup," "The team has won the game and lost it," and so on. Although at first glance such cases appear to be outside the scope of (D7), this is not so. Nevertheless, showing that they can be marked as contradictory on the basis of (D7) requires a more complicated discussion than we can afford here.[35] Instead, then, let us simply show that such cases can be marked as contradictory within a semantic theory of our type. If we look at the grammatical structure of these cases, we notice that they are constructed from two source sentences by using the conjunction-transformation; i.e., given two sentences of the form $S_1 = X - Y_1 - Z$ and $S_2 = X - Y_2 - Z$, where Y_1 and Y_2 are constituents of the same type in their respective sentences S_1 and S_2, we may construct a new sentence $S_3 = X - Y_1 + and + Y_2 - Z$.[36] Thus, the first of our examples is constructed from the two source sentences "The line is straight" and, "The line is not straight" ($X = the line is$, $Y_1 = straight$, $Y_2 = not straight$, and $Z =$ null element). Moreover, we notice that the two source sentences are inconsistent in the sense of (D9). Hence, we can mark the sentence "The line is straight and not straight" and

---

[34] This result should be taken into account in the controversy over the status of the law of double negation in the foundations of mathematics, specifically at the point at which some philosophers deny there is justification for double negation in the meaning of the word *not* in English. It can be argued on the basis of the material in the text that double negation has as strong support in the semantic structure of English as there is for simplication in the meaning of *and* in English.

[35] To show how this can be done involves using type two projection rules in such a way that one of the two conjoined sentence fragments has the path associated with it amalgamated with a path associated with the subject before the other's.

[36] N. Chomsky, *Syntactic Structures, op. cit.*

other cases of incompatible predication as contradictory by the rule that the conjunction of two inconsistent copula sentences is contradictory.[37]

This concludes our treatment of analyticity and contradiction in copula sentences, but the problem of analyticity and contradiction in natural language is by no means now solved. Although philosophers have raised and discussed this problem almost exclusively in terms of copula sentences, any complete treatment of analyticity and contradiction must also provide a basis for marking these properties in noncopula sentences, i.e., sentences in which the verb is transitive or intransitive. That a complete treatment of the problem must cover sentences of these types follows from the fact that the grammar makes analytic, synthetic, and contradictory sentences of each of these types available for semantic interpretation.

Analytic Sentences

(1) The man who runs every race runs every race.
(2) The owner of the team owns the team.
(3) The person who lent Sam the book lent the book to Sam.
(4) What costs lots of money costs lots of money.
(5) The sweating man sweats sometimes.
(6) The child who often sleeps sleeps often.

Contradictory Sentences

(1) The loser of the game we like best wins the game we like best.
(2) Those who play badly play well.
(3) The owner of the team does not own the team.
(4) The sweating man never sweats.
(5) Persons who do not lend books lend books.
(6) The child who sleeps often seldom sleeps.

These examples cannot be handled by the straightforward maneuver of changing the category of the variable S in ($D6$) to ($D8$) so that it ranges over sentences of any type, instead of just copula sentences. This is because such a change would lead to false predictions. For example, because of the antonymous words *old* and *young*, the sentence "Old men like young girls" will have a semantic element in the path associated with its noun-phrase subject that is antonymous with one in the path associated with its verb phrase, and thus, according to ($D7$), a semantic theory of English will predict that this sentence is contradictory when, in fact, it is synthetic. A more sophisticated treatment is necessary.

From the viewpoint of grammar, each of the above examples of analytic and contradictory noncopula sentences are constructed from two source sentences by the operation of a transformation that embeds one into the other. For example, the last of the sentences listed as analytic is constructed by the relative clause transformation by embedding the sentence "The child often sleeps"

---

[37] Also, we can mark the sentence "The line is straight or not straight" and other cases of exhaustive alternation as analytic by the rule that the disjunction of n-copula sentences is analytic if, and only if, each sentence introduces a different semantic element from the same antonymous n-tuple of semantic elements and every semantic element from this n-tuple is introduced by some embedded sentence.

in the form of the fragment *who often sleeps* into the matrix sentence "The child sleeps often" just after the shared noun phrase.[38] Likewise, the last of the sentences listed as contradictory is constructed by this transformation, but in this case the embedded sentence is "The child sleeps often" and the matrix sentence is "The child seldom sleeps." Moreover, from these examples we see that the embedded sentence and the matrix sentence for an analytic sentence are synonymous or else the reading of the embedded sentence contains no semantic elements not in the reading for the matrix sentence, i.e., the embedded sentence is redundant, e.g., "The child often sleeps" and "The child sleeps often," and that the embedded sentence and the matrix sentence for a contradictory sentence are inconsistent, e.g., "The child sleeps often" and "The child seldom sleeps." But, furthermore, the embedded sentence and the matrix sentence for a synthetic, transformationally compound sentence are neither synonymous nor inconsistent, e.g., "The old men like young girls" has as its embedded sentence "The men are old" and as its matrix "The men like young girls." Thus, in order to mark noncopula sentences as analytic, synthetic, and contradictory, we shall add the definitions:

> (*D*10) A transformationally compound sentence *S* is *analytic on a reading* if the matrix sentence and the sentence embedded into the matrix to construct *S* are paraphrases on a reading or if the embedded sentence is redundant.
>
> (*D*11) A transformationally compound sentence *S* is *contradictory on a reading* if the matrix sentence and the sentence embedded into the matrix to form *S* are inconsistent on a pair of readings.
>
> (*D*12) A transformationally compound sentence *S* is *synthetic on a reading* if the sentence *S* is neither analytic nor contradictory.[39]

We may now propose an explication of entailment—the relation that holds between the antecedent and the consequent of a conditional when the latter follows from the former by virtue of a meaning relation between them. The customary explicandum is the notion that a sentence is entailed by another if, and only if, the conditional that has the latter as its antecedent and the former as its consequent is analytic. However, the absence of an adequate theory of analyticity in natural language has frustrated all attempts to replace this explicandum by a satisfactory explicatum: with no formal means for identifying conditionals which are analytic, there can be no formal means of deciding whether one sentence entails another or not. But, since the present paper gives a theory of analyticity in natural language, we may look for an extension of this theory which covers conditional sentences and in this way provides a satisfactory explicatum for entailment.

---

[38] *Cf.* C. S. Smith, "A Class of Complex Modifiers in English," *Language*, XXXVII (1961), 342–65.

[39] There are many points about the implementation of these definitions for which this is neither the time nor the place, but it should be pointed out that both the matrix sentence and the sentence embedded in it must be of maximum size when the question of their synonymy or inconsistency comes up. *Cf.* N. Chomsky, "The Logical Basis of Linguistic Theory," *Proceedings of the Ninth International Congress of Linguists*, M.I.T. (1962), pp. 520–24.

The first step in providing such an explicatum is to set forth the definition:

(D13) The sentence S_1 entails the sentence S_2 if, and only if, the conditional "If S_1, then S_2" is analytic.

The second and final step is to set forth a definition (D14) of the term *analytic* which appears in (D13). The sentence S to which (D14) will apply must be of the form:

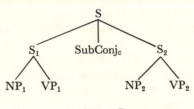

Figure 5

where S_1 is the antecedent of S (NP_1 being S_1's subject and VP_1 being S_1's main verb phrase), *SubConj$_c$* is a conditional subordinating conjunction, e.g., *If ...*, *then ... , ... implies ...* , and so on, and S_2 is the consequent of S (NP_2 being S_2's subject and VP_2 being S_2's main verb phrase).

(D14) A sentence S (having the form depicted in Fig. 5) is *analytic on the reading* $r_{1,2}$ if, and only if,

(a) it is the case that the reading r_1 for the whole sentence S_1 and the reading r_2 for the whole sentence S_2 which are amalgamated to form $r_{1,2}$ are, respectively, formed from the amalgamation of $r(NP_1)$ and $r(VP_1)$, where $r(NP_1)$ is the reading for NP_1 and $r(VP_1)$ is the reading for VP_1, and the amalgamation of $r(NP_2)$ and $r(VP_2)$, where $r(NP_2)$ is the reading of NP_2 and $r(VP_2)$ is the reading for VP_2 and

(b) it is the case that the relation between $r(NP_1)$ and $r(NP_2)$ and the relation between $r(VP_1)$ and $r(VP_2)$ is exactly that which (D6) specifies for p_1 and p_2, i.e., all semantic elements in $r(NP_2)$ are in $r(NP_1)$ and all semantic elements in $r(VP_2)$ are in $r(VP_1)$.

The following examples illustrate the type of sentences whose analyticity is adequate grounds for asserting the entailment of their consequent by their antecedent. We may use them to help explain (D14).

(1) If that person is a bachelor, then that person is male.
(2) If a spinster is foolish, then a woman is foolish.
(3) If a spinster is an aunt, then a woman is someone's relative.

The need to mark (1) as analytic shows that the relation between $r(VP_1)$ and $r(VP_2)$ must be that which (D6) requires of p_1 and p_2. While the need to mark (2) as analytic shows that the relation between $r(NP_1)$ and $r(NP_2)$ must be that which (D6) requires of p_1 and p_2—(3) is simply a mixed case.

Quine's complaint concerning previous attempts to draw the analytic-synthetic distinction has been that they are either circular because they assume notions that ought to be analyzed or empty because they offer no analysis whatever. Quine has demanded that the criterion we use for distinguishing between analytic and synthetic sentences avoid two traditional stumbling blocks. The criterion must not be circular: it must not require knowledge of the sentence's analyticity nor a knowledge of other semantic properties in analyticity's tight little circle. The criterion must not be a mere stipulation: it must provide an effective means of empirically justifying the attribution of analytic status to a sentence.

We now have such a criterion, but it is crucial to note, we have it only because we have a metatheory which characterizes the nature of a semantic theory. The metatheory tells us that a sentence S is analytic, synthetic, or contradictory depending on whether the semantic elements in p_1 and p_2 of S satisfy $(D6)$, $(D7)$, or $(D8)$.[40] A particular semantic theory of a natural language tells us, in turn, what semantic elements are in the path associated with the lexical items in S and hence what semantic elements are in the paths p_1 and p_2 of S. That the paths p_1 and p_2 of S have just the semantic elements that they need to have for S to satisfy $(D6)$ is, therefore, a matter of the correctness of the theory's dictionary entries for the lexical items in S and the correctness of the theory's projection rules that are employed to semantically interpret the constituent structure characterization of S. Both are needed to provide the derived paths p_1 and p_2. But their correctness, as Quine requires, is a matter that can be entirely settled independently of settling the particular question of S's analyticity. For the question of their correctness is a question about the adequacy of the semantic theory for marking the semantic ambiguity, anomaly, paraphrase relations, analyticity, and so on in the case of infinitely many sentences other than S, namely, those that contain some of the lexical items that are in S or those that are semantically interpreted by using some of the same projection rules that are used to obtain the derived paths p_1 and p_2 of S. Independently of an examination of S, the semantic theory can be empirically tested by comparing the claims that it makes about the semantic properties of sentences in a sample drawn from this infinite set with the linguistic intuitions of speakers. If the semantic interpretations of the theory assert that certain sentences are semantically ambiguous n-ways and they indeed are, that other sentences are anomalous and they are, that certain pairs are paraphrases and they are, and so on, then the theory is confirmed; otherwise disconfirmed. That a highly confirmed semantic theory predicts the analyticity of S is the only empirical justification that the claim that S is analytic can have, or needs. Finally, since a semantic theory's prediction that a particular sentence is analytic derives from a definition whose definiens refers solely to formal features of a semantically interpreted constituent structure characterization, there is no circularity in the way a semantic theory of the sort we have described here handles the classification and explanation of analytic sentences. For we not only provide a

---

[40] And if S is transformationally compound, depending on whether the semantic interpretations of the matrix sentence and the sentence embedded into the matrix sentence to form S satisfy $(D10)$, $(D11)$, or $(D12)$. The argument in the case of $(D10)$, $(D11)$, and $(D12)$ will be parallel; thus, it will be omitted.

recursive specification of the analytic sentences of a language but we also explain what formal structure it is claimed that a sentence has when a semantic theory predicts that the sentence is analytic.

The notion *analytic sentence* that we have explicated does not cover all the cases usually described as necessary truths. Thus, our explication explains why some necessary truths, viz., the analytic ones, are necessary, but it leaves open the question why those necessary truths that are not predicatively vacuous are necessary. Thus, the conception of analyticity and contradiction in natural language developed in this paper draws the analytic-synthetic distinction at essentially the point where Kant sought to draw it. Empiricists are thus returned from the fire of dogmatism to the frying pan of unanalyzed, synthetic necessary truths.

REFERENCE 2

INTRODUCTION

The question of *reference* is a specific instance of a general philosophical concern about the relation of words and the world—how is it possible to use *language* to talk about what is *not* language, the extra-linguistic world? Indeed, one historically important tradition hoped to find in an adequate theory of reference the full answer to the question of word-world relationships. On this account, the theory of reference was to constitute a theory of *meaning* as well. Sentences are combinations of words; they are made up of words. Each word stands for or names an object. The meaning of the word is the object for which it stands. Thus language achieves extra-linguistic import. In one variant or another, something like this theory has been a viable force in philosophy from Plato to the present.

As a general theory of word-world relations, this view, which we might call the *referential theory of meaning*, leaves much to be desired. On the face of it, the referential theory cannot be the *whole* story, for it is evident that some words do not behave, even tenuously, the way names behave. 'And', 'or', 'not', 'yes', and 'alas' will serve as examples. More deeply, it is not at all clear how a combination of *names* can be used to make an *assertion*, to say something about the world. A mere list of names—'Tom, Dick, Harry, Sam' for example —makes no *claim* which can be assessed as true or false.

A third difficulty with the referential theory of meaning moves us squarely into the center of the problems of reference (and illustrates, incidentally, once again the difficulty of isolating philosophical problems of language from other areas of philosophy). It is an apparent consequence of the referential theory that all true identity claims must be both necessary and uninformative. If 'the Morning Star' names the same object as 'the Evening Star'—viz, the planet

Venus—and if the *meaning* of a term is the object which it *names*, then

    (1) The Morning Star is identical to the Evening Star

must be *synonymous* with

    (2) The Morning Star is identical to the Morning Star.

Yet we should like to say that (2) is a necessary and uninformative truth, while (1) reports a significant empirical discovery of early Babylonian astronomy.

Again, there apparently are contexts in which the substitution of one term for another with identical *reference* may result in the production of a falsehood from a truth. For example, John may believe that Tegucigalpa is the capital of the Honduras. In fact, however, Tegucigalpa is the capital of Nicaragua. On the referential theory of meaning, John ought to believe, then, that the capital of Nicaragua is the capital of the Honduras—for, since 'Tegucigalpa' and 'the capital of Nicaragua' name the same entity, they have the *same* *meaning* and the substitution of one term for the other should leave meaning, and hence truth, unaltered. Yet it is entirely possible that John believe, even that he *know*, that Nicaragua and the Honduras have different capital cities.

Finally, even setting these difficulties aside and confining ourselves to terms which are ostensibly referential—proper names and so-called definite descriptions, noun phrases of the form '*the* such-and-such'——the referential theory of meaning remains highly problematic. For there are ostensibly referential terms to which *no* object corresponds What, for example, are we to make of 'Pegasus has wings', given that Pegasus is entirely mythical? Again, what can we say about 'The present king of France is bald', given that France is not presently a monarchy? Indeed, the referential theory of meaning apparently renders it impossible to make a true *negative existential* claim. For if it is meaningful to say that Pegasus, or the present king of France, does not exist, then some object must be named by, must constitute the *meaning* of, the term 'Pegasus', or 'the present king of France'. And surely such an object must in some sense *exist*, rendering our negative existential claim false.

Although the problems which we have been canvassing arise naturally in considering the referential theory of meaning, it is important to realize that, for the most part, they are independent of that theory and are not solved by its rejection. If, for example, we cannot make assertions about the world by combining names of objects, how *do* we succeed in making such assertions? If 'The Morning Star is identical to the Evening Star' does not say what 'The Morning Star is identical to the Morning Star' says, then what *does* it say? And if 'Pegasus does not exist' and 'The present king of France is bald' are not respectively about Pegasus and the present king of France—there being no such entities—what *are* they about? In virtue of what is the former true, and what are we to say of the latter? Is it true or false? These are some of the major questions with which any theory of reference must come to grips.

The following selections concentrate specifically on the status of ostensibly referential terms. RUSSELL advances the important thesis that definite descriptions are *incomplete symbols*, expressions which have *no* meaning considered in isolation but are only significant and definable in certain contexts. Thus, he holds that the question "For what does 'the present king of France' stand?" is a question which has *no* answer, but that to assert that the present king of France is bald is to make a claim which is meaningful and, in fact, *false*. In particular, Russell argues that to assert that the present king of France is bald is simply to assert that exactly one man is presently king of France *and* that this man is bald, a conjunction which is false by virtue of the falsity of its first conjunct—no man *is*, presently, king of France.

STRAWSON argues that Russell has overlooked the distinctions between a sentence and the *use* of a sentence, an expression and the *use* of an expression. On Strawson's account, the *expression* 'the present king of France' does not itself refer, but can be *used* by persons to refer to different individuals depending upon the time and circumstances of utterance. If, in uttering the sentence 'The present king of France is bald', a person fails to refer, claims Strawson, then he has not uttered a falsehood but rather he has failed to make *any* statement, failed to say anything which is either true or false.

DONNELLAN argues that both Strawson and Russell offer an oversimplified account of definite descriptions. On Donnellan's account, there are two uses of definite descriptions, uses which he terms 'attributive' and 'referential'. A description is used *attributively* when it is used to state something about *whoever* or *whatever* is the such-and-such. It is used *referentially* when it is intended to enable the hearer to *pick out* whom or what is being talked about *and* to say something about that person or thing. Russell, claims Donnellan, ignores altogether the referential use of definite descriptions, and Strawson, while recognizing referential uses, does not distinguish them properly from attributive uses and is thus led to incorrect conclusions concerning where failures of reference and consequent failures of truth-value occur.

Finally, SEARLE tackles the difficult problem of *proper names*. The problem turns on the question of whether a proper name has merely a *reference* or *denotation* or has, in addition, a *sense* or *connotation*. Neither answer appears fully satisfactory. If it is held that proper names denote but do not connote, we are faced with, among other things, the puzzles concerning identity, belief, and negative existential claims adumbrated earlier. But if it is claimed that every proper name has a sense in addition to a reference, it becomes appropriate to ask of a given proper name what *its* sense *is*, and to this question no answer seems suitable, for every proposal either renders ostensibly synthetic truths analytic or makes communication impossible by requiring that the name have different meanings for different persons and at different times or generates similar paradoxial consequences. Searle attempts to steer a path between these two groups of puzzles by isolating the unique *function* of proper names in our language.

Suggestions for Further Reading

Cartwright, R. L. "Negative Existentials." *The Journal of Philosophy*, LVII (1960), 629–39. Reprinted as Chapter 3, pp. 55–56 of Caton, cited below.

Caton, Charles E., ed. *Philosophy and Ordinary Language*. Urbana, Ill.: University of Illinois Press, 1963. Chapters 3, 5, and 8.

Donnellan, Keith. "Putting Humpty Dumpty Together Again." *Philosophical Review*, LXXVII (1968), 203–15. A reply to MacKay, cited below.

Frege, Gottlob. "On Sense and Reference." In Geach and Black, eds., *The Philosophical Writings of Gottlob Frege*. Oxford: Basil Blackwell, 1960.

Geach, Peter. "Russell's Theory of Descriptions." *Analysis*, X (1950), 84–88.

Linsky, Leonard. "Reference and Referents." Reprinted as Chapter 5, pp. 74–89 of Caton, cited above.

———. *Referring*. London: Routledge & Kegan Paul, Ltd., 1967.

MacKay, Alfred. "Mr. Donnellan and Humpty Dumpty on Referring." *Philosophical Review*, LXXVII, (1968), 197–202. A critique of selection 2.3.

Mill, J. S. *A System of Logic*, Book I. 8th ed. London, 1872. Contains some historically central criticisms of the referential theory of meaning.

Moore, G. E. "Russell's Theory of Descriptions." In Schillp, ed., *The Philosophy of Bertrand Russell*. Evanston: Northwestern University Press, 1944.

Quine, W. V. O. "Reference and Modality." *From a Logical Point of View*. New York: Harper Torchbooks, 1963. Chapter VIII, pp. 139–59.

———. *Word and Object*. Cambridge: MIT Press, 1960. Chapter 4.

Russell, Bertrand. "On Denoting." *Mind*, XIV (1905), 479–93, and variously reprinted. The first presentation of Russell's theory of descriptions.

———. "Mr. Strawson on Referring." *Mind*, LXVI (1957), 385–89. Russell's response to selection 2.2.

Ryle, Gilbert. "The Theory of Meaning." Reprinted as Chapter 8, pp. 128–53, of Caton, cited above.

BERTRAND RUSSELL

2.1 *Descriptions*

We [have] dealt [elsewhere] with the words *all* and *some*; in this [essay] we shall consider the word *the* in the singular, and ... we shall [also] consider the word *the* in the plural. It may be thought excessive to devote two chapters to

Reprinted from Bertrand Russell, *Introduction to Mathematical Philosophy* (London: George Allen and Unwin Ltd., 1919), Chapter XVI, pp. 167–80, by permission of the publisher.

one word, but to the philosophical mathematician it is a word of very great importance: like Browning's Grammarian with the enclitic δε, I would give the doctrine of this word if I were "dead from the waist down" and not merely in a prison.

We have already had occasion to mention "descriptive functions," *i.e.* such expressions as "the father of *x*" or "the sine of *x*." These are to be defined by first defining "descriptions."

A "description" may be of two sorts, definite and indefinite (or ambiguous). An indefinite description is a phrase of the form "a so-and-so," and a definite description is a phrase of the form "the so-and-so" (in the singular). Let us begin with the former.

"Who did you meet?" "I met a man." "That is a very indefinite description." We are therefore not departing from usage in our terminology. Our question is: What do I really assert when I assert "I met a man"? Let us assume, for the moment, that my assertion is true, and that in fact I met Jones. It is clear that what I assert is *not* "I met Jones." I may say "I met a man, but it was not Jones"; in that case, though I lie, I do not contradict myself, as I should do if when I say I met a man I really mean that I met Jones. It is clear also that the person to whom I am speaking can understand what I say, even if he is a foreigner and has never heard of Jones.

But we may go further: not only Jones, but no actual man, enters into my statement. This becomes obvious when the statement is false, since then there is no more reason why Jones should be supposed to enter into the proposition than why anyone else should. Indeed the statement would remain significant, though it could not possibly be true, even if there were no man at all. "I met a unicorn" or "I met a sea-serpent" is a perfectly significant assertion, if we know what it would be to be a unicorn or a sea-serpent, *i.e.* what is the definition of these fabulous monsters. Thus it is only what we may call the *concept* that enters into the proposition. In the case of "unicorn," for example, there is only the concept: there is not also, somewhere among the shades, something unreal which may be called "a unicorn." Therefore, since it is significant (though false) to say "I met a unicorn," it is clear that this proposition, rightly analysed, does not contain a constituent "a unicorn," though it does contain the concept "unicorn."

The question of "unreality," which confronts us at this point, is a very important one. Misled by grammar, the great majority of those logicians who have dealt with this question have dealt with it on mistaken lines. They have regarded grammatical form as a surer guide in analysis than, in fact, it is. And they have not known what differences in grammatical form are important. "I met Jones" and "I met a man" would count traditionally as propositions of the same form, but in actual fact they are of quite different forms: the first names an actual person, Jones; while the second involves a propositional function, and becomes, when made explicit: "The function 'I met *x* and *x* is human' is sometimes true." (It will be remembered that we adopted the convention of using "sometimes" as not implying more than once.) This proposition is obviously not of the form "I met x," which accounts for the existence of the proposition "I met a unicorn" in spite of the fact that there is no such thing as "a unicorn."

For want of the apparatus of propositional functions, many logicians have been driven to the conclusion that there are unreal objects. It is argued, *e.g.* by Meinong,[1] that we can speak about "the golden mountain," "the round square," and so on; we can make true propositions of which these are the subjects; hence they must have some kind of logical being, since otherwise the propositions in which they occur would be meaningless. In such theories, it seems to me, there is a failure of that feeling for reality which ought to be preserved even in the most abstract studies. Logic, I should maintain, must no more admit a unicorn than zoology can; for logic is concerned with the real world just as truly as zoology, though with its more abstract and general features. To say that unicorns have an existence in heraldry, or in literature, or in literature, or in imagination, is a most pitiful and paltry evasion. What exists in heraldry is not an animal, made of flesh and blood, moving and breathing of its own initiative. What exists is a picture, or a description in words. Similarly, to maintain that Hamlet, for example, exists in his own world, namely, in the world of Shakespeare's imagination, just as truly as (say) Napoleon existed in the ordinary world, is to say something deliberately confusing, or else confused to a degree which is scarcely credible. There is only one world, the "real" world: Shakespeare's imagination is part of it, and the thoughts that he had in writing Hamlet are real. So are the thoughts that we have in reading the play. But it is of the very essence of fiction that only the thoughts, feelings, etc., in Shakespeare and his readers are real, and that there is not, in addition to them, an objective Hamlet. When you have taken account of all the feelings roused by Napoleon in writers and readers of history, you have not touched the actual man; but in the case of Hamlet you have come to the end of him. If no one thought about Hamlet, there would be nothing left of him; if no one had thought about Napoleon, he would have soon seen to it that some one did. The sense of reality is vital in logic, and whoever juggles with it by pretending that Hamlet has another kind of reality is doing a disservice to thought. A robust sense of reality is very necessary in framing a correct analysis of propositions about unicorns, golden mountains, round squares, and other such pseudo-objects.

In obedience to the feeling of reality, we shall insist that, in the analysis of propositions, nothing "unreal" is to be admitted. But, after all, if there *is* nothing unreal, how, it may be asked, *could* we admit anything unreal? The reply is that, in dealing with propositions, we are dealing in the first instance with symbols, and if we attribute significance to groups of symbols which have no significance, we shall fall into the error of admitting unrealities, in the only sense in which this is possible, namely, as objects described. In the proposition "I met a unicorn," the whole four words together make a significant proposition, and the word "unicorn" by itself is significant, in just the same sense

---

[1] *Untersuchungen zur Gegenstandstheorie und Psychologie,* 1904.

as the word "man." But the *two* words "a unicorn" do not form a subordinate group having a meaning of its own. Thus if we falsely attribute meaning to these two words, we find ourselves saddled with "a unicorn," and with the problem how there can be such a thing in a world where there are no unicorns. "A unicorn" is an indefinite description which describes nothing. It is not an indefinite description which describes something unreal. Such a proposition as "x is unreal" only has meaning when "x" is a description, definite or indefinite; in that case the proposition will be true if "x" is a description which describes nothing. But whether the description "x" describes something or describes nothing, it is in any case not a constituent of the proposition in which it occurs; like "a unicorn" just now, it is not a subordinate group having a meaning of its own. All this results from the fact that, when "x" is a description, "x is unreal" or "x does not exist" is not nonsense, but is always significant and sometimes true.

We may now proceed to define generally the meaning of propositions which contain ambiguous descriptions. Suppose we wish to make some statement about "a so-and-so," where "so-and-so's" are those objects that have a certain property ϕ, *i.e.* those objects x for which the propositional function ϕx is true. (*E.g.* if we take "a man" as our instance of "a so-and-so," ϕx will be "x is human.") Let us now wish to assert the property ψ of "a so-and-so," *i.e.* we wish to assert that "a so-and-so" has that property which x has when ψx is true. (*E.g.* in the case of "I met a man," ψx will be "I met x.") Now the proposition that "a so-and-so" has the property ψ is *not* a proposition of the form "ψx." If it were, "a so-and-so" would have to be identical with x for a suitable x; and although (in a sense) this may be true in some cases, it is certainly not true in such a case as "a unicorn." It is just this fact, that the statement that a so-and-so has the property ψ is not of the form ψx, which makes it possible for "a so-and-so" to be, in a certain clearly definable sense, "unreal." The definition is as follows:—

The statement that "an object having the property ϕ has the property ψ"

means:

"The joint assertion of ϕx and ψx is not always false."

So far as logic goes, this is the same proposition as might be expressed by "some ϕ's are ψ's"; but rhetorically there is a difference, because in the one case there is a suggestion of singularity, and in the other case of plurality. This, however, is not the important point. The important point is that, when rightly analysed, propositions verbally about "a so-and-so" are found to contain no constituent represented by this phrase. And that is why such propositions can be significant even when there is no such thing as a so-and-so.

The definition of *existence*, as applied to ambiguous descriptions, results from what was said [elsewhere]. We say that "men exist" or "a man exists" if the propositional function "x is human" is sometimes true; and generally "a so-and-so" exists if "x is so-and-so" is sometimes true. We may put this in other language. The proposition "Socrates is a man" is no doubt *equivalent* to "Socrates is human," but it is not the very same proposition. The *is* of "Socrates is human" expresses the relation of subject and predicate; the *is* of "Socrates is a man" expresses identity. It is a disgrace to the human race that it has chosen to employ the same word "is" for these two entirely different ideas—a disgrace which a symbolic logical language of course remedies. The identity in "Socrates is a man" is identity between an object named (accepting "Socrates" as a name, subject to qualifications explained later) and an object ambiguously described. An object ambiguously described will "exist" when at least one such proposition is true, *i.e.* when there is at least one true proposition of the form "*x* is a so-and-so," where "*x*" is a name. It is characteristic of ambiguous (as opposed to definite) descriptions that there may be any number of true propositions of the above form—Socrates is a man, Plato is a man, etc. Thus "a man exists" follows from Socrates, or Plato, or anyone else. With definite descriptions, on the other hand, the corresponding form of proposition, namely, "*x* is the so-and-so" (where "*x*" is a name), can only be true for one value of *x* at most. This brings us to the subject of definite descriptions, which are to be defined in a way analogous to that employed for ambiguous descriptions, but rather more complicated.

We come now to the main subject of the present [discussion], namely, the definition of the word *the* (in the singular). One very important point about the definition of "a so-and-so" applies equally to "the so-and-so"; the definition to be sought is a definition of propositions in which this phrase occurs, not a definition of the phrase itself in isolation. In the case of "a so-and-so," this is fairly obvious: no one could suppose that "a man" was a definite object, which could be defined by itself. Socrates is a man, Plato is a man, Aristotle is a man, but we cannot infer that "a man" means the same as "Socrates" means and also the same as "Plato" means and also the same as "Aristotle" means, since these three names have different meanings. Nevertheless, when we have enumerated all the men in the world, there is nothing left of which we can say, "This is a man, and not only so, but it is *the* 'a man,' the quintessential entity that is just an indefinite man without being anybody in particular." It is of course quite clear that whatever there is in the world is definite: if it is a man it is one definite man and not any other. Thus there cannot be such an entity as "a man" to be found in the world, as opposed to specific men. And accordingly it is natural that we do not define "a man" itself, but only the propositions in which it occurs.

In the case of "the so-and-so" this is equally true, though at first sight less obvious. We may demonstrate that this must be the case, by a consideration of the difference between a *name* and a *definite description*. Take the proposition, "Scott is the author of *Waverley*." We have here a name, "Scott," and a description, "the author of *Waverley*," which are asserted to apply to the same person. The distinction between a name and all other symbols may be explained as follows:—

A name is a simple symbol whose meaning is something that can only occur as subject. . . . And a "simple" symbol is one which has no parts that are symbols. Thus "Scott" is a simple symbol, because, though it has parts (namely, separate letters), these parts are not symbols. On the other hand, "the author of *Waverley*" is not a simple symbol, because the separate words that compose the phrase are parts which are symbols. If, as may be the case, whatever *seems* to be an "individual" is really capable of further analysis, we shall have to content ourselves with what may be called "relative individuals," which will be terms that, throughout the context in question, are never analysed and never occur otherwise than as subjects. And in that case we shall have correspondingly to content ourselves with "relative names." From the standpoint of our present problem, namely, the definition of descriptions, this problem, whether these are absolute names or only relative names, may be ignored, since it concerns different stages in the hierarchy of "types," whereas we have to compare such couples as "Scott" and "the author of *Waverley*," which both apply to the same object, and do not raise the problem of types. We may, therefore, for the moment, treat names as capable of being absolute; nothing that we shall have to say will depend upon this assumption, but the wording may be a little shortened by it.

We have, then, two things to compare: (1) *a name*, which is a simple symbol, directly designating an individual which is its meaning, and having this meaning in its own right, independently of the meanings of all other words; (2) a *description*, which consists of several words, whose meanings are already fixed, and from which results whatever is to be taken as the "meaning" of the description.

A proposition containing a description is not identical with what that proposition becomes when a name is substituted, even if the name names the same object as the description describes. "Scott is the author of *Waverley*" is obviously a different proposition from "Scott is Scott": the first is a fact in literary history, the second a trivial truism. And if we put anyone other than Scott in place of "the author of *Waverley*," our proposition would become false, and would therefore certainly no longer be the same proposition. But, it may be said, our proposition is essentially of the same form as (say) "Scott is Sir Walter," in which two names are said to apply to the same person. The reply is that, if "Scott is Sir Walter" really means "the person named 'Scott' is the person named 'Sir Walter'," then the names are being used as descriptions: *i.e.* the individual, instead of being named, is being described as the person having that name. This is a way in which names are frequently used in practice, and there will, as a rule, be nothing in the phraseology to show whether they are being used in this way or *as* names. When a name is used directly, merely to indicate what we are speaking about, it is no part of the *fact* asserted, or of the falsehood if our assertion happens to be false: it is merely part of the symbolism by which we express our thought. What we want to express is something which might (for example) be translated into a foreign language; it is something for which the actual words are a vehicle, but of which they are no part. On the other hand, when we make a proposition about "the person called 'Scott'," the actual name "Scott" enters into what we are asserting, and not merely into the language used in making the assertion. Our proposition will now be a different one if we substitute "the person called 'Sir Walter'." But so long as we are using names *as* names, whether we say "Scott" or whether we say "Sir Walter" is as irrelevant to what we are asserting as whether we speak English or French. Thus so long as names are used *as* names, "Scott is Sir Walter" is the same trivial proposition as "Scott is Scott." This completes the proof that "Scott is the author of *Waverley*" is not the same proposition as results from substituting a name for "the author of *Waverley*," no matter what name may be substituted.

When we use a variable, and speak of a propositional function, ϕx say, the process of applying general statements about x to particular cases will consist in substituting a name for the letter "x," assuming that ϕ is a function which has individuals for its arguments. Suppose, for example, that ϕx is "always true"; let it be, say, the "law of identity," $x = x$. Then we may substitute for "x" any name we choose, and we shall obtain a true proposition. Assuming for the moment that "Socrates," "Plato," and "Aristotle" are names (a very rash assumption), we can infer from the law of identity that Socrates is Socrates, Plato is Plato, and Aristotle is Aristotle. But we shall commit a fallacy if we attempt to infer, without further premisses, that the author of *Waverley* is the author of *Waverley*. This results from what we have just proved, that, if we substitute a name for "the author of *Waverley*" in a proposition, the proposition we obtain is a different one. That is to say, applying the result to our present case: If "x" is a name, "$x = x$" is not the same proposition as "the author of *Waverley* is the author of *Waverley*," no matter what name "x" may be. Thus from the fact that all propositions of the form "$x = x$" are true we cannot infer, without more ado, that the author of *Waverley* is the author of *Waverley*. In fact, propositions of the form "the so-and-so is the so-and-so" are not always true: it is necessary that the so-and-so should *exist* (a term which will be explained shortly). It is false that the present King of France is the present King of France, or that the round square is the round square. When we substitute a description for a name, propositional functions which are "always true" may become false, if the description describes nothing. There is no mystery in this as soon as we realise (what was proved in the preceding paragraph) that when we substitute a description the result is not a value of the propositional function in question.

We are now in a position to define propositions in which a definite description occurs. The only thing that distinguishes "the so-and-so" from "a so-and-so" is the implication of uniqueness. We cannot speak of "*the* inhabitant of London," because inhabiting London is an attribute which is not unique. We cannot speak about "the present King of France," because there is none; but we can speak about "the present King of England." Thus propositions about "the so-and-so" always imply the corresponding propositions about "a so-and-so," with the addendum that there is not more than one so-and-so. Such a proposition as "Scott is the author of Waverley" could not be true if *Waverley* had never been written, or if several people had written it; and no more could any other proposition resulting from a propositional function x by the substitution of "the author of *Waverley*" for "x." We may say that "the author of *Waverley*" means "the value of x for which 'x wrote *Waverley*' is true." Thus the proposition "the author of *Waverley* was Scotch," for example, involves:

(1) "x wrote *Waverley*" is not always false;
(2) "if x and y wrote *Waverley*, x and y are identical" is always true;
(3) "if x wrote *Waverley* x was Scotch" is always true.

These three propositions, translated into ordinary language, state:

(1) at least one person wrote *Waverley*;
(2) at most one person wrote *Waverley*;
(3) whoever wrote *Waverley* was Scotch.

All these three are implied by "the author of *Waverley* was Scotch." Conversely, the three together (but no two of them) imply that the author of *Waverley* was Scotch. Hence the three together may be taken as defining what is meant by the proposition "the author of *Waverley* was Scotch."

We may somewhat simplify these three propositions. The first and second together are equivalent to: "There is a term c such that 'x wrote *Waverley*' is true when x is c and is false when x is not c." In other words, "There is a term c such that 'x wrote *Waverley*' is always equivalent to 'x is c'." (Two propositions are "equivalent" when both are true or both are false.) We have here, to begin with, two functions of x, "x wrote *Waverley*" and "x is c," and we form a function of c by considering the equivalence of these two functions of x for all values of x; we then proceed to assert that the resulting function of c is "sometimes true," *i.e.* that it is true for at least one value of c. (It obviously cannot be true for more than one value of c.) These two conditions together are defined as giving the meaning of "the author of *Waverley* exists."

We may now define "the term satisfying the function ϕx exists." This is the general form of which the above is a particular case. "The author of *Waverley*" is "the term satisfying the function 'x wrote *Waverley*'." And "the so-and-so" will always involve reference to some propositional function, namely, that which defines the property that makes a thing a so-and-so. Our definition is as follows:—

"The term satisfying the function ϕx exists" means:
"There is a term c such that ϕx is always equivalent to 'x is c'."

In order to define "the author of *Waverley* was Scotch," we have still to take account of the third of our three propositions, namely, "Whoever wrote *Waverley* was Scotch." This will be satisfied by merely adding that the c in question is to be Scotch. Thus "the author of *Waverley* was Scotch" is:

"There is a term c such that (1) 'x wrote *Waverley*' is always equivalent to 'x is c', (2) c is Scotch."

And generally: "the term satisfying ϕx satisfies ψx" is defined as meaning:

"There is a term c such that (1) ϕx is always equivalent to 'x is c', (2) ψc is true."

This is the definition of propositions in which descriptions occur.

It is possible to have much knowledge concerning a term described, *i.e.* to know many propositions concerning "the so-and-so," without actually knowing what the so-and-so is, *i.e.* without knowing any proposition of the form "*x* is the so-and-so," where "*x*" is a name. In a detective story propositions about "the man who did the deed" are accumulated, in the hope that ultimately they will suffice to demonstrate that it was A who did the deed. We may even go so far as to say that, in all such knowledge as can be expressed in words—with the exception of "this" and "that" and a few other words of which the meaning varies on different occasions—no names, in the strict sense, occur, but what seem like names are really descriptions. We may inquire significantly whether Homer existed, which we could not do if "Homer" were a name. The proposition "the so-and-so exists" is significant, whether true or false; but if *a* is the so-and-so (where "*a*" is a name), the words "*a* exists" are meaningless. It is only of descriptions—definite or indefinite—that existence can be significantly asserted; for, if "*a*" is a name, it *must* name something: what does not name anything is not a name, and therefore, if intended to be a name, is a symbol devoid of meaning, whereas a description, like "the present King of France," does not become incapable of occurring significantly merely on the ground that it describes nothing, the reason being that it is a *complex* symbol, of which the meaning is derived from that of its constituent symbols. And so, when we ask whether Homer existed, we are using the word "Homer" as an abbreviated description: we may replace it by (say) "the author of the *Iliad* and the *Odyssey*." The same considerations apply to almost all uses of what look like proper names.

When descriptions occur in propositions, it is necessary to distinguish what may be called "primary" and "secondary" occurrences. The abstract distinction is as follows. A description has a "primary" occurrence when the proposition in which it occurs results from substituting the description for "*x*" in some propositional function ϕx; a description has a "secondary" occurrence when the result of substituting the description for *x* in ϕx gives only *part* of the proposition concerned. An instance will make this clearer. Consider "the present King of France is bald." Here "the present King of France" has a primary occurrence, and the proposition is false. Every proposition in which a description which describes nothing has a primary occurrence is false. But now consider "the present King of France is not bald." This is ambiguous. If we are first to take "*x* is bald," then substitute "the present King of France" for "*x*," and then deny the result, the occurrence of "the present King of France" is secondary and our proposition is true; but if we are to take "*x* is not bald" and substitute "the present King of France" for "*x*," then "the present King of France" has a primary occurrence and the proposition is false. Confusion of primary and secondary occurrences is a ready source of fallacies where descriptions are concerned.

Descriptions occur in mathematics chiefly in the form of *descriptive functions*, *i.e.* "the term having the relation R to *y*," or "the R of *y*" as we may say, on the analogy of "the father of *y*" and similar phrases. To say "the father of *y* is rich," for example, is to say that the following propositional function of c: "c is rich, and 'x begat y' is always equivalent to 'x is c'," is "sometimes true," *i.e.* is true for at least one value of c. It obviously cannot be true for more than one value.

The theory of descriptions, briefly outlined in the present chapter, is of the utmost importance both in logic and in theory of knowledge. But for purposes of mathematics, the more philosophical parts of the theory are not essential, and have therefore been omitted in the above account, which has confined itself to the barest mathematical requisites.

P. F. STRAWSON

2.2 *On Referring*

We very commonly use expressions of certain kinds to mention or refer to some individual person or single object or particular event or place or process, in the course of doing what we should normally describe as making a statement about that person, object, place, event, or process. I shall call this way of using expressions the 'uniquely referring use'. The classes of expressions which are most commonly used in this way are: singular demonstrative pronouns ('this' and 'that'); proper names (*e.g.* 'Venice', 'Napoleon', 'John'); singular personal and impersonal pronouns ('he', 'she', 'I', 'you', 'it'); and phrases beginning with the definite article followed by a noun, qualified or unqualified, in the singular (*e.g.* 'the table', 'the old man', 'the king of France'). Any expression of any of these classes can occur as the subject of what would traditionally be regarded as a singular subject-predicate sentence; and would, so occurring, exemplify the use I wish to discuss.

I do not want to say that expressions belonging to these classes never have any other use than the one I want to discuss. On the contrary, it is obvious that they do. It is obvious that anyone who uttered the sentence, 'The whale is a mammal', would be using the expression 'the whale' in a way quite different from the way it would be used by anyone who had occasion seriously to utter the sentence, 'The whale struck the ship'. In the first sentence one is obviously *not* mentioning, and in the second sentence one obviously *is* mentioning, a particular whale. Again if I said, 'Napoleon was the greatest French soldier', I should be using the word 'Napoleon' to mention a certain individual, but I should not be using the phrase, 'the greatest French soldier', to mention an individual, but to say something about an individual I had already mentioned. It would be natural to say that in using this sentence I was talking *about* Napole-

Reprinted from *Mind*, LIX, No. 235 (1950), 320–44, by permission of the author and of *Mind*.

on and that what I was *saying* about him was that he was the greatest French soldier. But of course I *could* use the expression, 'the greatest French soldier', to mention an individual; for example, by saying: 'The greatest French soldier died in exile'. So it is obvious that at least some expressions belonging to the classes I mentioned *can* have uses other than the use I am anxious to discuss. Another thing I do not want to say is that in any given sentence there is never more than one expression used in the way I propose to discuss. On the contrary, it is obvious that there may be more than one. For example, it would be natural to say that, in seriously using the sentence, 'The whale struck the ship', I was saying something about both a certain whale and a certain ship, that I was using each of the expressions 'the whale' and 'the ship' to mention a particular object; or, in other words, that I was using each of these expressions in the uniquely referring ways. In general, however, I shall confine my attention to cases where an expression used in this way occurs as the grammatical subject of a sentence.

I think it is true to say that Russell's Theory of Descriptions, which is concerned with the last of the four classes of expressions I mentioned above (*i.e.* with expressions of the form 'the so-and-so'), is still widely accepted among logicians as giving a correct account of the use of such expressions in ordinary language. I want to show in the first place, that this theory, so regarded, embodies some fundamental mistakes.

What question or questions about phrases of the form 'the so-and-so' was the Theory of Descriptions designed to answer? I think that at least one of the questions may be illustrated as follows. Suppose someone were now to utter the sentence, 'The king of France is wise'. No one would say that the sentence which had been uttered was meaningless. Everyone would agree that it was significant. But everyone knows that there is not at present a king of France. One of the questions the Theory of Descriptions was designed to answer was the question: How can such a sentence as 'The king of France is wise' be significant even when there is nothing which answers to the description it contains, *i.e.*, in this case, nothing which answers to the description 'The king of France'? And one of the reasons why Russell thought it important to give a correct answer to this question was that he thought it important to show that another answer which might be given was wrong. The answer that he thought was wrong, and to which he was anxious to supply an alternative, might be exhibited as the conclusion of either of the following two fallacious arguments. Let us call the sentence 'The king of France is wise' the sentence S. Then the first argument is as follows:

(1) The phrase, 'the king of France', is the subject of the sentence S.
Therefore (2) if S is a significant sentence, S is a sentence *about* the king of France.
But (3) if there in no sense exists a king of France, the sentence is not about anything, and hence not about the king of France.
Therefore (4) since S is significant, there must in some sense (in some world) exist (or subsist) the king of France.

And the second argument is as follows:

(1) If S is significant, it is either true or false.
(2) S is true if the king of France is wise and false if the king of France is not wise.
(3) But the statement that the king of France is wise and the statement that the king of France is not wise are alike true only if there is (in some sense, in some world) something which is the king of France.

Hence (4) since S is significant, there follows the same conclusion as before.

These are fairly obviously bad arguments, and, as we should expect, Russell rejects them. The postulation of a world of strange entities, to which the king of France belongs, offends, he says, against 'that feeling for reality which ought to be preserved even in the most abstract studies'. The fact that Russell rejects these arguments is, however, less interesting than the extent to which, in reject- ing their conclusion, he concedes the more important of their principles. Let me refer to the phrase, 'the king of France', as the phrase D. Then I think Russell's reasons for rejecting these two arguments can be summarized as follows. The mistake arises, he says, from thinking that D, which is certainly the *grammatical* subject of S, is also the *logical* subject of S. But D is not the logical subject of S. In fact S, although grammatically it has a singular subject and a predicate, is not logically a subject-predicate sentence at all. The proposition it expresses is a complex kind of *existential* proposition, part of which might be described as a 'uniquely existential' proposition. To exhibit the logical form of the proposition, we should re-write the sentence in a logically appropriate grammatical form; in such a way that the deceptive similarity of S to a sentence expressing a subject-predicate proposition would disappear, and we should be safeguarded against arguments such as the bad ones I outlined above. Before recalling the details of Russell's analysis of S, let us notice what his answer, as I have so far given it, seems to imply. His answer seems to imply that in the case of a sentence which is similar to S in that (1) it is grammatically of the subject-predicate form and (2) its grammatical subject does not refer to any- thing, then the only alternative to its being meaningless is that it should not really (*i.e.* logically) be of the subject-predicate form at all, but of some quite different form. And this in its turn seems to imply that if there are any sentences which are genuinely of the subject-predicate form, then the very fact of their being significant, having a meaning, guarantees that there *is* something referred to by the logical (and grammatical) subject. Moreover, Russell's answer seems to imply that there are such sentences. For if it is true that one may be misled by the grammatical similarity of S to other sentences into thinking that it is logically of the subject-predicate form, then surely there must be other sentences grammatically similar to S, which *are* of the subject predicate form. To show not only that Russell's answer seems to imply these conclusions, but that he accepted at least the first two of them, it is enough to consider what he says about a class of expressions which he calls 'logically proper names' and contrasts with expressions, like D, which he calls 'definite descriptions'. Of logically proper names Russell says or implies the following things:

(1) That they and they alone can occur as subjects of sentences which are genuinely of the subject-predicate form.
(2) That an expression intended to be a logically proper name is *meaningless* unless there is some single object for which it stands: for the *meaning* of such an expression just is the individual object which the expression designates. To be a name at all, therefore, it *must* designate something.

It is easy to see that if anyone believes these two propositions, then the only way for him to save the significance of the sentence S is to deny that it is a logically subject-predicate sentence. Generally, we may say that Russell recognizes only two ways in which sentences which seem, from their grammatical structure, to be about some particular person or individual object or event, can be significant:

(1) The first is that their grammatical form should be misleading as to their logical form, and that they should be analysable, like S, as a special kind of existential sentence.
(2) The second is that their grammatical subject should be a logically proper name, of which the meaning is the individual thing it designates.

I think that Russell is unquestionably wrong in this, and that sentences which are significant, and which begin with an expression used in the uniquely referring way, fall into neither of these two classes. Expressions used in the uniquely referring way are never either logically proper names or descriptions, if what is meant by calling them 'descriptions' is that they are to be analysed in accordance with the model provided by Russell's Theory of Descriptions.

There are no logically proper names and there are no descriptions (in this sense).

Let us now consider the details of Russell's analysis. According to Russell, anyone who asserted S would be asserting that:

(1) There is a king of France.
(2) There is not more than one king of France.
(3) There is nothing which is king of France and is not wise.

It is easy to see both how Russell arrived at this analysis, and how it enables him to answer the question with which we began, viz. the question: How can the sentence S be significant when there is no king of France? The way in which he arrived at the analysis was clearly by asking himself what would be the circumstances in which we would say that anyone who uttered the sentence S had made a true assertion. And it does seem pretty clear, and I have no wish to dispute, that the sentences (1)–(3) above do describe circumstances which are at least *necessary* conditions of anyone making a true assertion by uttering the sentence S. But, as I hope to show, to say this is not at all the same thing as to say that Russell has given a correct account of the use of the sentence S or even that he has given an account which, though incomplete, is correct as far as it goes; and is certainly not at all the same thing as to say that the model translation provided is a correct model for all (or for any) singular sentences beginning with a phrase of the form 'the so-and-so'.

It is also easy to see how this analysis enables Russell to answer the question of how the sentence S can be significant, even when there is no king of France. For, if this analysis is correct, anyone who utters the sentence S to-day would be jointly asserting three propositions, one of which (viz. that there is a king of France) would be false; and since the conjunction of three propositions, of which one is false, is itself false, the assertion as a whole would be significant, but false. So neither of the bad arguments for subsistent entities would apply to such an assertion.

II

As a step towards showing that Russell's solution of his problem is mistaken, and towards providing the correct solution, I want now to draw certain distinctions. For this purpose I shall, for the remainder of this section, refer to an expression which has a uniquely referring use as 'an expression' for short; and to a sentence beginning with such an expression as 'a sentence' for short. The distinctions I shall draw are rather rough and ready, and, no doubt, difficult cases could be produced which would call for their refinement. But I think they will serve my purpose. The distinctions are between:

 (A1) a sentence,
 (A2) a use of a sentence,
 (A3) an utterance of a sentence,

and, correspondingly, between:

 (B1) an expression,
 (B2) a use of an expression,
 (B3) an utterance of an expression.

Consider again the sentence, 'The king of France is wise'. It is easy to imagine that this sentence was uttered at various times from, say, the beginning of the seventeenth century onwards, during the reigns of each successive French monarch; and easy to imagine that it was also uttered during the subsequent periods in which France was not a monarchy. Notice that it was natural for me to speak of 'the sentence' or 'this sentence' being uttered at various times during this period; or, in other words, that it would be natural and correct to speak of *one and the same* sentence being uttered on all these various occasions. It is in the sense in which it would be correct to speak of one and the same sentence being uttered on all these various occasions that I want to use the expression (A-1) 'a sentence'. There are, however, obvious differences between different *occasions of the use* of this sentence. For instance, if one man uttered it in the reign of Louis XIV and another man uttered it in the reign of Louis XV, it would be natural to say (to assume) that they were respectively talking about different people; and it might be held that the first man, in using the sentence, made a true assertion, while the second man, in using the same sentence, made a false assertion. If on the other hand two different men simultaneously uttered the sentence (*e.g.* if one wrote it and the other spoke it) during the reign of Louis XIV, it would be natural to say (assume) that they were both talking about the same person, and, in that case, in using the sentence, they *must* either both have made a true assertion or both have made a false assertion. And this illustrates what I mean by *a use* of a sentence. The two men who uttered the sentence, one in the reign of Louis XV and one in the reign of Louis XIV, each made a different use of the same sentence; whereas the two men who uttered the sentence simultaneously in the reign of Louis XIV, made the same use[1] of the same sentence. Obviously in the case of this sentence, and equally obviously in the case of many others, we cannot talk of *the sentence* being true or false, but only of its being used to make a true or false assertion, or (if this is preferred) to express a true or a false proposition. And equally obviously we cannot talk of *the sentence* being *about* a particular person, for the same sentence may be used at different times to talk about quite different particular persons, but only of *a use* of the sentence to talk about a particular person. Finally it will make sufficiently clear what I mean by an utterance of a sentence if I say that the two men who simultaneously uttered the sentence in the reign of Louis XIV made two different utterances of the same sentence, though they made the same *use* of the sentence.

If we now consider not the whole sentence, 'The king of France is wise', but that part of it which is the expression, 'the king of France', it is obvious that we can make analogous, though not identical distinctions between (1) the expression, (2) a use of the expression, and (3) an utterance of the expression. The distinctions will not be identical; we obviously cannot correctly talk of the expression 'the king of France' being used to express a true or false proposition, since in general only sentences can be used truly or falsely; and similarly it is only by using a sentence and not by using an expression alone, that you can talk about a particular person. Instead, we shall say in this case that you *use* the expression to *mention* or *refer to* a particular person in the course of using the sentence to talk about him. But obviously in this case, and a great many others, the *expression* (B1) cannot be said to mention, or refer to, anything, any more than the *sentence* can be said to be true or false. The same expression can have different mentioning-uses, as the same sentence can be used to make statements with different truth-values. 'Mentioning', or 'referring', is not something an expression does; it is something that someone can use an expression to do. Mentioning, or referring to, something is a characteristic of *a use* of an expression, just as 'being about' something, and truth-or-falsity, are characteristics of *a use* of a sentence.

A very different example may help to make these distinctions clearer. Consider another case of an expression which has a uniquely referring use, viz. the expresssion 'I'; and consider the sentence, 'I am hot'. Countless people

---

[1] This usage of 'use' is, of course, different from (*a*) the current usage in which 'use' (of a particular word, phrase, sentence) = (roughly) 'rules for using' = (roughly) 'meaning'; and from (*b*) my own usage in the phrase 'uniquely referring use of expressions' in which 'use' = (roughly) 'way of using'.

may use this same sentence; but it is logically impossible for two different people to make *the same use* of this sentence: or, if this is preferred, to use it to express the same proposition. The expression 'I' may correctly be used by (and only by) any one of innumerable people to refer to himself. To say this is to say something about the expression 'I': it is, in a sense, to give its meaning. This is the sort of thing that can be said about *expressions*. But it makes no sense to say of the *expression* 'I' that it refers to a particular person. This is the sort of thing that can be said only of a particular use of the expression.

Let me use 'type' as an abbreviation for 'sentence or expression'. Then I am not saying that there are sentences and expressions (types), *and* uses of them, *and* utterances of them, as there are ships *and* shoes *and* sealing-wax. I am saying that we cannot say *the same things* about types, uses of types, and utterances of types. And the fact is that we do talk about types; and that confusion is apt to result from the failure to notice the differences between what we can say about these and what we can say only about the *uses* of types. We are apt to fancy we are talking about sentences and expressions when we are talking about the uses of sentences and expressions.

This is what Russell does. Generally, as against Russell, I shall say this. Meaning (in at least one important sense) is a function of the sentence or expression; mentioning and referring and truth or falsity, are functions of the use of the sentence or expression. To give the meaning of an expression (in the sense in which I am using the word) is to give *general directions* for its use to refer to or mention particular objects or persons; to give the meaning of a sentence is to give *general directions* for its use in making true or false assertions. It is not to talk about any particular occasion of the use of the sentence or expression. The meaning of an expression cannot be identified with the object it is used, on a particular occasion, to refer to. The meaning of a sentence cannot be identified with the assertion it is used, on a particular occasion, to make. For to talk about the meaning of an expression or sentence is not to talk about its use on a particular occasion, but about the rules, habits, conventions governing its correct use, on all occasions, to refer or to assert. So the question of whether a sentence or expression *is significant or not* has nothing whatever to do with the question of whether the sentence, *uttered on a particular occasion*, is, on that occasion, being used to make a true-or-false assertion or not, or of whether the expression is, on that occasion, being used to refer to, or mention, anything at all.

The source of Russell's mistake was that he thought that referring or mentioning, if it occurred at all, must be meaning. He did not distinguish B1 from B2; he confused expressions with their use in a particular context; and so confused meaning with mentioning, with referring. If I talk about my handkerchief, I can, perhaps, produce the object I am referring to out of my pocket. I cannot produce the meaning of the expression, 'my handkerchief', out of my pocket. Because Russell confused meaning with mentioning, he thought that if there were any expressions having a uniquely referring use, which were what they seemed (*i.e.* logical subjects) and not something else in disguise, their meaning must *be* the particular object which they were used to refer to. Hence the troublesome mythology of the logically proper name. But if someone asks me the meaning of the expression 'this'—once Russell's favourite candidate for this status—I do not hand him the object I have just used the expression to refer to, adding at the same time that the meaning of the word changes every time it is used. Nor do I hand him all the objects it ever has been, or might be, used to refer to. I explain and illustrate the conventions governing the use of the expression. This *is* giving the meaning of the expression. It is quite different from giving (in any sense of giving) the object to which it refers; for the expression itself does not refer to anything; though it can be used, on different occasion, to refer to innumerable things. Now as a matter of fact there is, in English, a sense of the word 'mean' in which this word does approximate to 'indicate, mention or refer to'; *e.g.* when somebody (unpleasantly) says, 'I mean you'; or when I point and say, 'That's the one I mean.' But *the one I meant* is quite different from *the meaning of the expression* I used to talk of it. In this special sense of 'mean', it is people who mean, not expressions. People use expressions to refer to particular things. But the meaning of an expression is not the set of things or the single thing it may correctly be used to refer to: the meaning is the set of rules, habits, conventions for its use in referring.

It is the same with sentences: even more obviously so. Everyone knows that the sentence, 'The table is covered with books', is significant, and everyone knows what it means. But if I ask, 'What object is that sentence about?' I am asking an absurd question—a question which cannot be asked about the sentence, but only about some use of the sentence: and in this case the sentence has not been used to talk about something, it has only been taken as an example. In knowing what it means, you are knowing how it could correctly be used to talk about things: so knowing the meaning has nothing to do with knowing about any particular use of the sentence to talk about anything. Similarly, if I ask: 'Is the sentence true or false?' I am asking an absurd question, which becomes no less absurd if I add, 'It must be one or the other since it is significant'. The question is absurd, because the *sentence* is neither true nor false any more than it is *about* some object. Of course the fact that it is significant is the same as the fact that it *can* correctly be used to talk about something and that, in so using it, someone will be making a true or false assertion. And I will add that it will be used to make a true or false assertion *only* if the person using it *is* talking about something. If, when he utters it, he is not talking about anything, then his use is not a genuine one, but a spurious or pseudo-use: he is not making either a true or a false assertion, though he may think he is. And this points the way to the correct answer to the puzzle to which the Theory of Descriptions gives a fatally incorrect answer. The important point is that the question of whether the sentence is significant or not is quite independent of the question that can be raised about a particular use of it, viz. the question whether it is a genuine or a spurious use, whether it is being used to talk about something, or in make-believe, or as an example in philosophy. The question whether the sentence is significant or not is the question whether there exist such language habits, conventions or rules that the sentence logically could be used to talk about something; and is hence quite independent of the question whether it is being so used on a particular occasion.

III

Consider again the sentence, 'The king of France is wise', and the true and false things Russell says about it.

There are at least two true things which Russell would say about the sentence:

(1) The first is that it is significant; that if anyone were now to utter it, he would be uttering a significant sentence.
(2) The second is that anyone now uttering the sentence would be making a true assertion only if there in fact at present existed one and only one king of France, and if he were wise.

What are the false things which Russell would say about the sentence? They are:

(1) That anyone now uttering it would be making a true assertion or a false assertion;
(2) That part of what he would be asserting would be that there at present existed one and only one king of France.

I have already given some reasons for thinking that these two statements are incorrect. Now suppose someone were in fact to say to you with a perfectly serious air: 'The king of France is wise'. Would you say, 'That's untrue'? I think it is quite certain that you would not. But suppose he went on to *ask* you whether you thought that what he had just said was true, or was false; whether you agreed or disagreed with what he had just said. I think you would be inclined, with some hesitation, to say that you did not do either; that the question of whether his statement was true or false simply *did not arise*, because there was no such person as the king of France. You might, if he were obviously serious (had a dazed astray-in-the-centuries look), say something like: 'I'm afraid you must be under a misapprehension. France is not a monarchy. There is no king of France.' And this brings out the point that if a man seriously uttered the sentence, his uttering it would in some sense be *evidence* that he *believed* that there was a king of France. It would not be evidence for his believing this simply in the way in which a man's reaching for his raincoat is evidence for his believing that it is raining. But nor would it be evidence for his believing this in the way in which a man's saying, 'It's raining', is evidence for his believing that it is raining. We might put it as follows. To say 'The king of France is wise' is, in some sense of 'imply', to *imply* that there is a king of France. But this is a very special and odd sense of 'imply'. 'Implies' in this sense is certainly not equivalent to 'entails' (or 'logically implies'). And this comes out from the fact that when, in response to his statement, we say (as we should) 'There is no king of France', we should certainly *not* say we were *contradicting* the statement that the king of France is wise. We are certainly not saying that it is false. We are, rather, giving a reason for saying that the question of whether it is true or false simply does not arise.

And this is where the distinction I drew earlier can help us. The sentence, 'The king of France is wise', is certainly significant; but this does not mean that any particular use of it is true or false. We use it truly or falsely when we use it to talk about someone; when, in using the expression, 'The king of France', we are in fact mentioning someone. The fact that the sentence and the expression, respectively, are significant just is the fact that the sentence *could* be used, in certain circumstances, to say something true or false, that the expression *could* be used, in certain circumstances, to mention a particular person; and to know their meaning is to know what sort of circumstances these are. So when we utter the sentence without in fact mentioning anybody by the use of the phrase, 'The king of France', the sentence does not cease to be significant: we simply *fail* to say anything true or false because we simply fail to mention anybody by this particular use of that perfectly significant phrase. It is, if you like, a spurious use of the sentence, and a spurious use of the expression; though we may (or may not) mistakenly think it a genuine use.

And such spurious uses[2] are very familiar. Sophisticated romancing, sophisticated fiction[3] depend upon them. If I began, 'The king of France is wise', and went on, 'and he lives in a golden castle and has a hundred wives', and so on, a hearer would understand me perfectly well, without supposing *either* that I was talking about a particular person, *or* that I was making a false statement to the effect that there existed such a person as my words described. (It is worth adding that where the use of sentences and expressions is overtly fictional, the sense of the word 'about' may change. As Moore said, it is perfectly natural and correct to say that some of the statements in *Pickwick Papers* are *about* Mr. Pickwick. But where the use of sentences and expressions is not overtly fictional, this use of 'about' seems less correct; *i.e.* it would not *in general* be correct to say that a statement was about Mr. X or the so-and-so, unless there were such a person or thing. So it is where the romancing is in danger of being taken seriously that we might answer the question, 'Who is he talking about?' with 'He's not talking about anybody'; but, in saying this, we are not saying that what he is saying is either false or nonsense.)

Overtly fictional uses apart, however, I said just now that to use such an expression as 'The king of France' at the beginning of a sentence was, in some sense of 'imply', to imply that there was a king of France. When a man uses such an expression, he does not *assert*, nor does what he says *entail*, a uniquely existential proposition. But one of the conventional functions of the definite article is to act as a *signal* that a unique reference is being made—a signal, not a disguised assertion. When we begin a sentence with 'the such-and-such' the use of 'the' shows, but does not state, that we are, or intend to be, referring to one particular individual of the species 'such-and-such'. *Which* particular

---

[2] The choice of the word 'spurious' now seems to me unfortunate, at least for some non-standard uses. I should now prefer to call some of these 'secondary' uses.

[3] The unsophisticated kind begins: 'Once upon time there was . . .'

individual is a matter to be determined from context, time, place, and any other features of the situation of utterance. Now, whenever a man uses any expression, the presumption is that he thinks he is using it correctly: so when he uses the expression, 'the such-and-such', in a uniquely referring way, the presumption is that he thinks both that there is *some* individual of that species, and that the context of use will sufficiently determine which one he has in mind. To use the word 'the' in this way is then to imply (in the relevant sense of 'imply') that the existential conditions described by Russell are fulfilled. But to use 'the' in this way is not to *state* that those conditions are fulfilled. If I begin a sentence with an expression of the form, 'the so-and-so', and then am prevented from saying more, I have made no statement of any kind; but I may have succeeded in mentioning someone or something.

The uniquely existential assertion supposed by Russell to be part of any assertion in which a uniquely referring use is made of an expression of the form 'the so-and-so' is, he observes, a compound of two assertions. To say that there is a ϕ is to say something compatible with there being several ϕs; to say there is not more than one ϕ is to say something compatible with there being none. To say there is one ϕ and one only is to compound these two assertions. I have so far been concerned mostly with the alleged assertion of existence and less with the alleged assertion of uniqueness. An example which throws the emphasis on to the latter will serve to bring out more clearly the sense of 'implied' in which a uniquely existential assertion is implied, but not entailed, by the use of expressions in the uniquely referring way. Consider the sentence, 'The table is covered with books'. It is quite certain that in any normal use of this sentence, the expression 'the table' would be used to make a unique reference, *i.e.* to refer to some one table. It is a quite strict use of the definite article, in the sense in which Russell talks on p. 30 of *Principia Mathematica*, of using the article '*strictly*, so as to imply uniqueness'. On the same page Russell says that a phrase of the form 'the so-and-so', used strictly, 'will only have an application in the event of there being one so-and-so and no more'. Now it is obviously quite false that the phrase 'the table' in the sentence 'the table is covered with books', used normally, will 'only have an application in the event of there being one table and no more'. It is indeed tautologically true that, in such a use, the phrase will have an application only in the event of there being one table and no more *which is being referred to*, and that it will be understood to have an application only in the event of there being one table and no more which it is understood as being used to refer to. To use the sentence is not to assert, but it is (in the special sense discussed) to imply, that there is only one thing which is *both* of the kind specified (*i.e.* a table) *and is being referred to* by the speaker. It is obviously not to assert this. To refer is not to say you are referring. To say there is *some table or other* to which you are referring is not the same as referring to a particular table. We should have no use for such phrases as 'the individual I referred to' unless there were something which counted as referring. (It would make no sense to say you had pointed if there were nothing which counted as pointing.) So once more I draw the conclusion that referring to or mentioning a particular thing cannot be dissolved into any kind of assertion. To refer is not to assert, though you refer in order to go on to assert.

Let me now take an example of the uniquely referring use of an expression not of the form, 'the so-and-so'. Suppose I advance my hands, cautiously cupped towards someone, saying, as I do so, 'This is a fine red one.' He, looking into my hands and seeing nothing there, may say: 'What is? What are you talking about?' Or perhaps, 'But there's nothing in your hands.' Of course it would be absurd to say that, in saying 'But you've got nothing in your hands', he was *denying* or *contradicting* what I said. So 'this' is not a disguised description in Russell's sense. Nor is it a logically proper name. For one must know what the sentence means in order to react in that way to the utterance of it. It is precisely because the significance of the word 'this' is independent of any particular reference it may be used to make, though not independent of the way it may be used to refer, that I can, as in this example, use it to *pretend* to be referring to something.

The general moral of all this is that communication is much less a matter of explicit or disguised assertion than logicians used to suppose. The particular application of this general moral in which I am interested is its application to the case of making a unique reference. It is a part of the significance of expressions of the kind I am discussing that they can be used, in an immense variety of contexts, to make unique references. It is no part of their significance to assert that they are being so used or that the conditions of their being so used are fulfilled. So the wholly important distinction we are required to draw is between

(1) using an expression to make a unique reference; and
(2) asserting that there is one and only one individual which has certain characteristics (*e.g.* is of a certain kind, or stands in a certain relation to the speaker, or both).

This is, in other words, the distinction between

(1) sentences containing an expression used to indicate or mention or refer to a particular person or thing; and
(2) uniquely existential sentences.

What Russell does is progressively to assimilate more and more sentences of class (1) to sentences of class (2), and consequently to involve himself in insuperable difficulties about logical subjects, and about values for individual variables generally: difficulties which have led him finally to the logically disastrous theory of names developed in the *Enquiry into Meaning and Truth* and in *Human Knowledge*. That view of the meaning of logical-subject-expressions which provides the whole incentive to the Theory of Descriptions at the same time precludes the possibility of Russell's ever finding any satisfactory substitutes for those expressions which, beginning with substantival phrases, he progressively degrades from the status of logical subjects.[4] It is not simply, as is sometimes said, the fascination of the relation between a name and its bearer, that is the

---

[4] And this in spite of the danger-signal of that phrase, '*misleading* grammatical form'.

root of the trouble. Not even names come up to the impossible standard set. It is rather the combination of two more radical misconceptions: first, the failure to grasp the importance of the distinction (section II above) between what may be said of an expression and what may be said of a particular use of it; second, a failure to recognize the uniquely referring use of expressions for the harmless, necessary thing it is, distinct from, but complementary to, the predicative or ascriptive use of expressions. The expressions which can in fact occur as singular logical subjects are expressions of the class I listed at the outset (demonstratives, substantival phrases, proper names, pronouns): to say this is to say that these expressions, together with context (in the widest sense), are what one uses to make unique references. The point of the conventions governing the uses of such expressions is, along with the situation of utterance, to secure uniqueness of reference. But to do this, enough is enough. We do not, and we cannot, while referring, attain the point of complete explicitness at which the referring function is no longer performed. The actual unique reference made, if any, is a matter of the particular use in the particular context; the significance of the expression used is the set of rules or conventions which permit such references to be made. Hence we can, using significant expressions, pretend to refer, in make-believe or in fiction, or mistakenly think we are referring when we are not referring to anything.[5]

This shows the need for distinguishing two kinds (among many others) of linguistic conventions or rules: rules for referring, and rules for attributing and ascribing; and for an investigation of the former. If we recognize this distinction of use for what it is, we are on the way to solving a number of ancient logical and metaphysical puzzles.

My last two sections are concerned, but only in the barest outline, with these questions.

IV

One of the main purposes for which we use language is the purpose of stating facts about things and persons and events. If we want to fulfil this purpose, we must have some way of forestalling the question, 'What (who, which one) are you talking about?' as well as the question, 'What are you saying about it (him, her)?' The task of forestalling the first question is the referring (or identifying) task. The task of forestalling the second is the attributive (or descriptive or classificatory or ascriptive) task. In the conventional English sentence which is used to state, or to claim to state, a fact about an individual thing or person or event, the performance of these two tasks can be roughly and approximately assigned to separable expressions.[6] And in such a sentence, this assigning of

---

[5 This sentence now seems to me objectionable in a number of ways, notably because of an unexplicitly restrictive use of the word 'refer'. It could be more exactly phrased as follows: 'Hence we can, using significant expressions, refer in secondary ways, as in make-believe or in fiction, or mistakenly think we are referring to something in the primary way when we are not, in that way, referring to anything.']

[6 I neglect relational sentences; for these require, not a modification in the principle of what I say, but a complication of the detail.

expressions to their separate rôles corresponds to the conventional grammatical classification of subject and predicate. There is nothing sacrosanct about the employment of separable expressions for these two tasks. Other methods could be, and are, employed. There is, for instance, the method of uttering a single word or attributive phrase in the conspicuous presence of the object referred to; or that analogous method exemplified by, *e.g.*, the painting of the words 'unsafe for lorries' on a bridge, or the tying of a label reading 'first prize' on a vegetable marrow. Or one can imagine an elaborate game in which one never used an expression in the uniquely referring way at all, but uttered only uniquely existential sentences, trying to enable the hearer to identify what was being talked of by means of an accumulation of relative clauses. (This description of the purposes of the game shows in what sense it would be a game: this is not the normal use we make of existential sentences.) Two points require emphasis. The first is that the necessity of performing these two tasks in order to state particular facts requires no transcendental explanation: to call attention to it is partly to elucidate the meaning of the phrase, 'stating a fact'. The second is that even this elucidation is made in terms derivative from the grammar of the conventional singular sentence; that even the overtly functional, linguistic distinction between the identifying and attributive rôles that words may play in language is prompted by the fact that ordinary speech offers us separable expressions to which the different functions may be plausibly and approximately assigned. And this functional distinction has cast long philosophical shadows. The distinctions between particular and universal, between substance and quality, are such pseudo-material shadows, cast by the grammar of the conventional sentence, in which separable expressions play distinguishable rôles.[7]

To use a separate expression to perform the first of these tasks is to use an expression in the uniquely referring way. I want now to say something in general about the conventions of use for expressions used in this way, and to contrast them with conventions of ascriptive use. I then proceed to the brief illustration of these general remarks and to some further applications of them.

What in general is required for making a unique reference is, obviously, some device, or devices, for showing both *that* a unique reference is intended and *what* unique reference it is; some device requiring and enabling the hearer or reader to identify what is being talked about. In securing this result, the context of utterance is of an importance which it is almost impossible to exaggerate; and by 'context' I mean, at least, the time, the place, the situation, the identity of the speaker, the subjects which form the immediate focus of interest, and the personal histories of both the speaker and those he is addressing. Besides context, there is, of course, convention;—linguistic convention. But, except in the case of genuine proper names, of which I shall have more to say later, the fulfilment of more or less precisely stateable contextual conditions is *conventionally* (or, in a wide sense of the word, *logically*) required for

---

[[7] What is said or implied in the last two sentences of this paragraph no longer seems to me true, unless considerably qualified.]

the correct referring use of expressions in a sense in which this is not true of correct ascriptive uses. The requirement for the correct application of an expression in its ascriptive use to a certain thing is simply that the thing should be of a certain kind, have certain characteristics. The requirement for the correct application of an expression in its referring use to a certain thing is something over and above any requirement derived from such ascriptive meaning as the expression may have; it is, namely, the requirement that the thing should be in a certain relation to the speaker and to the context of utterance. Let me call this the contextual requirement. Thus, for example, in the limiting case of the word 'I' the contextual requirement is that the thing should be identical with the speaker; but in the case of most expressions which have a referring use this requirement cannot be so precisely specified. A further, and perfectly general, difference between conventions for referring and conventions for describing is one we have already encountered, viz. that the fulfilment of the conditions for a correct ascriptive use of an expression is a part of what is stated by such a use; but the fulfilment of the conditions for a correct referring use of an expression is never part of what is stated, though it is (in the relevant sense of 'implied') implied by such a use.

Conventions for referring have been neglected or misinterpreted by logicians. The reasons for this neglect are not hard to see, though they are hard to state briefly. Two of them are, roughly: (1) the preoccupation of most logicians with definitions; (2) the preoccupation of some logicians with formal systems. (1) A definition, in the most familiar sense, is a specification of the conditions of the correct ascriptive or classificatory use of an expression. Definitions take no account of contextual requirements. So that in so far as the search for the meaning or the search for the analysis of an expression is conceived as the search for the analysis of an expression is conceived as the search for a definition, the neglect or misinterpretation of conventions other than ascriptive is inevitable. Perhaps it would be better to say (for I do not wish to legislate about 'meaning' or 'analysis') that logicians have failed to notice that problems of use are wider than problems of analysis and meaning. (2) The influence of the preoccupation with mathematics and formal logic is most clearly seen (to take no more recent examples) in the cases of Leibniz and Russell. The constructor of calculuses, not concerned or required to make factual statements, approaches applied logic with a prejudice. It is natural that he should assume that the types of convention with whose adequacy in one field he is familiar should be really adequate, if only one could see how, in a quite different field—that of statements of fact. Thus we have Leibniz striving desperately to make the uniqueness of unique references a matter of logic in the narrow sense, and Russell striving desperately to do the same thing, in a different way, both for the implication of uniqueness and for that of existence.

It should be clear that the distinction I am trying to draw is primarily one between different rôles or parts that expressions may play in language, and not primarily one between different groups of expressions; for some expressions may appear in either rôle. Some of the kinds of words I shall speak of have predominantly, if not exclusively, a referring rôle. This is most obviously true of pronouns and ordinary proper names. Some can occur as wholes or parts of expressions which have a predominantly referring use, and as wholes or parts of expressions which have a predominantly ascriptive or classificatory use. The obvious cases are common nouns; or common nouns preceded by adjectives, including participial adjectives; or, less obviously, adjectives or participial adjectives alone. Expressions capable of having a referring use also differ from one another in at least the three following, not mutually independent, ways:

(1) They differ in the extent to which the reference they are used to make is dependent on the context of their utterance. Words like 'I' and 'it' stand at one end of this scale—the end of maximum dependence—and phrases like 'the author of *Waverley*' and 'the eighteenth king of France' at the other.

(2) They differ in the degree of 'descriptive meaning' they possess: by 'descriptive meaning' I intend 'conventional limitation, in application, to things of a certain general kind, or possessing certain general characteristics'. At one end of this scale stand the proper names we most commonly use in ordinary discourse; men, dogs, and motor-bicycles may be called 'Horace'. The pure name has no descriptive meaning (except such as it may acquire *as a result of* some one of its uses as a name). A word like 'he' has minimal descriptive meaning, but has some. Substantival phrases like 'the round table' have the maximum descriptive meaning. An interesting intermediate position is occupied by 'impure' proper names like 'The Round Table'—substantival phrases which have grown capital letters.

(3) Finally, they may be divided into the following two classes: (i) those of which the correct referring use is regulated by some *general* referring-cum-ascriptive conventions; (ii) those of which the correct referring use is regulated by no general conventions, either of the contextual or the ascriptive kind, but by conventions which are *ad hoc* for each particular use (though not for each particular utterance). To the first class belong both pronouns (which have the least descriptive meaning) and substantival phrases (which have the most). To the second class belong, roughly speaking, the most familiar kind of proper names. Ignorance of a man's name is not ignorance of the language. This is why we do not speak of the meaning of proper names. (But it won't do to say they are meaningless.) Again an intermediate position is occupied by such phrases as 'The Old Pretender'. Only an old pretender may be so referred to; but to know which old pretender is not to know a general, but an *ad hoc*, convention.

In the case of phrases of the form 'the so-and-so' used referringly, the use of 'the' together with the position of the phrase in the sentence (*i.e.* at the beginning, or following a transitive verb or preposition) acts as a signal *that* a unique reference is being made; and the following noun, or noun and adjective, together with the context of utterance, shows *what* unique reference is being made. In general the functional difference between common nouns and adjectives is that the former are naturally and commonly used referringly, while the latter are not commonly, or so naturally, used in this way, except as qualifying nouns; though they can be, and are, so used alone. And of course this functional difference is not independent of the descriptive force peculiar to each word.

In general we should expect the descriptive force of nouns to be such that they are more efficient tools for the job of showing what unique reference is intended when such a reference is signalized; and we should also expect the descriptive force of the words we naturally and commonly use to make unique references to mirror our interest in the salient, relatively permanent and behavioural characteristics of things. These two expectations are not independent of one another; and, if we look at the differences between the commoner sort of common nouns and the commoner sort of adjectives, we find them both fulfilled. These are differences of the kind that Locke quaintly reports, when he speaks of our ideas of substances being *collections* of simple ideas; when he says that 'powers make up a great part of our ideas of substances'; and when he goes on to contrast the identity of real and nominal essence in the case of simple ideas with their lack of identity and the shiftingness of the nominal essence in the case of substances. 'Substance' itself is the troublesome tribute Locke pays to his dim awareness of the difference in predominant linguistic function that lingered even when the noun had been expanded into a more or less indefinite string of adjectives. Russell repeats Locke's mistake with a difference when, admitting the inference from syntax to reality to the extent of feeling that he can get rid of this metaphysical unknown only if he can purify language of the referring function altogether, he draws up his programme for 'abolishing particulars'; a programme, in fact, for abolishing the distinction of logical use which I am here at pains to emphasize.

The contextual requirement for the referring use of pronouns may be stated with the greatest precision in some cases (*e.g.* 'I' and 'you') and only with the greatest vagueness in others ('it' and 'this'). I propose to say nothing further about pronouns, except to point to an additional symptom of the failure to recognize the uniquely referring use for what it is; the fact, namely, that certain logicians have actually sought to elucidate the nature of a variable by offering such *sentences* as 'he is sick', 'it is green', as examples of something in ordinary speech like a *sentential function*. Now of course it is true that the word 'he' may be used on different occasions to refer to different people or different animals: so may the word 'John' and the phrase 'the cat'. What deters such logicians from treating these two expressions as quasi-variables is, in the first case, the lingering superstition that a name is logically tied to a single individual, and, in the second case, the descriptive meaning of the word 'cat'. But 'he', which has a wide range of applications and minimal descriptive force, only acquires a use as a referring word. It is this fact, together with the failure to accord to expressions, used referringly, the place in logic which belongs to them (the place held open for the mythical logically proper name), that accounts for the misleading attempt to elucidate the nature of the variable by reference to such words as 'he', 'she', 'it'.

Of ordinary proper names it is sometimes said that they are essentially words each of which is used to refer to just one individual. This is obviously false. Many ordinary personal names—names *par excellence*—are correctly used to refer to numbers of people. An ordinary personal name is, roughly, a word, used referringly, of which the use is *not* dictated by any descriptive meaning the word may have, and is *not* prescribed by any such general rule for use as a referring expression (or a part of a referring expression) as we find in the case of such words as 'I', 'this' and 'the', but is governed by *ad hoc* conventions for each particular set of applications of the word to a given person. The important point is that the correctness of such applications does not follow from any *general* rule or convention for the use of the word as such. (The limit of absurdity and obvious circularity is reached in the attempt to treat names as disguised description in Russell's sense; for what is in the special sense implied, but not entailed, by my now referring to someone by name is simply the existence of someone, *now being referred to*, who is *conventionally referred to* by that name.) Even this feature of names, however, is only a symptom of the purpose for which they are employed. At present our choice of names is partly arbitrary, partly dependent on legal and social observances. It would be perfectly possible to have a thorough-going *system* of names, based *e.g.* on dates of birth, or on a minute classification of physiological and anatomical differences. But the success of any such system would depend entirely on the convenience of the resulting name-allotments for the purpose of making unique references; and this would depend on the multiplicity of the classifications used and the degree to which they cut haphazard across normal social groupings. Given a sufficient degree of both, the selectivity supplied by context would do the rest; just as is the case with our present naming habits. Had we such a system, we could use name-words descriptively (as we do at present, to a limited extent and in a different way, with some famous names) as well as referringly. But it is by criteria derived from consideration of the requirements of the referring task that we should assess the adequacy of any system of naming. From the naming point of view, no kind of classification would be better or worse than any other simply because of the kind of classification—natal or anatomical—that it was.

I have already mentioned the class of quasi-names, of substantival phrases which grow capital letters, and of which such phrases as 'the Glorious Revolution', 'the Great War', 'the Annunciation', 'the Round Table' are examples. While the descriptive meaning of the words which follow the definite article is still relevant to their referring rôle, the capital letters are a sign of that extra-logical selectivity in their referring use, which is characteristic of pure names. Such phrases are found in print or in writing when one member of some class of events or things is of quite outstanding interest in a certain society. These phrases are embryonic names. A phrase may, for obvious reasons, pass into, and out of, this class (*e.g.* 'the Great War').

V

I want to conclude by considering, all too briefly, three further problems about referring uses.

(*a*) *Indefinite references.*   Not all referring uses of singular expressions forestall the question 'What (who, which one) are you talking about?' There are some which either invite this question, or disclaim the intention or ability to answer it. Examples are such sentence-beginnings as 'A man told me that . . .' , 'Someone told me that . . .' The orthodox (Russellian) doctrine is that such sentences are existential, but not uniquely existential. This seems wrong in several ways. It is ludicrous to suggest that part of what is asserted is that the class of men or persons is not empty. Certainly this is *implied* in the by now familiar sense of implication; but the implication is also as much an implication of the *uniqueness* of the particular object of reference as when I begin a sentence with such a phrase as 'the table'. The difference between the use of the definite and indefinite articles is, very roughly, as follows. We use 'the' either when a previous reference has been made, and when 'the' signalizes that the same reference is being made; or when, in the absence of a previous indefinite reference, the context (including the hearer's assumed knowledge) is expected to enable the hearer to tell *what* reference is being made. We use 'a' either when these conditions are not fulfilled, or when, although a definite reference *could* be made, we wish to keep dark the identity of the individual to whom, or to which, we are referring. This is the *arch* use of such a phrase as 'a certain person' or 'someone'; where it could be expanded, not into 'someone, but you wouldn't (or I don't) know who' but into 'someone, but I'm not telling you who'.

(*b*) *Identification statements.*   By this label I intend statements like the following:

> (i*a*) That is the man who swam the channel twice on one day.
> (ii*a*) Napoleon was the man who ordered the execution of the Duc d'Enghien.

The puzzle about these statements is that their grammatical predicates do not seem to be used in a straightforwardly ascriptive way as are the grammatical predicates of the statements:

> (i*b*) That man swam the channel twice in one day.
> (ii*b*) Napoleon ordered the execution of the Duc d'Enghien.

But if, in order to avoid blurring the difference between (i*a*) and (i*b*) and (ii*a*) and (ii*b*), one says that the phrases which form the grammatical complements of (i*a*) and (ii*a*) are being used referringly, one becomes puzzled about what is being said in these sentences. We seem then to be referring to the same person twice over and either saying nothing about him and thus making no statement, or identifying him with himself and thus producing a trivial identity.

The bogy of triviality can be dismissed. This only arises for those who think of the object referred to by the use of an expression as its meaning, and thus think of the subject and complement of these sentences as meaning the same because they could be used to refer to the same person.

I think the differences between sentences in the (*a*) group and sentences in the (*b*) group can best be understood by considering the differences between the circumstances in which you would say (i*a*) and the circumstances in which you would say (i*b*). You would say (i*a*) instead of (i*b*) if you knew or believed that your hearer knew or believed that *someone* had swum the channel twice in one day. You say (i*a*) when you take your hearer to be in the position of one who can ask: 'Who swam the channel twice in one day?' (And in asking this, he is not saying that anyone did, though his asking it implies—in the relevant sense—that someone did.) Such sentences are like answers to such questions. They are better called 'identification-statements' than 'identities'. Sentence (i*a*) does not assert more or less than sentence (i*b*). It is just that you say (i*a*) to a man whom you take to know certain things that you take to be unknown to the man to whom you say (i*b*).

This is, in the barest essentials, the solution to Russell's puzzle about 'denoting phrases' joined by 'is'; one of the puzzles which he claims for the Theory of Descriptions the merit of solving.

(*c*) *The logic of subjects and predicates.*   Much of what I have said of the uniquely referring use of expressions can be extended, with suitable modifications, to the non-uniquely referring use of expressions; *i.e.* to some uses of expressions consisting of 'the', 'all the', 'all', 'some', 'some of the', etc. followed by a noun, qualified or unqualified, in the *plural;* to some uses of 'they', 'them', 'those', 'these'; and to conjunctions of names. Expressions of the first kind have a special interest. Roughly speaking, orthodox modern criticism, inspired by mathematical logic, of such traditional doctrines as that of the Square of Opposition and of some of the forms of the syllogism traditionally recognized as valid, rests on the familiar failure to recognize the special sense in which existential assertions may be implied by the referring use of expressions. The universal propositions of the fourfold schedule, it is said, must *either* be given a negatively existential interpretation (*e.g.* for A, 'there are no Xs which are not Ys') *or* they must be interpreted as conjunctions of negatively and positively existential statements of, *e.g.*, the form (for A) 'there are no Xs which are not Ys, and there are Xs'. The I and O forms are normally given a positively existential interpretation. It is then seen that, whichever of the above alternatives is selected, some of the traditional laws have to be abandoned. The dilemma, however, is a bogus one. If we interpret the propositions of the schedule as neither positively, nor negatively, nor positively *and* negatively, existential, but as sentences such that *the question of whether they are being used to make true or false assertions does not arise except when the existential condition is fulfilled for the subject term*, then all the traditional laws hold good together. And this interpretation is far closer to the most common uses of expressions beginning with 'all' and 'some' than is any Russellian alternative. For these expressions are most commonly used in the referring way. A literal-minded and childless man asked whether all his children are asleep will certainly not answer 'Yes' on the ground that he has none; but nor will he answer 'No' on this ground. Since he has no children, the question does not arise. To say this is not to say that I may not use the sentence, 'All my children are asleep', with the intention of letting someone know that I have children, or of deceiving him into thinking that I have. Nor is it any weakening of my thesis to concede that singular phrases of the form 'the so-and-so' may sometimes be used with a similar purpose. Neither Aristotelian nor Russellian rules give the exact logic of any expression of ordinary language; for ordinary language has no exact logic.

KEITH S. DONNELLAN

2.3 *Reference and Definite Descriptions*

I

Definite descriptions, I shall argue, have two possible functions. They are used to refer to what a speaker wishes to talk about, but they are also used quite differently. Moreover, a definite description occurring in one and the same sentence may, on different occasions of its use, function in either way. The failure to deal with this duality of function obscures the genuine referring use of definite descriptions. The best-known theories of definite descriptions, those of Russell and Strawson, I shall suggest, are both guilty of this. Before discussing this distinction in use, I will mention some features of these theories to which it is especially relevant.

On Russell's view a definite description may denote an entity: "if 'C' is a denoting phrase [as definite descriptions are by definition], it may happen that there is one entity x (there cannot be more than one) for which the proposition 'x is identical with C' is true. . . . We may then say that the entity x is the denotation of the phrase 'C'."[1] In using a definite description, then, a speaker may use an expression which denotes some entity, but this is the only relationship between that entity and the use of the definite description recognized by Russell. I shall argue, however, that there are two uses of definite descriptions. The definition of denotation given by Russell is applicable to both, but in one of these the definite description serves to do something more. I shall say that in this use the speaker uses the definite description to *refer* to something, and call this use the "referential use" of a definite description. Thus, if I am right, referring is not the same as denoting and the referential use of definite descriptions is not recognized on Russell's view.

Furthermore, on Russell's view the type of expression that comes closest to

---

Reprinted from *The Philosophical Review*, LXXV, No. 3 (1966), 281–304, by permission of the author and of *The Philosophical Review*.
[1] "On Denoting," reprinted in *Logic and Knowledge*, ed. by Robert C. Marsh (London, 1956), p. 51.

performing the function of the referential use of definite descriptions turns out, as one might suspect, to be a proper name (in "the narrow logical sense"). Many of the things said about proper names by Russell can, I think, be said about the referential use of definite descriptions without straining senses unduly. Thus the gulf Russell thought he saw between names and definite descriptions is narrower than he thought.

Strawson, on the other hand, certainly does recognize a referential use of definite definitions. But what I think he did not see is that a definite description may have a quite different role—may be used nonreferentially, even as it occurs in one and the same sentence. Strawson, it is true, points out nonreferential uses of definite descriptions,[2] but which use a definite description has seems to be for him a function of the kind of sentence in which it occurs; whereas, if I am right, there can be two possible uses of a definite description in the same sentence. Thus, in "On Referring," he says, speaking of expressions used to refer, "Any expression of any of these classes [one being that of definite descriptions] can occur as the subject of what would traditionally be regarded as a singular subject-predicate sentence; and would, so occurring, exemplify the use I wish to discuss."[3] So the definite description in, say, the sentence "The Republican candidate for president in 1968 will be a conservative" presumably exemplifies the referential use. But if I am right, we could not say this of the sentence in isolation from some particular occasion on which it is used to state something; and then it might or might not turn out that the definite description has a referential use.

Strawson and Russell seem to me to make a common assumption here about the question of how definite descriptions function: that we can ask how a definite description functions in some sentence independently of a particular occasion upon which it is used. This assumption is not really rejected in Strawson's arguments against Russell. Although he can sum up his position by saying, " 'Mentioning' or 'referring' is not something an expression does; it is something that someone can use an expression to do,"[4] he means by this to deny the radical view that a "genuine" referring expression *has* a referent, functions to refer, independent of the context of some use of the expression. The denial of this view, however, does not entail that definite descriptions cannot be identified as referring expressions in a sentence unless the sentence is being used. Just as we can speak of a function of a tool that is not at the moment performing its function, Strawson's view, I believe, allows us to speak of the referential function of a definite description in a sentence even when it is not being used. This, I hope to show, is a mistake.

A second assumption shared by Russell's and Strawson's account of definite descriptions is this. In many cases a person who uses a definite description can be said (in some sense) to presuppose or imply that something fits the

---

[2] "On Referring," reprinted in *Philosophy and Ordinary Language*, ed. by Charles C. Caton (Urbana, 1963), pp. 162–63. [See above, pp. 175–95.]

[3] *Ibid.*, p. 162.

[4] *Ibid.*, p. 170.

description.[5] If I state that the king is on his throne, I presuppose or imply that there is a king. (At any rate, this would be a natural thing to say for anyone who doubted that there is a king.) Both Russell and Strawson assume that where the presupposition or implication is false, the truth value of what the speaker says is affected. For Russell the statement made is false; for Strawson it has no truth value. Now if there are two uses of definite descriptions, it may be that the truth value is affected differently in each case by the falsity of the presupposition or implication. This is what I shall in fact argue. It will turn out, I believe, that one or the other of the two views, Russell's or Strawson's, may be correct about the nonreferential use of definite descriptions, but neither fits the referential use. This is not so surprising about Russell's view, since he did not recognize this use in any case, but it is surprising about Strawson's since the referential use is what he tries to explain and defend. Furthermore, on Strawson's account, the result of there being nothing which fits the description is a failure of reference.[6] This too, I believe, turns out not to be true about the referential use of definite descriptions.

II

There are some uses of definite descriptions which carry neither any hint of a referential use nor any presupposition or implication that something fits the description. In general, it seems, these are recognizable from the sentence frame in which the description occurs. These uses will not interest us, but it is necessary to point them out if only to set them aside.

An obvious example would be the sentence "The present king of France does not exist," used, say, to correct someone's mistaken impression that de Gaulle is the king of France.

A more interesting example is this. Suppose someone were to ask, "Is de Gaulle the king of France?" This is the natural form of words for a person to use who is in doubt as to whether de Gaulle is king or president of France. Given this background to the question, there seems to be no presupposition or implication that someone is the king of France. Nor is the person attempting to refer to someone by using the definite description. On the other hand, reverse the name and description in the question and the speaker probably would be thought to presuppose or imply this. "Is the king of France de Gaulle?" is the

---

[5] Here and elsewhere I use the disjunction "presuppose or imply" to avoid taking a stand that would side me with Russell or Strawson on the issue of what the relationship involved is. To take a stand here would be beside my main point as well as being misleading, since later on I shall argue that the presupposition or implication arises in a different way depending upon the use to which the definite description is put. This last also accounts for my use of the vagueness indicator, "in some sense."

[6] In a footnote added to the original version of "On Referring" (*op. cit.*, p. 181) Strawson seems to imply that where the presupposition is false, we still succeed in referring in a "secondary" way, which seems to mean "as we could be said to refer to fictional or make-believe things." But his view is still that we cannot refer in such a case in the "primary" way. This is, I believe, wrong. For a discussion of this modification of Strawson's view see Charles C. Caton, "Strawson on Referring," *Mind*, LXVIII (1959), 539–44.

natural question for one to ask who wonders whether it is de Gaulle rather than someone else who occupies the throne of France.[7]

Many times, however, the use of a definite description does carry a presupposition or implication that something fits the description. If definite descriptions do have a referring role, it will be here. But it is a mistake, I think, to try, as I believe both Russell and Strawson do, to settle this matter without further ado. What is needed, I believe, is the distinction I will now discuss.

III

I will call the two uses of definite descriptions I have in mind the attributive use and the referential use. A speaker who uses a definite description attributively in an assertion states something about whoever or whatever is the so-and-so. A speaker who uses a definite description referentially in an assertion, on the other hand, uses the description to enable his audience to pick out whom or what he is talking about and states something about that person or thing. In the first case the definite description might be said to occur essentially, for the speaker wishes to assert something about whatever or whoever fits that description; but in the referential use the definite description is merely one tool for doing a certain job—calling attention to a person or thing—and in general any other device for doing the same job, another description or a name, would do as well. In the attributive use, the attribute of being the so-and-so is all important, while it is not in the referential use.

To illustrate this distinction, in the case of a single sentence, consider the sentence, "Smith's murderer is insane." Suppose first that we come upon poor Smith foully murdered. From the brutal manner of the killing and the fact that Smith was the most lovable person in the world, we might exclaim, "Smith's murderer is insane." I will assume, to make it a simpler case, that in a quite ordinary sense we do not know who murdered Smith (though this is not in the end essential to the case). This, I shall say, is an attributive use of the definite description.

The contrast with such a use of the sentence is one of those situations in which we expect and intend our audience to realize whom we have in mind when we speak of Smith's murderer and, most importantly, to know that it is this person about whom we are going to say something.

For example, suppose that Jones has been charged with Smith's murder and has been placed on trial. Imagine that there is a discussion of Jones's odd behavior at his trial. We might sum up our impression of his behavior by saying, "Smith's murderer is insane." If someone asks to whom we are referring, by using this description, the answer here is "Jones." This, I shall say, is a referential use of the definite description.

That these two uses of the definite description in the same sentence are really quite different can perhaps best be brought out by considering the con-

---

[7] This is an adaptation of an example (used for a somewhat different purpose) given by Leonard Linsky in "Reference and Referents," in *Philosophy and Ordinary Language*, p. 80.

sequences of the assumption that Smith had no murderer (for example, he in fact committed suicide). In both situations, in using the definite description "Smith's murderer," the speaker in some sense presupposes or implies that there is a murderer. But when we hypothesize that the presupposition or implication is false, there are different results for the two uses. In both cases we have used the predicate "is insane," but in the first case, if there is no murderer, there is no person of whom it could be correctly said that we attributed insanity to him. Such a person could be identified (correctly) only in case someone fitted the description used. But in the second case, where the definite description is simply a means of identifying the person we want to talk about, it is quite possible for the correct identification to be made even though no one fits the description we used.[8] We were speaking about Jones even though he is not in fact Smith's murderer and, in the circumstances imagined, it was his behavior we were commenting upon. Jones might, for example, accuse us of saying false things of him in calling him insane and it would be no defense, I should think, that our description, "the murderer of Smith," failed to fit him.

It is, moreover, perfectly possible for our audience to know to whom we refer, in the second situation, even though they do not share our presupposition. A person hearing our comment in the context imagined might know we are talking about Jones even though he does not think Jones guilty.

Generalizing from this case, we can say, I think, that there are two uses of sentences of the form, "The ϕ is ψ." In the first, if nothing is the ϕ then nothing has been said to be ψ. In the second, the fact that nothing is the ϕ does not have this consequence.

With suitable changes the same difference in use can be formulated for uses of language other than assertions. Suppose one is at a party and, seeing an interesting-looking person holding a martini glass, one asks, "Who is the man drinking a martini?" If it should turn out that there is only water in the glass, one has nevertheless asked a question about a particular person, a question that it is possible for someone to answer. Contrast this with the use of the same question by the chairman of the local Teetotalers Union. He has just been informed that a man is drinking a martini at their annual party. He responds by asking his informant, "Who is the man drinking a martini?" In asking the question the chairman does not have some particular person in mind about whom he asks the question; if no one is drinking a martini, if the information is wrong, no person can be singled out as the person about whom the question was asked. Unlike the first case, the attribute of being the man drinking a martini is all-important, because if it is the attribute of no one, the chairman's question has no straightforward answer.

---

[8] In "Reference and Referents" (pp. 74–75, 80), Linsky correctly points out that one does not fail to refer simply because the description used does not in fact fit anything (or fits more than one thing). Thus he pinpoints one of the difficulties in Strawson's view. Here, however, I use this fact about referring to make a distinction I believe he does not draw, between two uses of definite descriptions. I later discuss that second passage from Linsky's paper.

This illustrates also another difference between the referential and the attributive use of definite descriptions. In the one case we have asked a question about a particular person or thing even though nothing fits the description we used; in the other this is not so. But also in the one case our question can be answered; in the other it cannot be. In the referential use of a definite description we may succeed in picking out a person or thing to ask a question about even though he or it does not really fit the description; but in the attributive use if nothing fits the description, no straightforward answer to the question can be given.

This further difference is also illustrated by commands or orders containing definite descriptions. Consider the order, "Bring me the book on the table." If "the book on the table" is being used referentially, it is possible to fulfill the order even though there is no book on the table. If, for example, there is a book *beside* the table, though there is none *on* it, one might bring that book back and ask the issuer of the order whether this is "the book you meant." And it may be. But imagine we are told that someone has laid a book on our prize antique table, where nothing should be put. The order, "Bring me the book on the table" cannot now be obeyed unless there is a book that has been placed on the table. There is no possibility of bringing back a book which was never on the table and having it be the one that was meant, because there is no book that in that sense was "meant." In the one case the definite description was a device for getting the other person to pick the right book; if he is able to pick the right book even though it does not satisfy the description, one still succeeds in his purpose. In the other case, there is, antecedently, no "right book" except one which fits the description; the attribute of being the book on the table is essential. Not only is there no book about which an order was issued, if there is no book on the table, but the order itself cannot be obeyed. When a definite description is used attributively in a command or question and nothing fits the description, the command cannot be obeyed and the question cannot be answered. This suggests some analogous consequence for assertions containing definite descriptions used attributively. Perhaps the analogous result is that the assertion is neither true nor false: this is Strawson's view of what happens when the presupposition of the use of a definite description is false. But if so, Strawson's view works not for definite descriptions used referentially, but for the quite different use, which I have called the attributive use.

I have tried to bring out the two uses of definite descriptions by pointing out the different consequences of supposing that nothing fits the description used. There are still other differences. One is this: when a definite description is used referentially, not only is there in some sense a presupposition or implication that someone or something fits the description, as there is also in the attributive use, but there is a quite different presupposition; the speaker presupposes of some *particular* someone or something that he or it fits the description. In asking, for example, "Who is the man drinking a martini?" where we mean to ask a question about that man over there, we are presupposing that that man over there is drinking a martini—not just that *someone* is a man drinking a martini. When we say, in a context where it is clear we are referring to Jones, "Smith's murderer is insane," we are presupposing that Jones is Smith's murderer. No such presupposition is present in the attributive use of definite descriptions. There is, of course, the presupposition that someone *or other* did the murder, but the speaker does not presuppose of someone in particular—Jones or Robinson, say—that he did it. What I mean by this second kind of presupposition that someone or something in particular fits the description—which is present in a referential use but not in an attributive use—can perhaps be seen more clearly by considering a member of the speaker's audience who believes that Smith was not murdered at all. Now in the case of the referential use of the description, "Smith's murderer," he could accuse the speaker of mistakenly presupposing both that someone or other is the murderer and that also Jones is the murderer, for even though he believes Jones not to have done the deed, he knows that the speaker was referring to Jones. But in the case of the attributive use, he can accuse the speaker of having only the first, less specific presupposition; he cannot pick out some person and claim that the speaker is presupposing that that person is Smith's murderer. Now the more particular presuppositions that we find present in referential uses are clearly not ones we can assign to a definite description in some particular sentence in isolation from a context of use. In order to know that a person presupposes that Jones is Smith's murderer in using the sentence "Smith's murderer is insane," we have to know that he is using the description referentially and also to whom he is referring. The sentence by itself does not tell us any of this.

IV

From the way in which I set up each of the previous examples it might be supposed that the important difference between the referential and the attributive use lies in the beliefs of the speaker. Does he believe of some particular person or thing that he or it fits the description used? In the Smith murder example, for instance, there was in the one case no belief as to who did the deed, whereas in the contrasting case it was believed that Jones did it. But this is, in fact, not an essential difference. It is possible for a definite description to be used attributively even though the speaker (and his audience) believes that a certain person or thing fits the description. And it is possible for a definite description to be used referentially where the speaker believes that nothing fits the description. It is true—and this is why, for simplicity, I set up the examples the way I did—that if a speaker does not believe that anything fits the description or does not believe that he is in a position to pick out what does fit the description, it is likely that he is not using it referentially. It is also true that if he and his audience would pick out some particular thing or person as fitting the description, then a use of the definite description is very likely referential. But these are only presumptions and not entailments.

To use the Smith murder case again, suppose that Jones is on trial for the murder and I and everyone else believe him guilty. Suppose that I comment that the murderer of Smith is insane, but instead of backing this up, as in the example previously used, by citing Jones's behavior in the dock, I go on to outline reasons for thinking that *anyone* who murdered poor Smith in that particularly horrible way must be insane. If now it turns out that Jones was not the murderer after all, but someone else was, I think I can claim to have been right if the true murderer is after all insane. Here, I think, I would be using the definite description attributively, even though I believe that a particular person fits the description.

It is also possible to think of cases in which the speaker does not believe that what he means to refer to by using the definite description fits the description, or to imagine cases in which the definite description is used referentially even though the speaker believes *nothing* fits the description. Admittedly, these cases may be parasitic on a more normal use; nevertheless, they are sufficient to show that such beliefs of the speaker are not decisive as to which use is made of a definite description.

Suppose the throne is occupied by a man I firmly believe to be not the king, but a usurper. Imagine also that his followers as firmly believe that he is the king. Suppose I wish to see this man. I might say to his minions, "Is the king in his countinghouse?" I succeed in referring to the man I wish to refer to without myself believing that he fits the description. It is not even necessary, moreover, to suppose that his followers believe him to be the king. If they are cynical about the whole thing, know he is not the king, I may still succeed in referring to the man I wish to refer to. Similarly, neither I nor the people I speak to may suppose that *anyone* is the king and, finally, each party may know that the other does not so suppose and yet the reference may go through.

V

Both the attributive and the referential use of definite descriptions seem to carry a presupposition or implication that there is something which fits the description. But the reasons for the existence of the presupposition or implication are different in the two cases.

There is a presumption that a person who uses a definite description referentially believes that what he wishes to refer to fits the description. Because the purpose of using the description is to get the audience to pick out or think of the right thing or person, one would normally choose a description that he believes the thing or person fits. Normally a misdescription of that to which one wants to refer would mislead the audience. Hence, there is a presumption that the speaker believes *something* fits the description—namely, that to which he refers.

When a definite description is used attributively, however, there is not the same possibility of misdescription. In the example of "Smith's murderer" used attributively, there was not the possibility of misdescribing Jones or anyone else; we were not referring to Jones nor to anyone else by using the description. The presumption that the speaker believes *someone* is Smith's murderer does not arise here from a more specific presumption that he believes Jones or Robinson or someone else whom he can name or identify is Smith's murderer.

The presupposition or implication is borne by a definite description used attributively because if nothing fits the description the linguistic purpose of the speech act will be thwarted. That is, the speaker will not succeed in saying something true, if he makes an assertion; he will not succeed in asking a question that can be answered, if he has asked a question; he will not succeed in issuing an order that can be obeyed, if he has issued an order. If one states that Smith's murderer is insane, when Smith has no murderer, and uses the definite description nonreferentially, then one fails to say anything *true*. If one issues the order "Bring me Smith's murderer" under similar circumstances, the order cannot be obeyed; nothing would count as obeying it.

When the definite description is used referentially, on the other hand, the presupposition or implication stems simply from the fact that normally a person tries to describe correctly what he wants to refer to because normally this is the best way to get his audience to recognize what he is referring to. As we have seen, it is possible for the linguistic purpose of the speech act to be accomplished in such a case even though nothing fits the description; it is possible to say something true or to ask a question that gets answered or to issue a command that gets obeyed. For when the definite description is used referentially, one's audience may succeed in seeing to what one refers even though neither it nor anything else fits the description.

VI

The result of the last section shows something to be wrong with the theories of both Russell and Strawson; for though they give differing accounts of the implication or presupposition involved, each gives only one. Yet, as I have argued, the presupposition or implication is present for a quite different reason, depending upon whether the definite description is used attributively or referentially, and exactly what presuppositions or implications are involved is also different. Moreover, neither theory seems a correct characterization of the referential use. On Russell's there is a logical entailment: "The ϕ is ψ" entails "There exists one and only one ϕ." Whether or not this is so for the attributive use, it does not seem true of the referential use of the definite description. The "implication" that something is the ϕ, as I have argued, does not amount to an entailment; it is more like a presumption based on what is *usually* true of the use of a definite description to refer. In any case, of course, Russell's theory does not show—what is true of the referential use—that the implication that *something* is the φ comes from the more specific implication that *what is being referred to* is the φ. Hence, as a theory of definite descriptions, Russell's view seems to apply, if at all, to the attributive use only.

Russell's definition of denoting (a definite description denotes an entity if that entity fits the description uniquely) is clearly applicable to either use of definite descriptions. Thus whether or not a definite description is used referentially or attributively, it may have a denotation. Hence, denoting and referring, as I have explicated the latter notion, are distinct and Russell's view recognizes only the former. It seems to me, moreover, that this is a welcome result, that denoting and referring should not be confused. If one tried to maintain that they are the same notion, one result would be that a speaker might be referring to something without knowing it. If someone said, for example, in 1960 before he had any idea that Mr. Goldwater would be the Repulican nominee in 1964, "The Republican candidate for president in 1964 will be a conservative," (perhaps on the basis of an analysis of the views of party leaders) the definite description here would *denote* Mr. Goldwater. But would we wish to say that the speaker had referred to, mentioned, or talked about Mr. Goldwater? I feel these terms would be out of place. Yet if we identify referring and denoting, it ought to be possible for it to turn out (after the Republican Convention) that the speaker had, unknown to himself, referred in 1960 to Mr. Goldwater. On my view, however, while the definite description used did *denote* Mr. Goldwater (using Russell's definition), the speaker used it *attributively* and did not *refer* to Mr. Goldwater.

Turning to Strawson's theory, it was supposed to demonstrate how definite descriptions are referential. But it goes too far in this direction. For there are nonreferential uses of definite descriptions also, even as they occur in one and the same sentence. I believe that Strawson's theory involves the following propositions:

   (1) If someone asserts that the φ is ψ he has not made a true or false statement
       if there is no φ.[9]

---

[9] In "A Reply to Mr. Sellars," *Philosophical Review*, LXIII (1954), 216–31, Strawson admits that we do not always refuse to ascribe truth to what a person says when the definite description he uses fails to fit anything (or fits more than one thing). To cite one of his examples, a person who said, "The United States Chamber of Deputies contains representatives of two major parties," would be allowed to have said something true even though he had used the wrong title. Strawson thinks this does not constitute a genuine problem for his view. He thinks that what we do in such cases, "where the speaker's intended reference is pretty clear, is simply to amend his statement in accordance with his guessed intentions and assess the amended statement for truth or falsity; we are not awarding a truth value at all to the original statement" (p. 230).

The notion of an "amended statement," however, will not do. We may note, first of all, that the sort of case Strawson has in mind could arise only when a definite description is used referentially. For the "amendment" is made by seeing the speaker's intended reference. But this could happen only if the speaker had an intended reference, a particular person or thing in mind, independent of the description he used. The cases Strawson has in mind are presumably not cases of slips of the tongue or the like; presumably they are cases in which a definite description is used because the speaker believes, though he is mistaken, that he is describing correctly what he wants to refer to. We supposedly amend the statement by knowing to what he intends to refer. But what description is to be used in the amended statement? In the

(2) If there is no ϕ then the speaker has failed to refer to anything.[10]

(3) The reason he has said nothing true or false is that he has failed to refer.

Each of these propositions is either false or, at best, applies to only one of the two uses of definite descriptions.

Proposition (1) is possibly true of the attributive use. In the example in which "Smith's murderer is insane" was said when Smith's body was first discovered, an attributive use of the definite description, there was no person to whom the speaker referred. If Smith had no murderer, nothing true was said. It is quite tempting to conclude, following Strawson, that nothing true *or* false was said. But where the definite description is used referentially, something true may well have been said. It is possible that something true was said of the person or thing referred to.[11]

Proposition (2) is, as we have seen, simply false. Where a definite description is used referentially it is perfectly possible to refer to something though nothing fits the description used.

The situation with proposition (3) is a bit more complicated. It ties together, on Strawson's view, the two strands given in (1) and (2). As an account of why, when the presupposition is false, nothing true or false has been stated, it clearly cannot work for the attributive use of definite descriptions, for the reason it supplies is that reference has failed. It does not then give the reason why, if indeed this is so, a speaker using a definite description attributively fails to say anything true or false if nothing fits the description. It does, however, raise a question about the referential use. Can reference fail when a definite description is used referentially?

I do not fail to refer merely because my audience does not correctly pick out what I am referring to. I can be referring to a particular man when I use the description "the man drinking a martini," even though the people to whom I speak fail to pick out the right person or any person at all. Nor, as we have stressed, do I fail to refer when nothing fits the description. But perhaps I fail

---

example, perhaps, we could use "the United States Congress." But this description might be one the speaker would not even accept as correctly describing what he wants to refer to, because he is misinformed about the correct title. Hence, this is not a case of deciding what the speaker meant to say as opposed to what he in fact said, for the speaker did not mean to say "the United States Congress." If this is so, then there is no bar to the "amended" statement containing any description that does correctly pick out what the speaker intended to refer to. It could be, e.g., "The lower house of the United States Congress." But this means that there is no one unique "amended" statement to be assessed for truth value. And, in fact, it should now be clear that the notion of the amended statement really plays no role anyway. For if we can arrive at the amended statement only by first knowing to what the speaker intended to refer, we can assess the truth of what he said simply by deciding whether what he intended to refer to has the properties he ascribed to it.

[10] As noted earlier (n. 6), Strawson may allow that one has possibly referred in a "secondary" way, but, if I am right, the fact that there is no ϕ does not preclude one from having referred in the same way one does if there is a ϕ.

[11] For a further discussion of the notion of saying something true *of* someone or something, see sec. VIII [p. 207].

to refer in some extreme circumstances, when there is nothing that *I* am willing to pick out as that to which I referred.

Suppose that I think I see at some distance a man walking and ask, "Is the man carrying a walking stick the professor of history?" We should perhaps distinguish four cases at this point. (a) There is a man carrying a walking stick; I have then referred to a person and asked a question about him that can be answered if my audience has the information. (b) The man over there is not carrying a walking stick, but an umbrella; I have still referred to someone and asked a question that can be answered, though if my audience sees that it is an umbrella and not a walking stick, they may also correct my apparently mistaken impression. (c) It is not a man at all, but a rock that looks like one; in this case, I think I still have referred to something, to the thing over there that happens to be a rock but that I took to be a man. But in this case it is not clear that my question can be answered correctly. This, I think, is not because I have failed to refer, but rather because, given the true nature of what I referred to, my question is not appropriate. A simple "No, that is not the professor of history" is at least a bit misleading if said by someone who realizes that I mistook a rock for a person. It may, therefore, be plausible to conclude that in such a case I have not asked a question to which there is a straightforwardly correct answer. But if this is true, it is not because nothing fits the description I used, but rather because what I referred to is a rock and my question has no correct answer when asked of a rock. (d) There is finally the case in which there is nothing at all where I thought there was a man with a walking stick; and perhaps here we have a genuine failure to refer at all, even though the description was used for the purpose of referring. There is no rock, nor anything else, to which I meant to refer; it was, perhaps, a trick of light that made me think there was a man there. I cannot say of anything, "That is what I was referring to, though I now see that it's not a man carrying a walking stick." This failure of reference, however, requires circumstances much more radical than the mere nonexistence of anything fitting the description used. It requires that there be nothing of which it can be said, "That is what he was referring to." Now perhaps also in such cases, if the speaker has asserted something, he fails to state anything true or false if there is nothing that can be identified as that to which he referred. But if so, the failure of reference and truth value does not come about merely because nothing fits the description he used. So (3) may be true of some cases of the referential use of definite descriptions; it may be true that a failure of reference results in a lack of truth value. But these cases are of a much more extreme sort than Strawson's theory implies.

I conclude, then, that neither Russell's nor Strawson's theory represents a correct account of the use of definite descriptions—Russell's because it ignores altogether the referential use, Strawson's because it fails to make the distinction between the referential and the attributive and mixes together truths about each (together with some things that are false).

VII

It does not seem possible to say categorically of a definite description in a particular sentence that it is a referring expression (of course, one could say this if he meant that it *might* be used to refer). In general, whether or not a definite description is used referentially or attributively is a function of the speaker's intentions in a particular case. "The murderer of Smith" may be used either way in the sentence "The murderer of Smith is insane." It does not appear plausible to account for this, either, as an ambiguity in the sentence. The grammatical structure of the sentence seems to me to be the same whether the description is used referentially or attributively: that is, it is not syntactically ambiguous. Nor does it seem at all attractive to suppose an ambiguity in the meaning of the words; it does not appear to be semantically ambiguous. (Perhaps we could say that the sentence is pragmatically ambiguous: the distinction between roles that the description plays is a function of the speaker's intentions.) These, of course, are intuitions; I do not have an argument for these conclusions. Nevertheless, the burden of proof is surely on the other side.

This, I think, means that the view, for example, that sentences can be divided up into predicates, logical operators, and referring expressions is not generally true. In the case of definite descriptions one cannot always assign the referential function in isolation from a particular occasion on which it is used.

There may be sentences in which a definite description can be used only attributively or only referentially. A sentence in which it seems that the definite description could be used only attributively would be "Point out the man who is drinking my martini." I am not so certain that any can be found in which the definite description can be used only referentially. Even if there are such sentences, it does not spoil the point that there are many sentences, apparently not ambiguous either syntactically or semantically, containing definite descriptions that can be used either way.

If it could be shown that the dual use of definite descriptions can be accounted for by the presence of an ambiguity, there is still a point to be made against the theories of Strawson and Russell. For neither, so far as I can see, has anything to say about the possibility of such an ambiguity and, in fact, neither seems compatible with such a possibility. Russell's does not recognize the possibility of the referring use, and Strawson's, as I have tried to show in the last section, combines elements from each use into one unitary account. Thus the view that there is an ambiguity in such sentences does not seem any more attractive to these positions.

VIII

Using a definite description referentially, a speaker may say something true even though the description correctly applies to nothing. The sense in which he may say something true is the sense in which he may say something true about someone or something. This sense is, I think, an interesting one that needs investigation. Isolating it is one of the by-products of the distinction between the attributive and referential uses of definite descriptions.

For one thing, it raises questions about the notion of a statement. This is brought out by considering a passage in a paper by Leonard Linsky in which he rightly makes the point that one can refer to someone although the definite description used does not correctly describe the person:

> ... said of a spinster that "Her husband is kind to her" is neither true nor false. But a speaker might very well be referring to someone using these words, for he may think that someone is the husband of the lady (who in fact is a spinster). Still, the statement is neither true nor false, for it presupposes that the lady has a husband, which she has not. This last refutes Strawson's thesis that if the presupposition of existence is not satisfied, the speaker has failed to refer.[12]

There is much that is right in this passage. But because Linsky does not make the distinction between the referential and the attributive uses of definite descriptions, it does not represent a wholly adequate account of the situation. A perhaps minor point about this passage is that Linsky apparently thinks it sufficient to establish that the speaker in his example is referring to someone by using the definite description "her husband," that he *believe* that someone is her husband. This will only approximate the truth provided that the "someone" in the description of the belief means "someone in particular" and is not merely the existential quantifier, "there is someone or other." For in both the attributive and the referential use the belief that someone *or other* is the husband of the lady is very likely to be present. If, for example, the speaker has just met the lady and, noticing her cheerfulness and radiant good health, makes his remark from his conviction that these attributes are always the result of having good husbands, he would be using the definite description attributively. Since she has no husband, there is no one to pick out as the person to whom he was referring. Nevertheless, the speaker believed that *someone or other* was her husband. On the other hand, if the use of "her husband" was simply a way of referring to a man the speaker has just met whom he assumed to be the lady's husband, he would have referred to that man even though neither he nor anyone else fits the description. I think it is likely that in this passage Linsky did mean by "someone," in his description of the belief, "someone in particular." But even then, as we have seen, we have neither a sufficient nor a necessary condition for a referential use of the definite description. A definite description can be used attributively even when the speaker believes that some particular thing or person fits the description, and it can be used referentially in the absence of this belief.

My main point, here, however, has to do with Linsky's view that because

---

[12] "Reference and Referents," p. 80. It should be clear that I agree with Linsky in holding that a speaker may refer even though the "presupposition of existence" is not satisfied. And I agree in thinking this an objection to Strawson's view. I think, however, that this point, among others, can be used to define two distinct uses of definite descriptions which, in turn, yields a more general criticism of Strawson. So, while I develop here a point of difference, which grows out of the distinction I want to make, I find myself in agreement with much of Linsky's article.

the presupposition is not satisfied, the *statement* is neither true nor false. This seems to me possibly correct *if* the definite description is thought of as being used attributively (depending upon whether we go with Strawson or Russell). But when we consider it as used referentially, this categorical assertion is no longer clearly correct. For the man the speaker referred to may indeed be kind to the spinster; the speaker may have said something true about that man. Now the difficulty is in the notion of "the statement." Suppose that we know that the lady is a spinster, but nevertheless know that the man referred to by the speaker is kind to her. It seems to me that we shall, on the one hand, want to hold that the speaker said something true, but be reluctant to express this by "It is true that her husband is kind to her."

This shows, I think, a difficulty in speaking simply about "the statement" when definite descriptions are used referentially. For the speaker stated something, in this example, about a particular person, and his statement, we may suppose, was true. Nevertheless, we should not like to agree with his statement by using the sentence he used; we should not like to identify the true statement via the speaker's words. The reason for this is not so hard to find. If we say, in this example, "It is true that her husband is kind to her," *we* are now using the definite description either attributively or referentially. But we should not be subscribing to what the original speaker truly said if we use the description attributively, for it was only in its function as referring to a particular person that the definite description yields the possibility of saying something true (since the lady has no husband). Our reluctance, however, to endorse the original speaker's statement by using the definite description referentially to refer to the same person stems from quite a different consideration. For if we too were laboring under the mistaken belief that this man was the lady's husband, we could agree with the original speaker using his exact words. (Moreover, it is possible, as we have seen, deliberately to use a definite description to refer to someone we believe not to fit the description.) Hence, our reluctance to use the original speaker's words does not arise from the fact that if we did we should not succeed in stating anything true or false. It rather stems from the fact that when a definite description is used referentially there is a presumption that the speaker believes that what he refers to fits the description. Since we, who know the lady to be a spinster, would not normally want to give the impression that we believe otherwise, we would not like to use the original speaker's way of referring to the man in question.

How then would we express agreement with the original speaker without involving ourselves in unwanted impressions about our beliefs? The answer shows another difference between the referential and attributive uses of definite descriptions and brings out an important point about genuine referring.

When a speaker says, "The ϕ is ψ," where "the ϕ" is used attributively, if there is no ϕ, we cannot correctly report the speaker as having said *of* this or that person or thing that it is ψ. But if the definite description is used referentially we can report the speaker as having attributed ψ to something. And *we* may refer to what the speaker referred to, using whatever description or name

suits our purpose. Thus, if a speaker says, "Her husband is kind to her," referring to the man he was just talking to, and if that man is Jones, we may report
him as having said *of Jones* that he is kind to her. If Jones is also the president
of the college, we may report the speaker as having said *of the president of the
college* that he is kind to her. And finally, if we are talking to Jones, we may
say, referring to the original speaker, "He said of you that *you* are kind to her."
It does not matter here whether or not the woman has a husband or whether,
if she does, Jones is her husband. If the original speaker referred to Jones, he
said of him that he is kind to her. Thus where the definite description is used
referentially, but does not fit what was referred to, we can report what a
speaker said and agree with him by using a description or name which does
fit. In doing so we need not, it is important to note, choose a description or
name which the original speaker would agree fits what he was referring to.
That is, we can report the speaker in the above case to have said truly of Jones
that he is kind to her even if the original speaker did not know that the man
he was referring to is named Jones or even if he thinks he is not named Jones.

Returning to what Linsky said in the passage quoted, he claimed that, were
someone to say "Her husband is kind to her," when she has no husband, *the
statement* would be neither true nor false. As I have said, this is a likely view
to hold if the definite description is being used attributively. But if it is being
used referentially it is not clear what is meant by "the statement." If we think
about what the speaker said about the person he referred to, then there is no
reason to suppose he has not said something true or false about him, even
though he is not the lady's husband. And Linsky's claim would be wrong.
On the other hand, if we do not identify the statement in this way, what is the
statement that the speaker made? To say that the statement he made was
that her husband is kind to her lands us in difficulties. For we have to decide
whether in using the definite description here in the identification of the
statement, we are using it attributively or referentially. If the former, then we
misrepresent the linguistic performance of the speaker; if the latter, then we
are ourselves referring to someone and reporting the speaker to have said
something of that person, in which case we are back to the possibility that
he did say something true or false of that person.

I am thus drawn to the conclusion that when a speaker uses a definite description referentially he may have stated something true or false even if nothing
fits the description, and that there is not a clear sense in which he has made
a statement which is neither true nor false.

IX

I want to end by a brief examination of a picture of what a genuine referring
expression is that one might derive from Russell's views. I want to suggest that
this picture is not so far wrong as one might suppose and that strange as this
may seem, some of the things we have said about the referential use of definite
descriptions are not foreign to this picture.

Genuine proper names, in Russell's sense, would refer to something without ascribing any properties to it. They would, one might say, refer to the thing itself, not simply the thing in so far as it falls under a certain description.[13] Now this would seem to Russell something a definite description could not do, for he assumed that if definite descriptions were capable of referring at all, they would refer to something only in so far as that thing satisfied the description. Not only have we seen this assumption to be false, however, but in the last section we saw something more. We saw that when a definite description is used referentially, a speaker can be reported as having said something *of* something. And in reporting what it was of which he said something we are not restricted to the description he used, or synonyms of it; we may ourselves refer to it using any descriptions, names, and so forth, that will do the job. Now this seems to give a sense in which we are concerned with the thing itself and not just the thing under a certain description, when we report the linguistic act of a speaker using a definite description referentially. That is, such a definite description comes closer to performing the function of Russell's proper names than certainly he supposed.

Secondly, Russell thought, I believe, that whenever we use descriptions, as opposed to proper names, we introduce an element of generality which ought to be absent if what we are doing is referring to some particular thing. This is clear from his analysis of sentences containing definite descriptions. One of the conclusions we are supposed to draw from that analysis is that such sentences express what are in reality completely general propositions: there is a ϕ and only one such and any ϕ is ψ. We might put this in a slightly different way. If there is anything which might be identified as reference here, it is reference in a very weak sense—namely, reference to *whatever* is the one and only one ϕ, if there is any such. Now this is something we might well say about the attributive use of definite descriptions, as should be evident from the previous discussion. But this lack of particularity is absent from the referential use of definite descriptions precisely because the description is here merely a device for getting one's audience to pick out or think of the thing to be spoken about, a device which may serve its function even if the description is incorrect. More importantly perhaps, in the referential use as opposed to the attributive, there is a *right* thing to be picked out by the audience and its being the right thing is not simply a function of its fitting the description.

---

[13] *Cf.* "The Philosophy of Logical Atomism," reprinted in *Logic and Knowledge*, p. 200.

JOHN R. SEARLE

2.4 *Proper Names*

Do proper names have senses? Frege[1] argues that they must have senses, for, he asks, how else can identity statements be other than trivially analytic. How, he asks, can a statement of the form a = b, if true, differ in cognitive value from a = a? His answer is that though "a" and "b" have the same referent they have or may have different *senses*, in which case the statement is true, though not analytically so. But this solution seems more appropriate where "a" and "b" are both nonsynonymous definite descriptions, or where one is a definite description and one is a proper name, than where both are proper names. Consider, for example, statements made with the following sentences:

(*a*) "Tully = Tully" is analytic.

But is

(*b*) "Tully = Cicero" synthetic?

If so, then each name must have a different sense, which seems at first sight most implausible, for we do not ordinarily think of proper names as having a sense at all in the way that predicates do; we do not, *e.g.* give definitions of proper names. But of course (*b*) gives us information not conveyed by (*a*). But is this information about words? The statement is not about words.

For the moment let us consider the view that (*b*) is, like (*a*), analytic. A statement is analytic if and only if it is true in virtue of linguistic rules alone, without any recourse to empirical investigation. The linguistic rules for using the name "Cicero" and the linguistic rules for using the name "Tully" are such that both names refer to, without describing, the same identical object; thus it seems the truth of the identity can be established solely by recourse to these rules and the statement is analytic. The sense in which the statement is informative is the sense in which any analytic statement is informative; it illustrates or exemplifies certain contingent facts about words, though it does not of course describe these facts. On this account the difference between (*a*) and (*b*) above is not as great as might at first seem. Both are analytically true, and both illustrate contingent facts about our use of symbols. Some philosophers claim that (*a*) is fundamentally different from (*b*) in that a statement using this form will be true for any arbitrary substitution of symbols replacing "Tully."[2] This, I wish to argue, is not so. The fact that the same mark refers to the same object on two different occasions of its use is a convenient but contingent usage, and indeed we can easily imagine situations where this

Reprinted from *Mind*, LXVII, No. 266 (1958), 166–73, by permission of the author and of the editor of *Mind*.

[1] *Translations from the Philosophical Writings of Gottlob Frege*, edited by Geach and Black, pp. 56 ff.

[2] W. V. Quine, *From a Logical Point of View*, esp. Chap. 2.

would not be the case. Suppose, *e.g.* we have a language in which the rules for using symbols are correlated not simply with a type-word, but with the order of its token appearances in the discourse. Some codes are like this. Suppose the first time an object is referred to in our discourse it is referred to by "x," the second time by "y," etc. For anyone who knows this code "x = y" is trivially analytic, but "x = x" is senseless. This example is designed to illustrate the similarity of (*a*) and (*b*) above; both are analytic and both give us information, though each gives us different information, about the use of words. The truth of the statements that Tully = Tully and Tully = Cicero both follow from linguistic rules. But the fact that the words "Tully = Tully" are used to express this identity is just as contingent as, though more universally conventional in our language than, the fact that the words "Tully = Cicero" are used to express the identity of the same object.

This analysis enables us to see how both (*a*) and (*b*) could be used to make analytic statements and how in such circumstances we could acquire different information from them, without forcing us to follow either of Frege's proposed solutions, *i.e.* that the two propositions are in some sense about words (*Begriffsschrift*) or his revised solution, that the terms have the same reference but different senses (*Sinn und Bedeutung*). But though this analysis enables us to see how a sentence like (*b*) *could* be used to make an analytic statement it does not follow that it could not also be used to make a synthetic statement. And indeed some identity statements using two proper names are clearly synthetic; people who argue that Shakespeare was Bacon are not advancing a thesis about language. In what follows I hope to examine the connection between proper names and their referents in such a manner as to show how both kinds of identity statement are possible and in so doing to show in what sense a proper name has a sense.

I have so far considered the view that the rules governing the use of a proper name are such that it is used to refer to and not to describe a particular object, that it has reference but not sense. But now let us ask how it comes about that we are able to refer to a particular object by using its name. How, for example, do we learn and teach the use of proper names? This seems quite simple—we identify the object, and, assuming that our student understands the general conventions governing proper names, we explain that this word is the name of that object. But unless our student already knows another proper name of the object, we can only *identify* the object (the necessary preliminary to teaching the name) by ostension or description; and, in both cases, we identify the object in virtue of certain of its characteristics. So now it seems as if the rules for a proper name must somehow be logically tied to particular characteristics of the object in such a way that the name has a sense as well as a reference; indeed, it seems it could not have a reference unless it did have a sense, for how, unless the name has a sense, is it to be correlated with the object?

Suppose someone answers this argument as follows: "The characteristics located in teaching the name are not the rules for using the proper name: they are simply pedagogic devices employed in teaching the name to someone

who does not know how to use it. Once our student has identified the object
to which the name applies he can forget or ignore these various descriptions
by means of which he identified the object, for they are not part of the sense
of the name; the name does not have a *sense*. Suppose, for example, that we
teach the name 'Aristotle' by explaining that it refers to a Greek philosopher
born in Stagira, and suppose that our student continues to use the name correctly, that he gathers more information about Aristotle, and so on. Let us
suppose it is discovered later on that Aristotle was not born in Stagira at all,
but in Thebes. We will not now say that the meaning of the name has changed,
or that Aristotle did not really exist at all. In short, explaining the use of a
name by citing characteristics of the object is not giving the rules for the name,
for the rules contain no descriptive content at all. They simply correlate the
name to the object independently of any descriptions of it."

But is the argument convincing? Suppose most or even all of our present
factual knowledge of Aristotle proved to be true of no one at all, or of several
prople living in scattered countries and in different centuries? Would we not
say for this reason that Aristotle did not exist after all, and that the name,
though it has a conventional sense, refers to no one at all? On the above
account, if anyone said that Aristotle did not exist, this must simply be another
way of saying that "Aristotle" denoted no objects, and nothing more; but if
anyone did say that Aristotle did not exist he might mean much more than
simply that the name does not denote anyone.[3] If, for example, we challenged
his statement by pointing out that a man named "Aristotle" lived in Hoboken
in 1903, he would not regard this as a relevant countercharge. We say of Cerberus
and Zeus that neither of them ever existed, without meaning that no object ever
bore these names, but only that certain kinds (descriptions) of objects never
existed and bore these names. So now it looks as though proper names do have
a sense necessarily but have a reference only contingently. They begin to look
more and more like shorthand and perhaps vague descriptions.

Let us summarise the two conflicting views under consideration: the first
asserts that proper names have essentially a reference but not a sense—proper
names denote but do not connote; the second asserts that they have essentially
a sense and only contingently a reference—they refer only on the condition
that one and only one object satisfies their sense.

These two views are paths leading to divergent and hoary metaphysical
systems. The first leads to ultimate objects of reference, the substances of the
scholastics and the *Gegenstände* of the *Tractatus*. The second leads to the identity
of indiscernibles, and variables of quantification as the only referential terms in
the language. The subject-predicate structure of the language suggests that
the first must be right, but the way we use and teach the use of proper names
suggests that it cannot be right: a philosophical problem.

Let us begin by examining the second. If it is asserted that every proper
name has a sense, it must be legitimate to demand of any name, "What is its

---

[3] *Cf.* Wittgenstein, *Philosophical Investigations*, para. 79.

sense?" If it is asserted that a proper name is a kind of shorthand description then we ought to be able to present the description in place of the proper name. But how are we to proceed with this? If we try to present a complete description of the object as the sense of a proper name, odd consequences would ensue, *e.g.* that any true statement about the object using the name as subject would be analytic, any false one self-contradictory, that the meaning of the name (and perhaps the identity of the object) would change every time there was any change at all in the object, that the name would have different meanings for different people, etc. So suppose we ask what are the necessary and sufficient conditions for applying a particular name to a particular object. Suppose for the sake of argument that we have independent means for locating an object; then what are the conditions for applying a name to it; what are the conditions for saying, *e.g.* "This is Aristotle"? At first sight these conditions seem to be simply that the object must be identical with an object originally christened by this name, so the sense of the name would consist in a statement or set of statements asserting the characteristics which constitute this identity. The sense of "This is Aristotle" might be, "This object is spatio-temporally continuous with an object originally named 'Aristotle'." But this will not suffice, for, as was already suggested, the force of "Aristotle" is greater than the force of "identical with an object named 'Aristotle'," for not just any object named "Aristotle" will do. "Aristotle" here refers to a particular object named "Aristotle," not to any. "Named 'Aristotle' " is a universal term, but "Aristotle," is a proper name, so "This is named 'Aristotle' " is at best a necessary but not a sufficient condition for the truth of "This is Aristotle." Briefly and trivially, it is not the identity of this with any object named "Aristotle," but rather its identity with Aristotle that constitutes the necessary and sufficient conditions for the truth of "This is Aristotle."

Perhaps we can resolve the conflict between the two views of the nature of proper names by asking what is the unique function of proper names in our language. To begin with, they mostly refer or purport to refer to particular objects; but of course other expressions, definite descriptions and demonstratives, perform this function as well. What then is the difference between proper names and other singular referring expressions? Unlike demonstratives, a proper name refers without presupposing any stage settings or any special contextual conditions surrounding the utterance of the expression. Unlike definite descriptions, they do not in general *specify* any characteristics at all of the objects to which they refer. "Scott" refers to the same object as does "the author of *Waverley*," but "Scott" specifies none of its characteristics, whereas "the author of *Waverley*" refers only in virtue of the fact that it does specify a characteristic. Let us examine this difference more closely. Following Strawson[4] we may say that referring uses of both proper names and definite descriptions presuppose the existence of one and only one object referred to. But as a proper name does not in general specify any characteristics of the object referred to, how

---

[4] "On Referring," *Mind* (1950). [See selection 2.2 above, pp. 175–95.]

then does it bring the reference off? How is a connection between name and object ever set up? This, which seems the crucial question, I want to answer by saying that though proper names do not normally assert or specify any characteristics, their referring uses nonetheless presuppose that the object to which they purport to refer has certain characteristics. But which ones? Suppose we ask the users of the name "Aristotle" to state what they regard as certain essential and established facts about him. Their answers would be a set of uniquely referring descriptive statements. Now what I am arguing is that the descriptive force of "This is Aristotle" is to assert that a sufficient but so far unspecified number of these statements are true of this object. Therefore, referring uses of "Aristotle" presuppose the existence of an object of whom a sufficient but so far unspecified number of these statements are true. To use a proper name referringly is to presuppose the truth of certain uniquely referring descriptive statements, but it is not ordinarily to assert these statements or even to indicate which exactly are presupposed. And herein lies most of the difficulty. The question of what constitutes the criteria for "Aristotle" is generally left open, indeed it seldom in fact arises, and when it does arise it is we, the users of the name, who decide more or less arbitrarily what these criteria shall be. If, for example, of the characteristics agreed to be true of Aristotle, half should be discovered to be true of one man and half true of another, which would we say was Aristotle? Neither? The question is not decided for us in advance.

But is this imprecision as to what characteristics exactly constitute the necessary and sufficient conditions for applying a proper name a mere accident, a product of linguistic slovenliness? Or does it derive from the functions which proper names perform for us? To ask for the criteria for applying the name "Aristotle" is to ask in the formal mode what Aristotle is; it is to ask for a set of identity criteria for the object Aristotle. "What is Aristotle?" and "What are the criteria for applying the name 'Aristotle'?" ask the same question, the former in the material mode, and the latter in the formal mode of speech. So if we came to agreement in advance of using the name on precisely what characteristics constituted the identity of Aristotle, our rules for using the name would be precise. But this precision would be achieved only at the cost of entailing some specific predicates by any referring use of the name. Indeed, the name itself would become superfluous for it would become logically equivalent to this set of descriptions. But if this were the case we would be in the position of only being able to refer to an object by describing it. Whereas in fact this is just what the institution of proper names enables us to avoid and what distinguishes proper names from descriptions. If the criteria for proper names were in all cases quite rigid and specific then a proper name would be nothing more than a shorthand for these criteria, a proper name would function exactly like an elaborate definite description. But the uniqueness and immense pragmatic convenience of proper names in our language lie precisely in the fact that they enable us to refer publicly to objects without being forced to raise issues and come to agreement on what descriptive characteristics exactly constitute the identity of the object. They function not as descriptions, but as pegs on which to hang descriptions. Thus the looseness of the criteria for proper names is a necessary condition for isolating the referring function from the describing function of language.

To put the same point differently, suppose we ask, "Why do we have proper names at all?" Obviously, to refer to individuals. "Yes, but descriptions could do that for us." But only at the cost of specifying identity conditions every time reference is made: suppose we agree to drop "Aristotle" and use, say, "the teacher of Alexander," then it is a necessary truth that the man referred to is Alexander's teacher—but it is a contingent fact that Aristotle ever went into pedagogy (though I am suggesting it is a necessary fact that Aristotle has the logical sum, inclusive disjunction, of properties commonly attributed to him: any individual not having at least some of these properties could not be Aristotle).

Of course it should not be thought that the only sort of looseness of identity criteria for individuals is that which I have described as peculiar to proper names. Referring uses of definite descriptions may raise problems concerning identity of quite different sorts. This is especially true of past tense definite descriptions. "This is the man who taught Alexander" may be said to entail, *e.g.* that this object is spatio-temporally continuous with the man teaching Alexander at another point in space-time: but someone might also argue that this man's spatio-temporal continuity is a contingent characteristic and not an identity criterion. And the logical nature of the connection of such characteristics with the man's identity may again be loose and undecided in advance of dispute. But this is quite another dimension of looseness than that which I cited as the looseness of the criteria for applying proper names and does not affect the distinction in function between definite descriptions and proper names, *viz.* that definite descriptions refer only in virtue of the fact that the criteria are not loose in the original sense, for they refer by telling us what the object is. But proper names refer without so far raising the issue of what the object is.

We are now in a position to explain how it is that "Aristotle" has a reference but does not describe, and yet the statement "Aristotle never existed" says more than that "Aristotle" was never used to refer to any object. The statement asserts that a sufficient number of the conventional presuppositions, descriptive statements, of referring uses of "Aristotle" are false. Precisely which statements are asserted to be false is not yet clear, for what precise conditions constitute the criteria for applying "Aristotle" is not yet laid down by the language.

We can now resolve our paradox: does a proper name have a sense? If this asks whether or not proper names are used to describe or specify characteristics of objects, the answer is "no." But if it asks whether or not proper names are logically connected with characteristics of the object to which they refer, the answer is "yes, in a loose sort of way." (This shows in part the poverty of a rigid sense-reference, denotation-connotation approach to problems in the theory of meaning.)

We might clarify these points by comparing paradigmatic proper names with degenerate proper names like "The Bank of England." For these latter, it seems the sense is given as straightforwardly as in a definite description; the presuppositions, as it were, rise to the surface. And a proper name may acquire a rigid descriptive use without having the verbal form of a description: God is just, omnipotent, omniscient, etc., *by definition* for believers. Of course the form may mislead us; the Holy Roman Empire was neither holy, nor Roman, etc., but it was nonetheless the Holy Roman Empire. Again it may be conventional to name only girls "Martha," but if I name my son "Martha" I may mislead, but I do not lie.

Now reconsider our original identity, "Tully = Cicero." A statement made using this sentence would, I suggest, be analytic for most people; the same descriptive presuppositions are associated with each name. But of course if the descriptive presuppositions were different it might be used to make a synthetic statement; it might even advance a historical discovery of the first importance.

PROPOSITIONS 3

INTRODUCTION

The study of propositions requires methods of investigation different from those appropriate to studying sentences and what they mean and utterances or statements. In large part, this difference results from that fact that we already have many intuitions about sentences, sentence meaning, and statements. We know, prior to formal linguistic or philosophical investigation, for example, that 'John drove his car to school' is a sentence, whereas 'drove car his to John school' is not. We also know that the former sentence is different from the sentence 'John rode his bicycle to school'. We can frequently recognize cases of synonymy, ambiguity, and anomaly. Further, we can often tell what counts for or against the correctness of a proposed definition for a word. While things may not be quite so neat when we turn to statements, statements are, nevertheless, not only things people make but things that people sometimes know they make, and an investigation of statements is aided by considering what people ordinarily regard as making a statement or making the same statement.

In contrast, one cannot reasonably expect to discover what propositions are by discovering what people ordinarily take them to be, for what propositions are and how they are to be distinguished from each other is determined, in large part, by what philosophers are, and have been, prepared to regard as propositions. 'Proposition' is a technical term of philosophy and, consequently, in studying propositions there is no alternative but to consider the roles propositions have been chosen to play in the history of philosophy. These roles may be roughly divided into three groups, which we shall call the *logical*, the *linguistic*, and the *psychological* accounts of propositions.

On the logical account of propositions, propositions have been regarded, first and foremost, as *truth-vehicles*. That is, propositions are taken to be either *the* things or *some* of the things which are true or false. There are several motivations for this view of propositions. One historically important motive has been to provide a subject matter for logic, something for logic to be about. Logic is, in the first instance, the study of inferences. Whether an inference is valid or invalid depends neither on the particular subject of discourse nor on the determinate mode of linguistic expression but solely upon the formal relations between premises and conclusion. Propositions may thus be conceived as sorts of entities which stand necessarily in such relations as entailment and contradiction, and it is these relations which constitute the grounds of valid and invalid inference and are reflected in particular linguistic embodiments. Something like this view of propositions is expressed by both CHURCH and GEACH.

A second motivation for the logical account of propositions is found in the classical correspondence theory of truth. On this view, truth is regarded as a relation between what is the case in the world, the *facts*, and the thing, whatever it is, which is true. Propositions have traditionally been cast in the role of the second term of this relation. Both the reasons for seeking a notion of propositions adequate to this role and some of the pitfalls such an account faces are explored by PITCHER.

The linguistic account of propositions treats propositions as the common content of what we say. On this view, two people have expressed the same proposition if they have said the same thing. As LEMMON points out, there are many ways of 'saying the same thing' as someone else. One traditional candidate for the sense of 'saying the same' relevant to distinguishing propositions has been synonymy. On this view, propositions are taken to be the meanings or senses of sentences. Two sentences will express the same proposition if they have the same meaning. As natural as this proposal has seemed, it is difficult to reconcile it with the logical account of propositions as truth-vehicles. If we allow, trivially, that a sentence is synonymous with itself, then the sentence 'Men have not yet walked on the moon' expresses the same proposition today as it did in 1948. Yet what would have been said in uttering the sentence in 1948 is true; what would be said in uttering it today is false. It seems hard to avoid saying, then, either that some proposition is both true and false or that propositions may change in truth-value from time to time and place to place. This line of argument is pursued in detail by LEMMON.

A second common version of the linguistic account identifies propositions with what is *asserted*. Two people express the same proposition if they assert the same thing. This avoids many of the obvious difficulties with the first version. Assertions are surely true or false, and we can comfortably hold that what was asserted by 'Men have not yet walked on the moon' in 1948 is different from what is asserted by it today. Yet while this version of the linguistic account accords well with the demands of a theory of truth, it conflicts seriously with the demands of a theory of inference and thus again seems not fully compatible with the desiderata imposed by the logical account. This point is persuasively argued by GEACH.

On a third version of the linguistic account, propositions are not only what people assert but the common contents of a wide variety of things people can do with words, (a wide variety of *speech acts;* see Section 7). Consider, for example, the utterances: 'That is the Sunday paper being delivered.' 'Here is the Sunday paper.' 'I promise to deliver the Sunday paper.' 'Would that the Sunday paper were delivered!' 'Has the Sunday paper been delivered?' Clearly there is some common content to all of these things. We might describe it as the idea of the Sunday paper's being delivered and identify this as a proposition. On this version of the linguistic account, a proposition is something we can, for example, assert, ask, tell, report, state, command, or promise.

One objection to this version of the linguistic account, stressed by PITCHER, is its *prima facie* incompatibility with the idea of propositions as truth-vehicles. After all, many of the utterances of which propositions are to be components are neither true nor false. As SEARLE's account helps to show, however, this objection does not carry much weight until we understand just *how* propositions are components of what we say and what sorts of components they are. Propositions are not parts of what we say in the way, for example, that words are parts of sentences. The relations between propositions and what we say are much more abstract and less well understood. So even if we grant that 'I promise to deliver the Sunday paper' is neither true nor false, it does not yet follow that the presumed component proposition about the Sunday paper's being delivered is neither true nor false.

Finally, let us look at the psychological account of propositions. On this view, propositions are thoughts or, more precisely, complete thoughts. A proposition is what someone is thinking when he is thinking that such-and-such. One major motivation of the psychological account has been to secure the language-independence of propositions. As CHURCH stresses, the proposition expressed by a bit of language must be invariant under translation. Propositions are not things that need to be expressed in particular words or even in a particular language. Rather a proposition is something which can be expressed by any of a variety of determinate linguistic forms. Suppose that Smith is thinking what he would express as 'Grass is green' and that Schleiermann is thinking what he would express as *'Gras ist grün'*. Then one plausible view is that Smith and Schleiermann are thinking the same thought. The psychological account identifies this thought with the proposition that grass is green. Propositions become neutral mental materials which are worked up into particular sayings or statings. (Something like this view is suggested by SEARLE's Principle of Expressibility: Whatever can be meant can be said.)

There are at least two ways in which propositions can be conceived of as mental entities. First, they may be regarded as subjective entities, part of the contents of a particular mind, like my headache last night or my intention to see all of Jane Fonda's movies. This view has been persuasively argued against by Gottlob Frege (1848–1925) and John Cook-Wilson (1849–1915). Some of the arguments are canvassed by CHURCH. Second, propositions may be regarded as objective. Neither the fact that they exist nor the distinguishing characteristics they possess depends on any mind at all. Rather, on this view, propositions are things that can enter into special mental relations with people and their minds. Paradigmatically, they are things that people can *think*.

This view of propositions suggests a connection between certain theories of the mental and our use of language. Since, in one important class of cases, we talk to say what we think, it seems natural to suppose that propositions in the psychological sense somehow underlie our use of language. We might suppose, for example, that first a proposition, or the representation of one, occurs in our mental processes and then is converted, by appropriate data processing transformations, into a sentence, the utterance of which is adequate on that occasion for expressing the relevant thought. Thus propositions on the psychological view have been thought to play an explanatory role in the account of our use of language. Whether this view, or something like it, has any plausibility, will be a central point of debate in Section 4.

Suggestions for Further Reading

Cartwright, Richard. "Propositions." In R. Butler, ed., *Analytic Philosophy*, Vol. 1. Oxford: Basil Blackwell, 1962.

Cook-Wilson, John. *Statement and Inference*. Oxford, 1926.

Frege, Gottlob. [1]. "Sense and Reference." *Philosophical Writings*, Geach and Black, eds. Oxford: Basil Blackwell, 1960.

———. [2]. "The Thought." *Mind*, n.s., LXV (1956). Reprinted in *Logic and Philosophy*, Iseminger, ed. New York: Appleton-Century-Crofts, 1968.

Goldberg, Bruce. "The Correspondence Hypothesis." *Philosophical Review*, LXXVII (1968). This article, ostensibly on the identity theory, may be read as an interesting attack on the psychological account of propositions, the main point being that there is nothing in common to all cases of thinking the same thought.

McCawley, James D. See entries in the bibliography for Section 4.

Mill, John Stuart. *System of Logic*. 8th ed. London, 1872. Especially Chapter IV.

Pap, Arthur. *Semantics and Necessary Truth*. New Haven: Yale University Press, 1958. Chapter 7.

Russell, Bertrand. "On Propositions, What They Are and How They Mean." In Marsh, ed., *Logic and Knowledge*. London: George Allen & Unwin, Ltd., 1956.

Searle, John. *Speech Acts*. Cambridge: Cambridge University Press, 1969.

Staal, J. F. "Analyticity." *Foundations of Language*, II (1967).

GEORGE PITCHER

3.1 *Propositions and the*
Correspondence Theory of Truth

People think and assert many things, some of which are true and others false.
(Many are neither true nor false; but that important fact can be ignored for
the present.) If a person thinks or asserts something true, what is there about
what he thinks or says that makes it true? What, in short, is truth? These
questions can seem unspeakably deep; they can also seem unspeakably trivial.
That is one good sign that they are philosophical. Another is that they are
puzzling. On the surface, they are not puzzling, but the deeper one goes, the
more puzzling they become.

The question "What is truth?" presents the aspect of a blank and very high
wall: one is reduced to staring at it helplessly. Abstract substantives often
produce this effect in philosophy. What we must evidently do is spurn the
noble but abstract noun in favor of the more humble adjective: 'truth', after
all, is just 'true' plus '-th'. Let us ask, then, What is it for something a person
says or thinks to be true? Some moves now at least seem possible. This freedom
affords only brief comfort, however; for the natural moves we are tempted to
make turn out either to be just wrong or to run into great obstacles.

For example: since 'true' is an adjective, one might naturally be tempted
to suppose that it designates a property. In "What she wore was magenta,"
'magenta' designates a property of what she wore; in "What he stepped on was
sticky," 'sticky' designates a property of what he stepped on; so why shouldn't
'true' in "What he said (or thought) was true" designate a property of what he
said (or thought)? G. E. Moore (1873–1958) succumbed to this temptation:
he admitted that he once held the view—on grounds, presumably, like those
which led him to the corresponding view about goodness—that truth is a
"simple unanalyzable property."[1] Bertrand Russell at one point asserted a
similar doctrine,[2] although as the grammatical illusion worked on him, he
saw two simple properties, truth and falsehood, where Moore had seen but
one: falsehood for Moore was the mere absence of truth, and so, like all evil,
nothing positive, but mere negation or deficiency.

But if falsehood is a deficiency, one thing that seems obvious is that the theory
of truth as a simple quality is itself sadly deficient. It has no shred of plausibility

Reprinted from the Introduction to *Truth*, George Pitcher, ed., © 1964, by permission of
Prentice-Hall, Inc., Englewood Cliffs, New Jersey.
[1] G. E. Moore, "Beliefs and Propositions," *Some Main Problems of Philosophy* (New York:
The Macmillan Company, 1953), p. 261.
[2] Bertrand Russell, "Meinong's Theory of Complexes and Assumptions," Part III, *Mind*,
XIII (1904), 423f.

for the important case of contingent truths (such as "John is in town," "It is raining"); because it implies that in order to discover that they are true, one has only to examine them to determine that they possess the requisite simple property, and that is absurd. And even in the case of necessary truths (such as "$2 + 2 = 4$"), where the view does at least have a measure of initial plausibility, it still leads to paradoxical results. For example, the question "What makes it true that $2 + 2 = 4$?" must surely make plain sense and have some kind of informative answer; yet according to the view under discussion it is a very strange question indeed and has no such answer. On the simple property view, the only possible kind of reply would be "It just *is*, that's all. What do you mean?" Similarly, assuming that yellowness is a simple property, the question "What makes this cloth yellow?" is a strange question to which the most appropriate answer is the uninformative one "It just *is*, that's all. What do you mean?" The question about yellowness, in fact, is actually far less strange than the corresponding one about truth would be, for it might mean "What substance is present in this cloth, or what chemical process is it subjected to, to make it yellow?," whereas on the simple property view of truth, there seems to be no such plausible way to construe the corresponding question about truth.[3] But surely questions of the form "What makes it true that S is P?," where "S is P" is a necessary truth, make perfectly good sense and have informative answers.

The basic dissatisfaction we feel with the simple property view can be put like this: it seems perfectly clear that what makes the thought that $2 + 2 = 4$ true cannot, as the view requires, be something inherent in the thought itself, as if the nature of the numbers 2 and 4 had nothing whatever to do with it; on the contrary, we are strongly inclined to suppose that what makes it true must be something about the numbers 2 and 4 and their relationship to one another. We think that what makes the thought true is the fact that $2 + 2$ *does* equal 4—however the expression 'the fact that . . .' is to be understood.

It appears, then, that we must shut our eyes to the misleading grammatical form of such sentences as "What he said is true" and "Your belief is true," which makes it look as though 'true' were the name of a property which may belong to what people say or think, and try to construe the predicate 'is true' in some more satisfactory way. The move which comes to mind at once, of course, is to construe it as designating a relation between what people assert or think, on the one hand, and something else—a fact, situation, state of affairs, event, or whatever—on the other; and the relation which seems to be called for is that of agreeing with, fitting, answering to—or, to use the traditional expression, corresponding to. A true thought, according to this account, is one that corresponds to a fact, situation, state of affairs, or whatever.

There can be no denying the attractiveness of this view: it seems to be just

---

[3] It might possibly be held that truth is a simple property attaching only to what Moore called *organic wholes* [See his *Principia Ethica* (London: Cambridge University Press, 1903), pp. 27ff.], in which case the question could be plausibly construed; but I do not see how the doctrine of organic wholes *could* be applied here in the area of truth.

right. It struck the great philosophers who first considered the problem of truth—viz., Plato and Aristotle—as so obviously the correct one that the question of possible alternatives to it never occurred to them.[4] And certainly if there were such a thing as the common-sense view of truth, it would be the correspondence theory. Common-sense views of this sort may all, in the end, be correct, once they are properly understood; and to call them "common-sense views" is to claim that at the outset they appear to be straightforwardly and undeniably correct. But between the outset and the end (when they are at last "properly understood")—that is to say, when they are in the hands of the philosophers—they inevitably run into tough sailing. Such, at any rate, is the fate of the correspondence theory of truth: philosophical arguments can make its initial plausibility seem to vanish into thin air.

The correspondence theory says: truth is a relation—that of correspondence —between what is said or thought and a fact or state of affairs in the world. Difficulties and perplexities arise concerning the nature of this relation and the nature of both its terms. Consider the first term of the relation, that to which the predicate 'true' is applied—namely, what is said or thought. I have been using the vague and ambiguous locution 'what is said or thought' mainly because it *is* vague and ambiguous enough to get by if it is not too carefully examined. But what exactly is meant by 'what is said or thought'? Suppose someone said truly "It is raining," so that what he said was true. He spoke or uttered the English sentence 'It is raining', but *that* is not what we want to call true. If instead of "It is raining" he had said "Il pleut" or "Es regnet," then in the sense of 'said' in which what he said was true, he would still have said the same thing, for these are just three ways of saying the same thing; but he would have uttered a different sentence. Therefore what he said, in the relevant sense—i.e., in the sense according to which what he said is *true*—is not the English sentence 'It is raining'. If one person says "It is raining," another "Il pleut," and a third "Es regnet," a correct answer to the question "What did he say?" would in each case be "He said that it is raining"—for each would have said *the same thing*. And it is this element which all three utterances have in common—this same thing that is said in all three cases—that is the real bearer of truth, not the different sentences which the speakers happen to utter.

But what *is* this common element? It is, evidently, the common idea behind each of the separate utterances, the common thought which each of the different sentences is used to express. Not, mind you, the thoughts qua individual acts of thinking that occur at certain definite times and in certain particular minds, for those are different individual events and what we want is some *one* thing which is common to them all. What we want is the identical *content* of these different acts of thinking, that *of which* they are all acts of thinking. This content of any number of possible individual thoughts has been called a *proposition:* and it has been held that propositions are the real bearers of truth (and falsity).

It seems sometimes to have been assumed as obvious that propositions must

---

[4] See Plato, *Sophist* 263B, and Aristotle, *Metaphysics*, Book IV, Chap. 7, 1011b 25–8.

be objective *entities*, on the ground that if two or more sentences all express the same thing, then of course there must be a thing which they all express. The same conviction was also reached as follows. When a person thinks or believes something, it is always a proposition that he thinks or believes. Hence, a proposition is an entity; for whenever a person thinks or believes something, there must *be* a thing that he thinks or believes.[5]

Propositions were thus often conceived to be timeless nonlinguistic entities capable of being apprehended, and of being believed or disbelieved, by any number of different minds. This conception of propositions encounters numerous difficulties, of which I shall discuss two kinds.

(a) We may begin by noting that there is a strong temptation to strip a proposition of any assertive force. Consider the following utterances: (i) The door is shut, (ii) Shut the door!, (iii) Is the door shut?, (iv) Oh, if the door were only shut!, (v) If the door is shut, then the picnic is off, (vi) The door is not shut, (vii) Either the door is shut or I've lost my mind. It is obvious that there is something in common to all these utterances, namely the idea, as we might put it, of the door's being shut. If we have no special prejudices in favor of categorical assertions and thus give no logical priority to utterances like (i), as against any of the other possible kinds, then we might naturally view the mere idea of the door's being shut as a kind of intelligible content or matter which minds can coolly contemplate and which utterances can embody with various different forms imposed upon it. Thus in (i), it is asserted that the content (the door's being shut) describes an actual state of affairs—the content is *asserted;* in (ii) the order is given that the content describe, in the near future, an actual state of affairs—the content is ordered; and so on. This intelligible content looks like our old friend the proposition, only stripped now of its assertive force.[6]

This way of regarding propositions seems right on at least one count: it makes asserting, ordering, questioning, and so on, actions which *people* perform by saying something, rather than actions which are mysteriously embodied, without any agent to perform them, in a wordless abstract entity that exists independently of human or other agents. Notice, however, that this new nonassertorial entity is *not*, although it may appear to be, the same thing as the proposition we began with. Propositions were introduced as the common ideas or thoughts which several different sentences may express. Such an idea or thought, however, contained an assertive element: in our example, it was the thought that it is raining—not the mere nonassertorial thought of its raining, but the assertorial thought that it *is* raining.

This new nonassertorial way of regarding propositions engenders difficulties. One could argue as follows, for example: (i) A mere intelligible content, such

---

[5] See Plato, *Theaetetus* 189A, and L. Wittgenstein, *Philosophical Investigations* (Oxford: Basil Blackwell & Mott, Ltd., 1953), Part I, Sec. 518.

[6] See C. I. Lewis, *An Analysis of Knowledge and Valuation* (La Salle, Ill.: Open Court Publishing Co., 1946), p. 49.

as "the door's being shut," cannot be true or false, since it makes no claim; it *asserts* (or *denies*) nothing. If someone were to assert (or deny) the content, by saying "The door is (or is not) shut," then his remark would indeed be true or false, but the content itself is neither. *Comment:* This plausible line of argument deprives the proposition of the very role for which it was invented—namely, that of being the sole bearer of truth (and falsity).[7]

To avoid this trouble, one might argue instead in the following way: (ii) Of course remarks, assertions, statements, and so on, can be true, but so can propositions. Propositions, on the present nonassertorial view, are the intelligible contents of remarks and hence, it may be said, are used to make true remarks; but both the propositions and the remarks are true. Consider this analogy: a die can be used to form star-shaped cookies, but both the cookie and the die are star-shaped[8]: why, then, should not a proposition and the remarks, statements, etc. it is used to make both be capable of truth? A true proposition will not be a true *assertion*, of course (just as the die is not a star-shaped cookie); it will be more like a true picture or representation of reality. *Comment:* For the present nonassertorial view of propositions, this line of reasoning is more satisfactory than the first, but it does introduce a kind of schizophrenia into the theory of truth, for it makes two radically different kinds of things the bearers of truth. Moreover, the sense in which remarks, assertions, and so on, are true seems to be somewhat different from that in which nonassertorial propositions are, if the latter are at all like pictures or representations. This dualistic result may not be fatal to the view under consideration, but it does make it untidy, at least.

(b) Whether propositions retain their assertive force or not, however, the very notion of a proposition as a timeless, wordless entity is fraught with well-known difficulties. How are we to conceive of this sort of entity? What, for example, are its constituents? The answer that immediately suggests itself, and indeed seems to be the only possible one, is that a proposition is composed of the meanings of the individual words or phrases making up the various different sentences which may be used to express it. The reasoning which lends support to this answer is the following: (i) Propositions were introduced in the first place as being what two or more sentences *with the same meaning* (e.g., 'It is raining', 'Il pleut', and 'Es regnet') have in common. Evidently, then, (ii) a proposition is the common meaning of all the sentences that can be used to express it. And so, (iii) a proposition must be composed of the meanings of the individual words or phrases which make up those sentences.

Let us accept this argument for the moment. Let us even swallow the camel of admitting the existence of Platonic meanings corresponding to each word. Still, there are some troublesome gnats to be strained at. First, if a proposition

---

[7] Hereafter I shall avoid the needless and annoying repetition of such expressions as 'and falsity', 'or falsehood', 'and false', and so on; they should, however, be understood, wherever appropriate.

[8] This analogy was suggested to me by Richard Rorty.

is to be formed, it is not enough that there simply *be* the Platonic meanings of the relevant individual words: the meanings must also be combined with one another. But what are the rules of combination, how is the combination supposed to be brought about, and what sort of complex entity is the result? Consider the corresponding problem at the level of words. In order to have a sentence, a group of individual words must be combined. But here we have a reasonably clear idea of how this is done: a person does it by writing (or speaking) the words one after another in accordance with the rules of syntax for the language, and the resulting complex entity is of a familiar sort. But it is not at all clear that we understand what is supposed to go on at the higher level of Platonic meanings. For example, are there rules of meaning-combination as there are rules of word-combination—rules of conceptual syntax? If so, what are they? When one tries to discover what they are, he sees either nothing or mere pale reflections of ordinary syntactical rules—and that ought to make us suspicious. And suppose there were such things as rules of conceptual syntax: what would it be to *combine* the individual Platonic meanings in accordance with the rules? Not writing them down next to each other or speaking them one after another; for one cannot write down or speak a meaning (in this sense of 'a meaning'). Are they then just eternally combined with each other in all the possible ways—thus constituting immutable conceptual facts in Plato's heaven—and does the mind, when it entertains a proposition, simply pick out for consideration one of these everlasting possible combinations? But then this account does not differ, except verbally, from saying that the individual Platonic meanings are *not* combined in themselves at all, and that the mind combines them by thinking them together in some as yet unexplained way, when it entertains propositions.

The foregoing difficulties need not, however, exercise us unduly, for the argument (i)–(iii) (of the last paragraph but one) which gave rise to them is not acceptable. Plausible as it may have seemed, it cannot be accepted, for both (i) and (ii) are false. (i) is false: propositions were introduced as the common content of what is said or asserted when in a number of utterances, the same thing is said or asserted. In the particular example I gave earlier, three sentences having the same meaning happened to be used: but this was not essential, for the same thing is often said or asserted by using sentences with different meanings. Sam Jones' brother says "My brother is sick"; the same Sam Jones' mother says, at the same time, "My son is sick"; and his son, at the same time, says "My father is sick." It is plausible to suppose that all three people asserted the same thing—i.e., expressed the same proposition—and yet no one could reasonably maintain that the three sentences they used all have the same meaning. And (ii) is false: if a proposition is the bearer of truth (and falsity), then it cannot be the meaning of a class of sentences, for, as Austin points out "We never say 'The meaning (or sense) of this sentence (or of these words) is true'." Again, although we can say of a proposition that it was asserted or denied, it makes no sense to say this of the meaning of a sentence.[9]

I conclude that the argument does not establish (iii). And, since the initial plausibility of (iii) derives entirely from (ii), which is false, I conclude also that (iii) is false. But if the meanings of words are not the constituents of propositions, what are? What *are* the constituents of what-a-person-asserts, the *content* of what he says? It seems difficult, or impossible, to answer. But this must surely be a great embarrassment to those who hold that propositions are real entities: if we cannot even begin to say what their constituents are, we hardly have a clear idea of what *they* are.

Here I shall cut short the unhappy tale of those woes which beset the correspondence theory of truth from the side of the alleged truth-bearers—viz., propositions: I want to get on to some other problematic features of the theory. But first it ought to be made clear that the troubles I have been discussing cannot in fairness be said to be troubles which *the* correspondence theory of truth encounters, as if the version of the theory presented so far in these pages were the only one there is. It is not. For one thing, many defenders of the theory have not conceived propositions to be entities such as I have described: propositions have also been held to be mental entities of one sort or another, to be linguistic entities of various sorts (e.g., declarative sentences or classes of such sentences), to be identical with the facts they describe—and they have been conceived in other ways as well. For another, many defenders of the theory have not even held that *propositions* are the bearers of truth at all: other leading candidates for this role have been beliefs, judgments, sentences, assertions, and statements. Needless to say, it will not be possible to explore here all these alternatives to the particular view I have been discussing. Some of them are not open, of course, to the objections I have raised, although they have troubles of their own. All I have tried to do is point out some typical *kinds* of problems which correspondence theories of truth, as traditionally conceived, encounter.

Puzzles about propositions are not confined to the correspondence theory alone: they can plague any theory of truth whatever. Now I turn to problems which are peculiar to the correspondence theory. I shall begin with the crucial notion of correspondence itself. It seems to me that there are two different kinds of correspondence which might be relevant to a theory of truth. The first amounts to little more than mere correlation of the members of two or more groups of things, in accordance with some rule(s) or principle(s). Consider, for example, what is meant when mathematicians speak of a one-to-one correspondence. The series of integers can be put into one-to-one correspondence with the series of even integers, as follows:

---

[9] I owe this point to R. Cartwright. See his "Propositions," in *Analytical Philosophy*, R. J. Butler, ed. (Oxford: Basil Blackwell & Mott, Ltd., 1962), p. 101. In this article, the points here under discussion, and related ones, are treated perceptively and thoroughly.

Series A (integers)	1	2	3	4	5	6 ... n
	↓	↓	↓	↓	↓	↓ ↓
Series B (even integers)	2	4	6	8	10	12 ... 2n

We may say that the 1 of Series A corresponds to the 2 of Series B, that the 12 of Series B corresponds to the 6 of Series A, and so on. What is involved here is the following: given any member x_i of one group, A, and the rule $y = 2x$, there is a unique member y_i of the other group, B, which satisfies this rule; and all it means to say that x_i corresponds to y_i (e.g., that the 1 of A corresponds to the 2 of B) is that x_i of group A and y_i of group B are correlated or paired off with one another in accordance with the stated rule. But without any indicated grouping or without some rule being either explicitly mentioned or tacitly understood, it hardly makes sense to speak of correspondence: what, for example, could be meant by claiming, out of the blue, that 1 corresponds to 2, or that 12 corresponds to 6? Again, if we were talking about forms of government, we might say that the British Parliament corresponds to our (American) Congress: and this would mean that the two can be paired off with one another in accordance with the principle that they serve (at least roughly) the same functions in their respective forms of government. This common kind of correspondence I shall call *correspondence-as-correlation*.

There is also another kind of correspondence. If two bits of paper each have a torn edge, so that when they are placed together the fit is perfect, then we can say that the two edges, or the two pieces of paper, exactly correspond. Again, if two witnesses are queried separately by the police about a shooting incident and they both tell exactly the same story, then their two accounts correspond perfectly—or correspond down to the last detail. The *Shorter Oxford English Dictionary* defines this sense of 'correspond' as follows: "To answer to something else in the way of fitness; to agree *with;* be conformable *to;* be congruous or in harmony *with.*" This kind of correspondence I shall call *correspondence-as-congruity*.

There seem to be two different senses of 'correspond' involved in 'correspondence-as-correlation' and 'correspondence-as-congruity'. This is indicated by the fact that all cases of correspondence-as-congruity can be qualified as perfect or exact, whereas this is not true of correspondence-as-correlation: for example, the 1 of Series A cannot sensibly be said to correspond perfectly (or imperfectly) with the 2 of Series B. To be sure, sometimes correspondence-as-correlation can be exact, but then the phrase 'corresponds exactly' means something different from what it means in connection with correspondence-as-congruity: thus the British Parliament *could* be said (no doubt inaccurately) to correspond exactly—but not, notice, *perfectly*—to the American Congress. But this would not mean that two legislative bodies "agree with" or are "conformable to" one another; it would mean that they perform exactly the same function in their respective forms of government.

Granted, then, that correspondence-as-correlation (where correspondence is a "weak" relation, a mere pairing of members of two or more groups in accordance with some principle) is to be distinguished from correspondence-as-

congruity (where correspondence is a "richer" relation of harmony or agreement between the two or more things), the question that now presents itself
is whether the correspondence theory construes truth as a relation of correspondence-as-correlation or as one of correspondence-as-congruity. There can
be little doubt that the main impetus of traditional correspondence theories
has been towards the latter interpretation: defenders of the theory tended to
think of a proposition and the fact it states as two separate complexes which
exactly fit each other. In the proposition "The cat is on the mat," 'the cat'
designates the cat, 'on' designates the relation of being on, and 'the mat' designates the mat: the proposition asserts that the first (the cat) and third (the mat)
in that order, are related by the second (the relation of being on). The fact
that the cat is on the mat consists of the cat and the mat, related so that the
former is on the latter. The agreement is perfect. Ludwig Wittgenstein (1889-
1951), who in his early *Tractatus Logico-Philosophicus*[10] worked out this conception of the correspondence theory more thoroughly than had ever been done
before, came to the conclusion that at least elementary propositions, those to
which all others are reducible by analysis, are perfect (logical) pictures of the
states of affairs they describe. The congruity that exists between a proposition
and the reality it describes is thus considered to be of the same intimate kind
as that which exists between a perfect representation of something and that of
which it is the representation.

The difficulties which the correspondence theory, conceived in this way,
encounters are enormous. I shall mention three of them, but discuss only the
first in any detail. It is obvious that if the view is even to get off the ground,
the real parts of a proposition must be at least roughly distinguishable, for it is
just in virtue of a connection between (a) the parts of the proposition and (b)
the parts of the fact it describes, that the proposition as a whole is congruent
with—i.e. , corresponds to—the fact as a whole. The first difficulty facing this
correspondence (-as-congruity) theory is that the problem of determining,
even roughly, how many constituents a proposition has is horribly difficult,
if not totally insoluble. As we have already seen (pp. 227–29), there is a tremendous problem about determining what *sort of thing* the constituents of a
proposition are: the initially most plausible view—namely, that they are the
meanings of words—turned out to be false, and no other plausible view presented itself. That troublesome question, however, can be by-passed in order to
discuss this new one—namely, the question of determining *how many* constituents a proposition has: for it is not always essential, in order to determine how
many x's there are, to know exactly what sort of thing x's are. In the present
case of propositions, in particular, it might seem obvious that even though the
constituents of a proposition cannot be identified with the meanings of the
words or phrases which make up a sentence that can be used to express it,
nevertheless there must be one constituent of a proposition (whatever its *nature*

---

[10] Translated by D. F. Pears and B. F. McGuinness (New York: The Humanities Press,
1961). This work was completed in 1918, and the first English translation appeared in 1922.

may be) corresponding to each main grammatical part of such a sentence. Perhaps it seems obvious, for example, that there are exactly three constituents of the proposition expressed by the sentence 'The cat is on the mat'—namely, those corresponding to the words 'the cat', 'the mat', and '——— is on ——— ———'. But difficulties immediately present themselves. There is a foreign language—I have just invented it—in which the proposition we express by saying "The cat is on the mat" is expressed by the one-word sentence 'Catamat'. Are we to say that when a speaker of this new language says "Catamat" he is expressing a proposition with only one constituent? But then how could that be the same proposition as the one we express by saying "The cat is on the mat," since ours has three constituents? Perhaps we are tempted to say that his proposition really has the same three constituents that ours does, since when he says "Catamat," what he means is that the cat (1) is on (2) the mat (3). This is true. But *he* can say, with as much justice, both (a) that when he says "Catamat," what he means is *catamat, and* (b) that when *we* say "The cat is on the mat," what we mean is *catamat*. So we are right back where we started. (See Wittgenstein, *Philosophical Investigations*, Part I, Secs. 19 and 20.)

What to do? (a) Are we to insist that the two sentences 'The cat is on the mat' and 'Catamat' both express the same proposition although conceding that the former has three constituents while the latter has only one? Identity of propositions would then have to be a matter not of the identity of their constituents, but rather of the identity of the facts or states of affairs they describe. But then since the correspondence (-as-congruity) of two things x and y involves some pairings of the respective parts of x and y, if one of these two propositions corresponds to the state of affairs, it is difficult to see how the other possibly could. This is difficult to see, at any rate, if one assumes, with most defenders of the correspondence theory, that states of affairs are real complex entities with a certain fixed number of constituents. One could try to reject that assumption: one could say that the proposition "The cat is on the mat" describes the state of affairs S_1 of the cat's being on the mat, which consists of three elements, while the proposition "Catamat" describes the state of affairs S_2 of cat'samat, which consists of only one element. But then the state of affairs S_1 could not without circularity be identified with S_2, as it must be if the suggestion under consideration is to stand. The reason for this is as follows: a state of affairs can only be picked out, in the end, by means of language. We can pick out S_1 only as that state of affairs which is described by the proposition expressed by the sentence 'The cat is on the mat'; and we can pick out S_2 only as that state of affairs which is described by the proposition expressed by the sentence 'Catamat'. Now we cannot without circularity go on to claim that S_1 and S_2 are the *same* state of affairs; because this claim could only be backed up by the contention that the propositions "The cat is on the mat" and "Catamat" are identical. But *ex hypothesi* these two propositions are themselves identical solely in virtue of their describing the same state of affairs.

(b) Shall we say, then, that the two sentences 'The cat is on the mat' and

'Catamat' express one and the same proposition, the number of whose constituents has no necessary connection with the number of expressions in either of the two sentences? But then *how* are we to determine this number? (c) Shall we abandon the search for the number of constituents of a proposition and contend that the question of how many constituents a proposition has is a wholly arbitrary one having no right answer? But then we would seem to be abandoning at the same time all hope of construing truth in terms of correspondence-as-congruity, since this kind of correspondence between two things seems to require the pairing of their respective parts.

The second kind of trouble with the correspondence-as-congruity theory arises from the fact that the most plausible candidate for the relation binding the respective parts of a proposition and the state of affairs it describes seems to be that of *designating, standing for,* or *denoting.* A denotative theory of meaning[11] is at least a natural adjunct to the correspondence theory of truth conceived in the present way, if it is not actually an essential part of it: the two were certainly intimately connected in Wittgenstein's *Tractatus.* But the unsatisfactoriness of any purely denotative theory of meaning is well-known, thanks largely to the later work, paradoxically enough, of Wittgenstein himself. The third set of difficulties facing the correspondence (-as-congruity) theory are those concerning the nature and hence the constituents of facts. . . .

It would appear that the only hope for the correspondence theory is not to view correspondence as a "rich" relation of congruity, but rather as a "weak" relation of mere correlation or pairing of individual propositions and facts. This version of the correspondence theory completely avoids the first two of the three kinds of difficulties encountered by the other version: there is no need for it to distinguish the parts of a proposition, and there is no necessity for it to embrace a denotative theory of meaning. It is, however, committed to an objective view of facts, or of some substitute for facts, and so is open to at least some of the criticisms on this score that the earlier version is. . . .

E. J. LEMMON

3.2   *Sentences, Statements, and Propositions*

In July 1950 there appeared an important article by P. F. Strawson entitled 'On Referring' [Strawson (1). See bibliography, p. 250.]. One of the aims of this paper was to show that Russell's theory of descriptions, inasmuch as

---

[11] I.e., one that construes the meaning of a term to be whatever it designates or denotes.

Reprinted from *British Analytical Philosophy*, B. Williams and A. Montifiore, eds. (New York: Humanities Press, Inc.; London: Routledge & Kegan Paul, Ltd., 1966), Chapter 4, pp. 87–107, by permission of the publishers.

it was designed to give an account of the use of definite descriptions (expressions of the form "the so-and-so") in ordinary language, embodied certain fundamental mistakes. In order to understand the mistakes that Strawson believed he had detected in Russell's theory, it will be as well to begin with a brief account of the theory itself.[1]

Consider the sentence:

(1) The present king of France is bald,

which contains as its grammatical subject the definite description "the present king of France." It would seem that this sentence is meaningful, and yet what exactly does it say about what? A natural answer is to reply that it says of some object, referred to by the phrase "the present king of France" that it has the property of being bald. For, if we were asked the same question about the similar sentence:

(2) Khruschev is bald,

we should naturally reply that it says of some object, referred to by the name "Khruschev," that it has the property of being bald. And yet this answer cannot be right in the case of (1), just because, in 1962 at least, there *is* no object referred to by the phrase "the present king of France," so that there does not, at the present time, seem to be *anything* for (1) to be about.

The difficulty here can be seen more clearly, perhaps, if we turn to another sentence containing the same definite description:

(3) The present king of France does not exist.

We are inclined to say not only that this sentence is meaningful, but also that it is *true*, even if, no doubt, oddly put; indeed, it seems to be precisely a way of putting the truth that there is no present unique king of France. But if we ask the question "What exactly does (3) say about what?," we again find it awkward to answer. For the natural reply—that it is about an object referred to by the phrase "the present king of France" to the effect that there is no such object—so far from making the sentence appear true, makes it appear not only false but actually self-contradictory: the sentence refers to an object and then claims that there is no such object to be referred to, on this analysis.

Russell's escape from the difficulty is to claim that, while (1) and (3) are *grammatically* very much like (2), all three being of the same grammatical subject-predicate form, this structure is *misleading* as to the actual content of (1) and (3). When submitted to a proper logical analysis, (1) and (3) turn out to be respectively a complex existential claim and the denial of an existential claim; the subject-predicate façade disappears. For (1) Russell proffers a logical analysis into:

(4) There is something which (*a*) is a present king of France, (*b*) is unique in being a present king of France and (*c*) is bald;

---

[1] The theory is most simply expounded in Russell. [See bibliography, p. 249.]

and for (3) an analysis into:

> (5) It is not the case that there is something which (*a*) is a present king of France, and (*b*) is unique in being a present king of France.

In these analyses, the definite description "the present king of France," which appeared to refer to some unique object, has disappeared, and the special force of the definite article "the" has been rendered by clause (*b*) in each case. It also follows from Russell's analysis that (3) is after all true, since (5) is evidently true; and that (1) is in fact *false*, since there is nothing which satisfies condition (*a*) of (4), and hence *a fortiori* nothing which satisfies all of conditions (*a*)–(*c*). It should be fairly easy to see from these examples how a Russell-type analysis can be applied to sentences of other kinds containing definite descriptions, in such a way that the definite descriptions are eliminated in favour of other less misleading locutions.

Strawson begins his attack on this theory by drawing attention to a class of expressions, which we shall call *uniquely referring expressions*, whose normal use in discourse is "to mention or refer to some individual person or single object or particular event or place or process" [Strawson (1), p. 320]. This class includes ordinary proper names ("Venice," "Napoleon"), demonstrative pronouns ("this," "that"), personal and impersonal pronouns ("I," "he," "it"), and definite descriptions. He then makes a distinction between (*a*) these expressions themselves, (*b*) a *use* of one of them and (*c*) an *utterance* of one of them; and correspondingly, between (*a*) a sentence (say, beginning with a uniquely referring expression, such as (1) and (2) above), (*b*) a use of a sentence and (*c*) an utterance of a sentence. For suppose a man to utter the sentence (1) during the reign of Louis XIV and again during the reign of Louis XV: then the same *sentence* will have been uttered, but it will have been put to different *uses* on the two occasions. For example, the statement made by using it on the first occasion may well have been true, while the statement made by using it on the second occasion may well have been false. This illustrates the contrast between (*a*) and (*b*), both for uniquely referring expressions and for sentences. Again, suppose that during the same reign simultaneously two men utter sentence (1). Both men, since they refer to the same king and say the same thing about him, will now have put the same sentence to the *same* use, and made the same statement, either true or false; but there will be two distinct *utterances* of sentence (1) and of the phrase "the present king of France." This illustrates the contrast between (*b*) and (*c*) in each case, as well as between (*a*) and (*c*).

The contrasts between (*a*), (*b*) and (*c*) do not always hinge on the time of utterance of expressions and sentences, as in the examples given. They may hinge on the place of utterance, or even on the person uttering. For example, two people *A* and *B* may both utter the same sentence:

> (6) I am hot,

but, if they do, will be putting it to different *uses*, since, such is the meaning of "I," *A* will be referring to *A* and *B* to *B*, so that *A*'s statement may well be true and *B*'s false. On the other hand, if *B* utters, not (6), but (addressing *A*):

(7) You are hot,

at the same time that *A* utters (6), then it is reasonable to say that *A* and *B* have now put different sentences to the same use, and made the same statement, either true or false. For both have referred to *A* and said the same thing about him.

It will be convenient to summarize Strawson's conclusions up to this point in the following two *dicta:* (α) the same sentence may be used in different contexts of utterance to make different statements, some true and some false; and (β) the same statement, either true or false, may be made by using different sentences in different contexts of utterance. (Similarly, the same uniquely referring expression may be used in different contexts of utterance to mention or refer to different things; and the same thing may be mentioned or referred to by using different uniquely referring expressions in different contexts.)

I am inclined to accept as true the *dicta* (α) and (β), though there remains some unclearness in the notion of "same statement" to which we shall return. But the conclusions which Strawson bases on these claims, and with which he hopes to refute Russell's theory of descriptions, may, I think, be doubted. He concludes that we cannot say *the same things* about sentences and their uses, or about uniquely referring expressions and their uses. In particular, *meaning* is a function of the sentence or expression, while truth and falsity and mentioning and referring are functions of the *use* of a sentence or expression. "To give the meaning of a sentence is to give *general directions* for its use in making true or false assertions" [Strawson (1), p. 327]. Hence we cannot, according to Strawson, ask the question "What is the sentence about?": this question can only be asked about some *use* of a sentence to make a statement. Similarly, we cannot ask the question "Is the sentence true or false?": it is the statements that we use the sentences to make that are true or false, and, indeed, a sentence such as (1) will be used to make a true or false statement only if the uniquely referring expression "the present king of France" is successfully used, in the context of utterance, to refer to some object, i.e. if there is, at the time of utterance, a unique king of France.

Strawson elsewhere [Strawson (3), p. 4] reinforces the point that truth and falsity are functions of statements not of sentences as follows: "We cannot identify that which is true or false (the statement) with the sentence used in making it; for the same sentence may be used to make quite different statements, some of them true and some of them false." Now this is, in fact, an unsatisfactory argument. It is as though one were to say that we cannot speak of a gate as having a definite colour, because the same gate may have different colours at different times. The proper consequence of *dictum* (α) is that, if we wish to speak of *sentences* as true or false, then this talk must be *relative to context of utterance,* just as talk of the colour of a gate is relative to date. Thus, we might say that sentence (1) is true at one date but false at another (as the gate is red at one date and green at another); and that sentence (6) is true, perhaps, on my lips but false on yours. Strawson's examples do not show that we cannot speak of the truth of falsity sentences: only that many sentences cannot be viewed as *absolutely* true or false.

And this is an important conclusion; for many logicians do seem, at least tacitly, to have supposed that sentences were all absolutely true or false. This is perhaps not surprising when we recall that modern logic is characteristically concerned with arguments in mathematics and the natural sciences, where there is good reason to suppose that sentences do not wait upon the context of utterance for their truth-value.[2] In fact, this contextual dependence is a much more deep-seated feature of sentences than one might at first sight suppose. Consider:

(8) Brutus killed Caesar.

We naturally say that this sentence is true if uttered today (though, of course, false if uttered in, say, 55 B.C.). But this is only because most contemporary contexts of utterance would disclose that the reference of the proper names "Brutus" and "Caesar" were the well-known Romans of that name. It is easy to imagine a contemporary context, in which the reference was to two dogs with the same names, such that (8) was in fact false. Our linguistic conventions are such that *no* ordinary proper names are uniquely assigned to a single object, so that there is always an element of contextual dependence in their reference and, consequently, in the truth-value of sentences containing them.

Let us now return to Strawson's attack on Russell. Strawson agrees with Russell that (1) is meaningful, and that anyone now uttering it would be saying something true only if there was at present a unique king of France; but he denies that anyone now uttering (1) would be saying anything true or false, and that part of what he would be saying would be that there was a unique present king of France. (Russell is committed to both these positions by the analysis into (4), as we have seen.) For Strawson, anyone uttering (1) today *fails* to refer successfully, his use of the sentence is a *spurious* use, and the question whether his statement is true or false fails to arise for just this reason [Strawson (1), pp. 329–31]. And he believes that Russell failed to see this just because he failed to make the distinction between sentences and their uses to make statements, and so assumed that the only alternative to a sentence's being true or false was for it to be meaningless.

If we bear in mind, however, that, while we accept Strawson's distinction between sentences and statements, we see no good reason to withhold the labels "true" and "false" from sentences because of it, we can recast Strawson's view of (1) as follows: the sentence (1), if uttered today, is *neither true nor false*, because the uniquely referring expression in it "the present king of France" has today no reference; and it is a prerequisite of sentence (1)'s being true or false that there be a unique king of France at its date of utterance, though

---

[2] "By the *truth value* of a sentence I understand the circumstance that it is true or false . . . For brevity I call the one the True, the other the False." Frege (1); Geach-Black, p. 63.

this is no part of what is claimed by (1).[3] But it is important to notice that this rephrasing of Strawson's position hinges not at all on the contrast between sentences and statements; this was pointed out by Quine [Quine (1)], who accepts Strawson's strictures on Russell's theory of descriptions regarded as an analysis of the ordinary use of such expressions, but is worried by the postulation of statements as opposed to sentences: "In appealing thus to 'statements' ... Mr. Strawson ... runs a certain risk. The risk is that of hypostatizing obscure entities, akin perhaps to 'propositions' or 'meanings' ... , and reading into them an explanatory value which is not there."

Now this raises several questions. Does the notion of a statement have any explanatory value? If it does (as seems at first sight so from Strawson's own examples), how do statements relate to propositions or meanings? Again, if Strawson's views about the "truth-valuelessness" of certain sentences in ordinary speech are correct, how is it that logicians (including Quine) can continue successfully to use Russell's theory of descriptions, as is certainly the case? These questions are interconnected, and we shall gain some insight into their solution by considering the position of Frege [Frege (1)], who puts forward a view in many respects similar to that of Strawson.

Frege begins his article "On Sense and Reference" with a puzzle about identity. Consider the two sentences:

> (9) The morning star is the morning star.
> (10) The morning star is the evening star.

We naturally say that (9) is a trivial truth of logic, an example indeed of the law of identity that $a = a$, while (10) is a far from trivial astronomical fact, dependent for its truth not on logic but on the way the world happens to be. Yet it is hard to see how they can be so different: for they are both *about* the same object, Venus, and say of it the same thing, that it is the morning star, i.e. that it is the evening star (which *is* the same thing since the morning star *is* the evening star). This puzzle is deeper than it looks, and Frege's way out is to distinguish between the *reference* of uniquely referring expressions and their sense.[4] Their reference is simply the object, if there is one, to which they

---

[3] If we do say that this is part of what (1) claims, as opposed to what it *presupposes*, then we are back, of course, to something like (4), and are forced to conclude that, since there is no present king of France, (1) today is actually false.

[4] Frege's distinction between *sense* and *reference* is closely related to Mill's between *connotation* and *denotation* [Mill]. But, while Frege applies his distinction only to uniquely referring expressions, Mill applies his to all terms or "names": roughly, the denotation of a term for Mill is the class of things of which the term is truly predicable (we all, for example, belong to the denotation of the term "human being"), and its connotation is the class of attributes which anything *has* to have in order to belong to its denotation (to be a human being one has to be rational, so that the attribute of rationality belongs to the connotation of "human being"). Thus "white" denotes any white thing, but connotes the attribute whiteness. Mill's distinction is in turn related to an older one, that between a term's *extension* and its *intension*: again roughly, by a term's intension is understood its meaning, whilst its extension is the class of *subspecies* of its denotation (in Mill's sense). Thus the *class* of whales belongs to the extension of the term "mammal"; any individual whale belongs to its denotation. I should add that these terms are used in varying ways by different authors.

uniquely refer. It is clear that the expressions "the morning star" and "the evening star" have the same reference, namely, the celestial object Venus. What the sense of an expression is is less clear, but examples may help. No one would say that "the morning star" *meant* the same as "the evening star," and so we may say that the two expressions have different senses. On the other hand, "the morning star" *does* have the same sense as its correct French translation "l'étoile du matin." Again, "the man whom Brutus killed" and "the man who invaded Britain in 55 B.C.," though they have the same reference, Caesar, have different senses, while "the man whom Brutus killed" and "the man who was killed by Brutus" have not only the same reference but also (presumably) the same sense. Frege nowhere *defines* sense, but he explains it as the *mode of presentation* of the object which is the reference.

It is similarly natural to speak of sentences as a whole as having a sense[5]: this will be, for example, what the sentence has in common with its correct translation into other languages. This sense will be a function of the sense of any expressions occurring in the sentence; Frege called it a *Gedanke*, but it is convenient to translate this "proposition" rather than "thought" in order to avoid misleading psychological implications [Church, p. 26]. Following Frege's terminology that uniquely referring expressions and sentences *express* their sense, we may say that a sentence expresses a proposition which is its sense.

Clearly, (γ) two different sentences may express the same proposition (have the same sense); clearly, also (δ) the same sentence, if it contains some ambiguous word or phrase, may have two different senses and so express two different propositions. These results are akin to Strawson's *dicta* (α) and (β) above, and we shall pursue this affinity later.

As to (9) and (10), we can say that, since all uniquely referring expressions in both have the same reference, they both have the same truth-value, namely, are both true, but that, nevertheless, since the *sense* of "the morning star" is different from that of "the evening star," (9) and (10) have different senses and express different propositions. Thus the puzzle about identity ceases to be puzzling.

Frege also draws attention to the fact that many uniquely referring expressions (one of his examples is "the least rapidly converging series," but "the present king of France" will do as well) have a perfectly clear sense but no reference. What of a sentence, such as (1) at least if uttered today, which contains such an expression? Then the sentence as a whole may have a perfectly clear sense (express unambiguously a proposition), but it will *lack a truth-value*, be neither true nor false.[6] This is exactly Strawson's position, as rephrased by us earlier.

---

[5] Frege also allows that sentences have a reference, and this turns out to be their truth-value; but this piece of doctrine need not concern us here.

[6] See Frege's discussion of "Odysseus was set ashore at Ithaca while sound asleep" [Frege (1), pp. 62–3]. Frege also says [p. 61], with Strawson, that the use of a uniquely referring expression *presupposes* a reference for it (*cf.* footnote 3).

However, there is a difference between Frege's position and Strawson's. Frege never makes clear, at least in "On Sense and Reference," that the reference of a uniquely referring expression may vary from context to context, even though the sense does not change[7]: witness Strawson's example of "the present king of France" uttered in different reigns. Indeed, he suggests rather the reverse, that to a given sense there will correspond a unique reference, when he writes [Frege (1), p. 58]: "The regular connection between a sign, its sense, and its reference is of such a kind that to the sign there corresponds a definite sense and to that in turn a definite reference." If Frege did believe that sense determined a unique reference in this manner, then he seems clearly to have been wrong: it is its sense *taken in conjunction with the context of utterance* that in general determines the reference of a uniquely referring expression.

We are now in a position to compare Frege's notion of a proposition (the sense of a sentence) with Strawson's notion of a statement (what sentences are used to make): both, of course, are to be viewed as distinct from sentences, which are merely taken to be sequences of words belonging to a given language; but how do they relate to one another? A little reflection shows, I think, that they are distinct notions. For consider again our original imaginary situation in which (1) was uttered in different reigns: there, we agreed, different *statements* were made because different kings were referred to; but, inasmuch as the *sense* of (1) remains unchanged at the different dates of utterance, the *proposition* expressed (in Frege's sense) is the same. And now suppose a different situation: let (1) be uttered during the reign of Louis XIV and let:

(11) The previous king of France was bald

be uttered during the reign of Louis XV. Here two distinct sentences have been used to make the *same* statement (Louis XIV has been referred to on both occasions, and the same thing said about him); but inasmuch as the two sentences are evidently not synonymous, two distinct propositions have been expressed.

Similar remarks apply to (6) and (7). No one would claim that these two sentences had the same meaning; hence they express different propositions; but they may be used in the right context to make the same statement. Conversely, if you and I both say (6), then, though we make different statements, we express the same proposition, since we use the same words in the same sense.

Despite the similarity, therefore, between (α) and (β) on the one hand, and (γ) and (δ) on the other, statements that sentences may be used to make are quite distinct from the propositions that they may express. (α) and (β) hinge on the fact that reference is partly determined by contextual factors; (γ) and (δ) are explained by the fact that languages contain synonymous and ambiguous terms. It should be fairly clear by now that, given two utterances, the questions whether these are of the same sentence, or of the same statement, or of the same proposition, are quite independent of one another. Admittedly,

---

[7] Contrast Frege (2).

in the examples given so far where the same proposition has been expressed on two different occasions, the same sentence has in fact been used; but by changing one of the utterances to an utterance of the correct French translation of the same sentence, we vary the sentence without changing the proposition.[8]

We have then, intuitively at least, three distinct notions: that of a sentence, that of a statement and that of a proposition. All three—sentences, statements and propositions—may be said to be true or false, though no doubt in different senses. A sentence may be said to be true (false), relative to a particular context of utterance, if, in that context, it is used to make a true (false) statement. A proposition may be said to be true (false) relative to context of utterance, if there is a sentence, true (false) relative to that context, which expresses it.

Of course, in the last paragraph I have taken it for granted that one understands what it is for a statement to be true or false, and defined a sense of "true" and "false" for sentences and propositions in terms of this understanding. It is arguable, however, that the ascription of truth and falsity to sentences is in fact more basic than their ascription to statements, if only because it seems difficult to identify uses of distinct sentences as making the *same* statement without already knowing that the sentences, in their respective contexts, have the same truth-value, though, in fact, a way of doing so will be suggested later on. Perhaps, therefore, we should suppose it known what it is for a sentence to be true (false), and define a statement as true (false) if there is a true (false) sentence which in some context can be used to make it. This puts both propositions and statements on the same footing with respect to sentences, but involves also the assumption that all propositions and statements are expressible by or can be made by the use of some sentence in some language. How reasonable is this assumption? What, for example, of the proposition (statement) that neutrinos have no mass? This was presumably as true in 500 B.C. as it is today, though no doubt not expressible in any language in use at that date. This objection seems to me specious: a suitable account of languages and the sentences belonging to them can ensure that the English sentence "Neutrinos have no mass" existed to express the proposition in question as surely in 500 B.C. as it does now, though the speakers at that time were, for historical reasons, unable to make use of it to this end.[9] Yet may there not be propositions or statements which no language will ever find the means to express? I think here we can say what we please: whether we postulate such

---

[8] The hardest situation to envisage is that of two distinct utterances of the same sentence to make the same statement, even though two distinct propositions are expressed. But it can be done. The interested reader should consult (δ) before trying to work out an example for himself.

[9] Or, if this seems paradoxical, we may take the "is" of "there is a sentence" in the above definitions to be timeless, i.e. equivalent to "was, is or will be." The view adopted here, that languages and the sentences belonging to them are timelessly given, is a common one among logicians (see, for example, Church, p. 27, footnote 72). The contrasting picture, that languages change in time, is no doubt needed by linguists and historians of ideas. That these two standpoints are not necessarily exclusive of one another, i.e. that different concepts of meaning may be useful in different fields of study, is argued in Cohen.

entities or not, in any case they can have, for obvious reasons, little interest for us.

Sentences, then, will vary in their truth-value, as we have seen, from context to context; so for that matter will propositions, as the senses of sentences. By contrast, statements are true or false once and for all. The statement that Brutus killed Caesar is true for all time,[10] even though the sentence (8), which in normal contexts today would be used to make it, may in other contexts be false.

If a sentence containing a uniquely referring expression is used in a context such that this expression lacks a reference, then, according to both Frege and Strawson (at least as rephrased), the sentence lacks a truth-value. But it still has a sense, so that in addition to true and false propositions we have to admit truth-valueless ones. Are we also to admit truth-valueless statements? This seems to be merely a matter of terminology: we may either say that in these special contexts no statement at all has been made, or that in them the statement made is neither true nor false. Strawson himself seems committed to the latter alternative [Strawson (3), p. 175], but the former seems just as viable as a form of expression; if we follow it, then all statements are either true or false, which may be viewed as a satisfactory consequence.

One merit of employing all three notions of sentence, statement and proposition is that it reveals a deep-seated ambiguity in the notion of *saying the same thing*. If I say "I am hot," and you say, to me, "You are hot," then in one sense we have said the same thing (made the same statement). If I say "I am hot," and you say "I am hot," then in a different sense we have said the same thing (uttered the same sentence). If I say "I am hot," and you, being French, say "J'ai chaud," then we have neither uttered the same sentence nor made the same statement; but there is still a sense in which we have said the same thing, namely, expressed the same proposition.

Another merit of employing the notion of proposition in addition to those of sentence and statement is that it enables us to give an account of such fairly common idioms as "it used to be true that . . ." and "it is no longer true that . . . ." Suppose we say:

(12) It used to be true that the population of London was under 4 million, but this is no longer true today.

Then what is it that used to be true and is no longer true? This cannot be a statement because, as we have seen, statements are timelessly true or false, and cannot change their truth-value. Nor can we say that (12) is about a certain *sentence*, say:

(13) The population of London is under 4 million,

---

[10] It was true, presumably, even before 44 B.C., when it might have been made by using the sentence "Brutus will kill Caesar." Here we brush by the problem of future contingents. There is space only for me to say that "Che sera sera" is a truth of logic, not a version of determinism.

to the effect that it was true at a certain date and is not true today. For sentences, as sequences of words, belong to some language, and if we wish to talk about them, we need to employ some special device for doing so, such as quotation marks. Thus (12) has to be contrasted with:

(14) "The population of London is under 4 million" used to be true, but is no longer true today,

in that (14) is a sentence, in English, about an English sentence, in a way that (12) is not. This point emerges clearly if we translate (12) and (14) into another language, say French; for a correct translation of (14) will leave the words inside the quotation marks *unchanged*, yielding a French sentence about an English sentence. It should be obvious that the "that"-clause in (12), as opposed to the quotation marks in (14), make reference to a *proposition*, namely, the proposition expressed by the English sentence (13), and the whole sentence says of this proposition that it used to be true, but is no longer so.

Incidentally, we here observe an ambiguity in the "that"-construction. While sentences are perhaps best referred to by the device of quotation marks, both statements and propositions can equally well be referred to by "that"-clauses,[11] and only a careful inspection of surrounding circumstances will reveal in general which is being spoken of. It is perhaps worth adding that the distinction between statements and propositions is only worth upholding in any case in connection with those sentences whose truth-value is contextually dependent. In the case of general sentences belonging to the natural sciences ("All ravens are black") or to mathematics ("$7 + 5 = 12$"), truth-value is timelessly given, and there seems little point and little sense in making a distinction here between the propositions expressed and the statements such sentences are used to make.

But this matter may be clearer when we have seen whether the notions of proposition and statement, so far discussed merely intuitively, can be defined with any rigour. For so far all we have really seen is that propositions in Frege's intuitive sense are distinct from statements in Strawson's, and that to uphold the distinction may help to clarify some puzzles. To these other questions we should now turn.

It must be admitted, in the first instance, that the ontological status of statements and propositions is peculiar. For they are certainly not linguistic entities, as sentences are—do not belong to a language—nor are they spatio-temporal particulars, locatable at a position in space-time, like physical objects or even events and processes. Thus, there is a *prima facie* case against postulating them, if only in accordance with Ockham's razor, unless we have to. On the other hand, as abstract objects, they are perhaps no worse than qualities

---

[11] So, for that matter, can *facts*. But perhaps facts are best construed as a kind of proposition or statement: see D. Mitchell, pp. 109–15.

(e.g. colours) or even works of art such as symphonies (as opposed to their performances, which no doubt are spatio-temporal events).

Whether the notion of proposition can ultimately be justified depends really on whether the notion of meaning or sense and the closely related notion of synonymy can be adequately defined. A vigorous attack on all these notions has been launched in recent years by Quine.[12] It would be beyond the scope of this paper even to attempt to meet Quine's criticisms, but a few rather scattered remarks may be in order.

In the first place, there is little doubt that we shall have a clear criterion for the identity of propositions if the notion of synonymy can be made clear. For we can say that two sentences S_1 and S_2 express the same proposition just in case they are synonymous. However, Quine argues [Quine (2), Ch. II, esp. paras. 14–16] that no firm empirical basis can be given to the general notion of synonymy, mainly on the grounds of a fundamental indeterminacy in the idea of translation from one language to another: different and incompatible translational schemes (which Quine calls analytical hypotheses) can be adopted which all fit the empirical linguistic data. Still, the situation here seems no worse than in science generally, where it is commonly the case that discrepant theories will fit all the facts—a choice is made rather on grounds of simplicity, elegance and the like. Quine himself admits [Quine (2), p. 75]:

> The indefinability of synonymy by reference to the methodology of analytical hypotheses is formally the same as the indefinability of truth by reference to scientific method. Also the consequences are parallel. Just as we may meaningfully speak of the truth of a sentence only within the terms of some theory, so on the whole we may meaningfully speak of interlinguistic synonymy only within the terms of some particular system of analytical hypotheses.

It seems to be a consequence of this view that, once a translational scheme is more or less agreed on (as is certainly the case between the familiar European languages, but may be less true in the case of, say, English and Hawaiian), we *may* speak profitably of synonymy. Of course, there is no doubt that the notion of synonymy is in need of proper clarification. But Quine has not shown that such clarification is unobtainable; rather he has revealed some of the difficulties that might stand in the way of it. It may, indeed, be some comfort that the notion of truth, with which few logicians or philosophers would wish to dispense, is only different in degree of clarity perhaps but not in kind from the notion of synonymy. I conclude that synonymy, as a basis for propositional identity, if unsatisfactory, is certainly not doomed by Quine's arguments. There is certainly, however, no room here to attempt to clarify the notion.

Later in the same book [Quine (2), Ch. VI, esp. paras. 40, 42, 43], Quine launches a new and separate attack on propositions, on the grounds that they are in any case theoretically dispensable. He claims first that any sentence

---

[12] See Quine (2), for the most recent onslaught: the related literature is cited in his bibliography.

(such as (1), (6) or (7)) which is dependent on context for its truth-value can be expanded, in a given context of utterance, into an *eternal sentence* which is not so dependent and will be absolutely true or false; examples of sentences which are already eternal sentences in this sense are, of course, theoretical sentences in mathematics and the sciences. The expansion consists in the first instance of replacing tensed verbs by tenseless ones, together with time-indicators; secondly, of replacing "indicator words" such as "I," "now" and "this," by exact and objective spatio-temporal references; and thirdly, of filling out incomplete descriptions and proper names so as to secure a unique for-all-time reference [Quine (2), p. 194]. It may, however, be doubted whether this expansion is in principle always possible; certainly Quine nowhere illustrates it. We have already seen that (8) is not in fact eternal, if only because there may be dogs called Brutus and Caesar. But even if we expanded (8) into:

(15) Brutus, the Roman Senator who lived from 85 to 42 B.C., killed Caesar, the Roman general who lived from 102 to 44 B.C.,

we are in theory no better off. For it is in principle still possible that there were two such senators or two such generals, or even two Romes. No such definite description or proper name, however "complete," carries a *logical* assurance of contextfree unique reference, which is what Quine's expansion seems to demand.[13]

However, we may leave this difficulty on one side for the moment. Supposing that the expansion into eternal sentences is possible, Quine contends that talk about propositions can in most contexts be replaced by talk about eternal sentences, so that there is no need to postulate the existence of the former. Several remarks are pertinent here. First, it is *statements* rather than *propositions* that eternal sentences might replace.[14] For eternal sentences, like statements but unlike propositions, are supposed to be timelessly true or false. Hence there is no reason to suppose that eternal sentences can hope to explain idioms such as those exemplified in (12). Propositions are in fact called in, as distinct from statements, precisely as the constant senses, from context to context, of *non*-eternal sentences. Secondly, it is not clear that eternal sentences will do in place of *statements*, just because eternal sentences belong to a language in a way that statements do not, so that distinctions such as that between (12) and (14) are obscured. A sentence to the effect that an eternal sentence is true is a sentence about a language, in a way that a sentence to the effect that the corresponding statement is true is not.[15] Thirdly, it is arguable that it is theoretically simpler to postulate the existence of statements as entities than to rely on a putative and complex translation into eternal sentences—provided, at least, that clear criteria for the identity of statements can be given.

---

[13] This argument is chiefly prompted by a similar line of thought in Strawson (2), Ch. 1, part 1.

[14] Quine concedes this at the beginning of para. 43 of Quine (2).

[15] Quine [Quine (2), 213–14] rejects this sort of argument, but only because it turns on the notion of synonymy.

It is to this problem, therefore, leaving propositions behind, that we shall now turn. What are sufficient and necessary conditions for two sentences uttered in different contexts to be used to make the same statement in Strawson's sense? Up to now, we have merely relied on examples, such as (6) and (7), and the intuitive notion that the sentences should both, in their separate ways, say the same thing about the same thing.

Let us consider, first of all, an example slightly different from (6) and (7). Suppose A says:

(16) The driver of the van had no hair,

and B says:

(17) Tom Jones was bald,

and the contexts of their utterances are such that they are both, the one by using a definite description and other by using a proper name, referring to the same person at the same date. Then, since to be bald is just to have no hair, we incline to say that they are both making the same statement by using different sentences in different contexts. Now to say that to be bald is to have no hair is to say that anyone is bald if, and only if, he has no hair. Let the context in which A utters (16) be c_1, and the context in which B utters (17) be c_2. Then sufficient and necessary conditions for (16) in c_1 to be used to make the same statement as (17) in c_2 are (a) that the reference in c_1 of "the driver of the van" be the same as the reference in c_2 of "Tom Jones," and (b) that anyone is bald if, and only if, he has no hair.

To generalize slightly: let $S(a)$ be a sentence containing the uniquely referring expression a, and $T(b)$ be a sentence containing the uniquely referring expression b. For any uniquely referring expression e let $rc(e)$ stand for the reference of e in context c. Then $S(a)$ in c_1 is used to make the same statement as $T(b)$ is used to make in c_2 if, and only if, $rc_1(a) = rc_2(b)$,[16] and for any x, $S(x)$ if, and only if, $T(x)$.

This definition is not completely correct as it stands, partly because of complexities concerning quotation-marks into which it would be tedious here to enter. A more serious defect is that it only takes account of sentences containing one uniquely referring expression each; but generalization to the case of many such is fairly straightforward.[17]

A consequence of the definition, as we should hope, is that $S(a)$ in c_1 is true if, and only if, $T(b)$ in c_2 is true, if they are used to make the same statement. For suppose $S(a)$ is true in c_1. Then, since, for any x, $S(x)$ if, and only if, $T(x)$, in particular $S(a)$ if, and only if, $T(a)$. Hence $T(a)$ is also true in c_1. But, since $rc_1(a) = rc_2(b)$, $T(b)$ will be true in c_2. The converse argument is similarly seen to hold. Thus, our criterion for the same statement is such that statements are absolutely true or false, a *desideratum* for the notion of statement.

---

[16] We use " = " here, as is logical practice, simply to mean "is the same as."

[17] To be explicit and formal, for a moment, $S(a_1, \ldots, a_n)$ in c_1 makes the same statement as $T(b_1, \ldots, b_n)$ in c_2 if, and only if, $rc_1(a_i) = rc_2(b_i)$ for $1 \leqslant i \leqslant n$ and, for any $x_1, \ldots, x_n$, $S(x_1, \ldots, x_n)$ if, and only if, $T(x_1, \ldots, x_n)$. The order in which uniquely referring expressions occur in the two sentences can be rearranged to suit this definition.

A word should be added concerning the matter of time-reference. For it to be the case that (16) and (17), in their respective contexts, are used to make the same statement it is clearly necessary that both A and B be referring to the same date. Hence, strictly, the sentences should be expanded by the insertion of words such as "yesterday" or "on 1st January 1962 A.D.," in order to include such a reference. But such words as "yesterday," "today," "then," "now" raise new problems for us. For suppose A to say at 10:15:

(18) Tom Jones is now bald,

and to utter the same sentence again at 10:30 on the same day. Has he made the same statement or not? We are inclined to say yes; but, given that by a near-miracle Tom Jones might have gone bald precisely between 10:15 and 10:30, this answer will apparently commit us to saying that the same statement may be false when first made by A, and true on the second occasion—a conclusion at conflict with our view that statements are timelessly true or false.

One solution is to say that "now," taken strictly, refers only to an instant of time, so that A's two utterances of (18) do indeed make different statements, since the reference of "now" changes with the time of utterance. But let us suppose that "now" may more loosely refer to a fairly indeterminate *period* of time surrounding the moment of utterance but sufficiently broad to include, let us say, 16 minutes each way; hence A's two utterances make the *same* statement by our present criteria, since his two "now"s refer to the same vague period. ("Today," "this afternoon," etc., do refer to periods in this way.) Then, in *that* sense of "now," it is not at all clear what the truth-value of (18) in *either* context is, in case Tom Jones loses his hair during the period in question: it is neither clearly false at 10:15, in view of what is about to happen, nor clearly true at 10:30, in view of what has just happened. And this unclearness is brought about by the inexactness of the predicate "bald" rather than by the vague reference of "now." If this inexactness is removed, then the truth-value of the sentence (18) in its two contexts of utterance will be settled in the same way, and we have again no exception to our conclusion that statements are timelessly true or false.

A rather tighter criterion for two sentences $S(a)$ and $T(b)$ to be used to make the same statement is to stipulate not merely that, for any x, $S(x)$ if, and only if, $T(x)$, but rather that it be *analytic* that, for any x, $S(x)$ if, and only if, $T(x)$. I shall not pursue this suggestion further here, but it is worth remarking that, while the notion of analyticity is as suspect from Quine's point of view as the notion of synonymy (with which it is indeed interdefinable), the actual criterion put forward above for the identity of statements contains, so far as I can see, no features with which Quine would quarrel. It is, in textbook jargon, a purely extensional rather than an intensional notion.

So far, I have argued that propositions are acceptable as entities if synonymy can be clarified sufficiently, and that this undertaking has not been shown by Quine to be hopeless; and that reasonable criteria for the identification of statements can also be put forward, so that they too, if we wish it, can be admitted into our ontology. There is a final question, raised earlier, which

I should like to discuss, concerning the admissibility of truth-valueless sentences, statements and propositions.

Let us admit, with Strawson, that for some sentences used in some contexts the question of the truth-value of the statements there made by using them can fail to arise, and that this will often if not always be the case where the sentence in question contains a uniquely referring expression which in that context fails to refer. We may say, with Quine, that such situations give rise to *truth-value gaps* [Quine (1), p. 439]. Then it is a standing tendency of modern formal logic, as exemplified in Russell's theory of descriptions, to close these gaps: to assign, that is to say, a definite truth-value, true or false, to sentences in this situation. Can this tendency be justified? Certainly not, of course, if it is one of the functions of formal logic faithfully to reflect every idiosyncracy of ordinary speech.

But formal logic is not called upon to do this. One of the aims of formal logic is to regularize and standardize the conditions under which sound argumentation takes place, and in situations where ordinary speech is unclear or undecided this very standardization may involve departures from familiar practice. So long as these are recognized as departures, so long, that is to say, as we admit that a formal analysis of an ordinary sentence is not necessarily equivalent to it in every respect, it is hard to see that harm is done.

In the particular case of uniquely referring expressions, it is a presumption of ordinary discourse that a speaker using one in a given context knows enough about the context to ensure that unique reference is in fact secured by his use of it. Thus, sentence (1) will only ordinarily be used by speakers in contexts in which there is in fact a unique king of France. And in such contexts Russell's analysis into (4) is entirely satisfactory: for it will render (1) true in case that unique king is bald, and false in case that unique king is not bald. If this presumption is not satisfied, then in ordinary speech we may say that the sentence is neither true nor false, while, as logicians following Russell, we shall say that it is false. It is almost possible to say that it is the speaker's own fault if what he says turns out to be false on logical analysis; for he should have made sure that there was a unique present king of France before uttering (1). One can say, in fact, that a certain logical fallacy is committed by someone who employs in a reasoning situation a uniquely referring expression which lacks a unique reference.[18]

It may be conceded that the logician has the right, in standardizing the conditions for sound argument, to depart to some extent from ordinary language, and yet be argued that any such departure should at least be justified. In the case in question, why is it more satisfactory to treat (1) as false when there is no unique king of France, rather than neither true nor false? The answer, I think, is very simple: the gain to the logician in closing truth-value gaps is that he is then able to treat *all sentences as true or false*—an assumption

---

[18] This fallacy is committed by Euclid, *Elements*, I, 1, who speaks of "the point at which the circles intersect" before he has shown that the circles in question intersect at all (in fact, they intersect at *two* points). The fallacy vitiates his proof, in fact.

which leads to an extremely simple logical structure. The familiar method of truth-table testing becomes available to him as a means of recognizing certain sentences as embodying logical laws, and so on. On the other hand, if the logician is to acknowledge truth-value gaps in his formal work, a considerable price in complexity has to be paid. And the desire to stay close to ordinary usage does not seem a sufficient motive for paying this price.[19]

If this *pragmatic* justification for the closing of truth-value gaps is felt to be worthy, we may accept Russell's theory of descriptions for purposes of logical analysis, and conclude that in logic we have no need for truth-valueless sentences, and consequently no need for truth-valueless propositions or statements either.[20] And we are finally able to see that the original dispute between Strawson and Russell rests on a misunderstanding: if Russell thought he was expounding the ordinary usage of definite descriptions, then probably he was wrong in much the way that Strawson describes; but this is in no way to impugn the utility of Russell's theory as a logical tool for the analysis of sentences used in serious argumentation. This utility has been demonstrated over and over again by the employment of the theory in the logical analysis of mathematical and scientific arguments.

Bibliographic References

Church, A. *Introduction to Mathematical Logic.* 2nd edition. Princeton, N.J.: Princeton University Press, 1956.

Cohen, L. J. *The Diversity of Meaning.* London: Methuen & Co. Ltd., 1962.

Frege, G. [1]. "Ueber Sinn und Bedeutung." *Zeitschrift fuer Philosophie und Philosophische Kritik,* C(1892), 25–50; English tr. ("On Sense and Reference") in Geach-Black, pp. 56–78.

———. [2]. "Die Gedanke." In *Beitäge zur Philosophie des Deutschen Idealismus,* (1919); English tr. ("The Thought: A Logical Inquiry") by A. and M. Quinton, *Mind,* LXV (1956), 289–311.

Geach, P. T. and M. Black. *Translations from the Philosophical Writings of Gottlob Frege.* Oxford: Basil Blackwell, 1952.

Mill, J. S. *A System of Logic.* London: Parker, 1843.

Mitchell, D. *Introduction to Logic.* London: Hutchinson & Co. (Publishers) Limited, 1962.

Quine, W. V. [1]. "Mr. Strawson on Logical Theory." *Mind,* LXII (1953), 433–51.

———. [2]. *Word and Object.* Cambridge: MIT Press, 1960.

Russell, B. A. W. "On Denoting." *Mind,* XIV (1905), 479–93.

---

[19] Similar observations are made in Cohen, pp. 250–1.

[20] This conclusion is exaggerated, of course; for we have not considered how to treat proper names (e.g. "Odysseus") which may ordinarily fail of reference; for a treatment of the problems raised by them, see Quine (2), para. 37.

Strawson, P. F. [1]. "On Referring." *Mind*, LIX (1950), 320–44.

———. [2] "Truth." *Proc. of the Aristotelian Society*, Supp. Vol., XXIV (1950), 129–56.

———. [3]. *Introduction to Logical Theory*. London: Methuen & Co. Ltd., 1952.

PETER GEACH

3.3 *Assertion*

A thought may have just the same content whether you assent to its truth or not; a proposition may occur in discourse now asserted, now unasserted, and yet be recognizably the same proposition. This may appear so obviously true as to be hardly worth saying; but we shall see it *is* worth saying, by contrast with erroneous theories of assertion, and also because a right view of assertion is fatal to well-known philosophical views on certain other topics.

I shall call this point about assertion *the Frege point*, after the logician who was the first (so far as I know) to make the point clearly and emphatically. In some of Frege's writings the point is made in the course of his expounding some highly disputable theories, about sense and reference and about propositions' being complex names of logical objects called "truth-values." But the dubiousness of these theories does not carry over to the Frege point itself. Admitting the Frege point does not logically commit us to these theories; as a matter of history, Frege already made the point in his youthful work, *Begriffsschrift*, many years before he had developed his theories of sense and reference. Those theories are more defensible than some philosophers allow; but to discuss them here would only obscure the main issue.

When I use the term "proposition," as I did just now, I mean a form of words in which something is propounded, put forward for consideration; it is surely clear that what is then put forward neither is *ipso facto* asserted nor gets altered in content by being asserted. Unfortunately, this use of "proposition," formerly a well-established one, has become liable to be misconstrued, for the word has been appropriated by certain theorists for a supposed realm of timeless abstract "intentional" objects, whose principle of individuation has thus far eluded capature in any clearly formulable criterion. Philosophers have weakly surrendered the term "proposition" to these theorists and cast around for some substitute; the ones they have come up with—"sentence" and "statement"—have been rather unhappy. It would be preferable to stick to the old use of "proposition," which has never quite gone out; if we need

Reprinted from *The Philosophical Review*, LXXIV, No. 4 (1965), 449–65, by permission of the author and of *The Philosophical Review*.

a substitute for "proposition" in the newfangled use, it will not be difficult to find one—let us say, "propositional content."

The use of "sentence" in the sense that "proposition" used to have often calls forth rather nagging objections. What is wrong with thus using "sentence" is quite a simple matter, and one is not likely to be misled once it has been pointed out: namely, that different occurrences of what is the same sentence by grammatical criteria may be different propositions by logical criteria. Moreover, the fact that "sentence" is a grammatical term makes it sound awkward as applied to logical or mathematical formulas, which could of course be naturally called "propositions." But nobody ought to plume himself on replacing "sentence" in this use by "statement"; for "statement" is a far more dangerously misleading term. It is obvious that our discourse may and does contain unasserted propositions; the notion of an unasserted statement may appear a contradiction in terms. If we want to allow for the possibility of a *statement's* being made nonassertorically, we have to strive against the natural use of the expressions "statement" and "making a statement," and the natural use may be too strong—*tamen usque recurret.*

This is not imaginary danger. In his essay *If, So, and Because* Professor Ryle actually uses the paradoxical sound of "unasserted statement" as a reason for censuring as deceptive the "code style" of the *modus ponens*: "if *p*, then *q*; but *p*, therefore *q*." The recurrences of the letters "*p*" and "*q*" suggest that a logician can recognize something identifiable which occurs now asserted, now unasserted; a statement, Ryle argues, cannot thus have two ways of occurring. Ryle even finds it a misleading feature of ordinary modern English that the same form of words may be used now to make a statement, now in an "if" or "then" clause; surely things would be clearer if we had to alter the mood or word order of clauses in framing a hypothetical.

A hypothetical statement, Ryle argues, cannot state a relation between two statements, because the antecedent and consequent clauses are not assertoric and thus not statements; statements are neither used nor mentioned in the hypothetical. Ryle toys with an idea of Cook-Wilson, who had similar worries, that a hypothetical asserts a relation between two questions; he decides against this, on the score that one who makes a hypothetical statement does not actually either pose or mention any questions. Ryle's final solution is that in a hypothetical the antecedent and consequent are indents or specifications for possible statements; they are no more themselves statements than a license to export bicycles is itself a bicycle—only confusion is easier because these clauses, like the statements for which they are indents, consist of words.

Thus far Ryle. His argument fully illustrates the dangers of "statement" as a logical term. If we speak rather of propositions, Ryle's difficulties vanish. What Ryle calls "making a hypothetical statement" is what I call "asserting a hypothetical proposition"; in making such an assertion the speaker is certainly putting forward the antecedent and consequent for consideration, so that they are undoubtedly propositions too, but he is of course not thus far stating or asserting them to be true.[1] He may then go on to assert the antecedent, and from this go on further to assert the consequent. This does not alter the force of either proposition; if in some languages the propositions need rewording when asserted, this is just an idiotism of idiom. The only thing that is wrong with the "code style" of the *modus ponens*—"if p then q; but p; therefore q"—is that we might profitably follow Frege in having an explicit assertion sign " $\vdash$ if p, then q; $\vdash p$; *ergo* $\vdash q$." (Here "p" and "q" are schematic propositional letters; any concrete interpretation of them as propositions yields a valid argument.)

Ryle argues that in "if p, then q; but p therefore q" the hypothetical is not a premise co-ordinate with "p," as the "code style" suggests, but is rather a license to perform the inference "p, therefore q" when you have the premise "p." His argument against the more conventional two-premise account of *modus ponens* is that if we needed to supply "if p, then q" as a premise for the inference of "q" from "p," then by parity of reasoning we should need to supply "if both p and if p then q, then q" as a premise for the inference of "q" from "p" and "if p then q"—and then we should have started on a vicious regress, the one made notorious by Lewis Carroll in "What the Tortoise Said to Achilles."

I do not think there is anything in this. Particular readings of "p" and "q" may make "p, therefore q" into a logically valid argument; but it is not in general logically valid, and if not, then no power in heaven or earth can issue me a "license" that makes it logically valid. On the other hand, "if p, then q; but p; therefore q" *is* logically valid; and this means precisely that the two premises "if p then q" and "p" are sufficient to yield the conclusion "q," so that there is no place for introducing an extra premise, and a regress never gets started.

The Frege point is thus something we need to grasp in order to understand *modus ponens*; it is no less needed in the doctrine of truth-functional connectives. Thus "p *aut* q" is true if and only if just one of the propositions represented by "p" and "q" is true, and "p *vel* q" is true if and only if at least one of them is true. (I use Latin words as connectives to dodge the idiotic but seemingly perennial discussion as to the "proper" meaning of "or" in ordinary language.) Now even if the proposition represented by "p *vel* q" or by "p *aut* q" is itself taken to be an asserted proposition, "p" will not be asserted in this context, and neither will "q"; so if we say that the truth value of the whole proposition is determined by the truth values of the disjuncts, we are committed to recognizing that the disjuncts have truth values independently of being actually asserted.

Oxford-trained philosophers often say nowadays that a sentence can have a truth value assigned to it only in that it is "used to make a statement" in

---

[1] A good instance of the tangles that the use of "statement" leads to is to be found on p. 88 of Strawson's *Introduction to Logical Theory* (London, 1952): "for each hypothetical statement," we are told, "there could be made just *one* statement which would be the antecedent"; but of course it *would not* be the antecedent if it were a statement.

a given context. If this were literally true, then a truth-functional account of "*p vel q*" or of "*p aut q*" would be impossible: for the disjunct clauses represented by "*p*" and "*q*" would not be being "used to make statements" in a context in which only the disjunction was asserted, and would thus not have any truth values for the truth value of the whole proposition to be a function of. This consequence is not often drawn: Strawson's *Logical Theory*, for example, does not raise this as a fundamental objection to the very idea of truth-functional logic, as on his own premises he might well do.

Nor can the idea of only statements' having truth values be reconciled with truth-functional logic by saying that the truth value of a disjunctive sentence used to make a statement in a given context is a function of the truth values that the disjuncts would have had if they had been separately used to make statements in the same context. For this is not even plausible unless we mean by "the truth values that the disjuncts would have had" those that they would have had if *without change of sense* they had been used to make statements in the given context. But if we can tell what truth values the disjuncts "would have had," given the force they actually have in the context of their occurrence, then a denial that they actually have truth values is quite empty; it just evinces a determination not to *call* unasserted propositions "true" or "false," and this is what Professor Antony Flew has aptly called a conventionalist sulk.

The truth-functional "and" occasions another error to those who miss the Frege point. Thinking in terms of statements, they see no need to recognize a conjunctive statement "*p* and *q*" as distinct from the pair of statements "*p*," "*q*"; if you recognize conjunctive propositions as a kind of proposition, you may as well say, Mill remarked, that a team of horses is a kind of horse or a street a kind of house. But it is clear that in contexts of the kind "*p* and *q*, or else *r*" or again "if *p* and *q*, then *r*," where we have a conjunction occurring unasserted, the conjunction is a single proposition, a logical unit, not a pair of separate propositions.

In another sort of case, however, we do get a pair of assertions rather than the assertion of a conjunctive proposition. Any statement containing a phrase of the form "the fact that *p*" is exponible as a pair of assertions, one of which asserts the content of the "that" clause. For example, an assertion "Jim is aware of the fact that his wife is unfaithful" is equivalent to the pair of assertions "Jim is convinced that his wife is unfaithful" and "Jim's wife is unfaithful."

We cannot analyze such an assertion as the assertion of a single conjunctive proposition—in our case, of "Jim is convinced that his wife is unfaithful, and Jim's wife is unfaithful." For this proposition conforms, as we might expect, to the law of excluded middle; it can be substituted for "*p*" in "either *p* or it is not the case that *p*" so as to get a logical truth. But we cannot so substitute "Jim is aware of the fact that his wife is unfaithful"; since "either Jim is aware of the fact (and so forth) or it is not the case that Jim is aware of the fact (and so forth)" is not a mere instance of excluded middle, but is something that can be admitted only by one who takes it to be a fact that Jim's wife is unfaithful. Like the original assertion about Jim, this is a double-barreled assertion; an assertion about Jim's wife gets smuggled in along with, and under cover of, an instance of the excluded middle.

This assertoric force of "the fact that" comes out even in requests, commands, questions, and so forth. If I ask, "Is Jim aware of the fact that his wife is deceiving him?" I am not just asking a question; I am asserting that Jim's wife is deceiving him. The question as I pose it cannot be properly answered "Yes" or "No" by someone who does not accept this assertion; a corresponding but unloaded question would be "Is Jim convinced that his wife is deceiving him?" In such cases, we do get a separate asserted proposition, which for clarity's sake ought to be separately enunciated; this points up the contrast with the genuine unity of a conjunctive proposition.

Negation often gets paired off with assertion as its polar opposite; this is another mistake over the Frege point—one exposed by Frege himself in his paper, *Negation*. Just as I can put forward a proposition "s" without asserting "s" as true, so I can put forward the negation of "s" without rejecting "s" as false—for example, when this negation occurs as part of a longer proposition, in a context, say, of the form "p and q, or else r and not s." Thus logic in any case demands the use of a negation sign which is not polarly opposed to the assertion sign and does not express rejection of what is negated; and when a proposition is rejected, we may equally well conceive this as asserting the negation of a proposition.

Indeed, there are serious objections to any other way of conceiving the matter. It is clear that "if not q, then r; but not q; therefore r" is a mere special case of the *modus ponens* "if p, then r; but p; therefore r." But if we regarded rejecting a proposition as different from asserting the negation of a proposition, we should have here two quite different logical forms; we might write these as follows, using Lukasiewicz' sign $\dashv$ for a rejection opposed to Frege's assertion $\vdash$:

$\vdash$ If not q, then r; $\dashv$ q; ergo $\vdash$ r.
$\vdash$ If p, then r; $\vdash$ p; ergo $\vdash$ r.

Plainly this is a futile complication. All we need in logic for assertion and negation is two signs—the assertion sign, and a negation which does *not* convey rejection (as in "if not q . . ."); whatever is more than these, as Frege says, cometh of evil.

Frege's logical doctrine suggests a parallel doctrine in the psychology of belief. Christians and Muslims have called each other unbelievers; but this does not mean that there are two polarly opposed activities or attitudes, believing and unbelieving, and that the point at issue is which side goes in for which; it is just that what Christians believe is opposed to what Muslims believe. Believing, like seeing, has no polar opposite, though contrary dogmas may be believed, as contrary colors may be seen. An incredulous man is not a man who goes in for unbelieving, but a man who believes the contrary of what people tell him.

On this view of beliefs, there will be a sharp difference between belief and appetitive or emotional attitudes; for love and hate, desire and aversion, pleasure and pain, are opposite as attitudes, not by being attitudes toward opposite objects. The distinction of "pro" and "contra," of favorable and unfavorable attitudes, has its place only in the realm of appetite, will, and passion, not in that of belief; this shows the error in treating religious beliefs as some sort of favorable attitude toward something.

I was speaking just now about assertoric sentences containing a phrase "the fact that p," which are to be expounded as pairs of asserted propositions, not as single propositions. A similar complication occurs in some other cases: thus, an assertoric sentence of the form "A has pointed out that p" is exponible as the double-barreled assertion of "A has maintained that p" and of "p" itself. Again (an example of Frege's), "A fancies that p" is exponible as the double-barreled assertion of "A thinks that p" and of "it is not the case that p." Assertions thus exponible will certainly retain part of their assertoric force when put, for example, into an "if" clause; thus, one who asserts, "If A is under the illusion that p, then q," does not mean "If A is under the impression that p, but it is not the case that p, then q"—rather, he both asserts, "It is not the case that p" and asserts, "If A is under the impression that p, then q." Notice that no such complication arises for the verb "know." Use of the expression "... knows that p" does not commit the speaker to asserting "p"; to adapt an example of Hintikka's, one who asserted in 1916, "If Russell knows that Wittgenstein is dead, then Wittgenstein is dead" would not himself be asserting, "Wittgenstein is dead."

In these special cases, we have an expression that endows a clause within a sentence (or the negation of such a clause) with an assertoric force that is, so to speak, inalienable, and is not canceled even by prefixing an "if" to the whole sentence in which the clause occurs. Apart from these special cases, which for simplicity's sake I shall henceforth ignore, there is no expression in ordinary language that regularly conveys assertoric force. The conjunction "if," which generally cancels all assertoric force in the "if" clause, can grammatically be prefixed to any sentence of assertoric form without altering its grammatical structure or even the way it sounds; somebody who fails to hear the first word of my "if" clause may actually mistake what I say for an assertion, so that like Alice I have to explain, "I only said 'if'."

In written or printed language, however, there is something of a clue to what is meant assertorically. There is a certain presumption—though of course it can be upset in various ways—that an author of a nonfictional work intends a sentence to be read as an assertion if it stands by itself between full stops and grammatically can be read as an assertion. The assertoric force of a sentence is thus shown by its *not* being enclosed in the context of a longer sentence.

Possibly there is something corresponding to this in the realm of thoughts; possibly a thought is assertoric in character unless it loses this character by occurring only as an element in a more complicated thought. In Spinoza's example, the boy whose mind is wholly occupied with the thought of a winged horse, and who lacks the adult background knowledge that rules out there being such a thing, cannot but assent to the thought of there being a winged horse. This would be a neat solution to the problem of how thought is related to judgment, but I do not insist on it; there may be fatal objections. Anyhow, if this theory is true, I need not recant anything I have so far said; it would still be true that a thought may occur now unasserted, now asserted, without change of content. But if I had to choose between this theory and the Frege point, this is what I would reject.

There have been a number of attempts to treat some expression of ordinary language as carrying with it the assertoric force. I think these attempts all miscarry; apart from the exceptional cases of double-barreled assertions, previously mentioned, there is no naturally used sign of assertion, but only the negative clue to assertoric force that I have just been discussing. That is why Frege had to devise a special sign.

Let us consider some attempts to read assertoric force into some ordinary expression. We want our assertions to be true, or to be taken for true; so it is natural to cast "it is true that . . ." for the role of assertion sign. But this will not do, for this expression may come in an unasserted clause without any change of meaning; nor is there any equivocation in an argument "it is true that p; and if it is true that p, then q; ergo q." Indeed, whether asserted or not, "it is true that p" is scarcely to be distinguished from the plain "p." This does not mean that "true" is a useless sign, for it is not always trivially eliminable— not, for example, from "what the policeman said is true" nor from "there is many a true word spoken in jest." But the identification of the assertoric force with the meaning of "it is true that . . ." is just a mistake.

Oddly enough, Frege himself committed a similar mistake in his *Begriffsschrift*. He regarded an unasserted proposition as a sign for the circumstance (*Umstand*) that so-and-so, and called his assertion sign a "common predicate" in all assertions—one predicating of the relevant "circumstance" that it actually obtains. But "the circumstance that p is one that actually obtains," like "it is true that p," hardly differs from plain "p," and any such proposition may unequivocally occur now asserted, now unasserted. In later works Frege saw his mistake, and gave up any attempt to explain the assertion sign by classifying it as a predicate, or as any other sort of sign; it is necessarily *sui generis*. For any other logical sign, if not superfluous, somehow modifies the content of a proposition; whereas this does not modify the content, but shows the proposition is being asserted.

Another concept often confused with assertoric force is the concept of existence. To be sure, people guilty of this confusion would say it is improper to speak of the concept of existence; for the assertion sign adds no concept, so their very confusion makes them deny that the verb "exists" or "there is" adds a concept either. What "there is an A" or "an A exists" adds over and above the bare term "an A" is not a concept, they say; rather, there is a transition from the bare concept of an *A* to a judgment, and it is the act of judgment that mirrors existence (or, they would perhaps prefer to say, being).

In recent philosophy the best-known advocate of this view is Gilson. Gilson fathers it on Aquinas; but I really do not see how it can be extracted from Aquinas' text. (Aquinas says a judgment is true when it says a thing is as it is; I suppose Gilson would read Aquinas as saying that a judgment is true when a thing IS as the judgment says the thing IS.) The actual provenance of Gilson's view seems to me to be different: he acknowledges an anticipation of it by Brentano, and there is an even clearer anticipation in Hume. "It is far from being true, that in every judgment which we form, we unite two different ideas; since in that proposition, *God is*, or indeed, any other, which regards existence, the idea of existence is no distinct idea, which we unite with that of the object . . . . The act of the mind exceeds not a single conception; and the only remarkable difference, which occurs on this occasion, is, when we join belief to the conception, and are persuaded of the truth of what we conceive" (*Treatise*, Book I, Section vii).

Be the doctrine whose it may, it is hopelessly erroneous. For one thing, an existential proposition, like any other proposition, may occur unasserted without change of content; we get this in such propositions as "either there is a Loch Ness monster or many observers have been unreliable," or, again, "if there are canals on Mars then Mars is inhabited." An existential proposition need not express a *judgment* of existence. And let no one retort that in such cases, just because there is no judgment, there is no existential proposition; for even the unasserted proposition "there is an *A*" is quite different in content from the bare term "an *A*." As Frege pointed out, we cannot substitute "there is a house" for "a house," in "Priam lived in a house of timber"; we cannot even substitute "there being a house." Again, as Aristotle pointed out, "goat-stag" by itself gives us nothing true or false, but "there is a goat-stag" does give us something false; and, we may add, the falsity of this proposition in no way depends on anybody's asserting it, or else we could not assert with truth, "It is false that there is a goat-stag," if nobody ever asserted there is.

In Buridan's *Sophismata* the point I have been making is brought out in an elegant ontological disproof of God's existence. Buridan points out that if I just say "a God" or "a horse" I have not yet said anything true or false, but if I add the verb "exists," then I have said something true or false; therefore, "a God exists" must signify something more than the bare term "a God" signifies. But, on the orthodox view, only after the world was created was there something more than God for the proposition "a God exists" to signify; therefore before the creation it did not signify anything more; therefore it was not true; therefore God did not then exist!

Of course, Buridan did not mean us to take this very seriously; there is in fact a patent equivocation in the use of "something more." Before the world was created, there would not be "something more" than God that could be signified by a name; but the sense in which "exists" in "a God exists" or "a horse exists" signifies "something more" than the grammatical subject is clearly not that it names another object. All the same, it does signify something more, in the sense of introducing a new *ratio* or concept into the proposition, whether the proposition is asserted or not.

The Hume-Brentano-Gilson thesis cannot be intelligibly stated if it is true; it claims that existence is unconceptualizable and can be grasped only in existential judgments, but this very claim is not an existential judgment and treats existence as conceptualizable. This suicide of a thesis might be called *Ludwig's self-mate*; but Wittgenstein at least ended his *Tractatus* by saying that now he must shut up, and he was fairly brief in coming to that conclusion.

Just as the "is" of existence has been supposed to carry assertoric force, so has the "is" of predication (which some people, two thousand years and more after Plato's *Sophist*, will wantonly confuse with the existential "is"). I can be brief about this; since the copulative verb "is" occurs in unasserted clauses, it cannot carry assertoric force. In fact, I should agree with Frege that the "is" of predication, *die blosse Copula*, has no force at all. There is no logical difference between the predicates "surpasses Frank at chess" and "better at chess than Frank"; the requirement of the latter for an "is" is mere idiom, and there is no such requirement in Russian nor in classical Greek (so that Aristotle can say casually that a predication is formed with or without the verb εἶναι "to be").

A more important and pervasive error has been the idea that the predicate itself carries the assertoric force: a predicate is often explained as what is *asserted* of something in a proposition. To be sure, someone who talks this way need not be ascribing assertoric force to the predicate; his "asserted" may be the German "*ausgesagt*" rather than "*behauptet*"; but his way of talking is ill advised and will certainly confuse people (as I found before I mended my own ways in the matter). And in many writers there is actual error on the point; here, indeed, one might well fear lest "mountainous error be too highly heapt for truth to overpeer." I shall not here try to state a correct view of predication; it is enough to point out that since one and the same unambiguous predicate may occur now in an asserted proposition, now in an unasserted clause, the predicate cannot have any inherent assertoric force. Again, if predicates have assertoric force, how can they ever be used in questions?

A recent example of this error about predicates may be found in Strawson's work *Individuals*. Rightly supposing that there is something important underlying the old distinction of subject and predicate, Strawson tries to explain the predicate as the term whose insertion into a proposition conveys assertoric force (in his own words: the term that is "introduced" in "the assertive or propositional style"). Strawson does indeed recognize that there are non-asserted occurrences of propositions; but he regards these as derivative, the asserted occurrences as primary, and is thus still able to think predicates can be characterized as the terms to which propositions in their primary occurrence owe their assertoric force.

Accepting the Frege point, we know that no term of any proposition gives the proposition assertoric force; for the same term might occur without any change of sense in an unasserted occurrence of the proposition. For predicates, the matter is especially clear: any predicate may be negatively predicated, and then, even if the proposition is asserted, the predicate is not being asserted of anything. Nor can negative predication be called a secondary use or occurrence of a predicate; "*P*" and "not *P*" are grasped together, and one is no more prior to the other than one side of a boundary line you draw is logically prior to the other side; as medievals said, *eadem est scientia oppositorum*.

What distinguishes predicates from subjects, I suggest, is not that they are assertoric in force, but that by negating a predicate we can get the negation of the proposition in which it was originally predicated (plainly, there is nothing analogous for subject terms). This feature of predicates was already brought out very clearly by Aristotle, but is wholly ignored by Strawson. All the same, it may be just because predicates are negatable that Strawson (with many others) came to think of them as bearing the assertoric force; if, as is often fancied, assertion and negation are Siamese twins, then they must share a home.

Predicates of a philosophically exciting sort have been badly misconstrued because assertoric force has been supposed to inhere in them. Theory after theory has been put forward to the effect that predicating some term "*P*"— which is always taken to mean: predicating "*P*" assertorically—is not describing an object as being *P* but some other "performance"; and the contrary view is labeled "the Descriptive Fallacy." All these theories are constructed on the same pattern and admit, as we shall see, of the same refutation.

The briefest statement of some of these theories ought to suffice. To call a kind of act bad is not to characterize or describe that kind of act but to condemn it. To say a proposition is true is not to describe it but to confirm or concede it. To say "He hit her" is not to state what happened, but to ascribe the act to him as a matter of legal or moral responsibility; and such an ascription is a verdict, not a statement, about him. To say "That looks red" is not to describe how a thing looks but to assert tentatively that it is red. Or again, the difference between a set of statements of sensible appearance and a statement that there is now, for example, an orange on the mantelpiece is supposed to be illuminated by considering a difference between a jury's accepting that all the evidence points to guilt and their actually delivering a verdict. To say "I know that *p*" is no statement about my own mental capacities, but is an act of warranting my hearer that *p*. And so on and so on.

Each of these theories is devised for a certain class of assertoric sentences; very often we find the theory will not even fit all of the class it was meant for. Thus, whatever plausibility there may be in analyzing "I know that Smith is the murderer" as "Smith is the murder—I warrant you that," no such analysis will fit "I know who is the murderer"; for here I do not even tell you, still less give you my warranty, who the murderer is. Again, "He hit her" is a very loaded example—what a swine to hit a woman!—but suppose "she" were a lioness that he shot? In that case, "He hit her" could be a mere bit of narrative and undoubtedly propositional in character; are we to suppose that the logical character of the utterance, its being or not being propositional at all, is radically affected if "she" is not a lioness but a woman?

But these particular objections are of minor interest. In all the kinds of case I have mentioned, the very same sentence can occur in an "if" clause; and to such occurrences the anti-descriptive theories will not apply. For example, in saying, "If what the policeman said is true, then . . . ," I am not confirming or agreeing with what the policeman said; in saying, "If he hit her, then . . . ," I am not ascribing the act to him, and still less giving some moral or legal verdict about him; in saying, "If that looks red, then . . . ," I am not even tentatively asserting that the thing is red.

Of course, the anti-descriptive theorist will reply that his theory was not meant to cover such cases—that the same form of words, after all, may have different uses on different occasions. This possibility of varying use, however, cannot be appealed to in cases where an ostensibly assertoric utterance "p" and "If p, then q" can be teamed up as premises for a *modus ponens*. Here, the two occurrences of "p," by itself and in the "if" clause, must have the same sense if the *modus ponens* is not to be vitiated by equivocation; and if any theorist alleges that at its ostensibly assertoric occurrence "p" is really no proposition at all, it is up to him to give an account of the role of "p" that will allow of its standing as a premise.

This task is pretty consistently shirked. For example, Austin would maintain that if I say assertorically, "I know Smith's Vermeer is a forgery," this is not an asserted proposition about me, but an act of warranting my hearers that the picture is a forgery. Austin never observed that this alleged nonproposition could function as a premise obeying ordinary logical rules, in inferences, like this:

> I know Smith's Vermeer is a forgery.
> I am no art expert.
> If I know Smith's Vermeer is a forgery, and I am no art expert, then Smith's Vermeer is a very clumsy forgery.
> *Ergo*, Smith's Vermeer is a very clumsy forgery.

Still less did Austin discuss *how* a nonproposition could be a premise. But failing such discussion, Austin's account of "I know" is valueless.

The theory that to call a kind of act "bad" is not to describe but to condemn it is open to similar objections. Let us consider this piece of moral reasoning:

> If doing a thing is bad, getting your little brother to do it is bad.
> Tormenting the cat is bad.
> *Ergo*, getting your little brother to torment the cat is bad.

The whole nerve of the reasoning is that "bad" should mean exactly the same at all four occurrences—should not, for example, shift from an evaluative to a descriptive or conventional or inverted-commas use. But in the major premise the speaker (a father, let us suppose) is certainly not uttering acts of condemnation: one could hardly take him to be condemning just *doing a thing*.

Here it is only fair to mention one exception to the bad practice of anti-descriptive theorists that I have just censured; for Mr. Hare does offer some sort of account of how acts of condemnation, though they are not propositions, can serve as premises. Hare argues forcibly that there is a logic of imperatives, although imperatives are not propositions; and he holds that condemnations like "tormenting the cat is bad" and imperatives like "Do not torment the cat" are alike in being species of prescriptive or action-guiding language. But we need not go into details of this; for Hare has offered us no imperative-logic model that even looks likely to yield an account of such moral reasoning as occurs in my example; and the fourfold unequivocal occurrence of "bad" in that example is enough to refute the act-of-condemnation theory.

Of course an *asserted* proposition in which "bad" is predicated may be *called* an act of condemnation. But this is of no philosophical interest; for then being an act of condemnation is nothing that can be put forward as an *alternative* to being a proposition. Moreover, this holds good only of asserted propositions, whereas "bad" may be predicated without change of force in unasserted clauses. The assertoric force attaches no more to "bad" than to other predicates.

The magnitude and variety of philosophical errors that result from not seeing the Frege point justifies a missonary zeal in the matter. When philosophers fail to see the Frege point, the reason, all too often, is that they have in general little regard for formal logic as a philosophical instrument; and this comes out in other ways too—as in M. Gilson's assertion that formal logic cannot cope with existential judgments, or in some Oxford philosophers' assertion that formal logic cannot cope with ordinary language. For myself, I think logicians have an all-purpose utility, as accountants have for all kinds of business; and resentment at an accountant's inquiries is not a healthy sign in any business. When a philosopher manifests annoyance at someone's seeking counter examples to a theory that runs smoothly enough for the philosopher's own chosen examples, he acts like a delinquent clerk: "Why should the accountant meddle with *that* book, when these other books are all right?" But logicians, like accountants, are paid to look out for discrepancies.

JOHN R. SEARLE

3.4   *Austin on Locutionary and Illocutionary Acts*

In attempting to explore Austin's notion of an *illocutionary act* I have found his corresponding notion of a *locutionary act* very unhelpful and have been forced to adopt a quite different distinction between illocutionary acts and propositional acts.[1] I think this difference is more than a matter of taxonomical preference and involves important philosophical issues—issues such as the nature of statements, the way truth and falsehood relate to statements, and the way what sentences mean relates to what speakers mean when they utter sentences. In this paper I want to explain my reasons for rejecting Austin's distinction and for introducing certain other distinctions, and in so doing to show how these questions bear on some of the larger philosophical issues.

I

The main theme of Austin's *How to Do Things With Words* is the replacement of the original distinction between performatives and constatives by a general theory of speech acts. The original distinction (the "special theory") was supposed to be a distinction between utterances which are statements or descriptions, and utterances which are acts, such as, for example, promises, apologies, bets, or warnings. It is supposed to be a distinction between utterances which are sayings and utterances which are doings. Austin shows in detail how attempts to make the distinction precise along these lines only show that it collapses. One is tempted to say that whereas constatives can be true or false, performatives cannot be true or false, but felicitous or infelicitous, depending on whether they are performed correctly, completely, and sincerely in accord with some antecedent set of conventions. But as Austin's careful researches show, certain performatives can be assessed as true or false (for example, warnings), and constatives can be assessed in the felicitous-infelicitous dimension as well (for example, an utterance of the sentence "All John's children are asleep" is infelicitous if John has no children). Eventually the conclusion becomes obvious: making a statement or giving a description is just as much performing an act as making a promise or giving a warning. What was originally supposed to be a special case of utterances (performatives) swallows the general case (constatives), which now turn out to be only certain kinds of

---

Reprinted from *The Philosophical Review*, LXXVII, No. 4 (1968), 405–24, by permission of the author and of *The Philosophical Review*.

[1] J. R. Searle, "What is a Speech Act?," in *Philosophy in America*, ed. by Max Black (London, 1965); and J. R. Searle, *Speech Acts, An Essay in the Philosophy of Language* (London: Cambridge University Press, 1969), Ch. 2. [See selection 7.4 below, pp. 614–28.]

speech acts among others. Statements, descriptions, and so forth are only other classes of illocutionary acts on all fours, as illocutionary acts, with promises, commands, apologies, bets, and warnings.

So far so good. But now Austin introduces a second distinction which will replace in the general theory what was hoped to be achieved by the performative-constative distinction in the special theory, the distinction between locutionary and illocutionary acts. As initially presented it is the distinction between uttering a sentence with a certain *meaning,* in one sense of "meaning" which Austin characterizes as "sense and reference" (the locutionary act) and uttering a sentence with a certain *force* (the illocutionary act). This can be illustrated by the following example. A serious literal utterance[2] by a single speaker of the sentence "I am going to do it" can be (can have the force of) a promise, a prediction, a threat, a warning, a statement of intention, and so forth. Yet the sentence is not ambiguous; it has one and only one literal meaning. It has one sense, and different utterances of it can have the same reference. Thus different utterances of the sentence with that literal meaning, given sameness of reference, can be one and only one locutionary act. They can be different locutionary tokens of one locutionary type. But those same utterances with the same sense and reference could be any of a number of different illocutionary forces, because, for example, one could be (could have the force of) a promise, while another was a prediction, yet another a threat, and so forth. Utterances which were different tokens of the same locutionary type could be tokens of different illocutionary types.

Now the first difficulty that one encounters with Austin's distinction is that it seems that it cannot be completely general, in the sense of marking off two mutually exclusive classes of acts, because for some sentences at least, meaning, in Austin's sense, determines (at least one) illocutionary force of the utterance of the sentence. Thus, though the sentence "I am going to do it" can be seriously uttered with its literal meaning in any number of illocutionary acts, what about the sentence "I hereby promise that I am going to do it"? Its serious and literal utterance must be a promise.[3] It may on occasion be other illocutionary acts as well, but it must at least be a promise—that is, an illocutionary act of a certain type. The meaning of the sentence determines an illocutionary force of its utterances in such a way that serious utterances of it with that literal meaning will have that particular force. The description of the act as a happily performed locutionary act, since it involves the meaning of the sentence, is already a description of the illocutionary act, since a particular illocutionary act is determined by that meaning. They are one and the same act. Uttering the sentence with a certain meaning is, Austin tells us, performing a certain locutionary act; uttering a sentence with a certain force is performing a certain illocutionary act; but where a certain force is part of

---

[2] I contrast "serious" utterances with play-acting, teaching a language, reciting poems, practicing pronunciation, etc., and I contrast "literal" with metaphorical, sarcastic, etc.

[3] Assuming that the act is successful, that is, that the conditions of successful utterance are satisfied.

the meaning, where the meaning uniquely determines a particular force, there are not two different acts but two different labels for the same act. Austin says that each is an abstraction from the total speech act, but the difficulty is that for a large class of cases—certainly all those involving the performative use of illocutionary verbs—there is no way of abstracting the locutionary act which does not catch an illocutionary act with it. Abstracting the meaning of the utterance will necessarily abstract an illocutionary force wherever that force is included in that meaning.

The *concept* of an utterance with a certain meaning (that is, the concept of a locutionary act) is indeed a different concept from the *concept* of an utterance with a certain force (that is, the concept of an illocutionary act).[4] But there are many sentences whose meaning is such as to determine that the serious utterance of the sentence with its literal meaning has a particular force. Hence the *class* of illocutionary acts will contain members of the *class* of locutionary acts. The concepts are different but they denote overlapping classes. For cases such as the performative use of illocutionary verbs the attempt to *abstract* the locutionary meaning from illocutionary force would be like abstracting unmarried men from bachelors. So our first tentative conclusion—we shall have to revise it later—is that the locutionary-illocutionary distinction is not completely general, because some locutionary acts are illocutionary acts.[5]

As it stands there is an easy, but in the end unsatisfactory, way out of this difficulty. A locutionary act is defined by Austin as the uttering of certain vocables with a certain sense and reference. But if that is absolutely all there is to the definition, then, it could be argued, the objection just raised is not really valid; because even for such cases as an utterance of "I hereby order you to leave" there is still a distinction between uttering the sentence with (that is, as having) a certain sense and reference on the one hand (the locutionary act) and actually bringing off a *successfully* performed illocutionary act. For example, I might utter the sentence to someone who does not hear me, and so I would not succeed in performing the illocutionary act of ordering him, even though I did perform a locutionary act since I uttered the sentence with its usual meaning (in Austin's terminology in such cases I fail to secure "illocutionary uptake"). Or to take a different example, I might not be in a position to issue orders to him, if, say, he is a general and I am a private (and so the "order" would again be "infelicitous," in Austin's terminology).

---

[4] Throughout this paper I use these as equivalent. But on one possible interpretation Austin meant to distinguish illocutionary acts of type F from utterances with illocutionary force F on the grounds that an utterance may have force F even though the purported act is not, as a whole, successful, and hence has not strictly speaking been performed. I grant that as a possible interpretation, but nothing in my arguments hinges on accepting my interpretation. The arguments are statable in essentially the same form on either interpretation.

[5] Austin was familiar with this difficulty. I discussed it with him in Hilary term of 1956, and he mentioned it briefly in his lectures of that term. It has also been discussed by L. J. Cohen, "Do Illocutionary Forces Exist," *Philosophical Quarterly*, XIV (1964), 118–37; and briefly by J. O. Urmson, "J. L. Austin," *Encyclopedia of Philosophy*, ed. by Edwards, Vol. I. Cohen unfortunately seems to conclude that there are no such things as illocutionary forces. This conclusion seems unwarranted.

So, one might argue, Austin's distinction between locutionary and illocutionary acts is still intact even for cases containing the performative use of illocutionary verbs. It is a distinction between the simple meaningful utterance and the successfully performed complete illocutionary act. The successfully performed illocutionary act requires all sorts of conditions not required by the locutionary act.

But this answer to my original objection is unsatisfactory for at least two reasons. First, it reduces the locutionary-illocutionary distinction to a distinction between trying and succeeding in performing an illocutionary act. Since the conditions of success for the performance of the act are—except for the general conditions on any kind of linguistic communication[6]—a function of the meaning of the sentence, then uttering that sentence seriously with its literal meaning will be at least purporting to perform an illocutionary act of giving an order. And the only distinction left for such sentences will be the distinction between that part of trying to perform an illocutionary act which consists in uttering the sentence seriously with its literal meaning, and actually succeeding in performing an illocutionary act, a much less interesting distinction than the original distinction between the locutionary act and the illocutionary act.[7]

But secondly, even if we adopt this way out it now leaves us with two quite different distinctions, for the distinction between this part of trying and actually succeeding is different from the original distinction between an utterance with a particular meaning and an utterance with a particular illocutionary force.

So, at this preliminary stage of our discussion, we find two quite different distinctions hiding under the locutionary-illocutionary cloak. One is an interesting but not completely general (in the sense of marking off two mutually exclusive classes) distinction between the meaning of an utterance and the force of the utterance, the second is a not so interesting but general distinction between a certain part of trying and succeeding in performing an illocutionary act.

II

All this, it seems to me, is still very tentative; and it is now time to probe deeper in an effort both to push the objection to the bottom and at the same time to do full justice to the subtlety of Austin's thought.

Austin analyzes the locutionary act into three parts. The *phonetic act* is the act of uttering certain noises, the *phatic act* is the act of uttering certain vocables or words, and the *rhetic act* is the act of using those vocables with a more or less definite sense and reference. Taken together, these constitute the locutionary act. Each of these is an "abstraction," as are indeed the locutionary and illocu-

---

[6] In part these conditions involve what I elsewhere call input-output conditions (Searle, *op. cit.*, ch. 3) and Austin calls conditions of illocutionary uptake (Austin, *op. cit.*, Lecture 9).

[7] Furthermore, Austin himself repeatedly insists that the distinction between "attempt and achievement" applies to all the kinds of acts. *Cf.*, e.g., *op. cit.*, p. 104.

tionary acts themselves. When he contrasts locutionary and illocutionary acts, Austin gives the following as examples of the contrast.

> Locution: He said to me "Shoot her!" meaning by "shoot" shoot and referring by "her" to *her*.
> Illocution: He urged (or advised, ordered, etc.) me to shoot her.
> Locution: He said to me, "You can't do that."
> Illocution: He protested against my doing it [pp. 101–102].

Notice that here he uses the *oratio recta* (direct quotation) form to identify locutionary acts and *oratio obliqua* (indirect quotation) to identify illocutionary acts. The sentence which identifies the locutionary act contains quotation marks, the sentence which identifies the illocutionary act does not. But on page 95, when discussing the internal structure of locutionary acts, he distinguishes within the locutionary act between the phatic act and the rhetic act, and here he identifies the phatic act by using the *oratio recta* form of quotation marks and identifies the rhetic act by using indirect quotation.

> He said "I shall be there" (phatic). He said he would be there (rhetic).
> He said "Get out" (phatic). He told me to get out (rhetic).
> He said "Is it in Oxford or Cambridge?" (phatic). He asked whether it was in Oxford or Cambridge (rhetic).

Prima facie it seems inconsistent to identify the locutionary act on one page by the use of direct quotation, contrasting it with the illocutionary act which is identified by the use of indirect quotation, and then on another page to identify the rhetic part of the locutionary act by the use of indirect quotation, contrasting it with another part of the locutionary act, the phatic act, which is identified by the use of direct quotation. But as Austin sees, it is not *necessarily* inconsistent, because since the locutionary act is defined as uttering a sentence with a certain sense and reference (meaning) then that sense and reference will determine an appropriate indirect speech form for reporting the locutionary act. For example, if the sentence is in the imperative, the sense of the imperative mood determines that the appropriate *oratio obliqua* form will be "He told me to" or some such; if it is in the interrogative, it will be "He asked me whether." Both of these are precisely examples Austin gives. But now notice a crucial difficulty with the indirect forms: the verb phrases in the reports of *rhetic* acts invariably contain *illocutionary* verbs. They are indeed very general illocutionary verbs, but they are illocutionary nonetheless. Consider "He told me to X." Does not the form "He told me to" cover a very general class of illocutionary forces, which includes such specific illocutionary forces as "He ordered, commanded, requested, urged, advised, me to"? The verbs in Austin's examples of indirect speech reports of rhetic acts are all illocutionary verbs of a very general kind, which stand in relation to the verbs in his reports of illocutionary acts as genus to species. That is, there are different species of the genus telling someone to do something—for example, ordering, requesting, commanding—but "tell . . . to . . ." is as much an illocutionary verb as any of these others, and a little reflection will show that it meets Austin's criteria for illocutionary verbs. In short, on close examination we discover that in characterizing rhetic acts, Austin has inadvertently characterized them as illocutionary acts. Furthermore, there is no way to give an indirect speech report of a rhetic act (performed in the utterance of a complete sentence) which does not turn the report into the report of an illocutionary act. Why is that?

We saw above that the original locutionary-illocutionary distinction is best designed to account for those cases where the meaning of the sentence is, so to speak, force-neutral—that is, where its literal utterance did not serve to distinguish a particular illocutionary force. But now further consideration will force us to the following conclusion: no sentence is completely force-neutral. Every sentence has some illocutionary force potential, if only of a very broad kind, built into its meaning. For example, even the most primitive of the old-fashioned grammatical categories of indicative, interrogative, and imperative sentences already contain determinants of illocutionary force. For this reason there is no specification of a locutionary act performed in the utterance of a complete sentence which will not determine the specification of an illocutionary act. Or, to put it more bluntly, on the characterization that Austin has so far given us of locutionary as opposed to illocutionary acts, there are (in the utterance of complete sentences) no rhetic acts as opposed to illocutionary acts at all. There are indeed phonetic acts of uttering certain noises, phatic acts of uttering certain vocables or words (and sentences), and illocutionary acts, such as making statements, asking questions, giving commands, but it does not seem that there are or can be acts of using those vocables in sentences with sense and reference which are not already (at least purported) illocutionary acts.

Austin might seem to be granting this when he says that to perform a locutionary act is in general and *eo ipso* to perform an illocutionary act (p. 98). But his point here is that each is only a separate *abstraction* from the total speech act. He still thinks that locutionary and illocutionary acts are separate and mutually exclusive abstractions. The point I am making now is that there is no way to abstract a rhetic act in the utterance of a complete sentence which does not abstract an illocutionary act as well, for a rhetic[8] act is always an illocutionary act of one kind or another.

In Section I we tentatively concluded that some members of the class of locutionary acts were members of the class of illocutionary acts. It now emerges that *all* the members of the class of locutionary acts (performed in the utterance of complete sentences) are members of the class of illocutionary acts, because every rhetic act, and hence every locutionary act, is an illocutionary act. The concepts *locutionary* act and *illocutionary* act are indeed different, just as the concepts *terrier* and *dog* are different. But the conceptual difference is not sufficient to establish a distinction between separate classes of acts, because just as every terrier is a dog, so every locutionary act is an illocutionary act. Since a rhetic act involves the utterance of a sentence with a certain meaning and the sentence

---

[8] It has to be emphasized that we are considering here (and throughout) utterances of whole sentences. If we confine ourselves to certain parts of sentences we shall be able to make a distinction. More of this in Sec. IV, pp. 272–75.

invariably as part of its meaning contains some indicator of illocutionary force, no utterance of a sentence with its meaning is completely force-neutral. Every serious literal utterance contains some indicators of force as part of meaning, which is to say that every rhetic act is an illocutionary act.

So if the distinction is construed, as I think it must be, as between mutually exclusive classes of acts, however abstract they may be, it collapses. There is still left a distinction between the literal meaning of a sentence and the intended force of its utterance (as illustrated by the example "I am going to do it") but that is only a special case of the distinction between literal meaning and intended meaning, between what the sentence means and what the speaker means in its utterance, and it has no special relevance to the general theory of illocutionary forces, because intended illocutionary force is only one of the aspects (sense and reference are others) in which intended speaker meaning may go beyond literal sentence meaning.

Austin sometimes talks as if in addition to the meaning of sentences there were a further set of conventions of illocutionary force; but in precisely those cases where there is a distinction between force and meaning, the force is not carried by a convention but by other features of the context, including the intentions of the speaker; and as soon as force is tied down by an explicit convention it becomes, or in general tends to become, part of meaning. For example, we have a convention that "How do you do?" is a greeting used when being introduced and not a question, but then that is part of the meaning of this idiom. Someone who thinks that this sentence is paraphrasable as "In what manner or condition do you perform?" or who takes it as permutable into such questions as "How does he do?" or "How do I do?" has not understood the meaning of this (contemporary English) idiom.

Where does that leave us now? Austin's original taxonomy included the following kinds of acts:

Locutionary   phonetic
                   phatic
                   rhetic
Illocutionary

What we really argued is that the rhetic act as originally characterized has to be eliminated and, with it, the locutionary act as originally characterized. So we are left with the following:

Phonetic
Phatic
Illocutionary

For any of these we can distinguish between trying and succeeding, so *that* distinction will not resurrect any special distinction between locutionary and illocutionary acts; and furthermore there is an additional distinction between what a speaker means by the utterance of a sentence and what that sentence means literally, but that distinction will not preserve a *general* distinction between locutionary meaning and illocutionary force, since the locutionary meaning of sentences always contains some illocutionary force potential, and hence the locutionary meaning of utterances determines (at least some) illocutionary force of utterances.

III

Underlying the objections I have been making to Austin's account are certain linguistic principles, which it seems to me will enable us to offer a diagnosis of what I am claiming are the limitations in that account. I shall state them baldly and then try to explain what they mean and what relevance they have to the present discussion.

1. Whatever can be meant can be said. I call this the Principle of Expressibility.
2. The meaning of a sentence is determined by the meanings of all its meaningful components.
3. The illocutionary forces of utterances may be more or less specific; and there are several different principles of distinction for distinguishing different types of illocutionary acts.

1. Often we mean more than we actually *say*. You ask me, "Are you going to the party?" I say, "Yes." But what I mean is "Yes, I am going to the party," not "Yes, it is a fine day." Similarly, I might say, "I'll come," and mean it as a promise—that is, mean it as I would mean "I hereby promise I will come," if I were uttering that sentence seriously and meaning literally what I said. Often I am unable to say exactly what I mean; even if I want to, because I do not know the words (if I am speaking French, say) or, worse yet, because there are no words or other linguistic devices for saying what I mean. But even in cases where I am unable to say exactly what I mean it is in principle possible to come to be able to say what I mean. I can, in principle if not in fact, always enrich my knowledge of the language I am speaking; or, more radically, if the language is not rich enough, if it simply lacks the resources for saying what I mean, I can, in principle at least, enrich the language. The general point, however, is that whatever one can mean one can, in principle if not in fact, say or come to be able to say. The lexical and syntactical resources of languages are indeed finite. But there are no limits in principle to their enrichment. I think this is an important principle, but I am not going to develop all of its consequences here.
2. The principle that the meaning of a sentence is entirely determined by the meanings of its meaningful parts I take as obviously true; what is not so obviously true, however, is that these include more than words (or morphemes) and surface word order. The meaningful components of a sentence include also its deep syntactic structure and the stress and intonation contour of its utterance. Words and word order are not the only elements which determine meaning.

3. The illocutionary forces of utterances may be more or less indeterminate. Suppose I ask you to do something for me. My utterance may be, for example, a request or an entreaty or a plea. Yet the description "I asked you to do it" is, though less specific than any of these, nonetheless a correct description. Furthermore, I may not at all know myself which of the specific possibilities I meant it as. My own intentions may have been indeterminate within this range (which is not to say that they can be completely indeterminate—that I may not know if it was a statement, an order, or a question). There are really two separate points here. One is that *descriptions* of illocutionary acts may be more or less determinate. The second and more important, which I now wish to emphasize, is that the acts themselves may be more or less definite and precise as to their illocutionary force.

One might think of illocutionary acts (and hence illocutionary verbs) as on a continuum of determinateness of specificity, but even this would not do full justice to the complexity of the situation, for under the rubric "illocutionary forces" are all sorts of different principles of distinction. Here, by way of example, are four different principles of distinction: the point or purpose of the act (for example, the difference between a question and a statement), the relative status of the speaker and hearer (for example, the difference between a command and a request), the degree of commitment undertaken (for example, the difference between an expression of intent and a promise), the conversational placing and role of the act (for example, the difference between a reply to what someone has said and an objection to what he has said).

Now how does all this relate to Austin's distinctions? Consider point 3 first. Austin was much impressed by the surface structure of natural languages, particularly English. The fact that he could get a list of "the third power of ten" illocutionary verbs was important to his conception of illocutionary acts. But there is nothing mutually *exclusive* about all the members of the list nor is the total list necessarily *exhaustive*. The same utterance may be correctly described by any number of different illocutionary verbs on the list, or the act may have been so special and precise in its intent that none of the existing words can quite characterize it exactly. If we think of illocutionary forces as existing on a continuum or continua of specificity (point 3), then the fact that our existing English verbs stop at certain points and not others on some continuum is a more or less contingent fact about English. It so happens that we have the word "promise," but we might not have had it. We might have had ten different words for different kinds of promises, or indeed we might instead have had only one word to cover our present classes of promises, vows, and pledges.

A neglect of point 3, then, seems one possible explanation of why Austin did not see that the supposedly locutionary verb phrases "tell someone to do something," "say that," "ask whether" are as much illocutionary verb phrases as "state that," "order someone to," or "promise someone that." They are indeed more general, but that makes their relation to the more specific verbs that of genus term to species term or determinable term to determinate term. It does not, as Austin seems to suggest (on p. 95),[9] make their denotation a different type of act altogether.

Now let us consider point 1. A commonplace of recent philosophizing about language has been the distinction between sentences and the speech acts performed in the utterances of those sentences. Valuable as this distinction is, there has also been a tendency to overemphasize it to the extent of neglecting the Principle of Expressibility. There is indeed a category distinction between the sentence and the illocutionary act performed in its utterance, but the illocutionary act or acts which can be performed in the utterance of a sentence are a function of the meaning of the sentence. And, more importantly, according to the Principle, for every illocutionary act one intends to perform, it is possible to utter a sentence the literal meaning of which is such as to determine that its serious literal utterance in an appropriate context will be a performance of that act. Austin's distinction between locutionary and illocutionary acts is supposed to be a distinction between uttering a sentence with a certain meaning, in the sense of sense and reference, and uttering it with a certain force; but according to the Principle, whenever one wishes to make an utterance with force F, it is always possible to utter a sentence the meaning of which expresses exactly force F, since if it is possible to mean (intend) that force it is possible to say that force literally. Often, of course, as I have noted, and as Austin emphasizes, the said-meaning and the meant-force come apart, but this is, though quite common, a contingent fact about the way we speak and not a conceptual truth about the concept of illocutionary force.

A neglect of the Principle of Expressibility (point 1) seems to be one of the reasons why Austin overestimated the distinction between meaning and force. It is a consequence of the Principle, together with the point that every sentence contains some determiners of illocutionary force, that the study of the meanings of sentences and the study of the illocutionary acts which could be performed in the utterances of sentences are not two different studies, but one and the same study from two different points of view. This is so because, to repeat, for every possible illocutionary act a speaker may wish to perform there is a possible sentence (or sequence of sentences) the serious literal utterance of which under appropriate circumstances would be a performance of that illocutionary act, and for every sentence some illocutionary force potential is included in the meaning of the sentence. So there could not, according to my analysis, be a general and mutually exclusive distinction between the meaning and the force of literal utterances, both because the force which the speaker intends can in principle always be given an exact expression in a sentence with a particular meaning, and because the meaning of every sentence already contains some determiners of illocutionary force.

A neglect of point 2 is also involved in our diagnosis. Austin characterized the rhetic act in terms of uttering a sentence with a certain sense and reference.

---

[9] In fact, "ask" crops up on p. 161 as well, as an example of an "expositive" illocutionary verb.

The difficulty, however, with this characterization is that the *terminology* of sense and reference inclines us to focus on words, or at most phrases as the bearers of sense and reference. But of course deep syntactic structure, stress, and intonation contour are bearers of meaning as well, as we noted in point 2. One of the possible reasons why Austin neglected the extent to which force was part of meaning is that his use of the Fregean terminology of sense and reference shifted the focus of emphasis away from some of the most common elements in the meaning of a sentence which determine the illocutionary force potential of the sentence: deep syntactic structure, stress, intonation contour (and, in written speech, punctuation). If one thinks of sentential meaning as a matter of sense and reference, and tacitly takes sense and reference as properties of words and phrases, then one is likely to neglect those elements of meaning which are not matters of words and phrases, and it is often precisely those elements which in virtue of their meaning are such crucial determinants of illocutionary force.

IV

Though I do not think Austin was completely successful in characterizing a locutionary-illocutionary distinction, there are certain real distinctions which underlie his effort. The first I mentioned is a distinction between that part of trying which consists solely in making a serious literal utterance and actually succeeding in performing an illocutionary act. The second is the distinction between what a sentence means and what the speaker may mean in uttering it, with the special case of serious literal utterance where the meaning of the sentence uttered does not completely exhaust the illocutionary intentions of the speaker in making the utterance. Now I wish to consider a third distinction which I think Austin had in mind.

He says (pp. 144–45):

> With the constative utterance, we abstract from the illocutionary (let alone the perlocutionary) aspects of the speech act, and we concentrate on the locutionary. ... With the performative utterance, we attend as much as possible to the illocutionary force of the utterance, and abstract from the dimension of correspondence with facts.

These and other remarks suggest to me that Austin may have had in mind the distinction between the content or, as some philosophers call it, the proposition, in an illocutionary act and the force or illocutionary type of the act.[10] Thus, for example, the proposition that I will leave may be a common content of different utterances with different illocutionary forces, for I can threaten, warn, state, predict, or promise that I will leave. We need to distinguish in the total illocutionary act the type of act from the content of the act. This distinction, in various forms, is by now common in philosophy and can be

---

[10] Austin once told me he thought a distinction could be made along these lines—but it is not clear that he intended the locutionary-illocutionary distinction to capture it.

found in philosophers as diverse as Frege, Hare, Lewis, and Meinong. If we wish to present this distinction in speech act terms (within a general theory of speech acts) a taxonomically promising way of doing it might be the following. We need to distinguish the illocutionary act from the propositional act— that is, the act of *expressing the proposition* (a phrase which is neutral as to illocutionary force). And the point of the distinction is that the identity conditions of the propositional act are not the same as the identity conditions of the total illocutionary act, since the same propositional act can occur in all sorts of different illocutionary acts. When we are concerned with so-called constatives we do indeed tend to concentrate on the propositional aspect rather than the illocutionary force, for it is the proposition which involves "correspondence with the facts." When we consider so-called performatives we attend as much as possible to the illocutionary force of the utterance (for example, "I know you *said* you'd come, but do you *promise*?").

Symbolically, we might represent the sentence as containing an illocutionary force-indicating device and a propositional content indicator. Thus:

$$F(p)$$

where the range of possible values for F will determine the range of illocutionary forces, and the p is a variable over the infinite range of possible propositions.[11] Notice that in this form the distinction is not subject to the objections we made to the original locutionary-illocutionary distinction. The propositional act is not represented, either in the symbolism or in natural languages, by the entire sentence, but only by those portions of the sentence which do not include the indicators of illocutionary force. Thus the propositional act is a genuine abstraction from the total illocutionary act, and so construed no propositional act is by itself an illocutionary act.

I do not know that this is one of the things Austin had in mind with the locutionary-illocutionary distinction, but the remarks quoted above suggest to me that it is (especially in connection with certain other remarks, such as his including "refer" among locutionary verbs; in my terminology referring is characteristically part of the propositional act, and referring expressions are portions of sentences, not whole sentences). But whether or not Austin ever intended this, it seems to me to be useful in its own right and to be one of the distinctions we need with which to supplant the original locutionary-illocutionary distinction.[12]

So far I have said that there are at least three different distinctions[13] which can be extracted from the locutionary-illocutionary distinction:

---

[11] Not all illocutionary acts would fit this model. E.g., "Hurrah for Manchester United" or "Down with Caesar" would be of the form $F(n)$, where n is replaceable by referring expressions.

[12] It is also a distinction I employ elsewhere (see references cited in n. 2).

[13] There is a fourth distinction, which I do not discuss here, between the illocutionary act performed by the speaker and what he implies in performing it. Cf. H. P. Grice, "The Causal Theory of Perception" (secs. 2–4), *Proceedings of the Aristotelian Society*, supp. vol. (1961); and J. R. Searle, "Assertions and Aberrations," *British Analytical Philosophy*, ed. by B. A. O. Williams and A. C. Montefiore (London, 1966), for some preliminary discussion of this distinction.

(1) The distinction between a certain aspect of trying and succeeding in performing an illocutionary act.

(2) The distinction between the literal meaning of the sentence and what the speaker means (by way of illocutionary force) when he utters it.

(3) The distinction between propositional acts and illocutionary acts.

I now want to use this last distinction in an examination of one of Austin's most important discoveries, the discovery that constatives are illocutionary acts as well as performatives, or, in short, the discovery that statements are speech acts.

The difficulty with this thesis as Austin presents it in *How to Do Things with Words* is that the word "statement" is structurally ambiguous. Like many nominalized verb forms it has what traditional grammarians call the act-object, or sometimes the process-product ambiguity. A modern transformational grammarian would say that it is structurally ambiguous as it has at least two different derivations from (phrase markers containing) the verb "state." "Statement" can mean either the *act of stating* or *what is stated*. (Possibly it has other meanings as well, but these are the most important for present purposes.) Here are two sentences in which these two meanings of "statement" are quite clearly distinct.

1. The statement of our position took all of the morning session.
2. The statement that all men are mortal is true.

Notice that you cannot say "The statement that all men are mortal took ten seconds." But you can say:

3. The statement of the statement that all men are mortal took ten seconds.

This just means that it took ten seconds to *make* the statement, or that the act of stating took ten seconds. Let us call these two senses the statement-act sense and the statement-object sense. Austin's discovery that statements are illocutionary acts holds for the act sense, but not for the object sense.

But that is not necessarily a weakness since the same distinction can be made for a great many other nominalized forms of the illocutionary verbs. The real significance of Austin's discovery is that "state" is an illocutionary verb like any other, and this leads us to the further observation that its nominalized forms share features with nominalized forms of illocutionary verbs; in particular in the "-ment" form "state" shares the act-object ambiguity. (As Austin might have said, it's the verb which wears the trousers.)[14]

The failure to take into account the structural ambiguity of "statement," however, had very important consequences for certain other parts of Austin's theory of language. For since statements are speech acts, and since statements can be true or false, it appears that that which is true or false is a speech act. But this inference is fallacious, as it involves a fallacy of ambiguity. Statement-acts are speech acts, and statement-objects (as well as propositions) are what

---

[14] To complicate matters further, not all literal utterances of "state" are connected with what philosophers call "statements" at all. Consider "State the question again, please" or "He restated his promise." Neither of these is a "constative."

can be true or false. And the view that it is the act of stating which is true or false is one of the most serious weaknesses of Austin's theory of truth.[15]

Confining ourselves to "constatives," the distinction between statement-acts and statement-objects can be explained in terms of our distinction between propositional content and illocutionary force as follows:

> The statement-act   = the act of stating.
>   = the act of stating a proposition.
>   = the act of expressing a proposition with a con-stative (I would prefer to call it "statemental") illocutionary force.
>   = the act of making a statement-object.
> The statement-object = what is stated (construed as stated).
>   = the proposition (construed as stated).

Propositions but not acts can be true or false; thus statement-objects but not statement-acts can be true or false. In the characterization of statement-object we have to add the phrase "construed as stated" because what is stated, the proposition, can also be the content of a question, of a promise, the antecedent of a hypothetical, and so forth. It is neutral as to the illocutionary force with which it is expressed, but statements are not neutral as to illocutionary force, so "statement" in its object sense is not synonymous with "proposition," but only with "proposition construed as stated."

So, to conclude this point, the distinction between the propositional act and the illocutionary act and the corresponding distinction between propositions and illocutions enables us to account for certain traditional problems in the notion of a statement. Statement-acts are illocutionary acts of stating. Statement-objects are propositions (construed as stated). The latter but not the former can be true or false. And it is the confusion between these which prevented Austin from seeing both that statements can be speech acts and that statements can be true or false, though acts cannot have truth values.

What is the outcome of our discussion of locutionary and illocutionary speech acts? We are left with:

> Phonetic acts
> Phatic acts
> Propositional acts
> Illocutionary acts

Propositional acts are all that we can salvage from the original conception of a rhetic act, in so far as we wish to distinguish rhetic acts from illocutionary acts. But whether or not Austin had them in mind, they are independently motivated and not subject to the objections we made to Austin's account of locutionary acts.

---

[15] As Strawson pointed out in the "Truth" symposium, *Proceedings of the Aristotelian Society*, supp. vol. (1950).

ALONZO CHURCH

3.5   *Propositions and Sentences*

The meaning of the word *proposition* has an interesting history. In Latin, *propositio* was originally a translation of the Greek πρότασις, and seems to have been used at first in the sense of premiss. But already by Boethius the word has come to be used in a sense which it long retained and which I can attempt to express in other words by speaking of a declarative sentence taken together with its meaning. Basically the same sense of the word as Boethius' is intended when Peter of Spain defines, "Propositio est oratio verum vel falsum significans indicando," and when post-scholastic traditional logicians define a proposition as a judgment expressed in words. (The mention of judgment in the definition of proposition is as far as I know postscholastic, but I think we may ignore it for our present purpose as being a minor change in the definition, not affecting in any essential way the questions with which we shall be concerned tonight.)

Though the terminology is by no means uniform among different writers, it seems fair on the whole to take Peter's definition of *propositio*, just quoted, as representative of the scholastic usage. However, some scholastic logicians use *enuntiatio*, either as an alternative to *propositio*, or in order to reserve the word *propositio* for use in some more special sense. And even Peter of Spain in another passage draws a certain distinction between *propositio* and *enuntiatio*.

Contrasted with this scholastic-traditional use of the word *proposition* is another use of the word which has arisen in more modern times, and which I shall distinguish by speaking of *proposition in the traditional sense* and *proposition in the abstract sense*. It is the latter, abstract, sense of *proposition* which is intended in the title of this lecture.

The difference between the two senses may be explained by supposing that we have before us an English declarative sentence, its translation into Latin, and its translation into German. In the traditional sense these are three different propositions. For though the three sentences have the same meaning (each in its own language), the words used are different in each case, and we must therefore, if we take the traditional definition seriously, speak of three propositions rather than one. In scholastic terminology, *propositio* is *oratio* of a certain kind, and *oratio* in turn is *vox* of a certain kind—to quote Peter of Spain again, *vox significativa ad placitum, cuius partes significant separatae*—and hence if the *vox*, the form of words, is different, the proposition must be said to be different, though all else be the same.

On the other hand, in the abstract sense, the English sentence and its two

Reprinted from A. Church, *The Problem of Universals* (Notre Dame, Indiana: University of Notre Dame Press, 1956), pp. 3–11, by permission of the publisher.

translations represent just one proposition. A proposition in the abstract sense, unlike the traditional proposition, may not be said to be of any language; it is not a form of words, and is not a linguistic entity of any kind except in the sense that it may be obtained by abstraction from language.

Of some logicians who write of propositions in the traditional sense or of judgments, I think it might reasonably be said that, in some vague way, and in spite of their explicit statement, what is really intended is the more abstract notion. For example in stating a particular syllogism, the minor term, having appeared in full in one of the premisses, may be represented in the conclusion only by a pronoun such as "it" or "he," or other non-essential changes may be made in the wording of a proposition without any indication that a new proposition has thereby resulted; the fact that no remark or justification is thought to be necessary for this seems to betray, if only by inadvertence, that the writer has in mind the meaning rather than the meaning plus the words. Again, I have heard it argued on behalf of Kant, who makes his logic treat of judgments (*Urtheile*), that what he intends thereby is not a psychological entity, an "act of the mind," but simply a proposition in the abstract sense, as distinguished from the traditional proposition, for which he uses *Satz*.

At any rate I believe that many have found awkward or unsatisfactory the traditional notion of proposition, with its dependence on the particular wording; and that for some purposes at least there is a clear need for the abstract notion—not the declarative sentence, but the content of meaning which is common to the sentence and its translations into other languages—not the particular judgment or thought but, as Frege writes in explaining his term *Gedanke*, the objective content of the thought which is capable of being the common property of many.

An explicit distinction between proposition in the traditional sense and proposition in the abstract sense first appears in Bolzano's *Wissenschaftslehre* of 1837. Bolzano's word is *Satz*, which indeed is the usual German translation of the Latin *propositio*, and the proposition in the abstract sense is distinguished by calling it *Satz an sich*.

In 1892, independently of Bolzano, propositions in the abstract sense were introduced by Frege under the name of *Gedanke*. For Frege, the *Gedanke* is the sense expressed by a declarative sentence (*Behauptungssatz*), as distinguished from the denotation of the sentence, which is its truth-value (i.e., either truth or falsehood).

The abstract notion of proposition appears again in Russell's *The Principles of Mathematics* in 1903. Russell does not mention Bolzano in this connection, but in discussing Frege he explains that Frege's *Gedanke* is approximately the same as his own *unasserted proposition*. Propositions in the abstract sense play an essential role in the *Principia Mathematica* of Whitehead and Russell, as originally written. And though Russell later repudiated the abstract notion—replacing it in *Introduction to Mathematical Philosophy* by a definition of *proposition* which closely follows Peter of Spain, and more recently by a psychological notion of proposition—writers such as Eaton, Cohen and Negal, Lewis and Langford, Carnap, and many others have followed the early Russell in employing the the word *proposition* in the abstract sense.

It should be added that although the use of the particular word *proposition* in this abstract sense is of modern origin, the notion itself is old. In fact the λεκτά of the Stoics are, wherever the λεκτόν of a declarative sentence is in question, propositions in the abstract sense.[1] And I am indebted to professor Bochenski for pointing out to me that the abstract notion appears again in the writings of the later scholastics, beginning with Gregory a Rimini, under the name of *complexe significabile*. Even John of St. Thomas still speaks of the "veritas complexa significata per enuntiationem" in what may be a reference to the *complexe significabile* (though the use of the word "veritas" is very odd in speaking of propositions whose signification may be false as well as true). But these ideas fell into oblivion, and had to be rediscovered in modern times by Bolzano, Frege, and Russell.

The word *sentence* is, of course, originally a term of grammar and linguistics. Its introduction into logic (where it is used to mean declarative sentence) is a recent innovation, and it still seems strange to many to find the word *sentence* where *proposition* might have been expected. I believe that the usage first arose in connection with translations from German into English, as the fact that the German has only one word *Satz* for both sentence and proposition had facilitated a shift in viewpoint on the part of certain logicians which became conspicuous only when the task of translation made it necessary to distinguish the two meanings of the German word. And certainly the use of the word *sentence* has often been the device of nominalistic logicians in order to repudiate propositions. Yet the word cannot be abandoned to the nominalists, as the very decision to use *proposition* in the abstract sense makes it necessary to have another word for the sentence as a purely syntactical entity, taken in abstraction from its meaning. Whatever may be one's philosophical prejudice, nominalistic or Platonistic or other, I believe that this terminology of sentence and proposition will be found superior to the older terminology that emphasizes and gives a special place to the composite entity, sentence plus (abstract) proposition.

The use of the word *propositio* for proposition in the abstract sense is attributed by Bolzano to Leibniz's *Dialogus de Connexione inter Res et Verba*. This would seem to be an exaggeration or a misunderstanding, as it does not appear in this dialogue that Leibniz intends any change in the traditional meaning of *propositio*. Nevertheless the dialogue is of interest in the present connection because it does set forth the essential considerations which tend to show that the duality of sentence and proposition provides a simpler and more satisfactory conceptual scheme than has yet been shown to be possible on a nominalistic basis.

The dialogue begins with A and B agreeing that truth must be supposed to

---

[1] It was brought out in the discussion, however, that the Stoics perhaps would not have allowed the existence of a λεκτόν except to correspond to a sentence actually uttered or at least considered by someone.

attach, not to thoughts (*cogitationes*) but to things (*res*). For example, if a thread of fixed length is to be laid upon a plane surface so as to enclose a maximum area, the shape must be a circle; and the truth of this, it is agreed, does not depend upon any one's having thought of it, as on the contrary it was true before geometers had proved it or any one had observed it. But, asks A, who seems to speak for Leibniz, can a *thing* be false? B answers that not the thing but some one's thought about it is false. But must it not be the same subject that is capable of truth and of falsehood, as may be seen by considering a case in which one is still in doubt as to whether considering a case in which one is still in doubt as to whether something is true or false? Thus we are led to say after all that truth must be of thoughts rather than things. How is this to be reconciled with the belief that that can be true which has been thought by no one and perhaps will not be? Leibniz's answer is that truth if neither of thoughts nor of things, but of possible thoughts, or possible propositions.

The remainder of the dialogue is then devoted to arguing that truth cannot be an arbitrary matter, depending upon human conventions about the definition and use of words. For there is but one geometry, the same for the Greeks, the Latins, and the Germans, though expressed in three different languages; and the results of an arithmetic calculation are the same, whether expressed in decimal or duodecimal notation. It is concluded that the basis of truth is not in the notation, not in the symbols or characters themselves, but in something in their use and interconnection which is not arbitrary, a certain relationship (*proportio*) of the characters among themselves and between the characters and things, which under transformation into a different language or notation either remains the same or is transformed into something suitably corresponding.

Leibniz is here very close to the notion of a proposition in the abstract sense, and it remained only for Bolzano to take the final step.

To be sure, instead of transmuting Leibniz's possible thoughts or possible propositions into abstract propositions, we might take them to be the possible sentences of some language, in the sense of all the sentences which the syntactical rules of the language allow as well-formed—whether or not the sentence has actually been written by any one or ever will be, and even if the sentence is so long that there is not space to write it within the confines of our (possibly finite) universe. This might not be wholly in disaccord with Leibniz's own ideas, since he maintains in the same dialogue that no distinct thought or reasoning is possible without words, signs, or characters of some sort. But so far as this device may have a nominalistic motivation, it is defeated by the fact that possible sentences in this sense are not particulars but universals, so that the purposes of nominalism are not served. Moreover if we consider, not the subject (or object) of truth, but rather the object of a belief or an assertion, I believe that the use of possible sentences in place of propositions in the abstract sense, in order to make a purely syntactical analysis, is unsatisfactory. I have tried to show this is a paper in *Analysis* ("On Carnap's analysis of Statements of Assertion and Belief," X, No. 5 [1950] which I will not discuss now except to express my opinion that, as far as the criticism in this paper concerns the particular analysis of belief statements by Carnap, rebuttals which have been offered are wide of the mark; and that the character of the criticism is such that it seems to leave very little possibility of a successful alternative analysis of belief statements along similar lines.

To return to Leibniz's argument—there are indeed some places in it at which an alternative course to that adopted may be possible or is at least worth consideration. The dialogue form may sometimes conceal this, as when the agreement by A and B that what is thought by no one might still be true tends to deter us from considering the tenability of the contrary opinion. But if we do question this basic assumption, we may then try the possibility of holding that only actual thoughts, or perhaps better, actual concrete sentences, are capable of truth or falsehood. The result is something like the Quine-Goodman finitistic nominalism, since there is possibly only a finite variety of concretely existing sentences—even if we consider the whole extent of past and future time, and even if we count sentences that have not been purposely written by any one but merely happen to exist somewhere and somewhen. On this basis it would seem to become impossible to make certain otherwise ordinary distinctions, such as the distinction between there being in principle no proof of a particular proposed mathematical theorem (for example the Gödel undecidable sentence) and there being no proof of it actually written out because all are too long. But even if we reconcile ourselves to the loss of such distinctions, it is clear from the work of Quine and Goodman that we must at the very best face a very difficult and complicated theory even in the formulation of logical syntax; and the difficulties will certainly be greater in the treatment of even an extensional semantics, and a fortiori, of such intensional questions as the logical analysis of belief statements. It is a familiar situation in mathematics generally, and in theoretical physics and other natural sciences, that a theory may be greatly simplified by incorporating into it additional entities beyond those which had originally to be dealt with, and I believe it to be a false economy which would forego simplification of a theory by such means. The notion of a concrete physical object, extended in space and persistent through time, is a case in point, as what had originally to be dealt with by the physical theories in which such objects appear was not these objects themselves but rather certain observations and physical experiences.[2] Indeed the justification would seem to be basically the same for extended physical objects in macrophysical theory and for ideal sentences in logical syntax: both are postulated entities—some may prefer to say inferred entities—without which the theory would be intolerably complex if not impossible.

There is one other point I would like to mention at which the nominalist might attempt to escape the course of Leibniz's argument. This is in the assumption that there is *something* which is the subject of truth—and I would add to this the assumption that there is something which is the object of assertion and

---

[2] Compare a remark made by Kurt Gödel in his paper, "Russell's Mathematical Logic," published in the volume *The Philosophy of Bertrand Russell* (Library of Living Philosophers).

of belief. The possibility must indeed by considered that the logical form is to be taken as different. But what has to be said here is that, with one exception, I know of no proposal of a different logical form than this for, say, belief statements which recommends itself as likely to be useful or tenable. There is therefore the chance that some new idea or new direction in the analysis of statements of truth and of assertion, belief, and the like might completely change the present situation.

The one exception I spoke of is the proposal of Israel Scheffler (*Analysis*, XIV, No. 4 [1954]) according to which names of propositions are to be eliminated in favor of certain predicates of inscriptions, which may be used to assert about an inscription in effect that it expresses such and such a proposition. Scheffler, writing in the context of the Quine-Goodman nominalism, speaks of predicates of inscriptions, i.e., of concrete particular occurrences of sentences, rather than of the ideal sentences of the usual logical syntax, and it seems that this may be essential to his proposal. In fact Scheffler supposes each inscription to have a unique meaning—determined by its context, inclusive of the language of which it forms a part—so that his propositional predicates (as I shall call them) can be taken as predicates of inscriptions only, without introducing the language as a second argument. And because this has the consequence that accidentally occurring inscriptions may not be considered, but only those that have been purposely written by some one in suitable context, the Quine-Goodman undertaking to reconstruct logical syntax on a finitistic basis (see *The Journal of Symbolic Logic*, XII, No. 4 [1947]) will certainly be rendered more difficult.

The propositional predicates must of course be either indivisible or at least not analyzable in any way that would reintroduce names of propositions (which would be replaceable by bindable variables). And the propositional predicates themselves must not be allowed to replace or be replaced by bindable variables. In this way Scheffler is able, on Quine's view, to avoid "ontological commitment" to propositions or to abstract entities named by the propositional predicates. But in consequence he is faced with the immediate difficulty that we do often want to make statements which, at least *prima facie*, require in their analysis the use of bound variables taking propositions as values. Examples are, "Church and Goodman have contradicted each other," "Goodman will speak about individuals," "Some assertions of Velikovsky are improbable," and the contention ascribed to Ramus, that all assertions of Aristotle are falsehoods. Of various methods that have occurred to me, to make an attempted nominalistic reproduction of these statements, perhaps the most plausible is to reconstrue them respectively as, "There exist inscriptions i_1 and i_2, such that i_1 has been uttered [spoken or written] by Church, i_2 has been uttered by Goodman, and i_1 and i_2 *are contradictory*," "There exist inscriptions which *are about individuals* and will be uttered by Goodman," "There exist inscriptions which are uttered by Velikovsky and *are improbable*," "All inscriptions uttered by Aristotle *are false*"—where the italicized predicates of inscriptions do not require the language as additional argument, in view of the assumption that the language is uniquely determined by the context. But if one attempts any extensive analysis of these predicates, and many others like them which immediately suggest themselves, it will be difficult to avoid restoring unwanted "ontological commitments." And if on the contrary a large number of these predicates are taken as unanalyzed or primitive, it may be difficult or impossible to provide (axiomatically) for the logical connections among them, between them and the propositional predicates, and between them and the syntactical make-up of the inscriptions they apply to in a specified language.

I conclude that Scheffler has not established his claim to have provided a workable substitute for propositions which is acceptable on the basis of finitistic nominalism. The possibility remains that the claim might be substantiated by a longer and more detailed development, including solutions of the difficulties just discussed and treatment of a compatible finitistic syntax. But objections to finitistic nominalism on the ground that the theory is too complicated in application would in any case not be removed.

It is necessary to consider also the question of an adaptation of Scheffler's device to ordinary non-finitistic syntax, in which sentences are treated rather than inscriptions. And as already suggested, there may be other choices of the logical form to be ascribed to a statement of belief, or the like, that are worth consideration. I want to urge in conclusion that various proposals for the analysis of such statements should be sought, and that those which appear promising should receive a detailed development by the logistic method, as being the only means by which the consequences of the proposal can be satisfactorily brought out and the discussion of it raised above the level of vague and pointless speculation. Sketches, informal suggestions, and general informal surveys such as that I have been making have their place, but in the end are futile, in view of the evident logical difficulty of the problem at hand, unless they issue in a detailed logistic formulation and study of at least one successful solution.

METHODOLOGY 4

INTRODUCTION

What should theories of language be like? What could they be like? These are the fundamental questions to be considered in this section. On one side of these questions, Noam CHOMSKY suggests that there are more worthwhile goals for a theory of language than those traditionally countenanced by linguists and psychologists. On the other side, W. V. O. QUINE and Gilbert HARMAN suggest that these more ambitious goals are unattainable. Quine's arguments against the attainability of these goals are quite general. In the article included here, Harman's primary interest is in attacking what he takes to be Chomsky's view of the psychological significance of theories of language. The view he attacks is one that is elaborated and defended in some detail by Jerrold KATZ in an article in this section.

In these selections, the issues are most often framed in terms of syntax, or in Quine's case, semantics. However, this is really an accidental feature of the dispute. Except, perhaps, for phonology, syntax is the easiest theory of language to discuss because it is the best understood. The semantic notions that Quine discusses are also rather natural ones to select, simply because they have been so much discussed by philosophers. The arguments presented, however, have great generality. They apply to any theory of language, no matter what its content may be.

Chomsky characterizes the dispute between himself and others such as Quine as one between rationalism and empiricism. We will not discuss the appropriateness of these terms. However, there are at least three distinct complex theses that make up what Chomsky calls empiricism, and it is worth discussing each separately. These three theses are epitomized by three men,

B. F. Skinner in psychology, Leonard Bloomfield in linguistics, and Quine in philosophy.

The thesis associated with Skinner is known as behaviorism. Perhaps the most significant feature of behaviorism is its claim that psychology, and by extension, linguistics, is about behavior, or about laws of behavior.[1] Underlying this claim is the view that behavior and physical events exhaust what we can observe, or at any rate, what we can directly observe. That being so, it is argued, what else is there for any discipline to be about? On this line, then, behavior and physical events are the data with which linguists and psychologists must deal.

But, of course, scientists do not just collect data. They also propound (or possibly even discover) laws. The next question, then, is what kind of laws could one formulate about these data? Several possibilities suggest themselves. First, we might formulate laws linking behavior with behavior. We might thus characterize organisms in terms of complexes of behavior which they exhibit.

Second, and more important for behaviorism, we might formulate laws that link behavior and physical events. An important subclass of such laws may serve as explanations of behavior, and perhaps also as bases for predicting it. To formulate such laws, we must first find a means of selecting a class of events which we may characterize as the experience to which a given organism is subjected. These events will represent all the forces which have acted on the organism to produce its present state or its complex of dispositions to behave. Thus, any bit of behavior the organism produces presumably has a cause, either external or internal, which lies in this set of experiences. We can explain the behavior if we can discover laws that link given pieces of behavior with given sets of experiences.

Although behaviorists in general do not seem to be very explicitly interested in describing the internal structures of organisms, we may view what they do and say as in fact incorporating certain claims about these internal structures.

The functions which describe the connection between experience and behavior can be regarded as describing the internal structure of the organism. It is this internal structure that determines that a given set of experiences produces the effect it does, rather than some other. Thus, behaviorists can be viewed as claiming that we may plausibly claim to have exhausted all the interesting properties of internal structure if we have described all the ways in which it mediates between experience and behavior.

Bloomfield represents a complementary position in linguistics. Like Skinner, he takes it that his data are restricted to behavior. Since his interest is in describing languages, he restricts himself to speech behavior. It is reasonable

---

[1] Pretheoretically, at least, it is certainly not always clear what is to count as behavior and what is not. Behaviorist views on what behavior is form quite an interesting part of behaviorism. However, these views are of secondary importance in developing the present dispute. Hence we will not examine them here.

to suppose that if a linguist wants to construct a grammar for a language, he must begin by compiling a corpus of data. On the view that the data are speech behavior, this corpus will consist of transcriptions of utterances produced by native speakers. Although linguists might perhaps set standards of simplicity and elegance if they wished, it is part of this view that ultimately the only fact that can count for or against the correctness of a particular grammar is the fact that on a particular occasion a given speaker produced a certain utterance. In particular, native speakers' grammatical intuitions are to be scrupulously ignored. The linguist is to be the expert at writing grammars, not the native speaker. What the native speaker says about the grammaticality of various strings or about the grammatical relations he perceives is of no interest.

On this view of grammar, then, the primary function of a grammar is to describe a particular corpus in a convenient way. It must rely on a lexicon and a small number of rules to construct all of the strings included in the corpus. It can, of course, be falsified by considering data outside the corpus. But since the data must be of the same sort as those in the corpus, the result is simply a grammar adequate for a larger corpus.

This suggests that grammars can be of a very simple form. To find a convenient set of rules for describing a corpus, one must first isolate parts of utterances which seem to be grammatically important. What makes them grammatically important for present purposes is roughly that they can occur in a wide variety of utterances. If we can isolate a number of such grammatically important parts, all of which can occur in utterances that are otherwise identical, then we can simplify the rules further. We can group all such parts into a grammatical class. For example, some traditional grammatical classes are noun phrase, verb phrase, noun, and adjectival phrase. In theory, each grammar must postulate its own set of such classes. Ultimately, every thing that the grammar marks as a part of a sentence should belong to just one such class. Finally, we can formulate our rules in terms of grammatical classes rather than individual parts of utterances.

What kinds of descriptions does such a grammar provide for sentences? To describe a sentence, one first segments it into its grammatically important parts and labels these according to the classes to which they belong. One then describes grammatical relations by stating which of these parts are included in which other parts.

It should be clear that, on this conception, the primary task of linguistics, outside of the study of particular languages, is to devise rigorous discovery procedures for grammars. These discovery procedures will be of two sorts. First there will be procedures for completing a corpus of data. We need to know how to seek our responsible native informants and what to ignore and what to transcribe from what they say. Second, we need procedures for operating on a corpus to construct a grammar.

When we have constructed a grammar for a particular language, what have we discovered about the people who speak it? On the present view, practically nothing. A grammar provides principles for the organization of sentences which are designed to be convenient for the linguist. These principles cannot be assumed to reflect anything about the ways in which native speakers organize data or how they speak and understand their language. So grammars tell us nothing about the mind. This view is perhaps more strongly antimentalistic than Skinner's. One of Skinner's aims is to avoid postulating what he calls "psychic fictions" such as minds. But if he succeeds in describing the way the organism mediates between experience and behavior, it is difficult to see how he has avoided saying something about the way the organism processes data. Grammar, on the other hand, is not concerned with laws that determine what organisms do. It simply provides one sort of description for some of the things they in fact do.

Bloomfield's antimentalism comes out most clearly, perhaps, in his views on linguistic universals. Suppose that we discover some facts about grammars that seem to be true of every grammar for every language we have studied. We thus discover that, despite the apparent diversity in speech behavior, the languages people speak are all the same in certain respects. This might incline us to think that we had discovered some deep and important species-specific traits of human beings. On Bloomfield's view, however, these universals of language can be regarded as nothing but accidents, caused either by our method of description or by the particular languages we chose to study. Linguistic universals are nothing but empirical generalizations which we should always be prepared to have overturned by the next language we study. We can never study every human language. Some are long dead. Others, for all we know, do not exist yet. Thus, linguistic universals can never be anything but generalizations of very little interest.

Quine's primary contribution to empiricism in linguistics consists of showing that a number of abstract epistemological problems, some of which have worried philosophers for centuries, apply to the question of establishing theories of languages. Quine argues that these are problems which should be taken quite seriously by linguists, so that a theory of language ought not to be taken as established or known until these problems are solved. Like Bloomfield, Quine's primary concern is with justification of theories, and more specifically, with a kind of justification that requires independent procedures for the confirmation of each of the claims a theory makes. Thus, on Quine's view, a theory should not include terms in its vocabulary unless these terms can be empirically grounded by means of definitions that are independent of the theory.

Quine's specific interest is in semantics, though his arguments are more general. We can get a good illustration of these views by considering a semantic notion like meaningfulness. Presumably, one of the tasks of a semantic theory (perhaps together with syntax) is to tell which strings of words are meaningful in a given language. Thus, some term such as 'meaningful' ought to be part of the vocabulary of the theory. But on Quine's view, a theory which includes such a term becomes unintelligible unless we can say independently of the theory what it is for something to be meaningful. Further, we ought to be able to specify it in a way that will allow us to construct *tests* for determining whether something is meaningful.

Like Skinner and Bloomfield, Quine takes the data of language to be speech behavior, or at least behavior. The epistemological difficulty then is that the kinds of theories linguists wish to construct are such that a large number of apparently distinct ones are logically compatible with *any* set of data.

Again, we will use semantics as an illustration. Consider two alternative theories of English. One theory claims that 'bachelor' is synonymous with 'unmarried man'. The other claims that these expressions are not synonymous, but rather that 'bachelor' is synonymous with 'married priest'. To confirm or disconfirm either theory, we must find appropriate data about the behavior of English speakers. Such data would presumably concern either the situations in which English-speakers utter the terms, or their reactions to hearing them. To oversimplify drastically, let us suppose that the data are that these speakers point to various people and apply one or another of the three terms to them. Suppose further, that the speakers apply the terms 'bachelor' and 'unmarried male' to the same set of people, and the term 'married priest' to a disjoint set of people. This is, of course, compatible with the thesis that the first theory is right and the second wrong. But it is also compatible with the reverse hypothesis. The native speakers may actually hold 'bachelor' to be synonymous with 'married priest' but be systematically mistaken about who the married priests are. Or these native speakers may be too polite to call a married priest a bachelor. They may employ that expression as a term of insult for unmarried males, whom they are inclined not to like.

A fundamental point at which Chomsky differs from Quine, Bloomfield, and Skinner is in allowing the linguist (and psychologist) a richer set of initial data than linguistically neutral, physical (e.g., phonetic) descriptions of pure behavior. In syntax, for example, the basic data admitted by Chomsky include pretheoretical facts about what is and what is not a *sentence* in the given language. Further relevant data may include *grammatical relations* which obtain between sentences and between parts of sentences.

What is and what is not a sentence, and which grammatical relations obtain and which don't is determined by what fluent speakers are prepared to recognize. In constructing a theory for a language of which the linguist is not himself a fluent speaker, it may be necessary to refer to some of the behavior of some groups of people as evidence for at least some of what fluent speakers are prepared to recognize. Since fluent speakers may be unaware of much of what, under proper conditions, they are prepared to recognize, behavior may be misleading as well and stand in need of interpretation. But these appeals to behavior as evidence are clearly different in kind from the systematic accumulation of a corpus of native utterances characterized phonetically and tagged with a physical or stimulus description of their context of occurrence.

One consequence of this view of linguistic data is a difference, at least between Chomsky and Skinner, on what theories of language ought to predict or account for. On Skinner's view a theory of language is concerned with predicting, or at least accounting for, speech behavior. On Chomsky's view, a grammar of a particular language is a finite means of representing the infinite number of sentences of that language that a fluent speaker is prepared to recognize and/or produce and the grammatical relations he is prepared to perceive in them. What it "predicts," insofar as it predicts at all, is what are and what are not the sentences of the language in question and what grammatical relations they contain. Predicting, or even accounting for, speech behavior is beyond the scope of any theory of language, since speech behavior may also be controlled by any of an indefinite number of factors that have nothing to do with language. For example, if I see a cow, I may say "There is a cow," but I may also say "Just like in Denmark," "I itch all over," "Is it not ugly?," "We could live off that for a week," or in fact, anything at all, as far as the rules of grammar (or of language) are concerned. I might even say "There is a dog." If I do, of course, I am wrong. Perhaps I have violated a rule of language, although that is far from clear. But by themselves these remarks have little bearing on whether I will say it or not. What I say will depend much more on my interests, intentions, strategies, etc., than on my mastery of grammar.

This example provides part of the point to Chomsky's distinction between competence and performance. Theories of language, on Chomsky's view, are theories of human competences. Grammar, for example, is a theory of what a speaker's mastery of the rules of grammar equips him to do. A theory of performance is a theory that may predict, but more likely would only explain, the fact that speakers (or perhaps only a speaker) behave as they do. Such a theory may very well presuppose a theory of competence, but is far from exhausted by it.

Another consequence of Chomsky's view of data about languages is that, particularly for those languages of which the linguist himself is a fluent speaker, there are a great deal of data already on hand. Thus, the problem of assembling, justifying, and confirming data becomes minimal. On the other hand, the problem of organizing the data on hand into some kind of coherent and adequate theory becomes both pressing and difficult. Thus, a linguist need not concern himself with devising rigorous test procedures for each of the claims of his theory, nor with providing definitions for its vocabulary of the sort demanded by Quine. What is of interest for linguistics is the justification of a theory as a whole. Such justification may depend on many considerations, both external and internal to the theory, but one can only justify a theory at all relative to some criterion of adequacy. Chomsky introduces two such criteria of great importance. A grammar may be regarded as descriptively adequate for a given language if it provides one and only one description for each sentence in that language. It thus represents the fluent speaker's competence in recognizing sentences. In addition to this competence, the fluent speaker has additional competences to recognize grammatical relations of certain sorts or to recognize grammatical descriptions of certain sorts as preferable to others. If a grammar adequately represents these additional syntactic competences, it has achieved what Chomsky calls explanatory adequacy.

Since the sort of theory Chomsky envisions is a theory of a human competence, it is reasonable to expect that the form of a successful theory would be determined to a great extent by what human beings are like. Thus Chomsky's view of linguistic universals is radically unlike that of Bloomfield. On Chomsky's view, a linguistic universal is not just a feature common to all languages linguists have happened to study. It is rather a feature common to all humanly possible languages, that is all languages which humans could learn and speak in roughly the way they normally do. Whether something is a linguistic universal, then, is determined by what sorts of languages humans are prepared to acquire. There may be many ways of determining what these sorts of languages are.

Finally, Chomsky differs from Skinner on the issue of how complex the mental structure underlying language acquisition must be. Skinner's decision to regard such a structure as a set of very general and simple dispositions to learn *tout court* seems to have been reached on largely *a priori* grounds. Chomsky argues that such decisions should be suggested by the facts. He claims that when we see the enormous complexity of what is to be acquired in learning language, and when we recognize certain gross facts about the ways it is learned, the following theses become plausible. First, human language acquisition devices are highly complex and innately determine a number of substantive principles about what the acquired language will be like. Second, these devices are species-specific, that is, they reflect special properties of human beings. Third, these devices are specific to the acquisition of language. They are not part of very general all-purpose problem-solving techniques or learning strategies.

Suggestions for Further Reading

Bloomfield, Leonard. *Language*. New York: Holt, 1933.

Chomsky, Noam. "A Review of B. F. Skinner's 'Verbal Behavior'." *Language*, XXXV, No. 1 (1959). Also in *The Structure of Language*, J. Fodor and J. Katz, eds. Englewood Cliffs, N.J.: Prentice-Hall, Inc., 1964.

————. "On the Notion 'Rule of Grammar'." Proceedings of the Twelfth Symposium in *Applied Mathematics*, XII (1961). Also in *The Structure of Language*.

————. *Cartesian Linguistics*. New York: Harper & Row, 1966.

————. "Linguistics and Philosophy." In S. Hook, ed., *Language and Philosophy*. New York: NYU Press, 1969, pp. 51–94.

————. "Deep Structure, Surface Structure and Semantic Interpretation." Reprinted by the Indiana University Linguistics Club, 1969.

Harman, Gilbert. "An Introduction to 'Translation and Meaning', Chapter Two of *Word and Object*." *Synthese*, XIX, No. 112 (December 1968), 14–26.

——. "Three Levels of Meaning." *The Journal of Philosophy*, LXV, No. 19 (October 1968), 590–602.

——. "Linguistic Competence and Empiricism." In S. Hook, ed., *Language and Philosophy*, pp. 143–51.

——. "Language, Thought and Communication." Forthcoming in *Minnesota Studies in the Philosophy of Science*.

Lees, Robert B. Review of *Syntactic Structures*. *Language*, XXXIII (July–September 1957), 355–407. Reprinted in Bobbs-Merrill Reprint Series in the Social Sciences.

McCawley, James D. "The Role of Semantics in a Grammar." In *Universals in Linguistic Theory*, ed. E. Bach and R. Harms. New York: Holt, Rinehart & Wilson, 1968, pp. 125–69.

——. "Concerning the Base Component of a Transformational Grammar." *Foundations of Language*, IV (1968), 243–69.

Postal, Paul. "Limitations of Phrase Structure Grammars." In J. Fodor and J. Katz, eds., *The Structure of Language*, pp. 137–51.

Rosenberg, Jay. "Synonymy and the Epistemology of Linguistics." *Inquiry*, X (1967), 405–20.

Skinner, B. F. *Verbal Behavior*. New York: Appleton-Century-Crofts, 1957.

WILLARD VAN ORMAN QUINE

4.1   *Translation and Meaning*

1. FIRST STEPS OF RADICAL TRANSLATION[1]

We have been reflecting in a general way on how surface irritations generate, through language, one's knowledge of the world. One is taught so to associate words with words and other stimulations that there emerges something recognizable as talk of things, and not to be distinguished from truth about the world. The voluminous and intricately structured talk that comes out bears little evident correspondence to the past and present barrage of non-verbal stimulation; yet it is to such stimulation that we must look for whatever empirical content there may be. In this chapter we shall consider how much of language can be made sense of in terms of its stimulus conditions, and what scope this leaves for empirically unconditioned variation in one's conceptual scheme.

A first uncritical way of picturing this scope for empirically unconditioned

---

Reprinted from W. V. O. Quine, *Word and Object*, Chapter 2, pp. 26–79, by permission of The M.I.T. Press, Cambridge, Massachusetts. Copyright © 1960 by The Massachusetts Institute of Technology.

[1] An interim draft of [this chapter] was published, with omissions, as "Meaning and Translation." Half of that essay survives verbatim here, comprising a scattered third of this chapter.

variation is as follows: two men could be just alike in all their dispositions to verbal behavior under all possible sensory stimulations, and yet the meanings or ideas expressed in their identically triggered and identically sounded utterances could diverge radically, for the two men, in a wide range of cases. To put the matter thus invites, however, the charge of meaninglessness: one may protest that a distinction of meaning unreflected in the totality of dispositions to verbal behavior is a distinction without a difference.

Sense can be made of the point by recasting it as follows: the infinite totality of sentences of any given speaker's language can be so permuted, or mapped onto itself, that (*a*) the totality of the speaker's dispositions to verbal behavior remains invariant, and yet (*b*) the mapping is no mere correlation of sentences with *equivalent* sentences, in any plausible sense of equivalence however loose. Sentences without number can diverge drastically from their respective correlates, yet the divergences can systematically so offset one another that the overall pattern of associations of sentences with one another and with non-verbal stimulation is preserved. The firmer the direct links of a sentence with non-verbal stimulation, of course, the less that sentence can diverge from its correlate under any such mapping.

The same point can be put less abstractly and more realistically by switching to translation. The thesis is then this: manuals for translating one language into another can be set up in divergent ways, all compatible with the totality of speech dispositions, yet incompatible with one another. In countless places they will diverge in giving, as their respective translations of a sentence of the one language, sentences of the other language which stand to each other in no plausible sort of equivalence however loose. The firmer the direct links of a sentence with non-verbal stimulation, of course, the less drastically its translations can diverge from one another from manual to manual. It is in this last form, as a principle of indeterminacy of translation, that I shall try to make the point plausible in the course of this chapter. But the chapter will run longer than it would if various of the concepts and considerations ancillary to this theme did not seem worthy of treatment also on their own account.

We are concerned here with language as the complex of present dispositions to verbal behavior, in which speakers of the same language have perforce come to resemble one another; not with the processes of acquistion, whose variations from individual to individual it is to the interests of communication to efface. The sentence 'That man shoots well', said while pointing to an unarmed man, has as present stimulation the glimpse of the marksman's familiar face. The contributory past stimulation includes past observations of the man's shooting, as well as remote episodes that trained the speaker in the use of the words. The past stimulation is thus commonly reckoned in part to the acquisition of language and in part to the acquisition of collateral information; however, this subsidiary dichotomy can await some indication of what it is good for and what general clues there are for it in observable verbal behavior. (*Cf.* sections 3, 6, 8.) Meanwhile what is before us is the going concern of verbal behavior and its currently observable correlations with stimulation. Reckon a man's current language by his current dispositions to respond verbally to current stimulation, and you automatically refer all past stimulation to the learning phase. Not but that even this way of drawing a boundary between language in acquisition and language in use has its fluctuations, inasmuch as we can consult our convenience in what bound we set to the length of stimulations counted as current. This bound, a working standard of what to count as specious present, I call the *modulus* of stimulation.

The recovery of a man's current language from his currently observed responses is the task of the linguist who, unaided by an interpreter, is out to penetrate and translate a language hitherto unknown. All the objective data he has to go on are the forces that he sees impinging on the native's surfaces and the observable behavior, vocal and otherwise, of the native. Such data evince native "meanings" only of the most objectively empirical or stimulus-linked variety. And yet the linguist apparently ends up with native "meanings" in some quite unrestricted sense; purported translations, anyway, of all possible native sentences.

Translation between kindred languages, e.g., Frisian and English, is aided by resemblance of cognate word forms. Translation between unrelated languages, e.g., Hungarian and English, may be aided by traditional equations that have evolved in step with a shared culture. What is relevant rather to our purposes is *radical* translation, i.e., translation of the language of a hitherto untouched people. The task is one that is not in practice undertaken in its extreme form, since a chain of interpreters of a sort can be recruited of marginal persons across the darkest archipelago. But the problem is the more nearly approximated the poorer the hints available from interpreters; thus attention to techniques of utterly radical translation has not been wanting.[2] I shall imagine that all help of interpreters is excluded. Incidentally I shall here ignore phonematic analysis, early though it would come in our field linguist's enterprise; for it does not affect the philosophical point I want to make.

The utterances first and most surely translated in such a case are ones keyed to present events that are conspicuous to the linguist and his informant. A rabbit scurries by, the native says 'Gavagai', and the linguist notes down the sentence 'Rabbit' (or 'Lo, a rabbit') as tentative translation, subject to testing in further cases. The linguist will at first refrain from putting words into his informant's mouth, if only for lack of words to put. When he can, though, the linguist has to supply native sentences for his informant's approval, despite the risk of slanting the data by suggestion. Otherwise he can do little with native terms that have references in common. For, suppose the native language includes sentences S_1, S_2, and S_3, really translatable respectively as 'Animal', 'White', and 'Rabbit'. Stimulus situations always differ, whether relevantly or not; and, just because volunteered responses come singly, the classes of situations under which the native happens to have volunteered S_1, S_2, and S_3, are of course mutually exclusive, despite the hidden actual meanings of the words. How then is the linguist to perceive that the native would have been

---

[2] See Pike, [*Phonemics: A Technique for Reducing Languages to Writing*].

willing to assent to S_1 in all the situations where he happened to volunteer S_3, and in some but perhaps not all of the situations where he happened to volunteer S_2? Only by taking the initiative and querying combinations of native sentences and stimulus situations so as to narrow down his guesses to his eventual satisfaction.

So we have the linguist asking 'Gavagai?' in each of various stimulatory situations, and noting each time whether the native assents, dissents, or neither. But how is he to recognize native assent and dissent when he sees or hears them? Gestures are not to be taken at face value; the Turks' are nearly the reverse of our own. What he must do is guess from observation and then see how well his guesses work. Thus suppose that in asking 'Gavagai?' and the like, in the conspicuous presence of rabbits and the like, he has elicited the responses 'Evet' and 'Yok' often enough to surmise that they may correspond to 'Yes' and 'No', but has no notion which is which. Then he tries the experiment of echoing the native's own volunteered pronouncements. If thereby he pretty regularly elicits 'Evet' rather than 'Yok', he is encouraged to take 'Evet' as 'Yes'. Also he tries responding with 'Evet' and 'Yok' to the native's remarks; the one that is the more serene in its effect is the better candidate for 'Yes'. However inconclusive these methods, they generate a working hypothesis. If extraordinary difficulties attend all his subsequent steps, the linguist may decide to discard that hypothesis and guess again.[3]

Let us then suppose the linguist has settled on what to treat as native signs of assent and dissent. He is thereupon in a position to accumulate inductive evidence for translating 'Gavagai' as the sentence 'Rabbit'. The general law for which he is assembling instances is roughly that the native will assent to 'Gavagai?' under just those stimulations under which we, if asked, would assent to 'Rabbit?'; and correspondingly for dissent.

But we can do somewhat more justice to what the linguist is after in such a case if, instead of speaking merely of stimulations under which the native will assent or dissent to the queried sentence, we speak in a more causal vein of stimulations that will *prompt* the native to assent or dissent to the queried sentence. For suppose the queried sentence were one rather to the effect that someone is away tracking a giraffe. All day long the native will assent to it whenever asked, under all manner of irrelevant attendant stimulations; and on another day he will dissent from it under the same irrelevant stimulations. It is important to know that in the case of 'Gavagai?' the rabbit-presenting stimulations actually prompt the assent, and that the others actually prompt the dissent.

In practice the linguist will usually settle these questions of causality, however tentatively, by intuitive judgment based on details of the native's behavior: his scanning movements, his sudden look of recognition, and the like. Also there are more formal considerations which, under favorable circumstances, can assure him of the prompting relation. If, just after the native has been

---

[3] See Firth, *Elements of Social Organization*, p. 23, on the analogous matter of identifying a gesture of greeting.

asked S and has assented or dissented, the linguist springs stimulation σ on him, asks S again, and gets the opposite verdict, then he may conclude that σ did the prompting.

Note that to prompt, in our sense, is not to elicit. What elicits the native's 'Evet' or 'Yok' is a combination: the prompting stimulation plus the ensuing query 'Gavagai?'.

2. STIMULATION AND STIMULUS MEANING

It is important to think of what prompts the native's assent to 'Gavagai?' as stimulations and not rabbits. Stimulation can remain the same though the rabbit be supplanted by a counterfeit. Conversely, stimulation can vary in its power to prompt assent to 'Gavagai' because of variations in angle, lighting, and color contrast, though the rabbit remain the same. In experimentally equating the uses of 'Gavagai' and 'Rabbit' it is stimulations that must be made to match, not animals.

A visual stimulation is perhaps best identified, for present purposes, with the pattern of chromatic irradiation of the eye. To look deep into the subject's head would be inappropriate even if feasible, for we want to keep clear of his idiosyncratic neural routings or private history of habit formation. We are after his socially inculcated linguistic usage, hence his responses to conditions normally subject to social assessment. Ocular irradiation *is* intersubjectively checked to some degree by society and linguist alike, by making allowances for the speaker's orientation and the relative disposition of objects.

In taking the visual stimulations as irradiation patterns we invest them with a fineness of detail beyond anything that our linguist can be called upon to check for. But this is all right. He can reasonably conjecture that the native would be prompted to assent to 'Gavagai' by the microscopically same irradiations that would prompt him, the linguist, to assent to 'Rabbit', even though this conjecture rests wholly on samples where the irradiations concerned can at best be hazarded merely to be pretty much alike.

It is not, however, adequate to think of the visual stimulations as momentary static irradiation patterns. To do so would obstruct examples which, unlike 'Rabbit', affirm movement. And it would make trouble even with examples like 'Rabbit', on another account: too much depends on what immediately precedes and follows a momentary irradiation. A momentary leporiform image flashed by some artifice in the midst of an otherwise rabbitless sequence might not prompt assent to 'Rabbit' even though the same image would have done so if ensconced in a more favorable sequence. The difficulty would thus arise that far from hoping to match the irradiation patterns favorable to 'Gavagai' with those favorable to 'Rabbit', we could not even say unequivocally of an irradiation pattern, of itself and without regard to those just before and after, that it is favorable to 'Rabbit' or that it is not.[4] Better, therefore, to take as the relevant stimulations not momentary irradiation patterns, but evolving

[4] This difficulty was raised by Davidson.

irradiation patterns of all durations up to some convenient limit or *modulus*. Furthermore we may think of the ideal experimental situation as one in which the desired ocular exposure concerned is preceded and followed by a blindfold.

In general the ocular irradiation patterns are best conceived in their spatial entirety. For there are examples such as 'Fine weather' which, unlike 'Rabbit', are not keyed to any readily segregated fragments of the scene. Also there are all those rabbit-free patterns that are wanted as prompting dissent from 'Rabbit'. And as for the patterns wanted as prompting assent to 'Rabbit', whole scenes will still serve better than selected portions might; for the difference between center and periphery, which is such an important determinant of visual attention, is then automatically allowed for. Total ocular irradiation patterns that differ in centering differ also in limits, and so are simply different patterns. One that shows the rabbit too peripherally simply will not be one that prompts assent to 'Gavagai' or 'Rabbit'.

Certain sentences of the type of 'Gavagai' are the sentences with which our jungle linguist must begin, and for these we now have before us the makings of a crude concept of empirical meaning. For meaning, supposedly, is what a sentence shares with its translation; and translation at the present stage turns solely on correlations with non-verbal stimulation.

Let us make this concept of meaning more explicit and give it a neutrally technical name. We may begin by defining the *affirmative stimulus meaning* of a sentence such as 'Gavagai', for a given speaker, as the class of all the stimulations (hence evolving ocular irradiation patterns between properly timed blindfoldings) that would prompt his assent. More explicitly, in view of the end of section 1, a stimulation σ belongs to the affirmative stimulus meaning of a sentence S for a given speaker if and only if there is a stimulation σ' such that if the speaker were given σ', then were asked S, then were given σ, and then were asked S again, he would dissent the first time and assent the second. We may define the *negative* stimulus meaning similarly with 'assent' and 'dissent' interchanged, and then define the *stimulus meaning* as the ordered pair of the two. We could refine the notion of stimulus meaning by distinguishing degrees of doubtfulness of assent and dissent, say by reaction time; but for the sake of fluent exposition let us forbear. The imagined equating of 'Gavagai' and 'Rabbit' can now be stated thus: they have the same stimulus meaning.

A stimulus meaning is the stimulus meaning of a sentence for a speaker at a date; for we must allow our speaker to change his ways. Also it varies with the modulus, or maximum duration recognized for stimulations. For, by increasing the modulus we supplement the stimulus meaning with some stimulations that were too long to count before. Fully ticketed, therefore, a stimulus meaning is the stimulus meaning *modulo n* seconds of sentence S for speaker a at time t.

The stimulations to be gathered into the stimulus meaning of a sentence have for vividness been thought of thus far as visual, unlike the queries that follow them. Actually, of course, we should bring the other senses in on a par with vision, identifying stimulations not with just ocular irradiation patterns but with these and the various barrages of other senses, separately and in all synchronous combinations. Perhaps we can pass over the detail of this.

The affirmative and negative stimulus meanings of a sentence (for a given speaker at a given time) are mutually exclusive. Granted, our subject might be prompted once by a given stimulation σ to assent to S, and later, by a recurrence of σ, to dissent from S; but then we would simply conclude that his meaning for S had changed. We would then reckon σ to his affirmative stimulus meaning of S as of the one date and to his negative stimulus meaning of S as of the other date.

Yet the affirmative and negative stimulus meanings do not determine each other; for many stimulations may be expected to belong to neither. In general, therefore, comparison of whole stimulus meanings can be a better basis for translations than comparison merely of affirmative stimulus meanings.

What now of that strong conditional, the 'would' in our definition of stimulus meaning? Its use here is no worse than its use when we explain '*x* is soluble in water' as meaning that *x* would dissolve if it were in water. What the strong conditional defines is a disposition, in this case a disposition to assent to or dissent from S when variously stimulated. The disposition may be presumed to be some subtle structural condition, like an allergy and like solubility; like an allergy, more particularly, in not being understood. The ontological status of dispositions, or the philosophical status of talk of dispositions, is a matter which I defer but meanwhile we are familiar enough in a general way with how one sets about guessing, from judicious tests and samples and observed uniformities, whether there is a disposition of a specified sort.

The stimulus meaning of a sentence for a subject sums up his disposition to assent to or dissent from the sentence in response to present stimulation. The stimulation is what activates the disposition, as opposed to what instills it (even though the stimulation chance to contribute somehow to the instilling of some further disposition).

Yet a stimulation must be conceived for these purposes not as a dated particular event but as a universal, a repeatable event form. We are to say not that two like stimulations have occurred, but that the same stimulation has recurred. Such an attitude is implied the moment we speak of sameness of stimulus meaning for two speakers. We could indeed overrule this consideration, if we liked, by readjusting our terminology. But there would be no point, for there remains elsewhere a compelling reason for taking the stimulations as universals; viz., the strong conditional in the definition of stimulus meaning. For, consider again the affirmative stimulus meaning of a sentence S: the class Σ of all those stimulations that *would* prompt assent to S. If the stimulations were taken as events rather than event forms, then Σ would have to be a class of events which largely did not and will not happen, but which would prompt assent to S if they were to happen. Whenever Σ contained one realized or unrealized particular stimulatory event σ, it would have to contain all other unrealized duplicates of σ; and how many are there of *these*? Certainly it is hopeless nonsense to talk thus of unrealized particulars and try to assemble them into classes. Unrealized entities have to be construed as universals.

We were impressed [earlier] with the interdependence of sentences. We may well have begun then to wonder whether meanings even of whole sentences (let alone shorter expressions) could reasonably be talked of at all, except relative to the other sentences of an inclusive theory. Such relativity would be awkward, since, conversely, the individual component sentences offer the only way into the theory. Now the notion of stimulus meaning partially resolves the predicament. It isolates a sort of net empirical import of each of various single sentences without regard to the containing theory, even though without loss of what the sentence owes to that containing theory. It is a device, as far as it goes, for exploring the fabric of interlocking sentences, a sentence at a time.

Between the notion of stimulus meaning and Carnap's remarks on empirical semantics[5] there are connections and differences worth noting. He suggests exploring the meaning of a term by asking the subject whether he would apply it under various imaginary circumstances, to be described to him. That approach has the virtue of preserving contrasts between such terms as 'goblin' and 'unicorn' despite the non-existence of contrasting instances in the world. Stimulus meaning has the same virtue, since there are stimulation patterns that would prompt assent to 'Unicorn?' and not to 'Goblin?'. Carnap's approach presupposes some decision as to what descriptions of imaginary circumstances are admissible; e.g., 'unicorn' would be not wanted in descriptions used in probing the meaning of 'unicorn'. He hints of appropriate restrictions for the purpose, mentioning "size, shape, color"; and my notion of stimulus meaning itself amounts to a firmer definition in that same direction. There remains a significant contrast in the uses the two of us make of subjunctive conditionals: I limit them to my investigator's considered judgment of what the informant would do if stimulated; Carnap has his investigator putting such conditionals to the judgment of the informant. Certainly my investigator would in practice ask the same questions as Carnap's investigator, as a quick way of estimating stimulus meanings, if language for such questions happened to be available. But stimulus meaning can be explored also at the first stages of radical translation, where Carnap's type of questionnaire is unavailable. On this score it is important, as we shall see in section 6, that my theory has to do primarily with sentences of a sort and not, like Carnap's, with terms.

3. OCCASION SENTENCES. INTRUSIVE INFORMATION

Occasion sentences, as against *standing* sentences, are sentences such as 'Gavagai', 'Red', 'It hurts', 'His face is dirty', which command assent or dissent only if queried after an appropriate prompting stimulation. Verdicts to stand-

---

[5] *Meaning and Necessity*, 2d ed., Suppl. D. See also Chisholm, *Perceiving*, pp. 175 ff., and his references.

ing sentences *can* be prompted too: stimulation implemented by an interferometer once prompted Michelson and Morley to dissent from the standing sentence 'There is ether drift', and a speaker's assent can be prompted yearly to 'The crocuses are out', daily to 'The *Times* has come'. But these standing sentences contrast with occasion sentences in that the subject may repeat his old assent or dissent unprompted by current stimulation when we ask him again on later occasions, whereas an occasion sentence commands assent or dissent only as prompted all over again by current stimulation. Standing sentences grade off toward occasion sentences as the interval between possible repromptings diminishes; and the occasion sentence is the extreme case where that interval is less than the modulus. Like the stimulus meanings themselves, the distinction between standing sentences and occasion sentences is relative to the modulus; an occasion sentence modulo n seconds can be a standing sentence modulo $n - 1$.

The stimulations belonging to neither the affirmative nor the negative stimulus meaning of an occasion sentence are just those that would inhibit a verdict on the queried sentence, whether through indecisiveness (as in the case of a poor glimpse) or through shocking the subject out of his wits. On the other hand the stimulations belonging to neither the affirmative nor the negative stimulus meaning of a standing sentence are of two sorts: besides the inhibitory ones there are the *irrelevant* ones, which neither prompt nor inhibit. Querying the sentence on the heels of such a stimulation would elicit a verdict, but always the one that the query would have elicited without the attendant stimulation; never a change of verdict.

The stimulus meaning is a full cross-section of the subject's evolving dispositions to assent to or dissent from a sentence, if the sentence is an occasion sentence; less so if it is a standing sentence. Standing sentences can differ among themselves in "meaning," by any intuitive account,[6] as freely as occasion sentences; but, the less susceptible they are to prompted assent and dissent, the fewer clues are present in stimulus meaning. The notion of stimulus meaning is thus most important for occasion sentences, and we shall limit our attention for a while to them.

Even for such favored occasion sentences as 'Gavagai' and 'Rabbit', actually, sameness of stimulus meaning has its shortcomings as a synonymy relation. The difficulty is that an informant's assent to or dissent from 'Gavagai?' can depend excessively on prior collateral information as a supplement to the present prompting stimulus. He may assent on the occasion of nothing better than an ill-glimpsed movement in the grass, because of his earlier observation, unknown to the linguist, of rabbits near the spot. Since the linguist would not on his own information be prompted by that same poor glimpse to assent to 'Rabbit?', we have here a discrepancy between the present stimulus meaning of 'Gavagai' for the informant and that of 'Rabbit' for the linguist.

---

[6] Twice I have been startled to find my use of 'intuitive' misconstrued as alluding to some special and mysterious avenue of knowledge. By an intuitive account I mean one in which terms are used in habitual ways, without reflecting on how they might be defined or what presuppositions they might conceal.

More persistent discrepancies of the same type can be imagined, affecting not one native but all, and not once but regularly. There may be a local rabbit-fly,[7] unknown to the linguist, and recognizable some way off by its long wings and erratic movements; and seeing such a fly in the neighborhood of an ill-glimpsed animal could help a native to recognize the latter as a rabbit. Ocular irradiations combining poor glimpses of rabbits with good ones of rabbit-flies would belong to the stimulus meaning of 'Gavagai' for natives generally, and not to that of 'Rabbit' for the linguist.

And, to be less fanciful, there are all those stimulations that incorporate verbal hints from native kibitzers. Thus suppose that the stimulation on the heels of which the informant is asked 'Gavagai?' is a composite stimulation presenting a bystander pointing to an ill-glimpsed object and saying 'Gavagai'. This composite stimulation will probably turn out to belong to the affirmative stimulus meaning of 'Gavagai' for the informant, and not to the stimulus meaning of 'Rabbit' for most English speakers, on whom the force of the by-stander's verbal intervention would be lost. Such cases would not fool our linguist, but they do count against defining synonymy as sameness of stimulus meaning. For we must remember that every sufficiently brief stimulation pattern, though it be one that never gets actualized or that the linguist would never use, still by definition belongs to the stimulus meaning of 'Gavagai' for a man at a given time if it is one that *would* prompt his assent at that time.

Intuitively the ideal would be to accord to the affirmative meaning of 'Gavagai' just those stimulations that would prompt assent to 'Gavagai?' on the strength purely of an understanding of 'Gavagai', unaided by collateral information: unaided by recent observation of rabbits near the spot, unaided by knowledge of the nature and habits of the rabbit-fly, unaided by conversance with the kibitzer's language. On the face of it there is a difficulty in excluding this third aid, considering our continuing dependence on the subject's understanding of 'Gavagai'. But also the trouble is more widespread. It is precisely that we have made no general experimental sense of a distinction between what goes into a native's learning to apply an expression and what goes into his learning supplementary matters about the objects concerned. True, the linguist can press such a distinction part way; he can filter out such idiosyncratic bits of collateral matter as the informant's recent observation of rabbits near the spot, by varying his times and his informants and so isolating a more stable and more social stimulus meaning as common denominator. But any socially shared information, such as that about the rabbit-fly or the ability to understand a bystander's remark, will continue to affect even that common denominator. There is no evident criterion whereby to strip such effects away and leave just the meaning of 'Gavagai' properly so-called—whatever meaning properly so-called may be. . . .

We have now seen that stimulus meaning as defined falls short in various ways of one's intuitive demands on "meaning" as undefined, and that sameness

---

[7] Here I am indebted to Davidson.

of stimulus meaning is too strict a relation to expect between a native occasion sentence and its translation—even in so benign a case as 'Gavagai' and 'Rabbit'. Yet stimulus meaning, by whatever name, may be properly looked upon still as the objective reality that the linguist has to probe when he undertakes radical translation. For the stimulus meaning of an occasion sentence is by definition the native's total battery of present dispositions to be prompted to assent to or to dissent from the sentence; and these dispositions are just what the linguist has to sample and estimate. We do best to revise not the notion of stimulus meaning, but only what we represent the linguist as doing with stimulus meanings. The fact is that he translates not by identity of stimulus meanings, but by significant approximation of stimulus meanings.

If he translates 'Gavagai' as 'Rabbit' despite the discrepancies in stimulus meaning imagined above, he does so because the stimulus meanings seem to coincide to an overwhelming degree and the discrepancies, so far as he finds them, seem best explained away or dismissed as effects of unidentified interferences. Some discrepancies he may sift out, as lately suggested, by varying his times and informants. Some, involving poor glimpses or shock or verbal intrusions, he would not even bother to bring to fulfillment by a querying of the sentence. Some, such as those involving the rabbit-fly, he will dismiss as effects of unidentified interferences if he does not encounter them often. In taking this last rather high line, clearly he is much influenced by his natural expectation that any people in rabbit country would have *some* brief expression that could in the long run be best translated simply as 'Rabbit'. He conjectures that the now-unexplained discrepancies between 'Gavagai' and 'Rabbit' are ones that may eventually be reconciled with his translation, after he has somehow got deep enough into the native language to ask sophisticated questions.

In practice, of course, the natural expectation that the natives will have a brief expression for 'Rabbit' counts overwhelmingly. The linguist hears 'Gavagai' once, in a situation where a rabbit seems to be the object of concern. He will then try 'Gavagai' for assent or dissent in a couple of situations designed perhaps to eliminate 'White' and 'Animal' as alternative translations, and will forthwith settle upon 'Rabbit' as translation without further experiment—though always in readiness to discover through some unsought experience that a revision is in order. I made the linguist preternaturally circumspect, and maximized his bad luck in respect of discrepant observations, in order to consider what theoretical bearing a native's collateral information can have upon the linguist's in fact wholly facile opening translation.

4. OBSERVATION SENTENCES

Some stimulus meanings are less susceptible than others to the influences of intrusive information. There is on this score a significant contrast between 'Red' and 'Rabbit' even when 'Red' is taken on a par with 'Rabbit' as announcing not a passing sense datum but an enduring objective trait of the physical object. True, there are extreme cases where we may be persuaded, by collateral information about odd lighting and juxtaposition, that something is really red that did not seem so or vice versa; but, despite such cases, there is less scope for collateral information in deciding whether a glimpsed thing is red than in deciding whether it is a rabbit. In the case of 'Red', therefore, sameness of stimulus meaning comes unusually close to what one intuitively expects of synonymy.

Color words are notoriously ill matched between remote languages, because of differences in customary grouping of shades. But this is no present problem; it means merely that there may well be no native occasion sentence, at least no reasonably simple one, with approximately the stimulus meaning of 'Red'. Again, even if there is one, there may still be a kind of trouble in equating it to 'Red', just because of the vagueness of color boundaries in both languages. But this again is no problem of collateral information; it is a difficulty that would remain even if a distinction between meaning and collateral information were successfully drawn. It can be coped with by a rough matching of statistical scatterings. The penumbra of vagueness of 'Red' consists of stimulations in respect of which the stimulus meanings of 'Red' tend to vary from speaker to speaker and from occasion to occasion; correspondingly for the penumbra of vagueness of the native sentence; and then 'Red' is a good translation to the extent that it resembles the native sentence umbra for umbra and penumbra for penumbra.

In terms of direct behavioral evidence, how do those fluctuations of stimulus meaning that are attributable to a penumbra of vagueness differ from those fluctuations of stimulus meaning (e.g. of 'Gavagai') that are laid to variations of collateral information from occasion to occasion? Partly in that the penumbral fluctuations increase rather smoothly as the stimulations grade off, while the fluctuations laid to collateral information are more irregular, suggesting intrusion of extraneous factors. But mainly in that each individual's assent or dissent tends to be marked by doubt and hesitation when the prompting stimulation belongs to the penumbra. If we were to complicate the notion of stimulus meaning to the extent of weighting each stimulation inversely according to reaction time (*cf.* section 2), then discrepancies in stimulus meaning from speaker to speaker would tend to count for little where due to vagueness, and for more where not.

If 'Red' is somewhat less susceptible than 'Rabbit' to the influences of intrusive information, there are other sentences that are vastly more so. An example is 'Bachelor'. An informant's assent to it is prompted genuinely enough by the sight of a face, yet it draws mainly on stored information and none on the prompting stimulation except as needed for recognizing the bachelor friend concerned. As one says in the uncritical jargon of meaning, the trouble with 'Bachelor' is that its meaning transcends the looks of the prompting faces and concerns matters that can be known only through other channels. 'Rabbit' is a little this way, as witness papier-mâché counterfeits; 'Bachelor' much more so. The stimulus meaning of 'Bachelor' cannot be treated as its "meaning" by any stretch of the imagination, unless perhaps accompanied by a stretch of the modulus.

A mark of the intrusion of collateral information, except when the information is generally shared as in the examples of the kibitzer and the rabbit-fly (section 3), was discrepancy in stimulus meaning from speaker to speaker of the same language. In a case like 'Bachelor', therefore, we may expect the discrepancies to be overwhelming; and indeed they are. For any two speakers whose social contacts are not virtually identical, the stimulus meanings of 'Bachelor' will diverge far more than those of 'Rabbit'.

The less susceptible the stimulus meaning of an occasion sentence is to the influences of collateral information, the less absurdity there is in thinking of the stimulus meaning of the sentence as the meaning of the sentence. Occasion sentences whose stimulus meanings vary none under the influence of collateral information may naturally be called *observation sentences*, and their stimulus meanings may without fear of contradiction be said to do full justice to their meanings. These are the occasion sentences that wear their meanings on their sleeves. Or, better, we may speak of degrees of observationality; for even the stimulus meaning of 'Red' can, we noted, be made to fluctuate a little from occasion to occasion by collateral information on lighting conditions. What we have is a gradation of observationality from one extreme, at 'Red' or above, to the other extreme at 'Bachelor' or below.

In the foregoing paragraph we have wallowed most unfastidiously in the conceptual slough of meaning and collateral information. But now it is interesting to note that what we have dredged out, a notion of degree of observationality, is not beyond cleaning up and rendering respectable. For, in behavioral terms, an occasion sentence may be said to be the more observational the more nearly its stimulus meanings for different speakers tend to coincide. Granted, this definition fails to give demerit marks for the effects of generally shared information, such as that about the rabbit-fly. But, as argued in section 3, I suspect that no systematic experimental sense is to be made of a distinction between usage due to meaning and usage due to generally shared collateral information.

The notion of observationality is relative to the modulus of stimulation. This is not to be wondered at, since the notion of stimulus meaning was relative to the modulus (*cf.* section 2), and so is the very distinction between habit formation and habit formed (*cf.* section 1). Observationality increases with the modulus, in the following way. A typical case of discrepancy between the stimulus meanings of 'Gavagai', for two natives, is the case where one native and not the other has lately seen rabbits near the spot that they are now viewing. An ill-glimpsed movement would now prompt the one native and not the other to assent to 'Gavagai?'. But if we make the modulus long enough to include as part of the one native's present stimulation his recent observation of rabbits near the spot, then what had been a discrepancy between stimulus meanings is a mere difference of stimulations: the one stimulation is such as would prompt either native to assent, and the other neither. Increase the modulus sufficiently to take in extended periods of learning about friends and you even increase the observationality of 'Bachelor'. But let us forget moduli again for a while, thus keeping our variables down.

We have defined observationality for occasion sentences somewhat vaguely, as degree of constancy of stimulus meaning from speaker to speaker. It would not do to use this definition generally among standing sentences, since the stimulus meaning of a standing sentence can show fair constancy from speaker to speaker for the wrong reason: mere sparseness of member stimulations. Among standing sentences that are well over toward the occasion end (*cf.* section 3), however, the notion of observationality works quite as well as among occasion sentences, and is significant in the same way; viz., the higher the observationality, the better we can get on with translation by stimulus meaning. We could hope, e.g., to translate 'The tide is out' by a rough matching of stimulus meanings; not so 'There is a famous novelist on board'.

Viewing the graded notion of observationality as the primary one, we may still speak of sentences simply as observation sentences when they are high in observationality. In a narrow sense, just 'Red' would qualify; in a wider sense, also 'Rabbit' and 'The tide is out'. It is for observation sentences in some such sense that the notion of stimulus meaning constitutes a reasonable notion of meaning.

To philosophers 'observation sentence' suggests the datum sentences of science. On this score our version is not amiss; for the observation sentences as we have identified them are just the occasion sentences on which there is pretty sure to be firm agreement on the part of well-placed observers. Thus they are just the sentences on which a scientist will tend to fall back when pressed by doubting colleagues. Moreover, the philosophical doctrine of infallibility of observation sentences is sustained under our version. For there is scope for error and dispute only insofar as the connections with experience whereby sentences are appraised are multifarious and indirect, mediated through time by theory in conflicting ways; there is none insofar as verdicts to a sentence are directly keyed to present stimulation. (This immunity to error is, however, like observationality itself, for us a matter of degree.) Our version of observation sentences departs from a philosophical tradition in allowing the sentences to be about ordinary things instead of requiring them to report sense data, but this departure has not lacked proponents.[8]

In estimating the stimulus meaning of a sentence for a speaker at a given time, the linguist is helped by varying the time and speaker. In choosing a translation, he is helped by comparing native speakers and so eliminating idiosyncrasies of stimulus meaning. Still the notion of stimulus meaning itself, as defined, depends on no multiplicity of speakers. Now the notion of obser-

[8] For remarks on this matter and references see von Mises, *Positivism*, pp. 91–95, 379. To the main theme of this paragraph I sense harmony in Strawson, *Individuals*, p. 212: "If any facts deserve ... to be called ... atomic facts, it is the facts stated by those propositions which demonstratively indicate the incidence of a general feature." For the propositions alluded to seem, in the light of adjacent text, to correspond pretty well to what I have called occasion sentences.

vationality, in contrast, is social. The behavioral definition offered for it above turns on similarities of stimulus meanings over the community.

What makes an occasion sentence low on observationality is, by definition, wide intersubjective variability of stimulus meaning. Language as a socially inculcated set of dispositions is substantially uniform over the community, but it is uniform in different ways for different sentences. If a sentence is one that (like 'Red' and 'Rabbit') is inculcated mostly by something like direct ostension, the uniformity will lie at the surface and there will be little variation in stimulus meaning; the sentence will be highly observational. If it is one that (like 'Bachelor') is inculcated through connections with other sentences, linking up thus indirectly with past stimulations of other sorts than those that serve directly to prompt present assent to the sentence, then its stimulus meaning will vary with the speakers' parts, and the sentence will count as very unobservational. The stimulus meaning of a very unobservational occasion sentence for a speaker is a product of two factors, a fairly standard set of sentence-to-sentence connections and a random personal history; hence the largely random character of the stimulus meaning from speaker to speaker.

Now this random character has the effect not only that the stimulus meaning of the sentence for one speaker will differ from the stimulus meaning of *that* sentence for other speakers. It will differ from the stimulus meaning also of any other discoverable sentence for other speakers, in the same language or any other. Granted, a great complex English sentence can be imagined whose stimulus meaning for one man matches, by sheer exhaustion of cases, another man's stimulus meaning of 'Bachelor'; but such a sentence would never be spotted, because nobody's stimulus meaning of 'Bachelor' would ever be suitably inventoried to begin with.

For, consider again how it was with 'Gavagai'. Here the stimulations belonging to the affirmative stimulus meaning share a distinctive trait that is salient, to us as well as to the native: the containing of rabbit glimpses. The trait is salient enough so that the linguist generalizes on it from samples: he expects the next glimpse of a rabbit to prompt assent to 'Gavagai' as past ones have. His generalization is repeatedly borne out, and he concludes with his conjecture that the native's whole stimulus meaning of 'Gavagai'—never experimentally exhausted, of course—will tend to match ours of 'Rabbit'. Now a similar effort with a non-observational native occasion sentence, of the type of our 'Bachelor', would have bogged down in its early stages. Sample stimulations belonging to the affirmative stimulus meaning of such a sentence, for the given native, would show no tempting common traits by which to conjecture further cases, or none but such as fail to hold up on further tries.

5. INTRASUBJECTIVE SYNONYMY OF OCCASION SENTENCES

Stimulus meaning remains defined without regard to observationality. But when applied to non-observational sentences like 'Bachelor' it bears little resemblance to what might reasonably be called meaning. Translation of

'Soltero' as 'Bachelor' manifestly cannot be predicated on identity of stimulus meanings between speakers; nor can synonymy of 'Bachelor' and 'Unmarried man'.

But curiously enough the stimulus meanings of 'Bachelor' and 'Unmarried man' are, despite all this, identical for any one speaker.[9] An individual would at any one time be prompted by the same stimulations to assent to 'Bachelor' and 'Unmarried man'; and similarly for dissent. *Stimulus synonymy*, or sameness of stimulus meaning, is as good a standard of synonymy for non-observational occasion sentences as for observation sentences as long as we stick to one speaker. For each speaker, 'Bachelor' and 'Unmarried man' are stimulus-synonymous without having the same meaning in any acceptably defined sense of 'meaning' (for stimulus meaning is, in the case of 'Bachelor', nothing of the kind). Very well; here is a case where we may welcome the synonymy and let the meaning go.

The one-speaker restriction presents no obstacle to saying that 'Bachelor' and 'Unmarried man' are stimulus-synonymous for the whole community, in the sense of being thus for each member. A practical extension even to the two-language case is not far to seek if a bilingual speaker is at hand. 'Bachelor' and 'Soltero' will be stimulus-synonymous for him. Taking him as a sample, we may treat 'Bachelor' and 'Soltero' as synonymous for the translation purposes of the two whole linguistic communities that he represents. Whether he is a good enough sample would be checked by observing the fluency of his communication in both communities and by comparing other bilinguals.

Section 4 left the linguist unable to guess the trend of the stimulus meaning of a non-observational occasion sentence from sample cases. We now see a way, though costly, in which he can still accomplish radical translation of such sentences. He can settle down and learn the native language directly as an infant might. Having thus become bilingual, he can translate the non-observational occasion sentences by introspected stimulus synonymy.

This step has the notable effect of initiating clear recognition of native falsehoods. As long as the linguist does no more than correlate the native's observation sentences with his own by stimulus meaning, he cannot discount any of the native's verdicts as false—unless *ad hoc*, most restrainedly, to simplify his correlations. But once he becomes bilingual and so transcends the observation sentences, he can bicker with the native as a brother.

Even short of going bilingual there is no difficulty in comparing two non-observational native sentences to see if they are intrasubjectively stimulus-synonymous for the native. The linguist can do this without having intuitively conjectured the trend of stimulus meaning of either sentence. He need merely

---

[9] It can be argued that this much-used example of synonymy has certain imperfections having to do with ages, divorce, and bachelors of arts. Another example much used in philosophy, 'brother' and 'male sibling', may be held to bog down under certain church usages. An example that is perhaps unassailable is 'mother's father' and 'maternal grandfather' (poetic connotations not being here in point), or 'widower' and 'man who lost his wife' (Jakobson). However, with this much by way of caveat against quibbling, perhaps we can keep to our conventional example and overlook its divagations.

query the sentences in parallel under random stimulations until he either hits a stimulation that prompts assent or dissent to one sentence and not to the other, or else is satisfied at last that he is not going to. A visiting Martian who never learns under what circumstances to apply 'Bachelor', or 'Unmarried man' either, can still find out by the above method that 'Bachelor' for one English speaker does not have the same stimulus meaning as 'Bachelor' for a different English speaker and that it has the same as 'Unmarried man' for the same speaker. He can, anyway, apart from one difficulty: there is no evident reason why it should occur to him thus blindly to try comparing 'Unmarried man' with 'Bachelor'. This difficulty makes the intrasubjective stimulus synonymy of non-observational occasion sentences less readily accessible to an alien linguist than the stimulus synonymy of observation sentences such as 'Gavagai' and 'Rabbit'. Still the linguist can examine for intrasubjective stimulus synonymy any pair of native occasion sentences that it occurs to him to wonder about; and we shall see in section 9 how indirect considerations can even suggest such pairs for examination.

Between the stimulus meaning of any sentence for one man and the stimulus meaning of the same or any other sentence for another man there are almost bound to be countless discrepancies in point of verbally contaminated stimulations, as long as one man understands a language that the other does not. The argument is that of the kibitzer case in section 3. The translating linguist had for this reason to discount verbally contaminated discrepancies. But intrasubjective comparisons are free of this trouble. Intrasubjectively we can even compare the occasion sentences 'Yes', 'Uh huh', and 'Quite' for stimulus synonymy, though the stimulations that enter into the stimulus meanings of these sentences are purely verbal in their relevant portions. A further advantage of the intrasubjective situation appears in the case of stimulations that would at a given time shock one speaker and not another into silence (cf. section 3), for clearly these will constitute no discrepancies intrasubjectively. Altogether the equating of stimulus meanings works out far better intrasubjectively than between subjects: it goes beyond observation sentences, it absorbs shock, and it better accommodates verbal stimulations.

Verbal stimulations can plague even the intrasubjective comparisons when they are stimulations of "second intention"—i.e., when besides consisting of words they are about words. Second-intention examples are the bane of theoretical linguistics, also apart from synonymy studies. Thus take the linguist engaged in distinguishing between those sequences of sounds or phonemes that can occur in English speech and those that cannot: all his excluded forms can return to confound him in second-intention English, as between quotation marks. Now some second-intention stimulations that could prompt a subject to assent to one of the queries 'Bachelor?' and 'Unmarried man?' to the exclusion of the other are as follows: a stimulation presenting the spelling of 'bachelor'; a stimulation presenting the words "rhymes with 'harried man'"; a stimulation presenting a glimpse of a bachelor friend together with a plea to redefine 'bachelor'. It is not easy to find a behavioral criterion of second-intention whereby to screen such cases, especially the last. . . .

Our success with 'Bachelor' and 'Unmarried man' has been sufficient, despite the impasse at second intention, to tempt us to overestimate how well intrasubjective stimulus synonymy withstands collateral information. By way of corrective, consider the Himalayan explorer who has learned to apply 'Everest' to a distant mountain seen from Tibet and 'Gaurisanker' to one seen from Nepal. As occasion sentences these words have mutually exclusive stimulus meanings for him until his explorations reveal, to the surprise of all concerned, that the peaks are identical. His discovery is painfully empirical, not lexicographic; nevertheless the stimulus meanings of 'Everest' and 'Gaurisanker' coincide for him thenceforward.[10]

Or again consider the occasion sentences 'Indian nickel' and 'Buffalo nickel'. These have distinct stimulus meanings for a boy for his first minute or two of passive acquaintance with these coins, and when he gets to turning them over the stimulus meanings tend to fuse.

Do they fully fuse? The question whether 'Indian nickel' and 'Buffalo nickel' have the same stimulus meaning for a given subject is the question whether any sequence of ocular irradiations or other stimulation (within the modulus), realized or not, *would* now prompt the subject to assent to or dissent from 'Indian nickel' and not 'Buffalo nickel' or vice versa. Among such stimulations are those that present, to all appearances, a coin whose obverse is like that of an Indian nickel but whose reverse bears some device other than the buffalo. Such stimulations can with a little felony even be realized. After a modulus-long examination of such a hybrid coin, a novice might conclude with surprise that there are after all two kinds of Indian nickel, while an expert, sure of his numismatics, might conclude that the coin must be fraudulent. For the expert, 'Indian nickel' and 'Buffalo nickel' are stimulus-synonymous; for the novice not.

The novice does believe and continues to believe, as the expert does, that all Indian nickels are buffalo nickels and vice versa; for the novice has not been and will not be actually subjected to the surprising stimulation described. But the mere fact that there is such a stimulation pattern and that the novice *would* now thus respond to it (whether we know it or not) is what, by definition, makes the stimulus meanings of 'Indian nickel' and 'Buffalo nickel' differ for the novice even as of now.

To keep our example pertinent we must abstract from what may be called the conniving mode of speech: the mode in which we knowingly speak of Olivier as Macbeth, of a statue of a horse as a horse, of a false nickel as a nickel. Even the expert would in practice speak of the prepared coin as "that Indian nickel with the whoozis on the back," adding that it was phony. Here we have a broader usage of 'nickel', under which nobody would seriously maintain

---

[10] I am indebted to Davidson for this point and to Schrödinger, *What Is Life?*, for the example. I am told that the example is wrong geographically.

even that all Indian nickels are in point of fact buffalo nickels and vice versa; whereas our purpose in the example is to examine two supposedly coextensive terms for sameness of stimulus meaning. In the example, therefore, read 'Indian nickel' and 'buffalo nickel' as 'real Indian nickel', 'real buffalo nickel'.

From the example we see that two terms can in fact be coextensive, or true of the same things, without being intrasubjectively stimulus-synonymous as occasion sentences. They can be believed coextensive without being, even for the believer, stimulus-synonymous as occasion sentences; witness 'Indian nickel' and 'Buffalo nickel' for the novice. But when as in the expert's case the belief is so firm that no pattern of stimulation (within the modulus) would suffice to dislodge it, they are stimulus-synonymous as occasion sentences.

So it is apparent that intrasubjective stimulus synonymy remains open to criticism, from intuitive preconceptions, for relating occasion sentences whose stimulus meanings coincide on account of collateral information. Now there is still a way of cutting out the effects of idiosyncratic information: we can hold out for virtual constancy over the community. In this social sense of stimulus synonymy, 'Indian nickel' and 'Buffalo nickel' would cease to count as stimulus-synonymous, because of such speakers as our novice; whereas 'Bachelors' and 'Unmarried man' might still rate as stimulus-synonymous even socially, as being intrasubjectively stimulus-synonymous for nearly everybody. There is still no screen against the effects of collateral information common to the community; but, as urged in section 3 I think that at that point the ideal becomes illusory.

6. SYNONYMY OF TERMS

In starting our consideration of meaning with sentences we have hewn the [earlier] line where it was stressed that words are learned only by abstraction from their roles in learned sentences. But there are one-word sentences, such as 'Red' and 'Rabbit'. Insofar as the concept of stimulus meaning may be said to constitute in some strained sense a meaning concept for these, it would seem to constitute a meaning concept for general terms like 'red' and 'rabbit'. This, however, is a mistake. Stimulus synonymy of the occasion sentences 'Gavagai' and 'Rabbit' does not even guarantee that 'gavagai' and 'rabbit' are coextensive terms, terms true of the same things.

For, consider 'gavagai'. Who knows but what the objects to which this term applies are not rabbits after all, but mere stages, or brief temporal segments, of rabbits? In either event the stimulus situations that prompt assent to 'Gavagai' would be the same as for 'Rabbit'. Or perhaps the objects to which 'gavagai' applies are all and sundry undetached parts of rabbits; again the stimulus meaning would register no difference. When from the sameness of stimulus meanings of 'Gavagai' and 'Rabbit' the linguist leaps to the conclusion that a gavagai is a whole enduring rabbit, he is just taking for granted that the native is enough like us to have a brief general term for rabbits and no brief general term for rabbit stages or parts.

A further alternative likewise compatible with the same old stimulus meaning is to take 'gavagai' as a singular term naming the fusion, in Goodman's sense, of all rabbits: that single though discontinuous portion of the spatiotemporal world that consists of rabbits. Thus even the distinction between general and singular terms is independent of stimulus meaning. The same point can be seen by considering, conversely, the singular term 'Bernard J. Ortcutt': it differs none in stimulus meaning from a general term true of each of the good dean's temporal segments, and none from a general term true of each of his spatial parts. And a still further alternative in the case of 'gavagai' is to take it as a singular term naming a recurring universal, rabbithood. The distinction between concrete and abstract object, as well as that between general and singular term, is independent of stimulus meaning.

Commonly we can translate something (e.g. 'for the sake of') into a given language though nothing in that language corresponds to certain of the component syllables. Just so the occasion sentence 'Gavagai' is translatable as saying that a rabbit is there, even if no part of 'Gavagai' nor anything at all in the native language quite corresponds to the term 'rabbit'. Synonymy of 'Gavagai' and 'Rabbit' as sentences turns on considerations of prompted assent; not so synonymy of them as terms. We are right to write 'Rabbit', instead of 'rabbit', as a signal that we are considering it in relation to what is synonymous with it as a sentence and not in relation to what is synonymous with it as a term.

Does it seem that the imagined indecision between rabbits, stages of rabbits, integral parts of rabbits, the rabbit fusion, and rabbithood must be due merely to some special fault in our formulation of stimulus meaning, and that it should be resoluble by a little supplementary pointing and questioning? Consider, then, how. Point to a rabbit and you have pointed to a stage of a rabbit, to an integral part of a rabbit, to the rabbit fusion, and to where rabbithood is manifested. Point to an integral part of a rabbit and you have pointed again to the remaining four sorts of things; and so on around. Nothing not distinguished in stimulus meaning itself is to be distinguished by pointing, unless the pointing is accompanied by questions of identity and diversity: 'Is this the same gavagai as that?', 'Do we have here one gavagai or two?'. Such questioning requires of the linguist a command of the native language far beyond anything that we have as yet seen how to account for. We cannot even say what native locutions to count as analogues of terms as we know them, much less equate them with ours term for term, except as we have also decided what native devices to view as doing in their devious ways the work of our own various auxiliaries to objective reference: our articles and pronouns, our singular and plural, our copula, our identity predicate.[11] The whole apparatus is interdependent, and the very notion of term is as provincial to our culture as are those associated devices. The native may achieve the same net effects through linguistic structures so different that any eventual construing of our devices in the native language

---

[11] Strawson is making this point when he writes that "feature-placing sentences do not introduce particulars into our discourse" ("Particular and General," *PAS*, LIV (1954), p. 244).

and vice versa can prove unnatural and largely arbitrary. (Cf. section 9.) Yet the net effects, the occasion sentences and not the terms, can match up in point of stimulus meanings as well as ever for all that. Occasion sentences and stimulus meaning are general coin; terms and reference are local to our conceptual scheme.[12]

It will perhaps be countered that there is no essential difficulty in spotting judgments of identity on the part of the jungle native, or even of a speechless animal. This is true enough for qualitative identity, better called resemblance. In an organism's susceptibility to the conditioning of responses we have plentiful criteria for his standards of resemblance of stimulations. But what is relevant to the preceding reflections is numerical identity. Two pointings may be pointings to a numerically identical rabbit, to numerically distinct rabbit parts, and to numerically distinct rabbit stages; the inscrutability lies not in resemblance, but in the anatomy of sentences. We could equate a native expression with any of the disparate English terms 'rabbit', 'rabbit stage', 'undetached rabbit part', etc., and still, by compensatorily juggling the translation of numerical identity and associated particles, preserve conformity to stimulus meanings of occasion sentences.[13]

Intrasubjective stimulus synonymy, for all its advantages over the two-speaker case, is similarly powerless to equate terms. Our Martian of section 5 can find as he did that 'Bachelor' and 'Unmarried man' are synonymous occasion sentences for the English speaker, but still either *term* to the exclusion of the other might, so far as he knows, apply not to men but to their stages or parts or even to a scattered concrete totality or an abstract attribute.

We saw in section 5 that coextensiveness of terms, or even believed coextensiveness, is not sufficient for their stimulus synonymy as occasion sentences. We now see also that it is not necessary. Where other languages than our own are involved, coextensiveness of terms is not a manifestly clearer notion than synonymy or translation itself; it is no clearer than the considerations, whatever they are (sections 9 and 10), that make for contextual translation of the identity predicate, the copula, and related particles.

Yet surely the main interest of the synonymy of 'Bachelor' and 'Unmarried man' as occasion sentences was the line it seemed to give on the synonymy of 'bachelor' and 'unmarried man' as terms. Now within English the situation is not beyond saving. To get synonymy of terms from synonymy of the corresponding occasion sentences we need only add a condition that will screen out such pairs as 'bachelor' and 'part of a bachelor'; and this we can do by requiring that the subject be prepared to assent to the standing sentence 'All *F*s are *G*s and vice versa', thinking of '*F*' and '*G*' as the terms in question. The definition becomes this: '*F*' and '*G*' are stimulus-synonymous as terms for a speaker at *t*

---

[12] Russell conceived of what he called "object words" as in effect occasion sentences (*An Inquiry into Meaning and Truth*, Ch. IV), but, like Carnap (see end of section 2, above), he failed to note the present point: that the use of a word as an occasion sentence, however determinate, does not fix the extension of the word as a term.

[13] On this theme see further sections 9 and 10.

if and only if as occasion sentences they have the same stimulus meaning for him at t and he would assent to 'All Fs are Gs and vice versa' if asked at t. But we can simplify this definition, by strengthening the latter part to make it assure the former part. Instead of just saying he would assent to 'All Fs are Gs and vice versa' as things stand at t, we can say he would still assent to it, if to anything, following any stimulation that might be imposed at t. (The 'if to anything' accommodates shock.) This strengthened condition assures that 'F' and 'G' will also agree in stimulus meaning as occasion sentences; for, if each stimulation would leave the subject prepared to assent to 'All Fs are Gs and vice versa' if to anything, then none would prompt him to assent to or dissent from one of 'F' and 'G' and not the other.[14]

For reasons evident in section 8, I call a sentence *stimulus-analytic* for a subject if he would assent to it, or nothing, after every stimulation (within the modulus). Our condition of stimulus synonymy of 'F' and 'G' as general terms then reduces to stimulus analyticity of 'All Fs are Gs and vice versa'. This condition has its parallel for singular terms, represented by 'a' and 'b'; viz., stimulus-analyticity of '$a = b$'. But note that our formulations apply only to English and to languages whose translations of 'all', 'are', and ' $=$ ' are somehow settled in advance. This limitation is to be expected in notions relating to terms.

Our simplification of the definition of term synonymy extends it to all terms, regardless of whether their objects are such that we could reasonably use the terms as occasion sentences. We must not conclude, from seeming appropriateness of the definition as applied to terms like 'rabbit', 'bachelor', and 'buffalo nickel', that it is as appropriate to the wider domain. However, let us leave that question and think further about the narrower domain.

Our version of synonymy makes the terms 'Indian nickel' and 'buffalo nickel' synonymous for the expert of section 5, and not for the novice. It is open to criticism, from intuitive preconceptions, for its equating of terms whose coextensiveness the subject has learned by exploration and experiment and not merely by encompassing their "meanings." Such, then, is the concept of stimulus synonymy of terms that comes out of stimulus synonymy of occasion sentences for individual speakers. We can still socialize the concept and so cut out the effects of idiosyncratic information, as we did for occasion sentences at the end of section 5: we can count just those terms as socially stimulus-synonymous that come out stimulus-synonymous for each individual speaker almost without exception. Socially, 'bachelor' and 'unmarried man' remain stimulus-synonymous while 'Indian nickel' and 'buffalo nickel' do not.

We welcome this consequence of socializing our concept of stimulus synonymy because our intuitive semantics[15] rates 'bachelor' and 'unmarried man' as synonymous, and probably 'Indian nickel' and 'buffalo nickel' not. But now what can have been the cause of those intuitive ratings themselves? Not, I think, any close analogue, however unconscious, of our present construction:

---

[14] Incoherent behavior is possible, but there is a limit to the bizarreness of exceptions worth allowing for in these behavioral formulations.

[15] See section 3, note 16.

not an implicit sociological guess that under extraordinary stimulation most people would hold 'bachelor' and 'unmarried man' coextensive while many would let 'Indian nickel' and 'buffalo nickel' diverge. A likelier place to seek the cause is in the difference between how we whose mother tongue is English learn 'bachelor' and how we learn 'Indian nickel'. We learn 'bachelor' by learning appropriate associations of words with words, and 'Indian nickel' by learning directly to associate the term with sample objects.[16] It is the difference, so central to Russell's philosophy, between description and acquaintance. It is kept before us in synchronic behavior as a difference between the non-observational occasion sentences, with their random variation in stimulus meaning from speaker to speaker, and observation sentences with their socially uniform stimulus meanings. (Cf. section 4.) One looks to 'unmarried man' as semantically anchoring 'bachelor' because there is no socially constant stimulus meaning to govern the use of the word; sever its tie with 'unmarried man' and you leave it no very evident social determination, hence no utility in communication.

'Brother', in its synonymy with 'male sibling', is essentially like 'bachelor' in its synonymy with 'unmarried man'. We learn 'brother' (in its accurate adult use) only by verbal connections with sentences about childbirth, and 'sibling' by verbal connections with 'brother' and 'sister'. The occasion sentences 'Brother' and 'Sibling' are non-observational: their stimulus meanings vary over society in as random a fashion as that of 'Bachelor', and it is only the few verbal links that give the terms the fixity needed in communication.

Many terms of systematic theoretical science are of a third sort. They are like 'bachelor' and 'brother' in having no socially constant stimulus meanings to govern their use; indeed such a term is commonly useless in the role of occasion sentence, so that there is no question of stimulus meaning. Yet they are unlike 'bachelor' and 'brother' in having a more complex network of verbal connections, so that no one tie seems crucial to communication. Thus it is that in theoretical science, unless as recast by semantics enthusiasts, distinctions between synonymies and "factual" equivalences are seldom sensed or claimed. Even the identity historically introduced into mechanics by defining 'momentum' as 'mass times velocity' takes its place in the network of connections on a par with the rest; if a physicist subsequently so revises mechanics that momentum fails to be proportional to velocity, the change will probably be seen as a change of theory and not peculiarly of meaning.[17] Synonymy intuitions do not emerge here, just because the terms are linked to the rest of language in more ways than words like 'bachelor' are.[18]

---

[16] To be precise about the example, we learn 'nickel' and 'Indian' in direct association with sample objects or likenesses, and then 'Indian nickel' is self-explanatory once we see one.

[17] See the last section of my "Carnap and Logical Truth."

[18] Putnam in "The Analytic and the Synthetic" [See selection 1.6 above, pp. 94–126.] has offered an illuminating account of the synonymy intuition in terms of a contrast between terms that connote clusters of traits and terms that do not. My account fits with his and perhaps adds to the explanation. His cases of clustering correspond to my observational terms such as 'Indian nickel' and theoretical terms such as 'momentum', as against 'bachelor'.

7. TRANSLATING LOGICAL CONNECTIVES

In sections 1 through 5 we accounted for radical translation of occasion sentences, by approximate identification of stimulus meanings. Now there is also a decidedly different domain that lends itself directly to radical translation: that of *truth functions* such as negation, logical conjunction, and alternation. For this purpose the sentences put to the native for assent or dissent may be occasion sentences and standing sentences indifferently. Those that are occasion sentences will have to be accompanied by a prompting stimulation, if assent or dissent is to be elicited; the standing sentences, on the other hand, can be put without props. Now by reference to assent and dissent we can state semantic criteria for truth functions; i.e., criteria for determining whether a given native idiom is to be construed as expressing the truth function in question. The semantic criterion of negation is that it turns any short sentence to which one will assent into a sentence from which one will dissent, and vice versa. That of conjunction is that it produces compounds to which (so long as the component sentences are short) one is prepared to assent always and only when one is prepared to assent to each component. That of alternation is similar with assent changed twice to dissent. . . .

When we find that a native construction fulfills one or another of these three semantic criteria, we can ask no more toward an understanding of it. Incidentally we can then translate the idiom into English as 'not', 'and', or 'or' as the case may be, but only subject to sundry humdrum provisos; for it is well known that these three English words do not represent negation, conjunction, and alternation exactly and unambiguously.

Any construction for compounding sentences from sentences is counted in logic as expressing a truth function if it fulfills this condition: the compound has a unique truth value (truth or falsity) for each assignment of truth values to the components. Semantic criteria can obviously be stated for all truth functions along the lines already followed for negation, conjunction, and alternation. . . .

8. SYNONYMOUS AND ANALYTIC SENTENCES

By its etymology, 'synonymous' applies to names. Though in use the term is intended simply to impute sameness of meaning, an effect of its etymology is seen in a tendency to invoke some other word, 'equivalent' or 'equipollent', for cases where both of the compared expressions are (unlike 'bachelor') verbally complex. My use of 'synonymous' is not thus restricted; I intend the word to carry the full generality of 'same in meaning', whatever that is. Indeed I have made no essential use of a distinction between word and phrase. Even the first object of translation, say 'Gavagai', may or may not in the end be parsed as a string of several words, depending on one's eventual choice of analytical hypotheses (sections 9, 10).

Taking this minor liberalization hereafter for granted, we still must distinguish between a broad and a narrow type of synonymy, or sameness of meaning, as applied to sentences. The broad one may be formulated in intuitive terms thus: the two sentences command assent concomitantly and dissent concomitantly, and this concomitance is due strictly to word usage rather than to how things happen in the world. One usually hears the matter described in terms rather of truth values than of assent and dissent; but I warp it over to the latter terms in order to maximize chances of making sense of the relation on the basis of verbal behavior.

For some purposes a narrower sort of synonymy of sentences is wanted, such as what Carnap calls intensional isomorphism, involving certain part-by-part correspondences of the sentences concerned. But such variant versions can be defined on the basis of the broader one. Synonymy of parts is defined by appeal to analogy of roles in synonymous wholes; then synonymy in the narrower sense is defined for the wholes by appeal to synonymy of homologous parts. So let us concentrate on the broader and more basic notion of sentence synonymy.

By talking in terms of assent and dissent here instead of in terms of truth values we introduce this difficulty: assent and dissent can be influenced by confusion due to a sentence's length and complexity. But this difficulty can be accommodated in the way sketched in section 5. Also it would be automatically taken care of under the program, just now mentioned, of deriving a relation of synonymy of sentence fragments and thence constructing a reformed synonymy relation for wholes. Let us pass over these points, for there is a more basic problem.

When the sentences are occasion sentences, the envisaged notion of synonymy is pretty well realized in intrasubjective stimulus synonymy, especially as socialized. For we can argue that only verbal habit can plausibly account for concomitant variation of two occasion sentences, in point of assent and dissent, over the whole gamut of possible stimulations. There are still the unscreened effects of community-wide collateral information, but there is no evident reason not to count such information simply as a determinant of the verbal habit (section 3). When the sentences are standing sentences which, like 'The *Times* has come', closely resemble occasion sentences in the variability of assent and dissent, stimulus synonymy still does pretty well.

But the less variable the standing sentences are in point of assent and dissent, the sparser their stimulus meanings will be and hence the more poorly stimulus synonymy will approximate to synonymy of the envisaged sort. For, however sparse its stimulus meaning, a sentence retains its connections with other sentences and plays its distinctive part in theories. The sparseness of its stimulus meaning is no sparseness of meaning intuitively speaking, but has the effect that stimulus meaning fails to do the sentence much justice.

By lengthening the modulus of stimulation we can enrich the stimulus meanings and so tighten the relation of stimulus synonymy; for, the longer the stimulations the better their chance of influencing assent and dissent. However, matters get out of hand when the modulus is excessive. Thus consider stimulus synonymy modulo a month. To say that two sentences are now so related is to say that any and every pattern of month-long stimulation, if begun now and terminated next month with a querying of the two sentences, would elicit the same verdict on both. The trouble is that there is no telling what to expect under fairly fantastic stimulation sequences of such duration. The subject might revise his theories in unforeseeable ways that would be claimed to change meanings of words. There is no reason to expect the concomitances of sentences under such circumstances to reflect present sameness of meaning in any intuitively plausible sense. Lengthening the modulus enriches stimulus meanings and tightens stimulus synonymy only as it diminishes scrutability of stimulus synonyms.

Stimulus synonymy, on an optimum modulus, is an approximation to what philosophers loosely call sameness of confirming experiences and of disconfirming experiences. It is an approximation to what it might mean "to speak of two statements as standing in the same germaneness-relation to the same particular experiences."[19] Where standing sentences are of highly unoccasional type, the inadequacy of stimulus synonymy to synonymy intuitively so-called is shared by the vaguer formulations just now noted. And it is shared by the proposal of Perkins and Singer, viz., that we compare sentences for synonymy by putting them to our informant for verification and seeing whether he proceeds similarly in both cases.[20] The trouble lies in the interconnections of sentences. If the business of a sentence can be exhausted by an account of the experiences that would confirm or disconfirm it as an isolated sentence in its own right, then the sentence is substantially an occasion sentence. The significant trait of other sentences is that experience is relevant to them largely in indirect ways, through the mediation of associated sentences. Alternatives emerge: experiences call for changing a theory, but do not indicate just where and how. Any of various systematic changes can accommodate the recalcitrant datum, and all the sentences affected by any of those possible alternative readjustments would evidently have to count as disconfirmed by that datum indiscriminately or not at all. Yet the sentences can be quite unlike with respect to content, intuitively speaking, or role in the containing theory.

Grice and Strawson try (*loc. cit.*) to meet this difficulty by defining S_1 and S_2 as synonymous when, for every assumption as to the truth values of other sentences, the same experiences confirm (and disconfirm) S_1 on that assumption as confirm (and disconfirm) S_2 on that assumption. Now instead of 'every assumption as to the truth values of other sentences' we can as well say simply 'every sentence S'; for S can be the logical conjunction of those "other sentences" in question or their negations. So S_1 and S_2 are defined to be synonymous when, for every S, the same experiences confirm (and disconfirm) S_1 on the hypothesis S as confirm (and disconfirm) S_2 on S. The notion of confirmatory and disconfirmatory experiences had a behavioral approximation in our notion of stimulus meaning; but can we relativize it thus to a hypothesis

---

[19]Grice and Strawson, "In Defense of a Dogma," p. 156. See selection 1.5 above, pp. 81–94.
[20] See Perkins and Singer, "Analyticity," *Journal of Philosophy*, XLVIII (1951). It is significant that their examples are occasion sentences.

S? I think we can; for confirmation or disconfirmation of S_1 on S is presumably confirmation or disconfirmation of the conditional sentence consisting of S as antecedent and S_1 as consequent. Then the proposed definition of synonymy becomes: S_1 and S_2 are synonymous if for every S the conditional compound of S and S_1 and that of S and S_2 are stimulus-synonymous. But now it is apparent that the definition fails to provide a tighter relation between S_1 and S_2 than stimulus synonymy. For, if S_1 and S_2 are stimulus-synonymous than *a fortiori* the conditionals are too.

A variant suggestion would be to define S_1 and S_2 as synonymous when, for every S, the logical conjunction of S and S_1 and that of S and S_2 are stimulus-synonymous. But this is yet more readily seen not to provide a tighter relation.

If either of these ventures had succeeded, the synonymy yielded would still have been strictly intralinguistic; for the auxiliary S, belonging to one language, gets joined to both S_1 and S_2. But the language would not have to be our own. For, by section 7, conjunction is translatable; and so is the conditional, if we take it in the material sense 'Not (p and not q)'.

The general relation of intrasubjective sentence synonymy thus unsuccessfully sought is interdefinable with another elusive notion of intuitive philosophical semantics: that of an *analytic* sentence. Here the intuitive notion is that the sentence is true purely by meaning and independently of collateral information: thus 'No bachelor is married', 'Pigs are pigs', and, by some accounts, '$2 + 2 = 4$'.[21] The interdefinitions run thus: sentences are synonymous if and only if their biconditional (formed by joining them with 'if and only if') is analytic, and a sentence is analytic if and only if synonymous with self-conditionals ('If p then p').

As synonymy of sentences is related to analyticity, so stimulus synonymy of sentences is related to stimulus analyticity (section 6).

Philosophical tradition hints of three nested categories of firm truths: the analytic, the *a priori*, and the necessary. Whether the first exhausts the second, and the second the third, are traditional matters of disagreement, though

---

[21] There is a small confusion that I should like to take this opportunity to resolve, though it lies aside from the main course of the present reflections. Those who talk confidently of analyticity have been known to disagree on the analyticity of the truths of arithmetic, but are about unanimous on that of the truths of logic. We who are less clear on the notion of analyticity may therefore seize upon the generally conceded analyticity of the truths of logic as a partial extensional clarification of analyticity; but to do this is not to embrace the analyticity of the truths of logic as an antecedently intelligible doctrine. I have been misunderstood on this score by Gewirth, *Journal of Philosophy*, L (1953), p. 406 n., and others. Contrast my "Truth by Convention." Not that all criticisms of my remarks on truths of logic turn on this misunderstanding. Pap's criticism in *Semantics and Necessary Truth*, p. 237 n., is another matter, and was answered anticipatorily in my "Carnap and Logical Truth," end of section IX (to which he had no access). Strawson's criticism in "Propositions, Concepts, and Logical Truths," *Philosophical Quarterly*, VII (1957), is another still, and an interesting one, which I cannot claim to have answered anywhere. —Speaking of "Truth by Convention," I would remark that my much-cited definition of logical truth therein was meant only as an improved exposition of a long-current idea. So I was not taken aback at Bar-Hillel's finding the idea in Bolzano; I was, though, at recently uncovering an anticipation of my specific exposition, in Ajdukiewicz.

none of the three has traditionally been defined in terms of detectable features of verbal behavior. Pressed nowadays for such a clarification, some who are content to take the three as identical have responded in this vein: the analytic sentences are those that we are prepared to affirm come what may. This comes to naught unless we independently circumscribe the 'what may'. Thus one may object that we would not adhere to 'No bachelor is married' if we found a married bachelor; and how are we to disallow his example without appealing to the very notion of analyticity we are trying to define? One way is to take 'come what may' as 'come what stimulation (section 2) may'; and this gives virtually the definition (section 6) of stimulus analyticity.[22]

We improved stimulus synonymy a bit by socializing it. We can do the same for analyticity, calling socially stimulus-analytic just the sentences that are stimulus-analytic for almost everybody. But analyticity in even this improved sense will apply as well to 'There have been black dogs' as to '2 + 2 = 4' and 'No bachelor is married'. Let us face it: our socialized stimulus synonymy and stimulus analyticity are still not behavioristic reconstructions of intuitive semantics, but only a behavioristic ersatz.

At the end of section 6 we speculated on what makes for the intuition of synonymy of terms. Similar considerations apply to intuitions of sentence synonymy and analyticity. Such an intuition figures in the case of analyticity despite the technical sound of the word; sentences like 'No unmarried man is married', 'No bachelor is married', and '2 + 2 = 4' have a feel that everyone appreciates. Moreover the notion of "assent come what may" gives no fair hint of the intuition involved. One's reaction to denials of sentences typically felt as analytic has more in it of one's reaction to ungrasped foreign sentences.[23] Where the sentence concerned is a law of logic, something of the ground of this reaction was discerned in section 7: dropping a logical law disrupts a pattern on which the communicative use of a logical particle heavily depends. Much the same applies to '2 + 2 = 4', and even to 'The parts of the parts of a thing are parts of the thing'. The key words here have countless further contexts to anchor their usage, but somehow we feel that if our interlocutor will not agree with us on these platitudes there is no depending on him in most of the further contexts containing the terms in question.

Examples like 'No bachelor is married' rate as analytic both directly on the vague count just now conjectured and by virtue of coming from logical truths by synonymy substitution.

If the mechanism of analyticity intuitions is substantially as I have vaguely suggested, they will in general tend to set in where bewilderment sets in as to what the man who denies the sentence can be talking about. This effect can be

---

[22] I am indebted to Davidson for the concept of stimulus analyticity, as well as for this observation concerning it. Mates also may be said to have taken a step in somewhat this direction, in his proposal of contrary-to-fact questionnaires ("Analytic sentences," *Philosophical Review*, LX (1951), 532).

[23] *Cf.* Grice and Strawson, "In Defense of a Dogma," pp. 150 f.

gradual and also cumulative.[24] The intuitions are blameless in their way, but it would be a mistake to look to them for a sweeping epistemological dichotomy between analytic truths as by-products of language and synthetic truths as reports on the world. I suspect that the notion of such a dichotomy only encourages confused impressions of how language relates to the world.[25] Stimulus analyticity, our strictly vegetarian imitation, is of course not here in question.

9. ANALYTICAL HYPOTHESES

We have had our linguist observing native utterances and their circumstances passively, to begin with, and then selectively querying native sentences for assent and dissent under varying circumstances. Let us sum up the possible yield of such methods. (1) Observation sentences can be translated. There is uncertainty, but the situation is the normal inductive one. (2) Truth functions can be translated. (3) Stimulus-analytic sentences can be recognized. So can the sentences of the opposite type, the "stimulus-contradictory" sentences, which command irreversible dissent. (4) Questions of intrasubjective stimulus synonymy of native occasion sentences even of non-observational kind can be settled if raised, but the sentences cannot translated.

And how does the linguist pass these bounds? In broad outline as follows. He segments heard utterances into conveniently short recurrent parts, and thus compiles a list of native "words." Various of these he hypothetically equates to English words and phrases, in such a way as to conform to (1)–(4). Such are his *analytical hypotheses*, as I call them. Their conformity to (1)–(4) is ideally

---

[21] Apostel and his associates have explored this matter experimentally by asking subjects to classify chosen sentences, with and without the guidance of prior headings. Their findings suggest a gradualism of intuitive analyticity. For earlier experimentation on synonymy intuitions see Naess, *Interpretation and Preciseness*. On gradualism see also Goodman, "On Likeness of Meaning," *Analysis*, (1949) and White, "The Analytic and the Synthetic," in Hook, Sidney, ed., *John Dewey: Philosopher of Science and Freedom* (New York: *The Dial Press*, 1950).

[25] The notion, reminiscent of Kant, is often uncritically assumed in modern epistemological writing. Sometimes it has been given a semblance of foundation in terms of "semantical rules" or "meaning postulates" (Carnap, *Meaning and Necessity*, especially 2d ed.), but these devices only assume the notion in a disguised form. (See my "Two Dogmas of Empiricism" and "Carnap and Logical Truth.") The notion has long had its doubters; Duhem's views in 1906, are scarcely congenial to it, and idealists have expressly scouted it. (See Gewirth *op. cit.* p. 399, for references.) My misgivings over the notion came out in a limited way in "Truth by Convention" (1936), and figured increasingly in my lectures at Harvard. Tarski and I long argued the point with Carnap there in 1939–40. Soon White was pursuing the matter with Goodman and me in triangular correspondence. Essays questioning the distinction issued from a number of pens, sometimes independently of the Harvard discussions; for instance Reid, "Analytic Statements in Semiosis," *Mind*, LII (1943). Carnap and White mentioned my position in their 1950 papers, but my published allusions to it were slight until in 1950 I was invited to address the American Philosophical Association on the issue, and so wrote "Two Dogmas." The ensuing controversy has run to many articles and several books. Besides items mentioned in notes of this section and section 6, see particularly Pasch, *Experience and the Analytic* (Part I), White (*Toward Reunion in Philosophy*, pp. 133–63), and Bennett, "Analytic–Synthetic," *PAS*, LIX (1959). The title of "Two Dogmas," by the way, has proved unfortunate in its unintended but very real suggestion that there is no empiricism without the dogmas in question; *cf.* e.g. Hofstadter, *Journal of Philosophy* LI (1954), 410, 413.

as follows. The sentence translations derivable from the analytical hypotheses are to include those already established under (1); they are to fit the prior translation of truth functions, as of (2); they are to carry sentences that are stimulus-analytic or stimulus-contradictory, according to (3), into English sentences that are likewise stimulus-analytic or stimulus-contradictory; and they are to carry sentence pairs that are stimulus-synonymous, according to (4), into English sentences that are likewise stimulus-synonymous.

The analytical hypotheses are begun, however tentatively, long before the work of (1)–(4) is finished, and they help guide the choice of examples for investigation under (1)–(4). This point is essential to (4), since without indirect hints through analytical hypotheses there is virtually no telling what pairs of non-observational sentences to try for intrasubjective stimulus synonymy.

Our recipe is overschematic. If the analytical hypotheses give some English platitude as translation of some native standing sentence, there would be encouragement in finding that the latter also commands general and unreflective assent among natives, even if neither is quite stimulus-analytic. Degrees of approximation to stimulus-analyticity, as well as degrees of observationality, would be allowed for in a truer account. And anyway the analytical hypotheses are not strictly required to conform to (1)–(4) with respect to quite every example; the neater the analytical hypotheses, the more tolerance.

Tolerance is bound to have been exercised if a native sentence, believed by the whole community with a firmness that no stimulus pattern of reasonable duration would suffice to shake, is translated as 'All rabbits are men reincarnate'. To translate a stimulus-analytic native sentence thus into an English sentence that is not stimulus-analytic is to invoke translator's license. I think this account gives such a translation quite the proper air: that of a bold departure, to be adopted only if its avoidance would seem to call for much more complicated analytical hypotheses. For certainly, the more absurd or exotic the beliefs imputed to a people, the more suspicious we are entitled to be of the translations; the myth of the prelogical people marks only the extreme. For translation theory, banal messages are the breath of life.

It may occur to the reader to try to derive from stimulus analyticity a finer analyticity concept by screening out sentences such as the native one about reincarnation, using this criterion: through indirect considerations they get translated into sentences of another language that are not stimulus-analytic. However, this criterion is illusory because of its relativity to analytical hypotheses, which, as stressed in succeeding pages, are not determinate functions of linguistic behavior.

Let us now get back to the analytical hypotheses for a more leisurely consideration of their form and content. They are not in general held to equational form. There is no need to insist that the native word be equated outright to any one English word or phrase. Certain contexts may be specified in which the word is to be translated one way and others in which the word is to be translated in another way. The equational form may be overlaid with supplementary semantical instructions *ad libitum*. Since there is no general positional correspondence between the words and phrases of one language and their translations in another, some analytical hypotheses will be needed also to explain syntactical constructions. These are usually described with help of auxiliary terms for various classes of native words and phrases. Taken together, the analytical hypotheses and auxiliary definitions constitute the linguist's jungle-to-English dictionary and grammar. The form they are given is immaterial because their purpose is not translation of words or constructions but translation of coherent discourse; single words and constructions come up for attention only as means to that end.

Nevertheless there is reason to draw particular attention to the simple form of analytical hypothesis which equates a native word or construction to a hypothetical English equivalent. For hypotheses need thinking up, and the typical case of thinking up is the case where the linguist apprehends a parallelism in function between some component fragment of a translated whole native sentence and some component word of the translation of the sentence. Only in some such way can we account for anyone's ever thinking to translate a native locution radically into English as a plural ending, or as the identity predicate ' = ', or as a categorical copula, or as any other part of our domestic apparatus of objective reference. It is only by such outright projection of prior linguistic habits that the linguist can find general terms in the native language at all, or, having found them, match them with his own; stimulus meanings never suffice to determine even what words are terms, if any, much less what terms are coextensive.

The method of analytical hypotheses is a way of catapulting oneself into the jungle language by the momentum of the home language. It is a way of grafting exotic shoots on to the old familiar bush until only the exotic meets the eye. From the point of view of a theory of translational meaning the most notable thing about the analytical hypotheses is that they exceed anything implicit in any native's dispositions to speech behavior. By bringing out analogies between sentences that have yielded to translation and others they extend the working limits of translation beyond where independent evidence can exist.

Not that (1)–(4) themselves cover all available evidence. For remember that we stated those only with reference to a linguist whose gathering of data proceeded by querying native sentences for assent and dissent under varying circumstances. A linguist can broaden his base, as remarked in section 5, by becoming bilingual. Point (1) is thereupon extended to this: (1') All occasion sentences can be translated. Point (4) drops as superfluous. But even our bilingual, when he brings off translations not allowed for under (1')–(3), must do so by essentially the method of analytical hypotheses, however unconscious. Thus suppose, unrealistically to begin with, that in learning the native language he had been able to simulate the infantile situation to the extent of keeping his past knowledge of languages out of account. Then, when as a bilingual he finally turns to his project of a jungle-to-English manual, he will have to project analytical hypotheses much as if his English personality were the linguist and his jungle personality the informant; the differences are just that he can introspect his experiments instead of staging them, that he has his notable inside track on non-observational occasion sentences, and that he will tend to feel his analytical hypotheses as obvious analogies when he is aware of them at all. Now of course the truth is that he would not have strictly simulated the infantile situation in learning the native language, but would have helped himself with analytical hypotheses all along the way; thus the elements of the situation would in practice be pretty inextricably scrambled. What with this circumstance and the fugitive nature of introspective method, we have been better off theorizing about meaning from the more primitive paradigm: that of the linguist who deals observably with the native informant as live collaborator rather than first ingesting him.

Whatever the details of its expository devices of word translation and syntactical paradigm, the linguist's finished jungle-to-English manual has as its net yield an infinite *semantic correlation* of sentences: the implicit specification of an English sentence, or various roughly interchangeable English sentences, for every one of the infinitely many possible jungle sentences. Most of the semantic correlation is supported only by analytical hypotheses, in their extension beyond the zone where independent evidence for translation is possible. That those unverifiable translations proceed without mishap must not be taken as pragmatic evidence of good lexicography, for mishap is impossible.

Thus let us recall section 6, where we saw that stimulus meaning was incapable of deciding among 'rabbit', 'rabbit stage', and various other terms as translations of 'gavagai'. If by analytical hypothesis we take 'are the same' as translation of some construction in the jungle language, we may proceed on that basis to question our informant about sameness of gavagais from occasion to occasion and so conclude that gavagais are rabbits and not stages. But if instead we take 'are stages of the same animal' as translation of that jungle construction, we will conclude from the same subsequent questioning of our informant that gavagais are rabbit stages. Both analytical hypotheses may be presumed possible. Both could doubtless be accommodated by compensatory variations in analytical hypotheses concerning other locutions, so as to conform equally to all independently discoverable translations of whole sentences and indeed all speech dispositions of all speakers concerned. And yet countless native sentences admitting no independent check, not falling under (1')–(3), may be expected to receive radically unlike and incompatible English renderings under the two systems.

There is an obstacle to offering an actual example of two such rival systems of analytical hypotheses. Known languages are known through unique systems of analytical hypotheses established in tradition or painfully arrived at by unique skilled linguists. To devise a contrasting system would require an entire duplicate enterprise of translation, unaided even by the usual hints from interpreters. Yet one has only to reflect on the nature of possible data and methods to appreciate the indeterminacy. Sentences translatable outright, translatable by independent evidence of stimulatory occasions, are sparse and must woefully under-determine the analytical hypotheses on which the translation of all further sentences depends. To project such hypotheses—beyond the independent-ly translatable sentences at all is in effect to impute our sense of linguistic analogy unverifiably to the native mind. Nor would the dictates even of our own sense of analogy tend to any intrinsic uniqueness; using what first comes to mind engenders an air of determinacy though freedom reign. There can be no doubt that rival systems of analytical hypotheses can fit the totality of speech behavior to perfection, and can fit the totality of dispositions to speech behavior as well, and still specify mutually incompatible translations of count-less sentences insusceptible of independent control.

10. ON FAILURE TO PERCEIVE THE INDETERMINACY

Thus the analytical hypotheses, and the grand synthetic one that they add up to, are only in an incomplete sense hypotheses. Contrast the case of transla-tion of the occasion sentence 'Gavagai' by similarity of stimulus meaning. This is a genuine hypothesis from sample observations, though possibly wrong. 'Gavagai' and 'There's a rabbit' have stimulus meanings for the two speakers, and these are roughly the same or significantly different, whether we guess right or not. On the other hand no such sense is made of the typical analytical hypothesis. The point is not that we cannot be sure whether the analytical hypothesis is right, but that there is not even, as there was in the case of 'Gavagai', an objective matter to be right or wrong about.

There are at least seven causes of failure to appreciate this point. One is that analytical hypotheses are confirmed in the field. . . . Another . . . is con-fusion of it with the more superficial reflection that uniqueness of grammatical systematization is not to be expected. . . .

A third cause of failure to appreciate the point is confusion of it with the platitude that uniqueness of translation is absurd. The indeterminacy that I mean is more radical. It is that rival systems of analytical hypotheses can con-form to all speech dispositions within each of the languages concerned and yet dictate, in countless cases, utterly disparate translations; not mere mutual paraphrases, but translations each of which would be excluded by the other system of translation. Two such translations might even be patently contrary in truth value, provided there is no stimulation that would encourage assent to either.

A fourth and major cause of failure to appreciate the point is a stubborn feeling that a true bilingual surely is in a position to make uniquely right correlations of sentences generally between his languages. This feeling is fostered by an uncritical mentalistic theory of ideas: each sentence and its admissible translations express an identical idea in the bilingual's mind. The feeling can also survive rejection of the ideas: one can protest still that the sentence and its translations all correspond to some identical even though unknown neural condition in the bilingual. Now let us grant that; it is only to say that the bilingual has his own private semantic correlation—in effect his private implicit system of analytical hypotheses—and that it is somehow in his nerves. My point remains; for my point is then that another bilingual could have a semantic correlation incompatible with the first bilingual's without deviating from the first bilingual in his speech dispositions within either language, except in his dispositions to translate.

A fifth cause is that linguists adhere to implicit supplementary canons that help to limit their choice of analytical hypotheses. . . . A sixth cause is that a few early analytical hypotheses carry the linguist so far. . . . A seventh cause is that in framing his analytical hypotheses the linguist is subject to practical constraints. . . .

Complete radical translation goes on, and analytical hypotheses are indispensable. Nor are they capricious; we have seen in outline how they are supported. May we not then say that in those very ways of thinking up and supporting the analytical hypotheses a sense *is* after all given to sameness of meaning of the expressions which those hypotheses equate? No. We could claim this only if no two conflicting sets of analytical hypotheses could be tied for first place on all theoretically accessible evidence. The indefinability of synonymy by reference to the methodology of analytical hypotheses is formally the same as the indefinability of truth by reference to scientific method. Also the consequences are parallel. Just as we may meaningfully speak of the truth of a sentence only within the terms of some theory or conceptual scheme, so on the whole we may meaningfully speak of interlinguistic synonymy only within the terms of some particular system of analytical hypotheses. . . .

Containment in the Low German continuum facilitated translation of Frisian into English (section 1), and containment in a continuum of cultural evolution facilitated translation of Hungarian into English. In facilitating translation these continuities encourage an illusion of subject matter: an illusion that our so readily intertranslatable sentences are diverse verbal embodiments of some intercultural proposition or meaning, when they are better seen as the merest variants of one and the same intracultural verbalism. The discontinuity of radical translation tries our meanings: really sets them over against their verbal embodiments, or, more typically, finds nothing there.

Observation sentences peel nicely; their meanings, stimulus meanings, emerge absolute and free of residual verbal taint. Similarly for occasion sentences more generally, since the linguist can go native. Theoretical sentences such as 'Neutrinos lack mass', or the law of entropy, or the constancy of the speed of light, are at the other extreme. It is of such sentences above all that Wittgenstein's dictum holds true: "Understanding a sentence means understanding a language."[26] Such sentences, and countless ones that lie intermediate between the two extremes, lack linguistically neutral meaning.

There is no telling how much of one's success with analytical hypotheses is due to real kinship of outlook on the part of the natives and ourselves, and how much of it is due to linguistic ingenuity or lucky coincidence. I am not sure that it even makes sense to ask. We may alternately wonder at the inscrutability

---

[26] *Blue and Brown Books*, p. 5. Perhaps the doctrine of indeterminacy of translation will have little air of paradox for readers familiar with Wittgenstein's latter-day remarks on meaning.

of the native mind and wonder at how very much like us the native is, where in the one case we have merely muffed the best translation and in the other case we have done a more thorough job of reading our own provincial modes into the native's speech. . . .

Our advantage with a compatriot is that with little deviation the automatic or homophonic (section 7) hypothesis of translation fills the bill. If we were perverse and ingenious we could scorn that hypothesis and devise other analytical hypotheses that would attribute unimagined views to our compatriot, while conforming to all his dispositions to verbal response to all possible stimulations. Thinking in terms of radical translation of exotic languages has helped make factors vivid, but the main lesson to be derived concerns the empirical slack in our own beliefs. For our own views could be revised into those attributed to the compatriot in the impractical joke imagined; no conflicts with experience could ever supervene, except such as would attend our present sensible views as well. To the same degree that the radical translation of sentences is underdetermined by the totality of dispositions to verbal behavior, our own theories and beliefs in general are under-determined by the totality of possible sensory evidence time without end. . . .

The indeterminacy of translation has been less generally appreciated than its somewhat protean domestic analogue. In mentalistic philosophy there is the familiar predicament of private worlds. In speculative neurology there is the circumstance that different neural hookups can account for identical verbal behavior. In language learning there is the multiplicity of individual histories capable of issuing in identical verbal behavior. Still one is ready to say of the domestic situation in all positivistic reasonableness that if two speakers match in all dispositions to verbal behavior there is no sense in imagining semantic differences between them. It is ironic that the interlinguistic case is less noticed, for it is just here that the semantic indeterminacy makes clear empirical sense.

NOAM CHOMSKY

4.2   *Methodological Preliminaries*

1. GENERATIVE GRAMMARS AS THEORIES OF LINGUISTIC COMPETENCE

This study will touch on a variety of topics in syntactic theory and English syntax, a few in some detail, several quite superficially, and none exhaustively. It will be concerned with the syntactic component of a generative grammar,

Reprinted from Noam Chomsky, *Aspects of the Theory of Syntax*, Chapter 1, pp. 3–59, by permission of The M.I.T. Press, Cambridge, Massachusetts. Copyright © 1965 by The Massachusetts Institute of Technology.

that is, with the rules that specify the well-formed strings of minimal syntactically functioning units (*formatives*) and assign structural information of various kinds both to these strings and to strings that deviate from well-formedness in certain respects.

The general framework within which this investigation will proceed has been presented in many places, and some familiarity with the theoretical and descriptive studies listed in the bibliography is presupposed. In this chapter, I shall survey briefly some of the main background assumptions, making no serious attempt here to justify them but only to sketch them clearly.

Linguistic theory is concerned primarily with an ideal speaker-listener, in a completely homogeneous speech-community, who knows its language perfectly and is unaffected by such grammatically irrelevant conditions as memory limitations, distractions, shifts of attention and interest, and errors (random or characteristic) in applying his knowledge of the language in actual performance. This seems to me to have been the position of the founders of modern general linguistics, and no cogent reason for modifying it has been offered. To study actual linguistic performance, we must consider the interaction of a variety of factors, of which the underlying competence of the speaker-hearer is only one. In this respect, study of language is no different from empirical investigation of other complex phenomena.

We thus make a fundamental distinction between *competence* (the speaker-hearer's knowledge of his language) and *performance* (the actual use of language in concrete situations). Only under the idealization set forth in the preceding paragraph is performance a direct reflection of competence. In actual fact, it obviously could not directly reflect competence. A record of natural speech will show numerous false starts, deviations from rules, changes of plan in mid-course, and so on. The problem for the linguist, as well as for the child learning the language, is to determine from the data of performance the underlying system of rules that has been mastered by the speaker-hearer and that he puts to use in actual performance. Hence, in the technical sense, linguistic theory is mentalistic, since it is concerned with discovering a mental reality underlying actual behavior. Observed use of language or hypothesized dispositions to respond, habits, and so on, may provide evidence as to the nature of this mental reality, but surely cannot constitute the actual subject matter of linguistics, if this is to be a serious discipline. The distinction I am noting here is related to the *langue-parole* distinction of Saussure; but it is necessary to reject his concept of *langue* as merely a systematic inventory of items and to return rather to the Humboldtian conception of underlying competence as a system of generative processes. . . .

A grammar of a language purports to be a description of the ideal speaker-hearer's intrinsic competence. If the grammar is, furthermore, perfectly explicit—in other words, if it does not rely on the intelligence of the understanding reader but rather provides an explicit analysis of his contribution—we may (somewhat redundantly) call it a *generative grammar*.

A fully adequate grammar must assign to each of an infinite range of sentences a structural description indicating how this sentence is understood by the ideal speaker-hearer. This is the traditional problem of descriptive linguistics, and traditional grammars give a wealth of information concerning structural descriptions of sentences. However, valuable as they obviously are, traditional grammars are deficient in that they leave unexpressed many of the basic regularities of the language with which they are concerned. This fact is particularly clear on the level of syntax, where no traditional or structuralist grammar goes beyond classification of particular examples to the stage of formulation of generative rules on any significant scale. An analysis of the best existing grammars will quickly reveal that this is a defect of principle, not just a matter of empirical detail or logical preciseness. Nevertheless, it seems obvious that the attempt to explore this largely uncharted territory can most profitably begin with a study of the kind of structural information presented by traditional grammars and the kind of linguistic processes that have been exhibited, however informally, in these grammars.

The limitations of traditional and structuralist grammars should be clearly appreciated. Although such grammars may contain full and explicit lists of exceptions and irregularities, they provide only examples and hints concerning the regular and productive syntactic processes. Traditional linguistic theory was not unaware of this fact. For example, James Beattie (1788) remarks that

> Languages, therefore, resemble men in this respect, that, though each has peculiarities, whereby it is distinguished from every other, yet all have certain qualities in common. The peculiarities of individual tongues are explained in their respective grammars and dictionaries. Those things, that all languages have in common, or that are necessary to every language, are treated of in a science, which some have called *Universal* or *Philosophical* grammar.

Somewhat earlier, Du Marsais defines universal and particular grammar in the following way (1729; quoted in Sahlin, 1928, pp. 29–30):

> Il y a dans la grammaire des observations qui conviennent à toutes les langues; ces observations forment ce qu'on appelle la grammaire générale: telles sont les remarques que l'on a faites sur les sons articulés, sur les lettres qui sont les signes de ces sons; sur la nature des mots, et sur les différentes manières dont ils doivent être ou arrangés ou terminés pour faire un sens. Outre ces observations générales, il y en a qui ne sont propres qu'à une langue particulière; et c'est ce qui forme les grammaires particulières de chaque langue.

Within traditional linguistic theory, furthermore, it was clearly understood that one of the qualities that all languages have in common is their "creative" aspect. Thus an essential property of language is that it provides the means for expressing indefinitely many thoughts and for reacting appropriately in an indefinite range of new situations. . . . The grammar of a particular language, then, is to be supplemented by a universal grammar that accommodates the creative aspect of language use and expresses the deep-seated regularities which, being universal, are omitted from the grammar itself. Therefore it is quite proper for a grammar to discuss only exceptions and irregularities in any detail. It is only when supplemented by a universal grammar that the grammar of a language provides a full account of the speaker-hearer's competence.

Modern linguistics, however, has not explicitly recognized the necessity for supplementing a "particular grammar" of a language by a universal grammar if it is to achieve descriptive adequacy. It has, in fact, characteristically rejected the study of universal grammar as misguided; and, as noted before, it has not attempted to deal with the creative aspect of language use. It thus suggests no way to overcome the fundamental descriptive inadequacy of structuralist grammars.

Another reason for the failure of traditional grammars, particular or universal, to attempt a precise statement of regular processes of sentence formation and sentence interpretation lay in the widely held belief that there is a "natural order of thoughts" that is mirrored by the order of words. Hence, the rules of sentence formation do not really belong to grammar but to some other subject in which the "order of thoughts" is studied. Thus in the *Grammaire générale et raisonnée* (Lancelot *et al.*, 1660) it is asserted that, aside from figurative speech, the sequence of words follows an "ordre naturel," which conforms "à l'expression naturelle de nos pensées." Consequently, few grammatical rules need be formulated beyond the rules of ellipsis, inversion, and so on, which determine the figurative use of language. The same view appears in many forms and variants. To mention just one additional example, in an interesting essay devoted largely to the question of how the simultaneous and sequential array of ideas is reflected in the order of words, Diderot concludes that French is unique among languages in the degree to which the order of words corresponds to the natural order of thoughts and ideas (Diderot, 1751). Thus "quel que soit l'ordre des termes dans une langue ancienne ou moderne, l'esprit de l'écrivain a suivi l'ordre didactique de la syntaxe française" (p. 390); "Nous disons les choses en français, comme l'esprit est forcé de les considérer en quelque langue qu'on écrive" (p. 371). With admirable consistency he goes on to conclude that "notre langue *pédestre* a sur les autres l'avantage de l'utile sur l'agréable" (p. 372); thus French is appropriate for the sciences, whereas Greek, Latin, Italian, and English "sont plus avantageuses pour les lettres." Moreover,

> le bons sens choisirait la langue française; mais ... l'imagination et les passions donneront la préférence aux langues anciennes et à celles de nos voisins ... il faut parler français dans la société et dans les écoles de philosophie; et grec, latin, anglais, dans les chaires et sur les théâtres; ... notre langue sera celle de la vérité, si jamais elle revient sur la terre; et ... la grecque, la latine et les autres seront les langues de la fable et du mensonge. Le français est fait pour instruire, éclairer et convaincre; le grec, le latin, l'italien, l'anglais, pour persuader, émouvoir et tromper: parlez grec, latin, italien au peuple; mais parlez français au sage (pp. 371–72).

In any event, insofar as the order of words is determined by factors independent of language, it is not necessary to describe it in a particular or universal grammar, and we therefore have principled grounds for excluding an explicit formulation of syntactic processes from grammar. It is worth noting that this naïve view of language structure persists to modern times in various forms, for example, in Saussure's image of a sequence of expressions corresponding to an amorphous sequence of concepts or in the common characterization of language use as merely a matter of use of words and phrases. . . .

But the fundamental reason for this inadequacy of traditional grammars is a more technical one. Although it was well understood that linguistic processes are in some sense "creative," the technical devices for expressing a system of recursive processes were simply not available until much more recently. In fact, a real understanding of how a language can (in Humboldt's words) "make infinite use of finite means" has developed only within the last thirty years, in the course of studies in the foundations of mathematics. Now that these insights are readily available it is possible to return to the problems that were raised, but not solved, in traditional linguistic theory, and to attempt an explicit formulation of the "creative" processes of language. There is, in short, no longer a technical barrier to the full-scale study of generative grammars.

Returning to the main theme, by a generative grammar I mean simply a system of rules that in some explicit and well-defined way assigns structural descriptions to sentences. Obviously, every speaker of a language has mastered and internalized a generative grammar that expresses his knowledge of his language. This is not to say that he is aware of the rules of the grammar or even that he can become aware of them, or that his statements about his intuitive knowledge of the language are necessarily accurate. Any interesting generative grammar will be dealing, for the most part, with mental processes that are far beyond the level of actual or even potential consciousness; furthermore, it is quite apparent that a speaker's reports and viewpoints about his behavior and his competence may be in error. Thus a generative grammar attempts to specify what the speaker actually knows, not what he may report about his knowledge. Similarly, a theory of visual perception would attempt to account for what a person actually sees and the mechanisms that determine this rather than his statements about what he sees and why, though these statements may provide useful, in fact, compelling evidence for such a theory.

To avoid what has been a continuing misunderstanding, it is perhaps worth while to reiterate that a generative grammar is not a model for a speaker or a hearer. It attempts to characterize in the most neutral possible terms the knowledge of the language that provides the basis for actual use of language by a speaker-hearer. When we speak of a grammar as generating a sentence with a certain structural description, we mean simply that the grammar assigns this structural description to the sentence. When we say that a sentence has a certain derivation with respect to a particular generative grammar, we say nothing about how the speaker or hearer might proceed, in some practical or efficient way, to construct such a derivation. These questions belong to the theory of language use—the theory of performance. No doubt, a reasonable model of language use will incorporate, as a basic component, the generative grammar that expresses the speaker-hearer's knowledge of the language; but this genera-tive grammar does not, in itself, prescribe the character or functioning of a perceptual model or a model of speech production. . . .

Confusion over this matter has been sufficiently persistent to suggest that a terminologcal change might be in order. Nevertheless, I think that the term "generative grammar" is completely appropriate, and have therefore continued to use it. The term "generate" is familiar in the sense intended here in logic, particularly in Post's theory of combinatorial systems. Furthermore, "generate" seems to be the most appropriate translation for Humboldt's term *erzeugen*, which he frequently uses, it seems, in essentially the sense here intended. Since this use of the term "generate" is well established both in logic and in the tradi-tion of linguistic theory, I can see no reason for a revision of terminology.

2. TOWARD A THEORY OF PERFORMANCE

There seems to be little reason to question the traditional view that investiga-tion of performance will proceed only so far as understanding of underlying competence permits. Furthermore, recent work on performance seems to give new support to this assumption. To my knowledge, the only concrete results that have been achieved and the only clear suggestions that have been put forth concerning the theory of performance, outside of phonetics, have come from studies of performance models that incorporate generative grammars of specific kinds—that is, from studies that have been based on assumptions about underlying competence. In particular, there are some suggestive observations concerning limitations on performance imposed by organization of memory and bounds on memory, and concerning the exploitation of grammatical devices to form deviant sentences of various types. The latter question is one to which we shall return. . . . To clarify the distinction between competence and performance, it may be useful to summarize briefly some of the suggestions and results that have appeared in the last few years in the study of performance models with limitations of memory, time, and access.

For the purposes of this discussion, let us use the term "acceptable" to refer to utterances that are perfectly natural and immediately comprehensible without paper-and-pencil analysis, and in no way bizarre or outlandish. Obvi-ously, acceptability will be a matter of degree, along various dimensions. One could go on to propose various operational tests to specify the notion more precisely (for example, rapidity, correctness, and uniformity of recall and recognition, normalcy of intonation). For present purposes, it is unnecessary to delimit it more carefully. To illustrate, the sentences of (1) are somewhat more acceptable, in the intended sense, than those of (2):

(1) (i) I called up the man who wrote the book that you told me about
    (ii) quite a few of the students who you met who come from New York are friends of mine
    (iii) John, Bill, Tom, and several of their friends visited us last night
(2) (i) I called the man who wrote the book that you told me about up

(ii) the man who the boy who the students recognized pointed out is a friend
of mine

The more acceptable sentences are those that are more likely to be produced, more easily understood, less clumsy, and in some sense more natural. The unacceptable sentences one would tend to avoid and replace by more acceptable variants, wherever possible, in actual discourse.

The notion "acceptable" is not to be confused with "grammatical." Acceptability is a concept that belongs to the study of performance, whereas grammaticalness belongs to the study of competence. The sentences of (2) are low on the scale of acceptability but high on the scale of grammaticalness, in the technical sense of this term. That is, the generative rules of the language assign an interpretation to them in exactly the way in which they assign an interpretation to the somewhat more acceptable sentences of (1). Like acceptability, grammaticalness is, no doubt, a matter of degree . . . , but the scales of grammaticalness and acceptability do not coincide. Grammaticalness is only one of many factors that interact to determine acceptability. Correspondingly, although one might propose various operational tests for acceptability, it is unlikely that a necessary and sufficient operational criterion might be invented for the much more abstract and far more important notion of grammaticalness. The unacceptable grammatical sentences often cannot be used, for reasons having to do, not with grammar, but rather with memory limitations, intonational and stylistic factors, "iconic" elements of discourse (for example, a tendency to place logical subject and object early rather than late . . .), and so on. Note that it would be quite impossible to characterize the unacceptable sentences in grammatical terms. For example, we cannot formulate particular rules of the grammar in such a way as to exclude them. Nor, obviously, can we exclude them by limiting the number of reapplications of grammatical rules in the generation of a sentence, since unacceptability can just as well arise from application of distinct rules, each being applied only once. In fact, it is clear that we can characterize unacceptable sentences only in terms of some "global" property of derivations and the structures they define—a property that is attributable, not to a particular rule, but rather to the way in which the rules interrelate in a derivation.

This observation suggests that the study of performance could profitably begin with an investigation of the acceptability of the simplest formal structures in grammatical sentences. The most obvious formal property of utterances is their bracketing into constituents of various types, that is, the "tree structure" associated with them. Among such structures we can distinguish various kinds —for example, those to which we give the following conventional technical names, for the purposes of this discussion:

(3) (i) nested constructions
(ii) self-embedded constructions
(iii) multiple-branching constructions

     (iv) left-branching constructions
     (v) right-branching constructions

The phrases *A* and *B* form a nested construction if *A* falls totally within *B*, with some nonnull element to its left within *B* and some nonnull element to its right within *B*. Thus the phrase "the man who wrote the book that you told me about" is nested in the phrase "called the man who wrote the book that you told me about up," in (2i). The phrase *A* is self-embedded in *B* if *A* is nested in *B* and, furthermore, *A* is a phrase of the same type as *B*. Thus "who the students recognized" is self-embedded in "who the boy who the students recognized pointed out," in (2ii), since both are relative clauses. Thus nesting has to do with bracketing, and self-embedding with labeling of brackets as well. A multiple-branching construction is one with no internal structure. In (1iii), the Subject Noun Phrase is multiple-branching, since "John," "Bill," "Tom," and "several of their friends" are its immediate constituents, and have no further association among themselves. In terms of bracketing, a multiple-branching construction has the form $[[A][B] \ldots [M]]$. A left-branching structure is of the form $[[[\ldots] \ldots] \ldots]$—for example, in English, such indefinitely iterable structures as $[[[[John]'s \ brother]'s \ father]'s \ uncle]$ or $[[[the \ man \ who \ you \ met] \ from \ Boston] \ who \ was \ on \ the \ train]$, or (1ii), which combines several kinds of left-branching. Right-branching structures are those with the opposite property—for example, the Direct-Object of (1i) or $[this \ is \ [the \ cat \ that \ caught \ [the \ rat \ that \ stole \ the \ cheese]]]$.

The effect of these superficial aspects of sentence structure on performance has been a topic of study since almost the very inception of recent work on generative grammar, and there are some suggestive observations concerning their role in determining acceptability (that is, their role in limiting performance). Summarizing this work briefly, the following observations seem plausible:

    (4) (i) repeated nesting contributes to unacceptability
      (ii) self-embedding contributes still more radically to unacceptability
     (iii) multiple-branching constructions are optimal in acceptability
     (iv) nesting of a long and complex element reduces acceptability
     (v) there are no clear examples of unacceptability involving only left-branching or only right-branching, although these constructions are unnatural in other ways—thus, for example, in reading the right-branching construction "this is the cat that caught the rat that stole the cheese," the intonation breaks are ordinarily inserted in the wrong places (that is, after "cat" and "rat," instead of where the main brackets appear)

In some measure, these phenomena are easily explained. Thus it is known . . . that an optimal perceptual device, even with a bounded memory, can accept unbounded left-branching and right-branching structures, though nested (hence ultimately self-embedded) structures go beyond its memory capacity. Thus case (4i) is simply a consequence of finiteness of memory, and the unacceptability of such examples as (2ii) raises no problem.

If (4ii) is correct, then we have evidence for a conclusion about organization of memory that goes beyond the triviality that it must be finite in size. An optimal finite perceptual device . . . need have no more difficulty with self-embedding than with other kinds of nesting . . . . To account for the greater unacceptability of self-embedding (assuming this to be a fact), we must add other conditions on the perceptual device beyond mere limitation of memory. We might assume, for example, that the perceptual device has a stock of analytic procedures available to it, one corresponding to each kind of phrase, and that it is organized in such a way that it is unable (or finds it difficult) to utilize a procedure φ while it is in the course of executing φ. This is not a necessary feature of a perceptual model, but it is a rather plausible one, and it would account for (4ii). . . .

The high acceptability of multiple-branching, as in case (4iii), is easily explained on the rather plausible assumption that the ratio of number of phrases to number of formatives (the node-to-terminal node ratio, in a tree-diagram of a sentence) is a rough measure of the amount of computation that has to be performed in analysis. Thus multiple coordination would be the simplest kind of construction for an analytic device—it would impose the least strain on memory. . . .

Case (4iv) suggests decay of memory, perhaps, but raises unsolved problems. . . .

Case (4v) follows from the result about optimal perceptual models mentioned earlier. But it is unclear why left- and right-branching structures should become unnatural after a certain point, if they actually do.

One might ask whether attention to less superficial aspects of grammatical structure than those of (3) could lead to somewhat deeper conclusions about performance models. This seems entirely possible. For example, . . . some syntactic and perceptual considerations [have been] adduced in support of a suggestion (which is, to be sure, highly speculative) as to the somewhat more detailed organization of a perceptual device. In general, it seems that the study of performance models incorporating generative grammars may be a fruitful study; furthermore, it is difficult to imagine any other basis on which a theory of performance might develop.

There has been a fair amount of criticism of work in generative grammar on the grounds that it slights study of performance in favor of study of underlying competence. The facts, however, seem to be that the only studies of performance, outside of phonetics . . . , are those carried out as a by-product of work in generative grammar. In particular, the study of memory limitations just summarized and the study of deviation from rules, as a stylistic device, to which we [shall] return . . . , have developed in this way. Furthermore, it seems that these lines of investigation can provide some insight into performance. Consequently, this criticism is unwarranted, and, furthermore, completely misdirected. It is the descriptivist limitation-in-principle to classification and organization of data, to "extracting patterns" from a corpus of observed speech, to describing "speech habits" or "habit structures," insofar as these may exist, etc., that precludes the development of a theory of actual performance.

3. THE ORGANIZATION OF A GENERATIVE GRAMMAR

Returning now to the question of competence and the generative grammars that purport to describe it, we stress again that knowledge of a language involves the implicit ability to understand indefinitely many sentences. Hence, a generative grammar must be a system of rules that can iterate to generate an indefinitely large number of structures. This system of rules can be analyzed into the three major components of a generative grammar: the syntactic, phonological, and semantic components.

The syntactic component specifies an infinite set of abstract formal objects, each of which incorporates all information relevant to a single interpretation of a particular sentence. Since I shall be concerned here only with the syntactic component, I shall use the term "sentence" to refer to strings of formatives rather than to strings of phones. It will be recalled that a string of formatives specifies a string of phones uniquely (up to free variation), but not conversely.

The phonological component of a grammar determines the phonetic form of a sentence generated by the syntactic rules. That is, it relates a structure generated by the syntactic component to a phonetically represented signal. The semantic component determines the semantic interpretation of a sentence. That is, it relates a structure generated by the syntactic component to a certain semantic representation. Both the phonological and semantic components are therefore purely interpretive. Each utilizes information provided by the syntactic component concerning formatives, their inherent properties, and their interrelations in a given sentence. Consequently, the syntactic component of a grammar must specify, for each sentence, a *deep structure* that determines its semantic interpretation and a *surface structure* that determines its phonetic interpretation. The first of these is interpreted by the semantic component; the second, by the phonological component.

It might be supposed that surface structure and deep structure will always be identical. In fact, one might briefly characterize the syntactic theories that have arisen in modern structural (taxonomic) linguistics as based on the assumption that deep and surface structures are actually the same. . . . The central idea of transformational grammar is that they are, in general, distinct and that the surface structure is determined by repeated application of certain formal operations called "grammatical transformations" to objects of a more elementary sort. If this is true (as I assume, henceforth), then the syntactic component must generate deep and surface structures, for each sentence, and must interrelate them. This is idea has been clarified substantially in recent work, in ways that will be described later. [Later] I shall present a specific and, in part, new proposal as to precisely how it should be formulated. For the moment, it is sufficient to observe that although the Immediate Constituent analysis (labeled bracketing) of an actual string of formatives may be adequate as an account of surface structure, it is certainly not adequate as an account of deep structure. My concern in this book is primarily with deep structure and, in particular, with the elementary objects of which deep structure is constituted.

To clarify exposition, I shall use the following terminology, with occasional revisions as the discussion proceeds.

The *base* of the syntactic component is a system of rules that generate a highly restricted (perhaps finite) set of *basic strings*, each with an associated structural description called a *base Phrase-marker*. These base Phrase-markers are the elementary units of which deep structures are constituted. I shall assume that no ambiguity is introduced by rules of the base. This assumption seems to me correct, but has no important consequences for what follows here, though it simplifies exposition. Underlying each sentence of the language there is a sequence of base Phrase-markers, each generated by the base of the syntactic component. I shall refer to this sequence as the *basis* of the sentence that it underlies.

In addition to its base, the syntactic component of a generative grammar contains a *transformational* subcomponent. This is concerned with generating a sentence, with its surface structure, from its basis. Some familiarity with the operation and effects of transformational rules is henceforth presupposed.

Since the base generates only a restricted set of base Phrase-markers, most sentences will have a sequence of such objects as an underlying basis. Among the sentences with a single base Phrase-marker as basis, we can delimit a proper subset called "kernel sentences." These are sentences of a particularly simple sort that involve a minimum of transformational apparatus in their generation. The notion "kernel sentence" has, I think, an important intuitive significance, but since kernel sentences play no distinctive role in generation or interpretation of sentences, I shall say nothing more about them here. One must be careful not to confuse kernel sentences with the basic strings that underlie them. The basic strings and base Phrase-markers do, it seems, play a distinctive and crucial role in language use.

Since transformations will not be considered here in detail, no careful distinction will be made, in the case of a sentence with a single element in its basis, between the basic string underlying this sentence and the sentence itself. In other words, at many points in the exposition I shall make the tacit simplifying (and contrary-to-fact) assumption that the underlying basic string *is* the sentence, in this case, and that the base Phrase-marker is the surface structure as well as the deep structure. I shall try to select examples in such a way as to minimize possible confusion, but the simplifying assumption should be borne in mind throughout.

4. JUSTIFICATION OF GRAMMARS

Before entering directly into an investigation of the syntactic component of a generative grammar, it is important to give some thought to several methodological questions of justification and adequacy.

There is, first of all, the question of how one is to obtain information about the speaker-hearer's competence, about his knowledge of the language. Like most facts of interest and importance, this is neither presented for direct observation nor extractable from data by inductive procedures of any known sort. Clearly, the actual data of linguistic performance will provide much evidence for determining the correctness of hypotheses about underlying linguistic structure, along with introspective reports (by the native speaker, or the linguist who has learned the language). This is the position that is universally adopted in practice, although there are methodological discussions that seem to imply a reluctance to use observed performance or introspective reports as evidence for some underlying reality.

In brief, it is unfortunately the case that no adequate formalizable techniques are known for obtaining reliable information concerning the facts of linguistic structure (nor is this particularly surprising). There are, in other words, very few reliable experimental or data-processing procedures for obtaining significant information concerning the linguistic intuition of the native speaker. It is important to bear in mind that when an operational procedure is proposed, it must be tested for adequacy (exactly as a theory of linguistic intuition—a grammar—must be tested for adequacy) by measuring it against the standard provided by the tacit knowledge that it attempts to specify and describe. Thus a proposed operational test for, say, segmentation into words, must meet the empirical condition of conforming, in a mass of crucial and clear cases, to the linguistic intuition of the native speaker concerning such elements. Otherwise, it is without value. The same, obviously, is true in the case of any proposed operational procedure or any proposed grammatical description. If operational procedures were available that met this test, we might be justified in relying on their results in unclear and difficult cases. This remains a hope for the future rather than a present reality, however. This is the objective situation of present-day linguistic work; allusions to presumably well-known "procedures of elicitation" or "objective methods" simply obscure the actual situation in which linguistic work must, for the present, proceed. Furthermore, there is no reason to expect that reliable operational criteria for the deeper and more important theoretical notions of linguistics (such as "grammaticalness" and "paraphrase") will ever be forthcoming.

Even though few reliable operational procedures have been developed, the theoretical (that is, grammatical) investigation of the knowledge of the native speaker can proceed perfectly well. The critical problem for grammatical theory today is not a paucity of evidence but rather the inadequacy of present theories of language to account for masses of evidence that are hardly open to serious question. The problem for the grammarian is to construct a description and, where possible, an explanation for the enormous mass of unquestionable data concerning the linguistic intuition of the native speaker (often, himself); the problem for one concerned with operational procedures is to develop tests that give the correct results and make relevant distinctions. Neither the study of grammar nor the attempt to develop useful tests is hampered by lack of evidence with which to check results, for the present. We may hope that these efforts will converge, but they must obviously converge on the tacit knowledge of the native speaker if they are to be of any significance.

One may ask whether the necessity for present-day linguistics to give such priority to introspective evidence and to the linguistic intuition of the native speaker excludes it from the domain of science. The answer to this essentially terminological question seems to have no bearing at all on any serious issue. At most, it determines how we shall denote the kind of research that can be effectively carried out in the present state of our technique and understanding. However, this terminological question actually does relate to a different issue of some interest, namely the question whether the important feature of the successful sciences has been their search for insight or their concern for objectivity. The social and behavioral sciences provide ample evidence that objectivity can be pursued with little consequent gain in insight and understanding. On the other hand, a good case can be made for the view that the natural sciences have, by and large, sought objectivity primarily insofar as it is a tool for gaining insight (for providing phenomena that can suggest or test deeper explanatory hypotheses).

In any event, at a given stage of investigation, one whose concern is for insight and understanding (rather than for objectivity as a goal in itself) must ask whether or to what extent a wider range and more exact description of phenomena is relevant to solving the problems that he faces. In linguistics, it seems to me that sharpening of the data by more objective tests is a matter of small importance for the problems at hand. One who disagrees with this estimate of the present situation in linguistics can justify his belief in the current importance of more objective operational tests by showing how they can lead to new and deeper understanding of linguistic structure. Perhaps the day will come when the kinds of data that we now can obtain in abundance will be insufficient to resolve deeper questions concerning the structure of language. However, many questions that can realistically and significantly be formulated today do not demand evidence of a kind that is unavailable or unattainable without significant improvements in objectivity of experimental technique.

Although there is no way to avoid the traditional assumption that the speaker-hearer's linguistic intuition is the ultimate standard that determines the accuracy of any proposed grammar, linguistic theory, or operational test, it must be emphasized, once again, that this tacit knowledge may very well not be immediately available to the user of the language. To eliminate what has seemed to some an air of paradox in this remark, let me illustrate with a few examples.

If a sentence such as "flying planes can be dangerous" is presented in an appropriately constructed context, the listener will interpret it immediately in a unique way, and will fail to detect the ambiguity. In fact, he may reject the second interpretation, when this is pointed out to him, as forced or un-natural (independently of which interpretation he originally selected under contextual pressure). Nevertheless, his intuitive knowledge of the language is clearly such that both of the interpretations (corresponding to "flying planes are dangerous" and "flying planes is dangerous") are assigned to the sentence by the grammar he has internalized in some form.

In the case just mentioned, the ambiguity may be fairly transparent. But consider such a sentence as

(5) I had a book stolen

Few hearers may be aware of the fact that their internalized grammar in fact provides at least three structural descriptions for this sentence. Nevertheless, this fact can be brought to consciousness by consideration of slight elaborations of sentence (5), for example: (i) "I had a book stolen from my car when I stupidly left the window open," that is, "someone stole a book from my car"; (ii) "I had a book stolen from his library by a professional thief who I hired to do the job," that is, "I had someone steal a book"; (iii) "I almost had a book stolen, but they caught me leaving the library with it," that is, "I had almost succeeded in stealing a book." In bringing to consciousness the triple ambiguity of (5) in this way, we present no new information to the hearer and teach him nothing new about his language but simply arrange matters in such a way that his linguistic intuition, previously obscured, becomes evident to him.

As a final illustration, consider the sentences

(6) I persuaded John to leave
(7) I expected John to leave

The first impression of the hearer may be that these sentences receive the same structural analysis. Even fairly careful thought may fail to show him that his internalized grammar assigns very different syntactic descriptions to these sentences. In fact, so far as I have been able to discover, no English grammar has pointed out the fundamental distinction between these two constructions. . . . However, it is clear that the sentences (6) and (7) are not parallel in struc-ture. The difference can be brought out by consideration of the sentences

(8) (i) I persuaded a specialist to examine John
    (ii) I persuaded John to be examined by a specialist
(9) (i) I expected a specialist to examine John
    (ii) I expected John to be examined by a specialist

The sentences (9i) and (9ii) are "cognitively synonymous": one is true if and only if the other is true. But no variety of even weak paraphrase holds between

(8i) and (8ii). Thus (8i) can be true or false quite independently of the truth or falsity of (8ii). Whatever difference of connotation or "topic" or emphasis one may find between (9i) and (9ii) is just the difference that exists between the active sentence "a specialist will examine John" and its passive counterpart "John will be examined by a specialist." This is not at all the case with respect to (8), however. In fact, the underlying deep structure for (6) and (8ii) must show that "John" is the Direct-Object of the Verb Phrase as well as the grammatical Subject of the embedded sentence. Furthermore, in (8ii) "John" is the logical Direct-Object of the embedded sentence, whereas in (8i) the phrase "a specialist" is the Direct-Object of the Verb Phrase and the logical Subject of the embedded sentence. In (7), (9i), and (9ii), however, the Noun Phrases "John," "a specialist," and "John," respectively, have no grammatical functions other than those that are internal to the embedded sentence; in particular, "John" is the logical Direct-Object and "a specialist" the logical Subject in the embedded sentences of (9). Thus the underlying deep structures for (8i), (8ii), (9i), and (9ii) are, respectively, the following:

> (10) (i) Noun Phrase—Verb—Noun Phrase—Sentence
> (*I—persuaded—a specialist—a specialist will examine John*)
> (ii) Noun Phrase—Verb—Noun Phrase—Sentence
> (*I—persuaded—John—a specialist will examine John*)
> (11) (i) Noun Phrase—Verb—Sentence
> (*I—expected—a specialist will examine John*)
> (ii) Noun Phrase—Verb—Sentence
> (*I—expected—a specialist will examine John*)

In the case of (10ii) and (11ii), the passive transformation will apply to the embedded sentence, and in all four cases other operations will give the final surface forms of (8) and (9). The important point in the present connection is that (8i) differs from (8ii) in underlying structure, although (9i) and (9ii) are essentially the same in underlying structure. This accounts for the difference in meaning. Notice, in support of this difference in analysis, that we can have "I persuaded John that (of the fact that) Sentence," but not "I expected John that (of the fact that) Sentence."

The example (6)–(7) serves to illustrate two important points. First, it shows how unrevealing surface structure may be as to underlying deep structure. Thus (6) and (7) are the same in surface structure, but very different in the deep structure that underlies them and determines their semantic interpretations. Second, it illustrates the elusiveness of the speaker's tacit knowledge. Until such examples as (8) and (9) are adduced, it may not be in the least clear to a speaker of English that the grammar that he has internalized in fact assigns very different syntactic analyses to the superficially analogous sentences (6) and (7).

In short, we must be careful not to overlook the fact that surface similarities may hide underlying distinctions of a fundamental nature, and that it may be necessary to guide and draw out the speaker's intuition in perhaps fairly subtle ways before we can determine what is the actual character of his knowledge of his language or of anything else. Neither point is new (the former is a commonplace of traditional linguistic theory and analytic philosophy; the latter is as old as Plato's *Meno*); both are too often overlooked.

A grammar can be regarded as a theory of a language; it is *descriptively adequate* to the extent that it correctly describes the intrinsic competence of the idealized native speaker. The structural descriptions assigned to sentences by the grammar, the distinctions that it makes between well-formed and deviant, and so on, must, for descriptive adequacy, correspond to the linguistic intuition of the native speaker (whether or not he may be immediately aware of this) in a substantial and significant class of crucial cases.

A linguistic theory must contain a definition of "grammar," that is, a specification of the class of potential grammars. We may, correspondingly, say that *a linguistic theory is descriptively adequate* if it makes a descriptively adequate grammar available for each natural language.

Although even descriptive adequacy on a large scale is by no means easy to approach, it is crucial for the productive development of linguistic theory that much higher goals than this be pursued. To facilitate the clear formulation of deeper questions, it is useful to consider the abstract problem of constructing an "acquisition model" for language, that is, a theory of language learning or grammar construction. Clearly, a child who has learned a language has developed an internal representation of a system of rules that determine how sentences are to be formed, used, and understood. Using the term "grammar" with a systematic ambiguity (to refer, first, to the native speaker's internally represented "theory of his language" and, second, to the linguist's account of this), we can say that the child has developed and internally represented a generative grammar, in the sense described. He has done this on the basis of observation of what we may call *primary linguistic data*. This must include examples of linguistic performance that are taken to be well-formed sentences, and may include also examples designated as nonsentences, and no doubt much other information of the sort that is required for language learning, whatever this may be (see pp. 343–44). On the basis of such data, the child constructs a grammar—that is, a theory of the language of which the well-formed sentences of the primary linguistic data constitute a small sample. To learn a language, then, the child must have a method for devising an appropriate grammar, given primary linguistic data. As a precondition for language learning, he must possess, first, a linguistic theory that specifies the form of the grammar of a possible human language, and, second, a strategy for selecting a grammar of the appropriate form that is compatible with the primary linguistic data. As a long-range task for general linguistics, we might set the problem of developing an account of this innate linguistic theory that provides the basis for language learning. (Note that we are again using the term "theory"—in this case "theory of language" rather than "theory of a particular language"—with a systematic ambiguity, to refer both to the child's innate predisposition to learn a language of a certain type and to the linguist's account of this.)

To the extent that a linguistic theory succeeds in selecting a descriptively adequate grammar on the basis of primary linguistic data, we can say that it meets the condition of *explanatory adequacy*. That is, to this extent, it offers an explanation for the intuition of the native speaker on the basis of an empirical hypothesis concerning the innate predisposition of the child to develop a certain kind of theory to deal with the evidence presented to him. Any such hypothesis can be falsified (all too easily, in actual fact) by showing that it fails to provide a descriptively adequate grammar for primary linguistic data from some other language—evidently the child is not predisposed to learn one language rather than another. It is supported when it does provide an adequate explanation for some aspect of linguistic structure, an account of the way in which such knowledge might have been obtained.

Clearly, it would be utopian to expect to achieve explanatory adequacy on a large scale in the present state of linguistics. Nevertheless, considerations of explanatory adequacy are often critical for advancing linguistic theory. Gross coverage of a large mass of data can often be attained by conflicting theories; for precisely this reason it is not, in itself, an achievement of any particular theoretical interest or importance. As in any other field, the important problem in linguistics is to discover a complex of data that differentiates between conflicting conceptions of linguistic structure in that one of these conflicting theories can describe these data only by *ad hoc* means whereas the other can explain it on the basis of some empirical assumption about the form of language. Such small-scale studies of explanatory adequacy have, in fact, provided most of the evidence that has any serious bearing on the nature of linguistic structure. Thus whether we are comparing radically different theories of grammar or trying to determine the correctness of some particular aspect of one such theory, it is questions of explanatory adequacy that must, quite often, bear the burden of justification. This remark is in no way inconsistent with the fact that explanatory adequacy on a large scale is out of reach, for the present. It simply brings out the highly tentative character of any attempt to justify an empirical claim about linguistic structure.

To summarize briefly, there are two respects in which one can speak of "justifying a generative grammar." On one level (that of descriptive adequacy), the grammar is justified to the extent that it correctly describes its object, namely the linguistic intuition—the tacit competence—of the native speaker. In this sense, the grammar is justified on *external* grounds, on grounds of correspondence to linguistic fact. On a much deeper and hence much more rarely attainable level (that of explanatory adequacy), a grammar is justified to the extent that it is a *principled* descriptively adequate system, in that the linguistic theory with which it is associated selects this grammar over others, given primary linguistic data with which all are compatible. In this sense, the grammar is justified on *internal* grounds, on grounds of its relation to a linguistic theory that constitutes an explanatory hypothesis about the form of language as such. The problem of internal justification—of explanatory adequacy—is essentially the problem of constructing a theory of language acquisition, an account of the specific innate abilities that make this achievement possible.

5. FORMAL AND SUBSTANTIVE UNIVERSALS

A theory of linguistic structure that aims for explanatory adequacy incorporates an account of linguistic universals, and it attributes tacit knowledge of these universals to the child. It proposes, then, that the child approaches the data with the presumption that they are drawn from a language of a certain antecedently well-defined type, his problem being to determine which of the (humanly) possible languages is that of the community in which he is placed. Language learning would be impossible unless this were the case. The important question is: What are the initial assumptions concerning the nature of language that the child brings to language learning, and how detailed and specific is the innate schema (the general definition of "grammar") that gradually becomes more explicit and differentiated as the child learns the language? For the present we cannot come at all close to making a hypothesis about innate schemata that is rich, detailed, and specific enough to account for the fact of language acquisition. Consequently, the main task of linguistic theory must be to develop an account of linguistic universals that, on the one hand, will not be falsified by the actual diversity of languages and, on the other, will be sufficiently rich and explicit to account for the rapidity and uniformity of language learning, and the remarkable complexity and range of the generative grammars that are the product of language learning.

The study of linguistic universals is the study of the properties of any generative grammar for a natural language. Particular assumptions about linguistic universals may pertain to either the syntactic, semantic, or phonological component, or to interrelations among the three components.

It is useful to classify linguistic universals as *formal* or *substantive*. A theory of substantive universals claims that items of a particular kind in any language must be drawn from a fixed class of items. For example, Jakobson's theory of distinctive features can be interpreted as making an assertion about substantive universals with respect to the phonological component of a generative grammar. It asserts that each output of this component consists of elements that are characterized in terms of some small number of fixed, universal, phonetic features (perhaps on the order of fifteen or twenty), each of which has a substantive acoustic-articulatory characterization independent of any particular language. Traditional universal grammar was also a theory of substantive universals, in this sense. It not only put forth interesting views as to the nature of universal phonetics, but also advanced the position that certain fixed syntactic categories (Noun, Verb, etc.) can be found in the syntactic representations of the sentences of any language, and that these provide the general underlying syntactic structure of each language. A theory of substantive semantic universals might hold for example, that certain designative functions must be carried out in a specified way in each language. Thus it might assert that each language will contain terms that designate persons or lexical items referring to certain specific kinds of objects, feelings, behavior, and so on.

It is also possible, however, to search for universal properties of a more abstract sort. Consider a claim that the grammar of every language meets certain specified formal conditions. The truth of this hypothesis would not in itself imply that any particular rule must appear in all or even in any two grammars. The property of having a grammar meeting a certain abstract condition might be called a *formal* linguistic universal, if shown to be a general property of natural languages. Recent attempts to specify the abstract conditions that a generative grammar must meet have produced a variety of proposals concerning formal universals, in this sense. For example, consider the proposal that the syntactic component of a grammar must contain transformational rules (these being operations of a highly special kind) mapping semantically interpreted deep structures into phonetically interpreted surface structures, or the proposal that the phonological component of a grammar consists of a sequence of rules, a subset of which may apply cyclically to successively more dominant constituents of the surface structure (a transformational cycle, in the sense of much recent work on phonology). Such proposals make claims of a quite different sort from the claim that certain substantive phonetic elements are available for phonetic representation in all languages, or that certain specific categories must be central to the syntax of all languages, or that certain semantic features or categories provide a universal framework for semantic description. Substantive universals such as these concern the vocabulary for the description of language; formal universals involve rather the character of the rules that appear in grammars and the ways in which they can be interconnected.

On the semantic level, too, it is possible to search for what might be called formal universals, in essentially the sense just described. Consider, for example, the assumption that proper names, in any language, must designate objects meeting a condition of spatiotemporal contiguity, and that the same is true of other terms designating objects; or the condition that the color words of any language must subdivide the color spectrum into continuous segments; or the condition that artifacts are defined in terms of certain human goals, needs, and functions instead of solely in terms of physical qualities. Formal constraints of this sort on a system of concepts may severely limit the choice (by the child, or the linguist) of a descriptive grammar, given primary linguistic data.

The existence of deep-seated formal universals, in the sense suggested by such examples as these, implies that all languages are cut to the same pattern, but does not imply that there is any point by point correspondence between particular languages. It does not, for example, imply that there must be some reasonable procedure for translating between languages.

In general, there is no doubt that a theory of language, regarded as a hypothesis about the innate "language-forming capacity" of humans, should concern itself with both substantive and formal universals. But whereas substantive universals have been the traditional concern of general linguistic theory, investigations of the abstract conditions that must be satisfied by any generative grammar have been undertaken only quite recently. They seem to offer extremely rich and varied possibilities for study in all aspects of grammar.

6. FURTHER REMARKS ON DESCRIPTIVE AND EXPLANATORY THEORIES

Let us consider with somewhat greater care just what is involved in the construction of an "acquisition model" for language. A child who is capable of language learning must have

(12) (i) a technique for representing input signals
    (ii) a way of representing structural information about these signals
    (iii) some initial delimitation of a class of possible hypotheses about language structure
    (iv) a method for determining what each such hypothesis implies with respect to each sentence
    (v) a method for selecting one of the (presumably, infinitely many) hypotheses that are allowed by (iii) and are compatible with the given primary linguistic data

Correspondingly, a theory of linguistic structure that aims for explanatory adequacy must contain

(13) (i) a universal phonetic theory that defines the notion "possible sentence"
    (ii) a definition of "structural description"
    (iii) a definition of "generative grammar"
    (iv) a method for determining the structural description of a sentence, given a grammar
    (v) a way of evaluating alternative proposed grammars

Putting the same requirements in somewhat different terms, we must require of such a linguistic theory that it provide for

(14) (i) an enumeration of the class $s_1, s_2, \ldots$ of possible sentences
    (ii) an enumeration of the class $SD_1, SD_2, \ldots$ of possible structural descriptions
    (iii) an enumeration of the class $G_1, G_2, \ldots$ of possible generative grammars
    (iv) specification of a function f such that $SD_{f(i,j)}$ is the structural description assigned to sentence s_i by grammar G_j, for arbitrary i,j
    (v) specification of a function m such that $m(i)$ is an integer associated with the grammar G_i as its value (with, let us say, lower value indicated by higher number)

Conditions of at least this strength are entailed by the decision to aim for explanatory adequacy.

A theory meeting these conditions would attempt to account for language learning in the following way. Consider first the nature of primary linguistic data. This consists of a finite amount of information about sentences, which, furthermore, must be rather restricted in scope, considering the time limitations that are in effect, and fairly degenerate in quality. . . . For example, certain signals might be accepted as properly formed sentences, while others are classed as nonsentences, as a result of correction of the learner's attempts on the part of the linguistic community. Furthermore, the conditions of use might be such as to require that structural descriptions be assigned to these objects in certain ways. That the latter is a prerequisite for language acquisition seems to follow from the widely accepted (but, for the moment, quite unsupported) view that there must be a partially semantic basis for the acquisition of syntax or for the justification of hypotheses about the syntactic component of a grammar. Incidentally, it is often not realized how strong a claim this is about the innate concept-forming abilities of the child and the system of linguistic universals that these abilities imply. Thus what is maintained, presumably, is that the child has an innate theory of potential structural descriptions that is sufficiently rich and fully developed so that he is able to determine, from a real situation in which a signal occurs, which structural descriptions may be appropriate to this signal, and also that he is able to do this in part in advance of any assumption as to the linguistic structure of this signal. To say that the assumption about innate capacity is extremely strong is, of course, not to say that it is incorrect. Let us, in any event, assume tentatively that the primary linguistic data consist of signals classified as sentences and nonsentences, and a partial and tentative pairing of signals with structural descriptions.

A language-acquisition device that meets conditions (i)–(iv) is capable of utilizing such primary linguistic data as the empirical basis for language learning. This device must search through the set of possible hypotheses $G_1, G_2, \ldots,$ which are available to it by virtue of condition (iii), and must select grammars that are compatible with the primary linguistic data, represented in terms of (i) and (ii). It is possible to test compatibility by virtue of the fact that the device meets condition (iv). The device would then select one of these potential grammars by the evaluation measure guaranteed by (v). The selected grammar now provides the device with a method for interpreting an arbitrary sentence, by virtue of (ii) and (iv). That is to say, the device has now constructed a theory of the language of which the primary linguistic data are a sample. The theory that the device has now selected and internally represented specifies its tacit competence, its knowledge of the language. The child who acquires a language in this way of course knows a great deal more than he has "learned." His knowledge of the language, as this is determined by his internalized grammar, goes far beyond the presented primary linguistic data and is in no sense an "inductive generalization" from these data.

This account of language learning can, obviously, be paraphrased directly as a description of how the linguist whose work is guided by a linguistic theory meeting conditions (i)–(v) would justify a grammar that he constructs for a language on the basis of given primary linguistic data.

Notice, incidentally, that care must be taken to distinguish several different ways in which primary linguistic data may be necessary for language learning. In part, such data determine to which of the possible languages (that is, the languages provided with grammars in accordance with the a priori constraint (iii)) the language learner is being exposed, and it is this function of the primary linguistic data that we are considering here. But such data may play an entirely different role as well; namely, certain kinds of data and experience may be required in order to set the language-acquisition device into operation, although they may not affect the manner of its functioning in the least. Thus it has been found that semantic reference may greatly facilitate performance in a syntax-learning experiment, even though it does not, apparently, affect the *manner* in which acquisition of syntax proceeds; that is, it plays no role in determining which hypotheses are selected by the learner. . . . Similarly, it would not be at all surprising to find that normal language learning requires use of language in real-life situations, in some way. But this, if true, would not be sufficient to show that information regarding situational context (in particular, a pairing of signals with structural descriptions that is at least in part prior to assumptions about syntactic structure) plays any role in determining how language is acquired, once the mechanism is put to work and the task of language learning is undertaken by the child. This distinction is quite familiar outside of the domain of language acquisition. For example, Richard Held has shown in numerous experiments that under certain circumstances reafferent stimulation (that is, stimulation resulting from voluntary activity) is a prerequisite to the development of a concept of visual space, although it may not determine the character of this concept. . . . Or, to take one of innumerable examples from studies of animal learning, it has been observed . . . that depth perception in lambs is considerably facilitated by mother-neonate contact, although again there is no reason to suppose that the nature of the lamb's "theory of visual space" depends on this contact.

In studying the actual character of learning, linguistic or otherwise, it is of course necessary to distinguish carefully between these two functions of external data—the function of initiating or facilitating the operation of innate mechanisms and the function of determining in part the direction that learning will take.

Returning now to the main theme, we shall call a theory of linguistic structure that meets conditions (i)–(v) an *explanatory theory*, and a theory that meets conditions (i)–(iv) a *descriptive theory*. In fact, a linguistic theory that is concerned only with descriptive adequacy will limit its attention to topics (i)–(iv). Such a theory must, in other words, make available a class of generative grammars containing, for each language, a descriptively adequate grammar of this language—a grammar that (by means of (iv)) assigns structural descriptions to sentences in accordance with the linguistic competence of the native speaker. A theory of language is empirically significant only to the extent that it meets conditions (i)–(iv). The further question of explanatory adequacy arises only in connection with a theory that also meets condition (v) (but see p. 346). In other words, it arises only to the extent that the theory provides a principled basis for selecting a descriptively adequate grammar on the basis of primary linguistic data by the use of a well-defined evaluation measure.

This account is misleading in one important respect. It suggests that to raise a descriprively adequate theory to the level of explanatory adequacy one needs only to define an appropriate evaluation measure. This is incorrect, however. A theory may be descriptively adequate, in the sense just defined, and yet provide such a wide range of potential grammars that there is no possibility of discovering a formal property distinguishing the descriptively adequate grammars, in general, from among the mass of grammars compatible with whatever data are available. In fact, the real problem is almost always to restrict the range of possible hypotheses by adding additional structure to the notion "generative grammar." For the construction of a reasonable acquisition model, it is necessary to reduce the class of attainable grammars compatible with given primary linguistic data to the point where selection among them can be made by a formal evaluation measure. This requires a precise and narrow delimitation of the notion "generative grammar"—a restrictive and rich hypothesis concerning the universal properties that determine the form of language, in the traditional sense of this term.

The same point can be put in a somewhat different way. Given a variety of descriptively adequate grammars for natural languages, we are interested in determining to what extent they are unique and to what extent there are deep underlying similarities among them that are attributable to the form of language as such. Real progress in linguistics consists in the discovery that certain features of given languages can be reduced to universal properties of language, and explained in terms of these deeper aspects of linguistic form. Thus the major endeavor of the linguist must be to enrich the theory of linguistic form by formulating more specific constraints and conditions on the notion "generative grammar." Where this can be done, particular grammars can be simplified by eliminating from them descriptive statements that are attributable to the general theory of grammar. . . . For example, if we conclude that the transformational cycle is a universal feature of the phonological component, it is unnecessary, in the grammar of English, to describe the manner of functioning of those phonological rules that involve syntactic structure. This description will now have been abstracted from the grammar of English and stated as a formal linguistic universal, as part of the theory of generative grammar. Obviously, this conclusion, if justified, would represent an important advance in the theory of language, since it would then have been shown that what appears to be a peculiarity of English is actually explicable in terms of a general and deep empirical assumption about the nature of language, an assumption that can be refuted, if false, by study of descriptively adequate grammars of other languages.

In short, the most serious problem that arises in the attempt to achieve explanatory adequacy is that of characterizing the notion "generative grammar" in a sufficiently rich, detailed, and highly structured way. A theory of grammar may be descriptively adequate and yet leave unexpressed major features that are defining properties of natural language and that distinguish natural languages from arbitrary symbolic systems. It is for just this reason that the attempt to achieve explanatory adequacy—the attempt to discover linguistic universals—is so crucial at every stage of understanding of linguistic structure, despite the fact that even descriptive adequacy on a broad scale may be an unrealized goal. It is not necessary to achieve descriptive adequacy before raising questions of explanatory adequacy. On the contrary, the crucial questions, the questions that have the greatest bearing on our concept of language and on descriptive practice as well, are almost always those involving explanatory adequacy with respect to particular aspects of language structure.

To acquire language, a child must devise a hypothesis compatible with presented data—he must select from the store of potential grammars a specific one that is appropriate to the data available to him. It is logically possible that the data might be sufficiently rich and the class of potential grammars sufficiently limited so that no more than a single permitted grammar will be compatible with the available data at the moment of successful language acquisition, in our idealized "instantaneous" model. . . . In this case, no evaluation procedure will be necessary as a part of linguistic theory—that is, as an innate property of an organism or a device capable of language acquisition. It is rather difficult to imagine how in detail this logical possibility might be realized, and all concrete attempts to formulate an empirically adequate linguistic theory certainly leave ample room for mutually inconsistent grammars, all compatible with primary data of any conceivable sort. All such theories therefore require supplementation by an evaluation measure if language acquisition is to be accounted for and selection of specific grammars is to be justified; and I shall continue to assume tentatively, as heretofore, that this is an empirical fact about the innate human *faculté de langage* and consequently about general linguistic theory as well.

7. ON EVALUATION PROCEDURES

The status of an evaluation procedure for grammars (see condition (v) of (12)–(14)) has often been misconstrued. It must first of all be kept clearly in mind that such a measure is not given a priori, in some manner. Rather, any proposal concerning such a measure is an empirical hypothesis about the nature of language. This is evident from the preceding discussion. Suppose that we have a descriptive theory, meeting conditions (i)–(iv) of (12)–(14) in some fixed way. Given primarily linguistic data D, different choices of an evaluation measure will assign quite different ranks to alternative hypotheses (alternative grammars) as to the language of which D is a sample, and will therefore lead to entirely different predictions as to how a person who learns a language on the basis of D will interpret new sentences not in D. Consequently, choice of an evaluation measure is an empirical matter, and particular proposals are correct or incorrect.

Perhaps confusion about this matter can be traced to the use of the term "simplicity measure" for particular proposed evaluation measures, it being assumed that "simplicity" is a general notion somehow understood in advance outside of linguistic theory. This is a misconception, however. In the context of this discussion, "simplicity" (that is, the evaluation measure m of (v)) is a notion to be defined within linguistic theory along with "grammar," "phoneme," etc. Choice of a simplicity measure is rather like determination of the value of a physical constant. We are given, in part, an empirical pairing of certain kinds of primary linguistic data with certain grammars that are in fact constructed by people presented with such data. A proposed simplicity measure constitutes part of the attempt to determine precisely the nature of this associa- tion. If a particular formulation of (i)–(iv) is assumed, and if pairs (D_1, G_1), (D_2, G_2), ... of primary linguistic data and descriptively adequate grammars are given, the problem of defining "simplicity" is just the problem of discovering how G_i is determined by D_i, for each i. Suppose, in other words, that we regard an acquisition model for language as an input-output device that determines a particular generative grammar as "output," given certain primary linguistic data as input. A proposed simplicity measure, taken together with a specifica- tion of (i)–(iv), constitutes a hypothesis concerning the nature of such a device. Choice of a simplicity measure is therefore an empirical matter with empirical consequences.

All of this has been said before. I repeat it at such length because it has been so grossly misunderstood.

It is also apparent that evaluation measures of the kinds that have been discussed in the literature on generative grammar cannot be used to compare different theories of grammar; comparison of a grammar from one class of proposed grammars with a grammar from another class, *by such a measure*, is utterly without sense. Rather, an evaluation measure of this kind is an essential part of a particular theory of grammar that aims at explanatory adequacy. It is true that there is a sense in which alternative theories of language (or alternative theories in other domains) can be compared as to simplicity and elegance. What we have been discussing here, however, is not this general question but rather the problem of comparing two theories of a language—two grammars of this language—in terms of a particular general linguistic theory. This is, then, a matter of formulating an explanatory theory of language; it is not to be confused with the problem of choosing among competing theories of language. Choice among competing theories of language is of course a fundamental question and should also be settled, insofar as possible, on empirical grounds of descriptive and explanatory adequacy. But it is not the question involved in the use of an evaluation measure in the attempt to achieve explana- tory adequacy.

As a concrete illustration, consider the question of whether the rules of a grammar should be unordered (let us call this the linguistic theory T_U) or ordered in some specific way (the theory T_O). A priori, there is no way to decide which of the two is correct. There is no known absolute sense of "sim- plicity" or "elegance," developed within linguistic theory or general episte- mology, in accordance with which T_U and T_O can be compared. It is quite meaningless, therefore, to maintain that in some absolute sense T_U is "simpler" than T_O or conversely. One can easily invent a general concept of "simplicity" that will prefer T_U to T_O, or T_O to T_U; in neither case will this concept have any known justification. Certain measures of evaluation have been proposed and in part empirically justified within linguistics—for example, minimization of feature specification ... or the measure based on abbreviatory notations (discussed on pp. 350f.). These measures do not apply, because they are internal to a specific linguistic theory and their empirical justification relies essentially on this fact. To choose between T_U and T_O, we must proceed in an entirely different way. We must ask whether T_U or T_O provides descriptively adequate grammars for natural languages, or leads to explanatory adequacy. This is a perfectly meaningful empirical question if the theories in question are stated with sufficient care. For example, if $T_U{}^S$ is the familiar theory of phrase structure grammar and $T_O{}^S$ is the same theory, with the further condition that the rules are linearly ordered and apply cyclically, with at least one rule $A \rightarrow X$ being obligatory for each category A, so as to guarantee that each cycle is nonvacuous, then it can be shown that $T_U{}^S$ and $T_O{}^S$ are incomparable in descriptive power (in "strong generative capacity"—see section 9 . . .). Consequently, we might ask whether natural languages in fact fall under $T_U{}^S$ or $T_O{}^S$, these being non-equivalent and empirically distinguishable theories. Or, supposing $T_U{}^P$ and $T_O{}^P$ to be theories of the phonological component (where $T_U{}^P$ holds phonological rules to be unordered and $T_O{}^P$ holds them to be partially ordered), it is easy to invent hypothetical "languages" for which significant generalizations are expressible in terms of $T_O{}^P$ but not $T_U{}^P$, or conversely. We can therefore try to determine whether there are significant generalizations that are expressible in terms of one but not the other theory in the case of empirically given languages. In principle, either result is possible; it is an entirely factual question, having to do with the properties of natural languages. We shall see later that $T_O{}^S$ is rather well motivated as a theory of the base, and strong arguments have been offered to show that $T_O{}^P$ is correct and $T_U{}^P$ is wrong, as a theory of phonological processes. . . . In both cases, the argument turns on the factual question of expressibility of linguistically significant generalizations in terms of one or the other theory, not on any presumed absolute sense of "simplicity" that might rank T_U and T_O relative to one another. Failure to appreciate this fact has led to a great deal of vacuous and pointless discussion.

Confusion about these questions may also have been engendered by the fact that there are several different senses in which one can talk of "justifying" a grammar, as noted on p. 340. To repeat the major point: on the one hand, the grammar can be justified on external grounds of descriptive adequacy—we may ask whether it states the facts about the language correctly, whether it predicts correctly how the idealized native speaker would understand arbitrary sentences and gives a correct account of the basis for this achievement; on the other hand, a grammar can be justified on internal grounds if, given an ex-planatory linguistic theory, it can be shown that this grammar is the highest-valued grammar permitted by the theory and compatible with given primary linguistic data. In the latter case, a principled basis is presented for the con-struction of this grammar, and it is therefore justified on much deeper empirical grounds. Both kinds of justification are of course necessary; it is important, however, not to confuse them. In the case of a linguistic theory that is merely descriptive, only one kind of justification can be given—namely, we can show that it permits grammars that meet the external condition of descriptive adequacy. It is only when all of the conditions (i)–(v) of (12)–(14) are met that the deeper question of internal justification can be raised.

It is also apparent that the discussion as to whether an evaluation measure is a "necessary" part of linguistic theory is quite without substance (see, however, pp. 346–47). If the linguist is content to formulate descriptions one way or another with little concern for justification, and if he does not intend to proceed from the study of facts about particular languages to an investigation of the characteristic properties of natural language as such, then construction of an evaluation procedure and the associated concerns that relate to explanatory adequacy need not concern him. In this case, since interest in justification has been abandoned, neither evidence nor argument (beyond minimal requirements of consistency) has any bearing on what the linguist presents as a linguistic description. On the other hand, if he wishes to achieve descriptive adequacy in his account of language structure, he must concern himself with the problem of developing an explanatory theory of the form of grammar, since this provides one of the main tools for arriving at a descriptively adequate grammar in any particular case. In other words, choice of a grammar for a particular language L will always be much underdetermined by the data drawn from L alone. Moreover, other relevant data (namely, successful grammars for other languages or successful fragments for other subparts of L) will be available to the linguist only if he possesses an explanatory theory. Such a theory limits the choice of grammar by the dual method of imposing formal conditions on grammar and providing an evaluation procedure to be applied for the language L with which he is now concerned. Both the formal conditions and the evaluation procedure can be empirically justified by their success in other cases. Hence, any far-reaching concern for descriptive adequacy must lead to an attempt to develop an explanatory theory that fulfills these dual functions, and concern with explanatory adequacy surely requires an investigation of evaluation procedures.

The major problem in constructing an evaluation measure for grammars is that of determining which generalizations about a language are significant ones; an evaluation measure must be selected in such a way as to favor these. We have a generalization when a set of rules about distinct items can be replaced by a single rule (or, more generally, partially identical rules) about the whole set, or when it can be shown that a "natural class" of items undergoes a certain process or set of similar processes. Thus, choice of an evaluation measure constitutes a decision as to what are "similar processes" and "natural classes"— in short, what are significant generalizations. The problem is to devise a procedure that will assign a numerical measure of valuation to a grammar in terms of the degree of linguistically significant generalization that this grammar achieves. The obvious numerical measure to be applied to a grammar is length, in terms of number of symbols. But if this is to be a meaningful measure, it is necessary to devise notations and to restrict the form of rules in such a way that significant considerations of complexity and generality are converted into considerations of length, so that real generalizations shorten the grammar and spurious ones do not. Thus it is the notational conventions used in presenting a grammar that define "significant generalization," if the evaluation measure is taken as length.

This is, in fact, the rationale behind the conventions for use of parentheses, brackets, etc., that have been adopted in explicit (that is, generative) grammars. . . . To take just one example, consider the analysis of the English Verbal Auxiliary. The facts are that such a phrase must contain Tense (which is, furthermore, *Past* or *Present*), and then may or may not contain a Modal and either the *Perfect* or *Progressive* Aspect (or both), where the elements must appear in the order just given. Using familiar notational conventions, we can state this rule in the following form:

(15) Aux → Tense (Modal) (*Perfect*) (*Progressive*)

(omitting details that are not relevant here). Rule (15) is an abbreviation for eight rules that analyze the element Aux into its eight possible forms. Stated in full, these eight rules would involve twenty symbols, whereas rule (15) involves four (not counting Aux, in both cases). The parenthesis notation, in this case, has the following meaning. It asserts that the difference between four and twenty symbols is a measure of the degree of linguistically significant generalization achieved in a language that has the forms given in list (16), for the Auxiliary Phrase, as compared with a language that has, for example, the forms given in list (17) as the representatives of this category:

(16) Tense, Tense⌢Modal, Tense⌢*Perfect*, Tense⌢*Progressive*, Tense⌢Modal⌢*Perfect*, Tense⌢Modal⌢*Progressive*, Tense⌢*Perfect*⌢*Progressive*, Tense⌢Modal⌢*Perfect*⌢*Progressive*

(17) Tense⌢Modal⌢*Perfect*⌢*Progressive*, Modal⌢*Perfect*⌢*Progressive*⌢Tense, *Perfect*⌢*Progressive*⌢Tense⌢Modal, *Progressive*⌢Tense⌢Modal⌢*Perfect*, Tense⌢*Perfect*, Modal⌢*Progressive*

In the case of both list (16) and list (17), twenty symbols are involved. List (16) abbreviates to rule (15) by the notational convention; list (17) cannot be abbreviated by this convention. Hence, adoption of the familiar notational conventions involving the use of parentheses amounts to a claim that there is a linguistically significant generalization underlying the set of forms in list (16) but not the set of forms in list (17). It amounts to the empirical hypothesis that regularities of the type exemplified in (16) are those found in natural languages, and are of the type that children learning a language will expect; whereas cyclic regularities of the type exemplified in (17), though perfectly genuine, abstractly, are not characteristic of natural language, are not of the type for which children will intuitively search in language materials, and are much more difficult for the language-learner to construct on the basis of scattered data or to use. What is claimed, then, is that when given scattered examples from (16), the language learner will construct the rule (15) generating the full set with their semantic interpretations, whereas when given scattered examples that could be subsumed under a cyclic rule, he will not incorporate this "generalization" in his grammar—he will not, for example, conclude from the existence of "yesterday John arrived" and "John arrived yesterday" that there is a third form "arrived yesterday John," or from the existence of "is John here" and "here is John" that there is a third form "John here is," etc. One might easily propose a different notational convention that would abbreviate list (17) to a shorter rule than list (16), thus making a different empirical assumption about what constitutes a linguistically significant generalization. There is no a priori reason for preferring the usual convention; it simply embodies a factual claim about the structure of natural language and the predisposition of the child to search for certain types of regularity in natural language.

The illustrative examples of the preceding paragraph must be regarded with some caution. It is the full set of notational conventions that constitute an evaluation procedure, in the manner outlined earlier. The factual content of an explanatory theory lies in its claim that the most highly valued grammar of the permitted form will be selected, on the basis of given data. Hence, descriptions of particular subsystems of the grammar must be evaluated in terms of their effect on the entire system of rules. The extent to which particular parts of the grammar can be selected independently of others is an empirical matter about which very little is known, at present. Although alternatives can be clearly formulated, deeper studies of particular languages than are presently available are needed to settle the questions that immediately arise when these extremely important issues are raised. To my knowledge, the only attempt to evaluate a fairly full and complex subsystem of a grammar is in Chomsky (1951), but even here all that is shown is that the value of the system is a "local maximum" in the sense that interchange of adjacent rules decreases value. The effect of modifications on a larger scale is not investigated. . . .

One special case of this general approach to evaluation that has been worked out in a particularly convincing way is the condition of minimization of distinctive feature specifications in the phonological component of the grammar. A very plausible argument can be given to the effect that this convention defines the notions of "natural class" and "significant generalization" that have been relied on implicitly in descriptive and comparative-historical phonological investigations, and that determine the intuitively given distinction between "phonologically possible" and "phonologically impossible" nonsense forms. . . . It is important to observe that the effectiveness of this particular evaluation measure is completely dependent on a strong assumption about the form of grammar, namely, the assumption that only feature notation is permitted. If phonemic notation is allowed in addition to feature notation, the measure gives absurd consequences, as Halle shows.

It is clear, then, that choice of notations and other conventions is not an arbitrary or "merely technical" matter, if length is to be taken as the measure of valuation for a grammar. It is, rather, a matter that has immediate and perhaps quite drastic empirical consequences. When particular notational devices are incorporated into a linguistic theory of the sort we are discussing, a certain empirical claim is made, implicitly, concerning natural language. It is implied that a person learning a language will attempt to formulate generalizations that can easily be expressed (that is, with few symbols) in terms of the notations available in this theory, and that he will select grammars containing these generalizations over other grammars that are also compatible with the given data but that contain different sorts of generalization, different concepts of "natural class," and so on. These may be very strong claims, and need by no means be true on any a priori grounds.

To avoid any possible lingering confusion on this matter, let me repeat once more that this discussion of language learning in terms of formulation of rules, hypotheses, etc., does not refer to conscious formulation and expression of these but rather to the process of arriving at an internal representation of a generative system, which can be appropriately described in these terms.

In brief, it is clear that no present-day theory of language can hope to attain explanatory adequacy beyond very restricted domains. In other words, we are very far from being able to present a system of formal and substantive linguistic universals that will be sufficiently rich and detailed to account for the facts of language learning. To advance linguistic theory in the direction of explanatory adequacy, we can attempt to refine the evaluation measure for grammars or to tighten the formal constraints on grammars so that it becomes more difficult to find a highly valued hypothesis compatible with primary linguistic data. There can be no doubt that present theories of grammar require modification in both of these ways, the latter, in general, being the more promising. Thus the most crucial problem for linguistic theory seems to be to abstract statements and generalizations from particular descriptively adequate grammars and, wherever possible, to attribute them to the general theory of linguistic structure, thus enriching this theory and imposing more structure on the schema for grammatical description. Whenever this is done, an assertion about a particular language is replaced by a corresponding assertion, from which the first follows, about language in general. If this formulation of a deeper hypothesis is incorrect, this fact should become evident when its effect on the description of other aspects of the language or the description of other languages is ascertained. In short, I am making the obvious comment that, wherever possible, general assumptions about the nature of language should be formulated from which particular features of the grammars of individual languages can be deduced. In this way, linguistic theory may move toward explanatory adequacy and contribute to the study of human mental processes and intellectual capacity—more specifically, to the determination of the abilities that make language learning possible under the empirically given limitations of time and data.

8. LINGUISTIC THEORY AND LANGUAGE LEARNING

In the preceding discussion, certain problems of linguistic theory have been formulated as questions about the construction of a hypothetical language-acquisition device. This seems a useful and suggestive framework within which to pose and consider these problems. We may think of the theorist as given an empirical pairing of collections of primary linguistic data associated with grammars that are constructed by the device on the basis of such data. Much information can be obtained about both the primary data that constitute the input and the grammar that is the "output" of such a device, and the theorist has the problem of determining the intrinsic properties of a device capable of mediating this input-output relation.

It may be of some interest to set this discussion in a somewhat more general and traditional framework. Historically, we can distinguish two general lines of approach to the problem of acquisition of knowledge, of which the problem of acquisition of language is a special and particularly informative case. The empiricist approach has assumed that the structure of the acquisition device is limited to certain elementary "peripheral processing mechanisms"—for example, in recent versions, an innate "quality space" with an innate "distance" defined on it . . . , a set of primitive unconditioned reflexes . . . , or, in the case of language, the set of all "aurally distinguishable components" of the full "auditory impression." . . . Beyond this, it assumes that the device has certain analytical data-processing mechanisms or inductive principles of a very elementary sort, for example, certain principles of association, weak principles of "generalization" involving gradients along the dimensions of the given quality space, or, in our case, taxonomic principles of segmentation and classification such as those that have been developed with some care in modern linguistics, in accordance with the Saussurian emphasis on the fundamental character of such principles. It is then assumed that a preliminary analysis of experience is provided by the peripheral processing mechanisms, and that one's concepts and knowledge, beyond this, are acquired by application of the available inductive principles to this initially analyzed experience. Such views can be formulated clearly in one way or another as empirical hypotheses about the nature of mind.

A rather different approach to the problem of acquisition of knowledge has been characteristic of rationalist speculation about mental processes. The rationalist approach holds that beyond the peripheral processing mechanisms, there are innate ideas and principles of various kinds that determine the form of the acquired knowledge in what may be a rather restricted and highly organized way. A condition for innate mechanisms to become activated is that appropriate stimulation be presented. Thus for Descartes (1647), the innate ideas are those arising from the faculty of thinking rather than from external objects:

> . . . nothing reaches our mind from external objects through the organs of sense beyond certain corporeal movements . . . but even these movements, and the figures which arise from them, are not conceived by us in the shape they assume in the organs of sense. . . . Hence it follows that the ideas of the movements and figures are themselves innate in us. So much the more must the ideas of pain, colour, sound and the like be innate, that our mind may, on occasion of certain corporeal movements, envisage these ideas, for they have no likeness to the corporeal movements . . . [p. 443].

Similarly, such notions as that things equal to the same thing are equal to each other are innate, since they cannot arise as necessary principles from "particular movements." In general,

> sight . . . presents nothing beyond pictures, and hearing nothing beyond voices or sounds, so that all these things that we think of, beyond these voices or pictures, as being symbolized by them, are presented to us by means of ideas which come from no other source than our faculty of thinking, and are accordingly together with that faculty innate in us, that is, always existing in us potentially; for existence in any faculty is not actual but merely potential existence, since the very word "faculty" designates nothing more or less than a potentiality. . . . [Thus ideas are innate in the sense that] in some families generosity is innate, in others certain diseases like gout or gravel, not that on this account the babes of these families suffer from these diseases in their mother's womb, but because they are born with a certain disposition or propensity for contracting them . . . [p. 442].

Still earlier, Lord Herbert (1624) maintains that innate ideas and principles "remain latent when their corresponding objects are not present, and even disappear and give no sign of their existence"; they "must be deemed not so much the outcome of experience as principles without which we should have no experience at all . . . [p. 132]." Without these principles, "we could have no experience at all nor be capable of observations"; "we should never come to distinguish between things, or to grasp any general nature . . . [p. 105]." These notions are extensively developed throughout seventeenth-century rationalist philosophy. To mention just one example, Cudworth (1731) gives an extensive argument in support of his view that "there are many ideas of the mind, which though the cogitations of them be often occasionally invited from the motion or appulse of sensible objects without made upon our bodies; yet notwithstanding the ideas themselves could not possibly be stamped or impressed upon the soul from them, because sense takes no cognizance at all of any such things in those corporeal objects, and therefore they must needs arise from the innate vigour and activity of the mind itself . . . [Book IV]." Even in Locke one finds essentially the same conception, as was pointed out by Leibniz and many commentators since.

In the Port-Royal *Logic* (Arnauld, 1662), the same point of view is expressed in the following way:

> It is false, therefore, that all our ideas come through sense. On the contrary, it may be affirmed that no idea which we have in our minds has taken its rise from sense, except on occasion of those movements which are made in the brain through sense, the impulse from sense giving occasion to the mind to form different ideas which it would not have formed without it, though these ideas have very rarely any resemblance to what takes place in the sense and in the brain; and there are at least a very great number of ideas which, having no connection with any bodily image, cannot, without manifest absurdity, be referred to sense . . . [Chapter 1].

In the same vein, Leibniz refuses to accept a sharp distinction between innate and learned:

> I agree that we learn ideas and innate truths either in considering their source or in verifying them through experience. . . . And I cannot admit this proposition: *all that one learns is not innate*. The truths of numbers are in us, yet nonetheless one learns them, either by drawing them from their source when we learn them through demonstrative proof (which shows that they are innate), or by testing them in examples, as do ordinary arithmeticians . . . [*New Essays*, p. 75]. [Thus] all arithmetic and all geometry are in us virtually, so that we can find them there if we consider attentively and set in order what we already have in the mind . . . [p. 78]. [In general,] we have an infinite amount of knowledge of which we are not always conscious, not even when we need it [p. 77]. The senses, although necessary for all our actual knowledge, are not sufficient to give it all to us, since the senses never give us anything but examples, i.e., particular or individual truths. Now all the examples which confirm a general truth, whatever their number, do not suffice to establish the universal necessity of that same truth . . . [pp. 42–43]. Necessary truths . . . must have principles whose proof does not depend on examples, nor consequently upon the testimony of the senses, although without the senses it would never have occurred to us to think of them. . . . It is true that we must not imagine that these eternal laws of the reason can be read in the soul as in an open book . . . but it is sufficient that they can be discovered in us by dint of attention, for which the senses furnish occasions, and successful experience serves to confirm reason . . . [p. 44]. [There are innate general principles that] enter into our thoughts, of which they form the soul and the connection. They are as necessary thereto as the muscles and sinews are for walking, although we do not at all think of them. The mind leans upon these principles every moment, but it does not come so easily to distinguish them and to represent them distinctly and separately, because that demands great attention to its acts. . . . Thus it is that one possesses many things without knowing it . . . [p. 74].

(as, for example, the Chinese possess articulate sounds, and therefore the basis for alphabetic writing, although they have not invented this).

Notice, incidentally, that throughout these classical discussions of the interplay between sense and mind in the formation of ideas, no sharp distinction is made between perception and acquisition, although there would be no inconsistency in the assumption that latent innate mental structures, once "activated," are then available for interpretation of the data of sense in a way in which they were not previously.

Applying this rationalist view to the special case of language learning, Humboldt . . . concludes that one cannot really teach language but can only present the conditions under which it will develop spontaneously in the mind in its own way. Thus the *form of a language*, the schema for its grammar, is to a large extent given, though it will not be available for use without appropriate experience to set the language-forming processes into operation. Like Leibniz, he reiterates the Platonistic view that, for the individual, learning is largely a matter of *Wiedererzeugung*, that is, of drawing out what is innate in the mind.

This view contrasts sharply with the empiricist notion (the prevailing modern view) that language is essentially an adventitious construct, taught by "conditioning" (as would be maintained, for example, by Skinner or Quine) or by drill and explicit explanation (as was claimed by Wittgenstein), or built up by elementary "data-processing" procedures (as modern linguistics typically maintains), but, in any event, relatively independent in its structure of any innate mental faculties.

In short, empiricist speculation has characteristically assumed that only the procedures and mechanisms for the acquisition of knowledge constitute an innate property of the mind. Thus for Hume, the method of "experimental reasoning" is a basic instinct in animals and humans, on a par with the instinct "which teaches a bird, with such exactness, the art of incubation, and the whole economy and order of its nursery"—it is derived "from the original hand of nature." . . . The form of knowledge, however, is otherwise quite free. On the other hand, rationalist speculation has assumed that the general form of a system of knowledge is fixed in advance as a disposition of the mind, and the function of experience is to cause this general schematic structure to be realized and more fully differentiated. To follow Leibniz's enlightening analogy, we may make

> . . . the comparison of a block of marble which has veins, rather than a block of marble wholly even, or of blank tablets, i.e., of what is called among philosophers a *tabula rasa*. For if the soul resembled these blank tablets, truths would be in us as the figure of Hercules is in the marble, when the marble is wholly indifferent to the reception of this figure or some other. But if there were veins in the block which should indicate the figure of Hercules rather than other figures, this block would be more determined thereto, and Hercules would be in it as in some sense innate, although it would be needful to discover these veins, to clear them by polishing, and by cutting away what prevents them from appearing. Thus it is that ideas and truths are for us innate, as inclinations, dispositions, habits, or natural potentialities, and not as actions; although these potentialities are always accompanied by some actions, often insensible, which correspond to them [Leibniz, *New Essays*, pp. 45–46].

It is not, of course, necessary to assume that empiricist and rationalist views can always be sharply distinguished and that these currents cannot cross. Nevertheless, it is historically accurate as well as heuristically valuable to distinguish these two very different approaches to the problem of acquisition of knowledge. Particular empiricist and rationalist views can be made quite precise and can then be presented as explicit hypotheses about acquisition of knowledge, in particular, about the innate structure of a language-acquisition device. In fact, it would not be inaccurate to describe the taxonomic, data-processing approach of modern linguistics as an empiricist view that contrasts with the essentially rationalist alternative proposed in recent theories of transformational grammar. Taxonomic linguistics is empiricist in its assumption that general linguistic theory consists only of a body of procedures for determining the grammar of a language from a corpus of data, the form of language being unspecified except insofar as restrictions on possible grammars are determined by this set of procedures. If we interpret taxonomic linguistics as making an empirical claim, this claim must be that the grammars that result from application of the postulated procedures to a sufficiently rich selection of data will be descriptively adequate—in other words, that the set of procedures can be regarded as constituting a hypothesis about the innate language-acquisition system. In contrast, the discussion of language acquisition in preceding sections was rationalistic in its assumption that various formal and substantive universals are intrinsic properties of the language-acquisition system, these providing a schema that is applied to data and that determines in a highly restricted way the general form and, in part, even the substantive features of the grammar that may emerge upon presentation of appropriate data. A general linguistic theory of the sort roughly described earlier, and elaborated in more detail in the following chapters and in other studies of transformational grammar, must therefore be regarded as a specific hypothesis, of an essentially rationalist cast, as to the nature of mental structures and processes. . . .

When such contrasting views are clearly formulated, we may ask, as an empirical question, which (if either) is correct. There is no a priori way to settle this issue. Where empiricist and rationalist views have been presented with sufficient care so that the question of correctness can be seriously raised, it cannot, for example, be maintained that in any clear sense one is "simpler" than the other in terms of its potential physical realization, and even if this could be shown, one way or the other, it would have no bearing on what is completely a factual issue. This factual question can be approached in several ways. In particular, restricting ourselves now to the question of language acquisition, we must bear in mind that any concrete empiricist proposal does impose certain conditions on the form of the grammars that can result from application of its inductive principles to primary data. We may therefore ask whether the grammars that these principles can provide, in principle, are at all close to those which we in fact discover when we investigate real languages. The same question can be asked about a concrete rationalist proposal. This has, in the past, proved to be a useful way to subject such hypotheses to one sort of empirical test.

If the answer to this question of adequacy-in-principle is positive, in either case, we can then turn to the question of feasibility: can the inductive procedures (in the empiricist case) or the mechanisms of elaboration and realization of innate schemata (in the rationalist case) succeed in producing grammars within the given constraints of time and access, and within the range of observed uniformity of output? In fact, the second question has rarely been raised in any serious way in connection with empiricist views . . . , since study of the first question has been sufficient to rule out whatever explicit proposals of an essentially empiricist character have emerged in modern discussions of language acquisition. The only proposals that are explicit enough to support serious study are those that have been developed within taxonomic linguistics. It seems to have been demonstrated beyond any reasonable doubt that, quite apart from any question of feasibility, methods of the sort that have been studied in taxonomic linguistics are intrinsically incapable of yielding the systems of grammatical knowledge that must be attributed to the speaker of a language. . . . In general, then, it seems to me correct to say that empiricist theories about language acquisition are refutable wherever they are clear, and that further empiricist speculations have been quite empty and uninformative. On the other hand, the rationalist approach exemplified by recent work in the theory of transformational grammar seems to have fairly productive, to be fully in accord with what is known about language, and to offer at least some hope of providing a hypothesis about the intrinsic structure of a language-acquisition system that will meet the condition of adequacy-in-principle and do so in a sufficiently narrow and interesting way so that the question of feasibility can, for the first time, be seriously raised.

One might seek other ways of testing particular hypotheses about a language-acquisition device. A theory that attributes possession of certain linguistic universals to a language-acquisition system, as a property to be realized under appropriate external conditions, implies that only certain kinds of symbolic systems can be acquired and used as languages by this device. Others should be beyond its language-acquisition capacity. Systems can certainly be invented that fail the conditions, formal and substantive, that have been proposed as tentative linguistic universals in, for example, Jakobsonian distinctive-feature theory or the theory of transformational grammar. In principle, one might try to determine whether invented systems that fail these conditions do pose inordinately difficult problems for language learning, and do fall beyond the domain for which the language-acquisition system is designed. As a concrete example, consider the fact that, according to the theory of transformational grammar, only certain kinds of formal operations on strings can appear in grammars—operations that, furthermore, have no a priori justification. For example, the permitted operations cannot be shown in any sense to be the most "simple" or "elementary" ones that might be invented. In fact, what might in general be considered "elementary operations" on strings do not qualify as grammatical transformations at all, while many of the operations that do qualify are far from elementary, in any general sense. Specifically, grammatical transformations are necessarily "structure-dependent" in that they manipulate substrings only in terms of their assignment to categories. Thus it is possible to formulate a transformation that can insert all or part of the Auxiliary Verb to the left of a Noun Phrase that precedes it, independently of what the length or internal complexity of the strings belonging to these categories may be. It is impossible, however, to formulate as a transformation such a simple operation as reflection of an arbitrary string (that is, replacement of any string $a_1 \ldots a_n$, where each a_i is a single symbol, by $a_n \ldots a_1$), or interchange of the $(2n - 1)^{\text{th}}$ word with the $2n^{\text{th}}$ word throughout a string of arbitrary length, or insertion of a symbol in the middle of a string of even length. Similarly, if the structural analyses that define transformations are restricted to Boolean conditions on *Analyzability*, as suggested later, it will be impossible to formulate many "structure-dependent" operations as transformations—for example, an operation that will iterate a symbol that is the left-most member of a category (impossible, short of listing all categories of the grammar in the structural analysis), or an operation that will iterate a symbol that belongs to as many rightmost as leftmost categories. Hence, one who proposes this theory would have to predict that although a language might form interrogatives, for example, by interchanging the order of certain categories (as in English), it could not form interrogatives by reflection, or interchange of odd and even words, or insertion of a marker in the middle of the sentence. Many other such predictions, none of them at all obvious in any a priori sense, can be deduced from any sufficiently explicit theory of linguistic universals that is attributed to a language-acquisition device as an intrinsic property. . . .

Notice that when we maintain that a system is not learnable by a language-acquisition device that mirrors human capacities, we do not imply that this system cannot be mastered by a human in some other way, if treated as a puzzle or intellectual exercise of some sort. The language-acquisition device is only one component of the total system of intellectual structures that can be applied to problem solving and concept formation; in other words, the *faculté de langage* is only one of the faculties of the mind. What one would expect, however, is that there should be a qualitative difference in the way in which an organism with a functional language-acquisition system will approach and deal with systems that are languagelike and others that are not.

The problem of mapping the intrinsic cognitive capacities of an organism and identifying the systems of belief and the organization of behavior that it can readily attain should be central to experimental psychology. However, the field has not developed in this way. Learning theory has, for the most part, concentrated on what seems a much more marginal topic, namely the question of species-independent regularities in acquisition of items of a "behavioral repertoire" under experimentally manipulable conditions. Consequently, it has necessarily directed its attention to tasks that are extrinsic to an organism's cognitive capacities—tasks that must be approached in a devious, indirect, and piecemeal fashion. In the course of this work, some incidental information has been obtained about the effect of intrinsic cognitive structure and intrinsic organization of behavior on what is learned, but this has rarely been the focus of serious attention (outside of ethology). The sporadic exceptions to this observation . . . are quite suggestive, as are many ethological studies of lower organisms. The general question and its many ramifications, however, remain in a primitive state.

In brief, it seems clear that the present situation with regard to the study of language learning is essentially as follows. We have a certain amount of evidence about the character of the generative grammars that must be the "output" of an acquisition model for language. This evidence shows clearly that taxonomic views of linguistic structure are inadequate and that knowledge of grammatical structure cannot arise by application of step-by-step inductive operations (segmentation, classification, substitution procedures, filling of slots in frames, association, etc.) of any sort that have yet been developed within linguistics, psychology, or philosophy. Further empiricist speculations contribute nothing that even faintly suggests a way of overcoming the intrinsic limitations of the methods that have so far been proposed and elaborated. In particular, such speculations have not provided any way to account for or even to express the fundamental fact about the normal use of language, namely the speaker's ability to produce and understand instantly new sentences that are not similar to those previously heard in any physically defined sense or in terms of any notion of frames or classes of elements, nor associated with those previously heard by conditioning, nor obtainable from them by any sort of "generalization" known to psychology or philosophy. It seems plain that language acquisition is based on the child's discovery of what from a formal point of view is a deep and abstract theory—a generative grammar of his language—many of the concepts and principles of which are only remotely related to experience by long and intricate chains of unconscious quasi-inferential steps. A consideration of the character of the grammar that is acquired, the degenerate quality and narrowly limited extent of the available data, the striking uniformity of the resulting grammars, and their independence of intelligence, motivation, and emotional state, over wide ranges of variation, leave little hope that much of the structure of the language can be learned by an organism initially uninformed as to its general character.

It is, for the present, impossible to formulate an assumption about initial, innate structure rich enough to account for the fact that grammatical knowledge is attained on the basis of the evidence available to the learner. Consequently, the empiricist effort to show how the assumptions about a language-acquisition device can be *reduced to a conceptual minimum* is quite misplaced. The real problem is that of developing a hypothesis about initial structure that is sufficiently rich to account for acquisition of language, yet not so rich as to be inconsistent with the known diversity of language. It is a matter of no concern and of only historical interest that such a hypothesis will evidently not satisfy the preconceptions about learning that derive from centuries of empiricist doctrine. These preconceptions are not only quite implausible, to begin with, but are without factual support and are hardly consistent with what little is known about how animals or humans construct a "theory of the external world."

It is clear why the view that all knowledge derives solely from the senses by elementary operations of association and "generalization" should have had much appeal in the context of eighteenth-century struggles for scientific naturalism. However, there is surely no reason today for taking seriously a position that attributes a complex human achievement entirely to months (or at most years) of experience, rather than to millions of years of evolution or to principles of neural organization that may be even more deeply grounded in physical law—a position that would, furthermore, yield the conclusion that man is, apparently, unique among animals in the way in which he acquires knowledge. Such a position is particularly implausible with regard to language, an aspect of the child's world that is a human creation and would naturally be expected to reflect intrinsic human capacity in its internal organization.

In short, the structure of particular may very well be largely determined by factors over which the individual has no conscious control and concerning which society may have little choice or freedom. On the basis of the best information now available, it seems reasonable to suppose that a child cannot help constructing a particular sort of transformational grammar to account for the data presented to him, any more than he can control his perception of solid objects or his attention to line and angle. Thus it may well be that the general features of language structure reflect, not so much the course of one's experience, but rather the general character of one's capacity to acquire knowledge—in the traditional sense, one's innate ideas and innate principles. It seems to me that the problem of clarifying this issue and sharpening our understanding of its many facets provides the most interesting and important reason for the study of descriptively adequate grammars and, beyond this, the formulation and justification of a general linguistic theory that meets the condition of explanatory adequacy. By pursuing this investigation, one may hope to give some real substance to the traditional belief that "the principles of grammar form an important, and very curious, part of the philosophy of the human mind" (Beattie, 1788).

9. GENERATIVE CAPACITY AND ITS LINGUISTIC RELEVANCE

It may be useful to make one additional methodological observation in connection with the topics discussed in the last few sections. Given a descriptive theory of language structure, we can distinguish its *weak generative capacity* from its *strong generative capacity* in the following way. Let us say that a grammar *weakly generates* a set of sentences and that it *strongly generates* a set of structural descriptions (recall that each structural description uniquely specifies a sentence, but not necessarily conversely), where both weak and strong generation are determined by the procedure f of (12iv) = (13iv) = (14iv). Suppose that the linguistic theory T provides the class of grammars $G_1, G_2, \ldots$, where G_i weakly generates the language L_i and strongly generates the system of structural descriptions Σ_i. Then the class $\{L_1, L_2, \ldots\}$ constitutes the *weak generative capacity* of T and the class $\{\Sigma_1, \Sigma_2, \ldots\}$ constitutes the *strong generative capacity* of T.

The study of strong generative capacity is related to the study of descriptive adequacy, in the sense defined. A grammar is descriptively adequate if it strongly generates the correct set of structural descriptions. A theory is descriptively adequate if its strong generative capacity includes the system of structural descriptions for each natural language; otherwise, it is descriptively inadequate. Thus inadequacy of strong generative capacity, on empirical grounds, shows that a theory of language is seriously defective. As we have observed, however, a theory of language that appears to be empirically adequate in terms of strong generative capacity is not necessarily of any particular theoretical interest, since the crucial question of explanatory adequacy goes beyond any consideration of strong generative capacity.

The study of weak generative capacity is of rather marginal linguistic interest. It is important only in those cases where some proposed theory fails even in weak generative capacity—that is, where there is some natural language even the *sentences* of which cannot be enumerated by any grammar permitted by this theory. In fact, it has been shown that certain fairly elementary theories (in particular, the theory of context-free phrase-structure grammar and the even weaker theory of finite-state grammar) do not have the weak generative capacity required for the description of natural language, and thus fail empirical tests of adequacy in a particularly surprising way. From this observation we must conclude that as linguistic theory progresses to a more adequate conception of grammatical structure, it will have to permit devices with a weak generative capacity that differs, in certain respects, from that of these severely defective systems.

It is important to note, however, that the fundamental defect of these systems is not their limitation in weak generative capacity but rather their many inadequacies in strong generative capacity. Postal's demonstration that the theory of context-free grammar (simple phrase-structure grammar) fails in weak generative capacity was preceded by over a half-dozen years of discussion of the strong generative capacity of this theory, which showed conclusively that it cannot achieve descriptive adequacy. Furthermore, these limitations in strong generative capacity carry over to the theory of context-sensitive phrase-structure grammar, which probably does not fail in weak generative capacity. Presumably, discussion of weak generative capacity marks only a very early and primitive stage of the study of generative grammar. Questions of real linguistic interest arise only when strong generative capacity (descriptive adequacy) and, more important, explanatory adequacy become the focus of discussion.

As observed earlier, the critical factor in the development of a fully adequate theory is the limitation of the class of possible grammars. Clearly, this limitation must be such as to meet empirical conditions on strong (and, a fortiori, weak) generative capacity, and, furthermore, such as to permit the condition of explanatory adequacy to be met when an appropriate evaluation measure is developed. But beyond this, the problem is to impose sufficient structure on the schema that defines "generative grammar" so that relatively few hypotheses will have to be tested by the evaluation measure, given primary linguistic data. We want the hypotheses compatible with fixed data to be "scattered" in value, so that choice among them can be made relatively easily. This requirement of "feasibility" is the major empirical constraint on a theory, once the conditions of descriptive and explanatory adequacy are met. It is important to keep the requirements of explanatory adequacy and feasibility in mind when weak and strong generative capacities of theories are studied as mathematical questions. Thus one can construct hierarchies of grammatical theories in terms of weak and strong generative capacity, but it is important to bear in mind that these hierarchies do *not* necessarily correspond to what is probably the empirically most significant dimension of increasing power of linguistic theory. This dimension is presumably to be defined in terms of the scattering in value of grammars compatible with fixed data. Along this empirically significant dimension, we should like to accept the least "powerful" theory that is empirically adequate. It might conceivably turn out that this theory is extremely powerful (perhaps even universal, that is, equivalent in generative capacity to the theory of Turing machines) along the dimension of weak generative capacity, and even along the dimension of strong generative capacity. It will not necessarily follow that it is very powerful (and hence to be discounted) in the dimension which is ultimately of real empirical significance.

In brief, mathematical study of formal properties of grammars is, very likely, an area of linguistics of great potential. It has already provided some insight into questions of empirical interest and will perhaps some day provide much deeper insights. But it is important to realize that the questions presently being studied are primarily determined by feasibility of mathematical study and it is important not to confuse this with the question of empirical significance.

Bibliographic References

Arnauld, A. and P. Nicole. *La Logique, ou l'art de penser*. 1662.

Beattie, J. *Theory of Language*. London, 1788.

Chomsky, N. *Morphophonemics of Modern Hebrew*. Unpublished Master's thesis, University of Pennsylvania, 1951.

Cudworth, R. *A Treatise Concerning Eternal and Immutable Morality*. Edited by E. Chandler. 1731.

Descartes, R. "Notes Directed Against a Certain Programme." 1647. In *The Philosophical Works of Descartes*. Translated by E. S. Haldane and G. T. Ross. Vol. I. New York: Dover, 1955.

Diderot, D. *Lettre sur les Sourds et Muets*. 1751. Page references are to J. Assezat, ed., *Oeuvres Complètes de Diderot*. Vol. I. Paris: Garnier Frères, 1875.

Du Marsais, C. Ch. *Les véritables principes de la grammaire*. 1729. On the dating of this manuscript, see Sahlin (1928), p. ix.

Herbert of Cherbury. *De Veritate*. 1624. Translated by M. H. Carré. University of Bristol Studies, No. 6., 1937.

Lancelot, C., A. Arnauld, *et al. Grammaire générale et raisonnée*. 1660.

Leibniz, G. W. *New Essays Concerning Human Understanding*. Translated by A. G. Langley. La Salle, Ill.: The Open Court Publishing Co., 1949.

Sahlin, G. *César Chesneau du Marsais et son rôle dans l'évolution de la grammaire générale*. Paris: Presses Universitaires, 1928.

JERROLD J. KATZ

4.3 *Mentalism in Linguistics*

Linguists who conceive of their science as a discipline which collects utterances and classifies their parts often pride themselves on their freedom from mentalism. But freedom from mentalism is an inherent feature of the taxonomic conception of linguistics, for, according to this conception, a linguist starts his investigation with observable physical events and at no stage imports anything else.

We may expand on this inherent freedom from mentalistic commitment as follows. Utterances are stretches of physical sound. Since the primary data for a taxonomic linguistic investigation is a set of utterances elicited from informants or obtained from texts, the linguist begins with observable physical events, sounds or inscriptions. At the first stage of classification—the cataloguing of phonemes on the basis of these stretches of sound or some grouping of them—the linguist erects classes of significant sounds. At the next stage he forms classes of sequences of phonemes, thus producing a catalog of the morphemes of the language. Finally he classifies sequences of morphemes as sentential constituents of various types. Even if at some point the linguist should also consider an aspect of the speaker himself (such as his intuitive judgments about well-formedness) or an aspect of the speaker's environment (such as what he is referring to), such consideration is restricted to just those aspects that are capable of being observed by anyone who cares to carry out the same investigation. Therefore, on the taxonomic conception of linguistics, there is nowhere from the beginning to the end of a linguistic investigation, any appeal to mental capacities or mental processes. Alternatively, the taxonomic conception is a very narrow form of reductionism, which holds that every linguistic construction, at any level, reduces ultimately, by purely classificational procedures, to physical segments of utterances.

This philosophy of linguistics is never explicitly defended in current literature, because the linguists who hold it generally assume that Bloomfield long ago conclusively refuted mentalism.[1] Hence a taxonomic linguist considers

---

Reprinted from *Language*, XL, No. 2 (1964), 124–37, by permission of the author and of the editor of *Language*.

[1] For obvious reasons, Bloomfield's own version of Bloomfieldian antimentalism is taken as my point of departure. But I could just as easily have taken any one of the many antimentalist positions found in the tradition of American behaviorist linguistics—for instance, with Twaddell's view of the psychological reality of linguistic concepts as expressed in his influential paper *On Defining the Phoneme, Language Monographs*, no. 16 (1935). There Twaddell writes:

"It is a work of supererogation to try to restate what Bloomfield has so well stated. For the sake of completeness, though, it may be justifiable to recapitulate the general principles which invalidate any 'mental' definition of the phoneme."

"Such a definition is invalid because (1) we have no right to guess about the linguistic workings of an inaccessible 'mind,' and (2) we can secure no advantage from such guesses. The linguistic processes of the 'mind' as such are quite simply unobservable; and introspection

it unnecessary to put forth arguments of his own against this doctrine. When he criticizes other linguists for subscribing to a mentalistic philosophy of linguistics or for adopting a mentalistic theory of linguistic structure, he relies on Bloomfield's critique of mentalism for support.

But when we look at Bloomfield's critique of mentalism and compare the doctrine he criticized with the doctrines that modern taxonomic linguists criticize for being mentalistic, we find, curiously enough, that the most influential of the latter turn out not to be the kind of doctrine that Bloomfield attacked. Bloomfield criticized, not mentalism in the contemporary sense of this term, but a highly theologized conception of mentalism, which very few who regard themselves as mentalists would have any desire to call their own. Typical of Bloomfield's criticism of mentalism is this[2]:

> The *mentalistic* theory . . . supposes that the variability of human conduct is due to the interference of some non-physical factor, a *spirit* or *will* or *mind* . . . that is present in every human being. This spirit, according to the mentalistic view, is entirely different from material things and accordingly follows some other kind of causation or perhaps none at all.

Here and in similar statements, Bloomfield makes it clear that he is criticizing mentalism because it renders prediction and explanation of linguistic behavior in terms of causal laws completely impossible. Since Bloomfield's critique applies only to a theologized version of mentalism, it follows that taxonomic linguists are not justified in appealing to Bloomfield's "refutation" to support their criticism of a version of mentalism according to which mental capacities and processes are subject to causal laws. Indeed, such a version of mentalism is wholly compatible with the doctrine Bloomfield called "mechanism."

There is, however, another feature of Bloomfield's discussion of mentalism which, though it can hardly be construed as a refutation of anything, does provide the taxonomic linguist with some basis in Bloomfield's work for his polemic against a nontheological version of mentalism. This feature is Bloomfield's endorsement of the empiricist viewpoint on scientific methodology. In this vein, he writes,[3]

> . . . we can distinguish science from other phases of human activity by agreeing that science shall deal only with events that are accessible in their time and place to any and all observers (strict *behaviorism*) or only with events that are

---

about linguistic processes is notoriously a fire in a wooden stove. Our only information about the 'mind' is derived from the behavior of the individual whom it inhabits. To interpret that behavior in terms of 'mind' is to commit the logical fallacy of 'explaining' a fact of unknown cause by giving that unknown cause a name, and then citing the name x as the cause of the fact. 'Mind' is indeed a summation of such x's, unknown causes of human behavior."

Other particularly explicit statements of the antimentalist viewpoint against which I intend to argue include C. F. Hockett, "Biophysics, Linguistics, and the Unity of Science," *American Scientist* (1948), 558–72; and a work as recent as R. M. W. Dixon, *Linguistic Science and Logic* (The Hague, 1963).

[2] L. Bloomfield, *Language* XXXII (New York, 1933).

[3] Bloomfield, "Linguistic Aspects of Science," *International Encyclopedia of Unified Science*, 1.231 (Chicago, 1938).

placed in coordinates of time and space (*mechanism*), or that science shall employ only such initial statements and predictions as lead to definite handling operations (*operationalism*), or only terms such as are derivable by rigid definition (*physicalism*).

The charge against mentalism made by those who cite Bloomfield in support of their dismissal of mentalism, then, is that mentalistic theories deal with events that do not meet the methodological demands of behaviorism, mechanism, operationalism, and physicalism. They believe the charge to be justified because they believe that a theory of linguistic structure which deals with such events is based on bad scientific methodology.

It is extremely important to note that Bloomfield goes on to say,[4]

> ... These several formulations [behaviorism, mechanism, operationalism, and physicalism], independently reached by different scientists, all lead to the same delimitation, and this delimitation does not restrict the subject matter of science but rather characterizes its method.

Bloomfield is here at pains to stress that the empiricist viewpoint on scientific methodology does not restrict the range or kind of phenomena that a scientist can describe and explain. The present paper denies just this claim. Against it, I argue two points. First, the taxonomic linguist's criticism of mentalistic theories for being based on bad scientific methodology fails through the inadequacy of the empiricist viewpoint on which it depends. That is, I shall argue that the empiricist viewpoint does not deserve to be the standard by which any conception of linguistics or any other science is judged. Second, a mentalistic theory is better than a taxonomic one because the delimitation imposed by the empiricist viewpoint, and accepted by taxonomic linguists, so severely restricts the character of a taxonomic theory that the range and kind of linguistic phenomena for which such a theory can account is considerably narrower than the range and kind that a mentalistic theory can handle. If these two points are both established, there should be an end to the criticizing of linguistic theories for being mentalistic; and, more significantly, there should be an end to taxonomic theories themselves.

One may formulate the controversy between taxonomic linguistics and mentalistic linguistics in terms of the following opposition. The linguist who adopts a causal conception of mentalism is contending that purely linguistic theories cannot succeed in predicting and explaining the facts of linguistic performance without making reference to the mental events, capacities, and processes of speakers, i.e., that linguistic theories must contain concepts which enable linguists to formulate the principles of mental operation that underlie speech. On the other hand, the linguist who adopts the taxonomic conception of linguistics is contending that purely linguistic theories can succeed in predicting and explaining the facts of linguistic performance.

It might appear that there is no way to settle this controversy short of some

---

[4] *Ibid.*, 231.

abstruse examination of the philosophical principles underlying the taxonomic and mentalistic positions, but this is false. The dispute can be settled simply by determining whether a taxonomic or a mentalistic theory is, in principle, better able to account for what is known about the general facts of linguistic phenomena. This determination can be made by showing that a mentalistic theory accounts for everything that a taxonomic theory accounts for, and, in addition and with no extension of the theory, for many things that the taxonomic theory must fail to account for. This is the spirit of Chomsky's criticisms of theories of grammar constructed within the taxonomic framework.[5] Unfortunately, Chomsky's arguments are often not taken in this way but are taken rather as trying to establish a new kind of taxonomic system.

The basic point of Chomsky's criticisms is that the failure of a taxonomic theory to handle the full range of facts about linguistic structure is due to the failure of such theories to concern themselves with mental capacities, events, and processes. The point which has been missed by those who interpret his arguments as trying to establish a new kind of taxonomic system is that only by introducing mentalistic concepts into our theories do we provide ourselves with the conceptual machinery which makes it possible to account for the full range of linguistic facts.

The general form of Chomsky's criticism of taxonomic linguistics is summarized as follows. The best kind of theory is one which systematizes the widest range of facts; hence a mentalistic theory is better than a taxonomic one because the former can handle any fact that the latter can handle, whereas the latter is unable to handle many kinds of facts that the former handles easily and naturally. The difference in the facts that these theories can handle is a direct function of the difference in the conceptual machinery they contain.

If it is to be shown that mentalism thus succeeds where taxonomic linguistics fails, it will be necessary to clarify certain features of the mentalist conception of linguistic theories. In particular, it must be made clear just what a mentalist means when he says that reference to mental states is a necessary aspect of any adequate linguistic theory, and just what status he intends mentalistic concepts to have. Unless his meaning is clarified, it will remain unclear whether it is the reference to mental states that is responsible for the margin of explanatory power by which mentalistic theories excel taxonomic theories. Unless the status of his concepts is clarified, it will remain open for the taxonomic linguist to claim that, although the mentalist says that his reference to mental states is a reference to things or events within the causal realm, the actual way in which this reference is made gives no clue how mental states might stand as causal antecedents of physical events like vocalization and speech sounds. These matters must be clarified in such a way that those who construe Chomsky's arguments as seeking to establish a new kind of taxonomic system cannot claim that the machinery in Chomsky's theories which produce the margin of ex-

---

[5] Cf. N. Chomsky, "A Transformational Approach to Syntax" and "Current Issues in Linguistic Theory," *The Structure of Language: Readings in the Philosophy of Language*, ed. by J. Fodor and J. J. Katz (Englewood Cliffs, N. J., Prentice-Hall, Inc., 1964).

planatory power by which they are more empirically successful have no psychological reality but are merely new kinds of data-cataloguing devices.

First, how can mental events like those referred to in mentalistic linguistic theories be links in the causal chain that contains also vocalizations and sound waves? To explain how speakers are able to communicate in their language, the mentalist hypothesizes that, underlying a speaker's ability to communicate, there is a highly complex mechanism which is essentially the same as that underlying the linguistic ability of other speakers. He thus views the process of linguistic communication as one in which such mechanisms operate to encode and decode verbal messages. The aim of theory construction in linguistics is taken to be the formulation of a theory that reveals the structure of this mechanism and explains the facts of linguistic communication by showing them to be behavioral consequences of the operation of a mechanism with just the structure that the formulated theory attributes to it.

The step of hypothesizing such a mechanism in the process of theory construction in linguistics is no different from hypothetical postulation in theory construction in any other branch of science where some component of the system about which we wish to gain understanding is inaccessible to observation. The linguist can no more look into the head of a fluent speaker than a physicist can directly observe photons or a biologist directly inspect the evolutionary events that produced the human species. The linguist, like the physicist and biologist, can only achieve scientific understanding by constructing a model of the system which contains a hypothesis about the structure of the components of the system that are not observable. If the logical consequences of the model match the observable behavior of the system and would not do so without the hypothesis, the scientist may say that this hypothesis accounts for the behavior of the system in terms of the behavior of the unobservable but causally efficient component. If the model is the simplest one which enables the scientist to derive all the known facts and predict previously unknown ones as effects of the hypothesized component, he can assert that his model correctly pictures the structure of the system and its unobservable components. In this way, a linguist can assert that his theory correctly represents the structure of the mechanism underlying the speaker's ability to communicate with other speakers.

This mechanism is, according to the mentalist linguist, a brain mechanism, a component of a neural system. It is inaccessible to observation in the sense that, even if the linguist could look inside a speaker's head, he would be unable to figure out the structure of the mechanism from the electrochemical events going on there. But, as I have just pointed out, this limitation does not doom the linguist's program of discovering the nature of the speaker's ability to communicate in language. Hence it cannot be taken as grounds for supposing that a linguistic theory is not about a brain mechanism and its concepts are not about mental states. It is perhaps because, from the behaviorist viewpoint, this observational inaccessibility of the neural mechanism represents the boundary of the subject matter of linguistics, that taxonomic linguists have denied that theoretical concepts in a linguistic theory can have psychological reality.

It would certainly explain why they have confined themselves to the corpus of elicitable utterances, behavioral responses to such utterances, and observable features of the context in which utterances occur, and why they have refused to regard the internal psychological properties of speakers as part of the subject matter of a linguistic theory.

Of course, the view that the reality of theoretical concepts in linguistics is mentalistic yet (in principle) irreducible to brain states, is a form of psychophysical dualism that a linguist should be reluctant to accept. But holding that brain states are observationally inaccessible and, at the same time, that linguistic constructions have an underlying psychological reality does not commit one to accepting such a dualism.

Let us suppose that the linguist constructs a theory by inferring hypothetically the characteristics of the mechanism underlying linguistic communication. His inference begins by positing a mechanism of which the observable events of linguistic communication are causal consequences. He invents a theory about the structure of this mechanism and the causal chain connecting the mechanism to observable events, to explain how these internal causes produce linguistic communication as their effect. Now it is clear that the linguist, though he claims that his theory describes a neurological mechanism, cannot immediately translate the theory into neurological terms, i.e. into talk about synapses, nerve fibers, and such. But—and this is the crucial point in showing that the mentalist is not a psychophysical dualist—this failure to have a ready neurological translation means only that he cannot yet specify what kind of physical realization of his theoretical description is inside the speaker's head. Since linguistics and neurophysiology are independent fields, it does not matter for the linguist what kind of physical realization is there. For the purpose of linguistic investigation, it is immaterial whether the mechanism inside the speaker's head is in reality a network of electronic relays, a mechanical system of cardboard flip-flops and rubber bands, or, for that matter, a group of homunculi industriously at work in a tiny office. All of these possibilities, and others, are on a par for the linguist as physical realizations of this mechanism, so long as each is isomorphic to the representation of linguistic structure given by the theory of the language. The critical distinction is, then, between an abstract, formal characterization of linguistic structure—the theory itself—and a physical system of some kind which instances this structure.[6] Discovering what kind of a physical system in the human brain instantiates the representation of structure given by a linguistic theory is the task of the neurophysiologist. The linguist's task is to provide a theory which represents the structure that any physical system must possess if it is to be capable of linguistic communication as we know it.

The theoretical constructions used by a mentalist linguist in building his theories are intended by him to have psychological reality. They do not, for

---

[6] *Cf.* H. Putnam, "Minds and machines," *Dimensions of Mind*, ed. by S. Hook (New York, 1960).

the linguist, require translation into neurophysiological terms, even though reference to mental states is construed as reference to brain states. This is why the events to which the mentalist's constructions refer can stand as links in the causal chain that contains vocalizations and sound waves as other links.

Why, now, do mentalistic linguistic theories excel taxonomic linguistic theories in descriptive and explanatory power, and why must mentalistic concepts be given credit for this excellence?

The three fundamental questions with which a synchronic description of a particular language deals are these:

(1) What is known by a speaker who is fluent in a natural language? That is, what facts about his language underlie his ability to communicate with others in that language?

(2) How is such linguistic knowledge put into operation to achieve communication? That is, how does a speaker use such linguistic knowledge to convey his thoughts, opinions, wishes, demands, questions, emotions, and so on to other speakers?

(3) How do speakers come to acquire this ability? That is, what innate dispositions and developmental processes are responsible for transforming a nonverbal infant into a fluent speaker?

An answer to (1) may be referred to as a "linguistic description."[7] A linguistic description has three components: syntactic, phonological, and semantic. If the linguistic description is a mentalistic theory, the syntactic component is a generative system which enumerates strings of minimally syntactically functioning units (which may be called formatives), together with a description of their syntactic structure. These structural descriptions, the output of the syntactic component in a linguistic description, are the input to both the phonological component and the semantic component. These two components are interpretative systems: the former interprets the abstract, formal descriptions of the syntactic structure of sentences as representations of vocal sound by assigning them a phonetic shape; the latter interprets them as meaningful messages. That is, the semantic component converts the outputs of the syntactic component into the messages that the sentences communicate to those who understand the language. The phonological and semantic components have no systematic connection with each other: one is concerned with pronunciation and the other with conceptualization.

An answer to (2) consists of at least two procedures. One is a "sentence recognition procedure," whose function is to assign to any given perceived utterance a phonetic representation, a syntactic description, and a semantic interpretation. The function of the other procedure is to choose an appropriate syntactic structure for any message that the speaker wishes to communicate and to provide a phonetic representation for that structure; it is a "sentence production procedure." Together, the two procedures determine how the

---

[7] For further discussion of this concept, *cf.* J. J. Katz and P. Postal, *An Integrated Theory of Linguistic Descriptions* (Cambridge, Mass., 1964).

knowledge of the language embodied in the linguistic description is used by a speaker to understand and produce sentences.

An answer to (3) is a theory of language acquisition. Such a theory explains how a nonverbal infant who is exposed in the normal way to a sample of sentences and nonsentences, and perhaps other data as well, comes to possess a linguistic description and procedures of sentence recognition and sentence production.

The first of the three questions is logically prior to the others. We must know what linguistic facts a speaker knows before we can say how those facts enable him to communicate and before we can say how he acquired them: linguistic description must precede inquiry into the nature of language use and acquisition. But this logical priority does not mean that the attempt to answer (2) and (3) must wait for a full answer to (1); rather, it means that substantive contributions toward an answer to (1) must be available in order that attempts to answer (2) and (3) can begin. Furthermore, it means—and this is critical— that the kind of answer that will be given, or sought, for (2) and (3) is determined by the kind of answer which is given or sought for (1). Since (2) is, in the same sense, logically prior to (3), the same applies to these two.

The basic fact about languages that a full answer to (1) must account for is that speakers can understand indefinitely many sentences never before encountered by them. So ubiquitous and commonplace is this fact that its theoretical significance is often missed: the very fact that almost every sentence we encounter is heard for the first time keeps us from fully appreciating how amazing it is that a fluent speaker is able to understand new sentences. But if we think about learning a foreign language, the theoretical significance of this feat becomes apparent immediately. We do not credit a person with mastery of a foreign language if he is only able to understand those sentences which he has been previously taught. The test of fluency is whether he can understand sentences that he has not been taught. The theoretical significance of understanding new sentences is that this ability is the test of whether one has mastery of a natural language.

To account for this feat in answering (1), the grammar must take the form of a system of rules which describe the structure of every sentence that a speaker would (in the absence of linguistically irrelevant psychological limitations) understand if he were to encounter it. Such rules must describe an infinite set of sentences because in a natural language there is no longest sentence. Given a sentence composed of n formatives, there is always another composed of $n + r$ formatives, formed from the first by various syntactic procedures, for instance by replacing a noun by a noun and a modifier which contains another noun, itself replaceable by a noun and a modifier, and so on. There will, of course, be a point at which still longer sentences cannot be either produced or understood by normal speakers in normal situations; but this limitation has to do with perceptual limits, the finite bound on memory storage, human mortality, and other linguistically inessential considerations. If we mistakenly identify these speech limitations with a finite-length limitation on what qualifies as a grammatical sentence of the language, we are forced to the absurd conclusion that, as such limitations are weakened (say, by the use of paper and pencil), either a new language is being used or the old one has undergone radical change.

This shows that a taxonomic grammar which describes only the sentences in a corpus fails to be empirically adequate: infinitely many grammatical sentences are left undescribed. Some taxonomic grammars are intended to describe the full set of sentences—that is, to segment and classify not only the sentences in a corpus but also of those that might be elicited and those that are of the same syntactic form as the elicited and elicitable sentences. But this should not obscure the theoretically more significant fact that such grammars are nonetheless put forth as data-cataloguing systems, the data being strings of syntactically well-formed formatives. Accordingly, their rules have no psychological reality, and cannot be construed as accounting for the knowledge that a speaker has which enables him to understand new sentences of his language. Furthermore, such rules cannot be the basis for an answer to (2), since an answer to (2) must relate the speaker's knowledge of the structure of sentences to procedures for applying this knowledge. For the same reason, such rules cannot be the basis for an answer to (3), since an answer to (3) is an input-output device which explains how a sample of sentences and nonsentences as input gives as output a linguistic description and procedures of sentence production and sentence recognition.

To show that a mentalistic theory of linguistic communication can succeed in answering (1), (2), and (3), and why mentalistic concepts are essential in giving it that power, we require an overall model which shows how the mechanism of linguistic communication operates in an actual situation. Such a model represents the most rudimentary form of the theory of linguistic communication which mentalists seek to construct, and is thus a first approximation toward an exact formulation of that theory in its fully sophisticated form. It should be stressed, however, that even as a first approximation such a model shares with the fully elaborated and precise theory the character and status of a hypothetically inferred theoretical construction.

Given that both speaker and hearer are equipped with a linguistic description and procedures for sentence production and recognition, we can reconstruct the communication situation in these terms. The speaker, for reasons that are biographically but not linguistically relevant, chooses some message he wants to convey to the hearer. He selects some thought he wishes to express to him, some command he wants to give him, or some question he needs to ask him. This message is, we may assume, in whatever form the semantic component of his linguistic description uses to represent the meaning content of thoughts, commands, questions, or the like. The speaker then uses the sentence production procedure to obtain an abstract syntactic structure having the proper conceptualization of his thought, command, or question as its semantic interpretation. This procedure helps him find a sentence that is suitable to the circumstances by rejecting all syntactic structures which, though they bear the proper semantic interpretation, are for sentences that are too long, syntactically too complicated, too pedantic, etc. After he has suitable syntactic structure, the speaker utilizes the phonological component of his linguistic description to produce a phonetic shape for it. This phonetic shape is encoded into a signal that causes the speaker's articulatory system to vocalize an utterance of the sentence. The sound waves of which these utterances consist are transmitted through the air and, after they reach the hearer's auditory system, are converted into a signal which is decoded into a phonetic shape. On the basis of that shape the hearer's sentence recognition procedure then provides a syntactic structure. That is, the procedure converts the signal produced by hearing the utterance into a phonetic shape whose physical realization is what reached the ear, and recovers the syntactic structure that the speaker originally chose as a formalization of his message. Once the hearer is in possession of this syntactic structure, he employs the semantic component of his linguistic description to obtain its semantic interpretation. He thus represents to himself the same message that the speaker wished to convey to him, and communication has taken place.

Although this model is phrased as if the processes described were conscious, no such assumption is involved. It is not an essential feature of mentalism that the processes postulated by the mentalist as going on inside a speaker's head should be open to the speaker's conscious awareness. This point alone ought to remove one source of opposition to mentalism in modern linguistics.

Within the framework of the above model of linguistic communication, every aspect of the mentalistic theory involves psychological reality. The linguistic description and the procedures of sentence production and recognition must correspond to independent mechanisms in the brain. Componential distinctions between the syntactic, phonological, and semantic components must rest on relevant differences between three neural submechanisms of the mechanism which stores the linguistic description. The rules of each component must have their psychological reality in the input-output operations of the computing machinery of this mechanism. The ordering of rules within a component must, contrary to the claims of Bloomfield and many others,[8] have its psychological reality in those features of this computing machinery which group such input-output operations and make the performance of operations in one group a precondition for those in another to be performed.

There are two further points concerning the superiority of a mentalistic theory. First, since the psychologist and the mentalistic linguist are construct-

---

[8] This, then, is the answer to Hockett's question about how to construe ordering otherwise than historically; cf. 'Two Models of Linguistic Description', *Word*, X (1954) 233: "... if it is said that the English past tense form *baked* is 'formed' from *bake* by a 'process' of 'suffixation', then no matter what disclaimer of historicity is made, it is impossible not to conclude that some kind of priority is being assigned to *bake* as against *baked* or the suffix. And if this priority is not historical, what is it?"

ing theories of the same kind, i.e. theories with the same kind of relation to the neurophysiology of the human brain, it follows that the linguist's theory is subject to the requirement that it harmonize with the psychologist's theories dealing with other human abilities and that it be consistent with the neurophysiologist's theories concerning the type of existing brain mechanisms. A linguistic theory that meets this requirement will have a wider range of facts into whose explanation it can enter and so will be a better theory than one which is otherwise equivalent to it in explanatory power. Such a theory enters into the explanation of many of those psychological theories with which it harmonizes. Theories of perception, theories of memory, of thinking, of learning, and other psychological theories leave open various questions about the effect of language on these processes and the effect of these processes on language; only a mentalistic theory of linguistic structure can hope to answer them. Further, by subjecting a linguistic theory to this requirement we make it more easily testable. For the requirement enables us to refute a linguistic theory if we can find psychological theories or facts that are inconsistent with it or neurophysiological accounts which describe brain structure in a way that precluded the linguistic theory from being isomorphic to any of the structures in the human brain. Again, a fruitful requirement like this can only be imposed on a mentalistic theory.

Second, a mentalistic theory also can provide a psychological reality for linguistic universals. Instead of linguistic universals being treated simply as common features of the linguistic description of every language, as they are in the taxonomic view, the fact that such common features are universal, i.e. are necessary features of natural languages, is explained in terms of the psychology of human language learners, the one constant feature among all the individual differences between speakers of different natural languages, and all the differences between the situations in which they learn to speak. One clear-cut sense of psychological reality for linguistic universals is that proposed by Chomsky.[9] According to Chomsky's account, there are two kinds of linguistic universals, substantive and formal. The formal universals are specifications of the form of the rules that appear in each of the components of any empirically successful linguistic description of a natural language; the substantive universals are theoretical terms which enter into the formulation of the rules of particular linguistics descriptions. Chomsky's hypothesis is that the child is innately equipped with a language-learning device that contains such linguistic universals and a simplicity principle; the latter enables him to acquire the simplest linguistic description of the form determined by the linguistic universals which accords with the sample of utterances he is exposed to. Linguistic universals thus have psychological reality as part of the internal structure of the innate mechanism responsible for a child's acquisition of a language. Such a hypothe-

---

[9] Chomsky, review of *Verbal Behavior* by B. F. Skinner, *Language*, XXXV (1959) 26–58.

sis, if true, explains why there should be a certain structure and content found in every language: they are found in every language because they are implanted by the innately given language-learning device that makes the acquisition of a natural language possible for normal humans.

Finally, why must this kind of psychological reality be attributed to the concepts of a mentalistic theory? Why can they not be regarded as mere fictions or as new kinds of data-cataloguing devices?

Bloomfield presents a particularly clear statement of the view against which I will argue. He writes,[10]

> We can describe the peculiarity of these plurals [*knives*, *mouths*, and *houses*] by saying that the final [f, θ, s] of the underlying singular is replaced by [v, ð, z] before the bound form is added. The word "before" in this statement means that the alternant of the bound form is the one appropriate to the substituted sound; thus, the plural of *knife* adds not [-s], but [-z]: "first" the [-f] is replaced by [-v], and "then" the appropriate alternant [-z] is added. The terms 'before', 'after', 'first', 'then', and so on, in such statements, tell the *descriptive order*. The actual sequence of constituents, and their structural order . . . are a part of the language, but the descriptive order of grammatical features is a fiction and results simply from our method of describing the forms; it goes without saying, for instance, that the speaker who says *knives*, does not "first" replace [f] by [v] and "then" add [-z], but merely utters a form (*knives*) which in certain features differs from a certain other form (namely, *knife*).

Bloomfield says that the speaker 'merely utters a form (*knives*)'. I have argued that in order to answer the three fundamental questions of linguistics, this is not enough; it is necessary to explain why the speaker says this rather than *knifes*. The mentalist, I have argued, explains this fact of English pluralization by crediting the speaker of English with a linguistic description that contains both the kind of rules and the kind of ordering restriction that Bloomfield mentions. The mentalist asserts that an English speaker says *knives* rather than *knifes* because sentences whose underlying syntactic form is . . . *knife + pl* . . . are produced by using such rules and ordering restrictions to pass from this syntactic form to its phonological realization *knives*. Presumably Bloomfield's answer to this would be that one need not treat such rules and ordering restrictions as psychologically real; they may be regarded as fictions and still enable us to correctly predict the way in which speakers of English pluralize.

Here is the crux of the issue. It is true that these features of the grammar may be regarded as fictions and still enable us to predict the facts of English pluralization; but what is required for prediction and what is required for explanation are two different things. A few examples show this quite dramatically. Suppose I have a betting system for the races that never fails to pick the winner. The system may be based on numerology, astrology, genealogy, or what have you. Suppose, further, that my system predicts that a certain horse will win in the third race, and he does. If any basis for correctly predicting an event is also an acceptable explanation for the event once it has occurred, then we are forced

---

[10] Bloomfield, *Language*, p. 213.

to the absurd conclusion that the horse won because my system predicted it. Again, suppose I predict that Jones will be sick because he drank my home brew, and it is known that 95 per cent of those who drink it become sick: is it an explanation of Jones's illness that he drank my home brew? Obviously not, since to explain why Jones became sick we must explain how he differs from the 5 per cent who can drink home brew without becoming sick.[11] The crucial question, then, is why we cannot explain linguistic facts if we treat the rules and ordering restrictions of a linguistic description as simply convenient fictions.

As described above, the mentalist explains the facts about a speaker's and hearer's linguistic performance in terms of a model that reconstructs the process by which a message is transmitted from the speaker to the hearer through the speaker's encoding the message in the form of an utterance and the hearer's decoding that utterance back to the speaker's original message. Such a model explains why an utterance has a certain linguistic property, and what function that property has in the process of communication, by locating the property in the causal chain which links the utterance on one side to the neurophysiological mechanisms that perform the encoding and articulation, on the other side to those that accomplish the perception and decoding. But if, with the taxonomic viewpoint, we interpret any of the elements of the mentalist's description of the process of communication as merely fictions, rather than references to neurophysiological links in such a causal chain, the whole explanation collapses. For that interpretation would amount to the claim that there are gaps in the causal chain. If there are gaps, we cannot account for the causal antecedents of a linguistic property and of its effects. The Bloomfieldian mode of interpreting features of a linguistic description is like contending that the pressure of a gas on the walls of its container is the effect of molecules striking the walls, and at the same time denying that a molecule is a real physical object. The hypothesis of a mechanism of linguistic communication, with the kind of structure attributed to it by an optimal linguistic description, can explain how linguistic communication takes place only if the mechanism and all its features have the same ontological status as the utterance itself. The hypothesized mechanism must be capable of affecting the articulatory system of a speaker so as to produce an utterance, and capable of being affected by the output of his receptor system when stimulated by an utterance. This implies, however (to stress it again), no commitment for the mentalist to any particular kind of physical realization for the linguistic description, except that whatever is inside the speaker's head must be capable of causal connection with the physical sounds that serve as the vehicle of linguistic communication.[12]

The taxonomic linguist assumes that only his conception and treatment of linguistics saves the linguist from countenancing such occult mental entities as a 'spirit' and 'soul'. The truth is, rather, that mentalism also—in the only

---

[11] *Cf.* S. Bromberger, *The Concept of Explanation* (Dissertation, Harvard University, 1960), for the first set of convincing examples of this kind to be proposed.

[12] For a general discussion of the fictionalist view of scientific theories, *cf.* Katz, "On The Existence of Theoretical Entities," in preparation.

sense of "mentalism" for which any serious claim to validity is made—avoids those occult entities. Both taxonomic and mentalist linguists deal exclusively with physically real events and structures. Both leave it to other sciences to determine the exact nature of the physical reality of the phenomena they theorize about. Just as the taxonomic linguist must leave it to the physicist to tell him about the physical reality of sound waves, and (if he is behavioristically inclined) to the physiologist to tell him about the physical reality of muscular contractions and glandular secretions, so the mentalist linguist must leave it to the neurophysiologist to tell him about the neurophysiological realization of his abstract linguistic description.

The actual difference between the taxonomic and the mentalistic conceptions of linguistics lies in what linguistic theories built on each of these conceptions can accomplish by way of answering questions (1), (2), and (3). We have found that the taxonomic linguist confines linguistic investigation to stating those facts about the structure of a natural language which can be formulated within the framework of a classificational system, while the mentalist goes far beyond this in seeking a full answer to all three questions. This difference is important: it justifies us in rejecting the taxonomic conception in favor of the mentalistic one. Taxonomic linguistics can only describe the utterances of a language; mentalistic linguistics not only can do this but can also explain how speakers communicate by using the utterances, and how the ability to communicate is acquired. Instead of the taxonomic linguist having a just complaint against the mentalist for appealing to occult entities, the mentalist has a just complaint against the taxonomic linguist for excluding from linguistics, a priori and arbitrarily, just what it is most important for this science to do. The freedom from mentalism inherent in the taxonomic conception of linguistics is its inherent weakness.

GILBERT HARMAN

4.4   *Psychological Aspects of the Theory of Syntax*

Noam Chomsky contends that the theory of transformational grammar* has important implications for certain psychological and philosophical issues. In particular, he attempts to show what these implications are for the theory of

---

Reprinted from *The Journal of Philosophy*, LXIV, No. 2 (February 2, 1967), 75–87, by permission of the author and of the editor of *The Journal of Philosophy*.

*Following Chomsky, I use the word "grammar" in a wide sense to include not only syntax but also phonology and semantics.

All page references are to Noam Chomsky, *Aspects of the Theory of Syntax*, Cambridge, Mass.: The M.I.T. Press, 1965.

what it is to know a language and for the dispute between "rationalism" and "empiricism" taken as theories of how one learns a language. Part I of this paper discusses his claim that in describing what it is to know a language we must make use of the notion of linguistic "competence." Part II discusses his claim that "empiricists" cannot give an adequate explanation of language learning. In both parts I try to show that Chomsky's claims rest on serious confusions and cannot be accepted as they stand.

I

Chomsky distinguishes a person's linguistic *competence* from his *performance*. Competence is "the speaker-hearer's knowledge of his language." Performance is "the actual use of language in concrete situations" (4). Now, there are two senses in which a person may be said to have knowledge of a language. A typical speaker, call him "Smith," knows how to understand other speakers of his language and to communicate with them, although he cannot describe his language very well. Smith has knowledge of the language in one sense. A linguist, Jones, knows about the language, knows that it is described by certain rules, etc. Jones has knowledge of the language in a second sense. Is competence supposed to be what Smith has or what Jones has?

Chomsky says, "A grammar of a language purports to be a description of the ideal speaker's intrinsic competence" (4). He also says that a grammar is "*descriptively adequate* to the extent that it correctly describes the intrinsic competence of the native speaker" (24). How can a grammar describe Smith's competence? If competence is knowing how to speak and understand a language and if the grammar describes that language, then the grammar indirectly describes Smith's competence as "the competence to speak and understand the language described by this grammar." But Chomsky does not refer only to such indirect description of Smith's competence. He also takes a grammar to describe competence as the knowledge that the language is described by the rules of the grammar. Since a speaker can rarely, if ever, say what the rules of his language are, Chomsky introduces a theory of *unconscious* knowledge about the language:

> Obviously every speaker of a language has mastered and internalized a genera-
> tive grammar that expresses his knowledge of the language. This is not to say
> that he is aware of the rules of the grammar or even that he can become aware
> of them, or that his statements about his intuitive knowledge are necessarily
> accurate. Any interesting generative grammar will be dealing, for the most part,
> with mental processes that are far beyond the level of actual or even potential
> consciousness (8).

Thus he says a grammar is "a theory of linguistic intuition" (19, 24, 26–27), where linguistic intuition is taken to be the same as "tacit competence" (26–27). A grammar specifies a speaker's "tacit knowledge" (19, 21, 27) or his "intuitive knowledge" (21). A speaker has "internalized" a grammar (8, 21, 24); i.e., he has "developed an internal representation of a system of rules" (25); he "has developed and internally represented a generative grammar" (25); he has arrived "at an internal representation of a generative system" (46).

Chomsky does not intend these remarks to be taken overly literally; and it is important to see this. Taken literally, he would be saying that we are to explain how it is that Smith knows how to speak and understand a language by citing his knowledge of another more basic language in which he has (unconsciously) "internally represented" the rules of the first language. (It does not seem to make sense to assume that Smith can represent rules without representing them in some language.) The main problem with such a literal interpretation of these remarks would be the implausibility of the resulting view. How, for example, would Smith understand the more basic language? In order to avoid either an infinite regress or a vicious circle, one would have to suppose that Smith can understand at least one language directly, without unconsciously knowing the rules for that language. But if this is admitted, there is no reason why Smith cannot know directly the language he speaks. Thus, literally interpreted, Chomsky's theory would almost certainly be false.

Similarly, on a literal interpretation of what Chomsky says about learning languages, Wittgenstein's remark about Augustine would apply to Chomsky's theory.

> And now, I think we can say: Augustine describes the learning of human language as if the child came into a strange country and did not understand the language of the country; that is, as if it already had a language, only not this one.[1]

Thus Chomsky says that the child learns a language on the basis of certain "primary linguistic data" (25). He proposes that

> ... the child approaches the data with the presumption that they are drawn from a language of a certain antecedently well-defined type, his problem being to determine which of the (humanly) possible languages is that of the community in which he is placed (27). ... On the basis of such data, the child constructs a grammar ... To learn a language, then, the child must ... possess a linguistic theory that specifies the form of a grammar of a possible human language (25). ... What are the initial assumptions that the child brings to language learning [?] (27) ... A child who is capable of language learning must have ... a technique for representing input signals ... a way of representing structural information about those signals (30).

Taken literally, Chomsky would be proposing that, before he learned any language, Smith had made a presumption about certain data; he had set himself a task; he possessed a theory; he made assumptions; he had techniques of representation. This would be possible only on the absurd assumption that before he learned his first natural language Smith already knew another language. So we could not accept Chomsky's proposal if it were to be taken literally.

In order to see just how Chomsky's remarks are to be interpreted, we must first understand how he conceives a theory of linguistic performance. He thinks there is a connection between theories of linguistic performance and "performance models":

> To my knowledge, the only concrete results that have been achieved and the only clear suggestions that have been put forth concerning the theory of perfor-

---

[1] Ludwig Wittgenstein, *Philosophical Investigations* (New York: The Macmillan Company, 1953), pp. 15–16.

mance, outside of phonetics, have come from firm studies of performance models that incorporate generative grammars of specific kinds . . . (10) In general it seems that the study of performance models incorporating generative grammars may be a fruitful study; furthermore, it is difficult to imagine any other basis on which a theory of performance might develop (15).

Such a model would be a device that duplicates certain aspects of the performance of what is modeled. Chomsky wants a theory of performance to describe how a model functions, but he does not require that the theory specify a physical realization of the model. Similarly, one might describe a computer by its program or flow chart without having to say whether it had vacuum tubes or transistors. Because of the abstract nature of the description of performance models and also because of a contrast he wants to make with "behavioristic theories," Chomsky calls theories incorporating performance models "mentalistic." His way of putting the point just made is:

> The mentalist . . . need make no assumptions about the possible physiological basis for the mental reality that he studies. In particular, he need not deny that there is such a basis. One would guess, rather, that it is the mentalistic studies that will ultimately be of greatest value for the investigations of neurophysiological mechanisms, since they alone are concerned with determining abstractly the properties that such mechanisms must exhibit and the functions they must perform (193).

Similarly, Chomsky identifies a theory of language learning with the construction of a language "acquisition model":

> To facilitate the clear formulation of deeper questions, it is useful to consider the abstract problem of constructing an "acquisition model" for language, that is, a theory of language learning or grammar construction (24–25).

Furthermore, it would seem that Chomsky intends the psychological remarks he makes about a child's learning of language to be interpreted as about such a model. The sentence immediately following that just cited is:

> Clearly, a child who has learned a language has developed an internal representation of a system of rules that determine how sentences are to be formed, used, and understood (25).

A few pages later he is more explicit:

> Let us consider with somewhat greater care just what is involved in the construction of an "acquisition model" for language. A child who is capable of language learning must have . . . a technique for representing input signals [etc.] (30).

Sometimes Chomsky speaks of what the child must do. At other times he speaks of what a "language acquisition device" must do. For example,

> This device must search through the set of possible hypotheses . . . and must select grammars that are compatible with the primary linguistic data (32).

Therefore, it seems reasonable to interpret Chomsky's psychological remarks as remarks about psychological models: models of linguistic performance and models of linguistic acquisition.

A mode is a device duplicating certain aspects of behavior. But whose behavior, and what aspects? Chomsky speaks of a performance model and a linguistic-acquisition model. These must be models of speakers rather than of linguists, of Smith rather than of Jones. Thus a performance model must duplicate something of what Smith does as an adult speaker, his communicating with others, etc., rather than something of what Jones does as a linguist, his giving analyses of particular sentences, etc. A language-acquisition model must duplicate Smith's ability, as a child, to learn a language after being exposed to it, rather than Jones's ability, as an adult, to discover a grammar of a language after some study of it.

An ideal performance model would be able to participate in conversations with human speakers. If linguistic behavior includes appropriate responses to perception, such as answering questions about what is seen, and if it also includes following orders, then a performance model would have to duplicate a considerable amount of a person's behavior. Furthermore, since most thinking is in language and is made possible by language, we might expect a linguistic-performance model to duplicate the kind of intelligent behavior that depends on such thought. In that case, there will be little difference between a linguistic-performance model and a general psychological model of a person.

Chomsky sometimes speaks as if a speaker-hearer, like Smith, knows (unconsciously) the grammatical rules of his language, although in fact typically only a linguist, like Jones, would know what these rules are. Chomsky also suggests that in learning his language Smith made use of a linguistic theory, although in fact only someone like Jones would have such a theory. Can such remarks be interpreted in terms of psychological models? Do we want the models to contain grammatical or linguistic theories?

It is clear that no good model of performance or linguistic acquisition will produce structural descriptions of sentences or grammatical theories of language as final output meant to duplicate Smith's linguistic behavior. But models might produce such things internally in the process of duplicating Smith's linguistic behavior. In interpreting sentences, the performance model might use rewrite rules to form structural descriptions of sentences to be interpreted. Such a performance model would contain a representation of the rules of the grammar. When Chomsky says the speaker has internalized a representation of grammatical rules, we may interpret him to mean that a performance model contains such a representation. Similarly, a linguistic-acquisition model must duplicate language-learning behavior. Such a model would be a device that, when exposed to a particular language, comes to be a performance model of a speaker of that language. Now, since we have taken the performance model to contain a representation of the relevant rules, the language-acquisition device must in part produce a representation of the relevant grammar when the device is exposed to a natural language.

A very general sketch of a performance model might be as in figure 1. Reasoning, etc., would be carried out in such a model using semantically interpreted structural descriptions (s.d.'s) of sentences rather than the sentences themselves. I have artificially separated things, e.g., by distinguishing perceptual input from phonetic input, in order to bring out some of the places where

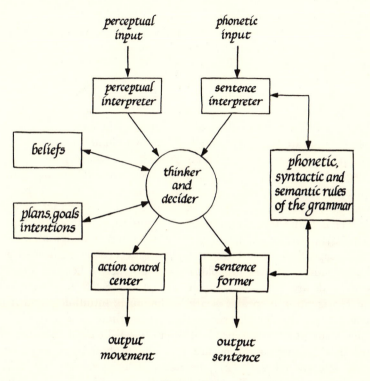

Figure 1

representations of grammatical rules might appear in such a model. This is somewhat misleading in that it disguises the influence of language on perception and thought, but this artificiality does not affect the following discussion.

Some of Chomsky's remarks about a speaker-hearer can now be interpreted. When he says a speaker has "an internal representation of a system of rules" (25), etc., he means that a performance model contains such a representation. (It is not obvious that every conceivable performance model need contain such a representation; but we have seen how a very natural performance model would.) Nevertheless, it is still not clear how to make sense of Chomsky's talk about linguistic competence, the speaker-hearer's "intuitive knowledge" of the rules of the grammar of his language. Should we say that the performance model, or some physical realization of the performance model, has tacit or intuitive knowledge of certain rules? What would that mean? Perhaps it would mean only that these rules are represented in the model.

In this connection it is useful to compare a linguistic-performance model with a model of a bicycle rider. The cyclist must keep balanced on the bicycle. Exactly what he needs to do in order to retain his balance will be dictated by certain principles of mechanics that he himself is unaware of. We might imagine that a model of a cyclist would contain representations of the relevant principles of mechanics and that it uses these principles in calculating what needs to be done so as to retain balance. Then, following Chomsky's model, we might say that the cyclist has an internal representation of the principles of mechanics. Should we go on to say that every cyclist has an intuitive or tacit knowledge of the principles of mechanics? This does not seem an illuminating way of talking about cyclists; and Chomsky's remarks about "tacit competence" (26–27) do not seem to provide an illuminating way of talking about speakers of a language.

I believe that Chomsky's notion of linguistic competence is best seen as the result of two separate but interacting factors. First Chomsky's use of the phrase 'tacit competence' betrays a confusion between the two sorts of knowledge of a language. Competence is knowledge in the sense of knowing how to do something; it is ability. It is not the sort of knowledge that can properly be described as "tacit." Tacit knowledge must be knowledge that something is the case. Second, and this abets the above confusion, speakers of a language do have something that might be thought of as tacit knowledge about the language. Thus, speakers can be brought to judge that certain sentences are ambiguous, that certain sentences are paraphrases of each other, or that certain strings of words are not grammatically acceptable. Such judgments are often taken as representing a speaker-hearer's "linguistic intuition"; and it is true, as Chomsky says, that for all practical purposes "there is no way to avoid the traditional assumption that a speaker-hearer's linguistic intuition is the ultimate standard that determines the accuracy of any proposed grammar, linguistic theory, or operational test" (21), *provided that 'linguistic intuition' refers to the intuitive judgments of speakers.* But notice that this sort of intuitive or unconscious knowledge is not the knowledge of particular rules of a transformational grammar. It is, as it were, knowledge about the output of such a grammar. Chomsky's tacit competence is, however, supposed to be knowledge of the particular rules of the grammar, the rules that are explicitly represented in a performance model. Therefore, linguistic competence cannot be identified with that type of unconscious knowledge speakers actually have. And it is only by identifying these two quite different things that Chomsky has been able to disguise his confusion between the two ways of knowing a language.

Thus, Chomsky's use of the phrase 'linguistic competence' embodies at least two confusions. He confuses knowing how with knowing that; and he confuses knowing that certain sentences are grammatically unacceptable, ambiguous, etc., with knowing the rules of the grammar by virtue of which sentences are unacceptable, ambiguous, etc. It follows that he has not shown the need for a notion resembling his "linguistic competence."

II

For philosophers, Chomsky's interesting claim is that facts about language support what he calls a "rationalist" theory of language learning as against an "empiricist" theory. In particular, he claims that transformational linguistics is incompatible with "empiricism." Unfortunately, much of his discussion of language learning is infected with his confusion about "linguistic competence." When these confusions are straightened out, it becomes clear that Chomsky gives us no reason to accept his claim about "empiricism."

For Chomsky, a theory of language learning concerns the linguistic-acquisition device. This device enables a potential performance model to become the performance model of a given language (e.g., as in figure 1) when exposed to people speaking that language. The device does this by seeing that the appropriate grammatical rules become represented in the performance model. How does the device do this?

According to Chomsky the device has available to it what he calls "primary linguistic data." The device considers various hypotheses about the grammar of the language, selecting the hypothesis best confirmed by the data.

> This device must search through the set of possible hypotheses ... and must select grammars that are compatible with the primary linguistic data ... The device would then select one of these potential grammars by [what Chomsky calls] the evaluation measure (32).

So the linguistic-acquisition device, as it were, *infers* that a certain grammar is the grammar of the language, given that the device has certain primary linguistic data.

This is, of course, highly oversimplified. Chomsky notes:

> Obviously, to construct an actual theory of language learning, it would be necessary to face several other very serious questions involving, for example, the gradual development of an appropriate hypothesis, simplification of the technique for finding a compatible hypothesis, and the continual accretion of linguistic skill and knowledge and the deepening of the analysis of language structure that may continue long after the basic form of the language has been mastered. What I am describing is an idealization in which only the moment of acquisition of the correct grammar is considered (202).

But even with this qualification, there is little to be said for the view that the machine's problem is that of inferring something from data. Consider, for example, what these data must be. As we shall see, Chomsky speaks as if the data were sample sentences of the language and possibly some other information. This is clearly wrong. Chomsky elsewhere in the book correctly points out: "A record of natural speech will show numerous false starts, deviations from rules, changes of plan in mid-course and so on" (4). The "data" a linguistic-acquisition device has will include "a record of natural speech" plus information about how the device can get along in conversation, etc., with the provisional rules it has. It is hard to think of the device as making an inference, unless one acknowledges that it not only infers what the grammar is but also infers a general theory of performance. What can be inferred from such data must provide an explanation of the data. And a hypothesis about grammar will not be sufficient for such an explanation. However, we have not envisioned the device as ever containing any representation of a theory of performance.

We have envisioned it as coming to contain only a representation of grammatical rules.

To "infer" the grammar from what "data" it really has, the device must already "know" something about the theory of performance. That is, the device must already have detailed information about the model represented in figure 1, above, excepting information about the actual grammatical rules represented in such a model. Since the device is taken as attached to a performance model, we may think of what it needs as "self-knowledge." Given a knowledge of its structure or of the structure of the performance model to which it is attached, given the information that models of other speakers of the language have the same structure, and given the "primary linguistic data," its problem is to discover the rules of grammar represented in the models of these other speakers.

This is certainly an artificial way of looking at the linguistic-acquisition device. We have seen in part I how misleading it is to say that a model has *knowledge* of those principles or statements represented in the model. What can it mean to ascribe "knowledge" to such a device, if we cannot even say that the knowledge in question is represented anywhere in the device? Perhaps we ought to suppose that the structure of the attached potential performance model itself represents the fact that performance models have such structure. Or perhaps we ought to suppose that the linguistic-acquisition device has an explicit representation of the structure of performance models. Chomsky does not even consider this problem. In any event, there is no reason to suppose any reasonable linguistic-acquisition device need make use of such representations. Surely it is more accurate to think of the device as a feedback mechanism that adjusts the rules represented in the attached potential performance model so as to maximize the way in which the resulting model gets along in conversation, etc.

Nevertheless, we must think of the linguistic-acquisition device as making inferences if there is to be any possibility of making sense of Chomsky's argument against "empiricism." Let us assume, then, that to say the device has information available to it is to say this information is explicitly represented in the device. Chomsky characterizes two positions on language as follows. The "empiricist" believes that the linguistic-acquisition device can arrive at correct grammatical rules by inductive inference from the primary linguistic data. The "rationalist" denies this and holds that the linguistic-acquisition device requires further "information" in addition to the primary linguistic data. Such further information consists of what Chomsky calls "innate ideas and principles" (48).

Whether or not empiricism, so defined, is defensible depends upon what is to count as inductive inference. On some interpretation of "inductive inference," empiricism can be ruled out directly, without appeal to transformational linguistics. On other interpretations, empiricism would not be incompatible with transformational linguistics. However, there does not seem to be any reasonable interpretation on which empiricism survives direct and relatively a priori refutation but is refuted by the appeal to transformational linguistics.

For example, suppose that inductive inference is taken as a process of generalization sharply to be distinguished from "theoretical inference." Suppose this distinction is made in such a way that, from primary linguistic data ("a record of natural speech," etc.) induction permits only rather weak generalization about unobserved speech and does not permit any inference about the theory of performance. Now, the linguistic-acquisition device must have information about the theory of performance if it is to infer the grammar from the primary linguistic data. The empiricist's device, by definition, does not have this information built into it, so it must infer a theory of performance from the data it has. If "induction" does not permit this inference, then the empiricist's device cannot even begin to discover the rules of grammar and is ruled out even before any appeal is made to the facts of transformational linguistics.

Chomsky must permit the empiricist's device at some point to have information about the structure of a performance model, given that he wants the failure of the device to be due to the facts of transformational linguistics. So, he must either (a) allow "induction" to include at least some theoretical inference or (b) maintain a strict distinction between induction and theoretical inference but permit the empiricist's device some initial information about performance models. Alternative (b) is not very promising. Where would one draw the line between what information the device can have and what it cannot have? Furthermore, given the emphasis in contemporary empiricism on the importance of theories in science, it would be quite unrealistic to define the empiricist's linguistic-acquisition device such that it could not make use of theoretical inference. Thus, Chomsky identifies Quine (47, 51) as one of the empiricists he has in mind; and Quine has certainly belabored the role of theory in any adequate account of human knowledge. Therefore, the empiricist device must be allowed to infer the truth of theories as well as generalizations, where this is appropriate, appropriateness being determined by certain principles of induction in a wide sense of "induction."

The same conclusion follows whether or not one agrees that it is necessary for the device to infer a whole theory of performance. In any event the device will need principles of theoretical inference. Weak principles of generalization would not even permit the inference of a corpus of sentences from a record of natural speech. Given the "data" possessed by the device, the notion of *sentence* is a theoretical notion.

Everything now depends on exactly what the principles of induction turn out to be. Empiricism cannot be refuted until they are specified. A resourceful empiricist, knowing some inductive logic, will deny that information from linguistics refutes his theory; instead he will take this information to reveal something about the correct set of inductive procedures. We know from Goodman's "New Riddle of Induction"[2] that any consistent set of inductive principles

---

[2] Nelson Goodman, *Fact, Fiction, and Forecast* (Cambridge, Mass.: Harvard University Press, 1955).

must favor certain generalizations over others. Therefore, one cannot support rationalism by showing that only languages with certain types of grammar (e.g., transformational grammar) are learnable, since an empiricist could reply that this shows only that the principles of induction used (which must be biased in favor of some hypotheses) are biased in favor of grammars of the designated types.

Chomsky's statement of his argument proceeds without mention of any of the complexities we have been considering. He asks "can the inductive procedures (in the empiricist case) . . . succeed in producing grammars within the given constraints of time and access, and within the range of observed uniformity of output?" (54) The answer to this question must depend on what counts as a legitimate inductive procedure. There is an enormous philosophical literature on induction. Chomsky ignores this literature. Instead he says,

> The only proposals that are explicit enough to support serious study are those that have been developed within taxonomic linguistics. It seems to have been demonstrated beyond any reasonable doubt that, quite apart from any question of feasibility, methods of the sort that have been studied in taxonomic linguistics are intrinsically incapable of yielding the systems of grammatical knowledge that must be attributed to the speaker of a language (54).

In this argument Chomsky muddles together all the things we have been concerned to distinguish.

First, the procedures of taxonomic linguistics are not relevant here. As Chomsky notes (52), taxonomic procedures are designed to determine the grammar of a language from a corpus of sentences of that language. But primary linguistic data do not consist in such a corpus. They contain a "record of natural speech" plus information about how the performance model has been getting along in conversations, etc., given its provisional grammatical rules. There is no way to apply taxonomic procedures to this sort of data.

Second, "taxonomic principles of segmentation and classification" (47) represent an anti-theoretical position in linguistics, a position that would sharply distinguish inductive generalization from theoretical "speculation" so as to do without the latter. As we have seen, if an empiricist is taken to deny the role of theory, the empiricist's linguistic-acquisition device cannot even get started, since its first task must be to formulate a theory of performance. This means the empiricist can be refuted without the need of any appeal to the facts of transformational linguistics.

Third, Chomsky thinks that taxonomic methods cannot yield correct grammars because they yield only "taxonomic," i.e., phrase-structure, grammars, and because the theory of phrase-structure grammar has supposedly been refuted by transformational linguistics.[3] But it is unclear to me that taxonomic principles of segmentation and classification would work even if the theory of phrase-structure grammar were right. I suspect the principles would not

---

[3] I do not believe in this refutation. See my articles: "Generative Grammars without Transformation Rules," *Language*, XXXIX (1963), 597–616; and "The Adequacy of Context-free Phrase-structure Grammars," to appear in *Word*.

work. The only connection I can see between taxonomic procedures and phrase-structure grammar is a tenuous historical one. People who have suggested taxonomic procedures are among those Chomsky takes to subscribe to the theory of phrase-structure grammar.

Fourth, it is not clear that taxonomic principles of segmentation and classification are the only empiricist proposals "explicit enough to support serious study" (54). Harris and Hiż's method of exploiting co-occurrence relationships is similar in spirit to the taxonomic procedures Chomsky is talking about; yet the method of co-occurrence cannot be associated with the theory of phrase-structure grammar. If anything, it must be associated with the theory of transformational grammar.[4]

Fifth, even if taxonomic procedures were of the relevant sort, if no other explicit empiricist procedures had been proposed, and if Chomsky could demonstrate the inadequacy of taxonomic procedures, that would not be enough to refute empiricism. Chomsky would have to show that no explicit empiricist procedure could be adequate. But, given the resourceful empiricist mentioned above, it does not seem possible that Chomsky could show any such thing, no matter what the facts about language turned out to be.

In short, Chomsky's discussion of rationalism and empiricism is as confused as his discussion of linguistic competence. He has certainly not shown that the facts of transformational linguistics defeat an empiricist theory of language learning.

---

[4] Zelig S. Harris, "Co-occurrence and Transformation in Linguistic Structure," *Language*, XXXIII (1957), 293–340. Henry Hiż, "Congrammaticality, Batteries of Transformations and Grammatical Categories," in Jakobson, ed., *Structure of Language and Its Mathematical Aspects, Proceedings of the Twelfth Symposium in Applied Mathematics* (Providence, R.I.: American Mathematical Society, 1961), 43–50.

THEORIES OF MEANING 5

INTRODUCTION

The philosophical discussion of meaning traditionally centers around three problems. The first concerns the specification of criteria of *meaningfulness*. What conditions must a sentence satisfy in order to *have a meaning*? The second is that of specifying conditions of *synonymy*. What are the criteria which two expressions (words or sentences) must satisfy in order to have *the same meaning*? (Some of the ramifications of this question were explored earlier. See selections 1.4 and 4.1.) The third problem is, in a sense, prior to the first or second. It is the problem of specifying *meanings* in general. Given an expression which *has* a meaning, what *is* its meaning? The last question can be read in either an ontological or an epistemological sense. On the ontological reading, it asks, first, whether meanings are entities and, second, if they are entities, what kind of entities they are. On the epistemological reading, the question asks for an account of the considerations to which we appeal in *determining* the meaning of an expression. In any case, one of the jobs which an adequate theory of meaning must do is to tell us, in a nontrivial way, what an account of meaning is an account *of*.

By a *theory of meaning*, we here intend the traditional attempt to lay out an account of meaning—criteria for determining meaningfulness, sameness of meaning, or particular meanings—in an *a priori* fashion. We contrast this approach with that developed in Section 6, following, where characterizations of meanings, meaningfulness, and synonymy are adjuncts of and outgrowths from a general semantic theory, derived from and grounded in the empirical investigation of languages. Theories of meaning, as we here use the expression, will generally be *reductive* in character and will attempt to give an account of meaning, synonymy, or meaningfulness in nonsemantic terms, or at least in terms that do not themselves belong to this family of concepts.

We have already, in the introduction to Section 2, examined one classical theory of meaning, the *referential theory* of meaning. Here the attempt was to reduce theory of meaning to the theory of reference. The referential theory holds, roughly, that a term is meaningful if it stands for an object, and that terms which stand for the same object have the same meaning since the meaning of a term *is* simply the object for which it stands. We canvassed a number of difficulties with this theory, perhaps the most striking of which was the problem of nonexistents—there are terms which, like 'Pegasus' and 'the present king of France', correspond to *no* object.

One traditional attempt to preserve the spirit, if not the letter, of the referential theory departs from the observation that, while Pegasus and the present king of France do not exist, our *ideas* of them most assuredly do. The *ideational theory* of meaning, then, holds that the meaning of a word is the idea produced by that word in the minds of speakers of a language. The theory of meaning, on this account, reduces to a branch of philosophical psychology, the philosophy of mind. The ideational theory finds explicit statement in the work of John Locke (1632–1704): "Words, in their primary or immediate signification, stand for nothing but *the ideas in the mind of him that uses them.*"

Ideas have been classically viewed on the model of mental images. So understood, the ideational theory was subjected to early criticism. René Descartes (1596–1650) argued that the mental image of a chiliagon (thousand-sided figure) did not differ significantly from the mental image of a figure with 1001 or 1012 or any other large number of sides. And George Berkeley (1685–1753) mounted a sustained attack on the notion of *general* ideas, arguing that, although 'triangle' surely has a meaning, we can have no idea of a triangle-in-general, a triangle which is neither right nor oblique, neither equilateral, isosceles, nor scalene.

The fullest contemporary critique of the ideational theory was produced by Ludwig Wittgenstein (1889–1951). He argued, not merely that ideas are, at best, an *accidental* accompaniment of linguistic phenomena, but also that, even were certain ideas found to occur *invariably* correlated with certain expressions, they could not do the jobs which philosophers have traditionally assigned meanings. Some of these Wittgensteinian criticisms are developed in the selection from WAISMANN.

Wittgenstein's positive account of meaning replaces the ideational theory with a theory of *meaning as use*. On this view, one determines the meaning of an expression by determining how the expression is *used* in the language, what its role is in linguistic activities regarded as part of a total "form of life." Waismann subscribes to this positive account as well, and arguments supporting it may be found in the selection here included.

ALSTON accepts the general view that an account of meaning reduces to an account of use. But he argues that the sense of 'use' in which this theory is correct is a technical sense and stands in need of explication. The kind of use which is relevant to considerations of meaning, he claims, concerns the contributions of expressions to the performance of certain *linguistic acts* which, following Austin, he terms 'illocutionary acts'. (For more on linguistic acts in general and illocutionary acts in particular, see Section 7.) On Alston's account, two expressions have the same meaning if the substitution of one for the other in a sentence leaves the *illocutionary act potential* of that sentence (the dispositions of speakers with respect to employing the sentence in the performance of illocutionary acts) unaltered.

A major concern of theories of meaning has always been to distinguish the meaningful from the meaningless, sense from nonsense. An important attempt along these lines is found in the *verifiability criterion* of meaningfulness, developed by the logical positivists beginning about 1930. On this view, intended as a consequence of the fundamental stance of empiricism, a sentence which is neither analytic nor contradictory is meaningful if and only if the putative assertion which it makes can, in principle, be subjected to *empirical test*, that is, if there are conceivable experiences tending to confirm or disconfirm the claim. The *meaning* of a sentence, then, will be exhausted by a specification of the conditions of its verification or falsification. This proposal has an intricate history which is explored in detail by HEMPEL.

One strength of the classical ideational theory lies in the relation it develops between an account of what an *expression* means and an account of what a *person* means (by an expression). GRICE explores, from a different angle, the possibility of reducing the former rubric to the latter. He argues that linguistic meaning (the meaning of expressions) is a species of a more general sort of meaning which he terms *nonnatural* meaning, meaning$_{NN}$. Nonnatural meaning, however, is to be grounded on a *natural* sense of meaning in which, paradigmatically, some natural *phenomenon* may properly be said to mean something as, e.g., red spots may mean measles. What a person *means to do* falls, according to Grice, within the category of natural meaning and provides the requisite grounding for nonnatural meaning. As what a person means to do is, roughly, what he intends, Grice proposes to analyze linguistic meaning in terms of the *intentions* of persons. Thus, "Sam meant$_{NN}$ something by x," on this account, is treated as essentially equivalent to "Sam *intended* his utterance of x to produce a certain effect in his audience by means of their recognition of his intention." This proposal is criticized by ZIFF, who suggests that Grice has confused the question of what a person meant *by an expression* with the question of what he meant *by uttering* the expression. While there may be a nonnatural sense of meaning, argues Ziff, it is a radical mistake to regard linguistic meaning as a species of meaning$_{NN}$.

Finally, DAVIDSON proposes that an account of sentence meaning is provided by an account of the *truth-conditions* of sentences. The referential theory of meaning having been shown inadequate, Davidson suggests that we assume that parts of sentences have meaning only in the "ontologically neutral sense of making a systematic contribution to the meaning of the sentence in which they occur." The essence of a theory of meaning, then, will be some systematic account of how the meaning of a sentence depends upon the meanings of its parts. It is just this, claims Davidson, which is accomplished by a specification of the truth-conditions of sentences. A theory of meaning for a language L can only show "how the meanings of sentences depend upon the meanings of words," he argues, if it contains a recursive definition of truth-in-L. His article surveys both progress toward that goal and obstacles yet to be overcome.

Suggestions for Further Reading

Ayer, A. J. *Language, Truth and Logic*. New York: Dover Publications, Inc., 1952. An important extended defense of the verifiability criterion of meaningfulness.

Berkeley, George. *Principles of Human Knowledge*. An early critique of the ideational theory of meaning as espoused by Locke, cited below, is included.

Carnap, Rudolf. "Testability and Meaning." In *Philosophy of Science*. III (1936), 419–71 and IV (1937), 1–40, and variously reprinted.

Grice, H. P. "Utterer's Meaning and Intentions." *Philosophical Review*, LXXVIII (1969), 147–77. A further development of selection 5.4.

Hallett, Garth. *Wittgenstein's Definition of Meaning as Use*. New York: Fordham University Press, 1967.

Hempel, C. G. "Empiricist Criteria of Cognitive Significance: Problems and Changes." In Hempel, *Aspects of Scientific Explanation*. New York: The Free Press, 1965. A fuller development of selection 5.3.

Locke, John. *An Essay Concerning Human Understanding*. Contains a defense of the ideational theory of meaning.

McCawley, James D. "Meaning and the Description of Language." Selection 6.2, below. Exhibits the emerging rapprochement between symbolic logic and transformational grammar envisioned by Davidson in selection 5.6.

Patton, T. E., and D. W. Stampe. "The Rudiments of Meaning: On Ziff on Grice." *Foundations of Language*, V (1962), 2–16.

Pitcher, George, ed. *Wittgenstein: The Philosophical Investigations*. New York: Doubleday & Company, Inc., 1966. A useful collection of interpretive and critical essays.

Tarski, Alfred. "The Semantic Conception of Truth." *Philosophy and Phenomenological Research*. IV (1944), 341–75, and variously reprinted.

Waismann, F. *The Principles of Linguistic Philosophy*. New York and London: The Macmillan Company and St. Martin's Press, 1965. Selection 5.1 is drawn from this volume.

Wittgenstein, L. *Philosophical Investigations*. New York: The Macmillan Company, 1953. See especially sections 1–88.

Ziff, Paul. *Semantic Analysis*. Ithaca: Cornell University Press, 1960.

F. WAISMANN

5.1   *Meaning*

1. SUBSTANTIVE AND SUBSTANCE

Remember the account which St. Augustine gives of the learning of language. In his words we are presented with a certain picture of the nature of human speech, namely this: the words of language name objects; sentences are combinations of such names.

In this picture of language we find the root of the idea: every word has a meaning. This meaning is co-ordinated with the word. It is the object for which the word stands.

This philosophic conception of meaning is indwelling in the primitive notion of the ways in which language works. [Elsewhere] we described various games that we play when learning language. In these games there occurs something which may be called a 'convention' or 'rule'. We say that the words have been given a meaning by virtue of these rules, or that they 'mean something'. We say, also, "Before we learned the game, the words had no meaning; but now, as a result of these rules, they have 'acquired a meaning'." Again, it may be said, "Teaching the rules of the game is tantamount to explaining the meaning of the words." It should be noticed that, in saying this, we introduce the word 'meaning' (and, 'mean') *in certain contexts* only. As long as we consider this 'natural usage', we never meet the idea of meaning in its enigmatic and almost mystifying aspect.

In considering such a game as that with the five cubes, one may divine how far the universal idea of meaning enshrouds language in mists which makes it impossible to see its features clearly. When we are asked, "How is it that the builder's man is able to carry out the command 'Five cubes!'?," we are inclined to reply, "Because he just understands what the words mean, because he has grasped their meaning." And in saying that we seem to refer to a definite mental process going on in his mind. This mental process seems to be what is really important, whereas the words are mere means to induce such processes in the mind. Without these processes the words seem dead. We picture to ourselves the relation between a word and what it means as if it were a psychological one; then we puzzle ourselves how it is that the mind has the miraculous capacity to perform things which no dead mechanism could perform, namely to *mean* something.

Now, one of the dangers of such a view is this: it makes us look for something which is the meaning. (This is particularly striking in the case that we mean something which does not exist.) This in itself is part of a general tendency which leads us, in the case of every substantive, to seek for an object

---

Reprinted from F. Waismann, *The Principles of Linguistic Philosophy*, edited by R. Harre (New York: St. Martin's Press, Inc.; London: Macmillan & Co. Ltd., 1965), by permission of the publishers.

which is designated by it. Here we are up against one of the sources of philosophical confusion. The strength of this propensity to hypostatization can still be studied in certain modes of thought that appeared in former stages of physics. Thus a force may readily be pictured as an unseen entity lurking in space and pulling like a stretched spring. In antiquity fire was conceived as an element. Likewise the features of substance were lent to energy, and the principle of conservation of energy interpreted as if there were in nature a subtle fluid that kept its identity through every change, and merely altered its form. And was it not ideas such as these which, partly masked by others, played a part in the hypothesis of a caloric fluid? Lord Salisbury once defined the ether as the nominative of the verb 'to undulate', thus expressing with the greatest terseness the conflict between thought and the spirit of language.

Is it really of so little consequence whether one philosopher finds in his language substantives like 'soul', 'ego', 'being', etc.? Would philosophers who grow up in a quite different domain of language, in which the functions of nouns were very much less developed, be found on the same paths of thought? A question such as "What is the number five?" cannot even be raised in Chinese, because 'five' can only occur in phrases such as 'five men', 'five houses', but never as subject in this language. Here we begin to see how deep an influence language can exercise on thought.

"Sleep is the gentler brother of Death." Such a saying instances the mythological use of nouns. And there is much in philosophy that suggests a pale reflection of mythology. "What is Time? What is this Being, made up of movement alone, without anything that moves?" (Schopenhauer).

One might compare our word-language with a script in which the letters are used for several purposes: sometimes for signifying sounds, sometimes for signifying accentuation, and sometimes as punctuation marks. Anyone regarding these characters as a notation of sounds might misinterpret them to mean that a single sound corresponded to every letter, as if the letters had not also quite different functions.

2. MEANINGS OF THE WORD 'MEANING'

Sometimes two words mean the same thing, e.g. 'riches' and 'wealth'; they are then used in the same way. The opposite of this case is that of a word with two different meanings. Let us take as an example of this, "Black is Black," when the one word refers to a person, the other to a colour. What is it that draws attention to the difference of meaning between the two? Obviously, it might be said, the fact that the two words obey different sets of grammatical rules. But this needs qualification, for there is really only one word there. Shall we then say that this one word obeys two different sets of rules? What could be meant by this? Let us consider an analogous case in chess. Can I lay down two different sets of rules for moving the queen? Surely only in the sense that I wish to describe two different sorts of games of chess and set down the descriptions side by side for comparison. But in a single game I cannot move this piece according to two different sets of instructions. The difficulty is resolved, however, when we see that we can simply introduce different words. If we express the proposition in question by the words "Mr. Black is black," we could well regard 'Mr. Black' as one word and 'black' as another one, or 'Black' as one and 'is black' as another. And this *is*, more or less, how we proceed when we want to explain to a child how one word can have many meanings (often by no means an easy task). We may say to him "Look here, Mr. Black strides up and down the room; the colour black cannot stride up and down." In this way we should have substituted for the one word two new expressions.

Let us recall for a moment the way we became clear as to the different meanings of the word 'is'.

Now we can say: a word '*a*' means different things in different contexts, if in the one case it can be replaced by '*b*' and in the other by '*c*' but not by '*b*'. Let us apply this generalization to the words 'meaning' and 'mean' themselves, by setting the following examples next one another:

  (i) His expression on Friday was full of meaning.
 (ii) He meant well.
(iii) There is much meaningless formality in everyday life.
 (iv) These clouds mean rain.
  (v) Your friendship means much to me.
 (vi) I meant him to go.
(vii) The superstitious ascribe a meaning to the purest accident.
(viii) In the light of this information the incident acquires a fresh meaning.
 (ix) These two words have the same meaning.

If the reader considers what other expressions are substitutable for the two words in the above sentences, he will gain some idea of the many senses in which they are used.

It is 'meaning' only in the sense of the last example which interests us here.

3. MEANING AS USE

We said that a word acquires meaning by the conventions of the game in which it occurs. But then we do not ask *what the meaning is*. The question in itself is, indeed, the expression of a misunderstanding of the substantive 'meaning'. It is already influenced by a misleading grammatical background; for in answer to a question "What is *x*?" we expect a sentence of the form "*x* is . . . ," supposed in some way to be equivalent to an ostensive definition ("*x* is *this*"). And now we are tempted to be on the lookout for some thing which is the meaning. This conception is strengthened by certain modes of expression in our language. When we say that two words have the same meaning, we may be inclined to think "So there is something owned by both," in the same way that we say "This house is owned by Smith and Jones." Speaking of meaning being *attached* to words is also misleading, because it sounds as if the meaning were a sort of magical entity, united to the word very much as the soul is to the body. But the meaning is not a soul in the body of the word, but what we call the 'meaning' manifests itself in the use of the word. The whole point of our explication could be summed up by saying "If you want to know what a word means, look and see how it is used."[1]

How should we, for example, explain to anyone what the word "naïve" means? We should, perhaps, first circumscribe the meaning with words which come fairly near to meaning the same as 'naïve'. We should say naïve means something like 'inexperienced, uncritical, unsuspicious, natural, not blasé, not over-worried with doubts', and so on. But then we should say "That does not exactly hit off what the word means," and should give an example of its use. We might tell an anecdote, describe a characteristic situation, and say "There, do you see, that man was naïve." What exactly does the word 'exactly' mean? Is there a definition for it? No; but in the very words of my question I have provided an instance of its use.

The reader can consider for himself examples such as 'perhaps', 'indeed', 'even', 'good gracious', 'bother', 'by dint of', etc.

If the usage of a word alters in the course of time its meaning alters also, e.g. 'villain' (originally = serf), 'awful', 'nice' (precise), 'simple', 'silly' (in Anglo-Saxon = blessed), 'lust' (innocent delight, as in Chaucer), 'luxury' (lasciviousness), 'naughty' (in Middle English = poor, needy; sixteenth–seventeenth centuries = wicked). In what else could a change of meaning consist, if not in a change of usage? Consider this moreover: a word is untranslatable if in the language into which it is to be translated there is no word used in exactly the same way. There are no English equivalents of, e.g., 'Gestalt', 'Weltanschauung', 'esprit', 'élan'. Life requires the continual birth of words of novel use, and so of new meanings, e.g. 'wireless', 'autarky', 'ironclad', 'expressionist', 'pointillistes', 'surrealist', 'Oblomovism', 'Pasteurization'.

It sounds so natural to say "every sign must signify something." Yet this idea will not survive serious examination. What does "Oh dear!" signify? Say we say "it does not mean anything"? If we want to explain it to anyone, we say, for instance, "Oh dear, it is raining again" in an appropriate tone of voice, and our hearer understands what it means. Some words might be designated as just 'vocal vents'. What does a full stop mean? It divides sentences. Here the meaning is the function performed. In the word 'meaning' we sum up the whole, often vastly complicated, mode of use of a sign.

Objection. But the use is surely only the outward form; the meaning is the inner reality that can only be understood from within.

Reply. Have we any means of describing the meaning of a sign without going into its use? Is giving the use only, so to speak, a roundabout way whereby to reach the meaning? If so, what is the other direct way? If the meaning is more than the use, in what does the difference consist? If I have taught someone how a word is used in different connections, different situations, and have taught the appropriate expression with which to speak it in each case, does he still not know its meaning? And what more should I do to enable him to perceive this meaning?

---

[1] Here again we develop an idea of Wittgenstein; *cf. Philosophical Investigations*, section 43.

"But could I not know the use of a word and nevertheless follow it mechanically without understanding it, as in a certain sense I do the singing of a bird? Could not the use for me always remain something outward, so that I can describe it without understanding?" It seems here as if the rules describe only in a purely external manner a use that must first be given meaning from within. Cases where this is so do sometimes occur. Consider the following example. A certain community agree to use the words of their language in a peculiar way, e.g. to put only words of the same number of syllables next one another; this might be a game. If someone came into the society who knew nothing of this arrangement, he would not understand what was going on. He might, in time, if he were a good observer, make out for himself the rules according to which the words were used and yet the sense of the whole arrangement might remain entirely obscure to him. But in this case what he does not understand is the *point* of the whole affair; which might lead him to suspect that he has only been watching a game. Hence we could put the question like this: "What distinguishes a game, as we have just described it, from actual language?" The answer may be put in a word: its integration into life. The words in a verbal game bear a far less close relation to life than words used in earnest. What is the difference, if the teacher on the one hand says (meaning it) 'Stand up', and on the other, in the English lesson says the same sentence as an example of a command? What distinguishes a chess game from an example of such a game, fencing from a duel?

If I see language against the background of life, if I follow exactly the parts played therein by the single words, does the kernel of the matter, the meaning, still escape me, leaving me only the outer shell of usage?

4. MEANING AND MENTAL IMAGE

The sentence "The meaning of a word is the inner reality" might be interpreted thus: "The meaning is the mental image." We do, in fact, often test our understanding of the meaning of a word by conjuring up an image of what it means. Most people if asked "Do you know what a merry-go-round is?" may well form a mental picture of a merry-go-round. But let us consider other cases before accepting this view. What do people think of when they hear the word 'Naples'? One may see a picture of the gulf with Vesuvius in front of him, another the map of Italy with Naples marked on it, a third only an image of the printed word. Those who know Naples picture it differently from those who do not, those who were there but a little time ago differently from those whose memories are faded. If all had the right to consider their own ideas of the city as constituting the meaning of the word 'Naples', it would mean something different for everyone and it would be impossible for any sentence in which it occurred to have a public meaning. Do only those who can picture to themselves such a figure understand the word 'icosahedron'? Is there anyone who can picture a chiliagon? What comes to the reader's mind on reading the expressions 'lien', 'conduct of civil suits'? It may be that these words give rise to certain definite images, but do such images constitute the meaning of the words? And how about words like 'electron', 'photon', 'quantum' that allow of no visual interpretation, nay even preclude it? Can it be maintained that there are special images for 'if', 'because', 'although' and 'so'?

At this point we might admit that in general the meaning of a word is nothing pictureable, and content ourselves with the narrower assertion that when a word stands for something pictureable its meaning is represented by the picture. Thus the meaning of the word 'red' would be the red colour of which I have an image. But, first of all, each person has a different image, while the meaning is the same for all. Moreover, the image that one associates with the word 'red' is not the meaning of the word, but an example of its use. (We may here think of Berkeley's question, whether it is possible to have a general image of a triangle—which is neither oblique, nor right-angled, equilateral, nor scalene, but all and none of these at once.) Finally, is it always true that whenever we hear the word 'red' we have a red image? Do we really represent to ourselves red and white when we say, for instance, "The War of the Red and White Roses"? Let the reader observe what goes on in him while he reads a book: does every colour word that he reads really call up a colour image? And if not, would he say that he has not understood what he read?

Why then are we tempted to say that the meaning is the image? I think for two reasons. In the first place, it is often the case that the occurrence of an image is the proof of understanding. Not being able to understand a word comes in a large number of cases simply to failing to have any idea that corresponds to it. (But is this so in all cases? Is it true of the concepts of physics?) The second reason is that images seem sometimes to guide us when we apply language; for instance, when we act on a command. Let us suppose someone has been told to fetch a gilly-flower out of the garden, and fulfils this order. We might ask "How could he know what to do if all that has happened is that he has heard certain words?" Here it is natural to answer that when he heard the words, he had an image of the flower which enabled him to look for it. Surely, we might say, it is the image which in this case fills the gap between word and action. In many cases this is so, but is it so in all? Suppose the injunction is to have an image of a certain shade of green, say emerald green. Is there here an image which acts as intermediary between the word and the required performance? But if so, having this image *is* the performance. Indeed, we might imagine that on hearing the words "emerald green" someone would first look up a colour pattern-book, look at the colour, and only then know what sort of image he has to conjure up. Could we not say in such a case that the pattern-book was what filled the gap between word and image?

Let us now consider what in fact happens when I send someone into the garden to pick a gilly-flower. There are various possibilities:

(i) I may give him a gilly-flower to make it clear what sort of flower it is I wish him to pick. He takes this pattern into the garden and compares flowers in the garden with it until he finds one of the same sort.

(ii) Instead of a real flower, I give him a picture of one, or a description in words (e.g. out of a gardener's handbook).

(iii) I show him a gilly-flower, and he goes to look for another by remembering what I showed him.

(iv) He has entirely forgotten in what circumstances he learned what a gilly-flower was, but he can evoke an image of one at will, by means of which he can fetch me one.

(v) He goes into the garden, looks around, and as soon as his glance lights on a gilly-flower he picks it. *Must* he at that moment have had a picture of a gilly-flower in his memory or in his imagination and compared it with what he was looking at? No, he may or may not have had one. It may be that he could not have imagined the flower beforehand, but nevertheless recognized it as soon as he saw it.

Let the reader make the attempt to visualize the letter G in Gothic script; if he is not trained, he will hardly succeed in doing so; but nevertheless he does recognize the letter at first sight when he sees it.

In daily life we often use words in this way. If someone says 'Turn off the light', I do it. Must I really have pictured to myself the whole process of turning off the light before I do it? Such a view would impose on us far too strenuous a mental exertion. It is, in fact, the case that a considerable part of communication is free from images.

Suppose that people could not hold an image in mind for longer than five minutes (that this were a psychological law), and that after this time the image was invariably forgotten. Would communication in these circumstances be impossible? And what would a language be like in these conditions? The words would practically never be accompanied by images. Would it, on this account, be correct to say they were devoid of meaning?

Such examples throw light on the view that a word has meaning only when it evokes some image in us. Imagination and memory images are characteristic of only one sort of use of words: in another use we may only be concerned with illustrations, samples, tables, etc. There is even a point in saying "Everything inside our minds can, for certain purposes, be replaced by something outside." Images can be replaced by pictures, calculations in our heads by calculations on paper, thinking by speaking, and conviction by a tone of conviction.

Compare now the following suggestions:

(i) The meaning of a word is the object to which it refers.

(ii) The meaning of a word is the image which we have when we speak, or hear the word.

(iii) The meaning of a word is the effects it has on a hearer. It is clear that none of these reaches the heart of the matter. And yet they force themselves upon the mind ever and again in philosophic literature. Let us, then, dwell for a moment on the question why one is tempted to reach after such an explanation. In the first place, because one wishes to embody in the definition what is important. The object referred to by a word and the image which accompanies it undoubtedly play a certain part in the use of the word. Secondly, we instinctively seek for what may be called a substantival definition of meaning: we want to find amongst the already existing substantives of language one that is synonymous with the word 'meaning'; that is to say, is used as the word 'meaning' is used; so we say either "The object referred to is the meaning" or "The idea is the meaning" or "The effects of a word are its meaning." If we *had* to give a substantival explanation of meaning the best we could do is to say, following Wittgenstein, "The meaning of a word is its use."

5. AN OBJECTION

The suggestion, that the explanation of a word consists in describing its use, might give rise to the following objection: If we answer the questions "What is style?", "What is culture?", "What is humour?" in the manner suggested, that is to say by displaying the use of these words through examples, are we not answering them in a merely superficial way? A good explanation gives us the feeling "Yes, that is right, here we have the essentials." The reply to our question may show profundity or shallowness. How is this compatible with our view? Should the explanation not disclose the deeper meaning which we dimly perceive behind those words?

But what is it that is sought by him who seeks the essence of culture? Does he want a definition? Or is he already familiar with the use of the word, and desirous of insight into the thing it denotes? If we gave a man who had just heard the word 'culture' for the first time Weininger's explanation, "Culture is a feeling for problems," would he then understand what the word means? And would he be in a position to use it correctly? Obviously not. Such explanations are flashes of light which, as it were, reveal for a moment an unsuspected connection, intelligible only to those who are already familiar with the meaning of the word.

The question "What is culture?" is in some respects similar to "What is heat?" This question can be understood in two ways. If it is about the meaning of the word 'heat', it is answered by a description of the use of this word. But it can also mean "What is the physical nature of heat?" To this question the answer would be "Irregular molecular movement." This is not a definition but a piece of scientific information.

WILLIAM P. ALSTON

5.2   *Meaning and Use*

There is a certain conviction about linguistic meaning which is widely shared today. This conviction might be expressed as follows. Somehow the concept of the meaning of a linguistic expression is to be elucidated in terms of the use of that expression, in terms of the way it is employed by the users of the language. To wit:

> . . . to know what an expression means is to know how it may and may not be employed . . .
>> Gilbert Ryle, "The Theory of Meaning," in *British Philosophy in the Mid-Century*, p. 255.

> Elucidating the meaning of a word is explaining how the word is used.
>> Patrick Nowell-Smith, *Ethics*, p. 67.

> The meaning of a word is simply the rules which govern its use, and to ask for its meaning is to ask for the rules.
>> J. L. Evans, "On Meaning and Verification," *Mind*, LXII, p. 9.

> To give the meaning of an expression . . . is to give *general directions* for its use to refer to or mention particular objects or persons; to give the meaning of a sentence is to give *general directions* for its use in making true or false assertions.
>> P. F. Strawson, "On Referring," *Mind*, LIX, p. 327.

> . . . to know the meaning of a sentence is to know how to use it, to know in what circumstances its use is correct or incorrect. . . . A sentence is meaningful if it has a use; we know its meaning if we *know* its use.
>> G. J. Warnock, "Verification and the Use of Language," *Revue Internationale de Philosophie*, V, p. 318.

And this conviction is not only held in the abstract. In the past fifteen years or so it has often been put into practice by way of investigating the use of one or another fundamental term, and a great deal of philosophical illumination has come out of these enterprises.

But despite the wide currency of the general conviction, and despite the numerous and wide-ranging investigations that have gone on under its aegis, no one has made a serious attempt to say, explicitly and in detail, what is to be meant by 'use' in these contexts, i.e., what is and what is not to count as revealing the *use* of a term. And still less has any serious attempt been made to say just how meaning is to be analyzed in terms of use, as so conceived. If we scrutinize attempts to spell out one or another feature of the use of a term, we shall find that a great many different sorts of facts about a term are mentioned. They include the conditions under which a sentence containing

---

Reprinted from *Philosophical Quarterly*, XIII, No. 51 (1963), 107–124, by permission of the author and of the editor of *Philosophical Quarterly*.

that word can or cannot be uttered, the circumstances which would make certain statements in which the word figures true or false, the sorts of sentential contexts into which the word can or cannot be inserted, the grammatical inflections of which it is or is not susceptible, the questions which can or cannot be asked concerning a particular application of the term, the responses which can or cannot appropriately be made to utterances in which it figures, the other expressions to which it is or is not equivalent, the sorts of performances which are typically carried out when the word (or a sentence containing the word) is uttered, the implications which sentences containing the word, or the utterance of such sentences, would have. And for each occurrence of such words as 'can' in the foregoing, we see a number of alternatives spread out before us—intelligibly, correctly, properly, appropriately—each of which raises a host of questions. It would be difficult to bring all such facts under a single rubric, and such incipient attempts as have been made are either patently inadequate or hopelessly sketchy or both. It does seem initially plausible to construe all this as the uncovering of various sorts of conditions for the *correct* use of the word in question, conditions having to do with either the linguistic or the extra-linguistic environment of the word. (*Cf.* the quotation from Warnock above.) And since one is correct or incorrect as he does or does not follow certain rules, this could equally well be put in terms of getting at the rules which govern the use of the word. But such a formulation is not of much use unless we do something to separate the sort of rules and the sort of correctness which is involved in use in this sense, from the sorts which are not. For it is only too obvious that many sorts of rules which govern linguistic activity have nothing to do with use in any sense of that term in which meaning could conceivably be a function of use. For example, many speakers recognize rules forbidding them to use certain racy or obscene words in certain circumstances, or rules forbidding them to use crude or vernacular locutions in certain social circles; and such rules could be said to define a certain mode of correctness. And yet the consideration of such rules does nothing to bring out the meaning of such words.

In this essay I want to make a beginning at elucidating a suitable sense for 'use' and indicating the way in which meaning is to be understood as a function of use in this sense. I think it may serve to clear the air somewhat if I first indicate some directions from which no help is to be expected. In view of the apparently widespread impression that when one says that meaning is a function of use he is using 'use' in a quite ordinary sense, it may repay us to examine the most prominent contexts in which 'use' is used in a relatively unproblematical and unpuzzling way in connection with linguistic expressions, in order to satisfy ourselves that none of them furnishes anything which will meet our present needs.

I

First consider the fact that the phrase, 'the use of x', as it is ordinarily used, fails to identify anything which an expression *has*, or which two expressions could be said to have in common. Ordinarily we speak of the use of a word, as of anything else, in the course of saying something about the fact of its employment—when, where, how frequent, etc.

> The use of 'presumably' is inappropriate at this point.
> The use of 'whom' at the beginning of a sentence is gradually dying out.
> The use of 'by crackey' is largely confined to rustics.

Compare:

> The use of sedatives is not indicated in his case.
> The use of the hand plough is dying out all over Europe.
> The use of automobiles in Russia is mostly limited to important officials.

It is clear that in such contexts 'The use of E' fails to designate anything which E has, and which it would share with any expression which had the same meaning, but fail to share with any expression which had a different meaning. If I were to ask one who had uttered the second sentence in the first list: "What is this use of 'whom' which is dying out, and what other expressions have the same use?", I would be missing the point of what he had said. In making that statement, he was not talking about something called 'the use of 'whom',' which could then be looked for in other surroundings. He was simply saying that people are using 'whom' at the beginning of a sentence less and less. Nor is the question, "What is the use of E?" any more fruitful. I suppose that "What is the use of 'sanguine'?" would mean, if anything, "What is the point of using 'sanguine'?", just as "What is the use of a typewriter?" would ordinarily be understood, if at all, as an awkward way of asking "What is the point of having (using) a typewriter?"; and this does not help.

Let us now look at some contexts in which we talk of the *way* an expression is used, or of *how* it is used. And let us consider what counts as a way of using an expression. Look at the adverbs we use to qualify 'A used E'.

> A used 'Communist' effectively.
> A used 'Yes sir' very insolently.
> A uses 'Presumably' frequently.

Clearly none of these ways has an important bearing on meaning. The fact that two words are both used frequently, effectively, or insolently does nothing to show that they have the same meaning. Looking at the corresponding question, "How is E used?", we might take anything which could serve as an answer to be a specification of a way of using E. It seems that such a question is normally concerned with the grammatical function of E. "How is 'albeit' used?" "As a conjunction." "How is 'ce' used?" "With forms of 'être' under certain conditions." Thus we could reasonably call 'as a conjunction', 'as a transitive verb', etc., ways of using expressions. But this won't do. Two words can both be used as a conjunction, or as a transitive verb, without having the same meaning.

We also speak of 'what E is used for', 'the use to which E is put', or 'the job E is used to perform'. But how do we specify what a word is used to do? It seems that the only cases in which we ordinarily make such specifications are of a rather special sort.

'And' is used to conjoin expressions of the same rank.

'Amen' is used to close a prayer.

'Ugh' is used to express disgust.

These are all cases in which it is impossible to teach someone the word by saying what it means, either because there is no approximately equivalent expression in the language ('and'), or because the exhibition of that expression would not be very helpful. (We might say " 'Amen' means *so be it*," but this would be misleading at best; for it would give no hint as to the special circumstances in which 'Amen' is appropriately used.)

II

From this survey I draw the conclusion that in non-technical talk about using words we are most unlikely to discover a sense of 'use' which is even a plausible candidate for a fundamental rôle in semantics. And if so, a technical sense will have to be constructed. If we consider some of the arguments which have led, or might lead, people to embrace the use-analysis, they might contain some clue to a sense of 'use' which one could use in carrying out the analysis. I shall consider three such arguments.

(1) "Since the meaning of a word is not a function of the physical properties of the word, and since a given pattern of sounds can have different meanings in different language-communities, or in the same language-community at different times, the meaning of a word must somehow be a function of the activity of language users, of what they do in their employments of the word." This argument may well lead us to suppose that meaning is a function of use in some sense, but in itself it will not help us to pin down that sense.

(2) "Specifications of meaning are commonly provided when we want to teach someone how to use the expression whose meaning we are specifying. Teaching someone how to use an expression is the native soil from which talk about meaning has grown. It is not, of course, the only sort of context in which one says what the meaning of a word is; there are also examinations, crossword puzzles, and many others. But it is the primary occasion for saying what a word means, and I would suppose that the other occasions are somehow derivative from it." Now this does strongly suggest that in telling someone what a word means we are putting him in a position to be able to use it, hence that knowing what it means is being able to use it, and hence that the meaning of the word is a function of how it is used. But all this, I fear, goes on the assumption that we already have an adequate understanding of what is involved in knowing how to use a word. I do not see how we could derive such an understanding from these considerations.

(3) "Ultimately a meaning-statement (a statement as to what a linguistic expression means) is to be tested by determining what people do in their employment of the expression in question. For in saying what the meaning of an expression is, what we do is not to designate some entity which could be

called the meaning of the expression, but rather to exhibit another expression which has some sort of equivalence with the first."[1]

For example:

'Procrastinate' means *put things off.*[2]
'Prognosis' means *forecast of the course and termination of a disease.*
'Redundant' means *superfluous.*
'Notwithstanding' means *in spite of.*

If this is granted, the next question obviously is: what sort of equivalence must two expressions have in order that one can be thus exhibited in specifying the meaning of the other?[3] It seems plausible to say that it is equivalence in the way they are used that is crucial, for reasons similar to those put forward in the first argument. And this suggests that a meaning statement is to be tested by examining people's employment of the expressions in question, to determine whether they are employed in the same way.

From this line of thought we can at least derive a suggestion as to how meaning is related to use, whatever use might turn out to be. We can sum up what has just been said in the following formula.

'x' means y (the meaning of 'x' is y) = df. 'x' and 'y' have the same use.

From this formula alone we get no help in trying to decide what meaning we should attach to 'use'. However, if we could make explicit just what we would look for if we set out to determine whether two expressions are used in the same way, that might give us a clue as to a proper interpretation for 'use'.

Consider the statement, " 'Procrastinate' means *put things off.*" I can test this statement, at least for my speech, as follows.[4] I review cases in which I would

---

[1] Arguments in support of this thesis are put forward in my essay, "The Quest for Meanings," *Mind*, LXXII, No. 285 (Jan. 1963).

[2] I should say something in explanation of my notation. I italicize what follows 'means' in order to indicate that there is something special about this occurrence of the expression. This is clear from the fact that we are neither using 'put things off', e.g., in the ordinary way (it is not functioning as a verb), nor are we referring to it in a way that would be marked by enclosing it in quotes. (This latter point can be seen by noting that we could not expand the sentence into: " 'Procrastinate' means the phrase, 'put things off'.") This type of occurrence, which I more or less arbitrarily call 'exhibiting', I take to be unique; and I believe that the only way to say what it is is to give the sort of elucidation of meaning-statements towards which I am working in this essay.

[3] 'Having the same meaning' or 'synonymous' seem to me to be naturally employed wherever, as in the foregoing, I would speak of 'having the sort of equivalence which enables one to be exhibited in specifying the meaning of the other'. However, one must be careful not to expect more from these phrases than they are intended to express. In using them I am not presupposing that I have specified, or can specify, something called 'a meaning' which they have in common. I shall freely avail myself of these phrases, but only as convenient and intuitively plausible abbreviations for the more cumbersome phrase.

[4] For the present I am limiting myself to investigations of the meaning the investigator himself attaches to expressions, or the way the investigator himself uses expressions. This is not different in principle from what would happen in an investigation of the way other speakers use the expressions, but the initial description of the latter would be very much more complicated unless the checks were very rough indeed. I feel justified in allowing myself this simplification because I am bringing in testing procedures at this point for their suggestive value only. Of course, ultimately we should have to consider how statements of meaning and use, as we shall have analyzed these terms, stand with respect to the possibility of inter-subjective testing.

say "You're always procrastinating," and determine whether I would use the sentence "You're always putting things off" to make just the same complaint. I think of cases in which I would say "Please don't put things off so much" and determine whether I would use the sentence "Please don't procrastinate so much" to make the same plea. I consider cases in which I say "Is he still procrastinating all the time?" and I determine whether I would use the sentence "Is he still putting things off all the time?" to ask the same question. And so on.

This suggests that a meaning-statement of the form, " 'x' means *y*" is to be tested by determining whether 'x' and 'y' can be substituted for each other in a wide variety of sentences without, in each case, changing the job(s) which the sentence is used to do, or, more precisely, without changing the suitability or potentiality of the sentence for performing whatever job(s) it was used to perform before the alteration. And since the "suitability" or "potentiality" of a sentence for the performance of a certain linguistic act is ultimately a function of the dispositions of the members of the community, a still more exact formulation would be this. The meaning-statement is justified to the extent that when 'x' is substituted for 'y' in a wide variety of sentences, and *vice versa*, the dispositions of members of the linguistic community with respect to employing sentences for the performance of linguistic actions is, in each case, roughly the same for the sentence produced by the alteration as for the sentence which was altered.

This in turn suggests the following way of conceiving use. First of all we shift our initial focus of attention from word-sized units to sentences. Even apart from the above considerations this is not an implausible move. The jobs which one might speak of using words to do, such as referring, denoting, and conjoining, have the status of incomplete aspects of actions, rather than of actions in their own right. One cannot, after bursting into a room, simply refer, denote, or conjoin, and then hastily depart. Referring or denoting is something one does in the course of performing a larger action-unit, such as making a request, admission, or prediction. It is therefore natural that we should begin the treatment of use with units the employment of each of which is sufficiently isolable to be treated as a complete action. I think it will be discovered that the smallest linguistic actions which are isolable in the concrete are all normally performed with the use of sentences. (Of course, we have to take into account the fact that any linguistic element can function, for the nonce, as a sentence-surrogate, as in one-word answers to questions, e.g., 'John' in answer to "Who was it that called?")

Having decided to begin with sentences, we can then define the notion of the use of a sentence as follows. ('s' and 't' will be used as sentence variables.)

The use of 's' = $_{df.}$ The linguistic act for the performance of which 's' is uttered.[5]

---

[5] This formulation, and those on the next few pages, are vastly over-simplified by the pretence that each expression has only one use and only one meaning. This pretence has been adopted in order to enable us to concentrate on other problems first and will be dropped in due course.

Thus the use of "Please pass the salt" is to request someone to pass some salt to the speaker; the use of "My battery is dead" is to tell someone that the speaker's battery is out of operation; the use of "How wonderful" is to express enthusiasm; and so on. Then if we recall the general formula relating meaning to use,

> IA. 'x' means $y =$ df. 'x' and 'y' have the same use.

we can expand this for sentences, in terms of the above definition of the use of a sentence, as follows.

> IB. 's' means $t =$ df. 's' and 't' are uttered for the performance of the same linguistic act.

For example, "A haint caint haint a haint" means *it is impossible for one supernatural spirit to inhabit another supernatural spirit.* This is to say that the sentences "A haint caint haint a haint" and "It is impossible for one supernatural spirit to inhabit another supernatural spirit" have the same use in the sense that they are employed to make the same assertion.

Some writers on this subject object to speaking of the meaning of a sentence.[6] They point out that sentences are not dictionary items, that one does not learn a new language sentence by sentence, etc. It think they are being over-scrupulous. One can understand the infrequency of talk about the meaning of sentences simply in terms of the fact that it is much more economical to present the semantics of a language in terms of word-sized units with their meanings, plus rules for combining them into sentences. And if this is the explanation, there is neither need for justification for denying that talk about the meaning of a sentence makes sense on those, admittedly rare, occasions when it comes up. Incidentally, the example given above is taken from one such occasion. A friend was playing for me a record of some Kentucky mountain ballads in which the sentence "A haint caint haint a haint" occurred, and my friend asked whether I knew what *that* meant. However, anyone who finds such talk distasteful can simply ignore the definition of sentential meaning. Nothing that is said about the meaning of words depends on it. (Although the discussion of word-meaning does depend on the notion of a sentence being used to perform a certain linguistic act.)

Focusing back down on words and other sentence-components[7] and continuing to follow the lead of the testing procedures outlined earlier, we can define having the same use for such units as follows, (using 'u' and 'v' as variables for sentence-components):

> 'u' has the same use as 'v' $=$ df. 'u' and 'v' can be substituted for each other in sentences without changing the linguistic act potentials of each of those sentences.

---

[6] See, e.g., Gilbert Ryle, "Use, Usage and Meaning," *Ar. Soc.* Suppl. Vol. XXXV (1961).

[7] For the sake of brevity I shall use the term 'word' alone, even where I intend what I am saying to apply to all meaningful sentence-components. I believe it will be clear where the addition is to be understood.

Substituting into the initial meaning-use formula, we get:

IC.   'u' means $v =$ df. 'u' and 'v' can be substituted for each other in sentences without changing the linguistic act potentials of each of those sentences.

III

I must pause at this point to consider two objections to these formulations, the consideration of which will reveal important aspects of our subject-matter. First, it is possible for you to tell me that two expressions have the same use (or the same meaning) without thereby telling me what either of them means. For example, you, as a native speaker of Japanese, might tell me that two expressions in that language have the same use, without telling me what either of them means. Similarly I could know, at least on authority, that two expressions have the same use without knowing what either of them means. But then something is wrong with our formula, according to which to say that 'u' and 'v' have the same use *is* to say what 'u' means.

I do not believe that this objection is as formidable as it appears at first sight, although in order to meet it we shall have to sacrifice the classic simplicity of the analysis. It seems to me that when one tells someone what an expression means, he is in effect telling him that two expressions have the same use; but he uses the meaning formulation only when he supposes that his hearer already knows how to use the second expression. Thus the meaning statement is subject to a presupposition which distinguishes it from the statement of equivalence of use. The ultimate reason for the presence of this presupposition is the fact, noted earlier, that specifications of meaning have the primary function of teaching someone how to use an expression. Pointing out that 'u' has the same use as 'v' will do nothing to help you master the use of 'u' unless you already know how to use 'v'. Once we make this complication explicit the difficulty vanishes. Rather than explicitly indicating this kind of presupposition on each occasion, I shall simply serve notice once for all that in each case the meaning-statement is to be taken to be equivalent to the use-statement only when the use-statement is taken with the presupposition that the hearer already knows how to use the second expression.

The second difficulty could be stated as follows. The sentences "I have just been to dinner at the White House" and "Heisenberg just asked me to write a preface to his latest book" would both be employed to impress the hearer; but one certainly would not say that they have the same meaning, nor would one exhibit one of these sentences in order to say what the other means. Nor would the fact that 'call' can be substituted for 'dinner' in the first sentence without altering its suitability for being used to impress the hearer, do anything to show that 'call' and 'dinner' have, even in part, the same meaning.

In reflecting on this difficulty one comes to recognize a fundamental distinction between two sorts of acts one could be said to perform by uttering a sentence (for the performance of which one could utter a sentence), one of which is usable in our definitions, the other of which is not. Consider the following lists.

I.	*II.*
report	bring x to learn that . . .
announce	persuade
predict	deceive
admit	encourage
opine	irritate
ask	frighten
reprimand	amuse
request	get x to do . . .
suggest	inspire
order	impress
propose	distract
express	get x to think about . . .
congratulate	relieve tension
promise	embarrass
thank	attract attention
exhort	bore

I am going to use the term 'illocutionary' to denote acts of the sort we have in the first list and 'perlocutionary' to denote acts of the sort we have in the second list. I borrow these terms from the late Professor John Austin's William James lectures, *How To Do Things With Words*. Austin chose these terms because he thought of the first sort of act as done *in* uttering a sentence, the second sort as done *by* uttering a sentence. Although I put less stock in this prepositional test than did Austin (who, indeed, put it forward only with many qualifications), the terms seem felicitous. However, it will be clear to readers of Austin that my distinction does not precisely parallel his; and it would be unfortunate if my terminological appropriation should lead anyone mistakenly to hold Austin responsible for my analysis.

These two classes of acts seem to me to differ in the following important ways.

(1) It is a necessary condition for the performance of a perlocutionary, but not an illocutionary, act, that the utterance have had a certain sort of result. I cannot be said to have brought you to learn something, to have moved you, frightened you, or irritated you, unless as a result of my utterance you have acquired some knowledge, have had certain feelings aroused, etc. But I could be said to have made a report, request, or admission, asked a question or offered congratulations, no matter what resulted from my utterance. I have still asked a question whether you answer it or not, or for that matter, whether or not you pay any attention to me or understand me.[8]

(2) A perlocutionary, but not an illocutionary, act can be performed without the use of language, or any other conventional device. I can bring you to

---

[8] It may be an arguable point whether I can be said to have made a request of you if you have failed to understand what I said. But even if I am wrong in supposing that I can, there would still remain a sharp difference between the two sorts of actions with respect to effects. For even if that particular sort of effect is necessary for illocutionaries, it is a general blanket requirement that does nothing to distinguish between one illocutionary and another. Whereas a perlocutionary act is made the particular act it is by the condition that a certain sort of result has occurred. It is the specific character of the result that distinguishes it from other perlocutionary acts.

learn that my battery is dead by manoeuvring you into trying to start the car yourself, and I can get you to pass the salt by simply looking around for it. But there is no way in which I can *report* that my battery is dead, or *request* you to pass the salt, without uttering a sentence or using some other conventional device, e.g., waving a flag according to a prearranged signal. This difference is closely connected with the first. It is because a perlocutionary act is logically dependent on the production of a state of affairs which is identifiable apart from the movements which produced it, that I can be said to perform that action whenever I do anything which results in that state of affairs. The result provides a sufficient distinguishing mark.

(3) Illocutionary acts are more fundamental than perlocutionary acts in the means-end hierarchy. I can request you to pass the salt in order to get you to pass the salt, or in order to irritate, distract, or amuse you. But I could hardly amuse you in order to request you to pass the salt, or get you to know that my battery is dead in order to report that my battery is dead.

A convenient rule-of-thumb (but no more than a rule-of-thumb) is provided by the fact that an illocutionary, but not a perlocutionary, act can in general be performed by the use of a sentence which includes a specification of the action performed. I can admit doing x by saying "I admit doing x." I can propose that we go to the concert by saying "I propose that we go to the concert." But perlocutionary acts resist this mould. In uttering "You're fine, how am I?", I may be amusing you; but I couldn't do the same thing by saying "I amuse you that you're fine, how am I?" If you were a fastidious and proud cook I might irritate you by saying "Please pass the salt," but I could not do the *same* thing (of a perlocutionary sort) by saying "I irritate you to please pass the salt." (Though this last utterance *might* irritate you in some way.)

The examples given earlier should make it clear that sameness of meaning cannot hang on sameness of perlocutionary act. On the other hand, I can find no cases in which sameness of meaning does not hang on sameness of illocutionary act. I therefore propose that the term 'linguistic act' in our definitions be restricted to illocutionary acts.

The notion of an illocutionary act is left in a rough state in this essay. It is obvious that if the sameness of the illocutionary act performed on two occasions, or the sameness of the illocutionary act usually performed by two sentences, is such a crucial notion in my account, it is of the first importance that I have reliable criteria of identity for illocutionary acts. And to develop these I should have to go beyond the largely negative characterization so far provided and determine the sorts of conditions which must be satisfied if one is to be truly said to have performed a certain illocutionary act. Of all the loose threads left dangling in this essay, this one has the highest priority.

IV

Having attained a measure of clarity concerning the sorts of acts involved, we can now turn to the task of correcting the oversimplification imposed on our definitions by the fiction that each expression has only one meaning and only one use. This is quite often not the case. "Can you reach the salt?" sometimes means *please pass the salt*, sometimes *are you able to reach as far as the salt?*, and perhaps sometimes *I challenge you to try to reach as far as the salt*. 'Sound' has a great many different meanings—*audible phenomenon, in good condition, long stretch of water, measure the depth of*, etc. Moreover, this unrealistic note in our definienda is reflected in the definiens. It is rarely the case that two sentences are used alike in every context, or that two expressions can be substituted for each other in every sentence without altering linguistic act potentials. Thus corresponding to the above case of sentence-multivocality we have the fact that "Can you reach the salt?" and "Please pass the salt" are used to perform the same linguistic act in many contexts but not in all. And corresponding to the case of word-multivocality cited above, we have the fact that 'sound' and 'audible phenomenon' can be substituted for each other in some sentential contexts without changing linguistic act potentials, e.g., in "Did you hear that . . . ?", but not in others, e.g., in "I've been sailing on the . . . ."

Thus if our account is not to be largely irrelevant to the facts, we must provide definition-schemas for kinds of meaning-statements which reflect the fact of multivocality. First, note that we often say, loosely, " 'u' means *v*" where, although there are other meanings, this is the chief or most prominent one. I suggest that we take care of this sort of case as follows.

IIA.   The chief meaning of 'x' is $y =$ df. 'x' and 'y' usually have the same use.

The expanded version for sentences would run:

IIB.   The chief meaning of 's' is $t =$ df. 's' and 't' are usually uttered in performing the same linguistic act.

And the expanded version for words would run:

IIC.   The chief meaning of 'u' is $v =$ df. 'u' and 'v' can be substituted for each other in most sentences without changing the linguistic act potentials of each sentence.

I am afraid that the terms 'most sentences' and 'usually', which occur in these definitions, promise more than they can provide. They can be given no mathematical interpretation, not even one as unspecific as 'over half'. Since we have no classification of contexts of utterance, or even any way of determining whether we are confronted with the same context on two different occasions, we cannot begin to say how many distinguishable contexts there are, and hence no sense can be attached to talk of any proportion of contexts. As for 'most sentences', no limit can be put on the number of sentence-types in a language, or even on the number of sentence-types in which a given word occurs; and so again there is no place for talk about a certain proportion of the total. (I take it to be clear that it would not do to understand 'most sentences' to mean *most sentence tokens which have actually occurred*; for this would make the results far too heavily influenced by the accidents of what has and has not happened to have been said. The same could be said for a similar proposal in the case of contexts.) We might understand 'most sentences' to mean *over half the sentence-types which have actually been employed*; but then we should have to weigh these types in terms of the frequency with which tokens of each of them occurs before we should be within hailing distance of what is needed. And the matter is further complicated by the fact that the prominence of a certain use is affected by factors other than the frequency of its occurrence, e.g., by how early in the course of learning the language it is generally acquired, or how important the topics are in respect to which it occurs. The most that can be said on this point is that the vagueness of the analysans nicely matches that of the analysandum.

This untidiness may well lead us to give up trying to introduce further refinements into the analysis of the notion of the chief meaning, and to concentrate instead on the notion of *a* meaning of an expression. In the light of the fact of multivocality this notion would seem to be the most fundamental one. *The* meaning of a univocal expression could be viewed as a limiting case, and talk of the chief meaning of a multivocal expression as a rough approximation which is good enough for certain working purposes. And with respect to the notion of *a* meaning it might seem that we could dispense with attempts to get at a suitable sense of 'most,' and simply say that all that is required for it to be the case that a meaning of 'u' is *v* is that 'u' and 'v' sometimes have the same use. But unfortunately this will not do because of the fact that in specifying a meaning of 'u' we want to exhibit another expression with which the use in question is clearly connected. If our other expression, 'v', only exceptionally had this use, we would not clearly identify it by exhibiting 'v'. It would not quite do to say, "A meaning of 'manage' is *run*"; even though it is true that 'manage' and 'run' sometimes have the same use. Hence we have to introduce the more stringent requirement that the use which 'x' and 'y' have in common is a use which 'y' usually has. Thus:

> IIIA.   A meaning of 'x' is $y =$ df. 'x' sometimes has the use which 'y' usually has.

Expanded for sentences this would read:

> IIIB.   A meaning of 's' is $t =$ df. 's' is sometimes used to perform the linguistic act which 't' is usually used to perform.

And expanded for words it would read:

> IIIC.   A meaning of 'u' is $v =$ df. In most sentences in which 'v' occurs 'u' can be substituted for it without changing the linguistic act potential of the sentence.

In this last definition the requirement that we choose a 'y' which usually has the meaning we wish to specify for 'x' is reflected in the specification of most of the sentences in which 'y' occurs. To say that 'u' sometimes, but not necessarily usually, has the use which 'v' usually has, is to say that 'u' can be substituted for 'v' in most 'v'-containing sentences, but not necessarily *vice versa*.

To say that 'x' has different meanings is to say that what is meant by 'x' on some occasions will differ from what is meant by 'x' on other occasions; in other words, it is to say that what the speaker means by 'x' on one occasion differs from what he meant by 'x' on another occasion. To round off the account I will suggest a pattern of analysis for such phrases.

IVA. What A (the speaker) meant by 'x' on O (a particular occasion) was *y* (What was meant by 'x' on O was *y*) = df. 'y' usually has the use which 'x' had on O.

Again we guarantee that the meaning-statement does bring out the meaning by requiring that 'y' usually have the use which is in question. This can be expanded for sentences as follows:

IVB. What A meant by 's' on O was *t* = df. The linguistic act which A performed on O by uttering 's' is the linguistic act which is usually performed by uttering 't'.

And for words the expanded version would be:

IVC. What A meant by 'u' on O was *v* = df. If we substitute 'v' for 'u' in the sentence which A uttered on O, the resulting sentence would usually be used to perform the linguistic act which A was performing on O.

For example, "When A said 'He was so mean to me', what she meant by 'mean' was *cruel*." On our account this becomes: "The sentence 'He was so cruel to me' would usually be used to make the complaint which A was making in uttering 'He was so mean to me'." Here the requirement that 'v' usually have the use to which we are trying to call attention cannot be reflected in an emphasis on substituting 'u' for 'v' rather than *vice versa*; for we are talking about a particular case in which 'u' rather than 'v' is being used, and so any substitution will have to be made into this context. Instead the requirement is reflected in the condition that the sentence resulting from the substitution of 'v' for 'u' be usually used to perform the act which is being performed on that occasion.

It seems that phrases like 'usually' and 'most sentences' are unavoidable in all these analyses. And so the chaotic state of these concepts is going to infect any meaning-talk. I shall shortly draw some morals from this fact, and other like facts.

V

I now want to call attention to certain difficulties attaching to these definitions, which in various ways show the meaning idiom not to be completely adequate for the subject matter with which it is designed to deal.

(1) Consider the fact that multivocality is not enough to prevent a statement of the form " 'u' and 'v' have the same use" from being wholly true. For it might be that even though 'u' has several different senses 'v' would have just the same range of senses, distributed over its occurrences in the same pattern. In that case it would be unqualifiedly true, despite the multivocality of 'u', to say that 'u' and 'v' could be substituted for each other in any sentence without altering the linguistic act potentialities of that sentence. And yet it would not clearly be correct in this case to say unqualifiedly that 'u' means *v*. It is not that this would be clearly incorrect; it is rather that we would not know what meaning-statement to make. It would not seem quite right to say that 'u' has *v* as its only meaning, for that would seem to imply that 'u'

has only one meaning. But on the other hand, it seems that nothing specific could be urged against that statement, for 'u' and 'v' are everywhere equivalent. The fact that meaning-talk is not forearmed against such a contingency suggests that underlying such talk there is an assumption that two expressions cannot be multivocal without diverging in their use at some point. And this assumption would seem to be justified, not only by the fact that it seems impossible to find a clear-cut example of this sort of thing, but also by the fact that multivocality is one important source of lack of synonymity. The fact that a given expression has a variety of uses makes it much more unlikely than it would have been otherwise that there should exist an exact synonym. The matching would have to be much more complex than it would if the expression were univocal. Hence I am not inclined to worry about the possibility of this kind of discrepancy in our definition.

(2) The multivocality of 'u' is no more a necessary than it is a sufficient condition of the failure of universal adequacy of the statement, " 'u' and 'v' have the same use." And this fact provides some actual cases of discrepancy between statements of this form and corresponding statements of the form, " 'u' means v." There are cases in which 'u' and 'v' are not everywhere inter-substitutable in the appropriate way, but where 'u' is not multivocal and where we would not be prepared to deny that 'u' has v as its only meaning. For example, " 'shiny' means *bright*." There are sentences in which a substitution of 'shiny' for 'bright' will not leave linguistic act potentialities unchanged, e.g., "He's a very bright student." And yet it seems that we should unhesitatingly affirm that the only meaning of 'shiny' is *bright*. Note that in this case 'bright' is multivocal, and that the failures in substitutability can be traced to that fact. Moreover, the failures have to do only with the substitution of 'shiny' for 'bright', not the reverse. I am inclined to think that in any case in which substitutability fails even though 'u' is univocal these conditions will hold. But even so the fact remains that we would be prepared to make an unqualified meaning-statement in cases in which unrestricted substitution is not possible. Of course this difficulty could be handled very simply by modifying the definiens to make it require substitutability of 'u' for 'v' only in most cases. But I am not happy about this. Remember that meaning-statements are used primarily to help someone acquire mastery of the expression whose meaning is being given. That is, we find an expression, 'v', which, we suppose, he already knows how to use, and we tell him, in effect, to use 'u' in the same way. Now if in such cases we are interested, as it seems clear we are interested, both in teaching him to use 'u' correctly himself, and in teaching him to understand employments of 'u' by others, then for the first purpose we need to give him an expression he already knows how to use for which 'u' can be substituted, and for the second purpose we need to give him an expression he already understands which can be substituted for 'u'. And this means that the meaning-statement is a reliable device for the purposes for which it is intended only to the extent that unrestricted substitution in both directions is possible. Thus failures of substitutability in either direction should lead to a

qualification of the meaning-statement. I think we can see why there is no modification when there are (minor) failures in substituting 'u' for 'v' only. Such failures indicate that there are uses of 'v' which 'u' does not have, but they do not necessarily indicate any plurality in the uses of 'u'. Therefore we do not want to say, on this basis, that *v* is only one of the meanings of 'u'. And this is the only qualification that is available, so long as we are restricted to the resources of ordinary meaning-talk. Here we seem to have a complication which the meaning idiom is incapable of expressing adequately.

(3) We have been talking as if whenever 'u' is substituted for 'v' in a sentence, the substitution either will or will not change the linguistic act potentials. But if we remember that any sentence can be used to perform more than one linguistic act, we will realize that a given substitution might conceivably alter the suitability of the sentence for performing some linguistic acts but not others. And this complicates matters. Perhaps in most cases the alteration is an all or nothing affair. But there are cases of the mixed sort. If, e.g., we substitute 'place where alcoholic drinks are served' for 'bar' in "I was admitted to the bar," we will leave unaffected the possibility that this sentence is used to report that one had been allowed to enter an establishment serving alcoholic beverages, but not the possibility that it is used to report that one has been granted the right to practice law. This complexity might be taken account of by modifying the definiens in each case to read "without *substantially* altering the linguistic act potentialities of the sentence in each case." Of course, there are various conceivable states of affairs in which this would not work. For example, it is conceivable, though it is not in fact the case, that in every sentence containing 'authentic', or in most such sentences, the substitution of 'genuine' for 'authentic' would alter at least one important linguistic act potential of the sentence, but leave at least one other important linguistic act potential unaffected. In that case it would not be true to say that in most sentences in which 'authentic' occurs, 'genuine' could be substituted for it without substantially altering the linguistic act potential of the sentence. And yet since a significant part of the linguistic act potential of each of these sentences would be unchanged by such a substitution, we might take this as indicating a significant overlap of meaning in the terms, and hence might want to say that one meaning of 'genuine' is *authentic*. I am not sure that this is a real possibility. But whether it is or not, it is noteworthy that here again we have certain complexities which cannot be adequately reflected in the meaning idiom.[9]

---

[9] It is maintained by some, e.g. by Paul Ziff in *Semantic Analysis*, Ithaca, N.Y., 1960, that there are cases in which at least rough equivalents of a word can be given, but in which it does not make sense to say that the word means so-and-so, e.g. 'tiger'. Ziff maintains that one would properly ask not "What does 'tiger' mean?", but rather "What is a tiger?". The class of cases for which this claim is made seems roughly to coincide with the class of terms which are such that no necessary and sufficient conditions for the application of the term can be given. The most plausible examples are all substantives. I do not wish to either accept or reject this position, though it seems plausible. I merely wish to point out that if it is justified it indicates still another limitation on the meaning idiom.

The general trend of these considerations (to which should be added the difficulties mentioned above concerning such terms as 'most' and 'usually' in the definitions) is to exhibit various respects in which talk about meaning, as it actually goes on, is vague, rough, and lacking in resources for reflecting all the significant distinctions within its subject-matter. It is clear that meaning-statements are dealing with sameness and difference of use among expressions, but it is also clear that they are dealing with this in a relatively unsubtle fashion. If we want analyses of meaning-statements which closely reflect their actual use, we are not going to get anything very fine-grained. If we want to talk in a more precise way about the facts that we are getting at in meaning-talk, the sameness of use idiom, as here developed, provides a more adequate instrument. In that idiom we can easily make such distinctions as that between failures of substitutability in the one direction or the other, and between the range of sentences in which substitution can be carried out and the extent to which substitution is possible in each of these sentences, distinctions which are obscured in the meaning idiom. We could then proceed to develop measures, along several different dimensions, of the extent to which two expressions have the same use.

Of course we could develop terms in the meaning idiom which would at least mark out segments of these dimensions and make that idiom more nearly adequate. But I doubt that the game is worth the candle. I feel that it is more fruitful to provide and refine analyses of meaning-statements just to the point at which it becomes clear what sort of claim is being made in meaning-statements, and then to pursue further refinements in the more supple use idiom. We should now be in a position to see that meaning-talk is a practically convenient approximation of the theoretically more fundamental statement in terms of sameness of use. In helping someone to learn to use an expression we find another which is approximately equivalent in use, and then, neglecting the various respects in which the two are or are not identical, and degrees of equivalence in each of these respects, we simply present the second expression as an equivalent, recognizing the complexity only to the extent of making some crude distinctions between *the* meaning, the chief meaning, and *a* meaning. It is clear why this is a useful procedure, but it is important to see that the very complexities which make the equivalence of use idiom unsuitable for everyday language learning make it vastly superior for semantic theory.

However, the sameness of use idiom has deficiencies of its own. For one thing, there are expressions for which, within the language, there are no synonyms, not even approximate ones, e.g., 'is' and 'and'. And this means that within the language we can neither say what they mean nor that they have the same use as some other expression. And yet we want to say that these words are meaningful or have a meaning; each of them plays an important and relatively consistent rôle in our talk, as much as other expressions which are not subject to this disability, e.g., 'albeit' or 'lid'. No doubt it is always, or almost always, possible to find some expression in another language which is approximately synonymous. But it seems odd that we should be forced to go outside the language to make explicit the function of these words. It is not that the other language, e.g., French, is richer in resources for talking about such matters. More generally, the presence or absence of an equivalent for a word in any given language seems to be an accident *vis-à-vis* the semantic status of that word; so that it should be possible to get at that semantic status without depending on such factors. This impression can be reinforced by considering the possibility of *inventing* an equivalent and, with luck, of getting it accepted into current use. In that case a meaning-statement, and a sameness of use statement, would then become possible without any significant change having occurred in the semantic status of the word in question.

Speaking of going outside the language to find an equivalent brings to mind an important defect of our analysis of 'same use' for words, viz., that it works only for intra-lingual equivalents. Remember that our analysis is in terms of substituting the two words for each other in a variety of sentences. This operation can be carried out only when the two words belong to the same language. If we try substituting 'eau' for 'water' in 'Give me some water', nothing happens; we draw a blank.

Both of these deficiencies would be remedied by developing a way of *specifying* the use which a given word has. That would free us from any dependence on the fact that there happens to exist an approximate synonym. Presumably it would be possible to specify (in English) the use(s) of 'and' or 'is', or any other expression which we would be inclined to call meaningful. And we can bring in inter-lingual judgments of sameness of use by first separately specifying the use of each word and then basing assertions of (degrees of) equivalence of use on that. This indicates that for these reasons, as well as for many others, the next major step in the direction pointed out by this essay (after a thorough analysis of the notion of an illocutionary act) will be the development of a satisfactory way of identifying and describing the use(s) of a particular word. This is almost virgin territory. There are various terms in current use which might be thought to mark out large categories of such uses—'denote', 'connote', 'refer', 'qualify', 'conjoin', etc.; but although some, especially 'refer', have received a great deal of discussion, some of it quite subtle, virtually nothing has been done in the direction of developing a general method for identifying, classifying and interrelating uses as a basis for semantic theory. At this point it can only be said that the difficulty of the enterprise is matched by its importance.

CARL G. HEMPEL

5.3   *Problems and Changes in the Empiricist Criterion of Meaning*

1. INTRODUCTION

The fundamental tenet of modern empiricism is the view that all non-analytic knowledge is based on experience. Let us call this thesis the principle of empiricism.[1] Contemporary logical empiricism has added[2] to it the maxim that a sentence makes a cognitively meaningful assertion, and thus can be said to be either true or false, only if it is either (1) analytic or self-contradictory or (2) capable, at least in principle, of experiential test. According to this so-called *empiricist criterion of cognitive meaning, or of cognitive significance*, many of the formulations of traditional metaphysics and large parts of epistemology are devoid of cognitive significance—however rich some of them may be in non-cognitive import by virtue of their emotive appeal or the moral inspiration they offer. Similarly certain doctrines which have been, at one time or another, formulated within empirical science or its border disciplines are so contrived as to be incapable of test by any conceivable evidence; they are therefore qualified as pseudohypotheses, which assert nothing, and which therefore have no explanatory or predictive force whatever. This verdict applies, for example, to the neovitalist speculations about entelechies or vital forces, and to the "telefinalist hypothesis" propounded by Lecomte du Noüy.[3]

The preceding formulations of the principle of empiricism and of the empiricist meaning criterion provide no more, however, than a general and rather vague characterization of a basic point of view, and they need therefore to be elucidated and amplified. And while in the earlier phases of its development, logical empiricism was to a large extent preoccupied with a critique of philosophic and scientific formulations by means of those fundamental principles, there has been in recent years an increasing concern with the positive tasks of analyzing in detail the logic and methodology of empirical science and of clarifying and restating the basic ideas of empiricism in the light of the insights thus obtained. In the present article, I propose to discuss

Reprinted from *Revue Internationale de Philosophie*, IV, No. 11 (1950), 41–63, by permission of the author and of the editor of *Revue Internationale de Philosophie*.

[1] This term is used by Benjamin [1941] in an examination of the foundations of empiricism. For a recent discussion of the basic ideas of empiricism see Russell [1948], Part Six.

[2] In his stimulating article, "Positivism," W. T. Stace argues, in effect, that the testability criterion of meaning is not logically entailed by the principle of empiricism. (See [Stace, 1944], especially section 11.) This is correct: According to the latter, a sentence expresses knowledge only if it is either analytic or corroborated by empirical evidence; the former goes further and identifies the domain of cognitively significant discourse with that of potential knowledge; i.e., it grants cognitive import only to sentences for which—unless they are either analytic or contradictory—a test by empirical evidence is conceivable.

[3] *Cf.* [du Noüy, 1947], Ch. XVI.

some of the problems this search has raised and some of the results it seems to have established.

2. CHANGES IN THE TESTABILITY CRITERION OF EMPIRICAL MEANING

As our formulation shows, the empiricist meaning criterion lays down the requirement of experiential testability for those among the cognitively meaningful sentences which are neither analytic nor contradictory; let us call them sentences with empirical meaning, or empirical significance. The concept of testability, which is to render precise the vague notion of being based—or rather baseable—on experience, has undergone several modifications which reflect an increasingly refined analysis of the structure of empirical knowledge. In the present section, let us examine the major stages of this development.

For convenience of exposition, we first introduce three auxiliary concepts, namely those of observable characteristic, of observation predicate, and of observation sentence. A property or a relation of physical objects will be called an *observable characteristic* if, under suitable circumstances, its presence or absence in a given instance can be ascertained through direct observation. Thus, the terms "green", "soft", "liquid", "longer than", designate observable characteristics, while "bivalent", "radioactive", "better electric conductor", and "introvert" do not. Terms which designate observable characteristics will be called *observation predicates*. Finally, by an *observation sentence* we shall understand any sentence which—correctly or incorrectly—asserts of one or more specifically named objects that they have, or that they lack, some specified observable characteristic. The following sentences, for example, meet this condition: "The Eiffel Tower is taller than the buildings in its vicinity," "The pointer of this instrument does not cover the point marked '3' on the scale," and even, "The largest dinosaur on exhibit in New York's Museum of Natural History had a blue tongue"; for this last sentence assigns to a specified object a characteristic—having a blue tongue—which is of such a kind that under suitable circumstances (e.g., in the case of my Chow dog) its presence or absence can be ascertained by direct observation. Our concept of observation sentence is intended to provide a precise interpretation of the vague idea of a sentence asserting something that is "in principle" ascertainable by direct observation, even though it may happen to be actually incapable of being observed by myself, perhaps also by my contemporaries, and possibly even by any human being who ever lived or will live. Any evidence that might be adduced in the test of an empirical hypothesis may now be thought of as being expressed in observation sentences of this kind.[4]

---

[4] Observation sentences of this kind belong to what Carnap has called the thing-language (*cf.*, e.g., [Carnap, 1938], pp. 52–53). That they are adequate to formulate the data which serve as the basis for empirical tests is clear in particular for the intersubjective testing procedures used in science as well as in large areas of empirical inquiry on the common-sense level. In epistemological discussions, it is frequently assumed that the ultimate evidence for beliefs about empirical matters consists in perceptions and sensations whose description calls for a phenomenalistic type of language. The specific problems connected with the phenomenalistic approach cannot be discussed here; but it should be mentioned that at any rate all the critical considerations presented in this article in regard to the testability criterion are applicable, *mutatis mutandis*, to the case of a phenomenalistic basis as well.

We now turn to the changes in the conception of testability, and thus of empirical meaning. In the early days of the Vienna Circle, a sentence was said to have empirical meaning if it was capable, at least in principle, of complete verification by observational evidence; i.e., if observational evidence could be described which, if actually obtained, would conclusively establish the truth of the sentence.[5] With the help of the concept of observation sentence, we can restate this requirement as follows: A sentence S has empirical meaning if and only if it is possible to indicate a finite set of observation sentences, $O_1, O_2, \ldots, O_n$, such that if these are true, then S is necessarily true, too. As stated, however, this condition is satisfied also if S is an analytic sentence or if the given observation sentences are logically incompatible with each other. By the following formulation, we rule these cases out and at the same time express the intended criterion more precisely:

(2.1) *Requirement of complete verifiability in principle:* A sentence has empirical meaning if and only if it is not analytic and follows logically from some finite and logically consistent class of observation sentence.[6]

---

[5] Originally, the permissible evidence was meant to be restricted to what is observable by the speaker and perhaps his fellow-beings during their life times. Thus construed, the criterion rules out, as cognitively meaningless, all statements about the distant future or the remote past, as has been pointed out, among others, by Ayer in [*Language, Truth and Logic*], Chapter 1; by Pap in [*Elements of Analytic Philosophy*], Chapter 13, esp. pp. 333 ff.; and by Russell in [*Human Knowledge*], pp. 445–47. This difficulty is avoided, however, if we permit the evidence to consist of any finite set of "logically possible observation data," each of them formulated in an observation sentence. Thus, e.g., the sentence S_1, "The tongue of the largest dinosaur in New York's Museum of Natural History was blue or black" is completely verifiable in our sense; for it is a logical consequence of the sentence S_2, "The tongue of the largest dinosaur in New York's Museum of Natural History was blue"; and this is an observation sentence, as has been shown above.

And if the concept of *verifiability in principle* and the more general concept of *confirmability in principle*, which will be considered later, are construed as referring to *logically possible evidence* as expressed by observation sentences, then it follows similarly that the class of statements which are verifiable, or at least confirmable, in principle includes such assertions as that the planet Neptune and the Antarctic Continent existed before they were discovered, and that atomic warfare, if not checked, may lead to the extermination of this planet. The objections which Russell (cf. [*Human Knowledge*], pp. 445 and 447) raises against the verifiability criterion by reference to those examples do not apply therefore if the criterion is understood in the manner here suggested. Incidentally, statements of the kind mentioned by Russell, which are not actually verifiable by any human being, were explicitly recognized as cognitively significant already by Schlick (in ["Meaning and Verification"], Part V), who argued that the impossibility of verifying them was "merely empirical." The characterization of verifiability with the help of the concept of observation sentence as suggested here might serve as a more explicit and rigorous statement of that conception.

[6] As has been frequently emphasized in empiricist literature, the term "verifiability" is to indicate, of course, the conceivability, or better, the logical possibility of evidence of an observational kind which, if actually encountered, would constitute conclusive evidence for the given sentence; it is not intended to mean the technical possibility of performing the tests needed to obtain such evidence, and even less does it mean the possibility of actually finding directly observable phenomena which constitute conclusive evidence for that sentence—which would be tantamount to the actual existence of such evidence and would thus imply the truth of the given sentence. Analogous remarks apply to the terms "falsifiability" and "confirmability." This point has been disregarded in some recent critical discussions of the verifiability criterion. Thus, e.g., Russell (cf. [*Human Knowledge*], p. 448) construes verifiability as the actual existence of a set of conclusively verifying occurrences. This conception, which has never been advocated

This criterion, however, has several serious defects. The first of those here to be mentioned has been pointed out by various writers:

(*a*) The verifiability requirement rules out all sentences of universal form and thus all statements purporting to express general laws; for these cannot be conclusively verified by any finite set of observational data. And since sentences of this type constitute an integral part of scientific theories, the verifiability requirement must be regarded as overly restrictive in this respect. Similarly, the criterion disqualifies all sentences such as "For any substance there exists some solvent", which contain both universal and existential quantifiers (i.e., occurrences of the terms "all" and "some" or their equivalents); for no sentences of this kind can be logically deduced from any finite set of observation sentences.

Two further defects of the verifiability requirement do not seem to have been widely noticed:

(*b*) Suppose that *S* is a sentence which satisfies the proposed criterion, whereas N is a sentence such as "The absolute is perfect", to which the criterion attributes no empirical meaning. Then the alternation SvN (i.e., the expression obtained by connecting the two sentences by the word "or"), likewise satisfies the criterion; for if S is a consequence of some finite class of observation sentences, then trivially SvN is a consequence of the same class. But clearly, the empiricist criterion of meaning is not intended to countenance sentences of this sort. In this respect, therefore, the requirement of complete verifiability is too inclusive.

(*c*) Let "P" be an observation predicate. Then the purely existential sentence "$(Ex)P(x)$" ("There exists at least one thing that has the property P") is completely verifiable, for it follows from any observation sentence asserting of some particular object that it has the property P. But its denial, being

---

by any logical empiricist, must naturally turn out to be inadequate since according to it the empirical meaningfulness of a sentence could not be established without gathering empirical evidence, and moreover enough of it to permit a conclusive proof of the sentences in question! It is not surprising, therefore, that his extraordinary interpretation of verifiability leads Russell to the conclusion: "In fact, that a proposition is verifiable is itself not verifiable" (*l. c.*). Actually, under the empiricist interpretation of complete verifiability, any statement asserting the verifiability of some sentence S whose text is quoted, is either analytic or contradictory; for the decision whether there exists a class of observation sentences which entail S, i.e., whether such observation sentences can be formulated, no matter whether they are true or false—that decision is a matter of pure logic and requires no factual information whatever.

A similar misunderstanding is in evidence in the following passage in which W. H. Werkmeister claims to characterize a view held by logical positivists: "A proposition is said to be 'true' when it is 'verifiable in principle'; i.e., when we know the conditions which, when realized, will make 'verification' possible (*cf.* Ayer)." (*Cf.* [*The Basis and Structure of Knowledge*], p. 145). The quoted thesis, which, again, was never held by any logical positivist, including Ayer, is in fact logically absurd. For we can readily describe conditions which, if realized, would verify the sentence "The outside of the Chrysler Building is painted a bright yellow"; but similarly, we can describe verifying conditions for its denial; hence, according to the quoted principle, both the sentence and its denial would have to be considered true. Incidentally, the passage under discussion does not accord with Werkmeister's perfectly correct observation, *l. c.*, p. 40, that verifiability is intended to characterize the meaning of a sentence—which shows that verifiability is meant to be a criterion of cognitive significance rather than of truth.

equivalent to the universal sentence "$(x) \sim P(x)$" ("Nothing has the property P") is clearly not completely verifiable, as follows from comment (a) above. Hence, under the criterion (2.1), the denials of certain empirically—and thus cognitively—significant sentences are empirically meaningless; and as they are neither analytic nor contradictory, they are cognitively meaningless. But however we may delimit the domain of significant discourse, we shall have to insist that if a sentence falls within that domain, then so must its denial. To put the matter more explicitly: The sentences to be qualified as cognitively meaningful are precisely those which can be significantly said to be either true or false. But then, adherence to (2.1) would engender a serious dilemma, as is shown by the consequence just mentioned: We would either have to give up the fundamental logical principle that if a sentence is true or false, then its denial is false or true, respectively (and thus cognitively significant); or else, we must deny, in a manner reminiscent of the intuitionistic conception of logic and mathematics, that "$(x) \sim P(x)$" is logically equivalent to the negation of "$(Ex) P (x)$". Clearly, the criterion (2.1), which has disqualified itself on several other counts, does not warrant such drastic measures for its preservation; hence, it has to be abandoned.[7]

Strictly analogous considerations apply to an alternative criterion, which makes complete falsifiability in principle the defining characteristic of empirical significance. Let us formulate this criterion as follows: A sentence has empirical meaning if and only if it is capable, in principle, of complete refutation by a finite number of observational data; or, more precisely:

(2.2) *Requirement of complete falsifiability in principle:* A sentence has empirical meaning if and only if its denial is not analytic and follows logically from some finite logically consistent class of observation sentences.[8]

This criterion qualifies a sentence as empirically meaningful if its denial satisfies the requirement of complete verifiability; as is to be expected, it is therefore inadequate on similar grounds as the latter:

(a) It rules out purely existential hypotheses, such as "There exists at least one unicorn", and all sentences whose formulation calls for mixed—i.e.,

---

[7] The arguments here adduced against the verifiability criterion also prove the inadequacy of a view closely related to it, namely that two sentences have the same cognitive significance if any set of observation sentences which would verify one of them would also verify the other, and conversely. Thus, e.g., under this criterion, any two general laws would have to be assigned the same cognitive significance, for no general law is verified by any set of observation sentences. The view just referred to must be clearly distinguished from a position which Russell examines in his critical discussion of the positivistic meaning criterion. It is "the theory that two propositions whose verified consequences are identical have the same significance" ([*Human Knowledge*], p. 448). This view is untenable indeed, for what consequences of a statement have actually been verified at a given time is obviously a matter of historical accident which cannot possibly serve to establish identity of cognitive significance. But I am not aware that any logical positivist ever subscribed to that "theory".

[8] The idea of using theoretical falsifiability by observational evidence as the "criterion of demarcation" separating empirical science from mathematics and logic on the one hand and from metaphysics on the other is due to K. Popper (*cf.* [*Logik der Forschung*], section 1-7 and 19-24; also see [*The Open Society and Its Enemies*], vol. II, pp. 282–85). Whether Popper would subscribe to the proposed restatement of the falsifiability criterion, I do not know.

universal and existential—quantification; for none of these can possibly be conclusively falsified by a finite number of observation sentences.

(*b*) If a sentence S is completely falsifiable whereas N is a sentence which is not, then their conjunction, S.N (i.e., the expression obtained by connecting the two sentences by the word "and") is completely falsifiable; for if the denial of S is entailed by some class of observation sentences, then the denial of S.N is, *a fortiori*, entailed by the same class. Thus, the criterion allows empirical significance to many sentences which an adequate empiricist criterion should rule out, such as, say "All swans are white and the absolute is perfect."

(c) If "P" is an observation predicate, then the assertion that all things have the property P is qualified as significant, but its denial, being equivalent to a purely existential hypothesis, is disqualified (*cf.* (*a*)). Hence, criterion (2.2) gives rise to the same dilemma as (2.1).

In sum, then, interpretations of the testability criterion in terms of complete verifiability or of complete falsifiability are inadequate because they are overly restrictive in one direction and overly inclusive in another, and because both of them require incisive changes in the fundamental principles of logic.

Several attempts have been made to avoid these difficulties by construing the testability criterion as demanding merely a partial and possibly indirect confirmability of empirical hypotheses by observational evidence.

(2.3) A formulation suggested by Ayer[9] is characteristic of these attempts to set up a clear and sufficiently comprehensive criterion of confirmability. It states, in effect, that a sentence S has empirical import if from S in conjunction with suitable subsidiary hypotheses it is possible to derive observation sentences which are not derivable from the subsidiary hypotheses alone.

This condition is suggested by a closer consideration of the logical structure of scientific testing; but it is much too liberal as it stands. Indeed, as Ayer himself has pointed out in the second edition of his book, *Language, Truth, and Logic*,[10] his criterion allows empirical import to any sentence whatever. Thus, e.g., if S is the sentence "The absolute is perfect", it suffices to choose as a subsidiary hypothesis the sentence "If the absolute is perfect then this apple is red" in order to make possible the deduction of the observation sentence "This apple is red", which clearly does not follow from the subsidiary hypothesis alone.[11]

---

[9] [*Language, Truth and Logic*], Ch. I.—The case against the requirements of verifiability and of falsifiability, and favor of a requirement of partial confirmability and disconfirmability is very clearly presented also by Pap in [*Elements of Analytic Philosophy*], Chapter 13.

[10] 2d ed., pp. 11–12.

[11] According to Stace (*cf.* ["Positivism"], p. 218), the criterion of partial and indirect testability, which he calls the positivist principle, presupposes (and thus logically entails) another principle, which he terms the *Principle of Observable Kinds*: "A sentence, in order to be significant, must assert or deny facts which are of a kind or class such that it is logically possible directly to observe some facts which are instances of that class or kind. And if a sentence purports to assert or deny facts which are of a class or kind such that it would be logically impossible directly to observe any instance of that class or kind, then the sentence is non-significant." I think the argument Stace offers to prove that this principle is entailed by the requirement of testability is inconclusive (mainly because of the incorrect tacit assumption that "on the transformation

(2.4) To meet this objection, Ayer has recently proposed a modified version of his testability criterion. The modification restricts, in effect, the subsidiary hypotheses mentioned in (2.3) to sentences which are either analytic or can independently be shown to be testable in the sense of the modified criterion.[12]

But it can readily be shown that this new criterion, like the requirement of complete falsifiability, allows empirical significance to any conjunction S.N, where S satisfies Ayer's criterion while N is a sentence such as "The absolute is perfect", which is to be disqualified by that criterion. Indeed: whatever consequences can be deduced from S with the help of permissible subsidiary hypotheses can also be deduced from S.N by means of the same subsidiary hypotheses, and as Ayer's new criterion is formulated essentially in terms of the deducibility of a certain type of consequence from the given sentence, it countenances S.N together with S. Another difficulty has been pointed out by Professor A. Church, who has shown[13] that if there are any three observation sentences none of which alone entails any of the others, then it follows for any sentence S whatsoever that either it or its denial has empirical import according to Ayer's revised criterion.

3. TRANSLATABILITY INTO AN EMPIRICIST LANGUAGE AS A NEW CRITERION OF COGNITIVE MEANING

I think it is useless to continue the search for an adequate criterion of testability in terms of deductive relationships to observation sentences. The past development of this search—of which we have considered the major stages—seems to warrant the expectation that as long as we try to set up a criterion of testability for individual sentences in a natural language, in terms of logical relationship to observation sentences, the result will be either too restrictive or too inclusive, or both. In particular it appears likely that such criteria would allow empirical import, in the manner of (2.1) (b) or of (2.2) (b), either to any alternation or to any conjunction of two sentences of which at least one is qualified as empirically meaningful; and this peculiarity has undesirable

---

view of deduction," the premises of a valid deductive argument must be necessary conditions for the conclusion (l. c., p. 225)). Without pressing this point any further, I should like to add here a remark on the principle of observable kinds itself. Professor Stace does not say how we are to determine what "facts" a given sentence asserts or denies, or indeed whether it asserts or denies any "facts" at all. Hence, the exact import of the principle remains unclear. No matter, however, how one might choose the criteria for the factual reference of sentences, this much seems certain: If a sentence expresses any fact at all, say f, then it satisfies the requirement laid down in the first sentence of the principle; for we can always form a class containing f together with the fact expressed by some observation sentence of our choice, which makes f a member of a class of facts at least one of which is capable, in principle, of direct observation. The first part of the principle of observable kinds is therefore all-inclusive, somewhat like Ayer's original formulation of the empiricist meaning criterion.

[12] This restriction is expressed in recursive form and involves no vicious circle. For the full statement of Ayers's criterion, see [Language, Truth and Logic], 2d edition, p. 13.

[13] Church, [Journal of Symbolic Logic], XIV (1949), 52–53].

consequences because the liberal grammatical rules of English as of any other natural language countenance as sentences certain expressions ("The absolute is perfect" was our illustration) which even by the most liberal empiricist standards make no assertion whatever; and these would then have to be permitted as components of empirically significant statements.

The predicament would not arise, of course, in an artificial language whose vocabulary and grammar were so chosen as to preclude altogether the possibility of forming sentences of any kind which the empiricist meaning criterion is intended to rule out. Let us call any such language an *empiricist language*. This reflection suggests an entirely different approach to our problem: Give a general characterization of the kind of language that would qualify as empiricist, and then lay down the following

(3.1) *Translatability criterion of cognitive meaning:* A sentence has cognitive meaning if and only if it is translatable into an empiricist language.

This conception of cognitive import, while perhaps not explicitly stated, seems to underlie much of the more recent work done by empiricist writers; as far as I can see it has its origin in Carnap's essay, *Testability and Meaning* (especially part IV).

As any language, so also any empiricist language can be characterized by indicating its vocabulary and the rules determining its logic; the latter include the syntactical rules according to which sentences may be formed by means of the given vocabulary. In effect, therefore, the translatability criterion proposes to characterize the cognitively meaningful sentences by the vocabulary out of which they may be constructed, and by the syntactical principles governing their construction. What sentences are singled out as cognitively significant will depend, accordingly, on the choice of the vocabulary and of the construction rules. Let us consider a specific possibility:

(3.2) We might qualify a language L as empiricist if it satisfies the following conditions:

(a) *The vocabulary of L contains:*

    (1) The customary locutions of logic which are used in the formulation of sentences; including in particular the expressions "not", "and", "or", "if ... then ... ", "all", "some", "the class of all things such that ... ", " ... is an element of class ... ";

    (2) Certain *observation predicates*. These will be said to constitute the basic empirical vocabulary of L;

    (3) Any expression definable by means of those referred to under (1) and (2).

(b) *The rules of sentence formation for L* are those laid down in some contemporary logical system such as *Principia Mathematica*.

Since all defined terms can be eliminated in favor of primitives, these rules stipulate in effect that a language L is empiricist if all its sentences are expressible, with the help of the usual logical locutions, in terms of observable characteristics of physical objects. Let us call any language of this sort a thing-language in the narrower sense. Alternatively, the basic empirical vocabulary of an empiricist language might be construed as consisting of phenomenalistic terms, each of them referring to some aspect of the phenomena of perception or sensation. The construction of adequate phenomenalistic languages, however, presents considerable difficulties,[14] and in recent empiricism, attention has been focussed primarily on the potentialities of languages whose basic empirical vocabulary consists of observation predicates; for the latter lend themselves more directly to the description of that type of intersubjective evidence which is invoked in the test of scientific hypotheses.

If we construe empiricist languages in the sense of (3.2), then translatability criterion (3.1) avoids all of the shortcomings pointed out in our discussion of earlier forms of the testability criterion:

(*a*) Our characterization of empiricist languages makes explicit provision for universal and existential quantification, i.e., for the use of the terms "all" and "some"; hence, no type of quantified statement is generally excluded from the realm of cognitively significant discourse;

(*b*) Sentences such as "The absolute is perfect" cannot be formulated in an empiricist language (*cf.* (*d*) below); hence there is no danger that a conjunction or alternation containing a sentence of that kind as a component might be qualified as cognitively significant;

(*c*) In a language L with syntactical rules conforming to *Principia Mathematica*, the denial of a sentence is always again a sentence of L. Hence, the translatability criterion does not lead to the consequence, which is entailed by both (2.1) and (2.2), that the denials of certain significant sentences are non-significant;

(*d*) Despite its comprehensiveness, the new criterion does not attribute cognitive meaning to *all* sentences; thus, e.g., the sentences "The absolute is perfect" and "Nothingness nothings" cannot be translated into an empiricist language because their key terms are not definable by means of purely logical expressions and observation terms.

4. THE PROBLEM OF DISPOSITION TERMS AND OF THEORETICAL CONSTRUCTS

Yet, the new criterion is still too restrictive—as are, incidentally, also its predecessors—in an important respect which now calls for consideration. If empiricist languages are defined in accordance with (3.2), then, as was noted above, the translatability criterion (3.1) allows cognitive import to a sentence only if its constitutive empirical terms are explicitly definable by means of observation predicates. But as we shall argue presently, many terms even of the physical sciences are not so definable; hence the criterion would oblige

---

[14] Important contributions to the problem have been made by Carnap, [*Der Logische Aufbau der Welt*] and by Goodman, [*The Structure of Appearance*].

us to reject, as devoid of cognitive import, all scientific hypotheses containing such terms—an altogether intolerable consequence.

The concept of temperature is a case in point. At first glance, it seems as though the phrase "Object x has a temperature of c degrees centigrade", or briefly "$T(x) = c$" could be defined by the following sentence, (D): $T(x) = c$ if and only if the following condition is satisfied: If a thermometer is in contact with x, then it registers c degrees on its scale.

Disregarding niceties, it may be granted that the definiens given here is formulated entirely in reference to observables. However, it has one highly questionable aspect: In *Principia Mathematica* and similar systems, the phrase "if p then q" is construed as being synonymous with "not p or q"; and under this so-called material interpretation of the conditional, a statement of the form "if p then q" is obviously true if (though not only if) the sentence standing in the place of "p" is false. If, therefore, the meaning of "if . . . then . . . " in the definiens of (D) is understood in the material sense, then that definiens is true if (though not only if) x is an object not in contact with a thermometer—no matter what numerical value we may give to c. And since the definiendum would be true under the same circumstances, the definition (D) would qualify as the assignment of any temperature value whatsoever to any object not in contact with a thermometer! Analogous considerations apply to such terms as "electrically charged", "magnetic", "intelligent", "electric resistance", etc., in short to all disposition terms, i.e., terms which express the disposition of one or more objects to react in a determinate way under specified circumstances: A definition of such terms by means of observation predicates cannot be effected in the manner of (D), however natural and obvious a mode of definition this may at first seem to be.[15]

There are two main directions in which a resolution of the difficulty might be sought. On the one hand, it could be argued that the definition of disposition terms in the manner of (D) is perfectly adequate provided that the phrase "if . . . then . . . " in the definiens is construed in the sense it is obviously intended to have, namely as implying, in the case of (D), that even if x is not actually in contact with a thermometer, still if it *were* in such contact, then the thermometer *would* register c degrees. In sentences such as this, the phrase "if . . . then . . . " is said to be used counterfactually; and it is in this "strong" sense, which implies a counterfactual conditional, that the definiens of (D) would have to be construed. This suggestion would provide an answer to the problem of defining disposition terms if it were not for the fact that no entirely satisfactory account of the exact meaning of counterfactual conditionals seems to be available at present. Thus, the first way out of the difficulty has the status of a program rather than that of a solution. The lack of an adequate

---

[15] This difficulty in the definition of disposition terms was first pointed out and analyzed by Carnap (in ["Testability and Meaning"]; see esp. section 7).

theory of counterfactual conditionals is all the more deplorable as such a theory is needed also for the analysis of the concept of general law in empirical science and of certain related ideas. A clarification of this cluster of problems constitutes at present one of the urgent desiderata in the logic and methodology of science.[16]

An alternative way of dealing with the definitional problems raised by disposition terms was suggested, and developed in detail, by Carnap. It consists in permitting the introduction of new terms, within an empiricist language, by means of so-called reduction sentences, which have the character of partial or conditional definitions.[17] Thus, e.g., the concept of temperature in our last illustration might be introduced by means of the following reduction sentence, (R): If a thermometer is in contact with an object x, then $T(x) = c$ if and only if the thermometer registers c degrees.

This rule, in which the conditional may be construed in the material sense, specifies the meaning of "temperature", i.e., of statements of the form "$T(x) = c$", only partially, namely in regard to those objects which are in contact with a thermometer; for all other objects, it simply leaves the meaning of "$T(x) = c$" undetermined. The specification of the meaning of "temperature" may then be gradually extended to cases not covered in (R) by laying down further reduction sentences, which reflect the measurement of temperature by devices other than thermometers.

Reduction sentences thus provide a means for the precise formulation of what is commonly referred to as operational definitions.[18] At the same time, they show that the latter are not definitions in the strict sense of the word, but rather partial specifications of meaning.

The preceding considerations suggest that in our characterization (3.2) of empiricist languages we broaden the provision a (3) by permitting in the vocabulary of L all those terms whose meaning can be specified in terms of the basic empirical vocabulary by means of definitions or reduction sentences. Languages satisfying this more inclusive criterion will be referred to as thing-languages in the wider sense.

[16] The concept of strict implication as introduced by C. I. Lewis would be of no avail for the interpretation of the strong "if ... then ..." as here understood, for it refers to a purely logical relationship of entailment, whereas the concept under consideration will, in general, represent a nomological relationship, i.e., one based on empirical laws. For recent discussions of the problems of counterfactuals and laws, see Langford [*Journal of Symbolic Logic*, VI (1941), 67–68]; Lewis [*An Analysis of Knowledge and Valuation*], pp. 210–230; Chisholm [*Mind*, LV (1946)]; Goodman [*Journal of Philosophy*, XLIV (1947)]; Reichenbach [*Elements of Symbolic Logic*], Chapter VIII; Hempel and Oppenheim [*Philosophy of Science*, XV (1948)], Part III; Popper [*Mind*, LVIII (1949)].

[17] *Cf.* Carnap [1936]; a brief elementary exposition of the central idea may be found in Carnap [1938], Part III. The partial definition (R) formulated above for the expression "$T(x) = c$" illustrates only the simplest type of reduction sentence, the so-called bilateral reduction sentence.

[18] On the concept of operational definition, which was developed by Bridgman, see, for example, Bridgman ([1927], [1938]) and Feigl ([1945]).

If the concept of empiricist language is broadened in this manner, then the translatability criterion (3.1) covers—as it should—also all those statements whose constituent empirical terms include "empirical constructs," i.e., terms which do not designate observables, but which can be introduced by reduction sentences on the basis of observation predicates.

Even in this generalized version, however, our criterion of cognitive meaning may not do justice to advanced scientific theories, which are formulated in terms of "theoretical constructs," such as the terms "absolute temperature," "gravitational potential," "electric field," "ψ function," etc. There are reasons to think that neither definitions nor reduction sentences are adequate to introduce these terms on the basis of observation predicates. Thus, e.g., if a system of reduction sentences for the concept of electric field were available, then—to oversimplify the point a little—it would be possible to describe, in terms of observable characteristics, some necessary and some sufficient conditions for the presence, in a given region, of an electric field of any mathematical description, however complex. Actually, however, such criteria can at best be given only for some sufficiently simple kinds of fields.

Now theories of the advanced type here referred to may be considered as hypothetico-deductive systems in which all statements are logical consequences of a set of fundamental assumptions. Fundamental as well as derived statements in such a system are formulated either in terms of certain theoretical constructs which are not defined within the system and thus play the rôle of primitives, or in terms of expressions defined by means of the latter. Thus, in their logical structure such systems equal the axiomatized uninterpreted systems studied in mathematics and logic. They acquire applicability to empirical subject matter, and thus the status of theories of empirical science, by virtue of an empirical interpretation. The latter is effected by a translation of some of the sentences of the theory—often derived rather than fundamental ones—into an empiricist language, which may contain both observation predicates and empirical constructs. And since the sentences which are thus given empirical meaning are logical consequences of the fundamental hypotheses of the theory, that translation effects, indirectly, a partial interpretation of the latter and of the constructs in terms of which they are formulated.[19]

In order to make translatability into an empiricist language an adequate criterion of cognitive import, we broaden therefore the concept of empiricist

---

[19] The distinction between a formal deductive system and the empirical theory resulting from it by an interpretation has been elaborated in detail by Reichenbach in his penetrating studies of the relations between pure and physical geometry; *cf.*, e.g., Reichenbach [*Philosophie der Raum-Zeit-Lehre*]. The method by means of which a formal system is given empirical content is characterized by Reichenbach as "coordinating definition" of the primitives in the theory by means of specific empirical concepts. As is suggested by our discussion of reduction and the interpretation of theoretical constructs, however, the process in question may have to be construed as a partial interpretation of the non-logical terms of the system rather than as a complete definition of the latter in terms of the concepts of a thing-language.

language so as to include thing-languages in the narrower and in the wider sense as well as all interpreted theoretical systems of the kind just referred to.[20] With this understanding, (3.1) may finally serve as a general criterion of cognitive meaning.

5. ON "THE MEANING" OF AN EMPIRICAL STATEMENT

In effect, the criterion thus arrived at qualifies a sentence as cognitively meaningful if its non-logical constituents refer, directly or in certain specified indirect ways, to observables. But it does not make any pronouncement on what "the meaning" of a cognitively significant sentence is, and in particular it neither says nor implies that that meaning can be exhaustively characterized by what the totality of possible tests would reveal in terms of observable phenomena. Indeed, *the content of a statement with empirical import cannot, in general, be exhaustively expressed by means of any class of observation sentences.*

For consider first, among the statements permitted by our criterion, any purely existential hypothesis or any statement involving mixed quantification. As was pointed out earlier, under (2.2) (*a*), statements of these kinds entail no observation sentences whatever; hence their content cannot be expressed by means of a class of observation sentences.

And secondly, even most statements of purely universal form (such as "All flamingoes are pink") entail observation sentences (such as "That thing is pink") only when combined with suitable other observation sentences (such as "That thing is a flamingo").

This last remark can be generalized: The use of empirical hypotheses for the prediction of observable phenomena requires, in practically all cases, the use of subsidiary empirical hypotheses.[21] Thus, e.g., the hypothesis that the agent of tuberculosis is rod-shaped does not by itself entail the consequence that upon looking at a tubercular sputum specimen through a microscope, rod-like shapes will be observed: a large number of subsidiary hypotheses, including the theory of the microscope, have to be used as additional premises in deducing that prediction.

Hence, what is sweepingly referred to as "the (cognitive) meaning" of a given scientific hypothesis cannot be adequately characterized in terms of potential observational evidence alone, nor can it be specified for the hypothesis taken in isolation: In order to understand "the meaning" of a hypothesis within an empiricist language, we have to know not merely what observation

---

[20] These systems have not been characterized here as fully and as precisely as would be desirable. Indeed, the exact character of the empirical interpretation of theoretical constructs and of the theories in which they function is in need of further investigation. Some problems which arise in this connection—such as whether, or in what sense, theoretical constructs may be said to denote—are obviously also of considerable epistemological interest. Some suggestions as to the interpretation of theoretical constructs may be found in Carnap [1939], section 24, and in Kaplan [*Journal of Philosophy*, XLIII (1946)]; for an excellent discussion of the epistemological aspects of the problem, see Feigl [*Philosophy of Science*, XVII (1950)].

[21] This point is clearly taken into consideration in Ayer's criteria of cognitive significance, which were discussed in section 2.

sentences it entails alone or in conjunction with subsidiary hypotheses, but also what other, non-observational, empirical sentences are entailed by it, what sentences in the given language would confirm or disconfirm it, and for what other hypotheses the given one would be confirmatory or disconfirmatory. In other words, the cognitive meaning of a statement in an empiricist language is reflected in the totality of its logical relationships to all other statements in that language and not to the observation sentences alone. In this sense, the statements of empirical science have a surplus meaning over and above what can be expressed in terms of relevant observation sentences.[22]

6. THE LOGICAL STATUS OF THE EMPIRICIST CRITERION OF MEANING

What kind of a sentence, it has often been asked, is the empiricist meaning criterion itself? Plainly it is not an empirical hypothesis; but it is not analytic or self-contradictory either; hence, when judged by its own standard, is it not devoid of cognitive meaning? In that case, what claim of soundness or validity could possibly be made for it?

One might think of construing the criterion as a definition which indicates what empiricists propose to understand by a cognitively significant sentence; thus understood, it would not have the character of an assertion and would be neither true nor false. But this conception would attribute to the criterion a measure of arbitrariness which cannot be reconciled with the heated controversies it has engendered and even less with the fact, repeatedly illustrated in the present article, that the changes in its specific content have always been determined by the objective of making the criterion a more adequate index of cognitive import. And this very objective illuminates the character of the empiricist criterion of meaning: It is intended to provide a clarification and *explication* of the idea of a sentence which makes an intelligible assertion.[23] This idea is admittedly vague, and it is the task of philosophic explication to replace it by a more precise concept. In view of this difference of precision we cannot demand, of course, that the "new" concept, the explicatum, be strictly synonymous with the old one, the explicandum.[24] How, then, are we to judge the adequacy of a proposed explication, as expressed in some specific criterion of cognitive meaning?

---

[22] For a fuller discussion of the issues here involved *cf.* Feigl [*Philosophy of Science*, XVII (1950)] . . . .

[23] In the preface to the second edition of his book, Ayer takes a very similar position: he holds that the testability criterion is a definition which, however, is not entirely arbitrary, because a sentence which did not satisfy the criterion "would not be capable of being understood in the sense in which either scientific hypotheses or common-sense statements are habitually understood" ([*Op. cit.*], p. 16).

[24] *Cf.* Carnap's characterization of explication in his article [*Philosophy and Phenomenological Research*, LII (1945)], which examines in outline the explication of the concept of probability. The Frege-Russell definition of integers as classes of equivalent classes, and the semantical definition of truth—*cf.* Tarski [*Philosophy and Phenomenological Research*, IV (1944)]—are outstanding examples of explication. For a lucid discussion of various aspects of logical analysis see Pap [*Op. cit.*], Chapter 17.

First of all, there exists a large class of sentences which are rather generally recognized as making intelligible assertions, and another large class of which this is more or less generally denied. We shall have to demand of an adequate explication that it take into account these spheres of common usage; hence an explication which, let us say, denies cognitive import to descriptions of past events or to generalizations expressed in terms of observables has to be rejected as inadequate. As we have seen, this first requirement of adequacy has played an important rôle in the development of the empiricist meaning criterion.

But an adequate explication of the concept of cognitively significant statement must satisfy yet another, even more important, requirement: Together with the explication of certain other concepts, such as those of confirmation and of probability, it has to provide the framework for a general theoretical account of the structure and the foundations of scientific knowledge. Explication, as here understood, is not a mere description of the accepted usages of the terms under consideration: it has to go beyond the limitations, ambiguities, and inconsistencies of common usage and has to show how we had better construe the meanings of those terms if we wish to arrive at a consistent and comprehensive theory of knowledge. This type of consideration, which has been largely influenced by a study of the structure of scientific theories, has prompted the more recent extensions of the empiricist meaning criterion. These extensions are designed to include in the realm of cognitive significance various types of sentences which might occur in advanced scientific theories, or which have to be admitted simply for the sake of systematic simplicity and uniformity,[25] but on whose cognitive significance or non-singificance a study of what the term "intelligible assertion" means in everyday discourse could hardly shed any light at all.

As a consequence, the empiricist criterion of meaning, like the result of any other explication, represents a linguistic proposal which itself is neither true nor false, but for which adequacy is claimed in two respects: First in the sense that the explication provides a reasonably close *analysis* of the commonly accepted meaning of the explicandum—and this claim implies an empirical assertion; and secondly in the sense that the explication achieves a *"rational reconstruction"* of the explicandum, i.e., that it provides, together perhaps with others explications, a general conceptual framework which permits a consistent and precise restatement and theoretical systematization of the contexts in which the explicandum is used—and this claim implies at least an assertion of a logical character.

Though a proposal in form, the empiricist criterion of meaning is therefore far from being an arbitrary definition; it is subject to revision if a violation

---

[25] Thus, e.g., our criterion qualifies as significant certain statements containing, say, thousands of existential or universal quantifiers—even though such sentences may never occur in every-day nor perhaps even in scientific discourse. For indeed, from a systematic point of view it would be arbitrary and unjustifiable to limit the class of significant statements to those containing no more than some fixed number of quantifiers. For further discussion of this point, *cf.* Carnap ["Testability and Meaning"], sections 17, 24, 25.

of the requirements of adequacy, or even a way of satisfying those requirements more fully, should be discovered. Indeed, it is to be hoped that before long some of the open problems encountered in the analysis of cognitive significance will be clarified and that then our last version of the empiricist meaning criterion will be replaced by another, more adequate one.

Bibliographic References

Ayer, A. J. *Language, Truth and Logic.* London: Oxford University Press, 1936; 2nd ed., London: Victor Gollancz, Ltd., 1946.

Benjamin, A. C. "Is Empiricism Self-refuting?" *Journal of Philosophy,* XXXVIII (1941).

Bridgman, P. W. *The Logic of Modern Physics.* New York: The Macmillan Company, 1927.

———. "Operational analysis." *Philosophy of Science,* V (1938).

Carnap, R. *Der Logische Aufbau der Welt.* Berlin, 1928.

———. "Testability and meaning." *Philosophy of Science,* III (1936), and IV (1937).

———. "Logical Foundations of the Unity of Science." *International Encyclopedia of Unified Science,* I, 1. Chicago: University of Chicago Press, 1938.

———. "Foundations of Logic and Mathematics." *International Encyclopedia of Unified Science,* I, 3. Chicago: University of Chicago Press, 1939.

———. "The Two Concepts of Probability." *Philosophy and Phenomenological Research,* V (1945).

Chisholm, R. M. "The Contrary-to-fact Conditional." *Mind,* LV (1946).

Church, A. Review of [Ayer], 2nd ed. *The Journal of Symbolic Logic,* XIV (1949), 52–53.

Feigl, H. "Operationism and scientific method." *The Psychological Review,* LII (1945). (Also reprinted in Feigl and Sellars, *Readings in Philosophical Analysis,* New York, 1949.)

———. "Existential Hypotheses; Realistic vs. Phenomenalistic Interpretations." *Philosophy of Science,* XVII (1950).

Goodman, N. "The problem of counterfactual conditionals." *Journal of Philosophy,* XLIV (1947).

———. *The Structure of Appearance.* Cambridge, Mass.: Harvard University Press, 1951.

Hempel, C. G. and P. Oppenheim. "Studies in the Logic of Explanation." *Philosophy of Science,* XV (1948).

Kaplan, A. "Definition and Specification of Meaning." *Journal of Philosophy,* XLIII (1946).

Langford, C. H. Review in *The Journal of Symbolic Logic,* VI (1941), 67–68.

Lecomte du Noüy. *Human Destiny.* New York, London, Toronto, 1947.

Lewis, C. I. *An Analysis of Knowledge and Valuation.* La Salle, Ill.: Open Court Publ., 1946.

Pap, A. *Elements of Analytic Philosophy.* New York: The Macmillan Company, 1949.

Popper, K. *Logik der Forschung.* Wien: Springer, 1935.

————. *The Open Society and its Enemies.* 2 Vols. London: Routledge & Kegan Paul Ltd. *Mind*, LVIII (1945).

Reichenbach, H. *Philosophie der Raum-Zeit-Lehre.* Berlin, 1928.

————. *Elements of Symbolic Logic.* New York: The Macmillan Company, 1947.

Russell, B. *Human Knowledge.* New York: Simon and Schuster, Inc., 1948.

Schlick, M. "Meaning and Verification." *Philosophical Review*, XLV (1936). (Also reprinted in Feigl and Sellars, *Readings in Philosophical Analysis*, New York, 1949.)

Stace, W. T. "Positivism" *Mind*, LIII (1944).

Tarski, A. "The Semantic Conception of Truth and the Foundations of Semantics." *Philosophy and Phenomenological Research*, IV (1944). (Also reprinted in Feigl and Sellars, *Readings in Philosophical Analysis*, New York, 1949.)

Werkmeister, W. H. *The Basis and Structure of Knowledge.* New York and London: Harper & Row, Publishers, 1948.

Whitehead, A. N. and B. Russell. *Principia Mathematica.* 3 Vols. 2nd ed. Cambridge, 1925–1927.

H. P. GRICE

5.4   *Meaning*

Consider the following sentences:

> "Those spots mean (meant) measles."
> "Those spots didn't mean anything to me, but to the doctor they meant measles."
> "The recent budget means that we shall have a hard year."

(1) I cannot say, "Those spots meant measles, but he hadn't got measles," and I cannot say, "The recent budget means that we shall have a hard year, but we shan't have." That is to say, in cases like the above, *x meant that p* and *x means that p* entail *p*.

(2) I cannot argue from "Those spots mean (meant) measles" to any conclusion about "what is (was) meant by those spots"; for example, I am not entitled to say, "What was meant by those spots was that he had measles." Equally I cannot draw from the statement about the recent budget the conclusion "What is meant by the recent budget is that we shall have a hard year."

(3) I cannot argue from "Those spots meant measles" to any conclusion to the effect that somebody or other meant by those spots so-and-so. *Mutatis mutandis*, the same is true of the sentence about the recent budget.

Reprinted from *The Philosophical Review*, LXVI, No. 3 (1957), 377–88, by permission of the author and of the editor of *The Philosophical Review*.

(4) For none of the above examples can a restatement be found in which the verb "mean" is followed by sentence or phrase in inverted commas. Thus "Those spots meant measles" cannot be reformulated as "Those spots meant 'measles' " or as "Those spots meant 'he has measles'."

(5) On the other hand, for all these examples an approximate restatement can be found beginning with the phrase "The fact that . . . "; for example, "The fact that he had those spots meant that he had measles" and "The fact that the recent budget was as it was means that we shall have a hard year."

Now contrast the above sentences with the following:

> "Those three rings on the bell (of the bus) mean that the 'bus is full'."
> "That remark, 'Smith couldn't get on without his trouble and strife', meant that Smith found his wife indispensable."

(1) I can use the first of these and go on to say, "But it isn't in fact full—the conductor has made a mistake"; and I can use the second and go on, "But in fact Smith deserted her seven years ago." That is to say, here *x means that p* and *x meant that p* do not entail *p*.

(2) I can argue from the first to some statement about "what is (was) meant" by the rings on the bell and from the second to some statement about "what is (was) meant" by the quoted remark.

(3) I can argue from the first sentence to the conclusion that somebody (viz., the conductor) meant, or at any rate should have meant, by the rings that the bus is full, and I can argue analogously for the second sentence.

(4) The first sentence can be restated in a form in which the verb "mean" is followed by a phrase in inverted commas, that is, "Those three rings on the bell mean 'the bus is full'." So also can the second sentence.

(5) Such a sentence as "The fact that the bell has been rung three times means that the bus is full" is not a restatement of the meaning of the first sentence. Both may be true, but they do not have, even approximately, the same meaning.

When the expressions "means," "means something," "means that" are used in the kind of way in which they are used in the first set of sentences, I shall speak of the sense, or senses, in which they are used, as the *natural* sense, or senses, of the expressions in question. When the expressions are used in the kind of way in which they are used in the second set of sentences, I shall speak of the sense, or senses, in which they are used, as the *nonnatural* sense, or senses, of the expressions in question. I shall use the abbreviation "means$_{NN}$" to distinguish the nonnatural sense or senses.

I propose, for convenience, also to include under the head of natural senses of "mean" such senses of "mean" as may be exemplified in sentences of the pattern "*A* means (meant) *to do* so-and-so (by *x*)," where *A* is a human agent. By contrast, as the previous examples show, I include under the head of nonnatural senses of "mean" any senses of "mean" found in sentences of the patterns "*A* means (meant) something by *x*" or "*A* means (meant) by *x* that . . . ." (This is overrigid; but it will serve as an indication.)

I do not want to maintain that *all* our uses of "mean" fall easily, obviously, and tidily into one of the two groups I have distinguished; but I think that in most cases we should be at least fairly strongly inclined to assimilate a use of "mean" to one group rather than to the other. The question which now arises is this: "What more can be said about the distinction between the cases where we should say that the word is applied in a natural sense and the cases where we should say that the word is applied in an nonnatural sense?" Asking this question will not of course prohibit us from trying to give an explanation of "meaning$_{NN}$" in terms of one or another natural sense of "mean."

This question about the distinction between natural and nonnatural meaning is, I think, what people are getting at when they display an interest in a distinction between "natural" and "conventional" signs. But I think my formulation is better. For some things which can mean$_{NN}$ something are not signs (e.g., words are not), and some are not conventional in any ordinary sense (e.g., certain gestures); while some things which mean naturally are not signs of what they mean (*cf.* the recent budget example).

I want first to consider briefly, and reject, what I might term a causal type of answer to the question, "What is meaning$_{NN}$?" We might try to say, for instance, more or less with C. L. Stevenson,[1] that for *x* to mean$_{NN}$ something, *x* must have (roughly) a tendency to produce in an audience some attitude (cognitive or otherwise) and a tendency, in the case of a speaker, to *be* produced *by* that attitude, these tendencies being dependent on "an elaborate process of conditioning attending the use of the sign in communication."[2] This clearly will not do.

(1) Let us consider a case where an utterance, if it qualifies at all as meaning$_{NN}$ something, will be of a descriptive or informative kind and the relevant attitude, therefore, will be a cognitive one, for example, a belief. (I use "utterance" as a neutral word to apply to any candidate for meaning$_{NN}$; it has a convenient act-object ambiguity.) It is no doubt the case that many people have a tendency to put on a tail coat when they think they are about to go to a dance, and it is no doubt also the case that many people, on seeing someone put on a tail coat, would conclude that the person in question was about to go to a dance. Does this satisfy us that putting on a tail coat means$_{NN}$ that one is about to go to a dance (or indeed means$_{NN}$ anything at all)? Obviously not. It is no help to refer to the qualifying phrase "dependent on an elaborate process of conditioning. . . ." For if all this means is that the response to the sight of a tail coat being put on is in some way learned or acquired, it will not exclude the present case from being one of meaning$_{NN}$. But if we have to take seriously the second part of the qualifying phrase ("attending the use of the sign in communication"), then the account of meaning$_{NN}$ is obviously circular. We might just as well say, "*X* has meaning$_{NN}$ if it is used in communication," which, though true, is not helpful.

---

[1] *Ethics and Language* (New Haven, 1944), Ch. iii.
[2] *Ibid.*, p. 57.

(2) If this is not enough, there is a difficulty—really the same difficulty, I think—which Stevenson recognizes: how we are to avoid saying, for example, that "Jones is tall" is part of what is meant by "Jones is an athlete," since to tell someone that Jones is an athlete would tend to make him believe that Jones is tall. Stevenson here resorts to invoking linguistic rules, namely, a permissive rule of language that "athletes may be nontall." This amounts to saying that we are not prohibited by rule from speaking of "nontall athletes." But why are we not prohibited? Not because it is not bad grammar, or is not impolite, and so on, but presumably because it is not meaningless (or, if this is too strong, does not in any way violate the rules of meaning for the expressions concerned). But this seems to involve us in another circle. Moreover, one wants to ask why, if it is legitimate to appeal here to rules to distinguish what is meant from what is suggested, this appeal was not made earlier, in the case of groans, for example, to deal with which Stevenson originally introduced the qualifying phrase about dependence on conditioning.

A further deficiency in a causal theory of the type just expounded seems to be that, even if we accept it as it stands, we are furnished with an analysis only of statements about the *standard* meaning, or the meaning in general, of a "sign." No provision is made for dealing with statements about what a particular speaker or writer means by a sign on a particular occasion (which may well diverge from the standard meaning of the sign); nor is it obvious how the theory could be adapted to make such provision. One might even go further in criticism and maintain that the causal theory ignores the fact that the meaning (in general) of a sign needs to be explained in terms of what users of the sign do (or should) mean by it on particular occasions; and so the latter notion, which is unexplained by the causal theory, is in fact the fundamental one. I am sympathetic to this more radical criticism, though I am aware that the point is controversial.

I do not propose to consider any further theories of the "causal-tendency" type. I suspect no such theory could avoid difficulties analogous to those I have outlined without utterly losing its claim to rank as a theory of this type.

I will now try a different and, I hope, more promising line. If we can elucidate the meaning of

"x meant$_{NN}$ something (on a particular occasion)" and
"x meant$_{NN}$ that so-and-so (on a particular occasion)"

and of

"A meant$_{NN}$ something by x (on a particular occasion)" and
"A meant$_{NN}$ by x that so-and-so (on a particular occasion),"

this might reasonably be expected to help us with

"x means$_{NN}$ (timeless) something (that so-and-so),"
"A means$_{NN}$ (timeless) by x something (that so-and-so),"

and with the explication of "means the same as," "understands," "entails," and so on. Let us for the moment pretend that we have to deal only with utterances which might be informative or descriptive.

A first shot would be to suggest that "x meant$_{NN}$ something" would be true if x was intended by its utterer to induce a belief in some "audience" and that to say what the belief was would be to say what x meant$_{NN}$. This will not do. I might leave B's handkerchief near the scene of a murder in order to induce the detective to believe that B was the murderer; but we should not want to say that the handkerchief (or my leaving it there) meant$_{NN}$ anything or that I had meant$_{NN}$ by leaving it that B was the murderer. Clearly we must at least add that, for x to have meant$_{NN}$ anything, not merely must it have been "uttered" with the intention of inducing a certain belief but also the utterer must have intended an "audience" to recognize the intention behind the utterance.

This, though perhaps better, is not good enough. Consider the following cases:

(1) Herod presents Salome with the head of St. John the Baptist on a charger.
(2) Feeling faint, a child lets its mother see how pale it is (hoping that she may draw her own conclusions and help).
(3) I leave the china my daughter has broken lying around for my wife to see.

Here we seem to have cases which satisfy the conditions so far given for meaning$_{NN}$. For example, Herod intended to make Salome believe that St. John the Baptist was dead and no doubt also intended Salome to recognize that he intended her to believe that St. John the Baptist was dead. Similarly for the other cases. Yet I certainly do not think that we should want to say that we have here cases of meaning$_{NN}$.

What we want to find is the difference between, for example, "deliberately and openly letting someone know" and "telling" and between "getting someone to think" and "telling."

The way out is perhaps as follows. Compare the following two cases:

(1) I show Mr. X a photograph of Mr. Y displaying undue familiarity to Mrs. X.
(2) I draw a picture of Mr. Y behaving in this manner and show it to Mr. X.

I find that I want to deny that in (1) the photograph (or my showing it to Mr. X) meant$_{NN}$ anything at all; while I want to assert that in (2) the picture (or my drawing and showing it) meant$_{NN}$ something (that Mr. Y had been unduly unfamiliar), or at least that I had meant$_{NN}$ by it that Mr. Y had been unduly familiar. What is the difference between the two cases? Surely that in case (1) Mr. X's recognition of my intention to make him believe that there is something between Mr. Y and Mrs. X is (more or less) irrelevant to the production of this effect by the photograph. Mr. X would be led by the photograph at least to suspect Mrs. X even if instead of showing it to him I had left it in his room by accident; and I (the photograph shower) would not be unaware of this. But it will make a difference to the effect of my picture on Mr. X whether or not he takes me to be intending to inform him (make him believe something) about Mrs. X, and not to be just doodling or trying to produce a work of art.

But now we seem to be landed in a further difficulty if we accept this account. For consider now, say, frowning. If I frown spontaneously, in the ordinary course of events, someone looking at me may well treat the frown as a natural sign of displeasure. But if I frown deliberately (to convey my displeasure), an onlooker may be expected, provided he recognizes my intention, *still* to conclude that I am displeased. Ought we not then to say, since it could not be expected to make any difference to the onlooker's reaction whether he regards my frown as spontaneous or as intended to be informative, that my frown (deliberate) does *not* mean$_{NN}$ anything? I think this difficulty can be met; for though in general a deliberate frown may have the same effect (as regards inducing belief in my displeasure) as a spontaneous frown, it can be expected to have the same effect only *provided* the audience takes it as intended to convey displeasure. That is, if we take away the recognition of intention, leaving the other circumstances (including the recognition of the frown as deliberate), the belief-producing tendency of the frown must be regarded as being impaired or destroyed.

Perhaps we may sum up what is necessary for A to mean something by x as follows. A must intend to induce by x a belief in an audience, and he must also intend his utterance to be recognized as so intended. But these intentions are not independent; the recognition is intended by A to play its part in inducing the belief, and if it does not do so something will have gone wrong with the fulfillment of A's intentions. Moreover, A's intending that the recognition should play this part implies, I think, that he assumes that there is some chance that it will in fact play this part, that he does not regard it as a foregone conclusion that the belief will be induced in the audience whether or not the intention behind the utterance is recognized. Shortly, perhaps, we may say that "A meant$_{NN}$ something by x" is roughly equivalent to "A uttered x with the intention of inducing a belief by means of the recognition of this intention." (This seems to involve a reflexive paradox, but it does not really do so.)

Now perhaps it is time to drop the pretense that we have to deal only with "informative" cases. Let us start with some examples of imperatives or quasi-imperatives. I have a very avaricious man in my room, and I want him to go; so I throw a pound note out of the window. Is there here any utterance with a meaning$_{NN}$? No, because in behaving as I did, I did not intend his recognition of my purpose to be in any way effective in getting him to go. This is parallel to the photograph case. If on the other hand I had pointed to the door or given him a little push, then my behavior might well be held to constitute a meaningful$_{NN}$ utterance, just because the recognition of my intention would be intended by me to be effective in speeding his departure. Another pair of cases would be (1) a policeman who stops a car by standing in its way and (2) a policeman who stops a car by waving.

Or, to turn briefly to another type of case, if as an examiner I fail a man, I may well cause him distress or indignation or humiliation; and if I am vindictive, I may intend this effect and even intend him to recognize my intention. But I should not be inclined to say that my failing him meant$_{NN}$ anything. On the other hand, if I cut someone in the street I do feel inclined to assimilate this to the cases of meaning$_{NN}$, and this inclination seems to me dependent on the fact that I could not reasonably expect him to be distressed (indignant, humiliated) unless he recognized my intention to affect him in this way. (*Cf.*, if my college stopped my salary altogether I should accuse them of ruining me; if they cut it by 2/6^d I might accuse them of insulting me; with some intermediate amounts I might not know quite what to say.)

Perhaps then we may make the following generalizations.

(1) "*A* meant$_{NN}$ something by *x*" is (roughly) equivalent to "*A* intended the utterance of *x* to produce some effect in an audience by means of the recognition of this intention"; and we may add that to ask what *A* meant is to ask for a specification of the intended effect (though, of course, it may not always be possible to get a straight answer involving a "that" clause, for example, "a belief that . . .").

(2) "*x* meant something" is (roughly) equivalent to "Somebody meant$_{NN}$ something by *x*." Here again there will be cases where this will not quite work. I feel inclined to say that (as regards traffic lights) the change to red meant$_{NN}$ that the traffic was to stop; but it would be very unnatural to say, "Somebody (e.g., the Corporation) meant$_{NN}$ by the red-light change that the traffic was to stop." Nevertheless, there seems to be *some* sort of reference to somebody's intentions.

(3) "*x* means$_{NN}$ (timeless) that so-and-so" might as a first shot be equated with some statement or disjunction of statements about what "people" (vague) intend (with equalifications about "recognition") to effect by *x*. I shall have a word to say about this.

Will any kind of intended effect do, or may there be cases where an effect is intended (with the required qualifications) and yet we should not want to talk of meaning$_{NN}$? Suppose I discovered some person so constituted that, when I told him that whenever I grunted in a special way I wanted him to blush or to incur some physical malady, thereafter whenever he recognized the grunt (and with it my intention), he did blush or incur the malady. Should we then want to say that the grunt meant$_{NN}$ something? I do not think so. This points to the fact that for *x* to have meaning$_{NN}$, the intended effect must be something which in some sense is within the control of the audience, or that in some sense of "reason" the recognition of the intention behind *x* is for the audience a reason and not merely a cause. It might look as if there is a sort of pun here ("reason for believing" and "reason for doing"), but I do not think this is serious. For though no doubt from one point of view questions about reasons for believing are questions about evidence and so quite different from questions about reasons for doing, nevertheless to recognize an utterer's intention in uttering *x* (descriptive utterance), to have a reason for believing that so-and-so, is at least quite like "having a motive for" accepting so-and-so. Decisions "that" seem to involve decisions "to" (and this is why we can "refuse to believe" and also be "compelled to believe").

(The "cutting" case needs slightly different treatment, for one cannot in any straightforward sense "decide" to be offended; but one can refuse to be offended.) It looks then as if the intended effect must be something within the control of the audience, or at least the *sort* of thing which is within its control.

One point before passing to an objection or two. I think it follows that from what I have said about the connection between meaning$_{NN}$ and recognition of intention that (insofar as I am right) only what I may call the primary intention of an utterer is relevant to the meaning$_{NN}$ of an utterance. For if I utter x, intending (with the aid of the recognition of this intention) to induce an effect E, and intend this effect E to lead to a further effect F, then insofar as the occurrence of F is thought to be dependent solely on E, I cannot regard F as in the least dependent on recognition of my intention to induce E. That is, if (say) I intend to get a man to do something by giving him some information, it cannot be regarded as relevant to the meaning$_{NN}$ of my utterance to describe what I intend him to do.

Now some question may be raised about my use, fairly free, of such words as "intention" and "recognition." I must disclaim any intention of peopling all our talking life with armies of complicated psychological occurrences. I do not hope to solve any philosophical puzzles about intending, but I do want briefly to argue that no special difficulties are raised by my use of the word "intention" in connection with meaning. First, there will be cases where an utterance is accompanied or preceded by a conscious "plan," or explicit formulation of intention (e.g., I declare how I am going to use x, or ask myself how to "get something across"). The presence of such an explicit "plan" obviously counts fairly heavily in favor of the utterer's intention (meaning) being as "planned"; though it is not, I think, conclusive; for example, a speaker who has declared an intention to use a familiar expression in an unfamiliar way may slip into the familiar use. Similarly in nonlinguistic cases: if we are asking about an agent's intention, a previous expression counts heavily; nevertheless, a man might plan to throw a letter in the dustbin and yet take it to the post; when lifting his hand he might "come to" and say *either* "I didn't intend to do this at all" *or* "I suppose I must have been intending to put it in."

Explicitly formulated linguistic (or quasi-linguistic) intentions are no doubt comparatively rare. In their absence we would seem to rely on very much the same kinds of criteria as we do in the case of nonlinguistic intentions where there is a general usage. An utterer is held to intend to convey what is normally conveyed (or normally intended to be conveyed), and we require a good reason for accepting that a particular use diverges from the general usage (e.g., he never knew or had forgotten the general usage). Similarly in nonlinguistic cases: we are presumed to intend the normal consequences of our actions.

Again, in cases where there is doubt, say, about which of two or more things an utterer intends to convey, we tend to refer to the context (linguistic or otherwise) of the utterance and ask which of the alternatives would be relevant to other things he is saying or doing, or which intention in a particular situation would fit in with some purpose he obviously has (e.g., a man who calls for a "pump" at a fire would not want a bicycle pump). Nonlinguistic parallels are obvious: context is a criterion in settling the question of why a man who has just put a cigarette in his mouth has put his hand in his pocket; relevance to an obvious end is a criterion in settling why a man is running away from a bull.

In certain linguistic cases we ask the utterer afterward about his intention, and in a few of these cases (the very difficult ones, like a philosopher asked to explain the meaning of an unclear passage in one of his works), the answer is not based on what he remembers but is more like a decision, a decision about how what he said is to be taken. 1 cannot find a nonlinguistic parallel here; but the case is so special as not to seem to contribute a vital difference.

All this is very obvious; but surely to show that the criteria for judging linguistic intentions are very like the criteria for judging nonlinguistic intentions is to show that linguistic intentions are very like nonlinguistic intentions.

PAUL ZIFF

5.5   *On H. P. Grice's Account of Meaning*

Because I believe the coin is counterfeit, because it seems to be gaining currency, I mean to examine and attempt to discredit an account of meaning circulated some time ago by H. P. Grice.[1]

Those among us concerned with problems of semantics are much concerned with the sense(s) or meaning(s) of the morpheme "mean" in (1) and (2):

    (1) The sentence 'Snow is white' means snow is white.
    (2) The adjective 'ungulate' means having hoofs.

Other senses or meanings of 'mean' are of interest in semantics primarily only in so far as they have some bearing on 'mean' in either (1) or (2).

Grice's paper is entitled "Meaning". It appears to be an account of meaning that is supposed to have some bearing on the senses of 'mean' in (1) and (2).

Grice apparently says that 'mean' in (1) and (2) is used in what he calls "nonnatural" senses of the verb. He uses the abbreviation 'mean-nn' to mark the "nonnatural" senses of 'mean'. He offers something of an analysis of 'mean-nn' (and of the morphological variants, 'mean-nn', 'means-nn', and so forth).

Reprinted from *Analysis*, XXVIII, No. 1 (October 1967), 1–8, by permission of the author and of the editor of *Analysis*.
[1] "Meaning", *The Philosophical Review*, LXVI, No. 3 (1957) 377–88. [See above, pp. 436–44.]

Does 'mean' in (1) or (2) have the sense(s) indicated by Grice's analysis?

It will simplify matters to adopt the following convention: when the expression 'mean-nn' (or any of its variants) is used here, that expression is to have the sense(s) indicated by and in conformance with Grice's analysis. The problem of this paper can then be stated in a simple way

Consider (1nn) and (2nn):

> (1nn) The sentence 'Snow is white' means-nn snow is white.
> (2nn) The adjective 'ungulate' means-nn having hoofs.

Is (1nn) simply a restatement of (1), (2nn) of (2)?

After an ingenious intricate discussion, Grice arrives at the following "generalizations" (p. 385):

> (i) '*A* meant-nn something by *x*' is (roughly) equivalent to '*A* intended the utterance of *x* to produce some effect in an audience by means of recognition of this intention'.
> (ii) '*x* meant-nn something' is (roughly) equivalent to 'Somebody meant-nn something by *x*'.
> (iii) '*x* means-nn (timeless) that so-and-so' might as first shot be equated with some statement or disjunction of statements about what "people" (vague) intend (with qualifications about "recognition") to effect by *x*.

It is indicated in the discussion that the letter '*A*' is supposed to be replaceable by the name of a person, that the letter '*x*' may be but need not be replaced by a sentence.

Thus it is evident that Grice's account is supposed to apply to sentence (1) and so to (1nn). Although he mentions words in the course of his discussion, none of the "generalizations" appear to apply to words. Thus apparently he is not concerned to supply, in the paper in question, an account of the sense of 'means' in (2). Consequently, I mean to forget about (2) and (2nn) and be concerned here only with (1) and (1nn)

Of the three "generalizations" stated, (iii) is the only one that directly applies to (1nn). Unfortunately, (iii) is not particularly pellucid. (Even so, what emerges from the fog will be sufficient to establish certain points.) Let us begin by examining (i) and (ii) in the hope of gaining insight into (iii).

On being inducted into the army, George is compelled to take a test designed to establish sanity. George is known to be an irritable academic. The test he is being given would be appropriate for morons. One of the questions asked is: 'What would you say if you were asked to identify yourself?' George replied to the officer asking the question by uttering (3):

> (3) Ugh ugh blugh blugh ugh blug blug.

According to the dictum of (i), George meant-nn something by (3): he intended the utterance of (3) to produce an effect in his audience by means of the recognition of his intention. The effect he intended was that of offending his audience. The accomplishment of this effect depended on the recognition of his intention. (The case in question is also in accordance with the various caveats noted by Grice in the course of his discussion: the officer testing George could "refuse to be offended", thus the intended effect was in some sense within the control of the audience; George's intention to offend was his "primary" intention; and so forth.) Consequently, as far as one can tell, (3) fills Grice's bill.

But even though it is clear that George meant-nn something by (3), it is equally clear that George did not mean anything by (3). Grice seems to have conflated and confused '*A* meant something by uttering *x*', which is true in a case like (3), with the quite different '*A* meant something by *x*', which is untrue in a case like (3).

The malady just noted in connection with (i) of course at once infects (ii). For even though it is clear that George meant-nn something by (3) and hence (3) meant-nn something, it is equally clear that (3) did not mean anything. Indeed, had (3) meant anything, that would have defeated George's purpose in uttering (3).

The preceding case admits of the following variation. On being given the test over again by another officer, instead of uttering (3), George uttered (4):

 (4) pi.hi.y pi.hi.y

Again in accordance with (i) we can say that George meant-nn something by by (4) and what he meant-nn was precisely what he meant-nn by (3). (For we may suppose that he had the same intention in each case, expected the same reaction, and so forth.)

But in this case, not only did George mean something by uttering (4), he also meant something by (4): even though he rightly expected his utterance to be treated as though it were mere noise, what he meant by (4), and what he said, was that he didn't know George was perversely speaking in Hopi.[2] (Here one need not confuse 'George did not mean what he said', which is true, for he did know the answer to the question, with the quite different 'George did not mean anything by (4)', which is untrue.)

That George meant-nn something by (4) is wholly irrelevant to the question whether George meant something by (4). And the fact that (4) meant-nn something (in virtue of (ii)) is wholly irrelevant to the question whether (4) meant anything. This should be obvious from the fact that what (4) meant had nothing whatever to do with what George intended to effect by uttering the utterance and hence had nothing whatever to do with what (4) meant-nn.

The curious character of (ii) can be further displayed by the following sort of cases. Consider (5):

 (5) Claudius murdered my father.

and let us conjure up three contexts of utterance: (a) George uttered a sentence token of type (5), thus he uttered (5a), in the course of a morning soliloquy; (b) George uttered another such token, (5b), in the afternoon in the course of a discussion with Josef; and (c) George uttered another such token, (5c), in the evening while delerious with fever. Now consider (6) and (6nn):

 (6) (5a) meant the same as (5b) which meant the same as
      (5c) which meant the same as (5a).

---

[2] See B. Whorf, *Language, Thought, and Reality* (Cambridge: The Technology Press, 1956), p. 114, for the phonetic significance of (4).

where (6nn) is the same as (6) save that for each occurrence of 'meant' in (6), (6nn) has an occurrence of 'meant-nn'. Thus (6) says that the three tokens in question all had the same meaning; (6nn) says that they all had the same meaning-nn.

Although (6) is true, according to Grice's account (6nn) must be false (here taking (6) and (6nn) to stand for statements). That this is so can be seen as follows.

According to (ii), a sentence S meant-nn something (roughly) if and only if somebody meant-nn something by it. Thus (5a), (5b), and (5c) meant-nn something (roughly) if and only if somebody meant-nn something by them.

Did anyone mean-nn anything by (5c)? Evidently not. For (5c) was uttered while George was delerious with fever, unaware of any audience. Hence (5c) was not intended to produce any effect in an audience. (Here one need not confuse 'What George said meant nothing', which may be true in one sense of 'what George said', with 'The expression which George uttered meant nothing', which is untrue.)

Did anyone mean-nn anything by (5b)? Presumably so. Since (5b) was uttered by George in the course of a discussion with Josef, if anything fits Grice's account, (5b) does.

Did anyone mean-nn anything by (5a)? It would seem not, for since George uttered (5a) in the course of a soliloquy, it could hardly have been intended to produce an effect in an audience. (But perhaps Grice would wish to maintain that, in so far as George was speaking to himself, he was his own audience. But then could he intend to produce an effect in himself by means of a recognition on his own part of his own intention? These are mysteries we may cheerfully bequeath to Mr. Grice.)

Evidently (6nn) is untrue even though (6) is true.

Sentence token (5c) exemplifies a case in which even though it was not true that the speaker meant anything by the token, the token nonetheless meant something. One can also produce cases in which a speaker did mean something by an utterance and yet the utterance itself did not mean anything.

George has had his head tampered with: electrodes have been inserted, plates mounted, and so forth. The effect was curious: when asked how he felt, George replied by uttering (7):

(7) Glyting elly beleg.

What he meant by (7), he later informed us, was that he felt fine. He said that, at the time, he had somehow believed that (7) was synonymous with 'I feel fine' and that everyone knew this.

According to (i), George meant-nn something by (7), and according to (ii), (7) must have meant-nn something. But (7) did not mean anything at all.

The preceding examples should suffice to indicate that Grice's equivalences (i) and (ii) are untenable. But their extraordinary character can be made even plainer by the following sort of case.

A man suddenly cried out 'Gleeg gleeg gleeg!', intending thereby to produce a certain effect in an audience by means of the recognition of his intention.

He wished to make his audience believe that it was snowing in Tibet. Of course he did not produce the effect he was after since no one recognized what his intention was. Nonetheless that he had such an intention became clear. Being deemed mad, he was turned over to a psychiatrist. He complained to the psychiatrist that when he cried 'Gleeg gleeg gleeg!' he had such an intention but no one recognized his intention and were they not mad not to do so.

According to Grice's equivalence (i), the madman meant-nn something by 'Gleeg gleeg gleeg!' and so, according to (ii), the madman's cry must have meant-nn something, presumably that it was snowing in Tibet. But the madman's cry did not mean anything at all; it certainly did not mean it was snowing in Tibet. Had it meant that, there would have been less reason to turn him over to a psychiatrist.

On Grice's account, good intentions suffice to convert nonsense to sense: the road to Babble is paved with such intentions.

It is time to turn to Grice's suggestion of an equivalence, (iii). Consider sentences (8), (9), and (9nn):

(8) He's a son of a stickleback fish.
(9) Sentence (9) means the male referred to is a son of a small scaleless fish (family Gasterosteidae) having two or more free spines in front of the dorsal fin.

where (9nn) is the same as (9) save that (as in (6nn)) 'means' has given way to 'means-nn'.

I take it that there is no reason whatever to suppose that the sense of 'means' in (9) differs in any way from the sense of 'means' in (1). Both (9) and (1) are simply of the form: sentence S means m. But if 'means' in (9) has precisely the same sense as 'means' in (1), it follows that (1nn) is not simply a restatement of (1). For (1) and (1nn) differ as (9) and (9nn) differ, and according to Grice's account, (9) and (9nn) are radically different. That this is so can be seen as follows.

I am inclined to suppose that (8) has been uttered only rarely. Nonetheless (taking (9) and (9nn) to stand for statements), I am reasonably certain that (9) is a reasonably correct statement of the meaning of (S) and I am being reasonable in being so certain.

If it is a correct statement of the meaning of (8), and if (9nn) is simply a restatement of (9), since (9nn) is, (9) must be equivalent to some statement or disjunction of statements about what "people" intend to effect by (8). So Grice evidently maintains; for despite its vagueness, that is what is indicated by (iii).

But the question 'What do people intend to effect by (8)?' would not be a sensible question. Since hardly anyone has ever uttered (8) before, or so I suppose, one can hardly ask what people intend to effect by it.

'Then what would people intend to effect by (8)?': the question is somewhat idle. What people would intend to effect by (8) is a matter about which one can only speculate, vaguely. However, since the obvious emendation of Grice's account invites such speculation, let us speculate.

What would people intend to effect by uttering (8)? Given the acoustic similarity between (8) and a familiar form of expression, given that stickle-backs are known to be tough fish, given that the sex of a fish is not readily determined by the uninitiated, most likely by uttering (8) people would thereby intend to denigrate a contextually indicated male person.

What people would intend to effect by (8) is a subject for profitless specula-tion. But if one must say something about the matter, I am inclined to suppose that (9nn) does not convey a correct account of what people would intend to effect by uttering (8). Thus (9nn) is presumably untrue.

If (9nn) were simply a restatement of (9), only a fool would profess to being even reasonably certain that (9) is a correct statement and it would be un-reasonable of him to be so certain. But I am reasonably certain that (9) is a correct statement of the meaning of (8) and I am not being unreasonable in being so certain. Therefore (9nn) cannot be simply a restatement of (9) and neither can (1nn) be simply a restatement of (1).

Before allowing Grice's analysis to rest in peace, the moral of its passing should be emphasised.

His suggestion is stated in terms of what people "intend", not in terms of what they "would intend". As such it obviously occasions difficulty with novel utterances. But matters are not at all improved by switching to what people "would intend".

For first, if a sentence is such that people in general simply would not utter it, then if they were to utter it, what they would intend to effect by uttering it might very well have nothing to do with the meaning of the sentence. What would a person intend to effect by uttering the sentence 'Snow is white and snow is white and snow is white and snow is white and snow is white'? I conjecture that a person uttering such a sentence would be either a philosopher or a linguist or an avant-garde novelist or a child at play or a Chinese torturer. What people would intend to effect by uttering such a sentence would most likely have nothing whatever to do with the meaning of the sentence.

Secondly, the switch to 'would' would be of help only if there were a con-structive method of determining what people would intend to effect by uttering an utterance. There is no such method. There is not likely to be any (at least in our lifetime).

Ignoring the futility of talking about what people "would intend" to effect by uttering an utterance, one need not ignore the fact that what people gen-erally in fact mean may be altogether irrelevant to a meaning of an utterance.

By the spoken utterance 'HE GAVE HIM HELL' people generally mean what is meant by the written utterance 'He gave him hell' and not what is meant by the written utterance 'He gave him Hell'. Quite possibly no one has ever said 'I saw the children shooting' meaning by that he saws children while he is shooting. That is nonetheless one of the meanings of that remarkably ambiguous sentence. Indefinitely many such examples could be supplied.

To be concerned with what people intend (or would intend) to effect by uttering an expression is to be concerned with the use of the expression. As I have elsewhere pointed out and argued at length, the use of an expression is determined by many factors, many of which have nothing (or have nothing directly) to do with its meaning: acoustic shape is one such factor, length another.[3]

Grice's analysis rings untrue. It was bound to; his alloy lacks the basic ingredient of meaning: a set of projective devices. The syntactic and semantic structure of any natural language is essentially recursive in character. What any given sentence means depends on what (various) other sentences in the language mean.

That people generally intend (or would intend) this or that by uttering an utterance has, at best, as much significance as a statement to the effect that when 'Pass the salt!' is uttered, generally people are eating, thus what I have elsewhere called the statement of a "regularity".[4] Not all regularities are semantically relevant: a regularity couched in terms of people's "intentions" is not likely to be.

But even if such regularities were somehow relevant, that would not matter much. A regularity is no more than a ladder which one climbs and then kicks away. An account of meaning constituted by (i), (ii), and (iii) never gets off the ground. There is no reason to suppose it can.[5]

DONALD DAVIDSON

5.6   *Truth and Meaning*

It is conceded by most philosophers of language, and recently even by some linguists, that a satisfactory theory of meaning must give an account of how the meanings of sentences depend upon the meanings of words. Unless such an account could be supplied for a particular language, it is argued, there would be no explaining the fact that we can learn the language: no explaining the fact that, on mastering a finite vocabulary and a finitely stated set of rules, we are prepared to produce and to understand any of a potential infinitude of sentences. I do not dispute these vague claims, in which I sense more than a kernel of truth.[1] Instead I want to ask what it is for a theory to give an account of the kind adumbrated.

One proposal is to begin by assigning some entity as meaning to each word

---

[3] See my *Semantic Analysis* (Ithaca: Cornell University Press, 1960).

[4] *Op. cit.*

[5] I am indebted to D. Stampe for useful criticisms of various points.

Reprinted from *Synthese*, XVII, No. 3 (1967), 304–323, by permission of the author and of the editor of *Synthese*.

[1] Elsewhere I have urged that it is a necessary condition, if a language is to be learnable, that it have only a finite number of semantical primitives: see "Theories of Meaning and Learnable Languages," in *Proceedings of the 1964 International Congress for Logic, Methodology and Philosophy of Science*, (Amsterdam: North-Holland Publishing Company, 1965), pp. 383–94.

(or other significant syntactical feature) of the sentence; thus we might assign Theaetetus to 'Theaetetus' and the property of flying to 'flies' in the sentence 'Theaetetus flies'. The problem then arises how the meaning of the sentence is generated from these meanings. Viewing concatenation as a significant piece of syntax, we may assign to it the relation of participating in or instantiating; however, it is obvious that we have here the start of an infinite regress. Frege sought to avoid the regress by saying that the entities corresponding to predicates (for example) are 'unsaturated' or 'incomplete' in contrast to the entities that correspond to names, but this doctrine seems to label a difficulty rather than solve it.

The point will emerge if we think for a moment of complex singular terms, to which Frege's theory applies along with sentences. Consider the expression 'the father of Annette'; how does the meaning of the whole depend on the meaning of the parts? The answer would seem to be that the meaning of 'the father of' is such that when this expression is prefixed to a singular term the result refers to the father of the person to whom the singular term refers. What part is played, in this account, by the unsaturated or incomplete entity for which 'the father of' stands? All we can think to say is that this entity 'yields' or 'gives' the father of x as value when the argument is x, or perhaps that this entity maps people onto their fathers. It may not be clear whether the entity for which 'the father of' is said to stand performs any genuine explanatory function as long as we stick to individual expressions; so think instead of the infinite class of expressions formed by writing 'the father of' zero or more times in front of 'Annette'. It is easy to supply a theory that tells, for an arbitrary one of these singular terms, what it refers to: if the term is 'Annette' it refers to Annette, while if the term is complex, consisting of 'the father of' prefixed to a singular term t, then it refers to the father of the person to whom t refers. It is obvious that no entity corresponding to 'the father of' is, or needs to be, mentioned in stating this theory.

It would be inappropriate to complain that this little theory *uses* the words 'the father of' in giving the reference of expressions containing those words. For the task was to give the meaning of all expressions in a certain infinite set on the basis of the meaning of the parts; it was not in the bargain also to give the meanings of the atomic parts. On the other hand, it is now evident that a satisfactory theory of the meanings of complex expressions may not require entities as meanings of all the parts. It behooves us then to rephrase our demand on a satisfactory theory of meaning so as not to suggest that individual words must have meanings at all, in any sense that transcends the fact that they have a systematic effect on the meanings of the sentences in which they occur. Actually, for the case at hand we can do better still in stating the criterion of success: what we wanted, and what we got, is a theory that entails every sentence of the form 't refers to x' where 't' is replaced by a structural description[2] of a singular term, and 'x' is replaced by that term itself. Further,

---

[2] A 'structural description' of an expression describes the expression as a concatenation of elements drawn from a fixed finite list (for example of words or letters).

our theory accomplishes this without appeal to any semantical concepts beyond the basic 'refers to'. Finally, the theory clearly suggests an effective procedure for determining, for any singular term in its universe, what that term refers to.

A theory with such evident merits deserves wider application. The device proposed by Frege to this end has a brilliant simplicity: count predicates as a special case of functional expressions, and sentences as a special case of complex singular terms. Now, however, a difficulty looms if we want to continue in our present (implicit) course of identifying the meaning of a singular term with its reference. The difficulty follows upon making two reasonable assumptions: that logically equivalent singular terms have the same reference; and that a singular term does not change its reference if a contained singular term is replaced by another with the same reference. But now suppose that 'R' and 'S' abbreviate any two sentences alike in truth value. Then the following four sentences have the same reference:

(1) R
(2) $\hat{x}(x = x.R) = \hat{x}(x = x)$
(3) $\hat{x}(x = x.S) = \hat{x}(x = x)$
(4) S

For (1) and (2) are logically equivalent, as are (3) and (4), while (3) differs from (2) only in containing the singular term '$\hat{x}(x = x.S)$' where (2) contains '$\hat{x}(x = x.R)$' and these refer to the same thing if S and R are alike in truth value. Hence any two sentences have the same reference if they have the same truth value.[3] And if the meaning of a sentences is what it refers to, all sentences alike in truth value must be synonymous—an intolerable result.

Apparently we must abandon the present approach as leading to a theory of meaning. This is the natural point at which to turn for help to the distinction between meaning and reference. The trouble, we are told, is that questions of reference are, in general, settled by extra-linguistic facts, questions of meaning not, and the facts can conflate the references of expressions that are not synonymous. If we want a theory that gives the meaning (as distinct from reference) of each sentence, we must start with the meaning (as distinct from reference) of the parts.

Up to here we have been following in Frege's footsteps; thanks to him, the path is well known and even well worn. But now, I would like to suggest, we have reached an impasse: the switch from reference to meaning leads to no useful account of how the meanings of sentences depend upon the meanings of the words (or other structural features) that compose them. Ask, for example, for the meaning of 'Theaetetus flies'. A Fregean answer might go something like this: given the meaning of 'Theaetetus' as argument, the meaning of 'flies' yields the meaning of 'Theaetetus flies' as value. The vacuity of this

---

[3] The argument is essentially Frege's. See A. Church, *Introduction to Mathematical Logic*, Vol. I (Princeton, 1956), pp. 24–25. It is perhaps worth mentioning that the argument does not depend on any particular identification of the entities to which sentences are supposed to refer.

answer is obvious. We wanted to know what the meaning of 'Theaetetus flies' is; it is no progress to be told that it is the meaning of 'Theaetetus flies'. This much we knew before any theory was in sight. In the bogus account just given, talk of the structure of the sentence and of the meanings of words was idle, for it played no role in producing the given description of the meaning of the sentence.

The contrast here between a real and pretended account will be plainer still if we ask for a theory, analogous to the miniature theory of reference of singular terms just sketched, but different in dealing with meanings in place of references. What analogy demands is a theory that has as consequences all sentences of the form '*s* means *m*' where '*s*' is replaced by a structural description of a sentence and '*m*' is replaced by a singular term that refers to the meaning of that sentence; a theory, moreover, that provides an effective method for arriving at the meaning of an arbitrary sentence structurally described. Clearly some more articulate way of referring to meanings than any we have seen is essential if these criteria are to be met.[4] Meanings as entities, or the related concept of synonymy, allow us to formulate the following rule relating sentences and their parts: sentences are synonymous whose corresponding parts are synonymous ('corresponding' here needs spelling out of course). And meanings as entities may, in theories such as Frege's, do duty, on occasion as references, thus losing their status as entities distinct from references. Paradoxically, the one thing meanings do not seem to do is oil the wheels of a theory of meaning—at least as long as we require of such a theory that it non-trivially give the meaning of every sentence in the language. My objection to meanings in the theory of meaning is not that they are abstract or that their identity conditions are obscure, but that they have no demonstrated use.

This is the place to scotch another hopeful thought. Suppose we have a satisfactory theory of syntax for our language, consisting of an effective method of telling, for an arbitrary expression, whether or not it is independently meaningful (i.e., a sentence), and assume as usual that this involves viewing each sentence as composed, in allowable ways, out of elements drawn from a fixed finite stock of atomic syntactical elements (roughly, words). The hopeful thought is that syntax, so conceived, will yield semantics when a dictionary giving the meaning of each syntactic atom is added. Hopes will be dashed, however, if semantics is to comprise a theory of meaning in our sense, for knowledge of the structural characteristics that make for meaningfulness in a sentence, plus knowledge of the meanings of the ultimate parts, does not add up to knowledge of what a sentence means. The point is easily illustrated by belief sentences. Their syntax is relatively unproblematic. Yet, adding a dictionary does not touch the standard semantic problem, which is that we

---

[4] It may be thought that Church, in "A Formulation of the Logic of Sense and Denotation," in *Structure, Method and Meaning: Essays in Honor of H. M. Sheffer*, ed. Henle, Kallen, and Langer, (New York: Liberal Arts Press, 1951), pp. 3–24, has given a theory of meaning that makes essential use of meanings as entities. But this is not the case: Church's logics of sense and denotation are interpreted as being about meanings, but they do not mention expressions and so cannot of course be theories of meaning in the sense now under discussion.

cannot account for even as much as the truth conditions of such sentences on the basis of what we know of the meanings of the words in them. The situation is not radically altered by refining the dictionary to indicate which meaning or meanings an ambiguous expression bears in each of its possible contexts; the problem of belief sentences persists after ambiguities are resolved.

The fact that recursive syntax with dictionary added is not necessarily recursive semantics has been obscured in some recent writing on linguistics by the intrusion of semantic criteria into the discussion of purportedly syntactic theories. The matter would boil down to a harmless difference over terminology if the semantic criteria were clear; but they are not. While there is agreement that it is the central task of semantics to give the semantic interpretation (the meaning) of every sentence in the language, nowhere in the linguistic literature will one find, so far as I know, a straightforward account of how a theory performs this task, or how to tell when it has been accomplished. The contrast with syntax is striking. The main job of a modest syntax is to characterize *meaningfulness* (or sentencehood). We may have as much confidence in the correctness of such a characterization as we have in the representativeness of our sample and our ability to say when particular expressions are meaningful (sentences). What clear and analogous task and test exist for semantics?[5]

We decided a while back not to assume that parts of sentences have meanings except in the ontologically neutral sense of making a systematic contribution to the meaning of the sentences in which they occur. Since postulating meanings has netted nothing, let us return to that insight. One direction in which it points is a certain holistic view of meaning. If sentences depend for their meaning on their structure, and we understand the meaning of each item in the structure only as an abstraction from the totality of sentences in which it features, then we can give the meaning of any sentence (or word) only by giving the meaning of every sentence (and word) in the language. Frege said that only in the context of a sentence does a word have meaning; in the same vein he might have added that only in the context of the language does a sentence (and therefore a word) have meaning.

This degree of holism was already implicit in the suggestion that an adequate theory of meaning must entail *all* sentences of the form '*s* means *m*'. But now, having found no more help in meanings of sentences than in meanings of words, let us ask whether we can get rid of the troublesome singular terms supposed to replace '*m*' and to refer to meanings. In a way, nothing could

---

[5] For a recent and instructive statement of the role of semantics in linguistics, see Noam Chomsky, "Topics in the Theory of Generative Grammar," in *Current Trends in Linguistics* ed. Thomas A. Sebeok, Vol. III (The Hague, 1966). In this article, Chomsky (1) emphasizes the central importance of semantics in linguistic theory, (2) argues for the superiority of transformational grammars over phrase structure grammars largely on the grounds that, although phrase structure grammars may be adequate to define sentencehood for (at least) some natural languages, they are inadequate as a foundation for semantics, and (3) comments repeatedly on the "rather primitive state" of the concepts of semantics and remarks that the notion of semantic interpretation "still resists any deep analysis."

be easier: just write '*s* means that *p*', and imagine '*p*' replaced by a sentence. Sentences, as we have seen, cannot name meanings, and sentences with 'that' prefixed are not names at all, unless we decide so. It looks as though we are in trouble on another count, however, for it is reasonable to expect that in wrestling with the logic of the apparently non-extensional 'means that' we will encounter problems as hard as, or perhaps identical with, the problems our theory is out to solve.

The only way I know to deal with this difficulty is simple, and radical. Anxiety that we are enmeshed in the intensional springs from using the words 'means that' as filling between description of sentence and sentence, but it may be that the success of our venture depends not on the filling but on what it fills. The theory will have done its work if it provides, for every sentence *s* in the language under study, a matching sentence (to replace '*p*') that, in some way yet to be made clear, 'gives the meaning' of *s*. One obvious candidate for matching sentence is just *s* itself, if the object language is contained in the metalanguage; otherwise a translation of *s* in the metalanguage. As a final bold step, let us try treating the position occupied by '*p*' extensionally: to implement this, sweep away the obscure 'means that', provide the sentence that replaces '*p*' with a proper sentential connective, and supply the description that replaces '*s*' with its own predicate. The plausible result is

   (*T*) *s* is *T* if and only if *p*.

What we require of a theory of meaning for a language *L* is that without appeal to any (further) semantical notions it place enough restrictions on the predicate 'is *T*' to entail all sentences got from schema *T* when '*s*' is replaced by a structural description of a sentence of *L* and '*p*' by that sentence.

Any two predicates satisfying this condition have the same extension,[6] so if the metalanguage is rich enough, nothing stands in the way of putting what I am calling a theory of meaning into the form of an explicit definition of a predicate 'is *T*'. But whether explicitly defined or recursively characterized, it is clear that the sentences to which the predicate 'is *T*' applies will be just the true sentences of *L*, for the condition we have placed on satisfactory theories of meaning is in essence Tarski's Convention *T* that tests the adequacy of a formal semantical definition of truth.[7]

The path to this point has been tortuous, but the conclusion may be stated simply: a theory of meaning for a language *L* shows 'how the meanings of sentences depend upon the meanings of words' if it contains a (recursive) definition of truth-in-L. And, so far at least, we have no other idea how to turn the trick. It is worth emphasizing that the concept of truth played no ostensible role in stating our original problem. That problem, upon refinement, led to the view that an adequate theory of meaning must characterize a predicate meeting certain conditions. It was in the nature of a discovery

---

[6] Assuming, of course, that the extension of these predicates is limited to the sentences of *L*.

[7] Alfred Tarski, "The Concept of Truth in Formalized Languages," in *Logic, Semantics, Metamathematics*, (Oxford, 1956), pp. 152–278.

that such a predicate would apply exactly to the true sentences. I hope that what I am doing may be described in part as defending the philosophical importance of Tarski's semantical concept of truth. But my defense is only distantly related, if at all, to the question whether the concept Tarski has shown how to define is the (or a) philosophically interesting conception of truth, or the question whether Tarski has cast any light on the ordinary use of such words as 'true' and 'truth'. It is a misfortune that dust from futile and confused battles over these questions has prevented those with a theoretical interest in language—philosophers, logicians, psychologists, and linguists alike —from recognizing in the semantical concept of truth (under whatever name) the sophisticated and powerful foundation of a competent theory of meaning.

There is no need to suppress, of course, the obvious connection between a definition of truth of the kind Tarski has shown how to construct, and the concept of meaning. It is this: the definition works by giving necessary and sufficient conditions for the truth of every sentence, and to give truth conditions is a way of giving the meaning of a sentence. To know the semantic concept of truth for a language is to know what it is for a sentence—any sentence—to be true, and this amounts, in one good sense we can give to the phrase, to understanding the language. This at any rate is my excuse for a feature of the present discussion that is apt to shock old hands: my freewheeling use of the word 'meaning', for what I call a theory of meaning has after all turned out to make no use of meanings, whether of sentences or of words. Indeed since a Tarski-type truth definition supplies all we have asked so far of a theory of meaning, it is clear that such a theory falls comfortably within what Quine terms the 'theory of reference' as distinguished from what he terms the 'theory of meaning'. So much to the good for what I call a theory of meaning, and so much, perhaps, against my so calling it.[8]

A theory of meaning (in my mildly perverse sense) is an empirical theory, and its ambition is to account for the workings of a natural language. Like any theory, it may be tested by comparing some of its consequences with the facts. In the present case this is easy, for the theory has been characterized as issuing in an infinite floor of sentences each giving the truth conditions of a sentence; we only need to ask, in selected cases, whether what the theory avers to be the truth conditions for a sentence really are. A typical test case might involve deciding whether the sentence 'Snow is white' *is* true if and only if snow is white. Not all cases will be so simple (for reasons to be sketched), but it is evident that this sort of test does not invite counting noses. A sharp conception of what constitutes a theory in this domain furnishes an exciting context for raising deep questions about when a theory of language is correct and how it is to be tried. But the difficulties are theoretical, not practical.

---

[8] But Quine may be quoted in support of my usage: " . . . in point of *meaning* . . . a word may be said to be determined to whatever extent the truth or falsehood of its contexts is determined." "Truth by Convention," first published in 1936; now in *The Ways of Paradox* (New York, 1966), p. 82. Since a truth definition determines the truth value of every sentence in the object language (relative to a sentence in the metalanguage), it determines the meaning of every word and sentence. This would seem to justify the title Theory of Meaning.

In application, the trouble is to get a theory that comes close to working; anyone can tell whether it is right.[9] One can see why this is so. The theory reveals nothing new about the conditions under which an individual sentence is true; it does not make those conditions any clearer than the sentence itself does. The work of the theory is in relating the known truth conditions of each sentence to those aspects ('words') of the sentence that recur in other sentences, and can be assigned identical roles in other sentences. Empirical power in such a theory depends on success in recovering the structure of a very complicated ability—the ability to speak and understand a language. We can tell easily enough when particular pronouncements of the theory comport with our understanding of the language; this is consistent with a feeble insight into the design of the machinery of our linguistic accomplishments.

The remarks of the last paragraph apply directly only to the special case where it is asumed that the language for which truth is being characterized is part of the language used and understood by the characterizer. Under these circumstances, the framer of a theory will as a matter of course avail himself when he can of the built-in convenience of a metalanguage with a sentence guaranteed equivalent to each sentence in the object language. Still, this fact ought not to con us into thinking a theory any more correct that entails " 'Snow is white' is true if and only if snow is white" than one that entails instead:

(S) 'Snow is white' is true if and only if grass is green,

provided, of course, we are as sure of the truth of (S) as we are of that of its more celebrated predecessor. Yet (S) may not encourage the same confidence that a theory that entails it deserves to be called a theory of meaning.

The threatened failure of nerve may be counteracted as follows. The grotesqueness of (S) is in itself nothing against a theory of which it is a consequence, provided the theory gives the correct results for every sentence (on the basis of its structure, there being no other way). It is not easy to see how (S) could be party to such an enterprise, but if it were—if, that is, (S) followed from a characterization of the predicate 'is true' that led to the invariable pairing of truths with truths and falsehoods with falsehoods—then there would not, I think, be anything essential to the idea of meaning that remained to be captured.

What appears to the right of the biconditional in sentences of the form '*s* is true if and only if *p*' when such sentences are consequences of a theory of truth plays its role in determining the meaning of *s* not by pretending synonymy but by adding one more brush-stroke to the picture which, taken as a whole, tells what there is to know of the meaning of *s*; this stroke is added by virtue of the fact that the sentence that replaces '*p*' is true if and only if *s* is.

It may help to reflect that (S) is acceptable, if it is, because we are inde-

---

[9] To give a single example: it is clearly a count in favor of a theory that it entails " 'Snow is white' is true if and only if snow is white." But to contrive a theory that entails this (and works for all related sentences) is not trivial. I do not know a theory that succeeds with this very case (the problem of "mass terms").

pendently sure of the truth of 'Snow is white' and 'Grass is green'; but in cases where we are unsure of the truth of a sentence, we can have confidence in a characterization of the truth predicate only if it pairs that sentence with one we have good reason to believe equivalent. It would be ill advised for someone who had any doubts about the color of snow or grass to accept a theory that yielded (S), even if his doubts were of equal degree, unless he thought the color of the one was tied to the color of the other. Omniscience can obviously afford more bizarre theories of meaning than ignorance; but then, omniscience has less need of communication.

It must be possible, of course, for the speaker of one language to construct a theory of meaning for the speaker of another, though in this case the empirical test of the correctness of the theory will no longer be trivial. As before, the aim of theory will be an infinite correlation of sentences alike in truth. But this time the theory-builder must not be assumed to have direct insight into likely equivalences between his own tongue and the alien. What he must do is find out, however he can, what sentences the alien holds true in his own tongue (or better, to what degree he holds them true). The linguist then will attempt to construct a characterization of truth-for-the-alien which yields, so far as possible, a mapping of sentences held true (or false) by the alien onto sentences held true (or false) by the linguist. Supposing no perfect fit is found, the residue of sentences held true translated by sentences held false (and vice versa) is the margin for error (foreign or domestic). Charity in interpreting the words and thoughts of others is unavoidable in another direction as well: just as we must maximize agreement, or risk not making sense of what the alien is talking about, so we must maximize the self-consistency we attribute to him, on pain of not understanding *him*. No single principle of optimum charity emerges; the constraints therefore determine no single theory. In a theory of radical translation (as Quine calls it) there is no completely disentangling questions of what the alien means from questions of what he believes. We do not know what someone means unless we know what he believes; we do not know what someone believes unless we know what he means. In radical translation we are able to break into this circle, if only incompletely, because we can sometimes tell that a person accedes to a sentence we do not understand.[10]

In the past few pages I have been asking how a theory of meaning that takes the form of a truth definition can be empirically tested, and have blithely ignored the prior question whether there is any serious chance such a theory can be given for a natural language. What are the prospects for a formal semantical theory of a natural language? Very poor, according to Tarski;

---

[10] This sketch of how a theory of meaning for an alien tongue can be tested obviously owes its inspiration to Quine's account of radical translation in Chapter II of *Word and Object* (New York, 1960). In suggesting that an acceptable theory of radical translation take the form of a recursive characterization of truth, I go beyond anything explicit in Quine. Toward the end of this paper, in the discussion of demonstratives, another strong point of agreement will turn up.

and I believe most logicians, philosophers of language and linguists agree.[11] Let me do what I can to dispel the pessimism. What I can in a general and programmatic way, of course; for here the proof of the pudding will certainly be in the proof of the right theorems.

Tarski concludes the first section of his classic essay on the concept of truth in formalized languages with the following remarks, which he italicizes:

> ... *The very possibility of a consistent use of the expression 'true sentence' which is in harmony with the laws of logic and the spirit of everyday language seems to be very questionable, and consequently the same doubt attaches to the possibility of constructing a correct definition of this expression.*[12]

Late in the same essay, he returns to the subject:

> ... the concept of truth (as well as other semantical concepts) when applied to colloquial language in conjunction with the normal laws of logic leads inevitably to confusions and contradictions. Whoever wishes, in spite of all difficulties, to pursue the semantics of colloquial language with the help of exact methods will be driven first to undertake the thankless task of a reform of this language. He will find it necessary to define its structure, to overcome the ambiguity of the terms which occur in it, and finally to split the language into a series of languages of greater and greater extent, each of which stands in the same relation to the next in which a formalized language stands to its metalanguage. It may, however be doubted whether the language of everyday life, after being 'rationalized' in this way, would still preserve its naturalness and whether it would not rather take on the characteristic features of the formalized languages.[13]

Two themes emerge: that the universal character of natural languages leads to contradiction (the semantic paradoxes), and that natural languages are too confused and amorphous to permit the direct application of formal methods. The first point deserves a serious answer, and I wish I had one. As it is, I will say only why I think we are justified in carrying on without having disinfected this particular source of conceptual anxiety. The semantic paradoxes arise when the range of the quantifiers in the object language is too generous in certain ways. But it is not really clear how unfair to Urdu or to Hindi it would be to view the range of their quantifiers as insufficient to yield an explicit definition of 'true-in-Urdu' or 'true-in-Hindi'. Or, to put the matter in another, if not more serious way, there may in the nature of the case always be something we grasp in understanding the language of another (the concept of truth) that we cannot communicate to him. In any case, most of the problems of general philosophical interest arise within a fragment of the relevant

---

[11] So far as I am aware, there has been very little discussion of whether a formal truth definition can be given for a natural language. But in a more general vein, several people have urged that the concepts of formal semantics be applied to natural language. See, for example, the contributions of Yehoshua Bar-Hillel and Evert Beth to *The Philosophy of Rudolph Carnap*, ed. Paul A. Schilpp, (La Salle, Ill., 1963), and Bar-Hillel's "Logical Syntax and Semantics," *Language*, XXX, 230–37.

[12] Tarski, *ibid.*, p. 165.

[13] *Ibid.*, p. 267.

natural language that may be conceived as containing very little set theory. Of course these comments do not meet the claim that natural languages are universal. But it seems to me this claim, now that we know such universality leads to paradox, is suspect.

Tarski's second point is that we would have to reform a natural language out of all recognition before we could apply formal semantical methods. If this is true, it is fatal to my project, for the task of a theory of meaning as I conceive it is not to change, improve or reform a language, but to describe and undertsand it. Let us look at the positive side. Tarski has shown the way to giving a theory for interpreted formal languages of various kinds; pick one as much like English as possible. Since this new language has been explained in English and contains much English we not only may, but I think must, view it as part of English for those who understand it. For this fragment of English we have, *ex hypothesi*, a theory of the required sort. Not only that, but in interpreting this adjunct of English in old English we necessarily gave hints connecting old and new. Wherever there are sentences of old English with the same truth conditions as sentences in the adjunct we may extend the theory to cover them. Much of what is called for is just to mechanize as far as possible what we now do by art when we put ordinary English into one or another canonical notation. The point is not that canonical notation is better than the rough original idiom, but rather that if we know what idiom the canonical notation is canonical *for*, we have as good a theory for the idiom as for its kept companion.

Philosophers have long been at the hard work of applying theory to ordinary language by the device of matching sentences in the vernacular with sentences for which they have a theory. Frege's massive contribution was to show how 'all', 'some', 'every', 'each', 'none', and associated pronouns, in some of their uses, could be tamed; for the first time, it was possible to dream of a formal semantics for a significant part of a natural language. This dream came true in a sharp way with the work of Tarski. It would be a shame to miss the fact that as a result of these two magnificent achievements, Frege's and Tarski's, we have gained a deep insight into the structure of our mother tongues. Philosophers of a logical bent have tended to start where the theory was and work out towards the complications of natural language. Contemporary linguists, with an aim that cannot easily be seen to be different, start with the ordinary and work toward a general theory. If either party is successful, there must be a meeting. Recent work by Chomsky and others is doing much to bring the complexities of natural languages within the scope of serious semantic theory. To give an example: suppose success in giving the truth conditions for some significant range of sentences in the active voice. Then with a formal procedure for transforming each such sentence into a corresponding sentence in the passive voice, the theory of truth could be extended in an obvious way to this new set of sentences.[14]

---

[14] The rapprochement I prospectively imagine between transformational grammar and a sound theory of meaning has been much advanced by a recent change in the conception of transformational grammar described by Chomsky in the article referred to above (note 5).

One problem touched on in passing by Tarski does not, at least in all its manifestations, have to be solved to get ahead with theory: the existence in natural languages of 'ambiguous terms'. As long as ambiguity does not affect grammatical form, and can be translated, ambiguity for ambiguity, into the metalanguage, a truth definition will not tell us any lies. The trouble, for systematic semantics, with the phrase 'believes that' in English is not its vagueness, ambiguity, or unsuitability for incorporation in a serious science: let our metalanguage be English, and all *these* problems will be translated without loss or gain into the metalanguage. But the central problem of the logical grammar of 'believes that' will remain to haunt us.

The example is suited to illustrating another, and related, point, for the discussion of belief sentences has been plagued by failure to observe a fundamental distinction between tasks: uncovering the logical grammar or form of sentences (which is in the province of a theory of meaning as I construe it), and the analysis of individual words or expressions (which are treated as primitive by the theory). Thus Carnap, in the first edition of *Meaning and Necessity*, suggested we render "John believes that the earth is round" as "John responds affirmatively to 'the earth is round' as an English sentence." He gave this up when Mates pointed out that John might respond affirmatively to one sentence and not to another no matter how close in meaning. But there is a confusion here from the start. The semantic structure of a belief sentence, according to this idea of Carnap's, is given by a three-place predicate with places reserved for expressions referring to a person, a sentence, and a language. It is a different sort of problem entirely to attempt an analysis of this predicate, perhaps along behavioristic lines. Not least among the merits of Tarski's conception of a theory of truth is that the purity of method it demands of us follows from the formulation of the problem itself, not from the self-imposed restraint of some adventitious philosophical puritanism.

I think it is hard to exaggerate the advantages to philosophy of language of bearing in mind this distinction between questions of logical form or grammar, and the analysis of individual concepts. Another example may help advertise the point.

If we suppose questions of logical grammar settled, sentences like 'Bardot is good' raise no special problems for a truth definition. The deep difference between descriptive and evaluative (emotive, expressive, etc.) terms do not show here. Even if we hold there is some important sense in which moral or evaluative sentences do not have a truth value (for example, because they

---

The structures generated by the phrase-structure part of the grammar, it has been realized for some time, are those suited to semantic interpretation; but this view is inconsistent with the idea, held by Chomsky until recently, that recursive operations are introduced only by the transformation rules. Chomsky now believes the phrase-structure rules are recursive. Since languages to which formal semantic methods directly and naturally apply are ones for which a (recursive) phrase-structure grammar is appropriate, it is clear that Chomsky's present picture of the relation between the structures generated by the phrase-structure part of the grammar, and the sentences of the language, is very much like the picture many logicians and philosophers have had of the relation between the richer formalized languages and ordinary language. (In these remarks I am indebted to Bruce Vermazen.)

cannot be 'verified'), we ought not to boggle at " 'Bardot is good' is true if and only if Bardot is good"; in a theory of truth, this consequence should follow with the rest, keeping track, as must be done, of the semantic location of such sentences in the language as a whole—of their relation to generalizations, their role in such compound sentences as 'Bardot is good and Bardot is foolish', and so on. What is special to evaluative words is simply not touched: the mystery is transferred from the word 'good' in the object-language to its translation in the metalanguage.

But 'good' as it features in 'Bardot is a good actress' is another matter. The problem is not that the translation of this sentence is not in the metalanguage—let us suppose it is. The problem is to frame a truth definition such that " 'Bardot is a good actress' is true if and only if Bardot is a good actress" —and all other sentences like it—are consequences. Obviously 'good actress' does not mean 'good and an actress'. We might think of taking 'is a good actress' as an unanalyzed predicate. This would obliterate all connection between 'is a good actress' and 'is a good mother', and it would give us no excuse to think of 'good', in these uses, as a word or semantic element. But worse, it would bar us from framing a truth definition at all, for there is no end to the predicates we would have to treat as logically simple (and hence accommodate in separate clauses in the definition of satisfaction): 'is a good companion to dogs', 'is a good 28-year-old conversationalist', and so forth. The problem is not peculiar to the case: it is the problem of attributive adjectives generally.

It is consistent with the attitude taken here to deem it usually a strategic error to undertake philosophical analysis of words or expressions which is not preceded by or at any rate accompanied by the attempt to get the logical grammar straight. For how can we have any confidence in our analyses of words like 'right', 'ought', 'can', and 'obliged', or the phrases we use to talk of actions, events and causes, when we do not know what (logical, semantical) parts of speech we have to deal with? I would say much the same about studies of the 'logic' of these and other words, and the sentences containing them. Whether the effort and ingenuity that has gone into the study of deontic logics, modal logics, imperative and erotetic logics has been largely futile or not cannot be known until we have acceptable semantic analyses of the sentences such systems purport to treat. Philosophers and logicians sometimes talk or work as if they were free to choose between, say, the truth-functional conditional and others, or free to introduce non-truth-functional sentential operators like 'Let it be the case that' or 'It ought to be the case that'. But in fact that decision is crucial. When we depart from idioms we can accomodate in a truth definition, we lapse into (or create) language for which we have no coherent semantical account—that is, no account at all of how such talk can be integrated into the language as a whole.

To return to our main theme: we have recognized that a theory of the kind proposed leaves the whole matter of what individual words mean exactly where it was. Even when the metalanguage is different from the object language, the theory exerts no pressure for improvement, clarification or analysis of individual words, except when, by accident of vocabulary, straightforward translation fails. Just as synonymy, as between expressions, goes generally untreated, so also synonymy of sentences, and analyticity. Even such sentences as 'A vixen is a female fox' bear no special tag unless it is our pleasure to provide it. A truth definition does not distinguish between analytic sentences and others, except for sentences that owe their truth to the presence alone of the constants that give the theory its grip on structure: the theory entails not only that these sentences are true but that they will remain true under all significant rewritings of their non-logical parts. A notion of logical truth thus given limited application, related notions of logical equivalence and entailment will tag along. It is hard to imagine how a theory of meaning could fail to read a logic into its object language to this degree; and to the extent that it does, our intuitions of logical truth, equivalence and entailment may be called upon in constructing and testing the theory.

I turn now to one more, and very large, fly in the ointment: the fact that the same sentence may at one time or in one mouth be true and at another time or in another mouth be false. Both logicians and those critical of formal methods here seem largely (though by no means universally) agreed that formal semantics and logic are incompetent to deal with the disturbances caused by demonstratives. Logicians have often reacted by downgrading natural language and trying to show how to get along without demonstratives; their critics react by downgrading logic and formal semantics. None of this can make me happy: clearly demonstratives cannot be eliminated from a natural langage without loss or radical change, so there is no choice but to accommodate theory to them.

No logical errors result if we simply treat demonstratives as constants[15]; neither do any problems arise for giving a semantic truth definition. " 'I am wise' is true if and only if I am wise," with its bland ignoring of the demonstrative element in 'I' comes off the assembly line along with " 'Socrates is wise' is true if and only if Socrates is wise" with *its* bland indifference to the demonstrative element in 'is wise' (the tense).

What suffers in this treatment of demonstratives is not the definition of a truth predicate, but the plausibility of the claim that what has been defined is truth. For this claim is acceptable only if the speaker and circumstances of utterance of each sentence mentioned in the definition is matched by the speaker and circumstances of utterance of the truth definition itself. It could also be fairly pointed out that part of understanding demonstratives is knowing the rules by which they adjust their reference to circumstance; assimilating demonstratives to constant terms obliterates this feature. These complaints

---

[15] Quine has good things to say about this in *Methods of Logic* (New York, 1950), see §8.

can be met, I think, though only by a fairly far-reaching revision in the theory of truth. I shall barely suggest how this could be done, but bare suggestion is all that is needed: the idea is technically trivial, and quite in line with work being done on the logic of the tenses.[16]

We could take truth to be a property, not of sentences, but of utterances, or speech acts, or ordered triples of sentences, times and persons; but it is simplest just to view truth as a relation between a sentence, a person, and a time. Under such treatment, ordinary logic as now read applies as usual, but only to sets of sentences relativized to the same speaker and time; further logical relations between sentences spoken at different times and by different speakers may be articulated by new axioms. Such is not my concern. The theory of meaning undergoes a systematic but not puzzling change: corresponding to each expression with a demonstrative element there must in the theory be a phrase that relates the truth conditions of sentences in which the expression occurs to changing times and speakers. Thus the theory will entail sentences like the following:

> 'I am tired' is true as (potentially) spoken by p at t if and only if p is tired at t.
> 'That book was stolen' is true as (potentially) spoken by p at t if and only if the book demonstrated by p at t is stolen prior to t.[17]

Plainly, this course does not show how to eliminate demonstratives; for example, there is no suggestion that 'the book demonstrated by the speaker' can be substituted ubiquitously for 'that book' *salva veritate*. The fact that demonstratives are amenable to formal treatment ought greatly to improve hopes for a serious semantics of natural language, for it is likely that many outstanding puzzles, such as the analysis of quotations or sentences about propositional attitudes, can be solved if we recognize a concealed demonstrative construction.

Now that we have relativized truth to times and speakers, it is appropriate to glance back at the problem of empirically testing a theory of meaning for an alien tongue. The essence of the method was, it will be remembered, to correlate held-true sentences with held-true sentences by way of a truth definition, and within the bounds of intelligible error. Now the picture must be elaborated to allow for the fact that sentences are true, and held true, only relative to a speaker and a time. The real task is therefore to translate each sentence by another that is true for the same speakers at the same times. Sentences with demonstratives obviously yield a very sensitive test of the correctness of a theory of meaning, and constitute the most direct link between language and the recurrent macroscopic objects of human interest and attention.[18]

---

[16] For an up-to-date bibliography, and discussion, see A. N. Prior, *Past, Present, and Future* (Oxford, 1967).

[17] There is more than an intimation of this approach to demonstratives and truth in Austin's 1950 article "Truth," reprinted in *Philosophical Papers* (Oxford, 1961). See pp. 89–90.

[18] These remarks clearly derive from Quine's idea that 'occasion sentences' (those with a demonstrative element) must play a central role in constructing a translation manual.

In this paper I have assumed that the speakers of a language can effectively determine the meaning or meanings of an arbitrary expression (if it has a meaning), and that it is the central task of a theory of meaning to show how this is possible. I have argued that a characterization of a truth predicate describes the required kind of structure, and provides a clear and testable criterion of an adequate semantics for a natural language. No doubt there are other reasonable demands that may be put on a theory of meaning. But a theory that does no more than define truth for a language comes far closer to constituting a complete theory of meaning than superficial analysis might suggest; so, at least, I have urged.

Since I think there is no alternative, I have taken an optimistic and programmatic view of the possibilities for a formal characterization of a truth predicate for a natural language. But it must be allowed that a staggering list of difficulties and conundrums remains. To name a few we do not know the logical form of counterfactual or subjunctive sentences; nor of sentences about probabilities and about causal relations; we have no good idea what the logical role of adverbs is, nor the role of attributive adjectives; we have no theory for mass terms like 'fire', 'water' and 'snow', nor for sentences about belief, perception and intention, nor for verbs of action that imply purpose. And finally, there are all the sentences that seem not to have truth values at all: the imperatives, optatives, interrogatives, and a host more. A comprehensive theory of meaning for a natural language must cope successfully with each of these problems.

SEMANTICS 6

INTRODUCTION

Traditionally, many varied enterprises have gone under the heading of semantics. However, as semantics has emerged as an independent and reasonably rigorous discipline, some rough kind of consensus on what it is about seems to have developed. At any rate, as it is to be understood for the purposes of this book, semantics is roughly a theory or theories of the meanings of words, phrases, and sentences in human languages. In this, semantics may be compared with *syntax*. Traditionally, the central category of syntax is that of a well-formed or *grammatical* utterance. By contrast, semantics is regarded as having as its basic category that of a significant or *meaningful* utterance. Very crudely, a grammatical utterance is one which is internally in order. Its parts (words) stand in proper relations to each other. A meaningful utterance is one which is externally in order. It stands in some interesting relation to the world (e.g., makes a claim about the world). These categories are not necessarily covariant. Chomsky provides "Colorless green ideas sleep furiously" as an example of an expression which is syntactically in order yet semantically anomalous, and "He don't want to go" is syntactically anomalous (at least in terms of classical English grammar) yet makes a determinate and understandable claim.

The primary goal of semantics is to adequately describe what words and expressions in languages mean, or may mean, when they are synonymous, when ambiguous, and so forth. Questions about what it is for something to be meaningful or for something to be an adequate account of the meaning of a word or expression are, initially, at least, of secondary importance. Of course, adequate semantic theories may contribute to the solution of such questions, and *caeteris paribus*, it would be desirable if they did so. On this account, semantics is to be contrasted with theories of meaning (see Section 5). The primary goal of theories of meaning is to provide necessary and sufficient conditions for meaningfulness, adequacy of accounts of meaning, and so forth. It is from such statements of conditions that adequate semantic theories are to follow.

As with grammar (*cf.* the introduction to Section 4), we can distinguish at the outset between two different kinds of semantic theories: universal and particular. A universal semantic theory would be a theory of meanings for human language in general. A particular semantic theory applies to a single language and would specify the meanings of all the well-formed expressions of that language. A universal theory would, to some degree, specify the form that each particular semantic theory must take. It might do this in a number of ways. For example, it might provide a vocabulary from which the vocabulary of each particular theory must be chosen. Or it might define a notion, such as 'possible sense of a sentence', which would restrict the output of each particular theory.

At present, there are several prominent ways of developing or modifying the notion of semantics presented above. One such way, which corresponds fairly closely to KATZ and FODOR's treatment of semantics, is to regard semantics as an *interpretive* theory of sentences. To understand what this means, we must first consider the notion of a *generative* theory. (See Chomsky's discussion in selection 4.2 above.) A generative theory of sentences for a particular language is a theory with a finite vocabulary of symbols and a finite set of rules for making constructions, called 'derivations', out of these symbols. Each such derivation provides a description of a sentence in the language. (More generally, a generative theory of any indefinitely large set of objects is one which, with finite means, provides a unique description for each of them.) The theory will be descriptively adequate just in case there exists a unique derivation, given the vocabulary and rules of the theory, for each sentence of the language in question. In addition, we may impose a higher standard of adequacy, called explanatory adequacy. A theory achieves explanatory adequacy if it best models a fluent speaker's competence to implicitly assign descriptions of a certain sort, that is, to recognize certain sorts of grammatical relations.

On the present conception of semantics, it is at least conceivable (Katz and Fodor claim it is true) that there could be an explanatorily adequate generative theory of sentences which failed to represent everything fluent speakers implicitly knew about them. It may be that some of the information fluent speakers are prepared to extract from sentences is not needed to distinguish optimally one from the other. To include this information in syntax would then be redundant. In that case, there is a need to construct a companion *interpretive* theory, that is, semantics, which attaches this extra information to each description of such a syntax.

As with generative theories, there may be a number of criteria of adequacy for interpretive theories. First, an interpretive theory of the sentences of a particular language may be adequate for describing specific competences of fluent speakers to recognize a number of specific properties of sentences. Katz and Fodor, for example, are interested in the notions of synonymy, paraphrase, ambiguity, and anomaly. A semantic theory will be adequate for describing, for instance, ambiguity if it marks each ambiguous sentence as such, and if it marks each sentence as ambiguous in the number of ways that it is so. It will be adequate for describing anomaly if it marks every anomalous sentence and no others as anomalous, and so on. This criterion of adequacy is essentially the one Katz and Fodor adopt, with the additional stipulation that the optimal theory be maximally simple and economical, in some not-fully-specified sense of those words.

The conception of semantics as an interpretive theory of sentences differs significantly from the traditional view of semantics in linguistics. In contrast to the traditional notion, there is, on the present view, no *a priori* way of deciding what information about sentences is syntactic and what is semantic. To decide this question, one must first have an adequate generative theory of sentences—a syntax. Whatever features of sentences are described by such a syntax will then be called syntactic. The rest, except for those which are phonological or graphemic, will be called semantic. On the traditional view, it is the job of semantics to describe semantic features of sentences—that is, those having to do with meaning—where it is presumably already well understood what these features are. This view led to disputes about the possibility or desirability of constructing a syntax without referring to semantic features. On the present conception of semantics, such disputes cannot arise.

In his article in this section, Charles FILLMORE accepts, for present purposes at least, the Katz-Fodor conception of semantics, but suggests a rather significant modification in their sketch of a theory. On Fillmore's modification, a semantic theory would not assign interpretations, at least directly, to every syntactically described sentence of the language. Instead, the theory would consist of two components. One component would assign interpretations to every member of some proper subset of sentences of the language. The other component would provide a set of rules, which he calls 'entailment rules', for interpreting the remaining sentences in terms of the sentences interpreted by the first component. Entailment rules provide us with the means for representing the fact that fluent speakers understand certain sentences in virtue of recognizing relations between their semantic interpretation and the semantic interpretations of certain other sentences which they are able to interpret directly.

There is an interesting parallel between Fillmore's two-component semantic theory and the distinction between phrase-structure and transformational components of a grammar. Roughly, the latter distinction arises as follows. First, there are certain reasonable restrictions on how items in the vocabulary of a grammar may be put together to form descriptions of sentences. These restrictions, although formalized by Chomsky, were generally agreed on by linguists for many years. Now, given these restrictions, it turns out that for purposes of generality, simplicity, and correctness in describing what a speaker knows about his language, it is necessary to divide a grammar into two parts.

First, certain grammatical relations may be marked directly in terms of the vocabulary of the theory. The rules for representing relations in this way are called the phrase-structure component of the grammar.

Second, however, there are significant grammatical relations that are not best represented in this way. These latter sorts are best represented in terms of relations between the constructions that are derivable in the phrase structure component of the grammar. The rules for forming constructions to represent such relations are called transformational rules.

Fillmore's entailment rules, then can be regarded as the semantic analogue of transformational rules in syntax. This suggests a number of ways in which Fillmore's proposal may be developed in the future.

McCawley suggests a more radical departure from the Katz-Fodor view of semantics. The most important of McCawley's claims is that every semantic feature of a word is necessary for determining grammaticality. In fact, certain aspects of grammaticality, roughly those having to do with the co-occurrence of words, are only determinable in terms of semantic features. If this claim is true, then it is no longer possible to regard semantics as an interpretive theory of sentences. There simply is no information left over for such a theory to represent.

If it is not to be an interpretive theory, what should semantics be? McCawley has several suggestions. First, he suggests that semantics should be an independent discipline. This does not require an accurate pretheoretical way of determining what information is semantic and what is not, any more than regarding syntax as an independent discipline requires a pretheoretical criterion for determining what is and what isn't a sentence. We can simply set about the business of constructing an adequate semantic theory, making use of what we do know about what words and sentences mean. Criteria for semantic information, if they remain of interest, may in part be determined by what such successful theories in fact look like.

Second, McCawley suggests that a semantic theory should have at least two components. The first component is a part of semantic theories of particular languages only. The second is a universal semantic theory. The component of particular theories is a dictionary. It provides a characterization of each word of the language which is adequate for both syntactic and semantic purposes. (On McCawley's view, these come to the same thing.) McCawley's view of a universal semantic theory on the other hand bears some resemblance to the Katz-Fodor view. Part of what such a theory contains is a universal vocabulary —that is, a vocabulary in terms of which descriptions of the meanings of words, etc. are to be given—from which the vocabulary for each particular semantic theory is to be chosen. In addition, however, the universal theory is to define some very general semantic notions. The most important of these is that of a humanly possible message. A humanly possible message is something that a sentence in some humanly possible language[1] might mean on a given reading.

---

[1] For an explanation of this notion, see the introduction to Section 4 and Chomsky, "Methodological Preliminaries," selection 4.2.

The universal theory is to define this notion by providing a generative theory of humanly possible messages.

Given his notion of semantics, McCawley goes on to speculate that the relation between semantics and syntax may be quite different from what it appears to be on the traditional transformational account. McCawley states this claim in two ways. First, he suggests that semantics may be generative and syntax interpretive. That is, semantics generates possible messages, which are then related to some particular sentence by rules for syntactic interpretation, that is, rules which tell what that message 'looks like' in the language in question. Second, McCawley suggests that the phrase-structure component of a transformational grammar may be unnecessary, and that its function may be performed by semantic theory. Both of these last claims have recently been argued against by Chomsky, the first on the grounds that it cannot be understood in any substantively interesting way, and the second on grounds of technical adequacy.

In the last article of this section, ZIFF raises some questions about the role of a semantic theory in determining the meanings of words and phrases. He provides a number of interesting cases in which utterances which presently strike us as anomalous, and must apparently be marked as anomalous by an adequate semantic theory, could become fully acceptable and non-deviant in the absence of any changes of meaning. This raises at least two questions. First, if a semantic theory does mark Ziff's examples as anomalous, to what extent does it contain facts about meaning, and to what extent does it contain information about the world? In what sense can we say that semantics tells us what things mean? Second, if a semantic theory does not mark such things as anomalous, then what could it loook like, and what would it tell us about how we are currently prepared to understand sentences? It is interesting to compare Ziff's examples with those brought up in raising questions about the analytic-synthetic distinction in Section 1.

Suggestions for Further Reading

NOTE: The articles by McCawley and Chomsky listed in Section 4 are relevant here as well.

Bolinger, Dwight. "The Atomization of Meaning." In Miron and Jakobovits, eds., *Readings in the Psychology of Language*. Englewood Cliffs, N.J.: Prentice-Hall, Inc., 1967.

Fillmore, Charles. "The Case for Case." In Bach and Harms, eds., *Universals in Linguistic Theory*. New York: Holt, Rinehart & Winston, 1968.

———. "Deictic Categories and the Meaning of 'Come'." In *Foundations of Language*, II (1966), 219–27.

———. "Lexical Entries for Verbs." In *Foundations of Language*, IV (1968), 373–93.

Katz, Jerrold J. *The Philosophy of Language*. New York: Harper & Row, Publishers, 1966.

————, and Paul M. Postal. *An Integrated Theory of Linguistic Descriptions*. Cambridge, Mass.: M.I.T. Press, 1964.

Weinreich, Uriel. "Explorations in Semantic Theory." In T. Sebeok, ed., *Current Trends in Linguistics*. Vol. III. The Hague: Mouton Publishers, 1966.

————. "On the Semantic Structure of Language." In J. Greenberg, ed., *Universals of Language*. Cambridge, Mass.: M.I.T. Press, 1966.

JERROLD J. KATZ / JERRY A. FODOR

6.1   *The Structure of a Semantic Theory*

This paper does not attempt to present a semantic theory of a natural language, but rather to characterize the abstract form of such a theory. A semantic theory of a natural language is part of a linguistic description of that language. Our problem, on the other hand, is part of the general theory of language, fully on a par with the problem of characterizing the structure of grammars of natural languages. A characterization of the abstract form of a semantic theory is a metatheory which answers such questions as: What is the domain of a semantic theory? What are the descriptive and explanatory goals of a semantic theory? What mechanisms are employed in pursuit of these goals? What are the empirical and methodological constraints upon a semantic theory?

Conceivably, differences between languages may preclude a uniform solution to the problem of finding an abstract characterization of the form of semantic theories. But this too is part of the problem. We want to know both what can be prescribed about semantic theories independent of differences between languages, or given certain truths about all languages, and what aspects of semantic theories vary with what aspects of particular natural languages. In the present paper, we approach the problem of abstractly characterizing the form of semantic theories by describing the structure of a semantic theory of English. There can be little doubt but that the results achieved will apply directly to semantic theories of languages closely related to English. The present investigation will also provide results that can be applied to semantic theories of languages unrelated to English and suggestions about how to proceed with the construction of such theories. But the question of the extent of their applicability to semantic theories of more distant languages will be left for subsequent investigation.

We may put our problem this way: What form should a semantic theory of a natural language take to accommodate in the most revealing way the facts

Reprinted from *Language*, XXXIX, No. 2 (1963), 170–210, by permission of the authors and of the editor of *Language*.

about the semantic structure of that language supplied by descriptive research? This question is of primary importance at the present stage of the development of semantics because semantics suffers not from a dearth of facts about meanings and meaning relations in natural languages, but, rather, from the lack of an adequate theory to organize, systematize, and generalize those facts. Facts about the semantics of natural languages have been contributed in abundance by many diverse fields including philosophy, linguistics, philology, psychology, and so on. Indeed, a compendium of such facts is readily available in any good dictionary. At present, however, the superabundance of facts obscures a clear view of their interrelations and of the principles providing their underlying structure.

This is not meant to deny that investigators in these fields have proposed semantic theories. But, in general, such theories have been either too loosely formulated or too weak in explanatory and descriptive power to account adequately for the available semantic facts. Moreover, taken together, these theories form a heterogeneous and disconnected assortment. Philosophical inquiry into the meaning and use of words has neither drawn upon nor contributed to semantic investigation in psychology and linguistics. Correspondingly, accounts of meaning proposed by linguists and psychologists cannot in any obvious way be connected with theories current in philosophy or with one another. In each case, the character of the theory and its constructs is so radically idiosyncratic, so peculiar to the realm of discourse from which it comes, that it is practically impossible to determine its relevance to theories and constructs from other realms of discourse. This becomes apparent from even the most cursory comparison of the work of such semantic theorists as Bloomfield, Carnap, Harris, Osgood, Quine, Russell, Skinner, Tarski, Wittgenstein, and Ziff. In the writings of these theorists, one finds explications of meaning based upon everything from patterns of retinal stimulation, to stimuli controlling verbal behavior, to affective factors in the response to words, to intensions, to sentential truth conditions, to conditions for nondeviant utterances, to distribution, to rules of use. As Chomsky has insightfully observed:

> Part of the difficulty with the theory of meaning is that "meaning" tends to be used as a catch-all term to include every aspect of language that we know very little about. Insofar as this is correct, we can expect various aspects of this theory to be claimed by other approaches to language in the course of their development.[1]

Such broad disagreement, extending not only to questions about the nature of meaning but even to questions about the kinds of considerations relevant to the construction of a semantic theory is attributable to the failure of investigators to deal seriously with metatheoretic questions about the abstract form of semantic theories. A characterization of the form of a semantic theory can be expected to accomplish the following. It defines the domain of a semantic

---

[1] N. Chomsky, *Syntactic Structures*, 2nd ed. ('s Gravenhage: L. Mouton & Co., 1962), p. 103, 10 *n*.

theory by telling us what phenomena a semantic theory seeks to describe and explain and what kinds of facts about them are theoretically relevant in semantic investigation. Also, characterizing the form of a semantic theory clarifies the goals of semantic description. Vaguely formulated goals can then be refined, and this can lead in turn to the discovery that certain putative goals are unacceptable, that others are interrelated, and that some take priority. Without such a clarification, competing theories of meaning are not even so much as comparable. With such clarification, the goals of semantic theory can be aligned with those of other areas of linguistics to afford an over-all picture of what an adequate description of a natural language describes. Further, by characterizing the form of semantic generalizations and of the manner in which they can systematically interrelate, a metatheory shows how semantic theories can effect a reduction of the superabundance of facts to manageable proportions by representing them in a system consisting of a small number of compact, interrelated generalizations. Finally, the metatheory determines the empirical and methodological constraints upon a semantic theory. Thus, it enables investigators to evaluate competing semantic theories by assessing the degree to which they satisfy such constraints. Inadequate conceptions of meaning can then be pushed to the point where their inadequacy becomes fully apparent.

THE PROJECTION PROBLEM

A full synchronic description of a natural language is a grammatical and semantic characterization of that language (where the term *grammatical* is construed broadly to include, besides syntax, phonology, phonemics, and morphology). Hence, a semantic theory must be constructed to have whatever properties are demanded by its role in linguistic description. Since, however, the goals of such description are reasonably well understood and since, in comparison to semantics, the nature of grammar has been clearly articulated, we may expect that, by studying the contribution semantics will be required to make to a synchronic description of a language, we can clarify the subject, the form of generalizations, the goals, and the empirical and methodological constraints of a semantic theory. Our first step toward determining the contribution a semantic theory is required to make toward a linguistic description of a natural language will be to delineate the contribution a grammar makes. Our aim is, in this way, to factor out the contribution of a semantic theory.

A fluent speaker's mastery of his language exhibits itself in his ability to produce and understand the sentences of his language, *including indefinitely many that are wholly novel to him* (i.e., his ability to produce and understand *any* sentence of his language[2]). The emphasis upon novel sentences is important. The most

---

[2] There are exceptions, such as sentences with technical words that the speaker does not know, sentences too long for the speaker to scan in his lifetime, and so on. But these exceptions are of no systematic importance. Analogously, a person's mastery of an algorithm for propositional calculus can be said to exhibit itself in his ability to mechanically decide whether *any* well-formed formula of propositional calculus is a tautology, even though some well-formed formulae are too long for human processing and so forth.

characteristic feature of language is its ability to make available an infinity of sentences from which the speaker can select appropriate and novel ones to use as the need arises. That is to say, what qualifies one as a fluent speaker is not the ability to imitate previously heard sentences but rather the ability to produce and understand sentences never before encountered. The striking fact about the use of language is the absence of repetition—almost every sentence uttered is uttered for the first time. This can be substantiated by checking texts for the number of times a sentence is repeated. It is exceedingly unlikely that even a single repetition of a sentence of reasonable length will be encountered.

A synchronic description of a natural language seeks to determine what a fluent speaker knows about the structure of his language that enables him to use and understand its sentences. Since a fluent speaker is able to use and understand any sentence drawn from the *infinite* set of sentences of his language, and since, at any time, he has only encountered a *finite* set of sentences, it follows that the speaker's knowledge of his language takes the form of rules which project the finite set of sentences he has fortuitously encountered to the infinite set of sentences of the language. A description of the language which adequately represents the speaker's linguistic knowledge must, accordingly, state these rules. The problem of formulating these rules we shall refer to as the *projection problem*.

This problem requires for its solution rules which project the infinite set of sentences in a way which mirrors the way speakers understand novel sentences. In encountering a novel sentence, the speaker is not encountering novel elements but only a novel combination of familiar elements. Since the set of sentences is infinite and each sentence is a different concatenation of morphemes, the fact that a speaker can understand any sentence must mean that the way he understands sentences he has never previously encountered is compositional: on the basis of his knowledge of the grammatical properties and the meanings of the morphemes of the language, the rules the speaker knows enable him to determine the meaning of a novel sentence in terms of the manner in which the parts of the sentence are composed to form the whole. Correspondingly, then, we can expect that a system of rules which solves the projection problem must reflect the compositional character of the speaker's linguistic skill.

A solution to the projection problem is certainly something less than a full theory of speech. In particular, it does not provide a theory of speech production (or recognition). The difference between a description of a language and a theory of speech production is the difference between asking for a characterization of the rules of language a speaker knows and asking for an account of how he actually applies such rules in speaking. Some things that are left out by the first theory but not by the second are: considerations of the psychological parameters of speech production (e.g., limitations of immediate memory, level of motivation, and so on); developmental accounts of the way the child becomes a fluent speaker (by conditioning? by the exploitation of innate mechanisms? by some combination of innate endowment and learning?). Although such problems about speech production lie outside the scope of a theory of a language, a theory of a language is essential to a theory of speech production. It is first necessary to know what is acquired and used before it is sensible to ask how it is acquired and used.

These considerations show that what is asked for when we ask for a description of a natural language is a solution to the projection problem for that language. If we are to discover the goals of semantics by subtracting from the goals of a description of a language whatever the grammar contributes to the solution of the projection problem, we must consider the contribution of grammar.

LINGUISTIC DESCRIPTION MINUS GRAMMAR
EQUALS SEMANTICS

The significance of transformational grammars for our present purposes is that they provide a solution for the grammatical aspect of the projection problem. (That is to say, transformational grammars answer the question: what does the speaker know about the phonological and syntactic structure of his language which enables him to use and understand any of its sentences, including those he has never previously heard?) They do so by providing rules which generate the sentences of the speaker's language. In particular, these rules generate infinitely many strings of morphemes which, although they are sentences of the language, have never been uttered by speakers. Moreover, a transformational grammar generates the sentences a speaker is, in principle, capable of understanding in such a way that their derivations provide their structural descriptions. Such descriptions specify: the elements out of which a sentence is constructed, the grammatical relations between these elements and between the higher constituents of the sentence, the relations between the sentence and other sentences of the language, and the ways the sentence is ambiguous together with an explanation of why it is ambiguous in these ways. Since it is this information about a novel sentence which the speaker knows and which enables him to understand its syntactic structure if and when he encounters the sentence, an adequate transformational grammar of a language *partially* solves the projection problem for the language.

A semantic theory of a language completes the solution of the projection problem for the language. Thus, semantics takes over the explanation of the speaker's ability to produce and understand infinitely many new sentences at the point where grammar leaves off. Since we wish to determine, when we have subtracted the problems in the description of a language properly belonging to grammar, what problems belong to semantics, we must begin by gaining some grasp of how much of the projection problem is left unsolved by an optimal grammar.

One way to appreciate how much of understanding sentences is left unexplained by grammar is to compare the grammatical characterizations of sentences to what we know about their semantic characterizations. If we do this, we notice that the grammar provides identical structural descriptions for sentences that are different in meaning and different structural descriptions for sentences that are identical in meaning. The former will be the case for all morphemically distinct substitution instances of a given sentential type. For example, "The dog bit the man" and "The cat bit the woman." The latter will be the case for all instances of sentential synonymy. For example, "The dog bit the man" and "The man was bitten by the dog."[3]

This indicates some of the types of problems that even an optimal grammar cannot deal with. In general, it is obvious that in no sense of meaning does the structural description the grammar assigns to a sentence specify either the meaning of the sentence or the meaning of its parts. Such considerations must now be made precise in order that we may apply our formula, *linguistic description minus grammar equals semantics*, to determine a lower bound on the domain of a semantic theory. Later in this section we will fix an upper bound by determining what problems lie outside the concerns of a complete linguistic description.

Grammars seek to describe the structure of a sentence *in isolation from its possible settings in linguistic discourse (written or verbal) or in nonlinguistic contexts (social or physical)*. The justification which permits the grammarian to study sentences in abstraction from the settings in which they have occurred or might occur is simply that the fluent speaker is able to construct and recognize syntactically well-formed sentences without recourse to information about settings, and this ability is what a grammar undertakes to reconstruct. Every facet of the fluent speaker's linguistic ability which a grammar reconstructs can be exercised independently of information about settings: this is true not only of the ability to produce and recognize sentences but also of the ability to determine syntactic relations between sentence types, to implicitly analyze the syntactic structure of sentences, and to detect grammatical ambiguities. Since, then, the knowledge a fluent speaker has of his language enables him to determine the grammatical structure of any sentence without reference to information about setting, grammar correspondingly forms an independent theory of this independent knowledge.

We may generalize to arrive at a sufficient condition for determining when an ability of speakers is the proper subject matter of a synchronic theory in linguistics. The generalization is this: *If speakers can employ an ability in apprehending the structure of any sentence in the infinite set of sentences of a language without reference to information about settings and without significant variation from speaker to speaker, then that ability is properly the subject matter of a synchronic theory in linguistics.*

The first question in determining the subject matter of a semantic theory is: can we find an ability which satisfies the antecedent of the above generalization, which is beyond the range of grammatical description and which is semantic in some reasonable sense? If we can, then that ability falls within the domain of a semantic theory.

In order to find such an ability, let us consider a communication situation

---

[3] Moreover, sentences that are given the same structural description can differ in that one may be semantically ambiguous or anomalous without the other being so. Compare, for example, "The bill is large," "The paint is silent," and "The street is wide," all of which receive the same structural description from the grammar.

so constructed that no information about setting can contribute to a speaker's understanding of a sentence encountered in that situation. Any extragrammatical ability a speaker can employ to understand the meaning of a sentence in such a situation will *ipso facto* be considered to require semantic explanation. The type of communication situation we shall consider is the following: a number of English speakers receive an anonymous letter containing only the English sentence *S*. We are interested in the difference between this type of situation and one in which the same anonymous letter is received by persons who do not speak English but are equipped with a completely adequate grammar of English. To investigate what the first group can do by way of comprehending the meaning of *S* that the second group cannot is to factor out the contribution of grammar to the understanding of sentences. We will only investigate aspects of linguistic ability which are invariant from individual to individual within each group. We thus assure that the abilities under investigation are a function not of idiosyncrasies of a speaker's personal history but only of his knowledge of his language.

Suppose *S* is the sentence "The bill is large." Speakers of English will agree that this sentence is ambiguous, i.e., that it has at least two readings: according to one, it means that some document demanding a sum of money to dispense a debt exceeds in size most such documents, and according to another, it means that the beak of a certain bird exceeds in bulk those of most similar birds. However, the fact that this sentence is ambiguous between these readings cannot be attributed to its syntactic structure since, syntactically, its structure on both readings is:

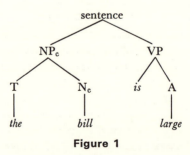

Figure 1

That is, the group who *do not* speak English but *are* equipped with a grammar can say no more about "The bill is large" than what is represented in Fig. 1. Thus, this sentence, which is marked as unambiguous by the grammar, will be understood as ambiguous by a fluent speaker. From this difference between the performances of the two groups, it follows that one facet of the speaker's ability that a semantic theory will have to reconstruct is that he can detect nonsyntactic ambiguities and characterize the content of each reading of a sentence.

Now suppose *S* is the sentence "The bill is large but need not be paid." Speakers of English will understand this sentence only on readings in which *bill* means an order to pay a sum of money to dispense a debt. This shows that a speaker can disambiguate parts of a sentence in terms of other parts and thereby determine the number of readings of a sentence. Thus, another facet of the speaker's semantic ability is that of determining the number of readings a sentence has by exploiting semantic relations in the sentence to eliminate potential ambiguities.

Now let S be the sentence "He painted the walls with silent paint." English speakers will at once recognize that this sentence is anomalous in some way. For example, they will distinguish it from such sentences as "He painted the walls with red paint" and "He painted the walls with silent rollers" by applying to it such epithets as *odd, peculiar, bizarre*, and the like. Although it is clear that the speaker does not have the explicit conceptual machinery to correctly characterize the difference between these sentences, his consistent use of such rough labels shows that he is aware of some sort of linguistic anomaly. But the group who do not speak English and are equipped only with a grammar will regard all these sentences as fully regular since there is no grammatical basis for distinguishing between them. Hence, another facet of the semantic ability of the speaker is that of detecting semantic anomalies. Correspondingly, a semantic theory will be needed to mark the distinction between semantically anomalous sentences and semantically regular sentences, insofar as this distinction is *not* coextensive with the distinction the grammar makes between ungrammatical and grammatical strings of morphemes.

Finally, whatever sentence the anonymous letter contains, as a rule, speakers of English can easily decide what sentences are paraphrases of it and what are not in the sense that they can answer such questions as: what does the letter say? does the letter say such-and-such? how can what the letter says be rephrased? This facet of the speaker's ability cannot be referred to his mastery of grammar either, for the group who are equipped with a grammar but who do not speak English will be unable to tell whether or not a sentence is a paraphrase of S. The reasons are simply that there need be no definite grammatical relation between a sentence and its paraphrases; e.g., "Two chairs are in the room" and "There are at least two things in the room and each is a chair"; and that where a definite grammatical relation obtains between a pair of sentences, neither need be a paraphrase of the other, e.g., "The ball was hit by the man" and "The ball was hit," "The man hit the ball," and "The man did not hit the ball."[4] Thus, still another facet of the speaker's semantic ability which must fall within the domain of a semantic theory is his paraphrasing skill.

We can now tentatively characterize the lower bound on the domain of a semantic theory since we have found an ability of speakers which cannot be accounted for by grammar, which is semantic in a reasonable sense and which enables speakers to apprehend the semantic structure of an infinite number of sentences without information about setting and independent of individual differences between speakers. We thus take the goals of a semantic theory to include at least the explication of each facet of this ability and of the interrelations between them.

---

[4] *Cf.* N. Chomsky, *op cit.*, Appendix II for the transformations which relate these sentences.

The speaker's exercise of this ability, which henceforth we shall refer to as *the ability to interpret sentences*, provides empirical data for the construction of a semantic theory, just as the construction of a grammar draws upon empirical data supplied by the exercise of the speaker's ability to distinguish well-formed sentences from ungrammatical strings, to recognize syntactic ambiguity, and to appreciate relations between sentence types. A semantic theory describes and explains the interpretative ability of speakers: by accounting for their performance in determining the number and content of the readings of a sentence; by detecting semantic anomalies; by deciding upon paraphrase relations between sentences; and by marking every other semantic property or relation that plays a role in this ability.

Having now fixed a lower bound on the domain of a semantic theory, our next step must be to fix an upper bound, thus uniquely determining the set of problems forming the domain of a semantic theory of a natural language.

Previous conceptions of semantics have usually defined the goals of a semantic description of a natural language in such a way that to achieve them a semantic theory would have to account for the manner in which settings determine how an utterance is understood. We shall now show that to set the goals of a semantic theory this high is to set them too high. Once we have shown that a semantic theory cannot be expected to account for the way settings determine how an utterance is understood, we will have fixed an upper bound on the domain of semantic theories. That is, we will have shown that a semantic theory is a theory of the speaker's ability to interpret the sentences of his language.

The abstract form of a theory of how settings control the understanding of utterances of sentences is as follows. Such a theory is a function F whose arguments are a sentence S, a grammatical description of S, GS, a semantic interpretation of S, IS (where IS is the set of possible readings of S), and an abstract characterization of a setting, C. $F(S, GS, IS, C)$ is:

(1) The particular reading in IS speakers of the language give S in settings of the type C, or

(2) An n-tuple ($n \geq 2$) of the readings from IS that speakers of the language give S if S is ambiguous n-ways in settings of type C, or

(3) The null element if speakers of the language give S none of the readings in IS when S occurs in settings of type C.

The value of $F(S, GS, IS, C)$ is (1) just in case C fully disambiguates S, i.e., C determines a unique reading from the one or more in IS; it is (2) just in case C fails to fully disambiguate S; it is (3) just in case an occurrence of S in C is token-odd.[5]

An example of each of these cases will clarify this abstract formulation by showing how a theory of this form would explicate the speaker's ability to choose the reading(s) a setting determines for a sentence occurring in it. As an example of case (1), consider the sentence "The shooting of the hunters was terrible." This sentence is ambiguous between the reading r_1 on which it

---

[5] Semantic type oddity is precluded by the assumption that IS contains at least one reading.

means that it was terrible that the hunters were shot and the reading r_2 on which it means that the marksmanship of the hunters was very bad. This ambiguity will be represented in *IS*. The theory *F* must decide which of these readings the sentence bears in settings which disambiguate it, and it must decide in which settings the sentence remains ambiguous. If, then, an utterance of the sentence occurs as an answer to the question "How good was the marksmanship of the hunters?" i.e., if *C* represents a situation in which the marksmanship of the hunters is clearly at issue, then, *ceteris paribus*, the value of *F* would have to be r_2.[6] Now consider case (2). An ambiguous sentence such as "He follows Marx" occurring in a setting in which it is clear that the speaker is remarking about intellectual history cannot bear the reading "he dogs the footsteps of Groucho." However, this setting leaves the sentence ambiguous between the readings "he is a disciple of Karl's" and "he postdates Karl." Thus, *F* will have to have these latter two readings as its value for this sentence and setting as arguments. Finally, let us consider case (3). Suppose the sentence "This is the happiest night of my life" is uttered during the middle of the day. Since this sentence is uttered in a setting lacking conditions which utterances of this sentence presuppose, the occurrence is a case of token-oddity. Thus, for this sentence-occurrence *F* must give the null element as its value, i.e., none of the readings this sentence has in *IS* are selected by *C*.

This, then, is the abstract form of a theory about the effect of setting upon the way speakers understand sentences. Any particular theory is complete just to the extent that it solves the problems incorporated in this abstract formulation. A complete theory of this kind is more powerful in principle than a theory of the semantic interpretation of sentences in isolation. But a theory of settings must contain a theory of semantic interpretation as a proper part because the readings that a speaker attributes to a sentence in a setting are a selection from among those that sentence has in isolation. It is clear that, *in general*, a sentence cannot have readings in a setting which it does not have in isolation. Of course, there are cases in which a sentence may have a reading for some speakers in some settings which it does not have in isolation for all speakers. But these cases are essentially idiomatic in the sense that meaning is determined either by special stipulation (passwords, nonce-senses, and so on) or by special rules (some codes, and the like) or by special information about the intentions of the speaker. If a theory of the selective effect of setting were required to deal with such cases, no such theory would be possible because any sentence may be made to mean anything you like simply by constructing the setting to include the appropriate stipulation.[7] Since, then, the readings that a speaker gives a sentence in setting are a selection from those the sentence

---

[6] In the case where a sentence has exactly one reading in *IS*, i.e., is unambiguous, that reading must be assigned to the sentence in each and every normal setting by the theory.

[7] Take the following example. Let *m* be a one-to-one mapping of the set of English sentences onto itself such that the image of each sentence is a sentence which differs in meaning from it. Then the sentence "The sentence *S* which immediately follows this sentence is to be understood as $m(S)$," is a setting such that the meaning of a sentence occurring in it is not one of the meanings of that sentence in isolation.

has in isolation, a theory of semantic interpretation is logically prior to a theory of the selective effect of setting.

The abstract formulation given above may be realized in the form of a theory of either of two kinds, depending on how the notion of setting is construed. One kind of theory of setting selection construes the setting of an utterance to be the nonlinguistic context in which the utterance occurs, i.e., the full socio-physical environment of the utterance. The other kind takes the setting of an utterance to be the linguistic context in which the utterance occurs, i.e., the written or spoken discourse of which the utterance is a part. We shall consider, in turn, the possibility of constructing a theory of each of these types.

The first kind of theory of setting selection seeks to account for the way in which aspects of the socio-physical world control the understanding of sentences. Differing varieties of this kind of theory may be obtained by varying the aspects of the socio-physical environment of which the rules of the theory are permitted to take account and by varying the spatio-temporal parameters of the environment. But clearly a necessary condition that any variety of this kind of theory must satisfy is that its construction of setting is so defined that it is able to represent all the nonlinguistic information required by speakers to understand sentences. Insofar as a theory fails to satisfy this condition, that theory is incomplete since there is some information which determines the way speakers understand a sentence but which the theory fails to represent as part of the setting of that sentence. If a theory fails to represent information which speakers actually utilize in understanding sentences, the theory fails to fully explain the mechanism by which such information contributes to the process of understanding.

However, a complete theory of this kind is not possible in principle because to satisfy the above necessary condition, it would be required that the theory represent *all* the knowledge speakers have about the world. That this is so can be seen from even a few examples which show how nonlinguistic information of any kind may be involved in the understanding of a sentence. Consider (1) "Our store sells alligator shoes" and (2) "Our store sells horse shoes." In normal settings (e.g., as signs in a store window, as newspaper advertisements), occurrences of (1) will be taken on the reading "our store sells shoes made from alligator skins" while (2) will be taken on the reading "our store sells shoes for horses." Notice, however, that (1) is open to the reading "our store sells shoes for alligators" and (2) is open to the reading "our store sells shoes made from the skin of horses." From this it follows that for a theory of setting selection to choose the correct reading for (1) it must represent the fact that, to date, alligators do not wear shoes, although shoes for people are sometimes made from alligator skin. Conversely, if the theory is to choose the correct reading for (2), it must represent the fact that horses wear shoes, although shoes for people are not made from the skin of horses. Other examples illustrate much the same point. Compare the three sentences: "Should we take junior back to the zoo?" "Should we take the lion back to the zoo?" "Should we take the bus back to the zoo?" Information which figures in the choice of the correct readings for these sentences includes the fact that lions, but not children and busses, are often kept in cages. Three further cases of the same sort are: "Can I put the wallpaper on?" and "Can I put the coat on?" "Joe jumped higher than the Empire State Building" and "Joe jumped higher than you;" "Black cats are unlucky" and "People who break mirrors are unlucky."[8]

For practically any item of information about the world, the reader will find it a relatively easy matter to construct an ambiguous sentence whose resolution in context requires the representation of that item.[9] Since a complete theory of setting selection must represent as part of the setting of an utterance any and every feature of the world which speakers need to determine the preferred reading of that utterance and since, as we have just seen, practically any item of information about the world is essential to some disambiguations, two conclusions follow. First, such a theory cannot in principle distinguish between the speaker's knowledge of his language and his knowledge of the world because, according to such a theory, part of the characterization of a *linguistic* ability is a representation of virtually all knowledge about the world speakers share. Second, since there is no serious possibility of systematizing all the knowledge of the world that speakers share and since a theory of the kind we have been discussing requires such a systematization, it is *ipso facto* not a serious model for semantics. However, none of these considerations is intended to rule out the possibility that, by placing relatively strong limitations on the information about the world that a theory can represent in the characterization of a setting, a *limited* theory of selection by socio-physical setting can be constructed. What these considerations do show is that a *complete* theory of this kind is not a possibility.

The second kind of realization of the abstract formulation of a theory of setting selection is one in which the setting of an occurrence of a sentence is construed as the written or spoken discourse of which the occurrence is a part. Such a theory has a strong and a weak version. The strong version requires that the theory interpret a discourse in the same way a fluent speaker would (i.e., mark the ambiguities the speaker marks, resolve the ambiguities the speaker resolves, detect the anomalous strings the speaker detects, recognize paraphrase relations the speaker recognizes, and do so both within and across sentence boundaries). Since, however, in so interpreting a discourse, a speaker may need to bring to bear virtually any information about the world that he and other speakers share, the argument given against a complete theory of selection by socio-physical setting applies equally against the strong version of a theory of selection by discourse. Thus, we need only consider the weak version.

The weak version of such a theory requires only that the theory interpret discourses just insofar as the interpretation is determined by grammatical and semantic relations which obtain within and among the sentences of the dis-

---

[8] The authors wish to express their gratitude to Mr. David Bellugi for referring them to *My Little Golden Book of Jokes* from which the above examples are drawn.

[9] The authors have convinced themselves of the truth of this claim by making it the basis of a party game. The game consists in one person supplying a fact, however obscure, and the others trying to construct a sentence which that fact disambiguates. Although this game is not remarkably amusing, it is surprisingly convincing.

course; i.e., it interprets discourses as would a fluent speaker afflicted with
amnesia for nonlinguistic facts but not with aphasia. Thus, such a theory seeks
to disambiguate sentences and sequences of sentences in terms of grammatical
and semantic relations between them and the sentences which form their setting in a discourse, to determine when an occurrence of a sentence or a sequence
of sentences is rendered anomalous by the sentences which form its setting in
a discourse, and to recognize paraphrase relations between pairs of sentences
and pairs of sequences of sentences in a discourse.[10]

But it is not at all clear that the weak version of theory of discourse-setting
selection has greater explanatory power in these respects than a theory of
semantic interpretation, since except for a few types of cases, discourse can be
treated as a single sentence in isolation by regarding sentence boundaries as
sentential connectives.[11] As a matter of fact, this is the natural treatment. In
the great majority of cases, the sentence break in discourse is simply *and*-con-
junction. (In others, it is *but, for, or,* and so on.)[12] Hence, for every discourse,
there is a single sentence which consists of the sequence of *n*-sentences that
comprises the discourse connected by the appropriate sentential connectives
and which exhibits the same semantic relations exhibited in the discourse. But
since the single sentence is, *ex hypothesi,* described by a theory of semantic interpretation, in every case in which a discourse can be treated as a single sentence,
a theory of semantic interpretation is as descriptively powerful as a theory of
setting selection.

---

[10] For examples of studies toward a theory of this kind, *Cf.* Z. S. Harris, "Discourse Analysis,"
Language, XXVI (1952), 1–30; and H. Herzberger, "Contextual Analysis," (doctoral dissertation, Princeton University, 1957).

[11] To illustrate this, let us consider the two-sentence discourse: "I shot the man with a gun,"
"If the man had had a gun too, he would have shot me first." The first sentence of this discourse is ambiguous in isolation, but not in this setting. But the problem of explaining this
disambiguation is the same as the problem of explaining why the single sentence "I shot the
man with a gun, but if the man had had a gun too, he would have shot me first," does not
have an ambiguous first clause. Likewise, consider the discourse, "I heard the noise," "The
noise was completely inaudible," and its single sentence equivalent, "I heard the noise, and the
noise was completely inaudible." In showing why the single sentence is anomalous, a theory
of semantic interpretation exhibits precisely those semantic relations in which the anomaly of
the discourse resides. This technique of replacing discourses or stretches in discourses with single
compound sentences, by using sentential connectives in place of sentence boundaries, clearly
has a very extensive application in reducing problems of setting selection to problems of semantic interpretation of sentences in isolation. Thus, given a theory of semantic interpretation,
it is unclear how much is left for a theory of setting selection to explain.

[12] Sometimes a discourse cannot be directly converted into a compound sentence in this way.
For example, the discourse "How are you feeling today?" "I am fine, thanks" does not convert
to "*How are you feeling today and I am fine, thanks" because the compound sentence is
ungrammatical. But the fact that sentences of different types cannot be run together in the
obvious way may not pose a serious problem because it is not at all clear that less obvious
conversions will not lead to a satisfactory treatment of such cases within a theory of semantic
interpretation. For example, we may convert the discourse just cited into the single sentence,
"*X* asked, 'How are you feeling today?' and *Y* replied, 'I am fine, thanks'." If such conversions can be carried out generally, then any problem about disambiguation, detection of
anomaly, and so on that can be raised and/or solved in a theory of setting selection can be raised
and/or solved by reference to an analogon in the theory of semantic interpretation. But even
if such conversions cannot be carried out generally, the most interesting and central cases
will still be within the range of a theory of semantic interpretation.

We opened the discussion of theories of setting selection in order to fix an upper bound on the domain of a semantic theory of a natural language. The result of the discussion is that, where such a theory is not reducible to a theory of semantic interpretation, it cannot be completed without systematizing all the knowledge about the world that speakers share and keeping such a systema- tization up-to-date as speakers come to share more knowledge. We remarked that a limited theory of how socio-physical setting determines how an utterance is understood is possible, but we pointed out that even then such a theory would blur the distinction between the speaker's knowledge of his language (his linguistic ability) and the speaker's knowledge of the world (his beliefs about matters of fact). Therefore, since it is unlikely that anything stronger than a theory of semantic interpretation is possible and since such a theory is an essential part of a linguistic description, it is eminently reasonable to fix the upper bound of a semantic theory of a natural language at the point where the requirements upon a theory of semantic interpretation are satisfied.

THE COMPONENTS OF A SEMANTIC THEORY

In the previous sections we have characterized the domain of a semantic investigation and circumscribed the descriptive and explanatory goals of a semantic theory of a natural language. Now we must determine what mecha- nisms a semantic theory employs in reconstructing the speaker's ability to interpret sentences in isolation. We have seen that this ability is systematic in that it enables the speaker to understand sentences he has never heard before and to produce novel sentences that other speakers understand in the way he understands them. To account for this ability, a semantic theory must be so formulated that its output matches the interpretive performance of a fluent speaker. In this section, we describe the form of semantic theories.

It is widely acknowledged and certainly true that one component of a seman- tic theory of a natural language is a dictionary of that language. The rationale for including a dictionary as a component of a semantic theory is based on two limitations of a grammatical description. First, a grammar cannot account for the fact that some sentences which differ *only* morphemically are inter- preted as different in meaning (e.g., "The tiger bit me" and "The mouse bit me"), while other sentences which differ only morphemically are interpreted as identical in meaning (e.g., "The oculist examined me" and "The eyedoctor examined me"). Second, a grammar cannot account for the fact that some sentences of radically different syntactic structure are synonymous (e.g., "Two chairs are in the room" and "There are at least two things in the room, and each is a chair"), while other syntactically different sentences are not. In each case, the interpretation of the sentences is determined in part by the meanings of their morphemes and by semantic relations among the morphemes. The rationale for including a dictionary as a component of a semantic theory is precisely to provide a representation of the semantic characteristics of mor- phemes necessary to account for the facts about sentences and their interrela- tions that the grammar leaves unexplained.

What has always been unclear about a semantic theory is what component(s) it contains besides a dictionary and how the components of a semantic theory relate to one another and to the grammar. We can find this out by asking in what respects a dictionary and grammar alone are not sufficient to match the fluent speaker's interpretations of sentences.

Let us imagine a fluent speaker of English presented with the infinite list of sentences and their structural descriptions generated by a grammar of English. Given an accurate dictionary of English, *which he applies by using his linguistic ability*, the fluent speaker can semantically interpret any sentence on the list under any of its grammatical derivations. He can determine the number and content of the readings of a sentence, tell whether or not a sentence is semantically anomalous, and decide which sentences on the list are paraphrases. Now contrast the fluent speaker's performance with the performance of a machine which *mechanically*[13] applies an English dictionary to a sentence on the list by associating with each morpheme of the sentence its dictionary entry. It is clear that the dictionary usually supplies more senses for a lexical item than it bears in almost any of its occurrences in sentences. But the machine will not be able to select the sense(s) the morpheme actually bears in a given sentential context, except insofar as the selection is already determined by the grammatical markers assigned to the morpheme in the derivation of the sentence. For example, the machine will be able to choose the correct sense of *seal* in "Seal the letter" insofar as the choice is determined by the fact that in this sentence *seal* is marked as a verb, and the correct sense of *seal* in "The seal is on the letter" insofar as the choice is determined by the fact that in this sentence *seal* is marked as a noun. But the machine will not be able to distinguish the correct sense of *seal* in "One of the oil seals in my car is leaking" from such incorrect senses as *a device bearing a design so made that it can impart an impression or an impression made by such a device* or *the material upon which the impression is made* or *an ornamental or commemorative stamp* and so forth, since all of these senses can apply to nominal occurrences of *seal*. What the machine is failing to do is to take account of or utilize the semantic relations between morphemes in a sentence. Thus, the machine cannot determine the correct number and content of readings of a sentence; nor can it distinguish semantically anomalous sentences from semantically regular ones. Since the machine will associate a dictionary entry with each morpheme in a sentence, it does not distinguish cases in which the sense of a morpheme or string of morphemes in a sentence precludes other morphemes in the sentence bearing *any* of the senses that the dictionary supplies for them. (E.g., the machine cannot distinguish "The wall is covered with silent paint" from "The wall is covered with fresh paint.") Finally, the machine cannot tell which sentences on the list are paraphrases of each other

---

[13] The qualification *mechanically* is important: it precludes the employment of linguistic skills not represented by the grammar or the dictionary. It is precisely the possession of such skills which distinguishes the fluent speaker from the nonspeaker equipped with a grammar and a dictionary. Hence, the degree to which the nonspeaker is permitted access to such skills is the degree to which we obscure what must be accounted for. Conversely, by prohibiting their employment, as we do by the qualification *mechanically*, we bring into clear relief just the skills that a semantic theory of a natural language must account for.

in any case except the one in which the sentences are of exactly the same syntactic structure and corresponding words in each sentence are either identical or synonymous.

The comparison between a fluent speaker and this machine reveals the respects in which a grammar and dictionary by themselves do not suffice to interpret sentences the way a speaker of the language does. What the fluent speaker has at his disposal which the machine does not are rules for applying the information in the dictionary which take account of semantic relations between morphemes and of the interaction between meaning and syntactic structure in determining the correct semantic interpretation for any of the infinitely many sentences the grammar generates. Thus, a semantic theory of a natural language must have such rules as one of its components if it is to match the speaker's interpretations of sentences.

We thus arrive at the following conception of a semantic theory. The basic fact that a semantic theory must explain is that a fluent speaker can determine the meaning of a sentence in terms of the meanings of its constituent lexical items. To explain this fact, a semantic theory must contain two components: a dictionary of the lexical items of the language and a system of rules (which we shall call *projection rules*) which operates on full grammatical descriptions of sentences and on dictionary entries to produce semantic interpretations for every sentence of the language. Such a theory would explain how the speaker applies dictionary information to sentences and would thus solve the projection problem for semantics by reconstructing the speaker's ability to interpret any of the infinitely many sentences of his language. The central problem for such a theory is that a dictionary usually supplies more senses for a lexical item than it bears in an occurrence in a given sentence, for a dictionary entry is a characterization of *every* sense a lexical item can bear in any sentence. Thus, the effect of the projection rules must be to select the appropriate sense of each lexical item in a sentence in order to provide the correct readings for each distinct grammatical structure of that sentence. The semantic interpretations assigned by the projection rules operating on grammatical and dictionary information must account in the following ways for the speaker's ability to understand sentences: they must mark each semantic ambiguity a speaker can detect; they must explain the source of the speaker's intuitions of anomaly when a sentence evokes them; they must suitably relate sentences speakers know to be paraphrases of each other.[14]

---

[14] The distinction between the dictionary and the rules for its application corresponds, in psychological terms, to a difference between mental processes. The dictionary is something that the speaker learns item by item, in a more or less rote fashion, and is something that he is constantly learning more of. Knowledge of the rules for applying the dictionary, on the other hand, is gained early and *in toto* and is exercised whenever a speaker uses his language. Correspondingly, the utilization of what is learned in learning a dictionary consists in recalling relatively independent bits of information. In the case of the rules, what is involved is the exercise of a faculty for coding and decoding linguistic information. The rules organize whatever systematic, nongrammatical information the speaker has about his language and are thus, in the strongest sense, essential to a knowledge of the language. To know a natural language, one *must* know these rules, but one need not know more than a small fraction of its vocabulary.

Pictured in this way, a semantic theory interprets the syntactic structure a grammatical description of a language reveals. This conception thus gives content to the notion that a semantic theory of a natural language is analogous to a model which interprets a formal system. Further, it explicates the exact sense of the doctrine that the meaning of a sentence is a function of the meanings of the parts of the sentence. The system of projection rules is just this function.

THE STRUCTURE AND EVALUATION OF DICTIONARY ENTRIES

We have seen that the two components of a semantic theory of a natural language are a dictionary and a set of projection rules. In the present section, we shall describe the form that a dictionary must take in a semantic theory, and we shall discuss how, in an empirical study of the semantics of a natural language, we can evaluate the adequacy of proposed dictionary entries for the lexical items of that language. The next section will describe the form of the projection rules.

From the viewpoint of a semantic theory, a dictionary entry consists of two parts: a grammatical portion which provides the parts-of-speech classification for the lexical item, and a semantic portion which represents each of the distinct senses the lexical item has in its occurrences as a given part of speech. (This leaves out much of what is conventionally found in a dictionary entry, e.g., pronunciation, etymology, chronology, and so forth. However, such information is not relevant to a synchronic semantic description of a language.) Thus, for example, the word *play* receives an entry which has grammatical and semantic components as follows:

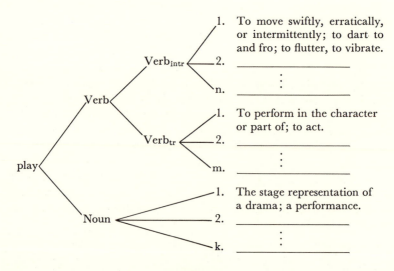

Figure 2

As pictured in Fig. 2, the grammatical portion classifies the syntactic roles the lexical item can play in sentences, while the semantic portion supplies one *sense* of the lexical item as the terminal element of each complete, distinct, descending path through the tree which represents the entry. The sense terminating each path can in turn be analyzed into two parts: a *sense-characterization* (which appears mandatorily) and a sequence of one or more synonyms (which appear optionally).

The central concept to be studied in this section is that of a sense-characterization of a lexical item. We can justify our concern with sense-characterizations to the exclusion of synonyms on the grounds that the concept *synonymity* can be reconstructed in terms of the concept *sense-characterization* but not vice versa. Therefore, the information about synonyms which a dictionary must provide can be given solely in terms of sense-characterizations but not vice versa. In particular, two lexical items have *n*-synonymous senses if and only if they have *n*-paths in common, and two lexical items are fully synonymous if and only if they have identical entries, i.e., every path of one is a path of the other. The explicit inclusion of synonyms in a dictionary entry, which is the common practice of conventional dictionaries, is a redundancy introduced to save the user the effort of discovering the synonyms of a lexical item by comparing its sense-characterizations with those of every other item in the dictionary. In short, the practice of listing the synonyms of an item is simply a technique of cross-reference. This follows from the fact that it must be a condition upon the adequacy of a dictionary that items which are synonymous in *n* of their senses have *n*-paths in common.

Dictionaries[15] give substantially the following entry for the word *bachelor*:

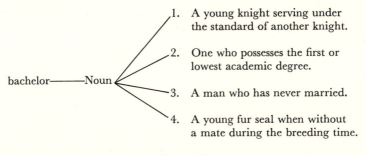

Figure 3

However, for reasons which will presently be made clear, the presentation of dictionary entries in the form exemplified in Figs. 2 and 3 is not adequate for a semantic theory. Instead, a semantic theory requires entries in a form exemplified in Fig. 4:

---

[15] Our sources for dictionary information throughout this paper have been *The Shorter Oxford English Dictionary* and *Webster's New Collegiate Dictionary*.

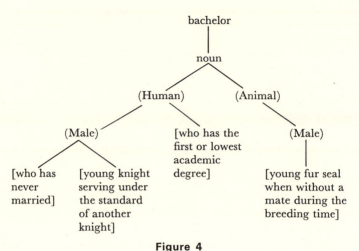

Figure 4

The unenclosed elements in Fig. 4 are *grammatical markers*, the elements enclosed in parentheses are what we shall call *semantic markers*; and the expressions enclosed in brackets are what we shall call *distinguishers*. We have already commented upon the function of grammatical markers. The semantic markers and distinguishers are used as the means by which we can decompose the meaning of a lexical item (on one sense) into its atomic concepts, thus enabling us to exhibit the semantic structure *in* a dictionary entry and the semantic relations *between* dictionary entries. That is, the semantic relations among the various senses of a lexical item and among the various senses of different lexical items are represented by formal relations between markers and distinguishers.

It is clear that any lexical information that a conventional dictionary entry can represent can also be represented by an entry in the normal form shown in Fig. 4. It is equally clear that any semantic relations that can be reconstructed from the former type of entry can also be reconstructed from the latter. For instance, distinct senses continue to be represented as distinct paths, synonymous senses of a lexical item continue to be represented in terms of identity of paths, and so on. However, there are semantic relations which can be reconstructed from entries in our normal form but not from entries in the conventional dictionary form. One such relation is that of *sex-antonymy*. This relation holds between the members of such pairs of words as *bachelor* and *spinster*, *man* and *woman*, *aunt* and *uncle*, *bride* and *groom*, *brother* and *sister*, *cow* and *bull*. What formally characterizes a sex-antonymous pair of words is that the members have identical paths except that where one has the semantic marker (*Male*) the other has the semantic marker (*Female*). Since there are indefinitely many important semantic relations which cannot be formally reconstructed from entries in the conventional dictionary form, this way of writing dictionary entries has a serious theoretical disadvantage. But this disadvantage is not the primary reason for introducing our normal form. The primary reason is that a formalization of the conventional dictionary entry is required in order to permit a formal statement of the projection rules. We will go into this in more detail later.

Semantic markers are the elements in terms of which semantic relations are expressed in a theory. Here there is a strong analogy to grammatical markers, since a grammatical marker (such as Noun, Verb, Adjective) is an element in terms of which syntactic relations are expressed. Thus, the semantic markers assigned to a lexical item in a dictionary entry are intended to reflect whatever systematic semantic relations hold between that item and the rest of the vocabulary of the language. On the other hand, the distinguishers assigned to a lexical item are intended to reflect what is idiosyncratic about the meaning of that item.[16] Generally speaking, a change in the system of semantic markers has extensive ramifications throughout the entire semantic theory, i.e., such a change radically alters the semantic relations which the theory claims obtain between indefinitely many words in the language. But a change in a distinguisher merely alters the relation between the item whose distinguisher has been changed and items which were its synonyms. For example, if the distinction between the markers (*Male*) and (*Female*) were obliterated in a semantic theory of English, not only would every pair of sex-antonymous words be represented as synonymous but the indefinitely many other semantic relations involving this distinction would also be incorrectly represented by the theory. In contrast, eliminating the distinguisher [*young fur seal when without a mate during the breeding time*] would merely prevent a theory from representing one sense of *bachelor* and whatever synonymity relations obtained between that sense of *bachelor* and certain senses of other words.

Branching under a semantic marker is sometimes singular but, very often, it is dyadic (or greater).[17] Since every path in a dictionary entry represents a distinct sense of a lexical item, a lexical item whose dictionary entry contains polyadic branching has more than one sense, i.e., is ambiguous. From the viewpoint of the semantic interpretation of sentences, polyadic branching represents the possibility of sentential semantic ambiguity in any sentence in which the ambiguous lexical item appears. For a necessary condition on the semantic ambiguity of a sentence is that it contain an ambiguous lexical item. But, clearly, this condition is not also sufficient since not all sentences containing ambiguous lexical items are themselves ambiguous. Consider the sentence "The stuff is light enough to carry." The dictionary entry for the word *light* exhibits branching into the semantic markers (*Color*) and (*Weight*). Such branching is required to account for the ambiguity of such sentences as "The stuff is light," "He wears a light suit in the summer," and so on. Since, however, "The stuff is light enough to carry" is unambiguous, it follows that the expression *enough to carry* somehow selects one of the paths in the dictionary entry

---

[16] This does not preclude the possibility that certain semantic relations among lexical items may be expressed in terms of interrelations between their distinguishers. Cases of such relations are those between color names.

[17] Of course, in the entries for some lexical items, there will be paths in which the lowest semantic marker dominates nothing, i.e., paths that do not terminate in distinguishers.

for *light* and excludes the other(s). Hence, the semantic interpretation of "The stuff is light enough to carry" must explain why the occurrence of *light* in this sentence is understood according to the sense in which *light* is a weight adjective.

In short, if a semantic theory is to predict correctly the number of ways speakers will take a sentence to be ambiguous and the precise content of each term of each ambiguity, then it must be able to determine every case in which a sentence containing ambiguous lexical items is itself ambiguous and every case in which selection resolves such ambiguities. But this, in turn, amounts to accepting the condition that a dictionary must be so constructed that every case of lexical ambiguity is represented by polyadic branching and that every case of selection can be represented as the exclusion (by some sentential material) of one or more branches. Semantic anomaly can then be construed as the limiting case of selection: the case where there is a lexical item in a sentence *all* of whose paths are excluded by selections due to other material in the sentence.

Given the principle that semantic relations are expressed in terms of semantic markers alone, we can see that the primary motivation for representing lexical information by semantic markers will be to permit a theory to express those semantic relations which determine selection and thereby to arrive at the correct set of readings for each sentence. That selection must be represented in terms of semantic markers follows from the fact that selection is a semantic relation between parts of a sentence together with the principle that all semantic relations are expressed by semantic markers. Thus, the markers in each entry in the dictionary must be sufficient to permit a reconstruction of the operation of the mechanisms of selection in each sentence in which the lexical item receiving that entry appears.

Another consequence of expressing semantic relations solely in terms of semantic markers is that distinguishers, when they appear in a path in a dictionary entry, must appear as terminal elements; i.e., there must be no branching under a distinguisher. If branching under a distinguisher were allowed, then the theory would posit at least one semantic relation which its dictionary fails to represent by semantic markers, viz., the one between the senses of the lexical item differentiated by that branching.

The distinction between markers and distinguishers is meant to coincide with the distinction between that part of the meaning of a lexical item which is systematic for the language and that part of the meaning of the item which is not. In order to describe the systematicity in the meaning of a lexical item, it is necessary to have theoretical constructs whose formal interrelations compactly represent this systematicity. The semantic markers *are* such theoretical constructs. The distinguishers, on the other hand, do not enter into theoretical relations within a semantic theory. The part of the meaning of a lexical item that a dictionary represents by a distinguisher is thus the part of which a semantic theory offers no general account.

We must now consider the basis on which to decide to represent some lexical information by semantic markers and other lexical information by distinguishers. We thus not only clarify the basis for such decisions, but clarify further the nature of markers and distinguishers.

In the last analysis, the decision to represent a piece of lexical information by semantic markers or by distinguishers can only be justified by showing that it leads to correct interpretations for sentences. What, therefore, must be explained is how such decisions effect the assignment of semantic interpretations and, conversely, how the requirement that a theory assign semantic interpretations correctly effects decisions about the way in which a piece of lexical information is represented.

A particular semantic theory of a natural language can *represent* only those sentential semantic ambiguities resulting from the occurrence of a lexical item for which the dictionary of the theory provides an entry which contains two or more paths. That is, the degree of semantic ambiguity a semantic interpretation assigns to a sentence is a function of the degree of branching within the entries for the lexical items appearing in the sentence, branching into markers, distinguishers, or a combination of both counting equally in determining degree of ambiguity. However, a particular semantic theory of a natural language can *resolve* only those sentential semantic ambiguities which result from the occurrence of lexical material associated with dictionary entries containing two or more paths that differ by at least one semantic marker. This limitation on a semantic theory's power to resolve ambiguities is a direct consequence of the fact that selection can operate only upon semantic markers. Hence, decisions to represent a piece of lexical information by markers or distinguishers determine in part what semantic ambiguities will be only marked in the semantic interpretation of sentences and what will be both marked and resolved.

The decision to represent a piece of lexical information by a marker or a distinguisher is controlled by two kinds of considerations. Since we wish to construct a semantic theory in such a way that its output matches the performance of a fluent speaker, we want the theory to represent in its semantic interpretations just those semantic ambiguities that the fluent speaker can mark and to resolve just those ambiguities that he can resolve. This will mean that in theory construction what lexical information is represented by markers and what is represented by distinguishers will be controlled by our evidence about the disambiguations a fluent speaker can make. Let us take as an example the case of the word *bachelor*. If the dictionary entry is as given in Fig. 4, every sentence in which *bachelor* appears will be represented as ambiguous between the senses given by the paths: *bachelor* → Noun → (*Human*) → (*Male*) → [*who has never married*]; and *bachelor* → Noun → (*Human*) → (*Male*) → [*young knight serving under the standard of another knight*]. Since this ambiguity of *bachelor* is represented only by a difference of distinguishers, there is no way that a theory whose dictionary contains this entry can resolve it. But though this is an absolute limitation on such a theory, it is not an absolute limitation on the construction of semantic theories in general. If we notice that fluent speakers do not take such sentences as "The old bachelor finally died" to be ambiguous, then we can construct our semantic theory to accommodate this simply by taking the lexical information that a bachelor in the second sense is necessarily young to be marker information rather than distinguisher information. This is done by adding the marker (*Young*) to the marker system and rewriting the dictionary entry for *bachelor* accordingly. (See Figure 5)

The second kind of consideration which controls what lexical information is included in the system of semantic markers is the desire for systematic economy. The addition of new semantic markers, as in the case above, is made in order to increase the precision and scope of a semantic theory, but in so doing it also increases the complexity of the theory's conceptual apparatus. Since allowing more complexity often coincides with greater precision and scope, the decision as to what lexical information to include in the marker system of a semantic theory should be made on the basis of a strategy which seeks to maximize systematic economy: the greatest possible conceptual economy with the greatest possible explanatory and descriptive power. If such decisions are optimally made, there should eventually come a point when increasing the complexity of a semantic theory by adding new markers no longer yields enough of an advantage in precision or scope to warrant the increase. At this point, the system of semantic markers should reflect exactly the systematic features of the semantic structure of the language.

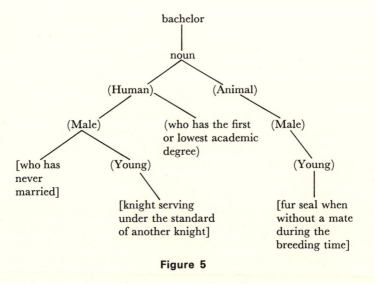

Figure 5

Thus far we have reconstructed four types of information which conventional dictionaries provide about a lexical item: its part of speech classification, its number of senses, its systematic semantic features, and its idiosyncratic features. There is one further type of information which conventional dictionaries give that is relevant to synchronic semantic description: information about the relation between features of certain combinations into which a lexical item may enter and the sense the item bears in those combinations. For example, consider *The Shorter Oxford English Dictionary* entry for the word *honest*: " . . . 3. of persons:

of good moral character, virtuous, upright, . . . of women: chaste, 'virtuous', . . . ". The "of persons" and "of women" are intended to indicate that the senses that follow them apply only under the conditions that they specify. That is, these specifications indicate that if the nominal head which *honest* modifies refers to a person without specification of sex, then *honest* has the meaning "of good moral character, virtuous, or upright," and if the nominal head refers to a woman, then *honest* means *either* "of good moral character, virtuous, or upright" *or* "chaste." Our reconstruction of this type of dictionary information must follow conventional dictionary procedure as far as it goes, but should go further in that the reconstruction should provide *all* the information necessary to determine selection and exclusion. Where the conventional dictionary, by using such devices as "of . . . ," tells us what a word means in certain combinations, our reconstruction must do this systematically and also provide a basis for determining what combinations are semantically acceptable and what are not.

For our reconstruction, we shall use left and right angles enclosing a Boolean function of syntactic or semantic markers. Such configurations of symbols will be affixed to the terminal element of a path (either the distinguisher or the last semantic marker if there is no distinguisher) and will be construed, relative to the projection rules, as providing a necessary and sufficient condition for a semantically acceptable combination. Thus, for example, the angle-material terminally affixed to the path of a modifier determines the applicability of *that* path of the modifier to a sense of a nominal head. In particular, a path in the dictionary entry for *honest* will be: *honest* → *Adjective* → (*Evaluative*) → (*Moral*) → [*innocent of illicit sexual intercourse*] [(*Human*) and (*Female*)]. This is to be construed as saying that an adjectival occurrence of *honest* receives the interpretation, (*Evaluative*) → (*Moral*) → [*innocent of illicit sexual intercourse*], just in case the head it modifies has a path containing both the semantic markers (*Human*) and (*Female*). How in actual practice a semantic theory utilizes angle-material to determine selection/exclusion relations to obtain semantic interpretations of sentences can only be made clear by the statement of the projection rules.

This concludes the characterization of our normal form for dictionary entries. A dictionary is, then, a list (ordered or not) of the lexical items of the language, each item being associated with an entry in our normal form. The question of whether the lexical items are to be words, morphemes, or some other unit, we do not attempt to decide here. However, certain considerations are relevant to this decision. The most important consideration is that we choose the unit that will enable us to describe the largest amount of the compositional structure of the language. As a rule, the meaning of a word is a compositional function of the meanings of its parts, and we would like to be able to capture this compositionality. An approach which directs us to choose as lexical items those syntactic units in terms of which we can reconstruct a maximum of compositional structure has, moreover, simplicity in its favor. Wherever we can use composition, dictionary entries are avoided. Thus, instead of having an entry for each verb which takes the prefix *de* and a separate entry for *de* plus that verb, we must choose our lexical units so that the dictionary need only contain an entry for *de* and an entry for the unprefixed form of each verb. This economy can be achieved because *de* + verb combinations are compositional wherever the verb is semantically marked as *(Process)* → *(Reversible Process)*.

It will be noticed that the dictionary is so formulated that all semantic properties and relations which are represented in entries are *formally* represented. This is required so that, given a formal statement of the projection rules (i.e., the application of the rules being defined solely in terms of the shapes of the symbols to which they apply and the operations the rules effect in producing their output being mechanical), the question of what semantic interpretation is assigned to a given sentence can be answered by formal computations without the aid of linguistic intuitions or insights. The need to have a formal semantic theory derives from the necessity of avoiding vacuity; for a semantic theory is vacuous to the extent that the speaker's intuitions or insights about semantic relations are essentially relied on in order that the rules of the theory apply correctly. Thus, it is uninformative to be told that an English sentence exhibits a semantic relation R just in case it satisfies the condition C if the condition C is so formulated that we cannot know C to be satisfied without essentially relying on a speaker's intuitive knowledge of semantic relations such as R. A formal theory is *ipso facto* not vacuous in this respect since no knowledge about semantic relations in any language is required to determine the correct application of its rules.[18]

Now we turn to the question of how the adequacy of dictionary entries can be evaluated. It is often assumed that a semantic theory must yield a feasible mechanical procedure which enables the linguist to actually construct a dictionary from information about the verbal behavior of speakers. Every proposal for such a procedure has, however, proven egregiously unsuccessful, and we believe this to be in the nature of the case. Likewise, we think that those theorists who have insisted upon a mechanical procedure for deciding whether or not a putative dictionary entry is optimal have set their aims too high; we regard the practical impossibility of such a decision procedure as also in the nature of the case. We shall not argue directly for these claims. We make them primarily to warn the reader against construing the conception of a semantic

---

[18] However, in order to utilize a semantic theory to enable a nonspeaker to understand sentences in the language it describes, the nonspeaker must understand the theory in the full sense in which this includes understanding the intended interpretation of the constructs of the theory and of their theoretical relations. But it is not necessary to understand the theory in that sense in order to derive the semantic interpretations the theory provides for sentences. This is guaranteed by the requirement that the theory be formal. The situation may be illuminated by an analogy to machine translation. Suppose we have a formal translation function which takes each sentence in a *source* language into its image in a *target* language. Given such a function, we can automatically associate the sentences of the two languages, and we can do so without appeal to linguistic intuitions about either language. But in order to use the function to *understand* the sentences of the target language, one must understand their images in the home language. Precisely the same situation obtains in the case of a semantic theory: the theory automatically associates an interpretation with each sentence, but this enables us to understand a sentence only insofar as we understand the theory which provides the interpretation.

theory proposed in this paper as either a mechanical discovery procedure or a mechanical decision procedure for dictionary entries.

However, this paper can be understood as proposing a conception of semantic theory which, *inter alia*, provides a procedure for determining which of two proposed dictionary entries is the best for a given language, but this evaluation procedure differs considerably from that usually envisioned by semantic theorists. On our conception, a dictionary is only one component of a semantic theory which has as its other component a set of projection rules for semantically interpreting sentences on the basis of the dictionary. Only the theory as a whole can be subjected to empirical test. This means that if a semantic theory gives incorrect interpretations for sentences, one must then decide whether to revise some dictionary entries, some projection rules, or some of each. Thus, questions of evaluation are to be raised primarily about entire semantic theories. Nonetheless, there is a derivative sense in which such questions can be raised about particular dictionary entries, viz., given projection rules and other dictionary entries that are sufficiently well established, which of the two candidate entries yields the best interpretations for sentences? This conception of evaluating dictionary entries differs from the usual one in that it makes such evaluations a matter of the degree to which the entry helps achieve the purpose of a dictionary within a theory of semantic interpretation. Semantic theorists usually conceive of such evaluation as effected by criteria which select the preferable of two entries *simply* on the basis of facts about the verbal behavior of speakers, thus overlooking the fact that it is the interpretation of sentences, not the construction of dictionaries, that is the objective of a semantic theory. Because they have overlooked this fact, their criteria for evaluating dictionary entries are invariably too weak in that these criteria fail to utilize systematic constraints on the semantic interpretation of sentences (matching the fluent speaker's ability to determine the number of readings of sentences, the content of the readings, and their paraphrase relations) in choosing a preferable dictionary entry.

The controls on a semantic theory of a natural language are, therefore, nothing more than the usual empirical and methodological constraints imposed upon any scientific theory: the requirement that a semantic theory match the fluent speaker's ability to interpret sentences is the particular form that the general methodological requirement that a scientific theory accord with the facts takes in the case of semantics. If certain consequences of a semantic theory conflict with the facts about the performance of fluent speakers, various revisions in the dictionary component, in the projection rule component, and in both must be tried out and compared to determine which solution best accommodates the available linguistic evidence.

THE PROJECTION RULE COMPONENT

We have seen that a grammar is a device which enumerates an infinite list of strings of morphemes, including every string that is a sentence and no string that is not, and assigns each sentence a structural description, i.e., grammatical markers specifying the elements out of which a string is constructed, their arrangement, and the syntactic relations holding between them. A sentence and its structural description provide the input to a semantic theory. A semantic theory has as its output a semantic interpretation of each sentence given it as input. We may picture the situation as in Fig. 6.

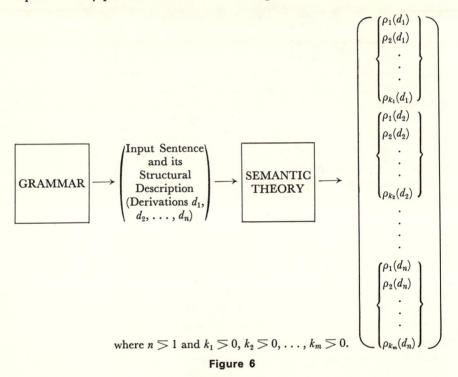

where $n \geqslant 1$ and $k_1 \geqslant 0, k_2 \geqslant 0, \ldots, k_m \geqslant 0$.

Figure 6

Fig. 6 shows the input to a semantic theory to be a sentence S together with a structural description consisting of the n-derivations of S, $d_1, d_2, \ldots, d_n$, one for each of the n-ways that S is grammatically ambiguous. The output of the semantic theory is shown as k_1 readings for d_1, k_2 readings for $d_2, \ldots, k_m$ readings for d_n, each reading corresponding to a term of a semantic (nongrammatical) ambiguity of S on some derivation. The schema $\rho_i(d_j)$ represents the ith reading of d_j (which the semantic theory supplies).

We can now characterize the notion *semantic interpretation of the sentence S* as the conjunction ψd_1 & ψd_2 & ... & ψd_n of the semantic interpretations of the n-derivations of S plus any statements about S that follow from conventions (1) to (8). The semantic interpretation of S *on the derivation* d_j is the output of the dictionary and projection rule components for S on d_j together with the statements about S on d_j that can be made on the basis of the conventions:

(1) If $k_1 + k_2 + \cdots + k_m = 1$, then S is unambiguous.
(2) If $k_1 + k_2 + \cdots + k_m > 1$, then S is $k_1 + k_2 + \cdots + k_m$ ways ambiguous.

(3) If $k_1 + k_2 + \cdots + k_m = 0$, then S is anomalous.

(4) If the set of readings assigned to the derivation d_j, $\rho_1(d_j)$, $\rho_2(d_j)$, $\ldots$, $\rho_{k_i}(d_j)$, has exactly one member, then S is unambiguous on d_j.

(5) If the set of readings assigned to the derivation d_j has more than one member, then S is k_i ways semantically ambiguous on d_j.

(6) If the set of readings assigned to d_j is null, then S is semantically anomalous on d_j.

(7) If S and another sentence P have at least one reading in common, then S and P are paraphrases on that reading.

(8) If S and P have all readings in common, then S and P are full paraphrases.

We can schematize the relation between the dictionary component and the projection rule component:

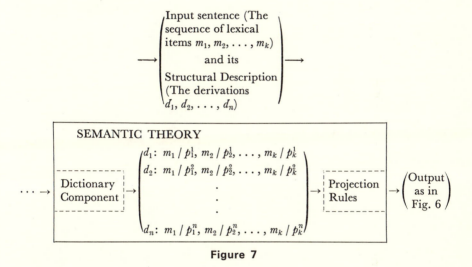

Figure 7

The input to the dictionary component consists of a sentence S represented by a sequence of lexical items, m_1, m_2, $\ldots$, m_k, and the set of derivations of S. The symbol, P^i_j, stands for a finite, non-null set of paths drawn from the dictionary entry for the lexical item m_j in S and such that any path in the dictionary entry for m_j is in the set just in case the path contains grammatical markers which assign m_j the syntactic role it has on the derivation d_i. The symbol, $/$, represents the association between a lexical item and a subset of the set of paths in its dictionary entry. The association is effected by the instruction (1) which, together with the dictionary, comprises the dictionary component:

(1) For each pair d_i and m_j, the path p in the entry for m_j is assigned to the set P^i_j if, and only if, p has as its initial subpath the sequence of grammatical markers $g_1, g_2, \ldots, g_r$ and the derivation d_i contains the path $g_1 \rightarrow g_2 \rightarrow \cdots \rightarrow g_r \rightarrow m_j$.

The instruction (1) chooses as relevant to the semantic interpretation of a sentence on a given derivation only those paths from the dictionary entries for each of the lexical items in the sentence which are compatible with the lower-level syntactic structure of the sentence on that derivation. The output of the dictionary component is thus a mapping of a finite, non-null set of paths onto each m_j for each d_i. This output, as Fig. 7 shows, is, in turn, the input to the projection rules.

We can now give a general picture of the operations whereby the projection rule component converts its input into a semantic interpretation. Each sentence the grammar makes available for semantic interpretation has associated with it n-derivations marking the n-ways in which it is structurally ambiguous. Each derivation marks constituent structure in a way that can be represented by a tree diagram. We shall employ such tree diagrams in the following pages, *but it is to be understood that projection rules can take account of information about the transformational history of a sentence which is not represented in a tree diagram.*

Figure 8 gives the derived constituent structure of the sentence "the man

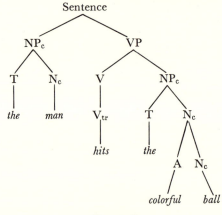

Figure 8

hits the colorfull ball."[19] The dictionary component associates sets of paths with such a tree in the manner specified by instruction (1). Thus, after the application of instruction (1), we have:

---

[19] It can be argued on grammatical grounds that the phrase *the colorful ball* should be represented simply as:

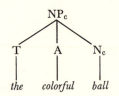

i.e., without the internal syntactic structure it is given in Fig. 8. This representation would not include the information (which will be required by the projection rules) that *colorful* is a modifier of the head *ball*. But the need for this sort of information does not commit us to the assumption that all branching in derived constituent structure trees is binary. For such information can be obtained by examining the transformational history of the sentence. This is a typical case of the way a projection rule can utilize information taken from the transformational history of the sentences to which it is applied.

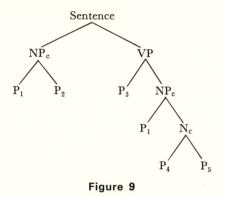

Figure 9

The marking of the lexical items *the, man, hits, the, colorful,* and *ball* as, respectively, Article, Noun concrete, Verb transitive, Article, Adjective, and Noun concrete, which at first glance may seem to have been lost in the application of instruction (1), is actually represented as the common initial subpath of every p in each P_j^i, e.g., P_3 is the set of paths all of whose members begin *hits* $\rightarrow V \rightarrow V_{tr}$.

The general way in which the projection rule component works is by proceeding from the bottom to the top of a constituent structure tree and effecting a series of amalgamations, starting with the output of instruction (1) and amalgamating sets of paths dominated by a grammatical marker, thus assigning a set of readings to the concatenation of lexical items under that marker by associating the result of the amalgamation with the marker until the highest marker *Sentence* is reached and associated with a set of readings. The projection rules amalgamate sets of paths dominated by a grammatical marker by combining elements from each of them to form a new set of paths which provides a set of readings for the sequence of lexical items under the grammatical marker. Amalgamation is an operation of joining elements from different sets of paths under a given grammatical marker just in case these elements satisfy the appropriate selection restrictions represented by material in angles.

Let us now give an example of how a semantic theory of English might interpret a sentence and, in this way, exhibit some of the projection rules for English.[20] As our example, we choose the sentence "the man hits the colorful ball" under the derivation given in Fig. 8.

The projection rule component receives this sentence and its derivation as input after instruction (1) has operated. (See Fig. 9.) The first step for the projection rule component is to amalgamate each set of paths under each of the grammatical markers which immediately dominates *only* sets of paths and to associate with the dominating marker the amalgam so obtained. Thus, in the case of Fig. 9, the first step is to amalgamate either P_4 and P_5 or P_1 and P_2, the order being immaterial.

---

[20] It should be made perfectly clear that the rules we shall give are not intended as contribution to a semantic theory of English but only as examples of the type of rules such a theory would employ.

Let us first take the amalgamation of P_4 and P_5. The paths comprising the set P_4 are:

$$P_4$$

(1) *Colorful* → Adjective → *(Color)* → *[Abounding in contrast or variety of bright colors]* $\langle(Physical\ Object)\ \text{v}\ (Social\ Activity)\rangle$

(2) *Colorful* → Adjective → *(Evaluative)* → *[Having distinctive character, vividness, or picturesqueness]* $\langle(Aesthetic\ Object)\ \text{v}\ (Social\ Activity)\rangle$

The paths comprising the set P_5 are:

$$P_5$$

(1) *Ball* → Noun concrete → *(Social Activity)* → *(Large)* → *(Assembly)* → *[For the purpose of social dancing]*

(2) *Ball* → Noun concrete → *(Physical Object)* → *[Having globular shape]*

(3) *Ball* → Noun concrete → *(Physical Object)* → *[Solid missile for projection by engine of war]*

P_41 is the sense of *colorful* in "The gift came in a colorful wrapper"; P_42 is the sense of *colorful* in "No novel is less colorful than Middlemarch, excepting Silas Marner"; P_51 is the sense of *ball* in "The queen danced at the French ambassador's ball"; P_52 is the sense of *ball* in "Tennis is played with a ball"; P_53 is the sense of *ball* in "The balls whistle free o'er the bright blue sea." It will be noticed that the sense of *ball* in "He plays ball better than Babe Ruth" is not represented by a path in P_5, although such a path is to be found in the dictionary entry for *ball*. This is because *ball*, when it means the game, is not a concrete noun and so instruction (1) eliminates the path which represents that sense.

The amalgamation of P_4 and P_5 is accomplished by the following projection rule:

(R_1)   Given two paths of the form

    (1)   Lexical String$_1$ → syntactic markers of head → (a_1) → (a_2) → $\cdots$ → (a_n) → [1] $\langle$set of strings of markers $\Omega_1\rangle$

    (2)   Lexical String$_2$ → syntactic markers of modifier → (b_1) → (b_2) → $\cdots$ → (b_m) → [2] $\langle$set of strings of markers $\Omega_2\rangle$

such that there is a substring σ of the string of syntactic or semantic head markers and $\sigma \in \Omega_2$. There is an amalgam of the form

Lexical String$_2$ + Lexical String$_1$ → dominating node marker → (a_1) → (a_2) → $\cdots$ → (a_n) → (b_1) → (b_2) $\cdots$ → (b_m) → [[2] [1]] $\langle\Omega_1\rangle$,

where any b_i is null when $(\exists a_i)\ (b_i = a_i)$ and [[2] [1]] is [1] when [2] = [1].[21]

The amalgam of P_4 and P_5 is the set of derived paths P_6:

$$P_6$$

(1) *Colorful* + *ball* → Noun concrete → *(Social Activity)* → *(Large)* → *(Assembly)* → *(Color)* → *[[Abounding in contrast or variety of bright colors] [For the purpose of social dancing]]*

(2) *Colorful* + *ball* → Noun concrete → *(Physical Object)* → *(Color)* → *[[Abounding in contrast or variety of bright colors] [Having globular shape]]*

---

[21] The reason why Ω_1 appears in the output of (R_1) is that some heads are, in turn, modifiers of other heads (e.g., adjectives are heads for adverbs and also modifiers for nouns in such cases as *(light [red] ball)*. In these cases, the conditions in Ω_1 will be required for selection.

(3) *Colorful + ball* → Noun concrete → (*Physical Object*) → (*Color*) → [[*Abounding in contrast or variety of bright colors*] [*Solid missile for projection by engine of war*]]

(4) *Colorful + Ball* → Noun concrete → (*Social Activity*) → (*Large*) → (*Assembly*) → (*Evaluative*) → [[*Having distinctive character, vividness, or picturesqueness*] [*For the purpose of social dancing*]]

There were six possible amalgamations from the combination of P_4 and P_5, but only four derived paths because, of the possible combinations of $P_4 2$ with elements of P_5, only the combination $P_4 2$ and $P_5 1$ satisfies the selection restriction ⟨(*Aesthetic Object* v (*Social Activity*)⟩. Thus, (R_1) predicts the semantic anomaly of *colorful + ball* on the reading where *colorful* has the sense represented by $P_4 2$ and *ball* has either the sense represented by $P_5 2$ or the sense represented by $P_5 3$. Another example of how (R_1) contributes to the formalization of the distinction between what is semantically acceptable and what is semantically anomalous is the following: The expression *spinster insecticide* would be regarded as anomalous by speakers of English, and this can be predicted on the basis of (R_1) and the dictionary entries for *spinster* and *insecticide*. The relevant path for *spinster* is: *spinster* → Adjective → (*Human*) → (*Adult*) → (*Female*) → [*Who has never married*]⟨(*Human*)⟩. On the basis of these paths, (R_1) assigns no reading to the expression *spinster insecticide*, (i.e. (R_1) predicts that *spinster insecticide* is semantically anomalous) because the path for *insecticide* does not contain the semantic marker (*Human*) which is necessary to satisfy the selection restriction associated with *spinster*.

The projection rule (R_1) introduces the semantic markers in the path of the modifier just below the string of semantic markers in the path of the head, eliminating from the path of the modifier semantic material already present in the path of the head and associating the distinguishers with one another. The operation of (R_1) corresponds closely to our intuitive notions of the nature of attribution. Attribution is the process of creating a new semantic unit compounded from a modifier and a head, whose semantic properties are those of the head, *except that the meaning of the compound is made more determinate than that of the head by the information the compound obtains from the modifier*. As Lees comments:

> We cannot get along with a single common noun to refer to a familiar common object, but must have at every moment modifiers with which to construct new more complex names to use for all the specific instances of that object which we encounter and talk about. Thus, we cannot, without extensive ambiguity, refer on every occasion to our favorite beverage by means of the single word *coffee*; instead we name its individual instances with such phrases as "my coffee," "that cold cup of coffee you left there," "some fresh coffee on the shelf," "a new brand of coffee," "pretty tasteless coffee," "Turkish coffee," and so on. There is no known limitation on the number of distinct objects for which we must at some time or other have distinctive names, and clearly no dictionary is large enough to contain them all, for a great many of the names which we employ have never before been uttered. Like full sentences themselves, there is no longest name, and there must consequently be an infinity of new names available for us to use when and if the need arises.[22]

---

[22] R. B. Lees, "The Grammar of English Nominalizations," *International Journal of American Linguistics*, XXVI, No. 3 (July 1960), xvii–xviii.

Although Lees is commenting on the grammar of nominal compounds, what he says applies equally well to their semantics and to the semantics of other modifier-head constructions. It is only because there is a systematic way of understanding the meaning of such constructions in terms of the meanings of their parts that the infinite stock of strings produced by the grammatical mechanism for creating new modifier-head constructions can be employed by speakers to refer to familiar objects.

As we have just mentioned, the meaning of a compound is more determinate than the meaning of its head in respect of the information the compound obtains from its modifier(s). Let us consider an example. The word *aunt* is indeterminate as to age (i.e., neither the sentence "My aunt is an infant" nor "My aunt is aged" has any special semantic properties), but *spinster*, as we have observed above, contains the semantic marker *(Adult)* in its path. This marker is carried over to the compound when (R_1) operates to produce an interpretation for *spinster aunt*. Thus, *spinster aunt* is made more determinate (with respect to age) than is *aunt*. This shows up in a comparison between the sentences "My spinster aunt is an infant" and "My spinster aunt is aged," the former of which is contradictory while the latter is not.

The limiting case, where the addition to the compound of semantic material from the modifier is zero, is of considerable theoretical significance. The compound *unmarried bachelor* is a case in point. The erasure clause in (R_1), i.e., "any b_i is null when $(\exists a_i)$ $(b_i = a_i)$ and $[[2][1]]$ is $[1]$ when $[2] = [1]$," tells us to delete from the path of the modifier any semantic material already represented in the path of the head. Thus, in forming the compound *unmarried bachelor* all the semantic information in the path of the modifier *unmarried* will be deleted so that the derived path for *unmarried bachelor* will contain no more than the semantic material which comes from the path for *bachelor*. The failure of the modifier to add semantic information would appear to account for the intuition that such expressions as *unmarried bachelor* are redundant and that, correspondingly, such statements as "Bachelors are unmarried" are *empty, tautological, vacuous, uninformative*. Thus, we have a new explanation of the analyticity of a classical type of analytic truth.[23] Moreover, this feature of the projection rules provides another empirical constraint on a semantic theory: if the theory characterizes an expression or sentence as redundant in the above sense, then the theory is confirmed if speakers take the expression or sentence in the appropriate way and is disconfirmed if they do not.

The next step in the semantic interpretation of "The man hits the colorful ball" is the amalgamation of P_1 and P_2. The entry for *the* in standard dictionaries is exceedingly complex primarily because the information required to make the correct selections among the various senses of *the* for its sentential occurrences is extremely complicated. Thus, we shall have to simplify and not try to represent all the information actually needed in the dictionary entry for *the*.

P_1 contains only the path: *the* → Noun phrase concrete → Definite Article

---

[23] *Cf.* J.J. Katz, "Analyticity and Contradiction in Natural Language" .... [See above, pp. 136–62.]

→ [*Some contextually definite*]. Other paths in the dictionary entry for *the*, viz., those corresponding to the generic senses of the definite article, are not assigned to P_1 by instruction (I) because only the above path contains the sequence of grammatical markers as its initial subpath which dominates *the* in the derivation in Fig. 8.[24] P_2 contains only the path: *man* → Noun concrete → Noun masculine → (*Physical Object*) → (*Human*) → (*Adult*) → (*Male*). Other paths in the dictionary entry for *man*, viz., the path corresponding to the sense of *man* in "Man is occasionally rational" and the path corresponding to the sense of *man* in "Every man on board ship was saved except an elderly couple," do not appear in P_2, the former because in that sense *man* is not a concrete noun and the latter because in that sense *man* is not a masculine noun. The rule which amalgamates P_1 and P_2 is:

(R_2) Given two paths of the form

   (1) Lexical String$_1$ → syntactic markers of noun → semantic markers of head → [1]
   (2) Lexical String$_2$ → syntactic markers of article → semantic markers of article → [2] ⟨set of strings of markers Ω⟩

   such that there is a substring σ of the string of syntactic or semantic nominal markers and $\sigma \in \Omega$. There is an amalgam of the form

   Lexical String$_2$ + Lexical String$_1$ → dominating node marker → semantic markers of article → [2] → semantic markers of noun → [1].

The application of (R_2) to P_1 and P_2 produces the derived path: *the* + *man* → Noun phrase concrete → [*Some contextually definite*] → (*Physical Object*) → (*Human*) → (*Adult*) → (*Male*). This path is the only member of the set P_7 shown in Fig. 10.

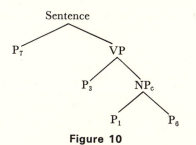

Figure 10

The amalgamation of P_1 and P_6 works in exactly the same way and yields P_8:

$$P_8$$

(1) *The* + *colorful* + *ball* → Noun phrase concrete → [*Some contextually definite*] → (*Social Activity*) → (*Large*) → (*Assembly*) → (*Color*) → [[*Abounding in contrast or variety of bright colors*] [*For the purpose of social dancing*]]

---

[24] In taking NP_c as part of the sequence of grammatical markers in the dictionary entry for *the*, we are not claiming that *the* is a concrete noun phrase, but only that it occurs as an element of a concrete noun phrase and that, when it does, it has the sense in P_1. This constitutes an extension of the notion of a "part of speech classification," but a natural and necessary one.

(2) *The + colorful + ball* → Noun phrase concrete → [*Some contextually definite*] → (*Physical Object*) → (*Color*) → [[*Abounding in contrast or variety of bright colors*] [*Having globular shape*]]

(3) *The + colorful + ball* → Noun phrase concrete → [*Some contextually definite*] → (*Physical Object*) → (*Color*) → [[*Abounding in contrast or variety of bright colors*] [*Solid missile for projection by engine of war*]]

(4) *The + colorful + ball* → Noun phrase concrete → [*Some contextually definite*] → (*Social activity*) → (*Large*) → (*Assembly*) → (*Evaluative*) → [[*Having distinctive character, vividness, or picturesqueness*] [*For the purpose of social dancing*]]

This leaves us with only the part of the constituent structure tree shown in Fig. 11 still to be interpreted.

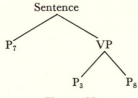

Figure 11

P_3 is as follows:

$$P_3$$

(1) *hits* → Verb → Verb transitive → (*Action*) → (*Instancy*) → (*Intensity*) → [*Collides with an impact*] ⟨SUBJECT: (*Higher Animal*) v (*Improper Part*) v (*Physical Object*), OBJECT: (*Physical Object*)⟩[25]

(2) *hits* → Verb → Verb transitive → (*Action*) → (*Instancy*) → (*Intensity*) → [*Strikes with a blow or missile*] ⟨SUBJECT: (*Human*) v (*Higher Animal*), OBJECT: (*Physical Object*), INSTRUMENTAL: (*Physical Object*)⟩

$P_3 1$ is the sense of *hits* in "The rock hits the ground with a thud." $P_3 2$ is the sense of *hits* in "The man hits the ground with a rock." It will be noticed that the representation of verbs includes between angles selection restrictions upon the subject and objects of the verb. This information is represented by markers of the form "SUBJECT: α," "OBJECT: β," and "INSTRUMENTAL: γ," where α, β, and γ, respectively, represent conditions on the paths associated with the subject, object and instrumental.

A few comments on this dictionary entry for *hits* as a transitive verb are necessary. We claim no more than rough accuracy for the above characterization. Our interest here, as throughout the present paper, is with prescribing the abstract form of a semantic theory rather than with actually writing one. Thus, the above characterization is intended primarily to illustrate how the

---

[25] Here some explanation is called for. *Instancy* is assigned to those verbs representing durationless events. Any sentence whose main verb is marked *Instancy* which is of the form "*Subject + Verb + ed + Object + for + numerical quantifier + measure of time*" will be understood to mean that the object was verbed more than once. Compare "He hit the ball for three hours" with "He studies the book for three hours." Next, *Intensity* is assigned to those verbs taking such adverbs as *hard, soft, gently*. Finally, the marker *Improper Part* is assigned to lexical items that represent wholes which the language contrasts with their parts.

results of a linguistic analysis are to be formally presented in order that the projection rules can utilize them. But we have tried to make our examples account for the fundamental semantic features. In the present case, the failure to mark an achievement sense of *hits* is not an oversight. We choose not to mark a special sense of *hits* in which it is an achievement verb because the behavior of *hits* diverges in significant ways from that of such paradigmatic achievement verbs as *sees* and *hears*. Thus, unlike "He hit the ball intentionally," "He saw the picture intentionally" is anomalous (except where it means that he went to see the picture intentionally), and "He heard the music intentionally" is anomalous (except where it means that he didn't *just* overhear the music). This is perhaps related to the fact that one can intentionally miss the ball, although one cannot in the relevant sense intentionally fail to hear the music. If, however, it should turn out that *hits* must be given a special, achievement sense, such a sense can be represented within the formalism of the present paper in a straightforward manner.

The projection rule which amalgamates P_3 and P_8 is:

(R_3) Given two paths of the form

    (1) Lexical String$_1$ → syntactic markers of main verb → semantic markers → [1] ⟨sets of strings of markers α, β⟩

    (2) Lexical String$_2$ → syntactic markers of object of main verb → Remainder of object path

such that there is a substring σ of the string of syntactic or semantic markers of the object and $\sigma \in \beta$. There is an amalgam of the form

Lexical String$_1$ + Lexical String$_2$ → dominating node marker → semantic markers of main verb → [1] → String analyzed *Remainder of object path* ⟨set of strings of markers α⟩

The application of (R_3) to P_3 and P_8 yields P_9.

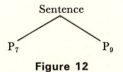

Figure 12

P_9 contains the following paths:

P_9

(1) *hits* + *the* + *colorful* + *ball* → VP → (Action) → (Instancy) → (Intensity) → [Collides with an impact] → [Some contextually definite] → (Physical Object) → (Color) → [[Abounding in contrast or variety of bright colors] [Having globular shape]] ⟨SUBJECT: (Higher Animal) v (Improper Part) v (Physical Object)⟩

(2) *hits* + *the* + *colorful* + *ball* → VP → (Action) → (Instancy) → (Intensity) → [Collides with an impact] → [Some contextually definite] → (Physical Object) → (Color) → [[Abounding in contrast or variety of bright colors] [Solid missile for projection by engine of war]] ⟨SUBJECT: (Higher Animal v (Improper Part) v (Physical Object)⟩

(3) *hits* + *the* + *colorful* + *ball* → VP → (Action) → (Instancy) → (Intensity) →

[*Strikes with a blow or missile*] → [*Some contextually definite*] → (*Physical Object*) → (*Color*) → [[*Abounding in contrast or variety of bright colors*] [*Having globular shape*]] ⟨SUBJECT: (*Human*) v (*Higher Animal*)⟩

(4) *hits + the + colorful + ball + VP* → (*Action*) → (*Instancy*) → (*Intensity*) → [*Strikes with a blow or missile*] → [*Some contextually definite*] → (*Physical Object*) → (*Color*) → [[*Abounding in contrast or variety of bright colors*] [*Solid missile for projection by engine of war*] ⟨SUBJECT: (*Human*) v (*Higher Animal*)⟩

Finally, the projection rule which operates on P_7 and P_9 to assign a set of readings to *Sentence* is:

(R_4) Given two paths of the form

   (1) Lexical String$_1$ → syntactic markers of verb phrase → Remainder of verb phrase path
   (2) Lexical String$_2$ → syntactic markers of subject → Remainder of subject path

such that there is a substring σ of the string of syntactic or semantic markers of the subject and $\sigma \, \epsilon \, \alpha$. There is an amalgam of the form

Lexical String$_2$ + Lexical String$_1$ → dominating node marker → String analyzed *Remainder of subject path* → String analyzed *Remainder of verb phrase path* deleting substring ⟨α⟩

The application of (R_4) to P_7 and P_9 yields the set P_{10}:

$$P_{10}$$

(1) *The + man + hits + the + colorful + ball* → *Sentence* → [*Some contextually definite*] → (*Physical Object*) → (*Human*) → (*Adult*) → (*Male*) → (*Action*) → (*Instancy*) → (*Intensity*) → [*Collides with an impact*] → [*Some contextually definite*] → (*Physical Object*) → (*Color*) → [[*Abounding in contrast or variety of bright colors*] [*Having globular shape*]]

(2) *The + man + hits + the + colorful + ball* → *Sentence* → [*Some contextually definite*] → (*Physical Object*) → (*Human*) → (*Adult*) → (*Male*) → (*Action*) → (*Instancy*) → (*Intensity*) → [*Collides with an impact*] → [*Some contextually definite*] → (*Physical Object*) → (*Color*) → [[*Abounding in contrast or variety of bright colors*] [*Solid missile for projection by engine of war*]]

(3) *The + man + hits + the + colorful + ball* → *Sentence* → [*Some contextually definite*] → (*Physical Object*) → (*Human*) → (*Adult*) → (*Male*) → (*Action*) → (*Instancy*) → (*Intensity*) → [*Strikes with a blow or missile*] → [*Some contextually definite*] → (*Physical Object*) → (*Color*) → [[*Abounding in contrast or variety of bright colors*] [*Having globular shape*]]

(4) *The + man + hits + the + colorful + ball* → *Sentence* → [*Some contextually definite*] → (*Physical Object*) → (*Human*) → (*Adult*) → (*Male*) → (*Action*) → (*Instancy*) → (*Intensity*) → [*Strikes with a blow or missile*] → [*Some contextually definite*] → (*Physical Object*) → (*Color*) → [[*Abounding in contrast or variety of bright colors*] [*Solid missile for projection by engine of war*]]

Therefore, a semantic theory of English containing rules and entries as given above characterizes the sentence "The man hits the colorful ball" as having the following semantic interpretation: the sentence is not semantically anomalous; it is four ways semantically ambiguous on the derivation in Fig. 8; each term corresponds to a reading in P_{10}; it is a paraphrase of any sentence which has one of the readings in P_{10}; and it is a full paraphrase of any sentence that has the set of readings P_{10} assigned to it. The semantic theory interprets the constituent structure tree in Fig. 8 in the way shown in Fig. 13, thus displaying which of the possible combinations of paths at a given node yielded derived paths for that node and which possible combinations were blocked. (See Figure 13.)

This completes our example of how a semantic theory of English might interpret a sentence generated by the grammar. Before we conclude our discussion of projection rules, we must consider the question of whether the projection rule component will contain types of projection rules different from the type employed above.

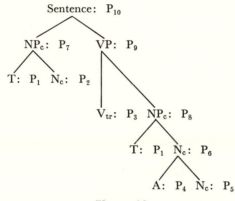

Figure 13

What is characteristic of rules (R_1) to (R_4) is that each rule operates on a part of a partially semantically interpreted constituent structure characterization, amalgamates paths from two sets of paths that are dominated by a particular node, and assigns to that node the set of amalgams as readings for the lexical string that the node dominates. Let us call such rules "type 1 projection rules." These rules must assign semantic interpretations to some of the sentences generated by the grammar, but they need not be the means by which EVERY sentence receives a semantic interpretation. We can conceive of another type of projection rule ("type 2 projection rules") in the following way. We restrict the application of type 1 projection rules to some formally determined proper subset of the set of sentences. Then we introduce type 2 projection rules to provide a semantic interpretation for every sentence that does not receive a semantic interpretation on the basis of type 1 projection rules. Since those sentences that the grammar produces without the aid of optional transformation, i.e., the kernel sentences, will be semantically interpreted by type 1 projection rules, the type 2 projection rules will assign semantic interpretations to sentences that are constructed with the use of optional transformations. Suppose S has been constructed from a certain set of source sentences by the optional transformation T. A type 2 rule is a rule which operates on the semantic interpretations of these source sentences and on either the derived constituent structure characterization of S or on the transformation T in order to produce a semantic interpretation of S. Type 2 projection rules should assign semantic interpretations in such a way as to reconstruct the manner in which the meaning of a sentence that is constructed by such a transformation T is a function of the meanings of each of the sentences used by T in S's construction.

The basic theoretical question that remains open here is just what proper subset of the set of sentences is semantically interpreted using type 1 projection rules only. One striking fact about transformations is that a great many of them (perhaps all) produce sentences that are identical in meaning to the sentence(s) out of which the transform was built.[26] In such cases, the semantic interpretation of the transformationally constructed sentence must be identical to the semantic interpretation(s) of the source sentence(s) at least with respect to the readings assigned at the sentence level. For example, sentences that are related to each other by the passive transformation, e.g., "The man eats cake" and "Cake is eaten by the man," have the same meaning, except perhaps in instances where quantifiers are involved.[27] For another example, sentence conjunctions, e.g., "The man ate the cake and candy" which comes from "The man ate the cake" and "The man ate the candy." Or, again, stylistic variants such as "There is something about it that puzzles me," "There is about it something that puzzles me," and "There is something that puzzles me about it." It would be theoretically most satisfying if we could take the position that transformations never change meaning. But such a generalization runs up against such cases as the question transformation, the imperative transformation, the negation transformation, and others. Such troublesome cases might be troublesome only because of an inadequacy in the way we are now formulating these transformations or these cases might represent a real departure from the otherwise uniform generalization that meaning is invariant under grammatical transformations. Until we can determine whether any transformations change meaning, and if some do, which do and which do not, we shall not know what sentences should be semantically interpreted with type 2 projection rules and how to formulate such rules.

Nevertheless, we can decide the cases that are clear. The set of sentences that will be semantically interpreted using type 1 projection rules include the sentences produced without the aid of optical transformations. Suppose we permit NO type 2 projection rule for any transformation that we know preserves meaning, and instead we introduce the convention that any sentences related by such a transformation T belongs to an equivalence class, all of whose members receive the same semantic interpretation. Then the facts that there will always be a kernel sentence in such an equivalence class and that every kernel

---

[26] For the background of this point, *cf.* J. A. Fodor, "Projection and Paraphrase in Semantics," *Analysis*, XXI, No. 4 (March 1961), 73–77; and J. J. Katz, "A Reply to 'Projection and Paraphrase in Semantics'," *Analysis*, XXII, No. 2 (Dec. 1961), 36–41.

[27] In these instances, too—if it is true that both active and passive have the same meaning because both are ambiguous.

sentence has a semantic interpretation on the basis of type 1 projection rules means that every nonkernel sentence in such an equivalence class automatically receives the semantic interpretation of its kernel co-member, which makes them all paraphrases as desired.

This treatment is by far the best method of marking paraphrase relations (and other semantic properties) among stylistic variants which result from the operation of a permutation transformation. This method avoids having a special type 2 rule in each such case: such special type 2 rules have no function except to state the empty fact that these transformations do not affect meaning. This method also avoids the use of type 1 rules on a sentence that is produced by a permutation transformation. This is very highly desirable because, since such transformations produce sentences with derived constituent structure characterizations having far less labeled bracketing than is found in the constituent structure characterization of the source sentence, it is generally the case that what labeled bracketing survives is too little to permit type 1 rules to be able to semantically interpret the derived sentence.

This treatment has the same merits in the cases of transformations that permute in such a way as to produce discontinuous elements in the transform and also in the cases of transformations that delete material. Thus, with this treatment we can most simply account for the paraphrase relations between (and other semantic properties of) such pairs as: "John looked up the rule" and "John looked the rule up"; and "Harry plays chess as well as Bill plays chess" and "Harry plays chess as well as Bill."

The possibility of type 2 projection rules presents two options for the construction of the projection rule component of a semantic theory. Either the projection rule component will consist of type 1 rules alone, or it will contain both type 1 and type 2 rules. The question whether type 2 rules will be required, and if so, to what extent, is a question to which no answer is possible here. Many considerations enter into answering it, including both methodological considerations such as conceptual economy, descriptive and explanatory power, and so on, and particular considerations concerning the structure of individual languages such as the degree to which transformational relations between sentences are independent of semantic relations between them.[28]

METATHEORY

In the present section, we shall discuss the theoretical perspective from which we have been treating the problem of characterizing the abstract form of a semantic theory. That is, we shall discuss the nature of semantic metatheory. We shall also consider some of the consequences of adopting an explicit metatheory in semantics.

---

[28] A more general and comprehensive discussion of this problem is to be found in J. J. Katz and P. Postal, *An Integrated Theory of Linguistic Descriptions* (Cambridge: M.I.T. Press, 1964).

There are two motivations for constructing an explicit metatheory for an area in linguistics, and thus for constructing an explicit metatheory for semantics.[29] First, the same scientific curiosity which makes us inquire into the semantic structure of individual languages *a fortiori* makes us interested in what is common in the semantic structure of families of language or of all languages. Thus, a metatheory for semantics must be a theory which represents semantic universals. Second, there must be *well-established* criteria for choosing among different semantic theories for the same language, where each theory is, as far as we can tell, compatible with the available evidence from fluent native speakers. But if a set of such criteria is to be well established, it must itself be shown to give desirable results with a wide variety of different languages, i.e., it must consistently choose, from language to language, the best semantic theory. Thus, a semantic theory must provide criteria for evaluating individual semantic theories and establish the adequacy of such criteria. We can incorporate both these motivations if we construct a metatheory which contains an enumeration of the semantic markers from which the theoretical vocabulary of each particular semantic theory is drawn and a specification of the form of the rules for a semantic theory of a natural language. For the enumeration and the specification provide both a representation of semantic universals and a basis on which to evaluate particular semantic theories (e.g., we may adopt the rule that the preferable theory is the one which is rated highest by a metric which compares rules in the specified form and chooses the one requiring the smallest number of markers from the enumeration given in the metatheory).

The semantic markers which we have utilized in our discussions of dictionary entries and projection rules are, of course, only examples. But if we imagine them functioning in a putative semantic theory of English, then the claim for them would have to be that they are drawn from the enumeration of markers provided by the methatheory, just as the claim for the projection rules would have to be that they are each instances of a form specified by the metatheory. Thus, a semantic marker is simply a theoretical construct which receives its interpretation in the semantic metatheory and is on a par with such scientific constructs as atom, gene, valence, and noun phrase. A marker such as (*Human*) or (*Color*) is, then, not an English word, but a construct represented by one.

A metatheory for semantics must, further, exhibit the relations between semantics and other areas of linguistics. We have discussed the relation between grammatical and semantic rules at some length. We must now consider the relation between grammatical and semantic markers.

Much confusion has been generated in the study of language by the search for a line between grammar and semantics. This is because what has been sought when students of language have tried to draw such a line is a criterion to determine when a concept expressing something about the structure of a language is syntactical and when it is semantical. But the trouble has always

---

[29] The conception of a metatheory for grammar, which he refers to as "linguistic theory." *Cf*. Chomsky, *op. cit.*, and *The Logical Structure of Linguistic Theory*, microfilmed, M.I.T.

been that every criterion proposed seems to be invalidated by examples of concepts which can, with apparently equal justice, be regarded as either syntactical or semantical. That is, there appears to be an overlap between the sets of syntactic and semantic markers. For example, such markers as *Male, Female, Human, Animal, Animate, Concrete, Abstract,* and so on, appear to fall in this overlap. But the confusion engendered in the search for a line between grammar and semantics is unwarranted because the overlap exists in name only.

This becomes clear once one ceases to search for a criterion to decide which markers are properly syntactic or semantic, and instead asks whether the line between grammatical and semantic markers can be drawn in terms of the theoretical functions they perform.[30] For example, in the grammar the distinction between abstract and concrete nouns is drawn in order to construct adequate rules for generating sentences containing nominalizations. According to Lees:

> ... there are certain restrictions on subject/predicate-nominal combinations based on abstractness (as well as perhaps on other lower-order nominal categories). There is a small class of (abstract) nouns which may appear on copula sentences opposite both nominalizations and concrete nominals: "the problem is that he went there," "the problem is his going there," "the problem is his tonsils," and the like for such nouns N_a as *problem, trouble, thing, reason, cause, question,* and so on. Nominalizations occur opposite only these latter nouns, while concrete nominals N_c occur opposite either other concretes or one of these latter abstract nouns N_a: "that he came home is the trouble," but not "*that he came home is that she left," or again: "his stomach is the cause," "his stomach is an organ," but not: "*his stomach is his having gone there."[31]

The distinction between mass and count nouns is, analogously, drawn in order to handle the syntactic relations between nouns and their articles and quantifiers, e.g., the mass noun *blood* in the singular takes *the* and *some* but not numerical quantifiers: "The blood was found" but not "*One blood was found." Likewise, the distinction between animate nouns and inanimate nouns and between masculine nouns and feminine nouns has to do (among other things) with pronoun agreement. For example, "The girl gave her own dress away," but not "*The girl gave his own dress away" or "*The girl gave its own dress away."

On the other hand, semantic markers are introduced to specify something about the meaning of lexical items. Thus, where it appears that a marker is common to both grammar and semantics, what is in fact the case is that there are two distinct markers having the same or similar names. This is most clear from the fact that it is often *not* the case that a lexical item receiving a certain grammatical marker also receives the corresponding semantic marker. For if we always assign a semantic marker when the corresponding grammatical

---

[30] It is not at all clear even that the request for such a criterion is a reasonable one. Would one ask for an analogous criterion to distinguish the concepts of physics and the concepts of chemistry?

[31] R. B. Lees, *op. cit.*, p. 14.

marker is assigned, then in many cases lexical items will be given the wrong sense characterizations. For instance, grammatically the words *ship, England, fortune,* and *fate* are marked feminine, but clearly they cannot receive the semantic marker (*Female*) if sentences are to receive the correct semantic interpretations. Again, such words as *pain, ache, twinge* must be marked as concrete nouns, but they cannot be marked as (*Physical Object*) if we are to account for such anomalies as "The pain weighs three pounds." Conversely, if we always assigned a grammatical marker whenever the corresponding semantic marker is assigned, then either the grammar will fail to generate some grammatical sentences or it will generate some ungrammatical strings, or it will fail to assign structure properly. For instance, semantically the nouns *child, baby,* and *infant* must be marked (*Human*) to obtain correct sense characterizations and correct semantic interpretations. But if they are marked as human nouns, the grammar will fail to generate such sentences as "The baby lost its rattle."

Thus, grammatical and semantic markers have different theoretical import. Grammatical markers have the function of marking the formal differences upon which the distinction between well-formed and ill-formed strings of morphemes rests, whereas semantic markers have the function of giving each well-formed string the conceptual content that permits them to be represented in terms of the message they communicate to speakers in normal situations. They are concerned with different kinds of selection and they express different aspects of the structure of a language. We can, therefore, justifiably regard semantic markers as theoretical constructs distinct from the markers employed in grammatical description.

JAMES D. McCAWLEY

6.2   *Meaning and the Description of Languages*

1. WHAT IS MEANING?

A language is a system which correlates meanings with sounds. To describe a language is thus to describe the way in which meanings are correlated with sounds in that language. A quick glance at a sample of the descriptions of languages which are avilable in print should make it clear to anyone that no one has as yet really succeeded in describing a language. There are many brilliant and insightful descriptions of portions of languages; for example, many languages have been described with great insight from the point of view of phonology (i.e. of the processes whereby the pronunciation of the words and

Reprinted from *Kotoba no uchū*, II, Nos. 9 (10–18), 10 (38–48), 11 (51–57), by permission of the author and of TEC Co., Ltd., Tokyo, Japan.

morphemes of the language is adjusted in accordance with the shape of the surrounding words or morphemes and the way in which those processes interact), for a large number of languages linguists have formulated worthwhile generalizations about the ways in which words may be combined into sentences, and there have been a fair number of interesting studies of the similarities and differences in meaning of selected words in a language. However, even in the case of a language such as English, which has been the subject of valuable and compendious studies by a large number of outstanding scholars, the published work still does not add up to anything approaching an adequate description of the way in which English correlates meanings with sounds.

One of the chief reasons for this lack of success is the fact that linguists are only beginning to understand how meanings can be described. While one can describe the sounds of languages by making up a list of the ways in which sounds may resemble or differ from each other and describing each sound by listing the properties on this list which it possesses (this is in essence the principle behind the International Phonetic Alphabet, which was constructed by listing the various "places of articulation," "manners of articulation," and "secondary articulations" which had been observed in various languages and creating an alphabetic symbol for each possible combination of such properties), such an approach is insufficient for the description of meaning, since the meaning of an utterance has a far more complex structure than the sound of an utterance does. The sound of an utterance can be regarded as simply a sequence of unit sounds and each of those sounds represented by a symbol such as an IPA letter; while in fact acoustically and articulatorily these "unit sounds" are not separate but overlap considerably, a representation as a sequence of symbols is perfectly adequate to represent the sound of an utterance for the purpose of the description of a language. However, the meaning of an utterance can in no sense be regarded as a sequence of "unit meanings." Many persons naively assume that since a sentence can be regarded as a sequence of words, its meaning is simply a sequence of meanings, namely the meanings of those words. However, the relation of the meaning of a sentence to its superficial form is in fact much more complicated. For example, to understand the English sentence

> John isn't rich, but he's handsome.

one must not only know the meaning of the element *n't* but must also know that it applies to "John is rich": the speaker is denying the proposition "John is rich" but is not denying the proposition "John is rich but he's handsome." On the other hand, the sentence

> John doesn't beat his wife because he loves her.

is ambiguous: *n't* may apply either to "John beats his wife" (in this case the sentence asserts that John does not beat his wife and states that the reason for his not beating her is that he loves her) or it may apply to "John beats his wife because he loves her" (in this case the sentence assumes that John beats his wife but states that the reason why he beats her is not that he loves her). To understand the sentence

> I don't think that John will arrive until Saturday.

one must know that *n't* does not apply to "*I think that John will arrive until Saturday," which is not even a possible sentence of English, but that the sentence has the same meaning as "I think that John won't arrive until Saturday" and must know that the combination *n't . . . until Saturday* means "on Saturday but not before Saturday." The sentence

> Harry called Arthur a goddam Communist.

is ambiguous: it may mean either that Harry used the term "goddam Communist" to refer to Arthur, which implies that Harry strongly dislikes Communists, or it may mean that Harry used the term "Communist" to refer to Arthur and that the speaker either strongly dislikes Communists or is surprised that Harry called Arthur a Communist; in the second meaning the sentence has no implication regarding Harry's feelings towards Communists.

These facts imply that to describe a meaning it is necessary not only to list "unit meanings" which are involved in it but also to indicate how various "unit meanings" are grouped together into more complex meanings, e.g. to show that the meaning of "John isn't rich" is in some sense a combination of the meaning of *n't* and meaning of *John is rich*. Moreover, these facts imply that the meaning of a sentence may involve items which do not appear in the superficial form of the sentence. For example, the second meaning of "Harry called Arthur a goddam Communist" has to do with the speaker of the sentence, even though no word such as *I* or *me* appears in the sentence.

2. LEVELS OF LINGUISTIC REPRESENTATION

So far I have referred to three ways in which an utterance may be viewed: as meaning, as sound, and as what I referred to as "superficial form." If these three ways of viewing an utterance play a role in linguistic description, then there must be three corresponding ways of representing each utterance: semantic representation, phonetic representation, and "surface syntactic representation." Above I spoke as if surface syntactic representation were merely a representation of the utterance as a sequence of morphemes or words. However, it will prove necessary to regard this mode of representation as also indicating the way in which these elements are grouped together into larger units and the syntactic categories to which these units belong, since both the grouping of elements and the categories affect how the utterance is pronounced. For example, "small boys' school" is pronounced with a relatively heavy stress on "small" if "boys'" and "school" are grouped together as a unit (with that pronunciation the expression means "small school for boys") but is pronounced with a relatively weak stress on "small" if "small" and "boys'" are grouped together as a unit (with this pronunciation the expression means "school for small boys"). The surface syntactic representation of a sentence may thus be considered to take the form of a tree diagram such as

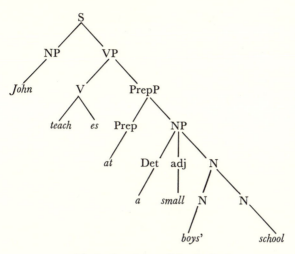

John teaches at a small boys' school

The lines in such a diagram represent the way in which smaller units are grouped into larger units; the labels indicate the categories to which the various units belong. Earlier I described phonetic representation in terms which, while highly imprecise, will suffice for the purposes of this paper. The nature of semantic representation is the principal topic of this paper; later in this paper I will make various concrete proposals concerning it, although these proposals will still fall far short of a complete theory of semantic representation.

These three "levels of representation" figure at least implicitly in virtually all descriptions of language which have been published. The version of transformational grammar presented in Noam Chomsky's *Aspects of the Theory of Syntax* (Cambridge, Mass.: M. I. T. Press, 1965) introduces a fourth "level of representation," the so-called "deep syntactic representation" or "deep structure." Chomsky's views, as presented in that work, may be summarized as follows:

1. A description of a language must specify what surface syntactic representations are possible and what semantic representation(s) is (are) correlated with each surface syntactic representation.

2. A language involves mechanisms corresponding to three systems of rules: a "base component," which specifies what the possible "deep syntactic representations" in that language are, a "transformational component," which converts each deep syntactic representation into the corresponding surface syntactic representation by subjecting it to a sequence of processes such as deletions, additions, and permutations, and a "semantic component," which in some manner or other (Chomsky does not specify what the rules of this component of the grammar are to look like or how they are to operate) associates to each deep syntactic representation a representation of its meaning.

3. Consequently, the "deep syntactic representation" of an utterance must contain sufficient information to determine both what its surface syntactic representation and its semantic representation will be.

6. The deep syntactic representation of a sentence is an object of the same formal nature as its surface syntactic representation, i.e. it can be represented by a tree diagram whose non-terminal nodes are labeled with syntactic category names and whose terminal nodes are labeled with some kind of "lexical material": either actual morphemes or abstract complexes of information which play a role in determining the superficial form of the sentence (e. g. in his discussion of German in *Aspects of the Theory of Syntax*, Chomsky proposes deep structures in which there are terminal nodes labeled "genitive case," "plural number," "feminine gender," even though these never occur separately in the superficial form of a sentence but only in items such as a single "genitive feminine plural" ending). The many intermediate stages involved in the conversion of deep syntactic representation into surface syntactic representation are naturally also of this same formal type.

3. CONCERNING THE STATUS OF "DEEP STRUCTURE"

Since the publication of *Aspects of the Theory of Syntax*, numerous scholars have been studying the syntax of several languages, especially English, within the framework of the four assumptions listed above. The more that these studies have advanced, the deeper that deep syntactic representations have become: virtually every advance achieved within this framework has required the setting up of deep structures which are further removed from the superficial form of sentences than had previously been thought to be necessary. For example, George Lakoff (*On the Nature of Syntactic Irregularity*, Indiana University dissertation, 1965) gave a most convincing argument that the sentence

John opened the door.

is not a simple sentence, as had been previously assumed, but indeed involves two embedded sentences; specifically, Lakoff argues that it must be derived from a structure which (neglecting the tense of the verb) has the form

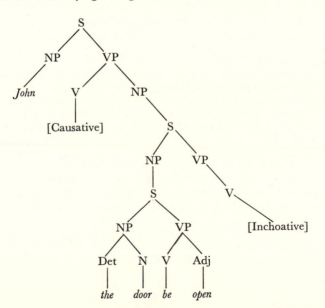

In this structure, [Inchoative] is an abstract element which combines with adjectives to form "verbs of change" such as are found in

Mary's face reddened. (= Mary's face became red)
The metal hardened. (= The metal became hard)

[Causative] is an abstract element which combines with verbs of change to form "verbs of causation," as in

The physicist hardened the metal. (= The physicist caused the metal to harden)
John stopped the car. (= John caused the car to stop)

One of Lakoff's most compelling arguments in favor of this analysis is the fact that when a verb of change or causation corresponds to an adjective which has a comparative degree (not all adjectives have a comparative degree; for example, one cannot say *Arthur is more male than Fred*), that verb is ambiguous between positive and comparative degree. Thus, *The metal hardened* may mean either "The metal became hard" or "The metal became harder"; *The physicist hardened the metal* may mean either "The physicist caused the metal to become hard" or "The physicist caused the metal to become harder." If these alternative meanings are to correspond to different deep structures (as required by point 3 above), it is necessary to set up a deep structure containing an adjective which may be in the positive degree for the one meaning and the comparative degree for the other meaning. A further compelling argument which Lakoff has discovered for this analysis is the possibility of saying

The physicist finally hardened the metal, but it took him six months to bring it about.

Without an analysis such as Lakoff's it is difficult to see how the second *it* could be explained: neither of the two noun-phrases which occur in the superficial form of "The physicist hardened the metal" could possibly be the antecedent of that *it*. However, Lakoff's analysis provides an antecedent for the *it*: the antecedent is the sentence which is the object of the abstract causative verb. For a second example, consider Rosenbaum's analysis of verbs such as *seem* (Peter S. Rosenbaum, *The Grammar of English Predicate Complement Constructions*, M. I. T. dissertation, 1965). The verbs *seem* and *want* occur in superficially similar sentences such as

John seems to know the answer.
John wants to know the answer.

However, *seem* differs from *want* in many respects: (1) The question "What does John want?" is possible but "*What does John seem?" is not; (2) The "cleft sentence" "What John wants is to know the answer" is possible but "*What John seems is to know the answer" is not; (3) *want* allows the infinitive to have a subject ("John wants Harry to win the prize") but *seem* does not (one cannot say "John seems Harry to win the prize"); and (4) *seem* allows *there* as its apparent subject ("There seems to be a man in the garden") but *want* does not ("*There wants to be a man in the garden"). Rosenbaum observed that all these facts are explained if *want* is regarded as a transitive verb with a sentence as its object and *seem* as an intransitive verb with a sentence as its subject in deep structure:

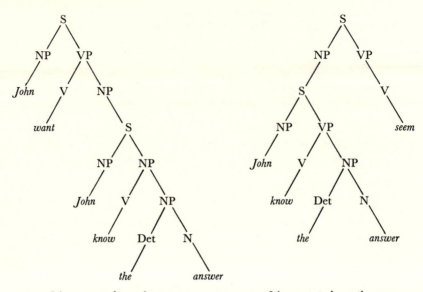

John wants to know the answer.   John seems to know the answer.

The superficial form of the first sentence is derived by a transformation which deletes the subject of the embedded sentence if it is identical to the subject of *want*; the superficial form of the second sentence is derived by a transformation which puts the verb-phrase of the embedded sentence after *seem*.

In many other cases besides these two, scholars working within the framework of *Aspects of the Theory of Syntax* have found it necessary to set up deep structures which are much further removed from the superficial form of sentences than are the structures postulated in *Aspects*. These structures not only are further removed from the superficial form of the sentences but are also much more similar to the semantic structures of the sentences in question. For example, "John opened the door" does indeed mean that John caused the door to become open, and "John seems to know the answer" does indeed mean that "John knows the answer" seems to be true.

Since the introduction of the notion "deep structure" by Chomsky, virtually every "deep structure" which has been postulated (excluding those which have been demonstrated simply to be wrong) has turned out not really to be a deep structure but to have underlying it a more abstract structure which could more appropriately be called the "deep structure" of the sentence in question. This fact raises the question of whether there indeed is such a thing as "deep structure." As an alternative to Chomsky's conception of linguistic structure, one could propose that in each language there is simply a single system of processes which convert the semantic representation of each sentence into its surface syntactic representation and that none of the intermediate stages in the con-

version of semantic representation into surface syntactic representation is entitled to any special status such as that which Chomsky ascribes to "deep structure." To decide whether Chomsky's conception of language or a conception
without a level of deep structure is correct, it is necessary to determine at
least in rough outlines what semantic representation must consist of, and on
the basis of that knowledge to answer the following two questions, which are
crucial for the choice between these two conceptions of language. (1) Are
semantic representations objects of a fundamentally different nature than
syntactic representations or can syntactic and semantic representations more
fruitfully be considered to be basically objects of the same type? (2) Does the
relationship between semantic representation and surface syntactic representation involve processes which are of two fundamentally different types and are
organised into two separate systems, corresponding to what Chomsky called
"transformation" and "semantic projection rules," or is there in fact no such
division of the processes which link the meaning of an utterance with its superficial form?

Later in this paper, I will give reasons for believing that semantic representation and syntactic representation are of essentially the same formal nature and
that the meanings of utterances are related to their superficial forms by a single
system of transformations of essentially the same type which figure in the syntactic theory of *Aspects*. However, in order to arrive at these conclusions, it will
be necessary for me first to say something about the system of representation
which I maintain will provide the general framework for the representation
of meaning, namely symbolic logic.

4. SYMBOLIC LOGIC AND THE REPRESENTATION OF MEANING

Symbolic logic developed in the latter half of the 19th century, chiefly through
the efforts of mathematicians who were interested in the logical foundations of
mathematics and for this purpose wished to have a system for representing the
content of propositions and for expressing relations between the content of
different propositions. Since these mathematicians were interested almost exclusively in propositions of mathematics and were generally extremely naive in
their beliefs about everyday uses of language, publications on symbolic logic
have largely ignored ordinary uses of language and have generally given a
hopelessly inadequate treatment to the small part of everyday language which
they have treated.[1] As a result of this, linguists have generally dismissed symbolic
logic as being of little relevance to the study of natural languages. However,
rather than simply dismissing symbolic logic outright, linguists would do well
to examine the question of whether symbolic logic is inherently incapable of
representing meanings adequately or whether the failure of attempts to express

---

[1] A notable exception is Hans Reichenbach, *Elements of Symbolic Logic* (New York: The
Macmillan Company, 1947), which can be recommended highly to linguists interested in
symbolic logic, even though its account of meaning is far from satisfactory. I apologize for the
profusion of symbolic logic formulas on the next few pages, which have a somewhat formidable
appearance; however, I know of no other way of representing the meanings in question.

meaning in terms of symbolic logic is due only to the investigators' naivete and ignorance about natural languages. I will argue below that symbolic logic, if enriched to allow the formal expression of certain linguistic devices which have been ignored in symbolic logic due to the fact that they play no role in propositions of mathematics, is a perfectly adequate general framework for the representation of meaning.

The following types of units have figured in symbolic logic:

(1) the propositional connectives $\wedge$ "and," $\vee$ "or," and $\neg$ "not." If p and q are two propositions, then $p \wedge q$ is the proposition that p and q are both true, $p \vee q$ is the proposition that at least one of p and q is true, and $\neg p$ is the proposition that p is false.

(2) individual constant symbols, which denote specific individuals (I will use lower-case letters with subscripts, e.g. x_1, x_9, a_{17} to represent individual constants).

(3) predicates, which denote properties and relationships (I will use symbols such as $f(x)$, $g(x, y)$, etc. to represent predicates).

(4) set symbols and the "quantifiers" $\vee$ ("for all") and $\exists$ ("there exists"); $\underset{x\epsilon M}{\vee} f(x)$ means that the property f is possessed by all members of the set M, e. g. if A is the set of all Americans, then $\underset{x\epsilon A}{\vee}$ (x is rich) is the proposition that all Americans are rich. $\underset{x\epsilon M}{\exists} f(x)$ means that there is at least one member of the set M which has the property f; for example $\underset{x\epsilon A}{\exists}$ (x is rich) is the proposition that at least one American is rich.

(5) descriptions of sets and individuals. $[x: f(x)]$ means the set of all things which possess the property f, e. g. [x: x is an American $\wedge$ x dislikes Lyndon Johnson] is the set of all Americans who dislike Lyndon Johnson; this set could alternatively be represented as [xϵA: dislikes Lyndon Johnson]. (ιx) (x murdered Abraham Lincoln) is used to represent "the individual who murdered Abraham Lincoln." $[x: f(x)]$ and $(\iota x) f(x)$ are really instances of the same thing: (ιx) is appropriate only in the case where exactly one individual possesses the property f, but just like $[x: f(x)]$ is indicates "that which possesses the property f." In addition, sets can be described by enumerating their members: $[x_1, x_2, x_3]$ denotes the set which has the members x_1, x_2, x_3 and no others.

All of these devices play an important role in natural languages:

(1) To my knowledge, all languages have ways of expressing the meanings of $\wedge$, $\vee$, and $\neg$, although one must be careful to note that in many languages the words used are more general than $\wedge$, $\vee$, and $\neg$. For example, the English word *and* may join not only propositions but indeed virtually any kind of items.

(2) Since processes such as pronominalization and the deletion that takes place in *John wants to know the answer* are contingent not only on two noun phrases containing the same words but on their being intended to refer to the same thing, it is necessary to regard each noun phrase as having a label attached to it corresponding to its "intended referent." Such labels, which Chomsky introduced in *Aspects* under the name "indices," include both individual constants and set constants.

(3) Predicates are expressed in natural languages by nouns, verbs, and adjectives:

> John is a fool.
> John is stupid.
> John loves Mary.

all express properties of the individual being referred to as *John*.

(4) Words such as *all* and expressions such as *at least one* are two members of a rather large class of expressions which are used to indicate not only the existence of an individual or a set but the absolute or relative number of members in that set, as in

> A *substantial fraction* of my friends are linguists.
> *Most* Americans watch television.

(5) Set and individual descriptions can be expressed in natural languages by noun phrases involving relative clauses. Set-description by enumerating the elements of the set is accomplished by the use of conjoined noun phrases, as in

> John, Tom, and Bill are similar.

There are many differences in meaning which appear to be expressible only in terms of these devices. For example, the sentence

> Those men saw themselves in the mirror.

is ambiguous between the senses (1) each of the men saw himself in the mirror, (2) the entire group of men saw the entire group in the mirror. It is difficult to imagine how these two meanings could be assigned different deep structures unless those deep structures contained something equivalent to the quantifiers which differ in the two meanings: (1) $\bigvee_{x \in M}$ (x saw x), (2) $\bigvee_{x \in M} \bigvee_{y \in M}$ (x saw y); or rather, using subscripts on verbs to represent events describable by those verbs,

(1) $\bigvee_{x \in M} \exists_{y(x)}$ (x see$_{y(x)}$ x in the mirror) (i. e. for each man there was an event in which he saw himself in the mirror),

(2) $\exists_{y} \bigvee_{x \in M} \bigvee_{z \in M}$ (x see$_y$ z in the mirror) (i. e. there was a single event in which each of the men saw all of the men in the mirror).

There are several published descriptions of pronominalization within the framework of transformational grammar[2], all of which derive personal and reflexive pronouns from full noun phrases which are identical to other noun phrases (e.g. John loves *himself* is derived from a deep structure having two occurrences of *John*, one as the subject of *love* and one as its object). However, such an analysis is impossible here, since if *themselves* is derived from an underlying repetition of those men, there is no way in which the deep structures of the two meanings of *Those men saw themselves in the mirror* could differ from each other. The same is also true of the deletion discussed above in connection with the sentence *John wants to know the answer.*

---

[2] R. B. Lees and E. S. Klima, "Rules for English Pronominalization," *Language*, XXXIX (1963), 17–28; John R. Ross, "On the Cyclic Nature of Pronominalization" in *To Honor Roman Jakobson: essays on the occasion of his seventieth birthday* (The Hague: Mouton Publishers, 1967); Ronald Langacker, "Pronominalization and the Chain of Command" in Riebel and Schane, eds., *Modern Studies in English: Readings in Transformational Grammar* (Englewood Cliffs, N. J.: Prentice-Hall, Inc., 1968), pp. 160–86.

One cannot say that

Everyone wants to get rich

arises from the deletion of *everyone*, since it is possible to say

Everyone wants everyone to get rich

which is very different in meaning from *Everyone wants to get rich*. The absence of a subject of the embedded sentence is determined not by whether the embedded sentence has as its subject a noun phrase identical to that which is the subject of *want*; it rather depends on a property of the semantic representation of the sentence, namely whether in that representation the index corresponding to the subject of the embedded sentence is the same as the index corresponding to the subject of *want*: the meaning of *Everyone wants to get rich* can be represented roughly as $\underset{x \in A}{\mathsf{V}}$ [x wants (x get rich)] and the meaning of *Everyone wants everyone to get rich* as $\underset{x \in A}{\mathsf{V}}$ [x wants ($\underset{y \in A}{\mathsf{V}}$ y get rich)], where A is the set of all human beings. These examples make it clear that if things with different meanings are to have different deep structures, the deep structures will have to contain something corresponding to quantifiers and those quantifiers will have to be allowed to occur at a different place in the deep structure from the index which they govern.

In addition, there are syntactic transformations which appear to be statable only in terms of a symbolic-logic-type representation. Consider, for example, the deletion transformation which gives rise to sentences such as

John knows Mary and so do I.
John is a lawyer and so is Harry.

The sentence

John loves his wife and so do I.

is ambiguous: *so do I* may mean either that I love my wife or that I love John's wife. Similarly,

John voted for himself and so did I.

may mean either that I voted for myself or that I voted for John. If the deletion transformation involved here simply deleted a repeated combination of words, it could derive these sentences from structures which also underlie *John loves his wife and I love his wife too* and *John voted for himself and I voted for him too* but not from structures which also underlie *John loves his wife and I love my wife too* and *John voted for himself and I voted for myself too*. The only way I know of stating this transformation correctly is to say that the deletion may take place only in a structure whose semantic representation is of the form $f(x_1) \wedge f(x_2)$. *John loves his wife* and *John voted for himself* can be interpreted as a property of x_1 (the index of *John*) in two ways. Let g(x) mean "x loves x's wife" and Let (hx) mean "x loves x_1's wife." Then the meaning of *John loves his wife and I love my wife too* can be represented as $g(x_1) \wedge g(x_2)$, where x_2 is the index of *I*, and the meaning of *John loves his wife and I love her too* can be represented as $(h\,x_1) \wedge h(x_2)$. Since both of these meanings meet the condition given above, both are subject to the deletion transformation, and both yield *John loves his wife and so do I. John voted for himself and so did I* works exactly the same way.

I thus conclude that all of the units and categories of symbolic logic play important roles both in the representation of meaning in natural languages and the formulation of syntactic transformations. However, are the units and categories of symbolic logic sufficient for these purposes? To be sufficient for the representation of meaning in natural languages, certain devices will have to be added to the normal repertoire of symbolic logic, specifically,

(1) It is necessary to admit predicates which assert properties not only of individuals but also of sets and propositions. Actually, $\wedge$, $\vee$, and $\neg$ are predicates of that type: $\neg$ is the property that the proposition to which it is applied is false, $\wedge$ is the property that the two propositions to which it is applied are both true, and $\vee$ is the property that at least one of the propositions to which it is applied is true. The discussion of *seem* in sec. 3 indicates that it too is a predicate which asserts property of a proposition, and there will be numerous other such predicates, for example the *may* of "John may have come on the 10:00 train" which asserts that the proposition "John came on the 10:00 train" may be true. Quantifiers and the other quantity expressions mentioned above can be regarded as expressing a relationship between a set and a predicate.

(2) It is incorrect to represent the meaning of, say, *The man kissed the woman* by a formula such as $(x_1$ kissed $x_2) \wedge (x_1$ is a man$) \wedge (x_2$ is a woman$)$, as is occasionally proposed. The meaning of such a sentence is not simply a conjunction of three terms but is rather something in which $(x_1$ is a man$)$ and $(x_2$ is a woman$)$ are in some sense subordinate to $(x_1$ kissed $x_2)$. This is made clear by the fact that the sentence

John denies that the man kissed the woman.

does not mean that John denied the proposition $(x_1$ kissed $x_2) \wedge (x_1$ is a man$) \wedge (x_2$ is a woman$)$; the denial of that proposition is the proposition $\neg (x_1$ kissed $x_2) \vee \neg (x_1$ is a man$) \vee \neg (x_2$ is a woman$)$. It rather means that John asserted the proposition $\neg (x_1$ kissed $x_2)$ and assumes that either the speaker or John is describing x_1 as *the man* and x_2 as *the woman*.

Point (2) relates to an extremely important way in which natural language differs from the propositions involved in mathematics. In mathematics one enumerates certain objects which he will talk about, defines other objects in terms of these objects, and confines himself to a discussion of objects which he has either postulated or denied and thus has assigned explicit names to; these names are in effect proper nouns. However, one does not begin a conversation by giving a list of postulates and definitions. He simply starts talking about whatever topic he feels like talking about and the bulk of the things he talks about will be things for which either there is no proper noun (e.g. there is no proper noun *Glarf* meaning "the third toe on Lyndon Johnson's left foot") or the speaker does not know any proper noun (e.g. one can perfectly well use an expression such as "the pretty redhead who you were talking to in the coffee shop" even if he does not know that girl's name. Moreover, people often talk about things which either do not exist or which they have identified incorrectly. Indices exist in the mind of the speaker rather than in the real world; they are conceptual entities which the individual speaker creates in interpreting his experience. Communication between different persons is possible because (1) different individuals often correctly identify things in the world or make similar incorrect identifications so that what one speaker says about an item in his mental picture of the universe, will jibe with something in his hearer's mental picture of the universe, and (2) the noun phrases which speakers use fulfill a function roughly comparable to that of postulates and definitions in mathematics: they state properties which the speaker assumes to be possessed by the conceptual entities involved in what he is saying and are used chiefly to give the listener sufficient information to identify the things that the speaker is talking about. I conclude that it is necessary for the meaning of an utterance to be divided into a "proposition" and a set of "NP-descriptions," e.g.

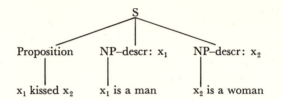

That such representations play a role in syntax is shown by an interesting class of ambiguities, which appear to have escaped notice until spring, 1967, when Paul Postal and George Lakoff began to investigate them. The sentence

> John said that he saw the woman who lives at 219 Main St.

may mean either that "the woman who lives at 219 Main St." is part of what John said in describing the woman he supposedly saw or it may mean that John said something such as "I saw Mary Wilson" and the speaker is describing Mary Wilson as "the woman who lives at 219 Main St." This ambiguity is brought out by the fact that the sentence can be continued in two ways, each of which allows only one of the two interpretations:

> . . . but the woman he saw really lives on Madison Ave.
> . . . but he doesn't know that she lives there.

Similarly, while it is in principle possible that the sentence

> John says that he didn't kiss the girl who he kissed.

is a report of John's having uttered the contradictory sentence "I didn't kiss the girl who I kissed," it is more likely to involve a statement such as "I didn't kiss Nancy" reported by a person who is convinced that John really did kiss Nancy. Similarly with

> John admits that he kissed the girl who he kissed.

These facts indicate that in certain kinds of embedded sentences the NP-descriptions relating to NP's in the embedded sentence may be either part of the embedded sentence or part of the main sentence. For example, the two meanings of the above example can be represented as

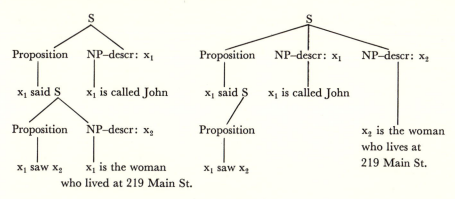

In the one case "the woman who lives at 219 Main St." is a part of what John said, in the other case it is not. Distinctions relating to what sentence an NP-description is a constituent of are also involved in sentences such as

Nancy wants to marry a Norwegian,

which may mean either that there is a Norwegian who Nancy wants to marry or that Nancy wants her future husband to be Norwegian although she hasn't yet found anyone to marry. In the first meaning, the NP-description *x is a Norwegian* is a constituent of the main sentence and in the second meaning it is a constituent of the sentence which is the underlying object of *want*. There is a similar ambiguity in

John wants to find the man who killed Harry.

In cases of multiple embeddings, it is possible to get multiple ambiguities corresponding to which of the sentences a given NP-description is a constituent of. For example,

John says that Nancy wants to marry a Norwegian

is ambiguous between the three senses (1) there is a person who John says Nancy wants to marry and who the speaker describes as a Norwegian, (2) John says that Nancy wants to marry a certain person and John describes that person as a Norwegian, and (3) John says that Nancy wants her future husband to be a Norwegian. It is difficult to see how these three senses could be assigned different deep structures unless those deep structures allowed noun-phrase descriptions to occur separate from the propositions which they are involved in and to be constituents of sentences in which those propositions are embedded.

The postulation of such deep structures would require English to have a transformation which substitutes each NP-description for an occurrence of the corresponding index. In each of the above diagrams, this transformation would substitute "the woman who lives at 219 Main St." for the single occurrence of x_2 and "John" for the first of the two occurrences of x_1. In this case, only the first occurrence of x_1 is a possible place for substitution "John": note that in

"He says that John saw the woman who lives at 219 Main St.," the "he" may not refer to John. However, in some cases it is possible to substitute an NP-description for any of several occurrences of the index in question, thus giving rise to alternate superficial forms such as

> After John left his apartment, he went to the bank.
> After he left his apartment, John went to the bank.

If deep structures such as the above are postulated, then pronominalization must be regarded in a quite different light than has hitherto been the case: pronominalization consists not of replacing repetitions of a noun phrase by pronous but rather of determining which occurrence of an index will have the corresponding noun-phrase description substituted for it. The occurrences of indices for which the substitution is not made are then filled in by pronouns. Note, incidentally that not all occurrences of an index are possible places for substituting the VP-description: the sentence

> After he left John's apartment, he went to the bank.

is not a variant of the above two (here the first *he* can only refer to someone other than John), and changes in word order affect the possibilities for substituting NP-descriptions: while

> John went to the bank after he left his apartment.

is synonymous with the original pair of sentences,

> He went to the bank after John left his apartment.

is not (here *he* can not refer to John). An explanation of the possibilities for pronominalization in these sentences is given in Ross (*op. cit.*) and Langacker (*op. cit.*). It is tempting to suggest that in the "deictic" use of pronouns (e.g. the sentence *Who is he?* in a situation where *he* does not refer to someone mentioned in a previous sentence but rather to someone who the speaker points out by a gesture) the NP-description consists not of lexical material but of the gesture which accompanies such pronouns, that the phonological reflex of a gesture is stress, and that substitution of the NP-description in this case causes the pronoun which arises to be stressed.

The underlying structures proposed in the last paragraph, incidentally, are extremely similar to the superficial form of sentences in many American Indian languages (see, e.g., G. H. Matthews, *Hidatsa Grammar* [The Hague, Mouton 1965]), where a clause consists of a sequence of noun phrases followed by a verb to which is prefixed a sequence of pronouns, one for each of the noun phrases. These languages have often been described as having a reduplication transformation which adds to the verb pronominal counterparts of all of the noun phrases in the clause. However, these languages could alternatively be described as simply lacking the NP-description substitution which English possesses. Since the indices within the "proposition" of each clause are not replaced by NP-descriptions, they are realized as pronouns.

It is necessary to impose a condition that in each semantic representation there be exactly one NP-description for each index in the representation and that that NP-description occur "higher" in the representation than all occurrences of the index in question. This condition makes it impossible to use a sentence such as

Napoleon admired Bonaparte

to express the proposition that Napoleon Bonaparte admired himself.

5. THE UNITY OF SYNTAX AND SEMANTICS

In the preceding section I have argued that to a very large extent the units and categories which play a role in semantic representation are exactly the units and categories which are involved in the formulation of the syntactic transformations which conditions 1–4 above would make necessary in a description of English. The symbolic logic formulas which I have used to represent meanings make widespread use of parentheses, whose sole function is to indicate the way in which items are grouped together into larger units; since grouping of items into larger units is precisely what is represented by the connections in tree diagrams such as appeared in sections 2 and 3 of this paper, semantic representations may likewise be considered to be trees. Since the rules for combining items into larger units in symbolic logic formulas must be stated in terms of categories such as "proposition," "predicate," and "index," these categories can be regarded as labels on the nodes of these trees. And since, as I noted in the preceding section, these categories all appear to correspond to syntactic categories, the same symbols (S, V, NP, etc.) may be used as node labels in semantic representation as are used in syntactic representations. Accordingly, semantic representations appear to be extremely close in formal nature to syntactic representations, so close in fact that it becomes essential to catalog the conceivable formal differences and determine whether those differences are real or apparent. The following appear to be the only possible formal differences between semantic and syntactic representations:

(1) The items in a syntactic representation must be assigned a linear order, whereas it is not obvious that linear ordering of items in a semantic representation makes any sense.

Whether this is a real difference between syntactic and semantic representations depends on whether things which have the same meaning must have the same semantic representation. If the synonymous sentences "John and Harry are similar" and "Harry and John are similar" are both to have the same semantic representation, that representation clearly would have to involve no ordering relation between *John* and *Harry*.

However, one could alternatively allow the same meaning to correspond to several different semantic representations and say that sameness of meaning corresponds not to sameness of semantic representation but rather to equivalence of semantic representation. In this view, semantic representations would have a linear ordering and there would be rules such as $p \lor q \equiv q \lor p$ for determining when two different semantic representations are equivalent. This, incidentally, is exactly the approach adopted in mathematics, where all formulas are assumed to have a linear ordering. I am not aware of any evidence which would favor a theory involving unordered semantic representations over a theory involving ordered semantic representations and equivalence relations. Until such evidence is found, the existence of an ordering relation among constituents cannot be accepted as a difference between syntactic and semantic representation.

(2) Syntactic representations involve lexical items from the language as their terminal nodes, whereas the terminal nodes in a semantic representation are semantic units rather than lexical units. If the intermediate representations between semantic representation and surface syntactic representation split neatly into two groups, those with only lexical items as their terminal nodes and those with only semantic items as their terminal nodes, it would indeed make sense to assert, as Chomsky does, that there is a level of "deep structure" which separates a semantic component of a language from a syntactic component; in that case, the insertion of lexical items into a sentence would all take place at a single point in the "derivational history" of each sentence, all that precedes that point being semantics and all that follows it being syntax. However, in actual fact, lexical insertion does not all take place at one point. Words such as *former* and *latter* cannot be chosen until after all transformations which change word order have been carried out. For example, in the sentence

It is obvious to John that Bill is a fool, and the former dislikes the latter.

former refers to John and *latter* to Bill even though the sentence is derived from a structure in which *that Bill is a fool* is the subject of *is obvious to John* and thus *Bill* precedes *John*. Moreover, the insertion of personal pronouns must take place at least two distinct points in a grammar. John R. Ross has pointed out (personal communication) that while one can say

Do you know John and Mary? He and she are a doctor and a teacher respectively.

one cannot say

Do you know John and Bill? He and he are a doctor and a teacher respectively.

but only

Do you know John and Bill? They are a doctor and a teacher respectively.

English has a rule that if two superficially identical noun phrases are conjoined they must be collapsed into a single noun phrase. This rule must apply after the pronouns *he*, *she*, etc. are inserted; but after the rule has applied it is necessary once more to insert pronouns in the places where this rule has collapsed conjoined identical pronouns into a single constituent.

In the case of derived items such as the verbs of change and causation discussed earlier, since the exact morphological process involved varies with the adjective in question (the causative verb *open* is superficially identical to the adjective *open*; the causative verb *redden* has the suffix *-en* added to the adjective *red*; the causative verb *liquefy* has the suffix *-efy* in place of the suffix of the adjective *liquid*; the causative verb *break* has a different vowel and lacks an ending which is present in the adjective broken[3] and since not all adjectives have corresponding inchoative and causative verbs (e.g. there is no such verb as *greenen* or *colden*), the form which results from combining an adjective with the abstract element [Inchoative] or [Causative] will in effect have to be listed in the dictionary of the language. This suggests that the inchoative transformation and causative transformation referred to earlier may profitably be regarded as processes which regroup semantic information prior to the insertion of lexical items. If this point of view is adopted, then one could perfectly well treat the two senses of *persuade* which occur in

> I persuaded John that the world is flat.
> I persuaded John to help me.

are the causatives of *believe* and *decide* respectively. On the basis of these various considerations, it seems plausible to hold that syntactic transformations and the insertion of lexical items, rather than being accomplished by separate components of a grammar, as Chomsky proposed in *Aspects*, are in fact intermingled within a single system of rules and that successive stages between the semantic representation of a sentence and its superficial form involve gradually more and more lexical material.

(3) There are many syntactic categories which appear to play no role in semantic representation, for example, verb-phrase, preposition, and prepositional phrase. In addition, grammatical gender and number, while often bearing some relationship to semantic distinctions of sex and number, are usually not identical to those semantic categories. To go into this question fully here would require far more space than can be spared in an article such as this. I will simply mention that Lakoff (*op. cit.*) and Fillmore ("The Case for Case" in Bach and Harms, eds., *Universals in Linguistic Theory*, New York: Holt, Rinehart & Winston, 1968), both working within the framework of a grammar with a level of deep structure, have given good reason for believing that the categories "prepositional phrase," "preposition," and "verb phrase" are unnecessary in deep structure and must be regarded as created by rules of the syntactic component. This means that even if there are separate systems of syntactic and semantic rules, the more superficial syntactic representations will contain a wider repertoire of categories than the deeper syntactic representations; consequently, the absence of certain syntactic categories from semantic representation provides no argument for the assertion that syntactic and semantic representation are different in nature.

In summary, I believe that these considerations indicate that syntactic and semantic representations are objects of the same formal nature, namely ordered trees whose non-terminal nodes are labeled by syntactic category symbols, and that in each language there is a single system of transformations which convert

---

[3] This treatment requires the adjective *broken* to be taken as syntactically more basic than the verb *break*. The fact that a form which is morphologically basic need not be syntactically basic was noted by Jespersen (*The Philosophy of Grammar*), who observed that from the point of view of syntax, *goodness* is to good as beauty is to beautiful.

semantic representations of sentences into their superficial form; these transformations include "lexical transformations," i.e. transformations which replace a portion of a tree by a lexical item. One may also draw the conclusion that syntax as a separate branch of linguistics simply does not exist: any generalizations about the way words can be combined in a language is merely the result of constraints on the ways in which semantic material may be combined and of the mechanisms which the language has for the conversion of semantic representations into the superficial forms of sentences.

6. PROBLEMS NOT DISCUSSED ABOVE

I do not wish to give the false impression that this article is an any sense a survey of semantics. It has been concerned solely with the question of how meanings can be represented and what the relationship of such representations to the description of languages is. Accordingly, I have failed to treat a great number of extremely interesting and important questions, for example,

(1) How do the meanings of words change as a language evolves?

(2) How does a child learn meanings in learning to speak his native language?

(3) What mechanisms are involved in phenomena such as metaphor, in which a speaker uses familiar words in meanings which they normally do not have, and why is it possible to understand such uses of language?

(4) To what extent are the units of semantic representation universal? Are there atomic predicates which play a role in representing meanings in all languages? If symbolic logic is a valid means of representing meanings in English, is it also a valid means of representing meanings in all other languages?

(5) To what extent does the lexicon of a language have a structure? Can one assert that the existence of certain words in a language implies the existence of certain other words, e. g. can one assert that every adjective has an antonym?

(6) Can all languages express the same ideas? One would be tempted to immediately answer "no," due to the obvious fact that languages often lack words for things unknown in the cultures in which they are spoken, e. g. Eskimo probably has no word for *pachinko* and Hottentot probably has no expression for "third-baseman." However, if one modifies the question slightly and asks whether all languages could express the same ideas if they were allowed to add words for all the things unknown in the cultures where they are spoken, the answer to the question ceases to be obvious. This question is of course closely related to question 4.

(7) To what extent does one's language affect his thinking? Even if all languages are capable of expressing the same thoughts, the rules of one language might make it difficult to express thoughts which are easy to express in another language. This conjecture is the celebrated "Whorf hypothesis," outlined by Benjamin Lee Whorf in *Language, Thought, and Reality* (Cambridge, Mass.: M. I. T. Press). The examples which Whorf gives in favor of his hypothesis are not convincing. However, there has been too little serious study of this topic to allow one to draw any conclusion concerning the correctness of Whorf's hypothesis. One minor respect in which Whorf's hypothesis appears

to be correct is that vocabulary may reinforce related beliefs and the terminology which one uses may lead one to retain beliefs which he might otherwise be less ready to retain; a case of this is discussed in James D. McCawley, "Sapir's 'Phonologic Representation'," *International Journal of American Linguistics*, XXXIII (1967), 106–111.

(8) To what extent is one's ability to learn lexical items conditioned by his knowledge of the world? It is doubtful that one could learn to use the word *banana* correctly unless he acquired a good deal of factual knowledge about bananas.

None of these problems has so far received an adequate solution; they are a small sample of the many crucial questions of linguistics and psychology which revolve about meaning.

CHARLES J. FILLMORE

6.3 *Entailment Rules in a Semantic Theory*

Occasionally during the past two or three decades descriptive linguists have asked themselves such questions as "What is the role of meaning in linguistic analysis?" and "What can linguistics contribute to our understanding of meaning?" The answers that have come up have generally been quite unencouraging. The answer to the first has usually been that meaning *should* have *no* role in making decisions in linguistic analysis, but, regrettably—our science is young —there are still many areas where meaning is called on to help us out. To the second question the answer has been that linguistics *should* be able to tell us something about meaning, but regrettably—our science is young—it hasn't really succeeded in doing so yet.

There have been times, however,—after making it clear that he was no longer talking as an "objective scientist"—when the descriptive linguist allowed himself to tell amusing anecdotes about semantic change or to describe interesting differences in the organization of concepts in different languages. And in such areas as systems of kinship terms—where, of course, he had a lot of help—he may even have been able to speak somewhat precisely.

With, these last activities as exceptions, the area of semantics was generally turned over to philosophers, psychologists, and cultists—people who were able to make precise and self-consistent observations about languages which nobody spoke, or to tell us amusing and revealing things about arbitrarily chosen words in some of the languages that people do speak.

Today, however, the picture has changed, largely because of the appearance of new conceptions in the theory of grammar. While the descriptive linguist

Used with the kind permission of the author.

conceived of his task as that of providing efficient procedures for labeling utterance segments and archiving utterances, the grammarian of today is interested in characterizing the ability of a speaker of a language to produce the sentences of his language and to perceive their grammatical structure. Semantic theories are now being constructed—based largely on the work of Noam Chomsky and Jerrold Katz—in an attempt to characterize the ability of speakers of a given language to assign semantic interpretations to sentences whose grammatical structure they perceive.

Various attempts are being made to integrate Chomsky's current version of grammar with the semantic theory of Katz and Fodor. A schema for one reasonable version of this integrated theory is given in Figure 1.

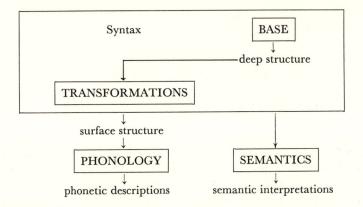

As is shown in the schema, the syntactic portion of a grammar contains two components, a base component and a transformational component. The base component specifies the underlying abstract forms of sentences—the so-called "deep structures"—and the transformational component converts these into forms directly related to actual utterances—the so-called "surface structures." The surface structures are mapped, by the phonological rules, into instructions for pronouncing the utterances.

The deep structure representation of a sentence is a string of lexical items organized to reveal grammatical categories (e.g. 'noun'), grammatical relations within the sentence (e.g. 'subject'), as well as the transformational structure of the sentence. That is, the grammatical base contains the recursive devices that account for the structure of complex and compound sentences, and introduces "markers" of the various sentence types—negative, passive, imperative, question, and the like. Each lexical item in the deep structure has associated with it, furthermore, both an assembly of semantic features corresponding to each possible reading (each sense) of the item, and a statement of the conditions under which each of these readings is selected.

A semantic theory, in this view, provides a system of rules for projecting from the deep-structure representation of sentences to one or more semantic interpretations, matching, if it is correct, the judgments of the speakers of the language. The capabilities of such a semantic theory can be summarized as follows:

First: Such a theory will assign identical semantic interpretations to synonymous expressions. For example, if the two sentences "The oculist is ill" and "The eye-doctor is sick" are synonymous, this fact will be revealed by a semantic theory which automatically assigns the same semantic interpretation to each of them. (Notice that because a system of semantic features has been posited, it is now possible to consider the existence or nonexistence of cases of *synonymy* as an empirical question. In certain previous conceptions of synchronic linguistics it was necessary to begin by assuming the nonexistence of exact synonyms. Now, however, the analyst is not free to decide in advance that there are no synonyms—this has become something which he needs to *find out*.)

Second: Within such a theory, those areas of vocabulary containing antonymous pairs of expressions will be identifiable in terms of the assignment of semantic features to lexical items. If several pairs of lexical items differ in only one pair of features, being otherwise identical, these pairs belong to a set of antonym pairs. As an example, pairs of words differing only in the selection of features that identify sex make up such a set—pairs like bull/cow, uncle/aunt, bachelor/spinster, etc.

Third: Such a theory provides for the context resolution of ambiguity. The conditions for interpreting each lexical item will determine which of several senses is appropriate in a given context. By consideration of these conditions, the semantic features of the verb "bark"—identifying, say, an activity of certain kinds of mammals—will, in a sentence like "The seal barked," rule out all but the "beast" interpretation of the polysemous word "seal." Similarly, that sense of "entertain" that involves feeding and singing songs to is disallowed in the expression "to entertain questions," because the word "entertain" in that sense requires an object which is semantically marked for animateness.

Fourth: Such a theory will provide ways of characterizing the analyticity of sentences. A sentence will be judged analytic, for example, if the semantic interpretation of the predicate is wholly contained in that of the subject. ("My father is a man.") A sentence with a relative clause on one of its nouns is analytic if the semantic interpretation of the sentence without the relative clause is wholly contained in the semantic interpretation of the relative clause. ("The people who speak English speak a language.") A conditional sentence is analytic if the semantic interpretation of the consequent is wholly contained in that of the antecedent. And so on.

Fifth: The deviance of semantically anomalous sentences will be marked, and the basis of their deviance will be accounted for. For instance, if a sentence like "My lap itches" is semantically deviant, a semantic theory will be expected to point out that while the verb "itch" requires a subject that can be interpreted as a body part, the noun "lap" cannot be so interpreted.

These remarks, I believe, fairly adequately represent the capabilities claimed for the Katz and Fodor semantic theory. Anyone interested in a discussion of the formal properties of such a theory and suggestions on the precise formulation of semantic rules should be referred to Jerrold Katz and Jerry Fodor, "The Structure of a Semantic Theory," in *The Structure of Language* edited by Jerry Fodor and Jerrold Katz.[1]

Now without suggesting that Katz and Fodor are unaware of its general inadequacies, I would like to discuss two specific failings of the theory—touching on one of them very briefly, dwelling at some length on the other.

The failure of this theory that comes most quickly to mind—and I am not the first to point this out—has to do with the interpretation of the so-called "relational" concepts. Briefly, it is not easy to see how any slight modification of the notion of "semantic feature" can lead to the correct interpretation of comparative sentences. In a sentence like "John is taller than Bill," a relation —an asymmetric relation—is understood to hold between John and Bill with respect to a certain dimension, namely height. The way in which the Katz and Fodor theory can be extended to take care of such relations is not obvious.

There seem to be semantic anomalies involving relational terms. I would insist, for example, that a sentence like "I am two years older than my father" is semantically odd. The deviance can be accounted for in some such way as the following: In the expression "my father," an asymmetric relation of precedence in time (among other things) is expressed between two objects. The comparative expression "older than" states another relation of precedence in time between the same two objects, and this relation is the reverse of and is incompatible with the first. Hence the anomaly.

The bizarreness of the sentence "I am two years older than my father" is quite different from whatever is odd about "My father is two years older than I am." If you hear the latter sentence, you may not believe it, or you may suspect that it was spoken by, say, a cat. But semantically, there is nothing wrong with it.

Another problem connected with relational concepts was pointed out by Sapir in his paper on "Grading." It has to do with the interpretation of relational concepts in which the second term of the relation is not expressed. The problem has been particularly puzzling to linguists who have sought simple-minded relations between morphemes and semantic units, because while "taller" is morphologically the adjective "tall" plus the comparative suffix "er," semantically the relational notion "taller than" is more basic than the notion "tall."

It seems to me that for a semantic theory to give a correct account of relational concepts we should expect the following:

First: The theory will intially assign a relational meaning to words like "tall." (Notice, however, that a sense relating only to the dimension 'height' will also be needed for "tall"—but not for "short"—as is seen in the way we understand such expressions as "six inches tall" or "this tall.")

Second: The theory will interpret such words by finding, in the grammatical context, the two terms of the relation, and it will record this relation, in some

---

[1] [See selection 6.1 above, pp. 472–514.]

way, as part of the interpretation of the sentence. One function of the comparative construction is to make the two terms of such a relation accessible.

THIRD: In those cases where the sentence does not contain a second term for the relation, the semantic theory will provide one, say the word "average."

Thus, "John is taller than Bill" will be taken care of in the first way, with "John" identified as the first term of the relation, "Bill" as the second. The sentence "John is tall," on the other hand, will be interpreted as "John is taller than average." In the sentence "John is tall," or "John is taller than average," the 'universe of discourse' of the word "average" is unspecified. There are, however, grammatical ways of identifying a universe of discourse for this word —as in a sentence like "He's tall for a pygmy."

A second type of semantic observation not provided for by the Katz and Fodor theory needs to be handled by what I call "entailment rules." If we call the rules provided by the Katz and Fodor theory, together with the rules I suggested for relational concepts, the "ordinary" semantic rules, entailment rules can be described, roughly, as operating in the following way: There is a sentence X which cannot by itself be interpreted by the ordinary semantic rules. Based on the grammatical structure of X, the entailment rules will convert X into a set of sentences[2] Y such that each of *these* sentences *can* be interpreted by the ordinary semantic rules. The semantic interpretation of the set of sentences Y, then, is provided as the semantic interpretation of the sentence X.

The semantic observations for which I will propose entailment rules will tie in with the observations on relational concepts at two or three points—the first being that the translation from "John is tall" into "John is taller than average" is perhaps best interpreted as resulting from an entailment rule.

As a first example of a situation calling for entailment rules, let us consider the way in which verbs like "know," "realize," and "be aware" are used in English. What difference, for example, do you perceive in the two sentences "I think that John is sick" and "I know that John is sick"? When I ask this question of my students, I am usually told at first that the difference relates to intensity of belief, degree of confidence, or the like. That this seems plausible at first is accounted for by the fact that in these sentences the subject is the speaker and the time of the sentence is the time of the utterance. When these features are varied, the important difference between these two verbs can be more adequately perceived.

Consider, for example, the third-person-subject sentences "Bill thinks that you were here" and "Bill knows that you were here." It's fairly clear, I think, that in these sentences we are not merely being told two different things about Bill. When used appropriately, the sentence "Bill knows that you were here" entails the sentence "You were here." The sentence with "thinks" does not.

This observation on "know" as compared with "think" accounts for the fact that "John thinks that he is a girl" is not semantically odd, while "John knows

---

[2] Perhaps the word 'proposition' should be used instead of 'sentence'. It is not necessary to an understanding of entailment rules that the elements of Y be realizable as sentences.

that he is a girl" is. "John knows that he is a girl" is semantically odd because it entails the semantically odd sentence "He is a girl."

The nature of the entailment rule for "know" can also be seen by varying the tense of the verb. If I say, for example, that "I thought Paris was the capital of Sweden," I am revealing only my past ignorance of geography. If I say "I knew that Paris was the capital of Sweden," I am also revealing my present ignorance, in spite of the past tense of the verb. That is because the sentence with "know" entails the sentence "Paris is the capital of Sweden."

The entailment rule for "know" can be formulated as follows:

$$X - V_k - that - S - Y \quad \textit{entails} \left\{ \begin{array}{l} X - V_k - that - S - Y \\ S \end{array} \right.$$

We recognize, first, a class of verbs V_k, a class including "know," "realize," and "be aware," but not including "think," "believe," or "be sure." The rule (which cannot be reapplied) states that the sentence embedded after V_k is entailed.

Notice that the rule refers only to the presence of a V_k, not to other grammatical properties of the sentence. This reflects the fact that the entailment is unchanged even when the verb itself is negated or questioned or the like. That is, I, the speaker, am claiming that "Bill is here" in all of the following sentences: "He doesn't know that Bill is here." "Does he know that Bill is here?" "Doesn't he know that Bill is here?"

(Before I leave the discussion of "know," I should say that in addition to the entailment difference, there is also a difference between "know" and "think" that *does* have to do with degree of confidence. I would say that apparent counterexamples of the rule for "know" are really instances of 'playing' with the word "know." This kind of play is indulged in, for instance, in certain cases where the entailed sentence is known to be false. There is a way of saying "I just *knew* Goldwater was going to get elected" where the meaning of complete confidence is conveyed in spite of the obvious falsity of the entailment.)

The next two examples of entailment situations involve uses of the word "even"—one in simple assertions, the other in comparative constructions. Consider the difference between the sentences "She reads Sanskrit" and "She even reads Sanskrit." The second tells us the same as the first, but it adds that this fact is somehow surprising. The contribution of the word "even" cannot be explained, it seems to me, by assigning it semantic features of the usual kind. I would say that the sentence "She even reads Sanskrit" is to be 'factored', so to speak, into two sentences, namely "She reads Sanskrit" and "One would expect that she does not read Sanskrit." One of the entailment rules in a semantic theory of English will carry out this 'factoring' operation.

Looking at another use of "even," consider the two sentences "John is taller than Bill" and "John is even taller than Bill." In the first sentence, John and Bill may both be giants or midgets—only their relative height is in question. In the second sentence, the presence of "even" entails that Bill is tall.

I would say that "John is even taller than Bill" entails the two sentences, "John is taller than Bill" and "Bill is tall." Recall that "Bill is tall," now, is to be interpreted as "Bill is taller than average."

To avoid giving the impression that we have to invent entailment rules for every situation in which the truth or appropriateness of one sentence is involved with the truth or appropriateness of other sentences, it may be wise to insert a brief 'aside' at this point to consider those many cases of intersentence inferences—or what have you—which are *not* to be handled in this way.

As our first example, we may consider the relation which holds between such sentences as "My parents were born in Sweden" and "My father was born in Sweden." The second is surely true whenever the first is true, but this is not something calling for the construction of an entailment rule. Relations of 'class inclusion' between lexical items may be quite adequately expressed within the limitations of the Katz and Fodor theory. The relationship between the two sentences, therefore, can be observed by simply comparing their semantic interpretations. The meaning of "father" includes the meaning of "parent." There is no need to introduce *rules* to express this relation over again.

Secondly, consider the two sentences "He is John's brother" and "John has a brother." It is obvious that the second sentence must be true whenever the first has been used appropriately, and it is true that this relationship is grammatically statable and could be formulated as an entailment rule. However, there are fairly convincing reasons for regarding the sentence "John has a brother" as the transformational source of the noun phrase "John's brother." A semantic theory operates on the deep structure of sentences; the deep structure of the sentence "He is John's brother" contains as one of its parts the sentence "John has a brother." There is no reason for a semantic theory to express, by means of a separate set of rules, the relation between a sentence and its transformational sources. The grammar of the language has already done that.

A third type of inference from one sentence to other sentences may be accounted for by referring to the speaker's and hearer's shared knowledge of the conditions under which anaphoric processes take place. As an illustration of this, consider the sentence "*He* doesn't swim, either." From the stressed pronoun and the word "either," one who knows English can infer that one male human fails to swim, and that at least one additional being fails to swim.

Now instead of saying that the information that somebody else doesn't swim is *part of the meaning of* "*He* doesn't swim, either," I would rather say that what we have here is—in a sense—an incomplete sentence and that the hearer knows what is necessary to complete it. A linguistic description of a language accounts for independently interpretable sentences. It does not account directly for a sentence like "*He* doesn't swim, either," but only for the larger sequences of which this can be a part. In the deep structure of these larger sequences, the information about someone else's inability to swim had to be explicitly present.

A final type of intersentence relationship that might be confused with the situation I am trying to deal with is what John Austin called "implications."

An example of an implication, in Austin's sense, is seen in the relation between the two sentences, "John is sick" and "I believe that John is sick." Here it's not utterances in isolation that are being examined, but the utterance "John is sick" on the part of a particular speaker at a particular time and the assumption that if the sentence had been used appropriately, it would also have been appropriate for the same speaker at the same time to have said, "I believe that John is sick."

This is more like an assumption of "good faith" that underlies speech communication in general than something which a semantic theory needs to explain. An assumption like this certainly need not be stated in the form of a rule which relates sentences to other sentences.

Now, class-inclusion relations, we have seen, can be taken care of in a Katz and Fodor semantic theory as presently conceived. The relation between a sentence and its transformational sources is made explicit in the grammar. Certain sentences are best thought of, from the point of view of an integrated theory of linguistic description, as incomplete sentences; semantic theory is to be held responsible only for independently interpretable sentences. And certain assumptions about the nonabuse of speech communication are *too* general to require expression in the form of semantic rules. These four situations present no problems to semantic theory, it is clear, but I believe the observations we came across in connection with the two uses of "even" do not fall into any of these types. I am convinced, therefore, that an adequate semantic theory needs to incorporate an essentially new type of rule to account for these observations.

Let's return now to the first observation on the word "even," and recall that the sentence "She even reads Sanskrit" entailed "One would expect that she does *not* read Sanskrit." If the original sentence had been, "She doesn't even read Sanskrit," the entailed sentence would have been "One would expect that she *does* read Sanskrit." It is true here and with several of the other entailment rules that we'll see, that if the original sentence is negative, one of the entailed sentences is positive; if the original sentence is positive, the entailed sentence is negative. This property I shall call 'sign-changing', and I'd like to deal with it by abstracting from the sentences the grammatical properties 'negativity/positivity', representing them in the rules with a variable 'α'. In a single entailment rule, then, if 'α' has one of these values, ' $-\alpha$' has the other. Using this notation, our first observation on "even" can be formulated in some such way as the following:

$$\alpha \text{ (NP + even + Aux + VP)} \quad \textit{entails} \Big\langle \begin{array}{l} \alpha \text{ (NP + Aux + VP)} \\ \text{One would expect that} \\ (-\alpha \text{ (NP + Aux + VP))} \end{array}$$

The entailed proposition can be represented more abstractly if 'expectation' can be presented as a modality on an entire sentence and if the syntactic element Aux (verbal auxiliary) can be considered as the first constituent of the remainder of the sentence. Our rule, now, can be rewritten as

$$\alpha \, (\text{Aux}(\text{NP} + \text{even} + \text{VP})) \quad \textit{entails} \begin{cases} \alpha \, (\text{Aux}(\text{NP} + \text{VP})) \\ \text{expectation} \, (- \, \alpha \, (\text{Aux}(\text{NP} + \text{VP}))) \end{cases}$$

A second example of a sign-changing rule involves the prepositional phrase which provides the 'universe of discourse' for interpreting relations whose second terms are unexpressed, as, e.g., in "He's tall for a pygmy." These "for"-phrases actually, however, do more than just that. If I say of someone that "She's smart for a girl," I am not telling you only of her rank among girls with respect to smartness—I have included a commentary on girls, namely that they are not, as a rule, smart. If I had said, "She's not smart for a girl," I would have been implying that girls *are* smart. "She's smart for a girl" entails "Girls are not smart." "She isn't smart for a girl" entails "Girls are smart," another sign-changing rule.

But now let's notice what happens when sentences of this last type contain the word "even." While "She's smart for a girl" entails that girls are not smart, "She's even smart for a girl" entails that girls are smart. What seems to be happening is that the word "even" calls into play a sign-changing rule which has the effect of reversing the sign of the entailment for the "for"-phrase. "She's even smart for a girl" entails that girls are smart. "She isn't even smart for a girl" entails that girls are not smart. This is a case where *two* sign-changing rules result in an entailed sentence that retains the sign of the original sentence.

An abundant source of entailment observations is supplied by the various types of conditional sentences. The rules for conditional sentences reveal some of the advantages of isolating the tenses and modalities from the remainder of the sentence, because semantically these features are associated with the conditional sentence as a whole, not with each clause separately. For one thing, conditional sentences are themselves essentially timeless. The auxiliaries in these sentences relate to the difference between neutral and counterfactual conditionals and to the time at which or during which the conditional relation is understood to hold, not to temporal aspects of the propositions contained in the conditional. We can represent the abstract structure of a neutral conditional sentence in such a form as

tense $(p \supset q)$

where the 'horseshoe' is to be read as, say, 'results in', in order to remind ourselves that the conditional relation of English is not that of material implication.

Thus, we could represent the neutral conditional sentence "If John comes, I go" as

general (John come $\supset$ I go)

or the sentence "If John comes, I'll go" as

future (John come $\supset$ I go).

I assume that the underlying grammatical structure of counterfactual conditionals will have some kind of a marker for identifying them as such. This marker will have the two-fold role of (a) triggering the transformations which provide counterfactual conditionals with the correct pair of auxiliaries ("If John *were* here, I *would go*," "If John *had been* here, I *would have gone*," etc.) and of (b) triggering the entailment rule which adds to the meaning of the conditional a sign-changed version of the antecedent—that is, which provides the information that the antecedent is false.

From the structure underlying "If John were there, I would go," the entailment rules in question would give us

      present (John be there ⊃ I go)
      negative (present (John be there));

and from "If John were not there, I would go" they would give us

      present ((negative (John be there)) ⊃ I go)
      positive (present (John be there));

and, to include an example of a past tense counterfactual conditional, we can see that "If John had come, I would have gone" entails

      past (John come ⊃ I go)
      negative (past (John come))

Conditional sentences the antecedents of which begin with "if only" entail a neutral conditional plus an optative comment on the antecedent. That is, "If only John comes, I'll go" entails

      future (John come ⊃ I go)
      optative (future (John come))

Conditional sentences whose antecedents begin with "even if"—the so-called 'concessive conditionals'—do not entail any actual conditional relations, but only, first, an expectation that a conditional relation holds, second, a denial of that conditional relation, and third, the information that the consequent is true. The 'expected' conditional has as its consequent a sign-changed version of the original consequent.

For example, "Even if John comes, I'll go" entails

      expectation (future (John come ⊃ negative (I go)))
      negative (future (John come ⊃ negative (I go)))
      future (I go)

Applying these relations to another example, we can see that the sentence, "Even if John doesn't come, I won't go" entails

      expectation (future (negative (John come) ⊃ I go))
      negative (future (negative (John come) ⊃ I go))
      negative (future (I go))

Recall now that in the analysis of conditional sentences we have found two sign-changing rules, one affecting the antecedent, and one affecting the consequent. Since it's possible to have both of these phenomena operating in the same sentence, a sentence like "Even if John had come, I would have gone" entails four things: (a) One would expect that John's coming would result in my not going. (b) It is not true that John's coming would result in my not going. (c) John did not come. and (d) I went. A sign-changed version of the consequent is found in the expected and denied conditional associated with "even"; a sign-changed version of the antecedent is found in the counterfactual entailment.

The result of applying entailment rules operating on past-tense counterfactual concessives can be formulated—this time by using two positivity/negativity variables, α and β—as follows:

even + if(α (past + have + en(NP + X))), β (past + will + have + en(NP' + Y))[3]

entails

(i)   expectation (past((α (NP + X)) $\supset$ $-$ β(NP' + Y)))
(ii)   negative (past((α (NP + X)) $\supset$ $-$ β (NP' + Y)))
(iii) $-$ α(past (NP + X))
(iv) β(past (NP' + Y))

Where both clauses are positive, we get:

even + if (positive(past + have + en(John + come))), positive(past + will + have + en(I + go))
("Even if John had come, I would have gone.")

entails

(i)   expectation (past ((positive (John come)) $\supset$ negative (I go)))
       ("One expects that John's coming would have resulted in my not going.")
(ii)   negative (past ((positive (John come)) $\supset$ negative (I go)))
       ("It is not true that John's coming would have resulted in my not going.")
(iii)   negative (past (John come))
       ("John did not come.")
(iv)   positive (past (I go))
       (" I went.")

Where both clauses are negative we get:

even + if (negative (past + have + en(John + come))), negative(past + will + have + en(I + go))
("Even if John hadn't come, I wouldn't have gone.")

entails

(i)   expectation (past ((negative (John come)) $\supset$ positive (I go)))
       ("One expects that John's not coming would have resulted in my going.")
(ii)   negative (past ((negative (John come)) $\supset$ positive (I go)))
       ("It is not true that John's not coming would have resulted in my going.")
(iii)   positive (past (John come))
       ("John came.")
(iv)   negative (past (I go))
       ("I didn't go.")

---

[3] The form of the Aux is given here in detail, although it is assumed that the deep structure of conditional sentences will specify, for the entire sentence, only the tense and whether it is counterfactual or neutral.

Where only the antecedent is negative, we get:

> even + if (negative(past + have + en (John + come))), positive(past + will + have + en(I + go))
> ("Even if John hadn't come, I would have gone.")

> > *entails*

    (i)   expectation (past ((negative (John come)) ⊃ negative (I go)))
             ("One expects that John's not coming would have resulted in my not going.")
    (ii) negative (past ((negative (John come)) ⊃ negative (I go)))
             ("It is not true that John's not coming would have resulted in my not going.")
    (iii) positive (past (John come))
             ("John came.")
    (iv) positive (past (I go))
             ("I went.")

Where only the consequent is negative, we get:

> even + if (positive (past + have + en(John + come))), negative (past + will + have(I + go))
> ("Even if John had come, I wouldn't have gone.")

> > *entails*

    (i)   expectation (past ((positive (John come)) ⊃ positive (I go)))
             ("One expects that John's coming would have resulted in my going.")
    (ii) negative (past ((positive (John come)) ⊃ positive (I go)))
             ("It is not true that John's coming would have resulted in my going.")
    (iii) negative (past (John come))
             ("John did not come.")
    (iv) negative (past (I went))
             ("I didn't go.")

What this discussion about conditionals means is that such notions as 'concessive' or 'counterfactual' are not primitive terms in the semantic theory but can themselves be analyzed in terms of such notions as 'conditional', 'negation', and 'expectation', all of them terms in the semantic theory which are needed on independent grounds. Our discussion could go on, showing, for example, that the types of 'provisional' relations associated with such conjunctions as 'unless' and 'provided that' may be similarly analyzed. Briefly "αA unless βB" entails "if − βB, αA" and "if βB, − αA." That is, "I'll go unless you go" is analyzed as "If you go, I won't go; if you don't go, I will go." "αA provided that βB" entails "if βB, αA" and "if − βB, − αA." That is, "I'll go provided that you go" is analyzed as "If you go, I'll go; if you don't go, I won't go."

The discussion of conditional sentences may seem like little more than a complicated way of talking about things that are intuitively well understood before we start. To show how entailment rules may be called on to shed light on new problems in semantic analysis, I would like to run through a series of arguments dealing with semantic properties of the pairs of words "come" vs. "go," and "bring" vs. "take." I'm interested in these words in contexts where they are semantically paired. The expression "go to school," will therefore not be considered in this discussion; and neither will the expression "take off" meaning "remove." It is not semantically paired with "bring off."

One proposal which has been made concerning these words has it that the semantic characterization of "come" and "bring" includes a feature shared by such words as "here" and "this," while in "go" and "take" there is a feature shared by "there" and "that." The proposal is that the features of place deixis obviously found in "this" and "that" are repeated in such pairs of words as "come" and "go." The features refer to relative proximity to the speaker, with a context variant in the case of verbs of motion indicating direction toward or away from the speaker.

This interpretation appears to be supported by the way we understand such sentences as "Please bring it here," "He came here this morning," "I'll go to your house tomorrow," "I took it there," and by the fact that we reject such sentences as "Please go here" or "Please take it here."

But what do I say when somebody calls me up on the telephone and asks me over? I say, "I'll come right over," not "I'll go right over"; "I'll bring something to drink," not "I'll take something to drink."

The suggestion that the features involved are merely deictic features referring to direction of movement with respect to the speaker at the moment of speaking, thus, has to be rejected.

A second proposal might be that while "go" and "take" involve movement away from the speaker, "come" and "bring" involve movement toward the place where the speaker will be when the action is completed. This new interpretation is supported by our earlier sentences—for example, "Please come here," "He brought it here"—and also by the troublesome sentences—"I'll bring it there" or "I'll come right over."

This proposal does nothing, however, to explain the difference between, say, "I'll bring it there" and "I'll take it there," since in both cases the speaker will be "there" after the action is completed. It is not a satisfactory account of the way we understand these sentences to say that in the one case information about the future location of the speaker is made explicit, in the other case it is not.

But a more important objection can be seen if we return to our telephone conversation. If I am not able to see my friend myself, I might get someone else to go. In such a case, I will say, "He'll come right over," or "She'll bring it to you," or the like. In these examples, the present or future location of the speaker is not involved at all.

Just to eliminate all possibilities before we resort to entailment rules, we might consider a third alternative, namely that the semantic feature common to "bring" and "come" has to do with the place where the hearer, not the speaker, will be after the action is completed. In "Please bring it here," "here" is where "you" will be after the bringing of it is done. In "I'll come to see you tonight," the "coming" is to where you will be. In "She'll bring it to you," the place to which she will bring it is the place where you will be.

Counterexamples to proposal three are easy to come by, and, in fact, have already been supplied. Clearly, in "She brought it here this morning," "your" location at that time is not in the picture at all. Equally obvious cases are those whose action involves both the speaker and the hearer. There is a difference between "Let's come to the library again tonight" and "Let's go to the library again tonight." And between "Please take me to the airport" and "Please bring me to the airport."

The fourth and final proposal is that these verbs bring into play various entailment rules—the details of which I have by no means worked out—and that, in the case of "come" and "bring," the entailments which are appropriate depend on the subject of the sentence.

Simplifying a little, I will limit the entailment observations related to these verbs to cases where the goal of movement is specified. I shall limit myself, in fact, to the cases where the goal of movement is either "here," "there," "to the airport" or "into the room." As we shall see, one of the effects of the entailment rules will be to change directional phrases such as these into the corresponding locational phrases. "Here" and "there" will be unaffected by this change, but "to the airport" and "into the room" will be changed to "at the airport" and "in the room" respectively.

The rule for "take" and "go" is relatively simple and is not affected by the subject. The location phrase (derived from the directional phrase) in a sentence with "take" or "go" is merely a place where *I am not*. That is, in such sentences as "I'll take it to the airport," "He went to the airport," "Please take it to the airport," the entailment is that "I am not at the airport."

$$\alpha(\text{Aux}(\text{NP} \begin{Bmatrix} \text{take} + \text{NP}' \\ \text{go} \end{Bmatrix} \text{Loc})) \quad entails \begin{cases} \text{same} \\ \text{negative (present(I + be + Loc*))} \end{cases}$$

Now we can say that by applying this rule to the sentence "Please take it here" we get the entailed sentence "I am not here," and the semantic rules for deictic categories will mark as anomalous all present-tense copular sentences with nonmatching deictic features for subject and predicate. The oddity of "Please take it here," thus, is another instance of 'secondary semantic oddity': "John knows that he is a girl" is semantically odd because the sentence it entails ("He is a girl") is odd. "Please take it here" is odd because the sentence it entails ("I am not here") is odd.

The rules for "come" and "bring," as I said, depend on the subject. Actually these verbs are ambiguous, because they involve a *choice* of entailments, one paralleling the rule for "go" and "take" but declaring that the place mentioned in the sentence is where *I am*, the other being somewhat more complicated. The most general form of the rule is as follows: (the negativity/positivity value of the sentence is not relevant to this rule and is therefore left unexpressed)

$$\text{Aux}(\text{NP} \begin{Bmatrix} \text{bring} + \text{NP}' \\ \text{come} \end{Bmatrix} \text{Loc}) \quad entails \begin{cases} \text{same} \\ \begin{cases} \text{Aux*(NP* + be + Loc*)} \\ \text{(present (I + be + Loc*))} \end{cases} \end{cases}$$

(The difference between Loc and Loc* is that Loc is a directional phrase, Loc* is the corresponding location phrase. Aux and Aux* will often be identical, but 'perfect' and 'progressive' will not be present in Aux*; that is, "He is bringing it to the station" does not entail "You are being at the station" but "You are at the station." The relation between NP and NP* can be stated as follows:

> NP* is "you" when NP is "I"
> NP* is "I" when NP is "you"
> (otherwise NP* is either "I" or "you".)

Notice that if these rules are correct, "come" or "bring" sentences with "I" or "you" as subject should be capable of two interpretations, unless one or both of the entailed sentences is anomalous. Thus, "I'll come to the airport early tomorrow" entails either that *you will be* at the airport or that *I am* at the airport now. These two interpretations fit, I believe, the two possible situations in which we could use that sentence. A sentence like "I'll come there," on the other hand, permits only the entailment that you will be there because "I am there" is anomalous.

To take an example with second person subject, notice that "You came to the airport" may entail either that I am at the airport now or that I was at the airport when you came. "You came there," however, is unambiguous, because while the entailment that *I was there* is acceptable, the other—that *I am there*—is not.

When the subject is something other than first or second persons, as shown by the rule, three interpretations are possible. That is, "He came to the airport" entails either that *you were* at the airport, that *I was* at the airport, or that *I am* at the airport now. All of these are acceptable.

I said that the details of these entailments were not thoroughly worked out, and that is certainly true. It is not clear to me, for instance, how the inclusive and exclusive senses of "we" are going to be taken care of. If "we" means "you and I," then "We came to the airport early today" has one interpretation. If it means "somebody else and I, but not you," it has two possible interpretations. Our theory will have to specify all three possibilities.

Another matter has to do with certain apparent differences in the applicability of these rules to "bring" and "come." You may have noticed that I used "come" in most of my recent examples. This is because there appears to be disagreement among speakers of English on certain uses of "bring." Imagine that you and I are here, and a friend of ours is in the hospital, and consider the appropriateness of my saying "Let's bring her some flowers." Many adult speakers of English would reject the sentence under these conditions, others would not. There is no such disagreement about the unacceptability, under the same conditions, of "Let's come to the hospital."

I conclude these remarks on entailments by admitting that my solutions are all extremely provisional; that I regard the positing of entailment rules as a last-resort matter; and that I have only suggested—have certainly not *provided*—a notation for these rules. I will be happy if any of these observations can be shown to be explainable by the 'ordinary semantic rules'. (I'll be embarrassed if they all can.)

One possible way of removing entailment rules is to invent transformational rules which, in each case, will show that the sentences I have worried about are transforms of the sentences which I said they entail. It might be possible to construct a transformation which will take the triplet of sentences "Mary is a girl," "Girls are not smart," and "Mary is smarter than the average girl" into the sentence "Mary is smart for a girl." Now we can say that the meaning of the sentence is a product of the meanings of its source sentences. The objection to this solution is that it amounts to constructing syntactic rules for the sake of preserving a questionable notion of semantic interpretation. The claim that the semantic interpretation of a sentence is a simple product of the semantic interpretation of its constituent sentences is a claim the truth of which should be discovered, not assumed in advance. The only way to discover if this claim is true is to have autonomous criteria for syntactic analysis.

The conclusion that a semantic theory needs at least some rules of the entailment type has introduced, at least for me, an important consideration in the performance of semantic analysis. I think we should continue to ask the old questions first—(1) What is the underlying grammatical structure of this sentence? (2) What semantic features can we assign to each lexical item such that the rules for amalgamating these sets of features within each constituent will account for the semantic interpretation of the sentence?

But when, after exploring all possible answers to these questions, certain problems remain unresolved, I now ask—(3) What do sentences like these entail?

PAUL ZIFF

6.4 *About What an Adequate Grammar Couldn't Do*

There is much that an adequate grammar of a natural language could not do, open an oyster, for example, but then, who would have thought it could? The pearls some hope to be disclosed by a grammar are of a rarer sort: insight into the structure of the language, an understanding of the linguistic capacities and behaviour of the native speakers, and so forth.

But along with its undoubted incapacity to open an oyster there is something else that an adequate grammar could not do which many do seem to suppose that it could, namely discriminate between ambiguous and unambiguous sentences. That it could not is what I shall try to show.

1. What an adequate grammar of a natural language could or could not do depends on what an adequate grammar is or would be. A grammar of course,

Reprinted from *Foundations of Language*, I, No. 1 (1965), 5–13, by permission of the author.

but when would it be adequate? Of this large question only a small part need be considered here.

There are various conditions of adequacy that one could seek to impose on a grammar with respect to ambiguity. So one might say (I): if a sentence is ambiguous then the grammar should provide more than one syntactic structural description for the sentence. Or (II): the grammar should provide more than one syntactic structural description for a sentence only if the sentence is ambiguous. Or (III): the grammar should provide more than one syntactic structural description for a sentence if and only if the sentence is ambiguous.

Conditions (I), (II), and (III) do not exhaust the possibilities. I mean to reject all three as unreasonable and offer in their place quite another. But for the moment there are other matters.

2. I would not suggest that anyone has suggested that condition (III) or condition (I) would be a reasonable condition to impose on a grammar with respect to ambiguity. It is conceivable that someone has but I don't know that.

Condition (II) has in fact been offered by Noam Chomsky. Thus, where "f is a function such that $f(i, j)$ is the set of structural descriptions of the sentence s_i that are provided by the grammar G_j," Chomsky says that "$f(i, j)$ should contain more than one structural description only if the sentence s_i is ambiguous—that is, this is a reasonable empirical condition, one of many, on the grammar of a language".[1]

3. If any of the conditions mentioned were acceptable as reasonable conditions on the adequacy of a grammar, my claim that an adequate grammar could not discriminate between ambiguous and unambiguous sentences would be either wholly or partially in error.

If condition (III) were fulfilled by a grammar, one could simply identify the set of ambiguous sentences of the language with the set of sentences having more than one structural description. The grammatical discrimination between ambiguous and unambiguous sentences would thus be complete. If condition (I) and not (II) were fulfilled, the set of ambiguous sentences would be a proper subset of the set of sentences having more than one syntactic structural description. Although this would not enable one to establish grammatically that a given sentence is ambiguous, it would in some cases enable one to establish grammatically that the sentence is not ambiguous. Thus the grammar would make at least a partial discrimination between ambiguous and unambiguous sentences. Conversely, if condition (II) and not (I) were fulfilled, the set of sentences having more than one syntactic structural description would be a proper subset of the set of ambiguous sentences. And though this would not enable one to establish grammatically that a given sentence is not ambiguous, if condition (II) were fulfilled in a nontrivial way, it would in some cases enable one to establish grammatically that the sentence is ambiguous. Thus again the grammar would make at least a partial discrimination between ambiguous and unambiguous sentences. (But see Section 6 below.)

---

[1] "On the Notion 'Rule of Grammar' ", *Structure of Language and Its Mathematical Aspects*, Proceedings of Symposia in Applied Mathematics (1961), pp. 6–24, here pp. 6–7.

But in maintaining that an adequate grammar could not discriminate between ambiguous and unambiguous sentences, I mean to say that there is not a single sentence with respect to which such a grammar would enable one to establish grammatically either that it is or that it is not ambiguous.

4. Condition (I) is that if a sentence is ambiguous then the grammar should provide more than one syntactic structural description for the sentence. That this would constitute an absurd demand to make on a grammar is no doubt obvious. But it is not irrelevant to consider precisely why.

The reason is not that no grammar could meet the condition. On the contrary, one could because one could easily construct one of the requisite sort. For example, consider the remark 'I saw a shark': since the remark can be, the sentence is said to be, ambiguous. Am I referring to the denizen of a pool or a poolroom? But nothing precludes the possibility of our constructing a (silly) grammar in which the word 'shark' is assigned to two distinct noun categories with the result that in that grammar the sentence 'I saw a shark' could be assigned two distinct syntactic structural descriptions in terms of the distinct noun categories.

5. There are at least two reasons why condition (I), and in consequence condition (III), would constitute an unreasonable demand to make on a grammar.

The first is that even though a grammar could fulfil condition (I), it could do so only at an extreme cost. A grammar could provide two distinct syntactic structural descriptions for a sentence like 'I saw a shark', but doing so would necessitate invoking an incredible number of wholly *ad hoc* categories, categories that would be of virtually no utility and would hardly figure elsewhere in the grammar.[2] Such a grammar would thus perversely gain in arbitrariness what it lost in simplicity.

The second reason why condition (I), and in consequence condition (III), would constitute an unreasonable demand to make on a grammar will be explained later in connection with a difficulty with condition (II).

6. Condition (II) is that the grammar should provide more than one syntactic structural description for a sentence only if the sentence is ambiguous. There are two cases to be considered for there are two different ways in which a grammar could fulfil this condition.

First, it could do so trivially simply by not providing more than one syntactic structural description for any sentence of the language. Secondly, the grammar could fulfil the condition in a nontrivial way, thus it would provide more than one syntactic structural description for some sentences of the language, each of which would in fact be ambiguous.

I shall consider the second case first, that in which a grammar fulfils the condition in a nontrivial way. It will not be difficult to see that the grammar will then inevitably be open to precisely the same objection already lodged against a grammar fulfilling condition (I): it will at best be arbitrary and complex owing to its unavoidable reliance on wholly *ad hoc* means.

---

[2] See my "About Ungrammaticalness", *Mind* (April 1964).

7. What is wanted here to begin with are examples of ambiguities and these are plentiful.

If I say 'I saw the shooting of the hunters' am I saying that I saw the hunters shooting or that I saw the hunters being shot? (Other alternatives we can presently ignore.) Again, 'He was shot by his sister': did his sister shoot him or was he shot alongside his sister? Still again, 'The man tore up the street': was the street torn up by the man or was it up the street that he tore? And one may think of such expressions as 'a large oyster bed', 'a small boys school', 'a rusty red knife', and so on.

8. It is and I shall later show that it is reasonable to expect that in an adequate grammar of English a sentence like 'I saw the shooting of the hunters' will be assigned (at least) two distinct syntactic structural descriptions. Assuming that the grammar fulfils condition (II) in a nontrivial way, we may assume that it provides (at least) two distinct syntactic structural descriptions for the sentence 'I saw the shooting of the hunters' and, in consequence, it may be inferred that that sentence is ambiguous. Since that sentence is ambiguous, all seems well, at least at first glance. But there are other cases to consider.

'I saw the shooting of the apes': is this sentence ambiguous? Did I see the apes being shot or the apes shooting? After all, apes might learn to handle firearms. So, yes, it is ambiguous. Intuitively speaking, it seems clear that the sentences 'I saw the shooting of the hunters' and 'I saw the shooting of the apes' have the same, or if not exactly the same then virtually the same, syntactic structure. Consequently if in the grammar one is, then both must be, assigned double syntactic structural descriptions. Since both sentences are ambiguous, this doesn't seem to pose any problem with respect to the fulfilment of condition (II). But now what shall we say about the sentence 'I saw the shooting of the elephants'?

9. If we stare at the following pairs of sentences we can see a difficulty staring out at us:

I saw the shooting of the children.
I saw the shooting of the elephants.

He was shot by the ape.
He was shot by the elephant.

The man tore up the street.
The man tore up the ticket.

I found a large oyster bed.
I found a succulent oyster bed.

They are visiting railroad men.
They are visiting railroad stations.

The first member of a pair is ambiguous, the second is not. Yet, intuitively speaking, each pair exemplifies the same or virtually the same syntactic structure.

If a grammar is to fulfil condition (II) in a nontrivial way it must provide more than one syntactic structural description for some sentences of the language but only those that are ambiguous. But this means that the grammar must assign different syntactic structures to some such pairs of sentences as those here listed. For it doesn't matter what example one takes: a mere morphological change can always suffice to eliminate the ambiguity supposedly being exemplified and supposedly attributable to the syntactic structure of the sentence.

10. Could a grammar fulfil condition (II) in a nontrivial way? Perhaps conceivably it could, but if it could, it could do so only by employing wholly *ad hoc* categories.

To consider but a single case, since the environment "I saw the shooting of the . . . " yields an ambiguous sentence when the blank is filled by 'hunters', 'men', 'children', 'apes', 'monkeys', etc. but not when the blank is filled by 'elephants', 'sows', 'eggs', 'meat', etc., one could arbitrarily invoke two special categories in terms of which one could hope to preclude the assignment of double syntactic structural descriptions in one case and not the other. But even this heroic measure would not suffice: there are further problems to cope with.

A word like 'hunters' would presumably have to be assigned to both categories in as much as the word can be used to refer either to persons or to horses and horses can't shoot. In any case it would be necessary to distinguish between the ambiguous 'I saw the shooting of the iron shod hunters' and the unambiguous 'I saw the shooting of the split hooved hunters', between the ambiguous 'I saw the shooting of the shouting hunters' and the unambiguous 'I saw the shooting of the whinnying hunters', and so on.

I believe we may safely conclude without further discussion that a grammar that fulfilled condition (II) in a nontrivial way would inevitably be sufficiently arbitrary and complex to warrant being disqualified as an adequate grammar of the language.

11. Suppose then a grammar fulfilled condition (II) trivially simply by not providing more than one syntactic structural description for any sentence of the language: could such a grammar qualify as an adequate grammar of the (English) language? The answer to this question can be found in connection with the second reason why conditions (I) and (III) must be rejected as constituting unreasonable demands on a grammar.

There are many ways of thinking about and viewing a grammar of a language, but it can hardly be denied that a grammar is directly and immediately primarily concerned with word arrangements, with sequences of words, with relations between words and words. A grammar is not, or not directly and immediately, primarily concerned with relations between words and nonlinguistic things.

The sentence 'I saw a shark' is ambiguous. But the ambiguity does not arise from and is not either directly or indirectly owing to the particular arrangement of the words in the sentence. Thus it would be unreasonable to suppose that the arrangement contributes to the ambiguity. This can be seen in the fact that, with a little but not over much stretching of the imagination, innumerable syntactically diverse sentences in which the word 'shark' is used can be or anyway can seem somewhat ambiguous.

So I believe we can say this: since the ambiguity of sentences like 'I saw a shark' is not of a type that falls within the province of grammar, it would be unreasonable to expect an adequate grammar of the language to deal with such cases. And the question then is: when is the ambiguity of a sentence of a type that does fall within the province of grammar?

12. There's an answer to this question that can be stated in general terms or there's no answer at all.

We are here concerned to evaluate, and if possible to formulate, a condition on the adequacy of a grammar, a condition that can be appealed to in the evaluation of a grammar. This means that it is necessary to answer the question in general terms eschewing all references to the particular categories of a particular grammar. This can be done.

13. Since ambiguity is not an uncommon feature of discourse it is not surprising that means are available in discourse for the resolution of ambiguities. Typically one queries the ambiguous sentence by posing alternatives. Thus one might query 'I saw a shark' with 'Do you mean a man or a fish?' But one can think of these alternatives as suggesting alternative rephrasals of the original sentence, and so one might ask "Do you mean 'I saw a man' or 'I saw a fish'?" Just so, one might query the ambiguous (written) sentence 'I found a large oyster bed' with "Does it mean 'I found a large bed of oysters' or 'I found a bed of large oysters'?"

But now consider the difference between the rephrasals of these two ambiguous sentences:

(1a) I saw a man.
(1b) I saw a fish.
(2a) I found a large bed of oysters.
(2b) I found a bed of large oysters.

The difference between (1a) and (1b) turns on and reduces to that between the words 'man' and 'fish'. It has nothing to do with the arrangement of words. But the difference between (2a) and (2b) is clearly a matter of the arrangement of words.

To take a more complex case, consider (3a) and (3b)

(3a) I saw the children shooting.
(3b) I saw the children being shot.

offered as rephrasals of 'I saw the shooting of the children'. Is the difference here a matter of the arrangement of words? The difference between (3a) and (3b) reduces to that between 'shooting' and 'being shot', thus it bears a superficial resemblance to that found between (1a) and (1b), the difference between 'man' and 'fish'. There are, however, semantic considerations that indicate that the resemblance is merely superficial, that the former difference is in fact indirectly a matter of the arrangement of words.

Sentences (3a) and (3b) may not be equivalent in truth value. Consequently the difference between them must be indicative of this possibility. Now consider (4) and (5):

> (4)   The children are shooting policemen.
> (5)   The children are being shot by policemen.

(4) and (5) clearly need not be equivalent in truth value just as (3a) and (3b), need not. The difference between them reduces to that between 'shooting' and 'being shot by'. But now consider (6).

> (6)   Policemen are shooting the children.

Unlike (4) and (5), (6) and (5) are equivalent in truth value. Nonetheless the apparent difference between (6) and (5) is the same as that between (4) and (5), namely that between 'shooting' and 'being shot by'. To account for the equivalence of truth values in one case, the possible lack of it in the other, we should be forced to conclude, and rightly, that the difference between 'shooting' and 'being shot' is in fact indirectly a matter of the arrangement of words, for (6) and (4) differ only in that.

14. I am inclined to suppose that the ambiguity of a sentence can sensibly be said to be of a type that falls within the province of grammar if and only if an arrangement of words contributes either directly or indirectly to the presence of the ambiguity. I am also inclined to suppose that a reasonable condition on the adequacy of a grammar would then be this: if the ambiguity of a sentence is of a type that falls within the province of grammar then the grammar should provide more than one syntactic structural description for that sentence.

A grammar that fulfilled this condition would then provide more than one syntactic structural description for a sentence like 'I saw the shooting of the hunters'. And no doubt in consequence it would also provide more than one syntactic structural description for the sentence 'I saw the shooting of the elephants' or even for 'I saw the shooting of the eggs'. But only a misconception of the nature of ambiguity could lead one to suppose that this would be an undesirable consequence.

15. A remark like 'I see a shark' is likely to be ambiguous only in a most unlikely sort of context. But because it can be we are or may be inclined to say that the sentence, which one employs to make the remark, is ambiguous. I think that what is important here is this: we say that a sentence-type is ambiguous if and only if there is or could be a semantically nondeviant token of the type that is ambiguous.[3] And this means that it may be desirable on occasion to distinguish between two quite different bases for the attribution of ambiguity. For one may attribute ambiguity to a sentence-type on the basis of the ambiguity of a semantically nondeviant token of the type. Or one may attribute ambiguity to a sentence-token on the basis of its being a token of an ambiguous sentence-type.

Thus if while pointing to a grim grey fish off the bow I say 'I see a shark',

---

[3] See my *Semantic Analysis* (Ithaca, N.Y.: Cornell University Press, 1960) for an explication of the concept of a semantically deviant utterance.

my remark is not likely to be ambiguous. The sentence-token I uttered was not ambiguous. However in so far as that token was a token of a type of which there is or could be a semantically nondeviant ambiguous token, there is a sense in which I could rightly be said to have said something ambiguous. Unless we take care here we may find ourselves saying that the sentence-token both is and is not ambiguous, which, though it may be true in a sense, is not necessarily the plainest way of putting things.

I shall say that a sentence-token is ambiguous if and only if in employing the token one is making an ambiguous remark, or comment, statement, observation, etc. I shall say that a sentence-type is ambiguous if and only if there is or could be a semantically nondeviant ambiguous token of the type. I shall say of any token of an ambiguous sentence-type (and of certain other tokens as well) that the token has a potential for ambiguity. Whether or not the potential is realized will of course depend on further factors. For example, even though 'I see a shark' conceivably is an ambiguous sentence-type, the token employed in the context previously indicated would hardly be ambiguous: owing to the character of the context, its potential for ambiguity could not be realized.

16. If we are to understand the linguistic source of ambiguity, we must attend to the source of a sentence's potential for ambiguity. Both 'I saw the shark' and 'I saw the shooting of the children' are ambiguous sentence-types. Consequently tokens of the types have a potential for ambiguity. But when we consider the two sentence-types we see at once that the source of the potential is different: in the first case, the source is morphological, in the second, syntactic. I shall accordingly speak of a morphological potential and of a syntactic potential for ambiguity.

For the realization of a morphological potential for ambiguity an appropriate context is required. But for the realization of a syntactic potential, both an appropriate morphemic constitution and an appropriate context are required. A token of the type 'I saw the shooting of the children' is ambiguous only if the token occurs in an appropriate context. It can be ambiguous because given its morphemic constitution its syntactic potential for ambiguity can be realized. On the other hand, a semantically nondeviant token of the type 'I saw the shooting of the elephants' cannot be ambiguous. But the reason is simply that such a token's potential for ambiguity cannot be realized owing to the nature of its morphemic constitution. From the fact that a sentence-type is not ambiguous, it does not follow that either the type or its tokens cannot sensibly be said to have a syntactic potential for ambiguity.

17. To attribute a syntactic potential for ambiguity to a sentence-type and to tokens of a sentence-type of which no semantically nondeviant token is ambiguous is to employ a form of projection, to operate in a systematic way. But that is only to be expected if one is concerned with grammar.

There is nothing particularly perplexing about the form of projection required here. The sentence-type 'I saw the shooting of the children' is ambiguous. Upon analysis we find that tokens of the type have a syntactic potential for ambiguity. We conclude that tokens of any sentence-type having the same syntactic structure as this sentence also have a syntactic potential for ambiguity. That many such sentence-types are not in fact ambiguous can then be explained in terms of their morphemic constitutions which serve to preclude the occurrence of an ambiguity.

Conversely, one can then explain certain matters that would otherwise go unexplained. For example, one need not be baffled by one's understanding of the following sequence of sentences found in a fairy tale: 'Did you see the shooting of the elephants? Yes, the elephants were using elephant guns'. The explanation is obvious: owing to the fact that the relevant sentence-token occurring in the fairy tale is semantically deviant, the restrictions imposed by the morphemic constitution of the sentence-type are overcome allowing the realization of the sentence's syntactic potential for ambiguity.

18. Could an adequate grammar discriminate between ambiguous and unambiguous sentences? Of course not.

If a grammar is to be an adequate grammar of the language then it should provide more than one structural description for all ambiguous sentences (types of course) whose ambiguity is of a type that falls within the province of grammar. Furthermore, the grammar cannot be largely arbitrary and arbitrarily complex. But any grammar meeting these requirements will inevitably fail to discriminate between ambiguous and unambiguous sentences.

That 'I saw the shooting of the apes' is, while 'I saw the shooting of the elephants' is not, ambiguous is not a grammatical fact. No sensible grammar could discriminate between such sentences. All that one can sensibly ask of a grammar is that it provide a means of discriminating between those sentences that do and those that don't have a syntactic potential for ambiguity.

That elephant guns are used on but not by elephants is an unfortunate fact, but the pain it causes a grammarian need be no greater than that of any other humanitarian.

SPEECH ACTS 7

INTRODUCTION

The publication of Strawson's "On Referring" in 1950 (selection 2.2 of this volume) may be conveniently taken as marking the beginning of the contemporary philosophical study of speech acts. In "On Referring", Strawson draws distinctions among a sentence, the *use* of a sentence, and the *utterance* of a sentence or, more generally, among an expression, the use of an expression, and the utterance of an expression. What these distinctions sharply focus attention on is the fact that speaking is something people *do*. Uttering a sentence is a bit of conduct, a public performance or action. *What* we are doing in uttering a sentence or in speaking, can, however, be made sense of in a number of very different ways. These accounts are not always best conducted in terms of grammatical or semantic characterizations of the sentences or expressions uttered, but often in terms of features of the utterance act itself. Here is one strong motive, then, for studying speech acts. Indeed, in one sense, the study of speech acts has been argued to be fundamental to *any* understanding of language. As Searle, for example, has stressed, the *basic* unit of linguistic communication is not an expression, word, or sentence considered abstractly as a syntactic or semantic entity, but the concrete production or issuance of an utterance in the performance of a public speech act. All linguistic communication necessarily involves such speech acts. Thus, it has been concluded, we have no choice, if we wish to understand language, but to undertake the serious study of the particular sort of *doing* which is *speaking*.

Not only is speaking something people do, however, but there are, in addition, a variety of other things—not, on the face of it, *linguistic*—which nonetheless may be done by people *in* or *by* speaking. This sort of consideration highlights a second motive for the study of speech acts, a motive that has been historically important in the development of contemporary philosophical theories. Many of the things we say fail to fit a particular philosophical model of making sense. The model in question is one suggested by some of the work of the logical positivists. Roughly, the idea behind this model is that we can only understand something insofar as we can understand what would count for or against its truth. Thus, to be meaningful something should be verifiable or falsifiable, confirmable or disconfirmable. (This position was explored in detail by Hempel in selection 5.3).

Unfortunately for this view of meaningfulness, even a casual study of the things we say reveals that many of them are not confirmable or disconfirmable, not because of practical or theoretical barriers to confirmation or disconfirmation, but because many of the things we say are not in the true-false line of work at all. Examples are, 'I promise to come to your house tonight', 'I do' as part of a marriage ceremony, and 'I name this baby 'Fred'.' In the first case, it is certainly possible to find out whether or not I *did* promise and, hence, to confirm or disconfirm the proposition that I *did* promise. But that is not to confirm or disconfirm what I say when I say 'I promise', for, in fact, I don't say anything true or false at all. What I do is, simply, promise. One indication of this is that the responses one might make to something that might be true or false do not fit here. Another is what happens in the case of insincerity. As for the first kind of evidence, consider some of the things which could be said in response to something that is clearly either true or false, for example, 'It is now raining'. We might say, 'What makes you think so?', 'How do you know?', 'I bet it isn't', 'Yes, you're quite right', and so on. But the same remarks seem inappropriate in promising. It sounds odd to say 'How do you know that you promise?', although there may be some strange cases where that could be an appropriate remark. Similarly, we do not normally say, 'I bet you don't promise', 'What makes you think you promise?', or 'Yes, you're quite right. You do promise. How did you know?'.

As for the second sort of evidence, when someone promises insincerely, he does something very close to lying, but something that differs from it in an important respect. If I say 'It's raining', and I am lying, then, generally speaking, it is not raining, or, at any rate, I do not believe that it is. But if I insincerely say 'I promise to come', then I have promised, and if I know what promising is, then I know that I have promised. And my promise is not in any clear sense *false* when what is promised fails to be the case, i.e., when I do not come. I have simply failed to *keep* my promise.

The examples given—promising, marrying, and christening—are examples of what AUSTIN originally regarded as *performatives*. Austin originally hoped that "performative" would turn out to mark a well-defined, grammatically specifiable class of things we can do by talking—as opposed to saying or stating something (*constative* functions of language)—but this early view was abandoned in favor of the more complex typology of locutionary, illocutionary, and perlocutionary acts found in the present selection. As originally studied, however, performative utterances have features which give rise to certain unique problems.

The first of these features is that, on the surface at least, most performatives look very much like statements. A performative utterance is typically the production of a sentence framed in the simple declarative present tense. As Austin pointed out, they "contain none of those verbal danger-signals which philosophers have by now detected or think they have detected (curious words like 'good' or 'all', suspect auxiliaries like 'ought' and 'can', and dubious constructions like the hypothetical)."[1] One natural thing to attempt, in light of this fact, is to distinguish performatives from one another, and from those things we say which *can* be true or false, not in terms of intrinsic—grammatical or syntactic—features, but in terms of the usual and conventional *effects* of performing them—what Austin calls 'illocutionary' forces. The attempt to set out this sort of schema for distinguishing and classifying *kinds* of speech acts forms the principal subject matter of the present selection from Austin. Whether such an attempt can succeed is discussed at length by Cohen.

The second problematic feature of performatives derives from the observation that in just these cases to utter a sentence is to do something *non*linguistic. On the face of it, this is a somewhat paradoxical claim. As Austin says "Are we then to say things like this: 'To marry is to say a few words', or 'Betting is simply saying something'? Such a doctrine sounds odd or even flippant at first, but with sufficient safeguards it may become not odd at all." Two facts alleviate the oddity. The first is that, in many cases, saying something is not the *only* way of performing the action in question. For example, I may, under appropriate conditions, bet by raising my hand or promise by nodding my head and winking. Second, not *every* case of saying the words is a case of performing the action in question. The words have no magical powers in themselves. They are merely ways of bringing something about in situations where, perhaps, much else has been and is being done as well.

These observations give rise to two further questions which are discussed in the selections that follow. The first is the question of the presuppositions of speech acts. What are the conditions that make it *possible* for a linguistic doing to be a nonlinguistic doing as well? This question is discussed in detail by Strawson and is addressed also in the selection from Searle. The second question is whether it is possible to specify necessary and sufficient conditions for the performance of a speech act of a given kind; for example, whether necessary and sufficient conditions can be specified for one's utterance of 'I promise' to constitute a case of promising, for the issuance utterance *itself* is neither necessary nor sufficient for promising to have occurred. This approach to the problem of speech acts is treated in detail both by Searle, from the standpoint of traditional philosophy of language, and by Travis, from the standpoint of contemporary transformational linguistics.

---

[1] J. L. Austin, *How to Do Things With Words* (London: Oxford University Press, 1962), pp. 4–5.

Suggestions for Further Reading

Austin, J. L. *How to Do Things With Words*. Cambridge, Mass.: Harvard University Press, and London: Clarendon Press, 1962.

———. "How to Talk—Some Simple Ways." *Philosophical Papers*. London: Oxford University Press, 1961, Chapter 8, pp. 181–200.

———. "Performative Utterances." *Philosophical Papers*. Chapter 10, pp. 220–40.

———. "Performatif–Constatif." In *Ordinary Language*. C. Caton, ed., Urbana: University of Illinois Press, 1963, Chapter 2, pp. 22–54.

Fingarette, Herbert. "Performatives." *American Philosophical Quarterly*, IV (1967), 39–48.

Geach, Peter. "Assertion." Selection 3.3 above, pp. 250–61.

———. "Ascriptivism." *Philosophical Review*, LXIX (1960), 221–25.

Hare, R. M. *The Language of Morals*. Chapter 2. London: Oxford University Press, 1952.

Searle, John. *Speech Acts*. Cambridge: Cambridge University Press, 1969.

———. "Meaning and Speech Acts." *Philosophical Review*, LXXI (1962), 423–32.

———. "Austin on Locutionary and Illocutionary Acts." Selection 3.4 above, pp. 262–75.

J. L. AUSTIN

7.1   *How to Do Things With Words*

I

In embarking on a programme of finding a list of explicit performative verbs, it seemed that we were going to find it not always easy to distinguish performative utterances from constative, and it therefore seemed expedient to go farther back for a while to fundamentals—to consider from the ground up how many senses there are in which to say something *is* to do something, or *in* saying something we do something, and even *by* saying something we do something. And we began by distinguishing a whole group of senses of "doing something" which are all included together when we say, what is obvious, that to say something is in the full normal sense to do something—which

Reprinted by permission of the publishers from J. L. Austin, *How to Do Things With Words*, Lectures 8, 9, and 11 (Cambridge, Mass.: Harvard University Press), and with the kind permission of the Clarendon Press, Oxford, England. Copyright 1962, by the President and Fellows of Harvard College.

includes the utterance of certain noises, the utterance of certain words in a certain construction, and the utterance of them with a certain "meaning" in the favourite philosophical sense of that word, i.e. with a certain sense and with a certain reference.

The act of "saying something" in this full normal sense I call, i.e. dub, the performance of a locutionary act, and the study of utterances thus far and in these respects the study of utterances thus far and in these respects the study of locutions, or of the full units of speech. Our interest in the locutionary act is, of course, principally to make quite plain what it is, in order to distinguish it from other acts with which we are going to be primarily concerned. Let me add merely that, of course, a great many further refinements would be possible and necessary if we were to discuss it for its own sake—refinements of very great importance not merely to philosophers but to, say, grammarians and phoneticians.

We have made three rough distinctions between the phonetic act, the phatic act, and the rhetic act. The phonetic act is merely the act of uttering certain noises. The phatic act is the uttering of certain vocables or words, i.e. noises of certain types, belonging to and as belonging to, a certain vocabulary, conforming to and as conforming to a certain grammar. The rhetic act is the performance of an act of using those vocables with a certain more-or-less definite sense and reference. Thus "He said 'The cat is on the mat'," reports a phatic act, whereas "He said that the cat was on the mat" reports a rhetic act. A similar contrast is illustrated by the pairs:

"He said 'I shall be there'," "He said he would be there";
"He said 'Get out'," "He told me to get out";
"He said 'Is it in Oxford or Cambridge?' "; "He asked whether it was in Oxford or Cambridge."

To pursue this for its own sake beyond our immediate requirements, I shall mention some general points worth remembering:

(1) Obviously, to perform a phatic I must perform a phonetic act, or, if you like, in performing one I am performing the other (not, however, that phatic acts are a sub-class of phonetic acts—as belonging to): but the converse is not true, for if a monkey makes a noise indistinguishable from "go" it is still not a phatic act.

(2) Obviously in the definition of the phatic act two things were lumped together: vocabulary and grammar. So we have not assigned a special name to the person who utters, for example, "cat thoroughly the if" or "the slithy toves did gyre." Yet a further point arising is the intonation as well as grammar and vocabulary.

(3) The phatic act, however, like the phonetic, is essentially mimicable, reproducible (including intonation, winks, gestures, &c.). One can mimic not merely the statement in quotation marks "She has lovely hair," but also the more complex fact that he said it like this: "She has lovely *hair*" (shrugs).

This is the "inverted commas" use of "said" as we get it in novels: every utterance can be just reproduced in inverted commas, or in inverted commas with "said he" or, more often, "said she," &c., after it.

But the rhetic act is the one we report, in the case of assertions, by saying "He said that the cat was on the mat," "He said he would go," "He said I was to go" (his words were "You are to go"). This is the so-called "indirect speech." If the sense or reference is *not* being taken as clear, then the whole or part is to be in quotation marks. Thus I might say: "He said I was to go to the 'minister', but he did not say which minister" or "I said that he was behaving badly and he replied that 'the higher you get the fewer'." We cannot, however, always use "said that" easily: we would say "told to," "advise to," &c., if he used the imperative mood, or such equivalent phrases as "said I was to," "said I should," &c. Compare such phrases as "bade me welcome" and "extended his apologies."

I add one further point about the rhetic act: of course sense and reference (naming and referring) themselves are here ancillary acts performed in performing the rhetic act. Thus we may say "I meant by 'bank' ... " and we say "by 'he' I was referring to ...." Can we perform a rhetic act without referring or without naming? In general it would seem that the answer is that we cannot, but there are puzzling cases. What is the reference in "all triangles have three sides"? Correspondingly, it is clear that we can perform a phatic act which is not a rhetic act, though not conversely. Thus we may repeat someone else's remark or mumble over some sentence, or we may read a Latin sentence without knowing the meaning of the words.

The question when one pheme or one rheme is the *same* as another, whether in the "type" or "token" sense, and the question what is one single pheme or rheme, do not so much matter here. But, of course, it is important to remember that the same pheme (token of the same type) may be used on different occasions of utterance with a different sense or reference, and so be a different rheme. When different phemes are used with the same sense and reference, we might speak of rhetically equivalent acts ("the same statement" in one sense) but not of the same rheme or rhetic acts (which are the same statement in another sense which involves using the same words).

The pheme is a unit of *language*: its typical fault is to be nonsense—meaningless. But the rheme is a unit of *speech*; its typical fault is to be vague or void or obscure, &c.

But though these matters are of much interest, they do not so far throw any light at all on our problem of the constative as opposed to the performative utterance. For example, it might be perfectly possible, with regard to an utterance, say "It is going to charge," to make entirely plain "what we were saying" in issuing the utterance, in all the senses so far distinguished, and yet not at all to have cleared up whether or not in issuing the utterance I was performing the act of *warning* or not. It may be perfectly clear what I mean by "It is going to charge" or "Shut the door," but not clear whether it is meant as a statement or warning, &c.

To perform a locutionary act is in general, we may say, also and *eo ipso* to perform an *illocutionary* act, as I propose to call it. To determine what illocutionary act is so performed we must determine in what way we are using the locution:

asking or answering a question,
giving some information or an assurance or a warning,
announcing a verdict or an intention,
pronouncing sentence,
making an appointment or an appeal or a criticism,
making an identification or giving a description,

and the numerous like. (I am not suggesting that this is a clearly defined class by any means.) There is nothing mysterious about our *eo ipso* here. The trouble rather is the number of different senses of so vague an expression as "in what way are we using it"—this may refer even to a locutionary act, and further to perlocutionary acts to which we shall come in a minute. When we perform a locutionary act, we use speech: but in what way precisely are we using it on this occasion? For there are very numerous functions of or ways in which we use speech, and it makes a great difference to our act in some sense—sense (B)[1]—in which way and which *sense* we were on this occasion "using" it. It makes a great difference whether we were advising, or merely suggesting, or actually ordering, whether we were strictly promising or only announcing a vague intention, and so forth. These issues penetrate a little but not without confusion into grammar (see above), but we constantly do debate them, in such terms as whether certain words (a certain locution) *had the force of* a question, or *ought to have been taken as* an estimate and so on.

I explained the performance of an act in this new and second sense as the performance of an "illocutionary" act, i.e. performance of an act *in* saying something as opposed to performance of an act *of* saying something; and I shall refer to the doctrine of the different types of function of language here in question as the doctrine of "illocutionary forces."

It may be said that for too long philosophers have neglected this study, treating all problems as problems of "locutionary usage," and indeed that [what I elsewhere call] the "descriptive fallacy" . . . commonly arises through mistaking a problem of the former kind for a problem of the latter kind. True, we are now getting out of this; for some years we have been realizing more and more clearly that the occasion of an utterance matters seriously, and that the words used are to some extent to be "explained" by the "context" in which they are designed to be or have actually been spoken in a linguistic interchange. Yet still perhaps we are too prone to give these explanations in terms of "the meanings of words." Admittedly we can use "meaning" also with reference to illocutionary force—"He meant it as an order," &c. But I want to distinguish *force* and meaning in the sense in which meaning is equivalent to sense and reference, just as it has become essential to distinguish sense and reference within meaning.

---

[1] See [next page].

Moreover, we have here an illustration of the different uses of the expression, "uses of language," or "use of a sentence," &c.—"use" is a hopelessly ambiguous or wide word, just as is the word "meaning," which it has become customary to deride. But "use," its supplanter, is not in much better case. We may entirely clear up the "use of a sentence" on a particular occasion, in the sense of the locutionary act, without yet touching upon its use in the sense of an *illocutionary* act.

Before refining any further on this notion of the illocutionary act, let us contrast both the locutionary *and* the illocutionary act with yet a third kind of act.

There is yet a further sense (C) in which to perform a locutionary act, and therein an illocutionary act, may also be to perform an act of another kind. Saying something will often, or even normally, produce certain consequential effects upon the feelings, thoughts, or actions of the audience, or of the speaker, or of other persons: and it may be done with the design, intention, or purpose of producing them; and we may then say, thinking of this, that the speaker has performed an act in the nomenclature of which reference is made either (C. *a*), only obliquely, or even (C. *b*), not at all, to the performance of the locutionary or illocutionary act. We shall call the performance of an act of this kind the performance of a *perlocutionary* act or *perlocution*. Let us not yet define this idea any more carefully—of course it needs it—but simply give examples:

(E. 1)
    Act (A)   or Locution
      He said to me "Shoot her!" meaning by "shoot" shoot and referring by "her" to *her*.

    Act (B)   or Illocution
      He urged (or advised, ordered, &c.) me to shoot her.

    Act (C. *a*)   or Perlocution
      He persuaded me to shoot her.

    Act (C. *b*)
      He got me to (or made me, &c.) shoot her.

(E. 2)
    Act (A)   or Locution
      He said to me, "You can't do that."

    Act (B)   or Illocution
      He protested against my doing it.

    Act (C. *a*)   or Perlocution
      He pulled me up, checked me.

    Act (C. *b*)
      He stopped me, he brought me to my senses, &c.
      He annoyed me.

We can similarly distinguish the locutionary act "he said that . . . " from the illocutionary act "he argued that . . . " and the perlocutionary act "he convinced me that . . . ."

It will be seen that the consequential effects of perlocutions are really consequences, which do not include such conventional effects as, for example, the speaker's being committed by his promise (which comes into the illocutionary act). Perhaps distinctions need drawing, as there is clearly a difference between what we feel to be the real production of real effects and what we regard as mere conventional consequences; we shall in any case return later to this.

We have here then roughly distinguished three kinds of acts—the locutionary, the illocutionary, and the perlocutionary.[2] Let us make some general comments on these three classes, leaving them still fairly rough. The first three points will be about "the use of language" again.

(1) Our interest in these lectures is essentially to fasten on the second, illocutionary act and contrast it with the other two. There is a constant tendency in philosophy to elide this in favour of one or other of the other two. Yet it is distinct from both. We have already seen how the expressions "meaning" and "use of sentence" can blur the distinction between locutionary and illocutionary acts. We now notice that to speak of the "use" of language can likewise blur the distinction between the illocutionary and perlocutionary act—so we will distinguish them more carefully in a minute. Speaking of the "use of 'language' for arguing or warning" looks just like speaking of "the use of 'language' for persuading, rousing, alarming"; yet the former may, for rough contrast, be said to be *conventional*, in the sense that at least it could be made explicit by the performative formula; but the latter could not. Thus we can say "I argue that" or "I warn you that" but we cannot say "I convince you that" or "I alarm you that." Further, we may entirely clear up whether someone was arguing or not without touching on the question whether he was convincing anyone or not.

(2) To take this farther, let us be quite clear that the expression "use of language" can cover other matters even more diverse than the illocutionary and perlocutionary acts. For example, we may speak of the "use of language" *for* something, e.g. for joking; and we may use "in" in a way different from the illocutionary "in," as when we say "in saying 'p' I was joking" or "acting a part" or "writing poetry"; or again we may speak of "a poetical use of language" as distinct from "the use of language in poetry." These references to "use of language" have nothing to do with the illocutionary act. For example, if I say "Go and catch a falling star," it may be quite clear what both the meaning and the force of my utterance is, but still wholly unresolved which of these other kinds of things I may be doing. There are parasitic uses of language, which are "not serious," not the "full normal use." The normal conditions of reference may be suspended, or no attempt made at a standard perlocutionary act, no attempt to make you do anything, as Walt Whitman does not seriously incite the eagle of liberty to soar.

(3) Furthermore, there may be some things we "do" in some connexion with saying something which do not seem to fall, intuitively at least, exactly

---

[2] [Here occurs in the manuscript a note made in 1958 which says: "(1) All this is not clear (2) and in all senses relevant ((A) and (B) as distinct from (C)) won't all utterances be performative?"]

into any of these roughly defined classes, or else seem to fall vaguely into more than one; but any way we do not at the outset feel so clear that they are as remote from our three acts as would be joking or writing poetry. For example, *insinuating*, as when we insinuate something in or by issuing some utterance, seems to involve some convention, as in the illocutionary act; but we cannot *say* "I insinuate . . . ," and it seems like implying to be a clever effect rather than a mere act. A further example is evincing emotion. We may evince emotion in or by issuing an utterance, as when we swear; but once again we have no use here for performative formulas and the other devices of illocutionary acts. We might say that we use swearing[3] *for* relieving our feelings. We must notice that the illocutionary act is a conventional act: an act done as conforming to a convention.

(4) Acts of all our three kinds necessitate, since they are the performing of actions, allowance being made for the ills that all action is heir to. We must systematically be prepared to distinguish between "the act of doing *x*," i.e. achieving *x*, and "the act of attempting to do *x*": for example, we must distinguish between warning and attempting to warn. We must expect infelicities here.

The next three points that arise do so importantly because our acts are *acts*.

(5) Since our acts are acts, we must always remember the distinction between producing effects or consequences which are intended or unintended; and (i) when the speaker intends to produce an effect it may nevertheless not occur, and (ii) when he does not intend to produce it or intends not to produce it it may nevertheless occur. To cope with complication (i) we invoke as before the distinction between attempt and achievement; to cope with complication (ii) we invoke the normal linguistic devices of disclaiming (adverbs like "unintentionally" and "so on") which we hold ready for personal use in all cases of doing actions.

(6) Furthermore, we must, of course, allow that as acts they may be things that we do not exactly *do*, in the sense that we did them, say, under duress or in any other such way. Other ways besides in which we may not fully do the action are given in (2) above.

(7) Finally we must meet the objection about our illocutionary and perlocutionary acts—namely that the notion of an act is unclear—by a general doctrine about action. We have the idea of an "act" as a fixed physical thing that we do, as distinguished from conventions and as distinguished from consequences. But

(*a*) the illocutionary act and even the locutionary act too may involve conventions: consider the example of doing obeisance. It is obeisance only because it is conventional and it is done only because it is conventional. Compare the distinction between kicking a wall and kicking a goal;

(*b*) the perlocutionary act may include what in a way are consequences, as when we say "By doing *x* I was doing *y*": we do bring in a greater or less

---

[3] "Swearing" is ambiguous: "I swear by Our Lady" *is* to swear by Our Lady: but "Bloody" is not to swear by Our Lady.

stretch of "consequences" always, some of which may be "unintentional." There is no restriction to the minimum physical act at all. That we can import an indefinitely long stretch of what might also be called the "consequences" of our act into the act itself is, or should be, a fundamental commonplace of the theory of our language about all "action" in general. Thus if asked "What did he do?," we may reply either "He shot the donkey" or "He fired a gun" or "He pulled the trigger" or "He moved his trigger finger," and all may be correct. So, to shorten the nursery story of the endeavours of the old woman to drive her pig home in time to get her old man's supper, we may in the last resort say that the cat drove or got the pig, or made the pig get, over the stile. If in such cases we *mention* both a B act (illocution) and a C act (perlocution) we shall say "*by* B-ing he C-ed" rather than "*in* B-ing . . . ." This is the reason for calling C a *per*locutionary act as distinct from an illocutionary act.

Next time we shall revert to the distinction between our three kinds of act, and to the expressions "in" and "by doing *x* I am doing *y*," with a view to getting the three classes and their members and non-members somewhat clearer. We shall see that just as the locutionary act embraces doing many things at once to be complete, so may the illocutionary and perlocutionary acts.

II

When it was suggested that we embark on a programme of making a list of explicit performative verbs, we ran into some difficulties over the matter of determining whether some utterance was or was not performative, or anyway, *purely* performative. It seemed expedient, therefore, to go back to fundamentals and consider how many senses there may be in which to say something is to do something, or in saying something we do something, or even *by* saying something we do something.

We first distinguished a group of things we do in saying something, which together we summed up by saying we perform a *locutionary act*, which is roughly equivalent to uttering a certain sentence with a certain sense and reference, which again is roughly equivalent to "meaning" in the traditional sense. Second, we said that we also perform *illocutionary acts* such as informing, ordering, warning, undertaking, &c., i.e. utterances which have a certain (conventional) force. Thirdly, we may also perform *perlocutionary acts*: what we bring about or achieve *by* saying something, such as convincing, persuading, deterring, and even, say, surprising or misleading. Here we have three, if not more, different senses or dimensions of the "use of a sentence" or of "the use of language" (and, of course, there are others also). All these three kinds of "actions" are, simply of course as actions, subject to the usual troubles and reservations about attempt as distinct from achievement, being intentional as distinct from being unintentional, and the like. We then said that we must consider these three kinds of act in greater detail.

We must distinguish the illocutionary from the perlocutionary act: for example we must distinguish "in saying it I was warning him" from "by saying it I convinced him, or surprised him, or got him to stop."

THE NEED TO DISTINGUISH "CONSEQUENCES"

It is the distinction between illocutions and perlocutions which seems likeliest to give trouble, and it is upon this that we shall now embark, taking in the distinction between illocutions and locutions by the way. It is certain that the perlocutionary sense of "doing an action" must somehow be ruled out as irrelevant to the sense in which an utterance, if the issuing of it is the "doing of an action," is a performative, at least if that is to be distinct from a constative. For clearly *any*, or almost any, perlocutionary act is liable to be brought off, in sufficiently special circumstances, by the issuing, with or without calculation, of any utterance whatsoever, and in particular by a straightforward constative utterance (if there is such an animal). You may, for example, deter me (C. *b*)[4] from doing something by informing me, perhaps guilelessly yet opportunely, what the consequences of doing it would in fact be: and this applies even to (C. *a*)[5] for you may convince me (C. *a*) that she is an adulteress by asking her whether it was not her handkerchief which was in *X's* bedroom,[6] or by stating that it was hers.

We have then to draw the line between an action we do (here an illocution) and its consequence. Now in general, and if the action is not one of saying something but a non-conventional "physical" action, this is an intricate matter. As we have seen, we can, or may like to think we can, class, by stages, more and more of what is initially and ordinarily included or possibly might be included under the name given to "our act" itself[7] as *really* only *consequences*, however little remote and however naturally to be anticipated, of our actual action in the supposed minimum physical sense, which will then transpire to be the making of some movement or movements with parts of our body (e.g. crooking our finger, which produced a movement of the trigger, which pro-

---

[4] and [5] See p. 564 for the significance of these references.

[6] That the giving of straightforward information produces, almost always, consequential effects upon action, is no more surprising than the converse, that the doing of any action (including the uttering of a performative) has regularly the consequence of making ourselves and others aware of facts. To do any act in a perceptible or detectable way is to afford ourselves and generally others also the opportunity of coming to know both (*a*) that we did it, and further (*b*) many other facts as to our motives, our character or what not which may be inferred from our having done it. If you hurl a tomato at a political meeting (or bawl "I protest" when someone else does—if that is performing an action) the consequence will probably be to make others aware that you object, and to make them think that you hold certain political beliefs: but this will not make either the throw or the shout true or false (though they may be, even deliberately, misleading). And by the same token, the production of any number of consequential effects will not prevent a constative utterance from *being* true or false.

[7] I do not here go into the question how far consequences may extend. The usual errors on this topic may be found in, for example, Moore's *Principia Ethica*.

duced . . . which produced the death of the donkey). There is, of course, much to be said about this which need not concern us here. But at least in the case of acts of saying something,

(1) *nomenclature* affords us an assistance which it generally withholds in the case of "physical" actions. For with physical actions we nearly always naturally name the action *not* in terms of what we are here calling the minimum physical act, but in terms which embrace a greater or less but indefinitely extensive range of what might be called its natural consequences (or, looking at it another way, the intention with which it was done).

We not merely do not use the notion of a minimum physical act (which is in any case doubtful) but we do not seem to have any class of names which distinguish physical acts from consequences: whereas with acts of saying something, the vocabulary of names for acts (B) seems expressly designed to mark a break at a certain regular point between the act (our saying something) and its consequences (which are usually not the *saying* of anything), or at any rate a great many of them.[8]

(2) Furthermore, we seem to derive some assistance from the special nature of acts of saying something by contrast with ordinary physical actions: for with these latter even the minimum physical action, which we are seeking to detach from its consequences, is, being a bodily movement, *in pari materia*[9] with at least many of its immediate and natural consequences, whereas, whatever the immediate and natural consequences of an act of saying something may be, they are at least not normally other further acts of saying something, whether more particularly on the speaker's own part or even on the part of others.[10] So that we have here a sort of regular natural break in the chain, which is wanting in the case of physical actions, and which is associated with the special class of names for illocutions.

But, it may be asked at this point, are not the consequences imported with the nomenclature of perlocutions really consequences of the acts (A), the locutions? Ought we not, in seeking to detach "all" consequences, to go right

---

[8] Note that if we suppose the minimum physical act to be movement of the body when we say "I moved my finger," the fact that the object moved *is* part of my body does in fact introduce a new sense of "moved." Thus I may be able to waggle my ears as a schoolboy does, or by grasping them between my finger and thumb, or move my foot either in the ordinary way or by manipulating with my hand when I have pins and needles. The ordinary use of "move" in such examples as "I moved my finger" is ultimate. We must not seek to go back behind it to 'pulling on my muscles' and the like.

[9] This *in pari materia* could be misleading to you. I do not mean, as was pointed out in the previous footnote, that my "moving my finger" is, metaphysically, in the least like "the trigger moving" which is its consequence, or like "my finger's moving the trigger." But "a movement of a trigger finger" is *in pari materia* with "a movement of a trigger."
Or we could put the matter in a most important other way by saying that the sense in which saying something produces effects on other persons, or *causes* things, is a fundamentally different sense of cause from that used in physical causation by pressure, &c. It has to operate through the conventions of language and is a matter of influence exerted by one person on another: this is probably the original sense of "cause."

[10] See below.

back beyond the illocution to the locution—and indeed to the act (A. *a*), the uttering of noises, which is a physical movement?[11] It has, of course, been admitted that to perform an illocutionary act is necessarily to perform a locutionary act: that, for example, to congratulate is necessarily to say certain words; and to say certain words is necessarily, at least in part, to make certain more or less indescribable movements with the vocal organs.[12] So that the divorce between "physical" actions and acts of saying something is not in all ways complete—there is some connexion. But (i) while this may be important in some connexions and contexts, it does not seem to prevent the drawing of *a* line for our present purposes where we want one, that is, between the completion of the illocutionary act and all consequences thereafter. And further (ii), much more important, we must avoid the idea, suggested above though not stated, that the illocutionary act is a *consequence* of the locutionary act, and even the idea that what is imported by the nomenclature of illocutions is an *additional* reference to *some* of the consequences of the locutions,[13] i.e. that to say "he urged me to" is to say that he said certain words and in addition that his saying them had *or* perhaps was intended to have certain consequences (? an effect upon me). We should not, if we were to insist for some reason and in some sense on "going back" from the illocution to the phonetic act (A. *a*), be going back to a minimum physical action via the chain of its consequences, in the way that we supposedly go back from the death of the rabbit to the movement of the trigger finger. The uttering of noises may be a consequence (physical) of the movement of the vocal organs, the breath, &c.: but the uttering of a word is *not* a consequence of the uttering of a noise, whether physical or otherwise. Nor is the uttering of words with a certain meaning a *consequence* of uttering the words, whether physical or otherwise. For that matter, even phatic (A. *b*) and rhetic (A. *c*) acts are not *consequences*, let alone physical consequences, of phonetic acts (A. *a*). What we do import by the use of the nomenclature of illocution is a reference, not to the consequences (at least in any ordinary sense) of the locution, but to the conventions of illocutionary force as bearing on the special circumstances of the occasion of the issuing of the utterance. We shall shortly return to the senses in which the successful or consummated performance of an illocutionary act *does* bring in "consequences" or "effects" in certain senses.[14]

---

[11] Or is it? We have already noted that "production of noises" is itself really a consequence of the minimum physical act of moving one's vocal organs.

[12] Still confining ourselves, for simplicity, to *spoken* utterance.

[13] Though see below.

[14] We may still feel tempted to ascribe some "primacy" to the locution as against the illocution, seeing that, given some individual rhetic act (A. *c*), there may yet be room for doubt as to how it should be described in the nomenclature of illocutions. Why after all should we label one *A* the other *B*? We may agree on the actual words that were uttered, and even also on the senses in which they were being used and on the realities to which they were being used to refer, and yet still disagree as to whether, in the circumstances, they amounted to an order or a threat or merely to advice or a warning. Yet after all, there is ample room, equally, for disagreement in individual cases as to how the rhetic act (A. *c*) should be described in the nomenclature of locutions (What did he really mean? To what person, time, or what not was

I have so far argued, then, that we can have hopes of isolating the illocutionary act from the perlocutionary as producing consequences, and that it is not itself a "consequence" of the locutionary act. Now, however, I must point out that the illocutionary act as distinct from the perlocutionary is connected with the production of effects in certain senses:

(1) Unless a certain effect is achieved, the illocutionary act will not have been happily, successfully performed. This is to be distinguished from saying that the illocutionary act is the achieving of a certain effect. I cannot be said to have warned an audience unless it hears what I say and takes what I say in a certain sense. An effect must be achieved on the audience if the illocutionary act is to be carried out. How should we best put it here? And how can we limit it? Generally the effect amounts to bringing about the understanding of the meaning and of the force of the locution. So the performance of an illocutionary act involves the securing of *uptake*.

(2) The illocutionary act "takes effect" in certain ways, as distinguished from producing consequences in the sense of bringing about states of affairs in the "normal" way, i.e. changes in the natural course of events. Thus "I name this ship the *Queen Elizabeth*" has the effect of naming or christening the ship; then certain subsequent acts such as referring to it as the *Generalissimo Stalin* will be out of order.

(3) We have said that many illocutionary acts invite by convention a response or sequel, which may be "one-way" or "two-way": thus we may distinguish arguing, ordering, promising, suggesting, and asking to, from offering, asking whether you will and asking "Yes or no?" If this response is accorded, or the sequel implemented, that requires a second act by the speaker or another person; and it is a commonplace of the consequence-language that this cannot be included under the initial stretch of action.

Generally we can, however, always say "I got him to" with such a word. This does make the act one ascribed to me and it is, when words are or maybe employed, a perlocutionary act. Thus we must distinguish "I ordered him and he obeyed" from "I *got him* to obey." The general implication of the latter is that other additional means were employed to produce this consequence as ascribable to me, inducements, and even very often personal influence amounting to duress; there is even very often an illocutionary act distinct from merely ordering, as when I say "I got him to do it by stating *x*."

---

he actually referring?): and indeed, we may often agree that his act was definitely one say, of ordering (illocution), while yet uncertain what it was he was meaning to order (locution). It is plausible to suppose that the act is at least as much "bound" to be describable as some more or less *definite* type of illocution as it is to be describable as some more or less definite locutionary act (A). Difficulties about conventions and intentions must arise in deciding upon the correct description whether of a locution or of an illocution: deliberate, or unintentional, ambiguity of meaning or reference is perhaps as common as deliberate or unintentional failure to make plain "how our words are to be taken" (in the illocutionary sense). Moreover, the whole apparatus of "explicit performatives" (see above) serves to obviate disagreements as to the description of illocutionary acts. It is much harder in fact to obviate disagreements as to the description of "locutionary acts." Each, however, is conventional and liable to need to have a "construction" put on it by judges.

So here are three ways in which illocutionary acts are bound up with effects; and these are all distinct from the producing of effects which is characteristic of the perlocutionary act.

We must distinguish actions which have a perlocutionary object (convince, persuade) from those which merely produce a perlocutionary sequel. Thus we may say "I tried to warn him but only succeeded in alarming him." What is the perlocutionary object of one illocution may be a sequel of another: for example, the perlocutionary object of warning, to alert someone, may be a sequel of a perlocutionary act which alarms someone. Again, deterrence may be the sequel of an illocution instead of the object of saying "Do not do it." Some perlocutionary acts always have sequels rather than objects, namely those where there is no illocutionary formula: thus I may surprise you or upset you or humiliate you by a locution, though there is no illocutionary formula "I surprise you by...," "I upset you by...," "I humiliate you by...."

It is characteristic of perlocutionary acts that the response achieved, or the sequel, can be achieved additionally or entirely by non-locutionary means: thus intimidation may be achieved by waving a stick or pointing a gun. Even in the cases of convincing, persuading, getting to obey and getting to believe, we may achieve the response non-verbally. However, this alone is not enough to distinguish illocutionary acts, since we can for example warn or order or appoint or give or protest or apologize by non-verbal means and these are illocutionary acts. Thus we may cock a snook or hurl a tomato by way of protest.

More important is the question whether perlocutionary acts may always achieve their response or sequel by non-conventional means. Certainly we can achieve some sequels of perlocutionary acts by entirely non-conventional means (or as we say "unconventional" means), by acts which are not conventional at all, or not for that purpose; thus I may persuade some one by gently swinging a big stick or gently mentioning that his aged parents are still in the Third Reich. Strictly speaking, there cannot be an illocutionary act unless the means employed are conventional, and so the means for achieving its ends non-verbally must be conventional. But it is difficult to say where conventions begin and end; thus I may warn him by swinging a stick or I may give him something by merely handing it to him. But if I warn him by swinging a stick, then swinging my stick is a warning: he would know very well what I meant: it may seem an unmistakable threatening gesture. Similar difficulties arise over giving tacit consent to some arrangement, or promising tacitly, or voting by a show of hands. But the fact remains that many illocutionary acts cannot be performed except by saying something. This is true of stating, informing (as distinct from showing), arguing, giving estimates, reckoning, and finding (in the legal sense); it is true of the great majority of verdictives and expositives as opposed to many exercitives and commissives.

III

When we originally contrasted the performative with the constative utterance we said that

(1) the performative should be doing something as opposed to just saying something; and

(2) the performative is happy or unhappy as opposed to true or false.

Were these distinctions really sound? Our subsequent discussion of doing and saying certainly seems to point to the conclusion that whenever I "say" anything (except perhaps a mere exclamation like "damn" or "ouch") I shall be performing both locutionary and illocutionary acts, and these two kinds of acts seem to be the very things which we tried to use as a means of distinguishing, under the names of "doing" and "saying," performatives from constatives. If we are in general always doing both things, how can our distinction survive?

Let us first reconsider the contrast from the side of constative utterances: Of these, we were content to refer to "statements" as the typical or paradigm case. Would it be correct to say that when we state something

(1) we are doing something as well as and distinct from just saying something, and

(2) our utterance is liable to be happy or unhappy (as well as, if you will, true or false)?

(1) Surely to state is every bit as much to perform an illocutionary act as, say, to warn or to pronounce. Of course it is not to perform an act in some specially physical way, other than in so far as it involves, when verbal, the making of movements of vocal organs; but then nor, as we have seen, is to warn, to protest, to promise or to name. "Stating" seems to meet all the criteria we had for distinguishing the illocutionary act. Consider such an unexceptionable remark as the following:

> In saying that it was raining, I was not betting or arguing or warning: I was simply stating it as a fact.

Here "stating" is put absolutely on a level with arguing, betting, and warning. Or again:

> In saying that it was leading to unemployment, I was not warning or protesting: I was simply stating the facts.

Or to take a different type of test also used earlier, surely

> I state that he did not do it

is exactly on a level with

> I argue that he did not do it,
> I suggest that he did not do it,
> I bet that he did not do it, &c.

If I simply use the primary or non-explicit form of utterance:

> He did not do it

we may make explicit what we were doing in saying this, or specify the illocutionary force of the utterance, equally by saying any of the above three (or more) things.

Moreover, although the utterance "He did not do it" is often issued as a statement, and is then undoubtedly true or false (*this* is if anything is), it does not seem possible to say that it differs from "I state that he did not do it" in this respect. If someone says "I state that he did not do it," we investigate the truth of his statement in just the same way as if he had said "He did not do it" *simpliciter*, when we took that to be, as we naturally often should, a statement. That is, to say "I state that he did not" is to make the very same statement as to say "He did not": it is not to make a different statement about what "I" state (except in exceptional cases: the historic and habitual present, &c.). As notoriously, when I say even "I think he did it" someone is being rude if he says "That's a statement about you": and this *might* conceivably be about myself, whereas the statement could not. So that there is no necessary conflict between

- (*a*) our issuing the utterance being the doing of something,
- (*b*) our utterance being true or false.

For that matter compare, for example, "I warn you that it is going to charge," where likewise it is both a warning and true or false that it is going to charge; and that comes in in appraising the warning just as much as, though not quite in the same way as, in appraising the statement.

On mere inspection, "I state that" does not appear to differ in any essential way from "I maintain that" (to say which is to maintain that), "I inform you that," "I testify that " &c. Possibly some "essential" differences may yet be established between such verbs: but nothing has been done towards this yet.

(2) Moreover, if we think of the second alleged contrast, according to which performatives are happy or unhappy and statements true or false, again from the side of supposed constative utterances, notably statements, we find that statements *are* liable to every kind of infelicity to which performatives are liable. Let us look back again and consider whether statements are not liable to precisely the same disabilities as, say, warnings by way of what we called "infelicities"—that is various disabilities which make an utterance unhappy without, however, making it true or false.

We have already noted that sense in which saying or stating "The cat is on the mat" implies that I believe that the cat is on the mat. This is parallel to the sense—is the same sense—as that in which "I promise to be there" implies that I intend to be there and that I believe I shall be able to be there. So the statement is liable to the *insincerity* form of infelicity; and even to the *breach* form of infelicity in this sense, that saying or stating that the cat is on the mat commits me to saying or stating "The mat is underneath the cat" just as much as the performative "I define X as Y" (in the *fiat* sense say) commits me to using those terms in special ways in future discourse, and we can see how this is connected with such acts as promising. This means that statements can give rise to infelicities of our two Γ kinds.

Now what about infelicities of the A and B kinds, which rendered the act—warning, undertaking, &c.—null and void?: can a thing that looks like a statement be null and void just as much as a putative contract? The answer seems to be Yes, importantly. The first cases are A. 1 and A. 2, where there is no convention (or not an accepted convention) or where the circumstances are not appropriate for its invocation by the speaker. Many infelicities of just this type do infect statements.

We have already noticed the case of a putative statement *presupposing* (as it is called) the existence of that which it refers to; if no such thing exists, "the statement" is not about anything. Now some say that in these circumstances, if, for example, someone asserts that the present King of France is bald, "the question whether he is bald does not arise"; but it is better to say that the putative statement is null and void, exactly as when I say that I sell you something but it is not mine or (having been burnt) is not any longer in existence. Contracts often are void because the objects they are about do not exist, which involves a breakdown of reference (total ambiguity).

But it is important to notice also that "statements" too are liable to infelicity of this kind in other ways also parallel to contracts, promises, warnings, &c. Just as we often say, for example, "You cannot order me," in the sense "You have not the right to order me," which is equivalent to saying that you are not in the appropriate position to do so: so often there are things you cannot state—have no right to state—are not in a position to state. You *cannot* now state how many people there are in the next room; if you say "There are fifty people in the next room," I can only regard you as guessing or conjecturing (just as sometimes you are not ordering me, which would be inconceivable, but possibly asking me to rather impolitely, so here you are "hazarding a guess" rather oddly). Here there is something you might, in other circumstances, be in a position to state; but what about statements about other persons' feelings or about the future? Is a forecast or even a prediction about, say, persons' behaviour really a statement? It is important to take the speech-situation as a whole.

Just as sometimes we cannot appoint but only confirm an appointment already made, so sometimes we cannot state but only confirm a statement already made.

Putative statements are also liable to infelicities of type B, flaws, and hitches. Somebody "says something he did not really mean"—uses the wrong word—says "the cat is on the mat" when he meant to say "bat." Other similar trivialities arise—or rather not entirely trivialities; because it is possible to discuss such utterances entirely in terms of meaning or sense and reference and so get confused about them, though they are really easy to understand.

Once we realize that what we have to study is *not* the sentence but the issuing of an utterance in a speech situation, there can hardly be any longer a possibility of not seeing that stating is performing an act. Moreover, comparing stating to what we have said about the illocutionary act, it is an act to which, just as much as to other illocutionary acts, it is essential to "secure uptake": the doubt about whether I stated something if it was not heard or understood is just the same as the doubt about whether I warned *sotto voce* or protested if someone did not take it as a protest, &c. And statements do "take effect" just as much as "namings," say: if I have stated something, then that commits

me to other statements: other statements made by me will be in order or out
of order. Also some statements or remarks made by you will be henceforward
contradicting me or not contradicting me, rebutting me or not rebutting me,
and so forth. If perhaps a statement does not invite a response, that is not
essential to all illocutionary acts anyway. And certainly in stating we are or
may be performing perlocutionary acts of all kinds.

The most that might be argued, and with some plausibility, is that there
is no perlocutionary *object* specifically associated with stating, as there is with
informing, arguing, &c.; and this comparative purity may be one reason why
we give "statements" a certain special position. But this certainly would not
justify giving, say, "descriptions," if properly used, a similar priority, and it is
in any case true of many illocutionary acts.

However, looking at the matter from the side of performatives, we may still
feel that they lack something which statements have, even if, as we have
shown, the converse is not so. Performatives are, of course, incidentally saying
something as well as doing something, but we may feel that they are not essentially true or false as statements are. We may feel that there is here a dimension in which we judge, assess, or appraise the constative utterance (granting
as a preliminary that it is felicitous) which does not arise with non-constative
or performative utterances. Let us agree that all these circumstances of situation have to be in order for me to have succeeded in stating something, yet
when I have, *the* question arises, was what I stated true or false? And this we
feel, speaking in popular terms, is now the question of whether the statement
"corresponds with the facts." With this I agree: attempts to say that the use
of the expression "is true" is equivalent to endorsing or the like are no good.
So we have here a new dimension of criticism of the accomplished statement.

But now

(1) doesn't just such a similar objective assessment of the accomplished utterance
arise, at least in many cases, with other utterances which seem typically
performative; and

(2) is not this account of statements a little over-simplified?

First, there is an obvious slide towards truth or falsity in the case of, for
example, verdictives, such as estimating, finding, and pronouncing. Thus
we may:

estimate	rightly or wrongly	for example, that it is half past two,
find	correctly or incorrectly	for example, that he is guilty,
pronounce	correctly or incorrectly	for example, that the batsman is out.

We shall not say "truly" in the case of verdictives, but we shall certainly address
ourselves to the same question; and such adverbs as "rightly," "wrongly,"
"correctly," and "incorrectly" are used with statements too.

Or again there is a parallel between inferring and arguing soundly or
validly and stating truly. It is not just a question of whether he did argue or
infer but also of whether he had a right to, and did he succeed. Warning and
advising may be done correctly or incorrectly, well or badly. Similar considera-

tions arise about praise, blame, and congratulation. Blame is not in order, if, say, you have done the same thing yourself; and the question always arises whether the praise, blame, or congratulation was merited or unmerited: it is not enough to say that you have blamed him and there's an end on't—still one act is, with reason, preferred to another. The question whether praise and blame are merited is quite different from the question whether they are opportune, and the same distinction can be made in the case of advice. It is a different thing to say that advice is good or bad from saying that it is opportune or inopportune, though the timing of advice is more important to its goodness than the timing of blame is to its being merited.

Can we be sure that stating truly is a different *class* of assessment from arguing soundly, advising well, judging fairly, and blaming justifiably? Do these not have something to do in complicated ways with facts? The same is true also of exercitives such as naming, appointing, bequeathing, and betting. Facts come in as well as our knowledge or opinion about facts.

Well, of course, attempts are constantly made to effect this distinction. The soundness of arguments (if they are not deductive arguments which are "valid") and the meritedness of blame are not objective matters, it is alleged; or in warning, we are told, we should distinguish the "statement" that the bull is about to charge from the warning itself. But consider also for a moment whether the question of truth or falsity is so very objective. We ask: "Is it a *fair* statement?", and are the good reasons and good evidence for stating and saying so very different from the good reasons and evidence for performative acts like arguing, warning, and judging? Is the constative, then, always true or false? When a constative is confronted with the facts, we in fact appraise it in ways involving the employment of a vast array of terms which overlap with those that we use in the appraisal of performatives. In real life, as opposed to the simple situations envisaged in logical theory, one cannot always answer in a simple manner whether it is true or false.

Suppose that we confront "France is hexagonal" with the facts, in this case, I suppose, with France, is it true or false? Well, if you like, up to a point; of course I can see what you mean by saying that it is true for certain intents and purposes. It is good enough for a top-ranking general, perhaps, but not for a geographer. "Naturally it is pretty rough," we should say, "and pretty good as a pretty rough statement." But then someone says: "But is it true or is it false? I don't mind whether it is rough or not; of course it's rough, but it has to be true or false—it's a statement, isn't it?" How can one answer this question, whether it is true or false that France is hexagonal? It is just rough, and that is the right and final answer to the question of the relation of "France is hexagonal" to France. It is a rough description; it is not a true or a false one.

Again, in the case of stating truly or falsely, just as much as in the case of advising well or badly, the intents and purposes of the utterance and its context are important; what is judged true in a school book may not be so judged in a work of historical research. Consider the constative, "Lord Raglan won the battle of Alma," remembering that Alma was a soldier's battle if ever there was one and that Lord Raglan's orders were never transmitted to some of his subordinates. Did Lord Raglan then win the battle of Alma or did he not? Of course in some contexts, perhaps in a school book, it is perfectly justifiable to say so—it is something of an exaggeration, maybe, and there would be no question of giving Raglan a medal for it. As "France is hexagonal" is rough, so "Lord Raglan won the battle of Alma" is exaggerated and suitable to some contexts and not to others; it would be pointless to insist on its truth or falsity.

Thirdly, let us consider the question whether it is true that all snow geese migrate to Labrador, given that perhaps one maimed one sometimes fails when migrating to get quite the whole way. Faced with such problems, many have claimed, with much justice, that utterances such as those beginning "All . . ." are prescriptive definitions or advice to adopt a rule. But what rule? This idea arises partly through not understanding the reference of such statements, which is limited to the known; we cannot quite make the simple statement that the truth of statements depends on facts as distinct from knowledge of facts. Suppose that before Australia is discovered X says "All swans are white." If you later find a black swan in Australia, is X refuted? Is his statement false now? Not necessarily: he will take it back but he could say "I wasn't talking about swans absolutely everywhere; for example, I was not making a statement about possible swans on Mars." Reference depends on knowledge at the time of utterance.

The truth or falsity of statements is affected by what they leave out or put in and by their being misleading, and so on. Thus, for example, descriptions, which are said to be true or false or, if you like, are "statements," are surely liable to these criticisms, since they are selective and uttered for a purpose. It is essential to realize that "true" and "false," like "free" and "unfree," do not stand for anything simple at all; but only for a general dimension of being a right or proper thing to say as opposed to a wrong thing, in these circumstances, to this audience, for these purposes and with these intentions.

In general we may say this: with both statements (and, for example, descriptions) *and* warnings, &c., the question of whether, granting that you did warn and had the right to warn, did state, or did advise, you were *right* to state or warn or advise, can arise—not in the sense of whether it was opportune or expedient, but whether, on the facts and your knowledge of the facts and the purposes for which you were speaking, and so on, this was the proper thing to say.

This doctrine is quite different from much that the pragmatists have said, to the effect that the true is what works, &c. The truth or falsity of a statement depends not merely on the meanings of words but on what act you were performing in what circumstances.

What then finally is left of the distinction of the performative and constative utterance? Really we may say that what we had in mind here was this:

(*a*) With the constative utterance, we abstract from the illocutionary (let alone the perlocutionary) aspects of the speech act, and we concentrate on the locutionary: moreover, we use an over-simplified notion of correspondence with the facts—over-simplified because essentially it brings in the illocutionary aspect. We aim at the ideal of what would be right to say in all circumstances, for any purpose, to any audience, &c. Perhaps this is sometimes realized.

(*b*) With the performative utterance, we attend as much as possible to the illocutionary force of the utterance, and abstract from the dimension of correspondence with facts.

Perhaps neither of these abstractions is so very expedient: perhaps we have here not really two poles, but rather an historical development. Now in certain cases, perhaps with mathematical formulas in physics books as examples of constatives, or with the issuing of simple executive orders or the giving of simple names, say, as examples of performatives, we approximate in real life to finding such things. It was examples of this kind, like "I apologize," and "The cat is on the mat," said for no conceivable reason, extreme marginal cases, that gave rise to the idea of two distinct utterances. But the real conclusion must surely be that we need (*a*) to distinguish between locutionary and illocutionary acts, and (*b*) specially and critically to establish with respect to each kind of illocutionary act—warnings, estimates, verdicts, statements, and descriptions—what if any is the specific way in which they are intended, first to be in order or not in order, and second, to be "right" or "wrong"; what terms of appraisal and disappraisal are used for each and what they mean. This is a wide field and certainly will not lead to a simple distinction of "true" and "false"; nor will it lead to a distinction of statements from the rest, for stating is only one among very numerous speech acts of the illocutionary class.

Furthermore, in general the locutionary act as much as the illocutionary is an abstraction only: every genuine speech act is both. (This is similar to the way in which the phatic act, the rhetic act, &c., are mere abstractions.) But, of course, typically we distinguish different abstracted "acts" by means of the possible slips between cup and lip, that is, in this case, the different types of nonsense which may be engendered in performing them. We may compare with this point what was said in the opening lecture about the classification of kinds of nonsense.

L. JONATHAN COHEN

7.2   *Do Illocutionary Forces Exist?*

I

If the late Professor J. L. Austin had survived to publish the substance of his
William James Lectures himself, he would no doubt have made many alterations in them. With his brilliant sharpness of intellect he would probably have
eliminated more flaws than most of his critics will ever see. But, tragic as it is,
we have only a posthumously published version of those lectures, and it is
to this version, carefully put together by J. O. Urmson under the title *How
to Do Things With Words* (Oxford, 1962), that criticism must perforce be
directed. I wish to argue that the concept of illocutionary force developed
therein is empty.

According to Austin every act of speaking, except perhaps a mere exclamation like "damn" or "ouch," is both a locutionary and an illocutionary act.
Qua locutionary it is, as it were, three acts in one: the (phonetic) act of uttering
certain noises; the (phatic) act of uttering certain vocables or words belonging
to and as belonging to a certain vocabulary, in a certain grammatical construction, with a certain intonation, etc.; and the (rhetic) act of using those
vocables with a certain more or less definite sense and reference. Austin takes
"sense and reference" here on the strength of current views, as he puts it,
and all he says about them directly is that together they are equivalent to
"meaning." But he does remark also that phatic acts may be reported by
direct quotation, as in "He said 'The cat is on the mat'," while rhetic acts are
reported in indirect discourse. The product of a phatic act is a unit of language,
and its typical fault is to be meaningless, while the product of a rhetic act is
a unit of speech, and its typical fault is to be vague or void or obscure, etc.
Austin claims that to perform such a three-in-one locutionary act is in general
also, and *eo ipso*, to perform an illocutionary act. In order to determine what
illocutionary act is so performed, says Austin, we must determine in what way
we are using the locution. E.g., are we asking or answering a question? Are
we giving some information or assurance or a warning? Are we announcing
a verdict or an intention? Are we pronouncing sentence? Are we making
an appointment or an appeal or a criticism? Or are we making an identification or giving a description? Austin gives the name of "illocutionary forces"
to those different types of function that language has in the performance of
an illocutionary act. It is as essential, he suggests, to distinguish force from
meaning, as it is to distinguish sense from reference within meaning. (In
three passages, pp. 115 n., 124, and 129, Austin treats the rheme as the total

Reprinted from *Philosophical Quarterly*, XIV, No. 55 (1964),118–37, by permission of the
author and of the editor of *Philosophical Quarterly*.

speech-act, but the inconsistency between these passages and pp. 92–97 is unimportant for the purposes of this article.)

Moreover, in addition to the performance of the locutionary act *of* saying something, and the performance of an illocutionary act *in* saying something, we may at the same time perform a perlocutionary act *by* saying something. Austin calls an act of speaking perlocutionary so far as it produces certain intended or unintended effects upon the feelings, thoughts, or actions of the audience, of the speaker, or of other persons. E.g., while "He urged me to shoot her" would describe an illocutionary act, "He persuaded me to shoot her" would describe a perlocutionary one. Austin claims that, just as expressions like "meaning" and "use of sentence" can blur the distinction between locutionary and illocutionary acts, so too to speak of the "use" of language can blur the distinction between the illocutionary and the perlocutionary act. Speaking of the "use of language for arguing or warning" looks just like speaking of the "use of language for persuading, rousing, alarming." Yet the former may, for rough contrast, be said to be *conventional*, he claims, in the sense that at least it could be made explicit by a performative formula, while the latter could not. Thus we can say, performatively, "I argue that" or "I warn you that," but we cannot say "I convince you that" or "I alarm you that." Austin points out, too, that the expression "the use of language" can cover other matters even more diverse than what he calls illocutionary and perlocutionary acts. We may speak of the use of language *in* poetry or *for* joking, and we can also use language to make insinuations or to express our feelings, as in swearing.

Austin thinks that the distinction between illocutions and perlocutions is the one likeliest to give trouble, and seeks at some length to clarify the extent to which the use of the prepositions "in" and "by" in sentences of the form "In/by saying *x* I was doing *y*" may afford a criterion for making this distinction. But since I shall be primarily concerned with the locutionary-illocutionary distinction it will suffice here to mention how Austin emphasizes that the illocutionary act is in no way the consequence of the locutionary act, nor does it consist in the production of consequences. Rather, to perform an illocutionary act is necessarily to perform a locutionary act—to congratulate is necessarily to say certain words. What we do import, he says, by the use of the nomenclature of illocution is a reference, not to the consequences (at least in any ordinary sense) of the locution, but to the conventions of illocutionary force as bearing on the special circumstances of the utterance. Any, or almost any perlocutionary act is liable to be brought off, in sufficiently special circumstances, by the issuing, with or without calculation, of any utterance whatsoever. But the range of illocutionary acts that may be brought off by a given utterance is restricted by the conventions of illocutionary force. Austin does insist, however, that the performance of an illocutionary act involves "the securing of uptake." A man cannot be said to have warned an audience, Austin claims, unless it hears what he says and takes what he says in a certain sense. Also an illocutionary act may take effect in certain ways other than the bringing about of changes in the natural course of events. Thus naming a ship

"Queen Elizabeth" has the effect of putting out of order any later references to it by another name. And certain illocutionary acts, such as questions, may characteristically invite responses. But any normal production of consequences in speech is a perlocutionary act.

Though the term "perlocutionary" is Austin's own invention, the existence of what Austin calls perlocutionary acts is commonly accepted and, indeed, undeniable. In different circumstances utterances with the same meaning can have such vastly different effects on their hearers that it is obviously wrong to identify any part of the meaning of an utterance with its actual effect on its hearers. Obviously the same piece of information about a rise in fat stock prices may cheer farmers quite as much as it distresses butchers. Indeed, we only need a special term "perlocutionary" to cover this aspect of people's utterances if Austin is right in thinking that, besides having a meaning and an effect, an utterance may also have what he calls an illocutionary force. The line between meaning and effect is in general clear enough. But, as Austin's own work shows, great difficulties arise, and the need for technical terminology is felt, as soon as room is sought for an utterance to have a "force" as well as a meaning and an effect. I want to argue that this technical terminology is unnecessary, because no utterance can have any such force. I shall approach the problem indirectly, by first examining Austin's concept of meaning.

II

Austin's own account of "meaning" here is unfortunately rather unhelpful since, though he equates meaning with sense and reference, he does not tell us which of the many current views about "sense" and "reference" he shares. Certainly he cannot just have meant by "meaning" that in virtue of which an utterance is true or false. So many of the utterances with which he deals are not of a kind that can be either true or false. They are questions, commands, curses, resignations, namings, etc., instead. Moreover, even Strawson's distinction (*Introduction to Logical Theory*, 1952, p. 145) between the referring role expressions may have in statements, and the ascriptive, descriptive or classificatory role, will not quite suit Austin's purposes. Strawson's distinction is between the reference and the sense of words or phrases, while Austin's desire to contrast the meaning of an utterance with its illocutionary force suggests that by "sense" and "reference" he mainly means the sense and reference of a whole utterance, not of its component words or phrases. Indeed, if Austin had meant to cite the sense and reference of an utterance's component words or phrases he could hardly have considered these two factors sufficient to determine the meaning of a whole utterance for his purposes. He would have had to cite sense, reference *and word-order* instead, for he could hardly have wanted to ascribe the same meaning to "George hit John" and "John hit George." Frege, of course, did extend his distinction to whole statements. But Frege's theory has three considerable disadvantages for Austin's purposes. According to Frege (*Translations from the Philosophical Writings*, ed. P. Geach and M. Black, 1952, p. 68) when a subordinate clause with "that" occurs after such words as "command," "ask," etc., the reference of the clause is to a command, request, etc. So that when—to use Austin's term—the illocutionary force of "Retreat!" is made explicit in "I command that you retreat," this illocutionary force ceases to exist as such, contrary to what Austin suggests, and disappears into the reference. Moreover, even with regard to statements Austin would be led into the paradoxical position of holding that a statement's illocutionary force can never be made explicit without changing its meaning. According to Frege "My age is 40" would have a different sense and reference from "I state that my age is 40." Worse still, if Austin uses "meaning" as equivalent to Frege's "sense and reference," then one cannot know the meaning of a statement on Austin's view unless one knows its truth-value, since Frege took the normal reference of a statement to be its truth-value. This hardly jibes with Austin's claim that the utterance of vocables with a more or less definite sense and reference is normally reported in indirect discourse. When we report "He said that the cat was on the mat" we do not commit ourselves as to the truth or falsity of the remark reported.

Indeed in some respects it seems doubtful whether Austin can have had any clear idea of meaning at all here. Two of his tenets on the subject are very difficult to reconcile. On the one hand he tells us that, except perhaps for exclamations, every utterance is both a locutionary and an illocutionary act. Presumably therefore every utterance, on his view, has both meaning and illocutionary force. On the other hand Austin suggests that when we have an explicit performative we also have an illocutionary act. When we say "I warn you that" or "I order you to" as an explicit performative, we perform the illocutionary act of warning or ordering, respectively. But what locutionary act do we then perform? What is the meaning of our utterance, as distinct from its illocutionary force?

It is tempting at first to suppose that in Austin's view the meaning of our utterance is found solely in the clause that follows the performative prefix. The meaning would then lie in the clause "your haystack is on fire," when the whole utterance was "I warn you that your haystack is on fire," or in the clause "go to London" when the whole utterance was "I order you to go to London." It would then be plausible to claim that these utterances have precisely the same meaning and illocutionary force as their respective subordinate clauses might have had if uttered alone and without the benefit of performative prefix. Their only difference from the latter kind of utterance would be in having their illocutionary force rendered explicit. But unfortunately there are at least three objections to interpreting Austin's theory in this way.

First, it is not at all clear why one should not suppose the expression "I warn you that" to refer both to the speaker and to the addressee of the utterance; and if the personal pronouns "I" and "you" enable it to have this reference one might also suspect the verb "warn" to give it a sense. Secondly, it is difficult to see how the addition of such a performative prefix can make no difference to the locutionary act performed, since this act is in part defined

in terms of the (phonetic) act of uttering certain noises and the (phatic) act
of uttering units of a certain vocabulary in conformity to a certain grammar.
Thus viewed the locutionary act of uttering "I warn you that your haystack
is on fire" must be of a different kind from that of uttering just "Your haystack
is on fire." Perhaps Austin would have claimed here that though the phonetic
and phatic acts are different the rhetic act is the same. But an accurate interpreter, assigned the job of rendering the explicit meanings into French, would
certainly give different versions for the two utterances.

Neither of these two objections is conclusive. Austin might have wanted to
maintain the view, paradoxical though it may be, that personal pronouns do
not have a referring role in performative prefixes and that in his use of
"meaning" a necessary difference in accurate translations does not entail
difference of meaning. But there is a more serious objection. If every illocutionary act is also a locutionary one, then the performative utterance of "I
protest" (said as the chairman refuses to let you speak) or of "I apologize"
(said as you accidentally tread on someone's toes) or of "I withdraw," "I congratulate you," "I thank you," "I bless you," "I take your side," "I nominate
you," or of any other such self-sufficient expression, must have a meaning as
well as an illocutionary force. But if these potentially performative expressions can have a meaning when uttered alone one can hardly suppose that
they lose this meaning when subordinate clauses are added, as in "I protest
that I have not been allowed to speak" or "I thank you for helping me."
One is thus forced to the conclusion that on Austin's view the meaning of an
utterance like "I warn you that your haystack is on fire" is not to be found
solely in its subordinate clause.

In what way then does the illocutionary force of such an utterance differ
from that part of its meaning which belongs to it in virtue of its performative
prefix? When you say "I protest," you are not describing your protest nor
reporting it. You are just protesting. If your utterance is to be assigned a
meaning of any kind, this meaning must be of a performative kind. The
meaning lies solely in the making of the protest. This emerges quite clearly
if we judge the meaning by an accurate interpreter's translation. But it also
emerges even if we accept Austin's own thesis that the meaning of a locutionary act is reported in indirect discourse. For we can report your utterance
not only by "You protested," but also by "You said you protested," as Austin
remarks elsewhere ("Truth," *Proceedings of the Aristotelian Society* Supp. Vol.
XXIV, 1950, p. 125). It is thus clear that wherever explicitly performative
expressions are used, the illocutionary force, if such a thing exists at all, cannot
be distinguished from the meaning.

But even where explicitly performative expressions do not occur the term
"illocutionary force" turns out to be just as otiose. After all, if the utterance
"Your haystack is on fire" gives a warning that is rendered explicit by "I
warn you that your haystack is on fire," and if the warning is part of the
meaning of the latter utterance, it is hardly unreasonable to suppose that the

warning is also part of the former utterance's meaning, though inexplicitly so. If one says "He caught a large one" and is asked to be more explicit, one might say "James landed a trout more than ten pounds in weight," and certainly then it is meaning—sense and reference, if you like—that has been made explicit. What reason is there for supposing that it is illocutionary force, rather than meaning, that has been rendered explicit in "I warn you that your haystack is on fire"?

It is no use arguing that meaning is said to be rendered explicit only when the sense or reference of individual expressions within the utterance is vague, ambiguous or otherwise uncertain. It may instead be the whole grammatical structure of an utterance that prevents its meaning from being fully explicit. For example, the meaning of "He asks, whether it is raining or snowing" might be made explicit either by "He asks his question irrespective of whether it is raining or snowing" or by "His question is whether it is raining or snowing." Similarly it is pretty clear that if you address the English sentence "Is it raining?" to your friend, as he looks out of the window, your meaning would be made even more explicit if you added, a moment later, "I ask whether it is raining." Asking a question, with or without benefit of performative, is on Austin's view a typical illocutionary act. Yet even in your first utterance ("Is it raining?"), let alone in your second ("I ask whether it is raining"), it is impossible to distinguish illocutionary force from meaning. What on earth could be the meaning of your locutionary act other than to ask whether it is raining?

Austin thinks it plausible, as indeed it is, that explicit performatives are a later development in the history of language. In primitive languages, he suggests, it would not yet be clear, nor possible to distinguish, which we were in fact doing of various things that (in accordance with later distinctions) we might be doing. E.g. "Bull" or "Thunder" in a primitive language of one-word utterances could be a warning, or information, or prediction, etc. Clarification of such utterances is as much a creative act, in the development of language, as a discovery or prediction. Austin gives a long list of other linguistic devices which may also help clarification here, though the explicit performative is the most successful device: verb-mood ("Shut it—I should" resembles the performative "I advise you to shut it"), tone of voice, cadence, emphasis (*cf.* the difference between uttering the sounds "It's going to charge" as a warning or as a report), adverbs and adverbial phrases (e.g. adding "without fail" to "I shall" in making a promise), connecting particles ("therefore" resembles "I conclude that"), and so on. Austin seems to hold that all such devices clarify illocutionary force, not meaning. But on this view there can be no difference of meaning at all between such utterances as "It must have rained, because the streets are wet" and "It must have rained, therefore the streets are wet." Yet most ordinary speakers of English, let alone linguists and interpreters, would be very surprised indeed to hear that such a pair of utterances have the same meaning. Indeed there is no reason to suppose that particles like "therefore" must have different functions in the utterance of categorical sentences from those they have in the utterance of conditional ones. But in a conditional sentence like the second part of "The streets are wet: if therefore it has rained the rivers will rise" we cannot substitute a performative occurrence of "I conclude that" for "therefore." We must suppose that this particle has a meaning, function or use in such utterances, and whatever meaning it has there it can just as well have also in "It must have rained, therefore the streets are wet." It is not that we use "therefore" with the force of "I conclude that," as Austin asserts, but rather we use "I conclude that" with the meaning of "therefore." An analogous point may be made against exclusively performative accounts of "is true" (*cf.* Jonathan Cohen, "Mr. Strawson's Analysis of Truth," *Analysis*, X, 1950, 136 ff., and more generally P. T. Geach, "Ascriptivism," *Philosophical Review*, LXIX, 1960, 221 ff., and J. R. Searle, "Meaning and Speech Acts," *Philosophical Review*, LXXI, 1962, 423 ff.: W. D. Ross made a similar point against Carnap's "command" theory of moral judgment in *Foundations of Ethics*, 1939, pp. 33–4).

Austin seeks to distinguish between the clarification of meaning and the clarification of illocutionary force. Precision is the objective of the former, explicitness of the latter. Measurement was the most successful device ever invented, he says, for developing precision, just as performatives are the most successful device for developing explicitness. But this particular distinction between precision and explicitness must stand or fall with the distinction between meaning and illocutionary force. It cannot reinforce that distinction because it has no independent support. Admittedly we speak of replacing vague quantitative descriptions by precise measurements. But we also speak of replacing implicit references to a particular person, say, by explicit ones. E.g. "Wearers of green dinner-jackets ought to apologize to the committee" may be rendered explicit by "George ought to apologize to the committee." Moreover, just as explicitness is sometimes needed with regard to the sense or reference of particular terms, so too precision is sometimes sought with regard to the meaning of a whole utterance. Logical or causal connections are more precisely expressed by conditional, disjunctive, or conjunctive sentences than by the vaguer device of paratactic construction.

Austin's theory of illocutions fares no better if we consider the use of the prepositions "in" and "by" in sentences of the form "In/by saying x I was doing y" as a criterion for distinguishing between illocutionary force and perlocutionary effect. So far as the use of these prepositions does afford such a criterion it also affords one for distinguishing between meaning and effect. When you remark "In saying that I was praising his memory, not his intelligence," you are obviously clarifying meaning. So why not also when you remark "In saying that I was praising, not blaming, him"? Austin suggests that where the use is not illocutionary "in saying" is replaceable by "in speaking of," or "in using the expression," or "by the word." But these additional tests will not serve his purpose. For we can describe what Austin would call illocutionary force by remarking "In speaking of that (viz. his achievement as a political radical) I was praising, not blaming him." We can also describe illocutionary force by remarking "In using the word 'radical' to describe him I was praising, not blaming, him" or "In using the word 'warn' (viz. in 'I warn you') I was threatening, not premonishing." Moreover, there are cases where we cannot describe what Austin would call meaning by such a phrase as "in using the word," e.g. "In saying that (viz. 'He showed remarkable knowledge of the text') I was praising his memory, not his intelligence." Thus the availability of the "In/by saying *x* I was doing *y*" criterion as a way of marking off perlocutionary effect from something else is no reason for supposing that that something else must be illocutionary force rather than meaning.

Austin also claims that we can warn or intend to warn, command or intend to command, sympathize or intend to sympathize, and perform many other illocutionary acts, though not all, without the use of language at all. But few would be unwilling to concede that within particular communities many gestures and postures come to be as meaningful as linguistic utterances.

In short, what Austin calls the illocutionary force of an utterance is that aspect of its meaning which is either conveyed by its explicitly performative prefix, if it has one, or might have been so conveyed by the use of such an expression. Any attempt to prise off this aspect of meaning, and regard it not as meaning but as something else, leads to paradox and confusion. It blurs the continuity and similarity between questions about meaning at different levels, and puts unnecessary conceptual obstacles in the path of those who wish to study the various ways in which as a culture becomes richer and more sophisticated its languages become able to express more and more subtly diverse shades of meaning.

III

What could have led Austin to put forward so erroneous a theory? Perhaps several different factors combine to make the theory seem plausible, though probably not all of them influenced Austin himself.

First, there are many strings of English words that can have vastly different meanings according to the intonation with which they are uttered. E.g. " it is raining" may be uttered as a question, with a rising intonation, or as a statement, with a falling one. If English sentences are grammatically ordered strings of English words, and if it makes sense to discuss the meanings of English sentences, as grammarians, lexicographers and logicians often do, then it looks as though any individual utterance of "it is raining" may be ascribed both a meaning, derived immediately from the meaning of the English sentence "it is raining," and also an illocutionary force depending on such variable factors as the intonation with which the sentence has been uttered. But on a stricter phonetic analysis here we have not just one sentence of spoken English, but at least two (*cf.* L. Bloomfield, *Language*, 1958, pp. 170 ff., or B. Bloch and L. Trager, *Outline of Linguistic Analysis*, 1942, p. 52).

The difference between a rising and a falling intonation has as much of a right to affect the classification of individual utterances into English sentences as has the difference of sound between "raining" and "hailing." There are pitch phonemes as well as vowel and consonant ones. So that attention to the meaning of the sentence-type cannot justify a distinction between the meaning and the illocutionary force of such utterances.

Secondly, what is, from any familiar grammatical point of view, exactly the same sentence may be uttered with a wide range of meanings. For instance, "You are very kind" may be said as praise, as thanks or as a piece of character assessment, and "Go to London tomorrow!" may be said as a command, an order, a request, a recommendation or a piece of advice. So far as it is possible to determine the precise nature of the utterance, without having it rendered explicit by a performative expression, we determine this by reference to what else is said both before and after the utterance, both by the speaker and by other parties to the conversation, and also by reference to the non-linguistic circumstances of the utterance, such as whether or not someone has just performed a service for the speaker or whether or not the speaker has any authority, status or contractual power vis-à-vis his audience. Here again it seems as though the individual utterance has not only a meaning, derived immediately from the general meaning of the sentence-type—the highest common factor, as it were, of all the sentence-type's possible uses—but also an illocutionary force, dependent upon its own, rather more special, circumstances. But it is no peculiarity of what Austin marks off as illocutionary forces that they are often determined only by reference to such contextual considerations. Exactly the same is also often true of what Austin himself would undoubtedly have regarded as meanings. The meaning of "He hit her" is, according to Austin, the sense and reference of such an utterance. But the reference of personal pronouns depends on their context of utterance. "They're all gold" means something different when said by someone looking at the clouds in a sunset from what it means when said by someone looking at a tray of cutlery. In one case the colour is being described, in another the material. "He's lost his case" means one thing when said on a railway platform, another in the antechamber of a law-court, though phonetically it is the same sentence in both cases. If we do not suppose in these cases that the context-dependent element in the commonly accepted meaning of the utterance is not *stricto sensu* meaning at all, then we should treat any utterance of "Go to London tomorrow!" analogously. That some such utterances command rather than advise, or recommend rather than request, is a feature of their respective meanings and not something that should be distinguished from their meaning under a label like "illocutionary force."

Thirdly, English sentences of certain patterns are so commonly uttered with one particular kind of meaning that when they are uttered with another meaning—either in a technical usage confined to some particular kind of profession or social institution, like a law-court, or in a usage that anyone can employ—this may appear as an addition rather than as an alternative to their common meaning. For example, the sentence "I wish you good after-noon" has a pattern commonly found in utterances that announce wishes. But it might well be uttered in dismissal of its audience and not as a wish at all. In such a case one may be tempted wrongly to suppose that the utterance has the sentence-pattern's common role as a basic meaning, and the dismissal as an additional feature, its illocutionary force, dependent partly on this basic meaning and partly on contextual circumstances. No doubt there are often also cases in which the common meaning is present alongside the special one— where, for example, the utterance is both a wish and a dismissal. In those cases the meaning is a genuinely compound one. But if this is not so—if the utterance is not a wish at all but only a dismissal—there is no need to suppose that it retains any of the sentence's original, common meaning. When one remarks of a sunset "They're all gold," one is not describing the material of which the clouds are composed as well as the colour they have momentarily taken on. To object to such a remark "You're wrong: they're minute droplets of moisture" would be just a bad joke, a pun of a peculiarly feeble kind. Nor would it be any better a joke for the man who is dismissed with "I wish you good afternoon" to reply "You're a hypocrite: you don't wish me that at all." And, if he cannot sensibly reply thus, then how can we distinguish the illocu-tionary force of the dismissal from its meaning?

A fourth factor that contributes to making Austin's theory seem plausible is that people often do not succeed in producing utterances that are as clear and definite in meaning as they are intended to be. A man may say "Go to London tomorrow!" and intend it as a request, though in the context there is nothing to determine whether it is a request, an order, a recommendation or a piece of advice. If the man is called upon to clarify himself, he might say "I request you to go to London tomorrow" or, more likely, just "It's a request," rather than "I intended it as a request," at least if he still wishes to make the request. It then seems plausible to suggest that the force of the original utter-ance is distinguishable from its meaning, on the ground that what was under-stood at once was the meaning and what was in doubt until it had been clarified was the force. But it would in general be better practice to say explicitly how much of the intended meaning was understood at once and how much was not. It is just this that even on Austin's view we should have to say in a case like "He hit her," where the utterance has exactly the meaning its speaker intends except for the fact that it is not yet clear whether "he" refers here to her husband or to her lover. And similarly if we know that an utterance was intended as either a recommendation or a piece of advice, but definitely not as an order or a request, Austin's meaning-force distinction will not help us so much. Nor would it help a man who did not know the meaning of "admonish" when a judicial authority said "We hereby admonish you." For if that utterance really had a force as well as a meaning then at least one could not know the meaning without knowing the force. Nor again is it of much use to be able to say about an utterance in a foreign language that one understood its force but not its meaning. What one would normally want to say in such a situation is that one knew it was a question though ignorant of what was asked, or that one knew it was an order though ignorant of what was ordered—as one might say that one knew it reported an assault on her though ignorant who was said to have committed it. Certainly Austin himself distinguishes between the illocutionary act intended and the illocutionary act performed. But my point is that this is no more than a special case of the distinction between meaning intended and meaning expressed.

Fifthly, there is the difference between attempted namings, vetoes, excommunications, contracts, conclusions, etc., and successful ones. Unsuccessful attempts go a little bit further than unachieved intentions. If the director's wife says "I name this ship *Queen Philippa*" and then fails to press hard enough on the button releasing the champagne bottle, she may be described as having tried unsuccessfully to name the ship. Yet her utterance was clearly meaningful. So there seems to be a difference worth noting between the meaning her utterance actually had and the illocutionary force it only just failed to have. Similarly, if a circle-squaring kind of mathematician tries to deduce a contradiction in number theory, there seems to be a difference between the meaning of his final utterance "I conclude that two is not equal to two" and the illocutionary force—the force of being a genuine conclusion—that this utterance fails to have.

Here Austin's own doctrine of infelicities, as he calls them, is relevant. The performances of the director's wife and the circle-squaring mathematician are unhappy. This naming ceremony had a flaw in it, and this mathematician's proof was invalid. But need we say more of most other naming ceremonies or mathematical proofs than that they go off without a hitch or are valid? Perhaps difficulty is sometimes caused here by the existence of two senses for all illocutionary verbs like "conclude," "name," etc. We can say either "He concluded that . . . , though he was not entitled to" or "He tried to conclude that . . . , though he did not succeed," and either "She named the ship . . . , but the ceremony was invalid" or "She tried to name the ship . . . , but bungled the ceremony." There is, as it were, both a happy-or-unhappy sense of these verbs and also a happy one. In the former we either leave it open whether the attempt was successful or imply that it was not: in the latter we imply that it was. Sometimes Austin seems to suggest that in the explicitly performative use of these verbs their sense is always the happy-or-unhappy one. For sometimes he seems to suggest that with regard to any explicitly performative utterance it is always an open question whether or not it is unhappy, and this cannot be an open question in the happy sense. In its happy sense the verb's utterance is either happy, or is not genuinely performative at all because circumstances conspire to prevent its use from being the performance that in another mood, tense, or person it would describe. At other times Austin seems to suggest that if circumstances are inappropriate for the utterance of such word as "I bet ten bob on the favourite," then no act of betting should be deemed to have been performed. If this is how all explicitly performative utterances are to be regarded, then Austin seems to be suggesting here that the performative use of a verb is always in what I have called its happy sense, because if the verb were used in its happy-or-unhappy sense there would in fact be a performative utterance even where the circumstances were inappropriate. But so long as the happy-or-unhappy sense is also available for performative use it is impossible to defend Austin's concept of illocutionary force by saying that it is what distinguishes genuine betting, naming, concluding, etc., utterances from faulty ones, since the latter too can have such a force.

Austin held that illocutionary acts consist in the production of consequences just insofar as all illocutionary acts must secure uptake and performances like namings may have an effect on how it is in order to call somebody or something. This is in any case a rather untidy exception to Austin's general principle that only perlocutionary acts consist in the production of consequences. Moreover, once the happy-or-unhappy sense of Austin's illocutionary verbs has been firmly distinguished from their happy sense the need for him to suppose a consequential element in illocutionary acts disappears altogether, since the supposed consequential element is present only in those illocutionary acts that are happy in the appropriate respects. Only if a naming-utterance is ceremonially valid does it have the effect of putting out of order any later references to the ship by another name. Only if the farmer hears and understands me when I say "I warn you that your haystack is on fire"—only then has my attempt at warning come off. In the happy-or-unhappy sense of "warn" I can say, without contradicting myself, "I warned him by shouting in his ear though he was too deaf to hear," but in the happy sense I can only say "I tried to warn him by shouting in his ear though I failed because he was too deaf." For a speaker's utterance to be a warning in the happy-or-unhappy sense what is required is that it should be *of a kind that he could reasonably expect* to secure uptake. I cannot warn a man fifty yards away by whispering. But a warning, in this sense, does not actually have to *achieve* uptake. Thus it is quite possible to preserve the general principle that the meaning of an utterance does not include any of its effects even if we regard naming, warning, concluding, etc., as aspects of meaning, provided that we concern ourselves here only with the happy-or-unhappy senses of these verbs or with the corresponding "try," "seek," "attempt," "endeavour," etc. expressions, as with "I am trying to warn you." These are the only usages in which these verbs may occur in an exclusively performative phrase. When used in their happy senses they must normally be supposed instead, if in the first person present indicative active, both to perform an act of the appropriate happy-or-unhappy variety and also to imply the occurrence of circumstances, consequential or otherwise, that render this performance a happy one.

A sixth factor that may perhaps sometimes play a part in making Austin's theory seem plausible is that it is often necessary to distinguish between what is said and the act of saying it. For instance, suppose a civil servant says to a journalist "The alpha rockets are useless." What the civil servant says may be fully justifiable on the evidence of the rockets' tests. But his saying it to the journalist may nevertheless be quite unjustifiable because it is a breach of security that can serve no useful purpose. Suppose further that the journalist is somewhat puzzled about the utterance. He may then be unclear either about what the civil servant said or about his saying it, and just as in the former case he requires clarification about meaning, so in the latter he seems to require clarification about something—call it "force"?—that stands to the civil servant's speech-act in roughly the same relation as meaning stands to what the civil servant said. If what the civil servant said may be true or false in virtue of its meaning, the act of saying it must surely have something else, its force, in virtue of which it can be justified or unjustified, valid or invalid, happy or unhappy.

But we have to be careful about what can count as force here. If by the question of force is meant nothing but whether the utterance is a report, or warning, or prediction, or criticism, etc., then we do not need a special term "force." All that is at stake is how to describe the speech-act as a whole in virtue of the meaning of what was said. Determine the meaning fully, paying due regard to contextual circumstances that affect meaning, and you already have all the information you need in order to make this description, and it is in virtue of this description that the act is either happy or unhappy. Of course there are also many other aspects of the civil servant's speech-act about which the journalist might also be puzzled. Was it legal or illegal? moral or immoral? serious or facetious? What was its motive? its immediate effect? its probable long-term consequences? The variety of questions that can be asked here testifies to the importance of distinguishing what is said from the act of saying it. But this distinction cannot itself support Austin's distinction between meaning and force. Indeed Austin himself, by speaking of locutionary acts (that have meaning) as well as of illocutionary ones (that have force), makes it quite clear that this is not how he himself would seek to defend his theory.

Seventhly, people often say things like "In warning them of the danger he was committing himself to their cause." In such a case the original utterance, which warned of the danger, might merely have been "There is a plot to kill you," and it seems rather paradoxical to suggest that "I commit myself to your cause" could have been part of the meaning of this utterance in any everyday sense of "meaning." Accordingly it might seem plausible to hold that, if "he was committing himself to their cause" does not give the meaning of the original utterance, it must give its force. So too, for example, the force of a man's utterance might be supposed to be given when we remark "In stating that he knew his speed he was admitting his guilt."

But the trouble here is that, at least on Austin's theory, we have already given the forces of these utterances when we say "In *warning* them . . ." or "In *stating* that . . . ." We are in effect referring to the utterances by means of what Austin would call their forces. Are we to suppose, therefore, a second-order force, as it were? But if so we shall need to suppose third-, fourth-, fifth-order forces, and so on, for we might also be in a position to say "In committing himself to their cause he was condemning his own past actions," "In condemning his own past actions he was repudiating his previous beliefs," "In repudiating his previous beliefs he was making the obvious deductions from what had happened," and so on indefinitely. And, quite apart from the complexity of having to accept all these illocutionary meta-forces, meta-meta-forces, meta-meta-meta-forces, etc., as well as Austin's original illocutionary force, there is the trouble that these higher-order forces cannot be made explicit in the same way as the lowest-order one normally can be. The element of warning in the above-mentioned utterance "There is a plot to kill you" may be made explicit by prefixing the performative "I warn you that" to the same sentence. But the element of commitment is only made explicit by prefixing "I commit myself" to quite a different expression. Similarly the element of statement in the above-mentioned utterance, "I know my speed was 90 m.p.h.," may be made explicit by prefixing "I hereby state that" to this very sentence. But the element of admission is only made explicit by prefixing "I admit that" to the sentence "I am guilty of driving dangerously." Certainly there are some kinds of first-order force that cannot be made explicit quite so easily. In the case of naming, defining, analysing, calling, etc., the appropriate performative verb has to be prefixed to an expression of somewhat altered grammatical construction. Instead of saying "This ship is to be *Queen Philippa*" one might say "I name this ship *Queen Philippa*." But though the grammatical construction is altered here the key words remain the same, which is not the case with what I have provisionally called higher-order forces. Indeed not only do the key words differ in these cases, but a wholly different kind of speech-act may be involved—even a speech-act that requires a different mood of the verb, as with "In advising them to desert he was raising the question of how to escape from the camp." Furthermore, it is obvious that in sufficiently suitable circumstances almost any two speech-acts whatever can be related together in this way. The relationship is thus more like that present in what Austin called perlocutionary acts, since he insisted that the range of illocutionary acts that may be brought off by a given utterance is conventionally restricted. But the speech-acts described in these statements are not perlocutionary either, because their production of effects is not at stake.

It is clear then, though Austin does not discuss the problem, that these are not illocutionary forces in his sense at all and that their common occurrence lends no support to his theory. Instead, they are most appropriately described as the implications of speech-acts, where a speech-act is said to imply that p if and only if the speech-act gives its audience sufficient reason to take it that p but it is not part of the utterance's meaning that p. Thus in warning certain people that there is a plot to kill them a man might be said to imply his commitment to their cause. If the words "by implication" are inserted before "committing" in the statement "In warning them of the danger he was committing himself to their cause," the effect is to clarify the meaning of the statement, not to alter it. Indeed, once we recognize the existence of such implications, which cannot be illocutionary forces, we see that no small part of the evidence for Austin's theory disappears. Austinians are naturally reluctant to suppose that, when a man asks a question in saying "I would like to know the time," the question is part of his utterance's meaning. It now appears that perhaps they are *sometimes* right, but not because the questioning is to be classified instead under the heading of "illocutionary force," as they would have it. They are right because the question was merely implied. The man's utterance genuinely described what he wanted to know though his speech-act implied that he was asking the time.

There may well be many other factors that contribute to the plausibility of Austin's theory. I shall mention here only one other, making eight in all. The word "performative" does not occur in that portion of Austin's paper "Other Minds" (*Proceedings of the Aristotelian Society* Supp. Vol. XX, (1946), 169–75) in which he first published a discussion of performative usage. But he does discuss phrases and expressions there rather than utterances, and his later application of the term "performative" to whole utterances (explicit in the first chapter of *How to Do Things With Words*) is an unfortunate deviation that may play some part in making the theory of illocutionary forces seem plausible. For as soon as one sees that the whole of the communication achieved by saying "I promise to go" may also, in appropriate contexts, be achieved by saying "I shall go," it is reasonable to suppose that if the former utterance is to be called performative in virtue of the promise it makes, so too must the latter be. The only difference will be that the former is explicitly performative and the latter inexplicitly so. By parity of reasoning, if a witness's utterance "I state that he hit her" is performative, then his statement "He hit her" is also performative, though again inexplicitly so. But if even statements like "He hit her" are performative, then all normal utterances are, and the descriptive value of the term has been eroded by a typically philosophical inflation. If all events turn out to be mental (or all material), a new and difficult issue arises as to what can then be meant by the term "mental" (or "material"), since within its domain of predictability no contrast is available between the mental and the non-mental (or between the material and non-material). Similarly "performative" can now no longer serve as a classificatory term, such that some but not all members of its domain may be correctly labelled with it. No wonder then that the need is felt to introduce a new term—a term with a different domain. Inflation often leads to the introduction of a new currency. If all utterances turn out to be performative, then instead of distinguishing some utterances from others it looks as though we have to distinguish one aspect of every utterance from another. We have to regard all utterances as dual, as it were. Every speech-act is said to be really two acts, not just one, and new terms are introduced, "locutionary" and "illocutionary," with these symbiotic acts as their domain. Finally, to round out the dualism, meaning is associated with locutionary acts, force with illocutionary ones. But all this philosophical inflation, and consequential coining of new technical terms, can be avoided if we keep "performative" as a term applicable to verbs, verb-uses, particles, adverbs, phrases or meanings rather than to sentences or whole utterances. We can then make all the further distinctions we need between, say, what is explicitly performative (e.g. "I promise"), semiexplicitly performative (e.g. "Without fail"), inexplicitly performative (e.g. "I shall") or not performative at all (e.g. "that I shall go"). There is no need now for the locutionary-illocutionary distinction.

IV

What reply could be made to these criticisms of Austin's theory? The most likely reply I foresee would run something like this:

"You have pointed out one or two minor inconsistencies or omissions in Austin's exposition, but in all important respects you really agree with him. Admittedly the thesis that every utterance has distinct locutionary and illocutionary aspect may need to be modified in the case of explicitly performative verb-usage, and perhaps in one or two other cases as well. Admittedly the thesis that illocutionary acts involve the securing of uptake rests on a confusion between two different senses of certain verbs. But you yourself state the core of Austin's theory when you say that the illocutionary force of an utterance is that aspect of its meaning which is either conveyed by its explicitly performative prefix, if it has one, or might have been so conveyed by the use of such an expression. The only difference is that Austin made his point clearer by using the word 'meaning' in a narrower sense, so that force stood out as something co-ordinate with meaning rather than as one special form or aspect of it."

But this is a vital difference. It is, for instance, directly responsible for such paradoxical features of Austin's theory as that even explicitly performative utterances have distinct locutionary and illocutionary aspects. It may tend to obscure, as we have seen, the continuity and similarity between certain kinds of context-dependence in linguistic usage, and it may also tend to obscure the fact that performativeness is just as much tied as reference is to particular parts of speech, particular kinds of idiom, and particular features of grammar. Moreover, Austin's co-ordination of force with meaning wrongly suggests that the dissimilarity between reference and sense is somehow less than that between force, or performative function, and sense, whereas in at least one important respect the latter dissimilarity is less than the former. For consider. We gather what things or people an utterance refers to, in a given context, primarily by attending to its demonstratives, proper names, personal pronouns, definite descriptions, etc. We gather what force the utterance has by attending, in the same context, primarily to its connecting particles, adverbs, verb-mood, explicitly performative verb-use, word-order, etc. But whereas the reference of many sentences, like "He met her there yesterday," changes on almost every occasion of its utterance, the range of forces a sentence may have is much more stable. A sentence keeps on having one or other of the same range of forces again and again, whereas many of its references never recur, especially if it includes some such word as "now" or "yesterday." And in this respect "force" is much more like "sense" than "reference" is, if we accept any of the familiar definitions of "sense" that make it a contributory element within the whole meaning of an utterance rather than just identical with that meaning. The sense of a word like "gold" or of a sentence like "He lost his case" normally varies only within a certain limited range. There is thus a better case for grouping sense and force together as meaning, so as to distinguish this meaning from reference, than there is for Austin's grouping of sense and reference together as meaning so as to distinguish the latter from force. Not only would the less variable be distinguished in this way from the more variable, but also we should not then be surprised to find that in some cases, such as explicit performatives, there is no clear difference at all between sense and force.

In short, the merit of Austin's book lies in the insight it affords into the wealth and variety of performative meaning. His introduction of the concept of illocutionary force achieves nothing but to obscure the nature of this insight. We need the term "performative" but not the term "illocutionary," and we must use "performative" as an adjective applicable to verbs, verb-uses, parti-cles, adverbs, phrases or meanings, but not to whole utterances or to sentences *qua* sentences. "Performative" is thus co-ordinate with "predicative," "referen-tial," etc., not with "statement-making" or "constative."

"What then," it may be asked, "is to become of the campaign against the descriptivist fallacy or against the fact-value dichotomy? Austin's theory of illocutionary force was at least in part designed to emphasize how very few of our utterances are really either statements, on the one hand, or evaluations, on the other. Thus he discusses at length the many other ways in which utter-ances can be appraised for felicity or infelicity besides the consideration of truth-values that may be appropriate in a narrow range of cases, and he urges philosophers who are interested in the word 'good' to form a complete list of those illocutionary acts of which commending, grading, etc., are isolated specimens. The case for Austin's theory of illocutionary force seems much stronger when that theory is viewed in the light of the support it affords to the campaign against descriptivist, or face-value, oversimplification."

Certainly nothing I have said so far can lend support to the view that statements are commoner than they in fact are. Any genuine difference of illocutionary force that Austin claimed to exist between some utterances and others—any difference that can be rendered explicit by the use of different performative verbs—reappears on my account of speech-acts as a difference of meaning. Nevertheless I suspect that Austin may have been unduly hard on the way in which many philosophers have used the term "statement," and it is a pity that he does not consider this term in any detail. It is worth while distinguishing (very briefly for present purposes: the problem is really a very much larger one, of course) at least three senses of the word:—

(1) In one sense to describe a man as having stated something is to describe him both as having said it and as being somehow committed to it. He can state a problem, a request, an evaluation, a recommendation, etc., as well

as a fact. But stating is more than just saying. There is nothing odd about an utterance like "What I *say* now is . . . , though I don't want to be held to that view of the situation." But there is something a little odd about "What I *state* now is . . . , though I don't want to be held to that view of the situation." In this sense motorists make statements to the police after road accidents, and in times of crisis politicians issue statements to the press. Such statements are to be contrasted with conjectures, asides, insinuations, hints, suggestions, etc.; and the verb "to state" is to be contrasted with the corresponding verbs. A wise man therefore considers very carefully the terms in which he is going to make a statement, though not everyone who makes a statement is wise. Moreover, since there is this personal commitment of the speaker involved in the making of statements, two motorists' statements may agree in every particular and yet be regarded as quite different statements. Or the same politician may make one statement on Tuesday and another, in identical terms, on Friday. Statements in this sense are differentiated by their time or place of utterance and by their authorship, as well as by their content, since we may be interested to know who is or was committed to what, and when.

(2) The word "statement" is also commonly used as a technical term in logic. Roughly, a statement in this sense is defined by the axioms of the propositional calculus, when the connectives of that calculus are given their usual interpretation as logical constants. Statements are those substitution-instances for variables of the calculus that make its theorems come out true under such an interpretation. Of course there are notorious difficulties about this definition. Must a statement be either true or false? Does every utterance of sentences like "The king of France is bald," or "All Cretans are liars," make a statement? How are statements related to sentences? and so on. I have discussed some of these problems elsewhere (*The Diversity of Meaning*, 1962, pp. 141 ff. and 229 ff.), but they are unimportant here. What is important for present purposes is that in this sense the word "statement" does not denote a kind of speech-act at all, but is a technical term of logical analysis. It is to be contrasted with "predicate," "term," "operator," "connective," etc., rather than with "conjecture," "aside," "insinuation," "hint," "suggestion," etc. There is very little work that the verb "to state" can do in any closely related sense, and scarcely any at all in the first person present indicative active. Nor can one ask for *the* time, place or authorship of a statement in this sense, because such statements are differentiated by their wording and meaning only, and not by their circumstances of utterance. They are just logical counters—the kind of thing that can occur now as the conclusion of one man's argument, now as the premiss of another. They can also occur just as well in an idle surmise as in a piece of sworn testimony. Hence the people who utter them may or may not thereby commit themselves to their truth. It all depends on the mode of utterance.

(3) Philosophers have also often found it convenient to use the word "statement" in a sense parasitical on (2). They have often called any speech-act

a statement if its content can be regarded for logical purposes as a statement in sense (2). In this sense most conjectures, asides, suggestions, insinuations and hints are just as much statements as are many statements in sense (1), but there are also many statements in sense (1) that are not statements in sense (3). The contrast is now with questions, commands, exclamations, etc. Moreover, in virtue of its utility in the simplification and systematization of logical theory, the "true-or-false" dichotomy is commonly extended to cover all or most statements in sense (3) too, and becomes their paramount mode of appraisal, rather than "accurate-or-inaccurate," "correct-or-incorrect," "right-or-wrong," etc. Perhaps sometimes philosophers have been a little careless in failing to distinguish sense (3) from sense (1). But it is difficult to see how sense (3) can be in any way objectionable. It has a useful generality which can make it a convenient tool of philosophical theorizing, whereas sense (1) is of no more philosophical interest than thousands of other names for special kinds of speech-act. Certainly there is no merit at all in the charge that philosophers who have used sense (3) have committed a malapropism. It is too easy to find mistakes in what philosophers have said about statements if it is assumed that the word "statement" has only one legitimate sense, as Austin sometimes seems to assume.

Moreover, the statement-evaluation dichotomy, whatever it may be, is as erroneous on my view as on Austin's. In sense (1) of "statement" stating is only one among very many kinds of speech-act that may be concerned with values. In sense (3), on the other hand, stating is a general kind of speech-act of which evaluating is a species—just one species among very many others— since we can perfectly well treat "It is wicked to kill for pleasure" or "He has a good chance of winning" as substitution-instances for the variables of the propositional calculus. Indeed there is a case for saying that Austin's recommendation about the word "good" is itself a hangover from the fact-value dichotomy. He seems to suggest that there is a particular group of illocutionary acts among those he mentions, in the performance of which alone the word "good" occurs. But I have hardly been able to find any speech-act mentioned by Austin that cannot rely strongly on the word "good" for its performance on certain occasions. We can use it equally well in what he calls verdictives, like the umpire's ruling "That was a good service"; exercitives, like the dismissal "Good riddance to you"; commissives, like the promise "In all good faith I say that I shall"; behabitives, like the thanks "It was good of you"; and expositives like the concession "It is a good point of theirs that . . . ." This fact, and the arguments of Geach and Searle already mentioned, tend to suggest that we shall get more light about "good" from studying what Austin would call the sense of utterances in which it occurs than from studying their force. "Good" is a predicative, not a performative, word, even in fundamental value-judgments, insofar as it can be a substitution-instance for any predicate variable of quantification theory, whereas an explicitly performative expression cannot. This problem, too, is a very large one, of course. But my account of speech-acts does not anticipate its solution. My account leaves moral philosophers quite free to discuss the kind of contribution which "good" makes to the meanings of utterances in which it occurs: how far is its role performative, how far predicative? Campaigns against descriptivism, muddle-headed though they often are, have nothing to lose by rejecting Austin's theory of illocutionary force.

P. F. STRAWSON

7.3 *Intention and Convention in Speech Acts*

I

In this paper I want to discuss some questions regarding J. L. Austin's notions of the illocutionary force of an utterance and of the illocutionary act which a speaker performs in making an utterance.[1]

There are two preliminary matters I must mention, if only to get them out of the way. Austin contrasts what he calls the "normal" or "serious" use of speech with what he calls "etiolated" or "parasitical" uses. His doctrine of illocutionary force relates essentially to the normal or serious use of speech and not, or not directly, to etiolated or parasitical uses; and so it will be with my comments on his doctrine. I am not suggesting that the distinction between the normal or serious use of speech and the secondary uses which he calls etiolated or parasitical is so clear as to call for no further examination; but I shall take it that there is such a distinction to be drawn and I shall not here further examine it.

My second preliminary remark concerns another distinction, or pair of distinctions, which Austin draws. Austin distinguishes the illocutionary force of an utterance from what he calls its "meaning" and distinguishes between the illocutionary and the locutionary acts performed in issuing the utterance. Doubts may be felt about the second term of each of these distinctions. It may be felt that Austin has not made clear just what abstractions from the total speech act he intends to make by means of his notions of meaning and of locutionary act. Although this is a question on which I have views, it is not what the present paper is about. Whatever doubts may be entertained about Austin's notions of meaning and of locutionary act, it is enough for present purposes to be able to say, as I think we clearly can, the following about

Reprinted from *The Philosophical Review*, LXXIII, No. 4 (1964), 439–60, by permission of the author and of the editor of *The Philosophical Review*.

[1] J. L. Austin, *How to Do Things With Words* (Oxford: Clarendon Press, 1962). [See selection 7.1 above, pp. 560–79.]

their relation to the notion of illocutionary force. The meaning of a (serious) utterance, as conceived by Austin, always embodies some limitation on its possible force, and sometimes—as, for example, in some cases where an explicit performative formula, like "I apologize," is used—the meaning of an utterance may exhaust its force; that is, there may be no more to the force than there is to the meaning; but very often the meaning, though it limits, does not exhaust, the force. Similarly, there may sometimes be no more to say about the illocutionary force of an utterance than we already know if we know what locutionary act has been performed; but very often there is more to know about the illocutionary force of an utterance than we know in knowing what locutionary act has been performed.

So much for these two preliminaries. Now I shall proceed to assemble from the text some indications as to what Austin means by the force of an utterance and as to what he means by an illocutionary act. These two notions are not so closely related that to know the force of an utterance is the same thing as to know what illocutionary act was actually performed in issuing it. For if an utterance with the illocutionary force of, say, a warning is not understood in this way (that is, as a warning) by the audience to which it is addressed, then (it is held) the illocutionary act of warning cannot be said to have been actually performed. "The performance of an illocutionary act involves the securing of uptake"; that is, it involves "bringing about the understanding of the meaning and of the force of the locution."[2] Perhaps we may express the relation by saying that to know the force of an utterance is the same thing as to know what illocutionary act, *if any*, was actually performed in issuing it. Austin gives many examples and lists of words which help us to form at least a fair intuitive notion of what is meant by "illocutionary force" and "illocutionary act." Besides these, he gives us certain general clues to these ideas, which may be grouped, as follows, under four heads:

1. Given that we know (in Austin's sense) the meaning of an utterance, there may still be a further question as to *how what was said was meant* by the speaker, or as to *how the words spoken were used*, or as to *how the utterance was to be taken* or *ought to have been taken*. In order to know the illocutionary force of the utterance, we must know the answer to this further question.

2. A locutionary act is an act *of* saying something; an illocutionary act is an act we perform *in* saying something. It is what we *do*, *in* saying what we *say*. Austin does not regard this characterization as by any means a satisfactory test for identifying kinds of illocutionary acts since, so regarded, it would admit many kinds of acts which he wishes to exclude from the class.

3. It is a sufficient, though not, I think, a necessary, condition of a verb's being the name of a *kind* of illocutionary act that it can figure, in the first person present indicative, as what Austin calls an explicit performative. (This latter notion I shall assume to be familiar and perspicuous.)

4. The illocutionary act is "a conventional act; an act done as conforming

---

[2] I refer later to the need for qualification of this doctrine.

to a convention." As such, it is to be sharply contrasted with the producing of certain effects, intended or otherwise, by means of an utterance. This producing of effects, though it too can often be ascribed *as an act* to the speaker (his *perlocutionary* act), is in no way a conventional act. Austin reverts many times to the "conventional" nature of the illocutionary act and speakes also of "conventions of illocutionary force." Indeed, he remarks that though acts which can properly be called by the same names as illocutionary acts—for example, acts of warning—can be brought off nonverbally, without the use of words, yet, in order to be properly called by these names, such acts must be *conventional* nonverbal acts.

II

I shall assume that we are clear enough about the intended application of Austin's notions of illocutionary force and illocutionary act to be able to criticize, by reference to cases, his general doctrines regarding those notions. It is the general doctrine I listed last above—the doctrine that an utterance's having such and such a force is a matter of convention—that I shall take as the starting point of inquiry. Usually this doctrine is affirmed in a quite unqualified way. But just once there occurs an interestingly qualified statement of it. Austin says, of the use of language with a certain illocutionary force, that "it may . . . be said to be *conventional* in the sense that at least it could be made explicit by the performative formula." The remark has a certain authority in that it is the first explicit statement of the conventional nature of the illocutionary act. I shall refer to it later.

Meanwhile let us consider the doctrine in its unqualified form. Why does Austin say that the illocutionary act is a conventional act, an act done as conforming to a convention? I must first mention, and neutralize, two possible sources of confusion. (It may seem an excess of precaution to do so. I apologize to those who find it so.) First, we may agree (or not dispute) that any speech act is, as such, at least in part a conventional act. The performance of any *speech* act involves at least the observance or exploitation of some *linguistic* conventions, and every illocutionary act is a speech act. But it is absolutely clear that this is not the point that Austin is making in declaring the illocutionary act to be a conventional act. We must refer, Austin would say, to linguistic conventions to determine what *locutionary* act has been performed in the making of an utterance, to determine what the *meaning* of the utterance is. The doctrine now before us is the further doctrine that where force is *not* exhausted by meaning, the fact that an utterance has the further unexhausted force it has is also a matter of convention; or, where it is exhausted by meaning, the fact *that* it is, is a matter of convention. It is not just as being a speech act that an illocutionary act—for example, of warning—is conventional. A nonverbal act of warning is, Austin maintains, conventionally such in just the same way as an illocutionary—that is, verbal—act of warning is conventionally such.

Second, we must dismiss as irrelevant the fact that it can properly be said to be a matter of convention that an act of, for example, warning is correctly called by this name. For if this were held to be a ground for saying that illocutionary acts were conventional acts, then any describable act whatever would, as correctly described, be a conventional act.

The contention that illocutionary force is a matter of convention is easily seen to be correct in a great number of cases. For very many kinds of human transaction involving speech are governed and in part constituted by what we easily recognize as established conventions of procedure additional to the conventions governing the *meanings* of our utterances. Thus the fact that the word "guilty" is pronounced by the foreman of the jury in court at the proper moment constitutes his utterance as the act of bringing in a verdict; and that this is so is certainly a matter of the conventional procedures of the law. Similarly, it is a matter of convention that if the appropriate umpire pronounces a batsman "out," he thereby performs the act of *giving the man out*, which no player or spectator shouting "Out!" can do. Austin gives other examples, and there are doubtless many more which could be given, where there clearly exist statable conventions, relating to the circumstances of utterance, such that an utterance with a certain meaning, pronounced by the appropriate person in the appropriate circumstances, has the force it has *as* conforming to those conventions. Examples of illocutionary acts of which this is true can be found not only in the sphere of social institutions which have a legal point (like the marriage ceremony and the law courts themselves) or of activities governed by a definite set of rules (like cricket and games generally) but in many other relations of human life. The act of *introducing*, performed by uttering the words "This is Mr. Smith," may be said to be an act performed as conforming to a convention. The act of surrendering, performed by saying "*Kamerad!*" and throwing up your arms when confronted with a bayonet, may be said to be (to have become) an act performed as conforming to an accepted convention, a conventional act.

But it seems equally clear that, although the circumstances of utterance are always relevant to the determination of the illocutionary force of an utterance, there are many cases in which it is not as conforming to an accepted *convention* of any kind (other than those linguistic conventions which help to fix the meaning of the utterance) that an illocutionary act is performed. It seems clear, that is, that there are many cases in which the illocutionary force of an utterance, though not exhausted by its meaning, is not owed to any *conventions* other than those which help to give it its meaning. Surely there may be cases in which to utter the words "The ice over there is very thin" to a skater is to issue a warning (is to say something with the *force* of a warning) without its being the case that there is any stable convention at all (other than those which bear on the nature of the *locutionary* act) such that the speaker's act can be said to be an act done as conforming to that convention.

Here is another example. We can readily imagine circumstances in which an utterance of the words "Don't go" would be correctly described not as a request or an order, but as an entreaty. I do not want to deny that there may be conventional postures or procedures for entreating: one can, for example, kneel down, raise one's arms and *say*, "I entreat you." But I do want to deny that an act of entreaty can be performed only as conforming to some such conventions. What makes X's words to Y an *entreaty* not to go is something—complex enough, no doubt—relating to X's situation, attitude to Y, manner, and current intention. There are questions here which we must discuss later. But to suppose that there is always and necessarily a convention conformed to would be like supposing that there could be no love affairs which did not proceed on lines laid down in the *Roman de la Rose* or that every dispute between men must follow the pattern specified in Touchstone's speech about the countercheck quarrelsome and the lie direct.

Another example. In the course of a philosophical discussion (or, for that matter, a debate on policy) one speaker *raises an objection* to what the previous speaker has just said. X says (or proposes) that p and Y *objects* that q. Y's utterance has the force of an objection to X's assertion (or proposal) that p. But where is the *convention* that constitutes it an objection? That Y's utterance has the force of an objection may lie partly in the character of the dispute and of X's contention (or proposal) and it certainly lies partly, in Y's *view* of these things, in the bearing which he takes the proposition that q to have on the doctrine (or proposal) that p. But although there may be, there does not have to be, any convention involved other than those linguistic conventions which help to fix the meanings of the utterances.

I do not think it necessary to give further examples. It seems perfectly clear that, if at least we take the expressions "convention" and "conventional" in the most natural way, the doctrine of the conventional nature of the illocutionary act does not hold generally. Some illocutionary acts are conventional; others are not (except in so far as they are locutionary acts). Why then does Austin repeatedly affirm the contrary? It is unlikely that he has made the simple mistake of generalizing from some cases to all. It is much more likely that he is moved by some further, and fundamental, feature of illocutionary acts, which it must be our business to discover. Even though we may decide that the description "conventional" is not appropriately used, we may presume it worth our while to look for the reason for using it. Here we may recall that oddly qualified remark that the performance of an illocutionary act, or the use of a sentence with a certain illocutionary force, "may be said to be conventional in the sense that at least it *could* be made explicit by the performative formula." On this we may first, and with justice, be inclined to comment that there is no such *sense* of "being conventional," that if this is a *sense* of anything to the purpose, it is a sense of "being *capable* of being conventional." But although this is a proper comment on the remark, we should not simply dismiss the remark with this comment. Whatever it is that leads Austin to call illocutionary acts in general "conventional" must be closely connected with whatever it is about such acts as warning, entreating, apologizing, advising, that accounts for the fact that *they* at least *could* be made explicit by the use of the corresponding first-person performative form. So we must ask what it is about them that accounts for this fact. Obviously it will not do to answer simply that they are acts which can be performed by the use of words. So are many (perlocutionary) acts, like convincing, dissuading, alarming, and amusing, for which, as Austin points out, there is no corresponding first-person *performative* formula. So we need some further explanation.

III

I think a concept we may find helpful at this point is one introduced by H. P. Grice in his valuable article on *Meaning* (*Philosophical Review*, LXVII, 1957) [See selection 5.4 above, pp. 436–44], namely, the concept of *someone's nonnaturally meaning something by an utterance*. The concept does not apply only to speech acts—that is, to cases where that by which someone nonnaturally means something is a *linguistic* utterance. It is of more general application. But it will be convenient to refer to that by which someone, S, nonnaturally means something as S's *utterance*. The explanation of the introduced concept is given in terms of the concept of intention. S nonnaturally means something by an utterance x if S intends (i_1) to produce by uttering x a certain response (r) in an audience A and intends (i_2) that A shall recognize S's intention (i_1) and intends (i_3) that this recognition on the part of A of S's intention (i_1) shall function as A's reason, or a part of his reason, for his response r. (The word "response," though more convenient in some ways than Grice's "effect," is not ideal. It is intended to cover cognitive and affective states or attitudes as well as actions.) It is, evidently, an important feature of this definition that the securing of the response r is intended to be mediated by the securing of another (and always cognitive) effect in A; namely, recognition of S's intention to secure response r.

Grice's analysis of his concept is fairly complex. But I think a little reflection shows that it is not quite complex enough for his purpose. Grice's analysis is undoubtedly offered as an analysis of a situation in which one person is trying, in a sense of the word "communicate" fundamental to any theory of meaning, to communicate with another. But it is possible to imagine a situation in which Grice's three conditions would be satisfied by a person S and yet, in this important sense of "communicate," it would not be the case that S could be said to be trying to communicate by means of his production of x with the person A in whom he was trying to produce the response r. I proceed to describe such a situation.

S intends by a certain action to induce in A the belief that p; so he satisfies condition (i_1). He arranges convincing-looking "evidence" that p, in a place where A is bound to see it. He does this, knowing that A is watching him at work, but *knowing also that* A *does not know that* S *knows that* A *is watching him at work*. He realizes that A will not take the *arranged* "evidence" as genuine or natural evidence that p, but realizes, and indeed intends, that A will take his arranging of it as grounds for thinking that he, S, intends to induce in A

the belief that p. That is, he intends A to recognize his (i_1) intention. So S satisfies condition (i_2). He knows that A has general grounds for thinking that S would not wish to make him, A, think that p unless it were known to S to be the case that p; and hence that A's recognition of his $(S$'s$)$ intention to induce in A the belief that p will in fact seem to A a sufficient reason for believing that p. And he intends that A's recognition of his intention (i_1) should function in just this way. So he satisfies condition (i_3).

S, then, satisfies all Grice's conditions. But this is clearly not a case of attempted *communication* in the sense which (I think it is fair to assume) Grice is seeking to elucidate. A will indeed take S to be trying to bring it about that A is aware of some fact; but he will not take S as trying, in the colloquial sense, to "let him know" something (or to "tell" him something). But unless S at least brings it about that A takes him (S) to be trying to let him (A) know something, he has not succeeded in communicating with A; and if, as in our example, he has not even *tried* to bring this about, then he has not even *tried* to communicate with A. It seems a minimum further condition of his trying to do this that he should not only intend A to recognize his intention to get A to think that p, but that he should also *intend A to recognize his intention to get A to recognize his intention* to get A to think that p.

We might approximate more closely to the communication situation if we changed the example by supposing it not only clear to both A and S that A was watching S at work, but also clear to them both that it *was* clear to them both. I shall content myself, however, with drawing from the actually considered example the conclusion that we must add to Grice's conditions the further condition that S should have the further intention (i_4) that A should recognize his intention (i_2). It is possible that further argument could be produced to show that even adding this condition is not *sufficient* to constitute the case as one of attempted communication. But I shall rest content for the moment with the fact that this addition at least is necessary.

Now we might have expected in Grice's paper an account of what it is for A to *understand* something by an utterance x, an account complementary to the account of what it is for S to *mean* something by an utterance x. Grice in fact gives no such account, and I shall suggest a way of at least partially supplying this lack. I say "at least partially" because the uncertainty as to the sufficiency of even the modified conditions for S's nonnaturally *meaning* something by an utterance x is reflected in a corresponding uncertainty in the sufficiency of conditions for A's understanding. But again we may be content for the moment with necessary conditions. I suggest, then, that for A (in the appropriate sense of "understand") to understand *something* by utterance x, it is necessary (and perhaps sufficient) that there should be *some* complex intention of the (i_2) form, described above, which A takes S to have, and that for A to understand the utterance correctly, it is necessary that A should take S to have *the* complex intention of the (i_2) form which S does have. In other words, if A is to understand the utterance correctly, S's (i_4) intention and hence his (i_2) intention must be fulfilled. Of course it does not follow from the fulfillment of these intentions that his (i_1) intention is fulfilled; nor, consequently, that his (i_3) intention is fulfilled.

It is at this point, it seems, that we may hope to find a possible point of connection with Austin's terminology of "securing uptake." If we do find such a point of connection, we also find a possible starting point for an at least partial analysis of the notions of illocutionary force and of the illocutionary act. For to secure uptake is to secure understanding of (meaning and) illocutionary force; and securing understanding of illocutionary force is said by Austin to be an essential element in bringing off the illocutionary act. It is true that this doctrine of Austin's may be objected to.[3] For surely a man may, for example, actually have made such and such a bequest, or gift, even if no one ever reads his will or instrument of gift. We may be tempted to say instead that at least *the aim, if not the achievement,* of securing uptake is an essential element in the performance of the illocutionary act. To this, too, there is an objection. Might not a man really have made a gift, in due form, and take some satisfaction in the thought, even if he had no expectations of the fact ever being known? But this objection at most forces on us an amendment to which we are in any case obliged[4]: namely, that the aim, if not the achievement, of securing uptake is essentially *a standard, if not an invariable,* element in the performance of the illocutionary act. So the analysis of the aim of securing uptake remains an essential element in the analysis of the notion of the illocutionary act.

IV

Let us, then, make a tentative identification—to be subsequently qualified and revised—of Austin's notion of uptake with that at least partially analyzed notion of understanding (on the part of an audience) which I introduced just now as complementary to Grice's concept of somebody nonnaturally meaning something by an utterance. Since the notion of audience understanding is introduced by way of a fuller (though partial) analysis than any which Austin gives of the notion of uptake, the identification is equivalent to a tentative (and partial) analysis of the notion of uptake and hence of the notions of illocutionary act and illocutionary force. If the identification were correct, then it would follow that to say something with a certain illocutionary force is at least (in the standard case) to have a certain complex intention of the (i_4) form described in setting out and modifying Grice's doctrine.

Next we test the adequacy and explanatory power of this partial analysis by seeing how far it helps to explain other features of Austin's doctrine regarding illocutionary acts. There are two points at which we shall apply this test. One is the point at which Austin maintains that the production of an utterance with a certain illocutionary force is a conventional act in that

---

[3] I owe the objections which follow to Professor Hart.

[4] For an illocutionary act *may* be performed *altogether* unintentionally. See the example about redoubling at bridge, p. 612 below.

unconventional sense of "conventional" which he glosses in terms of general suitability for being made explicit with the help of an explicitly performative formula. The other is the point at which Austin considers the possibility of a general characterization of the illocutionary act as what we *do*, *in* saying what we say. He remarks on the unsatisfactoriness of this characterization in that it would admit as illocutionary acts what are not such; and we may see whether the suggested analysis helps to explain the exclusion from the class of illocutionary acts of those acts falling under this characterization which Austin wishes to exclude. These points are closely connected with each other.

First, then, we take the point about the general suitability of an illocutionary act for performance with the help of the explicitly performative formula for that act. The explanation of this feature of illocutionary acts has two phases; it consists of, first, as general, and then a special, point about intention. The first point may be roughly expressed by saying that in general a man can speak of his intention in performing an action with a kind of authority which he cannot command in predicting its outcome. What he intends in doing something is up to him in a way in which the results of his doing it are not, or not only, up to him. But we are concerned not with just any intention to produce any kind of effect by acting, but with a very special kind of case. We are concerned with the case in which there is not simply an intention to produce a certain response in an audience, but an intention to produce that response by means of recognition on the part of the audience of the intention to produce that response, this recognition to serve as part of the reason that the audience has for its response, and the intention that this recognition should occur being itself intended to be recognized. The speaker, then, not only has the general authority on the subject of his intention that any agent has; he also has a motive, inseparable from the nature of his act, for making that intention clear. For he will not have secured understanding of the illocutionary force of his utterance, he will not have performed the act of communication he sets out to perform, unless his complex intention is grasped. Now clearly, for the enterprise to be possible at all, there must exist, or he must find, means of making the intention clear. If there exists any conventional linguistic means of doing so, the speaker has both a right to use, and a motive for using, those means. One such means, available sometimes, which comes very close to the employment of the explicit performative form, would be to attach, or subjoin, to the substance of the message what looks like a force-elucidating *comment* on it, which may or may not have the form of a self-ascription. Thus we have phrases like "This is only a suggestion" or "I'm only making a suggestion"; or again "That was a warning" or "I'm warning you." For using such phrases, I repeat, the speaker has the *authority* that anyone has to speak on the subject of his intentions and the *motive* that I have tried to show is inseparable from an act of communication.

From such phrases as these—which have, *in appearance*, the character of comments on utterances other than themselves—to the explicit performative formula the step is only a short one. My reason for *qualifying* the remark that such phrases have the character of comments on utterances other than themselves is this. We are considering the case in which the subjoined quasi-comment is addressed to the same audience as the utterance on which it is a quasi-comment. Since it is *part* of the speaker's audience-directed intention to make clear the character of his utterance as, for example, a warning, and since the subjoined quasi-comment directly subserves this intention, it is better to view the case, appearances notwithstanding, *not* as a case in which we have two utterances, one commenting on the other, but as a case of a single unitary speech act. Crudely, the addition of the quasi-comment "That was a warning" is *part* of the total act of warning. The effect of the short step to the explicitly performative formula is simply to bring appearances into line with reality. When that short step is taken, we no longer have, even in appearance, two utterances, one a comment on the other, but a single utterance in which the first-person performative verb *manifestly* has that peculiar logical character of which Austin rightly made so much, and which we may express in the present context by saying that the verb serves not exactly to *ascribe* an intention to the speaker but rather, in Austin's phrase, to *make explicit* the type of communication intention with which the speaker speaks, the type of force which the utterance has.

The above might be said to be a deduction of the general possibility and utility of the explicitly performative formula for the cases of illocutionary acts not essentially conventional. It may be objected that the deduction fails to show that the intentions rendered explicit by the use of performative formulae *in general* must be of just the complex form described, and hence fails to justify the claim that just this kind of intention lies at the core of all illocutionary acts. And indeed we shall see that this claim would be mistaken. But before discussing why, we shall make a further application of the analysis at the second testing point I mentioned. That is, we shall see what power it has to explain why some of the things we may be *doing, in* saying what we say, are not illocutionary acts and could not be rendered explicit by the use of the performative formula.

Among the things mentioned by Austin which we might be doing in saying things, but which are not illocutionary acts, I shall consider the two examples of (1) showing off and (2) insinuating. Now when we show off, we are certainly trying to produce an effect on the audience: we talk, indeed, for effect; we try to impress, to evoke the response of admiration. But it is no part of the intention to secure the effect *by means of* the recognition of the intention to secure it. It is no part of our total intention to secure recognition of the intention to produce the effect at all. On the contrary: recognition of the intention might militate against securing the effect and promote an opposite effect, for example, disgust.

This leads on to a further general point not explicitly considered by Austin, but satisfactorily explained by the analysis under consideration. In saying to an audience what we do say, we very often intend not only to produce the primary response *r* by means of audience recognition of the intention to produce that response, but to produce further effects by means of the production of the primary response r. Thus my further purpose in informing you that p (that is, aiming to produce in you the primary cognitive response of knowledge or belief that p) may be to bring it about thereby that you adopt a certain line of conduct or a certain attitude In saying what I say, then, part of what I am *doing* is trying to influence your attitudes or conduct in a certain way. Does this part of what I am doing in saying what I say contribute to determining the character of the illocutionary act I perform? And if not, why not? If we take the first question strictly as introduced and posed, the answer to it is "No." The reason for the answer follows from the analysis. We have no complex intention (i_4) that there should be recognition of an intention (i_2) that there should be recognition of an intention (i_1) that the further effect should be produced; for it is no part of our intention that the further effect should be produced by way of recognition of our intention that it should be; the production in the audience of belief that p is intended to be itself the means whereby his attitude or conduct is to be influenced. We secure uptake, perform the act of communication that we set out to perform, if the audience understands us as *informing* him that p. Although it is true that, in saying what we say, we are in fact *trying* to produce the further effect—this is part of what we are doing, whether we succeed in producing the effect or not—yet this does not enter into the characterization of the illocutionary act. With this case we have to contrast the case in which, instead of aiming at primary response and a further effect the latter to be secured through the former alone, we aim at a complex primary response. Thus in the case where I do not simply inform, but warn, you that p, among the intentions I intend you to recognize (and intend you to recognize as intended to be recognized) are not only the intention to secure your belief that p, but the intention to secure that you are on your guard against p-perils. The difference (one of the differences) between showing off and warning is that your recognition of my intention to put you on your guard may well contribute to putting you on your guard, whereas your recognition of my intention to impress you is not likely to contribute to my impressing you (or not in the way I intended).[5]

Insinuating fails, for a different reason, to be a type of illocutionary act. An essential feature of the intentions which make up the illocutionary complex is their overtness. They have, one might say, essential avowability. This is, in one respect, a logically embarrassing feature. We have noticed already how we had to meet the threat of a counterexample to Grice's analysis of the communicative act in terms of three types of intention—(i_1), (i_2), and (i_3)— by the addition of a further intention (i_4) that an intention (i_2) should be recognized. We have no proof, however, that the resulting enlarged set of

---

[5] Perhaps trying to impress might sometimes have an illocutionary character. For I might try to impress you with my *effrontery*, intending you to recognize this intention and intending your recognition of it to function as part of your reason for being impressed, and so forth. But then I am not *merely* trying to impress you; I am *inviting* you to be impressed. I owe this point to Mr. B. F. McGuinness.

conditions is a complete analysis. Ingenuity might show it was not; and the way seems open to a regressive series of intentions that intentions should be recognized. While I do not think there is anything necessarily objectionable in this, it does suggest that the complete and rounded-off set of conditions aimed at in a conventional analysis is not easily and certainly attainable in these terms. That is why I speak of the feature in question as logically embarrassing. At the same time it enables us easily to dispose of insinuating as a candidate for the status of a type of illocutionary act. The whole point of insinuating is that the audience is to *suspect*, but not more than suspect, the intention, for example, to induce or disclose a certain belief. The intention one has in insinuating is essentially nonavowable.

Now let us take stock a little. We tentatively laid it down as a necessary condition of securing understanding of the illocutionary force of an utterance that the speaker should succeed in bringing it about that the audience took him, in issuing his utterance, to have a complex intention of a certain kind, namely the intention that the audience should recognize (and recognize as intended to be recognized) his intention to induce a certain response in the audience. The suggestion has, as we have just seen, certain explanatory merits. Nevertheless we cannot claim general application for it as even a partial analysis of the notions of illocutionary force and illocutionary act. Let us look at some reasons why not.

V

I remarked earlier that the words "Don't go" may have the force, *inter alia*, either of a request or of an entreaty. In either case the primary intention of the utterance (if we presume the words to be uttered with the *sense* "Don't go *away*") is that of inducing the person addressed to stay where he is. His staying where he is is the primary response aimed at. But the only other intentions mentioned in our scheme of partial analysis relate directly or indirectly to recognition of the primary intention. So how, in terms of that scheme, are we to account for the variation in illocutionary force between requests and entreaties?

This question does not appear to raise a major difficulty for the scheme. The scheme, it seems, merely requires supplementing and enriching. *Entreaty*, for example, is a matter of trying to secure the primary response not merely through audience recognition of the intention to secure it, but through audience recognition of a complex attitude of which this primary intention forms an integral part. A wish that someone should stay may be held in different ways: passionately or lightly, confidently or desperately; and it may, for different reasons, be part of a speaker's intention to secure recognition of *how* he holds it. The most obvious reason, in the case of entreaty, is the belief, or hope, that such a revelation is more likely to secure the fulfillment of the primary intention.

But one may not only request and entreat; one may *order* someone to stay where he is. The words "Don't go" may have the illocutionary force of an order. Can we so simply accommodate in our scheme *this* variation in illocutionary force? Well, we can accommodate it; though not so simply. We can say that a man who issues an order typically intends his utterance to secure a certain response, that he intends this intention to be recognized, and its recognition to be a reason for the response, that he intends the utterance to be recognized as issued in a certain social context such that certain social rules or conventions apply to the issuing of utterances in this context and such that certain consequences may follow in the event of the primary response not being secured, that he intends *this* intention too to be recognized, and finally that he intends the recognition of these last features to function as an element in the reasons for the response on the part of the audience.

Evidently, in this case, unlike the case of entreaty, the scheme has to be extended to make room for explicit reference to social convention. It can, with some strain, be so extended. But as we move further into the region of institutionalized procedures, the strain becomes too much for the scheme to bear. On the one hand, one of its basic features—namely, the reference to an intention to secure a definite response in an audience (over and above the securing of uptake)—has to be dropped. On the other, the reference to social conventions of procedure assumes a very much greater importance. Consider an umpire giving a batsman out, a jury bringing in a verdict of guilty, a judge pronouncing sentence, a player redoubling at bridge, a priest or a civil officer pronouncing a couple man and wife. Can we say that the umpire's primary intention is to secure a certain response (say, retiring to the pavilion) from a certain audience (say, the batsman), the jurymen's to secure a certain response (say, the pronouncing of sentence) from a certain audience (say, the judge), and then build the rest of our account around this, as we did, with some strain, in the case of the order? Not with plausibility. It is not even possible, in other than a formal sense, to isolate, among all the participants in the procedure (trial, marriage, game) to which the utterance belongs, a particular audience to whom the utterance can be said to be addressed.

Does this mean that the approach I suggested to the elucidation of the notion of illocutionary force is entirely mistaken? I do not think so. Rather, we must distinguish types of case; and then see what, if anything, is common to the types we have distinguished. What we initially take from Grice—with modifications—is an at least partially analytical account of an act of communication, an act which might indeed be performed nonverbally and yet exhibit all the essential characteristics of a (nonverbal) equivalent of an illocutionary act. We gain more than this. For the account enables us to understand how such an act may be linguistically conventionalized right up to the point at which illocutionary force is exhausted by meaning (in Austin's sense); and in this understanding the notion of wholly overt or essentially avowable intention plays an essential part. Evidently, in these cases, the illocutionary act itself is not *essentially* a conventional act, an act done as conforming to a convention; it may be that the act is conventional, done as conforming to a convention, only in so far as *the means used to perform it* are conventional. To speak only of those conventional means which are also *linguistic* means, the extent to which the act is one done as conforming to conventions may depend solely on the extent to which conventional linguistic meaning exhausts illocutionary force.

At the other end of the scale—the end, we may say, from which Austin began—we have illocutionary acts which *are* essentially conventional. The examples I mentioned just now will serve—marrying, redoubling, giving out, pronouncing sentence, bringing in a verdict. Such acts could have no existence outside the rule- or convention-governed practices and procedures of which they essentially form parts. Let us take the standard case in which the participants in these procedures know the rules and their roles, and are trying to play the game and not wreck it. Then they are presented with occasions on which they have to, or may, perform an illocutionary act which forms part of, or furthers, the practice or procedure as a whole; and sometimes they have to make a decision within a restricted range of alternatives (for example, to pass or redouble, to pronounce sentence of imprisonment for some period not exceeding a certain limit). Between the case of such acts as these and the case of the illocutionary act not essentially conventional, there is an important likeness and an important difference. The likeness resides in the fact that, in the case of an utterance belonging to a convention-governed practice or procedure, the speaker's utterance is standardly *intended* to further, or affect the course of, the practice in question in some one of the alternative ways open, and intended to be recognized as so intended. I do not mean that such an act could *never* be performed *unintentionally*. A player might let slip the word "redouble" without *meaning* to redouble; but if the circumstances are appropriate and the play strict, then he *has* redoubled (or he may be *held* to have redoubled). But a player who continually did this sort of thing would not be asked to play again, except by sharpers. Forms can take charge, in the absence of appropriate intention; but when they do, the case is *essentially* deviant or nonstandard. There is present in the standard case, that is to say, the same element of wholly overt and avowable intention as in the case of the act not essentially conventional.

The difference is a more complicated affair. We have, in these cases, an act which is conventional in two connected ways. First, if things go in accordance with the rules of the procedure in question, the act of furthering the practice in the way intended is an act required or permitted by those rules, an act done as falling under the rules. Second, the act is identified as the act it is just because it is performed by the utterance of a form of words conventional for the performance of that act. Hence the speaker's utterance is not only *intended* to further, or affect the course of, the practice in question in a certain conventional way; in the absence of any breach of the conventional conditions for furthering the procedure in this way, it cannot fail to do so.

And here we have the contrast between the two types of case. In the case of an illocutionary act of a kind not essentially conventional, the act of communication is performed if *uptake* is secured, if the utterance is taken to be issued with the complex overt intention with which it is issued. But even though the act of communication is performed, the wholly overt intention which lies at the core of the intention complex may, *without any breach of rules or conventions*, be frustrated. The audience response (belief, action, or attitude) may simply not be forthcoming. It is different with the utterance which forms part of a wholly convention-governed procedure. Granted that uptake is secured, then any frustration of the wholly overt intention of the utterance (the intention to further the procedure in a certain way) must be attributable to a breach of rule or convention. The speaker who abides by the conventions can avowably have the intention to further the procedure in the way to which his current linguistic act is conventionally appropriated *only* if he takes it that the conventional conditions for so furthering it are satisfied and hence takes it *that his utterance will not only reveal his intentions but give them effect*. There is nothing parallel to this in the case of the illocutionary act of a kind not essentially conventional. In both cases, we may say, speakers assume the responsibility for making their intentions overt. In one case (the case of the convention-constituted procedure) the speaker who uses the explicitly performative form also explicitly assumes the responsibility for making his overt intention effective. But in the other case the speaker cannot, in the speech act itself, explicitly assume any such responsibility. For there are not conditions which can conventionally guarantee the effectiveness of his overt intention. Whether it is effective or not is something that rests with his audience. In the one case, therefore, the explicitly performative form *may* be the name of the very act which is performed if and only if the speaker's overt intention is effective; but in the other case it cannot be the name of this act. But of course—and I shall recur to this thought—the sharp contrast I have here drawn between two extreme types of case must not blind us to the existence of intermediate types.

Acts belonging to convention-constituted procedures of the kind I have just referred to form an important part of human communication. But they do not form the whole nor, we may think, the most fundamental part. It would be a mistake to take them as the model for understanding the notion of illocutionary force in general, as Austin perhaps shows some tendency to do when he both insists that the illocutionary act is essentially a conventional act and connects this claim with the possibility of making the act explicit by the use of the performative formula. It would equally be a mistake, as we have seen, to generalize the account of illocutionary force derived from Grice's analysis; for this would involve holding, falsely, that the complex overt intention manifested in any illocutionary act always includes the intention to secure a certain definite response or reaction in an audience over and above that which is necessarily secured if the illocutionary force of the utterance is understood. Nevertheless, we can perhaps extract from our consideration of two contrasting types of case something which is common to them both and to all the other types which lie between them. For the illocutionary force of an utterance is essentially something that is intended to be understood. And the understanding of the force of an utterance in all cases involves recognizing what may be called broadly an audience-directed intention and recognizing it as wholly overt, as intended to be recognized. It is perhaps this fact which lies at the

To perform illocutionary acts is to engage in a rule-governed form of behaviour. I shall argue that such things as asking questions or making statements are rule-governed in ways quite similar to those in which getting a base hit in baseball or moving a knight in chess are rule-governed forms of acts. I intend therefore to explicate the notion of an illocutionary act by stating a set of necessary and sufficient conditions for the performance of a particular kind of illocutionary act, and extracting from it a set of semantical rules for the use of the expression (or syntactic device) which marks the utterance as an illocutionary act of that kind. If I am successful in stating the conditions and the corresponding rules for even one kind of illocutionary act, that will provide us with a pattern for analysing other kinds of acts and consequently for explicating the notion in general. But in order to set the stage for actually stating conditions and extracting rules for performing an illocutionary act I have to discuss three other preliminary notions: *rules*, *propositions*, and *meaning*. I shall confine my discussion of these notions to those aspects which are essential to my main purposes in this paper, but, even so, what I wish to say concerning each of these notions, if it were to be at all complete, would require a paper for each; however, sometimes it may be worth sacrificing thoroughness for the sake of scope and I shall therefore be very brief.

II. RULES

In recent years there has been in the philosophy of language considerable discussion involving the notion of rules for the use of expressions. Some philosophers have even said that knowing the meaning of a word is simply a matter of knowing the rules for its use or employment. One disquieting feature of such discussions is that no philosopher, to my knowledge at least, has ever given anything like an adequate formulation of the rules for the use of even one expression. If meaning is a matter of rules of use, surely we ought to be able to state the rules for the use of expressions in a way which would explicate the meaning of those expressions. Certain other philosophers, dismayed perhaps by the failure of their colleagues to produce any rules, have denied the fashionable view that meaning is a matter of rules and have asserted that there are no semantical rules of the proposed kind at all. I am inclined to think that this scepticism is premature and stems from a failure to distinguish different sorts of rules, in a way which I shall now attempt to explain.

I distinguish between two sorts of rules: Some regulate antecedently existing forms of behaviour; for example, the rules of etiquette regulate interpersonal relationships, but these relationships exist independently of the rules of etiquette. Some rules on the other hand do not merely regulate but create or define new forms of behaviour. The rules of football, for example, do not merely regulate the game of football but as it were create the possibility of or define that activity. The activity of playing football is constituted by acting in accordance with these rules; football has no existence apart from these rules. I call the latter kind of rules constitutive rules and the former kind regulative rules. Regulative rules regulate a pre-existing activity, an activity whose existence is logically independent of the existence of the rules. Constitutive rules constitute (and also regulate) an activity the existence of which is logically dependent on the rules.[2]

Regulative rules characteristically take the form of or can be paraphrased as imperatives, e.g. 'When cutting food hold the knife in the right hand', or 'Officers are to wear ties at dinner'. Some constitutive rules take quite a different form, e.g. a checkmate is made if the king is attacked in such a way that no move will leave it unattacked; a touchdown is scored when a player crosses the opponents' goal line in possession of the ball while a play is in progress. If our paradigms of rules are imperative regulative rules, such non-imperative constitutive rules are likely to strike us as extremely curious and hardly even as rules at all. Notice that they are almost tautological in character, for what the 'rule' seems to offer is a partial definition of 'checkmate' or 'touchdown'. But, of course, this quasi-tautological character is a necessary consequence of their being constitutive rules: the rules concerning touchdowns must define the notion of 'touchdown' in the same way that the rules concerning football define 'football'. That, for example, a touchdown can be scored in such and such ways and counts six points can appear sometimes as a rule, sometimes as an analytic truth; and that it can be construed as a tautology is a clue to the fact that the rule in question is a constitutive one. Regulative rules generally have the form 'Do X' or 'If Y do X'. Some members of the set of constitutive rules have this form but some also have the form 'X counts as Y'.[3]

The failure to perceive this is of some importance in philosophy. Thus, e.g., some philosophers ask 'How can a promise create an obligation?' A similar question would be 'How can a touchdown create six points?' And as they stand both questions can only be answered by stating a rule of the form 'X counts as Y'.

I am inclined to think that both the failure of some philosophers to state rules for the use of expressions and the scepticism of other philosophers concerning the existence of any such rules stem at least in part from a failure to recognize the distinctions between constitutive and regulative rules. The model or paradigm of a rule which most philosophers have is that of a regulative rule, and if one looks in semantics for purely regulative rules one is not likely to find anything interesting from the point of view of logical analysis. There are no doubt social rules of the form 'One ought not to utter obscenities at formal gatherings', but that hardly seems a rule of the sort that is crucial in explicating the semantics of a language. The hypothesis that lies behind the present paper is that the semantics of a language can be regarded as a series of systems of constitutive rules and that illocutionary acts are acts performed in accordance with these sets of constitutive rules. One of the aims of this

---

[2] This distinction occurs in J. Rawls, "Two Concepts of Rules," *Philosophical Review* (1955), and J. R. Searle, "How to Derive 'Ought' from 'Is'," *Philosophical Review* (1964).

[3] The formulation 'X counts as Y' was originally suggested to me by Max Black.

paper is to formulate a set of constitutive rules for a certain kind of speech act. And if what I have said concerning constitutive rules is correct, we should not be surprised if not all these rules take the form of imperative rules. Indeed we shall see that the rules fall into several different categories, none of which is quite like the rules of etiquette. The effort to state the rules for an illocutionary act can also be regarded as a kind of test of the hypothesis that there are constitutive rules underlying speech acts. If we are unable to give any satisfactory rule formulations, our failure could be construed as partially disconfirming evidence against the hypothesis.

III. PROPOSITIONS

Different illocutionary acts often have features in common with each other. Consider utterances of the following sentences:

    (1) Will John leave the room?
    (2) John will leave the room.
    (3) John, leave the room!
    (4) Would that John left the room.
    (5) If John will leave the room, I will leave also.

Utterances of each of these on a given occasion would characteristically be performances of different illocutionary acts. The first would, characteristically, be a question, the second an assertion about the future, that is, a prediction, the third a request or order, the fourth an expression of a wish, and the fifth a hypothetical expression of intention. Yet in the performance of each the speaker would characteristically perform some subsidiary acts which are common to all five illocutionary acts. In the utterance of each the speaker *refers* to a particular person John and *predicates* the act of leaving the room of that person. In no case is that all he does, but in every case it is a part of what he does. I shall say, therefore, that in each of these cases, although the illocutionary acts are different, at least some of the non-illocutionary acts of reference and predication are the same.

The reference to some person John and predication of the same thing of him in each of these illocutionary acts inclines me to say that there is a common *content* in each of them. Something expressible by the clause 'that John will leave the room' seems to be a common feature of all. We could, with not too much distortion, write each of these sentences in a way which would isolate this common feature: 'I assert that John will leave the room', 'I ask whether John will leave the room', etc.

For lack of a better word I propose to call this common content a proposition, and I shall describe this feature of these illocutionary acts by saying that in the utterance of each of (1)–(5) the speaker expresses the proposition that John will leave the room. Notice that I do not say that the sentence expresses the proposition; I do not know how sentences could perform acts of that kind. But I shall say that in the utterance of the sentence the speaker expresses a proposition. Notice also that I am distinguishing between a proposition and an assertion or statement of that proposition. The proposition that John will leave the room is expressed in the utterance of all of (1)–(5) but only in (2) is that proposition asserted. An assertion is an illocutionary act, but a proposition is not an act at all, although the act of expressing a proposition is a part of performing certain illocutionary acts.

I might summarise this by saying that I am distinguishing between the illocutionary act and the propositional content of an illocutionary act. Of course, not all illocutionary acts have a propositional content, for example, an utterance of 'Hurrah!' or 'Ouch!' does not. In one version or another this distinction is an old one and has been marked in different ways by authors as diverse as Frege, Sheffer, Lewis, Reichenbach and Hare, to mention only a few.

From a semantical point of view we can distinguish between the propositional indicator in the sentence and the indicator of illocutionary force. That is, for a large class of sentences used to perform illocutionary acts, we can say for the purpose of our analysis that the sentence has two (not necessarily separate) parts, the proposition indicating element and the function indicating device.[4] The function indicating device shows how the proposition is to be taken, or, to put it in another way, what illocutionary force the utterance is to have, that is, what illocutionary act the speaker is performing in the utterance of the sentence. Function indicating devices in English include word order, stress, intonation contour, punctuation, the mood of the verb, and finally a set of so-called performative verbs: I may indicate the kind of illocutionary act I am performing by beginning the sentence with 'I apologize', 'I warn', 'I state', etc. Often in actual speech situations the context will make it clear what the illocutionary force of the utterance is, without its being necessary to invoke the appropriate function indicating device.

If this semantical distinction is of any real importance, it seems likely that it should have some syntactical analogue, and certain recent developments in transformational grammar tend to support the view that it does. In the underlying phrase marker of a sentence there is a distinction between those elements which correspond to the function indicating device and those which correspond to the propositional content.

The distinction between the function indicating device and the proposition indicating device will prove very useful to us in giving an analysis of an illocutionary act. Since the same proposition can be common to all sorts of illocutionary acts, we can separate our analysis of the proposition from our analysis of kinds of illocutionary acts. I think there are rules for expressing propositions, rules for such things as reference and predication, but those rules can be discussed independently of the rules for function indicating. In this paper

---

[4] In the sentence 'I promise that I will come' the function indicating device and the propositional element are separate. In the sentence 'I promise to come', which means the same as the first and is derived from it by certain transformations, the two elements are not separate.

I shall not attempt to discuss propositional rules but shall concentrate on rules for using certain kinds of function indicating devices.

IV. MEANING

Speech acts are characteristically performed in the utterance of sounds or the making of marks. What is the difference between *just* uttering sounds or making marks and performing a speech act? One difference is that the sounds or marks one makes in the performance of a speech act are characteristically said to *have meaning*, and a second related difference is that one is characteristically said to *mean something* by those sounds or marks. Characteristically when one speaks one means something by what one says, and what one says, the string of morphemes that one emits, is characteristically said to have a meaning. Here, incidentally, is another point at which our analogy between performing speech acts and playing games breaks down. The pieces in a game like chess are not characteristically said to have a meaning, and furthermore when one makes a move one is not characteristically said to mean anything by that move.

But what is it for one to mean something by what one says, and what is it for something to have a meaning? To answer the first of these questions I propose to borrow and revise some ideas of Paul Grice. In an article entitled "Meaning,"[5] Grice gives the following analysis of one sense of the notion of 'meaning' To say that A meant something by x is to say that 'A intended the utterance of x to produce some effect in an audience by means of the recognition of this intention'. This seems to me a useful start on an analysis of meaning, first because it shows the close relationship between the notion of meaning and the notion of intention, and secondly because it captures something which is, I think, essential to speaking a language: In speaking a language I attempt to communicate things to my hearer by means of getting him to recognize my intention to communicate just those things. For example, characteristically, when I make an assertion, I attempt to communicate to and convince my hearer of the truth of a certain proposition; and the means I employ to do this are to utter certain sounds, which utterance I intend to produce in him the desired effect by means of his recognition of my intention to produce just that effect. I shall illustrate this with an example. I might on the one hand attempt to get you to believe that I am French by speaking French all the time, dressing in the French manner, showing wild enthusiasm for de Gaulle, and cultivating French acquaintances. But I might on the other hand attempt to get you to believe that I am French by simply telling you that I am French. Now, what is the difference between these two ways of my attempting to get you to believe that I am French? One crucial difference is that in the second case I attempt to get you to believe that I am French by getting you to recognize that it is my purported intention to get you to believe

---

[5] *Philosophical Review*, 1957. [See selection 5.4 above, pp. 436–44.]

just that. That is one of the things involved in telling you that I am French. But of course if I try to get you to believe that I am French by putting on the act I described, then your recognition of my intention to produce in you the belief that I am French is not the means I am employing. Indeed in this case you would, I think, become rather suspicious if you recognized my intention.

However valuable this analysis of meaning is, it seems to me to be in certain respects defective. First of all, it fails to distinguish the different kinds of effects —perlocutionary versus illocutionary—that one may intend to produce in one's hearers, and it further fails to show the way in which these different kinds of effects are related to the notion of meaning. A second defect is that it fails to account for the extent to which meaning is a matter of rules or conventions. That is, this account of meaning does not show the connection between one's meaning something by what one says and what that which one says actually means in the language. In order to illustrate this point I now wish to present a counter-example to this analysis of meaning. The point of the counter-example will be to illustrate the connection between what a speaker means and what the words he utters mean.

Suppose that I am an American soldier in the Second World War and that I am captured by Italian troops. And suppose also that I wish to get these troops to believe that I am a German officer in order to get them to release me. What I would like to do is to tell them in German or Italian that I am a German officer. But let us suppose I don't know enough German or Italian to do that. So I, as it were, attempt to put on a show of telling them that I am a German officer by reciting those few bits of German that I know, trusting that they don't know enough German to see through my plan. Let us suppose I know only one line of German, which I remember from a poem I had to memorize in a high school German course. Therefore I, a captured American, address my Italian captors with the following sentence: 'Kennst du das Land, wo die Zitronen blühen?' Now, let us describe the situation in Gricean terms. I intend to produce a certain effect in them, namely, the effect of believing that I am a German officer; and I intend to produce this effect by means of their recognition of my intention. I intend that they should think that I am trying to tell them is that I am a German officer. But does it follow from this account that when I say 'Kennst du das Land . . .' etc., what I mean is, 'I am a German officer?' Not only does it not follow, but in this case it seems plainly false that when I utter the German sentence what I mean is 'I am a German officer', or even 'Ich bin ein deutscher Offizier', because what the words mean is, 'Knowest thou the land where the lemon trees bloom?' Of course, I want my captors to be deceived into thinking that what I mean is "I am a German officer," but part of what is involved in the deception is getting them to think that that is what the words which I utter mean in German. At one point in the *Philosophical Investigations* Wittgenstein says "Say 'it's cold here' and mean 'it's warm here'. "[6] The reason we are unable

---

[6] *Philosophical Investigations* (Oxford, 1953), para. 510.

to do this is that what we can mean is a function of what we are saying. Meaning is more than a matter of intention, it is also a matter of convention.

Grice's account can be amended to deal with counter-examples of this kind. We have here a case where I am trying to produce a certain effect by means of the recognition of my intention to produce that effect, but the device I use to produce this effect is one which is conventionally, by the rules governing the use of that device, used as a means of producing quite different illocutionary effects. We must therefore reformulate the Gricean account of meaning in such a way as to make it clear that one's meaning something when one says something is more than just contingently related to what the sentence means in the language one is speaking. In our analysis of illocutionary acts, we must capture both the intentional and the conventional aspects and especially the relationship between them. In the performance of an illocutionary act the speaker intends to produce a certain effect by means of getting the hearer to recognize his intention to produce that effect, and furthermore, if he is using words literally, he intends this recognition to be achieved in virtue of the fact that the rules for using the expressions he utters associate the expressions with the production of that effect. It is this *combination* of elements which we shall need to express in our analysis of the illocutionary act.

V. HOW TO PROMISE

I shall now attempt to give an analysis of the illocutionary act of promising. In order to do this I shall ask what conditions are necessary and sufficient for the act of promising to have been performed in the utterance of a given sentence. I shall attempt to answer this question by stating these conditions as a set of propositions such that the conjunction of the members of the set entails the proposition that a speaker made a promise, and the proposition that the speaker made a promise entails this conjunction. Thus each condition will be a necessary condition for the performance of the act of promising, and taken collectively the set of conditions will be a sufficient condition for the act to have been performed.

If we get such a set of conditions we can extract from them a set of rules for the use of the function indicating device. The method here is analogous to discovering the rules of chess by asking oneself what are the necessary and sufficient conditions under which one can be said to have correctly moved a knight or castled or check-mated a player, etc. We are in the position of someone who has learned to play chess without ever having the rules formulated and who wants such a formulation. We learned how to play the game of illocutionary acts, but in general it was done without an explicit formulation of the rules, and the first step in getting such a formulation is to set out the conditions for the performance of a particular illocutionary act. Our inquiry will therefore serve a double philosophical purpose. By stating a set of conditions for the performance of a particular illocutionary act we shall have offered a partial explication of that notion and shall also have paved the way for the second step, the formulation of the rules.

I find the statement of the conditions very difficult to do, and I am not entirely satisfied with the list I am about to present. One reason for the difficulty is that the notion of a promise, like most notions in ordinary language, does not have absolutely strict rules. There are all sorts of odd, deviant, and borderline promises; and counter-examples, more or less bizarre, can be produced against my analysis. I am inclined to think we shall not be able to get a set of knock down necessary and sufficient conditions that will exactly mirror the ordinary use of the word 'promise'. I am confining my discussion, therefore, to the centre of the concept of promising and ignoring the fringe, borderline, and partially defective cases. I also confine my discussion to full-blown explicit promises and ignore promises made by elliptical turns of phrase, hints, metaphors, etc.

Another difficulty arises from my desire to state the conditions without certain forms of circularity. I want to give a list of conditions for the performance of a certain illocutionary act, which do not themselves mention the performance of any illocutionary acts. I need to satisfy this condition in order to offer an explication of the notion of an illocutionary act in general, otherwise I should simply be showing the relation between different illocutionary acts. However, although there will be no reference to illocutionary *acts*, certain illocutionary *concepts* will appear in the analysans as well as in the analysandum; and I think this form of circularity is unavoidable because of the nature of constitutive rules.

In the presentation of the conditions I shall first consider the case of a sincere promise and then show how to modify the conditions to allow for insincere promises. As our inquiry is semantical rather than syntactical, I shall simply assume the existence of grammatically well-formed sentences.

Given that a speaker S utters as sentence T in the presence of a hearer H, then, in the utterance of T, S sincerely (and non-defectively) promises that p to H if and only if:

(1) *Normal Input and Output Conditions obtain.*

I use the terms 'input' and 'output' to cover the large and indefinite range of conditions under which any kind of serious linguistic communication is possible. 'Output' covers the conditions for intelligible speaking and 'input' covers the conditions for understanding. Together they include such things as that the speaker and hearer both know how to speak the language; both are conscious of what they are doing; the speaker is not acting under duress or threats; they have no physical impediments to communication, such as deafness, aphasia, or laryngitis; they are not acting in a play or telling jokes, etc.

(2) *S expresses that p in the utterance of T.*

This condition isolates the propositional content from the rest of the speech act and enables us to concentrate on the peculiarities of promising in the rest of the analysis.

(3) *In expressing that p, S predicates a future act A of S.*

In the case of promising the function indicating device is an expression whose scope includes certain features of the proposition. In a promise an act must be predicated of the speaker and it cannot be a past act. I cannot promise to have done something, and I cannot promise that someone else will do something. (Although I can promise to see that he will do it.) The notion of an act, as I am construing it for present purposes, includes refraining from acts, performing series of acts, and may also include states and conditions: I may promise not to do something, I may promise to do something repeatedly, and I may promise to be or remain in a certain state or condition. I call conditions (2) and (3) the *propositional content conditions.*

(4) *H would prefer S's doing A to his not doing A, and S believes*
   H would prefer his doing A to his not doing A.

One crucial distinction between promises on the one hand and threats on the other is that a promise is a pledge to do something for you, not to you, but a threat is a pledge to do something to you, not for you. A promise is defective if the thing promised is something the promisee does not want done; and it is further defective if the promisor does not believe the promisee wants it done, since a non-defective promise must be intended as a promise and not as a threat or warning. I think both halves of this double condition are necessary in order to avoid fairly obvious counter-examples.

One can, however, think of apparent counter-examples to this condition as stated. Suppose I say to a lazy student 'If you don't hand in your paper on time I promise you I will give you a failing grade in the course'. Is this utterance a promise? I am inclined to think not; we would more naturally describe it as a warning or possibly even a threat But why then is it possible to use the locution 'I promise' in such a case? I think we use it here because 'I promise' and 'I hereby promise' are among the strongest function indicating devices for *commitment* provided by the English language For that reason we often use these expressions in the performance of speech acts which are not strictly speaking promises but in which we wish to emphasize our commitment. To illustrate this, consider another apparent counter-example to the analysis along different lines. Sometimes, more commonly I think in the United States than in England, one hears people say 'I promise' when making an emphatic assertion. Suppose, for example, I accuse you of having stolen the money. I say, 'You stole that money, didn't you?' You reply 'No, I didn't, I promise you I didn't'. Did you make a promise in this case? I find it very unnatural to describe your utterance as a promise. This utterance would be more aptly described as an emphatic denial, and we can explain the occurrence of the function indicating device 'I promise' as derivative from genuine promises and serving here as an expression adding emphasis to your denial.

In general the point stated in condition (4) is that if a purported promise is to be non-defective the thing promised must be something the hearer wants done, or considers to be in his interest, or would prefer being done to not being done, etc.; and the speaker must be aware of or believe or know, etc. that this is the case. I think a more elegant and exact formulation of this condition would require the introduction of technical terminology.

(5) *It is not obvious to both S and H that S will do A in the normal course of events.*

This condition is an instance of a general condition on many different kinds of illocutionary acts to the effect that the act must have a point. For example, if I make a request to someone to do something which it is obvious that he is already doing or is about to do, then my request is pointless and to that extent defective. In an actual speech situation, listeners, knowing the rules for performing illocutionary acts, will assume that this condition is satisfied. Suppose, for example, that in the course of a public speech I say to a member of my audience 'Look here, Smith, pay attention to what I am saying'. In order to make sense of this utterance the audience will have to assume that Smith has not been paying attention or at any rate that it is not obvious that he has been paying attention, that the question of his paying attention has arisen in some way; because a condition for making a request is that it is not obvious that the hearer is doing or about to do the thing requested.

Similarly with promises. It is out of order for me to promise to do something that it is obvious I am going to do anyhow. If I do seem to be making such a promise, the only way my audience can make sense of my utterance is to assume that I believe that it is not obvious that I am going to do the thing promised. A happily married man who promises his wife he will not desert her in the next week is likely to provide more anxiety than comfort.

Parenthetically I think this condition is an instance of the sort of phenomenon stated in Zipf's law. I think there is operating in our language, as in most forms of human behaviour, a principle of least effort, in this case a principle of maximum illocutionary ends with minimum phonetic effort; and I think condition (5) is an instance of it.

I call conditions such as (4) and (5) *preparatory conditions*. They are *sine quibus non* of happy promising, but they do not yet state the essential feature.

(6) *S intends to do A.*

The most important distinction between sincere and insincere promises is that in the case of the sincere promise the speaker intends to do the act promised, in the case of the insincere promise he does not intend to do the act. Also in sincere promises the speaker believes it is possible for him to do the act (or to refrain from doing it), but I think the proposition that he intends to do it entails that he thinks it is possible to do (or refrain from doing) it, so I am not stating that as an extra condition. I call this condition the *sincerity condition.*

(7) *S intends that the utterance of T will place him under an obligation to do A.*

The essential feature of a promise is that it is the undertaking of an obligation to perform a certain act. I think that this condition distinguishes promises (and other members of the same family such as vows) from other kinds of speech acts. Notice that in the statement of the condition we only specify the speaker's intention; further conditions will make clear how that intention is realized. It is clear, however, that having this intention is a necessary condition of making a promise; for if a speaker can demonstrate that he did not have this intention in a given utterance, he can prove that the utterance was not a promise. We know, for example, that Mr. Pickwick did not promise to marry the woman because we know he did not have the appropriate intention. I call this the *essential condition*.

> (8) *S intends that the utterance of T will produce in H a belief that conditions* (6) *and* (7) *obtain by means of the recognition of the intention to produce that belief, and he intends this recognition to be achieved by means of the recognition of the sentence as one conventionally used to produce such beliefs.*

This captures our amended Gricean analysis of what it is for the speaker to mean to make a promise. The speaker intends to produce a certain illocutionary effect by means of getting the hearer to recognize his intention to produce that effect, and he also intends this recognition to be achieved in virtue of the fact that the lexical and syntactical character of the item he utters conventionally associates it with producing that effect.

Strictly speaking this condition could be formulated as part of condition (1), but it is of enough philosophical interest to be worth stating separately. I find it troublesome for the following reason. If my original objection to Grice is really valid, then surely, one might say, all these iterated intentions are superfluous; all that is necessary is that the speaker should seriously utter a sentence. The production of all these effects is simply a consequence of the hearer's knowledge of what the sentence means, which in turn is a consequence of his knowledge of the language, which is assumed by the speaker at the outset. I think the correct reply to this objection is that condition (8) explicates what it is for the speaker to "seriously" utter the sentence, i.e. to utter it and mean it, but I am not completely confident about either the force of the objection or of the reply.

> (9) *The semantical rules of the dialect spoken by S and H are such that T is correctly and sincerely uttered if and only if conditions* (1)–(8) *obtain.*

This condition is intended to make clear that the sentence uttered is one which by the semantical rules of the language is used to make a promise. Taken together with condition (8), it eliminates counter-examples like the captured soldier example considered earlier. Exactly what the formulation of the rules, is, we shall soon see.

So far we have considered only the case of a sincere promise. But insincere promises are promises nonetheless, and we now need to show how to modify the conditions to allow for them. In making an insincere promise the speaker does not have all the intentions and beliefs he has when making a sincere promise. However, he purports to have them. Indeed it is because he purports to have intentions and beliefs which he does not have that we describe his act as insincere. So to allow for insincere promises we need only to revise our conditions to state that the speaker takes responsibility for having the beliefs and intentions rather than stating that he actually has them. A clue that the speaker does take such responsibility is the fact that he could not say without absurdity, e.g. 'I promise to do *A* but I do not intend to do *A*'. To say 'I promise to do *A*' is to take responsibility for intending to do *A*, and this condition holds whether the utterance was sincere or insincere. To allow for the possibility of an insincere promise then we have only to revise condition (6) so that it states not that the speaker intends to do *A*, but that he takes responsibility for intending to do *A*, and to avoid the charge of circularity I shall phrase this as follows:

(6*) *S intends that the utterance of T will make him responsible for intending to do A.*

Thus amended (and with 'sincerely' dropped from our analysandum and from condition (9)), our analysis is neutral on the question whether the promise was sincere or insincere

VI. RULES FOR THE USE OF THE FUNCTION INDICATING DEVICE

Our next task is to extract from our set of conditions a set of rules for the use of the function indicating device. Obviously not all of our conditions are equally relevant to this task. Condition (1) and conditions of the forms (8) and (9) apply generally to all kinds of normal illocutionary acts and are not peculiar to promising. Rules for the function indicating device for promising are to be found corresponding to conditions (2)–(7).

The semantical rules for the use of any function indicating device *P* for promising are:

Rule 1. P is to be uttered only in the context of a sentence (or larger stretch of discourse) the utterance of which predicates some future act *A* of the speaker *S*.

I call this the *propositional content rule*. It is derived from the propositional content conditions (2) and (3).

Rule 2. P is to be uttered only if the hearer *H* would prefer *S*'s doing *A* to his not doing *A*, and *S* believes *H* would prefer *S*'s doing *A* to his not doing *A*.

Rule 3. P is to be uttered only if it is not obvious to both *S* and *H* that *S* will do *A* in the normal course of events.

I call rules (2) and (3) *preparatory rules*. They are derived from the preparatory conditions (4) and (5).

Rule 4. P is to be uttered only if *S* intends to do *A*.

I call this the *sincerity rule*. It is derived from the sincerity condition (6).

Rule 5. The utterance of *P* counts as the undertaking of an obligation to do *A*.

I call this the *essential rule*.

These rules are ordered: Rules 2–5 apply only if Rule 1 is satisfied, and Rule 5 applies only if Rules 2 and 3 are satisfied as well.

Notice that whereas rules 1–4 take the form of quasi-imperatives, i.e. they are of the form: utter *P* only if *x*, rule 5 is of the form: the utterance of *P* counts as *Y*. Thus rule 5 is of the kind peculiar to systems of constitutive rules which I discussed in section II.

Notice also that the rather tiresome analogy with games is holding up remarkably well. If we ask ourselves under what conditions a player could be said to move a knight correctly, we would find preparatory conditions, such as that it must be his turn to move, as well as the essential condition stating the actual positions the knight can move to. I think that there is even a sincerity rule for competitive games, the rule that each side tries to win. I suggest that the team which "throws" the game is behaving in a way closely analogous to the speaker who lies or makes false promises. Of course, there usually are no propositional content rules for games, because games do not, by and large, represent states of affairs.

If this analysis is of any general interest beyond the case of promising then it would seem that these distinctions should carry over into other types of speech act, and I think a little reflection will show that they do. Consider, e.g., giving an order. The preparatory conditions include that the speaker should be in a position of authority over the hearer, the sincerity condition is that the speaker wants the ordered act done, and the essential condition has to do with the fact that the utterance is an attempt to get the hearer to do it. For assertions, the preparatory conditions include the fact that the hearer must have some basis for supposing the asserted proposition is true, the sincerity condition is that he must believe it to be true, and the essential condition has to do with the fact that the utterance is an attempt to inform the hearer and convince him of its truth. Greetings are a much simpler kind of speech act, but even here some of the distinctions apply. In the utterance of 'Hello' there is no propositional content and no sincerity condition. The preparatory condition is that the speaker must have just encountered the hearer, and the essential rule is that the utterance indicates courteous recognition of the hearer.

A proposal for further research then is to carry out a similar analysis of other types of speech acts. Not only would this give us an analysis of concepts interesting in themselves, but the comparison of different analyses would deepen our understanding of the whole subject and incidentally provide a basis for a more serious taxonomy than any of the usual facile categories such as evaluative versus descriptive, or cognitive versus emotive.

CHARLES TRAVIS

7.5   *A Generative Theory of Illocutions*

I

Two things, if anything, are clear in philosophy of language today. First, in recent years linguists have substantially increased their ability to discover and state precisely formulated and systematically connected facts about sentences. Second, many vastly interesting facts about language are not about sentences at all. But though it is clear, since J. L. Austin, at least, that this latter claim is true, our knowledge of such further facts remains sketchy and anecdotal. It is *prima facie* interesting then, to apply to this further linguistic data some of the notions which have proven fruitful in studying sentences.

One distinction that has been helpful in studying sentences is the distinction between generative, interpretive, and recognition theories. It seems plausible that, as with sentences, all three sorts of theories will be needed for a full understanding of further facts about language as well. This paper will develop the notion of a generative theory of illocutions, and provide some idea of what such a theory might look like.

A generative theory, as it is to be understood here, is a theory which, with finite means, provides descriptions for each member of a nonfinite set of things. A generative theory may be said to be a generative theory of a particular human competence if it provides exactly one description for each of the infinite, or indefinitely large number of things which those with the competence are thereby prepared to recognize and/or treat in some characteristic manner. We may view a generative theory as one sort of device which, with finite means, draws one or more distinctions which some specifiable class of people are equipped to draw in an indefinitely large number of cases. For example, a syntax of a given language is a generative theory which distinguishes between sentences and nonsentences of that language. It does so by containing exactly one representation for each sentence of the language.

In general, the requirement of finite means implies that the theory will consist of a finite vocabulary and a finite number of rules for operating on that vocabulary to derive a potentially infinite number of descriptions. A generative theory, then, distinguishes between the objects it treats (for example, English sentences) and other things in that something is characterizable as the appropriate sort of object (e.g., an English sentence), according to the theory, just in case a description of it is derivable in the theory. A history of the rules employed in the derivation within a given theory of some object will constitute the structural description assigned to that object by the theory.

A generative theory of illocutions for a language will, with finite means, provide a unique representation for each of the indefinite number of acts of saying something which a fluent speaker is prepared to recognize, to recognize as an instance of using the language, and to understand in a characteristic way. It will thus draw a distinction between full acts of saying something and other human actions. Every utterance which is an act of using the language will have a representation in the theory. Any two acts which are represented differently in the theory will be such that they are to be understood differently in the language in question. This means that any fluent speaker who fully understands them will understand them differently.

Following Chomsky, we will distinguish two goals which a theory may strive to achieve, that of descriptive and that of explanatory adequacy. A generative theory of illocutions for some language will have achieved descriptive adequacy when it has met the goals already set for it above. In addition, it will have achieved explanatory adequacy when it provides its descriptions in the best-motivated way. This means that it must account for a range of competences possessed by a fluent speaker beyond that of simply recognizing speech acts. Its descriptions must illuminate the relations the fluent speaker recognizes between one speech act and another, and it must distinguish speech acts by referring to features that the fluent speaker is best prepared to find in them, that is, by making distinctions that he will most easily recognize.

II

Before carrying the investigation further, it will be helpful to consider two questions. First, what, in general, is the subject matter of a generative theory of illocutions? Second, what is peculiar about the way in which a generative theory treats the facts that it does?

The descriptions provided by a generative theory of illocutions contain exactly enough information for the theory to describe two utterances differently just in case in uttering them two different illocutions would be performed. We will take this to be equivalent to the following. Suppose the theory provides two different descriptions, A and B. Then, if x produces an utterance fitting A and y produces an utterance fitting B, then x and y are to be understood as in some respect having said different things or more simply x and y are to be understood differently.[1] Thus the theory is to be the widest sort of generative theory of linguistic intuitions.

Let us consider some examples of the sort of information which is to be included in this theory on the above criterion. First, suppose John and Sam both said "Tom went to the bank," but John meant 'bank' in the sense of 'financial institution', whereas Sam meant it in the sense of 'side of the river'. Then in one respect, at least, what John said was different from what Sam said. The generative theory then, will have to mark differences in the senses of words and sentences. Part of the description provided for an utterance by

---

[1] Of course this is only a criterion of descriptive adequacy. There may be many sets of descriptions which satisfy it. To achieve explanatory adequacy, which is also a goal of the present undertaking, the information must be arranged in the way which best illuminates the relations between parts of it recognized by the fluent speaker. This is the justification for including nodes such as those in a preliminary subcategorization as well as *REF* and *UD* (see Section III).

the theory will be a specification of the sense of the sentence produced in uttering it. Second, suppose John and Sam both said "The bank was closed," and they both meant by 'bank' 'financial institution', but John was referring to the First National Bank, while Sam was referring to the Security Trust Bank. Again in one respect what they said was different. Part of the description of an utterance, then, will contain a specification of the reference made in uttering it. What the specification must be like is determined by the distinctions it must mark.

Third, suppose that George and Quinton both say "France is hexagonal," but George is the chief cartographer of Rand McNally who is describing how to draw a map while Quinton is a General who is laying out a campaign. Following Austin, we will take it that George and Quinton are also to be understood differently, since George is to be taken as saying something false, whereas Quinton is only to be taken as saying something rough which may then be good enough for the purpose or not. Here there is not just one obvious way of marking the distinction. One way, however, is to mark utterances according to whether or not they are assessable as true or false.

Now let us consider a difficult case. Suppose Harold and Roger each makes a statement. They utter different sentences which, however, are synonomous on the intended reading. All of the referring parts of the sentences are to be taken as making the same references. In each case, the statements are to be assessed as true or false. Is there any respect in which Harold and Roger have said different things? Trivially, of course, they have. For suppose Harold said, "Oculists eye blondes" and Roger said, "Eye doctors eye blondes." Surely what is between the quotes in each case is different. In that respect, at least, Harold and Roger said different things.

There are also less trivial ways in which statements sharing all the common features of Harold's and Roger's may require being understood differently. Consider the following dialogue:

"Are oculists really the same as eye doctors, or is an oculist a species of eye doctor?"

"I don't know. It might help if we at least knew whether all eye doctors are oculists."

"How can we find out?"

"Well, there is one curious fact about oculists. Oculists eye blondes."

The final statement in this dialogue is surely not to be interpreted in the same way the statement "Eye doctors eye blondes" would be. One might want to chalk up the difference here to the fact that the participants in this dialogue are somewhat ignorant of English. But that need not be the case. Suppose in their empirical investigation they discover a species of eye doctor whose only contact with eyes is in making certain alterations in neural paths by means of a complex laser beam device. Does English dictate that he is an oculist? That is certainly far from clear. So content may be affected in fairly deep ways by choice of lexical items. To specify an illocution, then, we must specify a sentence with a given syntactic structure and lexical content.

Of course, the information which we gather from someone's saying something on a given occasion may be of many sorts. There are an indefinite number of ways we may, and sometimes do, take an utterance. Intuitively, much of this information, and many facts about how we take utterances ought not to be included in a theory of linguistic descriptions. First, if it is all to be included, then there seem to be no clear bounds to the scope of the theory, hence little prospect for success. Second, many of these facts are not part of understanding how an utterance is to be understood in a language. They are not about, and do not follow from, the regularities of a language or the devices it provides for us to speak in it. Rather, they follow from regularities or facts about particular speakers and hearers or from the general background knowledge they may possess in particular situations. Let us consider examples of such information and see just how it is kept out of a generative theory of illocutions.

(1). When John said, "I don't have to see every film Godard makes," we understood that he had been working too hard.
(2). When he said, "John is tired," I understood that I ought not to ask John to go to the movies.
(3). When he said, "John is tired," he meant that I ought not to ask John to go to the movies.
(4). When farmer Brown said, "The crops are dry," we understood that his corn was suffering.

There are many reasons why such information ought not to be included in a theory whose aim is to distinguish ways in which utterances are to be understood in a language. One such reason becomes apparent if we consider what happens when someone fails to understand the above utterances in the specified way. For example, suppose that in (3) the remark is addressed to someone who says "Oh, I didn't know that," and then immediately invites John to the movies. Clearly the hearer has missed the point of the remark. So we might say that he failed to understand the significance of (or reason for) making it, or even that he failed to understand the significance of its being the case that John is tired. But he hasn't thereby failed to understand what was said. Had he failed to understand that, he could not have made false inferences about the significance of John's being tired, since he would not know that the utterance was to be taken as asserting that. On the other hand, had the hearer taken the remark to be about John Smith, when in fact it was about John Robinson, then, although he doesn't know that John Robinson should be left alone, he hasn't failed to get the point of the remark. He has simply failed to fully understand what was said, that is, he doesn't know what information the remark conveyed.

Sometimes, of course, one can know what the point of an utterance is without understanding it. For example, if Smith knows no Italian, and someone screams at him an Italian equivalent of "John is tired," with appropriate gestures, and with intentions as in (3), Smith may understand that he is to leave John alone, though he hasn't any idea what was said. But this does not show us how to identify the things that may be said in Italian.

The information in the examples (1) to (4) may also be distinguished from information which is to be included in the theory by distinguishing between possibilities of misleading and possibilities of misinforming. If farmer Brown's corn is the only healthy crop in the area, he may mislead people about the state of his corn by saying "The crops are dry." But if he says this to a visiting committee of agricultural experts, knowing that the crops in the area are well irrigated, but cagily thinking of the crops in Outer Mongolia, then he has misinformed, rather than misled the experts.

Finally, there is an important consideration about what it would take to represent the extra information in (1) to (4). In (1), for example, what John's utterance led us to understand about him is what we might express by saying "John has been working too hard." What is needed to represent that information is roughly the same as what is needed to specify the relevant way in which this utterance is to be understood. We understand that John has been working too hard in the appropriate sense of those words, where 'John' is to be understood as making a particular reference, and so on. In such cases of understanding, then, there is some other utterance[2] which is to be understood in English as expressing what we understand.

The relation between the information in (1) to (4) and a generative theory of illocutions is quite different from that between the information treated in that theory and a theory, such as semantics, which leaves some of that information out of account. Roughly, semantics is about the meanings of words and sentences. Thus it fails to say anything about the references we may make with words. It doesn't represent the fact that a particular utterance of "John is tired" refers to John Smith. Unlike the above case, however, no sentence is to be understood in English as expressing or meaning what we understand here. Rather, a number of sentences, such as " 'John' refers to John Smith" may be used to assert it.

These tests seem to be useful guides. They are not intended to define the subject matter. Possibly, there just isn't an *a priori* sharp line between what the theory treats and what it does not. But it is clear what to say in a large number of cases. This is enough to get the theory started. Once it is started, we may find that we don't always need an *a priori* clear line.

But given that we now have a reasonable understanding of what the theory is about, how does a generative theory differ from the usual approach to these facts? Typically, philosophers who study illocutions, or some of their ingredients, such as references, approach them through a very different set of questions. For example, it is common to ask "What are the necessary and sufficient conditions for the performance (successful) (happy) of a speech act of a given sort?", or "When should we say that a speech act of a given sort was performed?" or "What are the necessary and sufficient conditions for successfully referring?" This approach is illustrated by the following remarks by John Searle.[3]

---

[2] Not necessarily unique.

[3] "What Is a Speech Act?," in Max Black, ed., *Philosophy in America*, pp. 222–23. [See above, pp. 614–28.]

> I intend, therefore, to explicate the notion of an illocutionary act by stating a set of necessary and sufficient conditions for the performance of a particular kind of illocutionary act and extracting from it a set of semantical rules for the use of the expression (or syntactic device) which marks the utterance as an illocutionary act of that kind. If I am successful in stating those conditions, and the corresponding rules for even one kind of illocutionary act, that will provide us with a pattern for analyzing other kinds of acts and consequently explicating the notion in general.

If we had a complete theory of the sorts of rules and conditions that Searle describes, then it could be applied to the problem of formulating a generative theory in several ways. First, it would provide us with a rigorous procedure for determining a set of data out of which the generative theory is to be formulated. That is, we would have precise and explicit criteria for determining what the theory is about. Second, we would have a rigorous procedure for testing the theory. We could see whether the descriptions it generated fit any utterances, and if so, which ones. This might give us a good indication whether the theory was drawing the right distinctions or not.

The present investigation into illocutions is proceeding on the assumption that it may be profitable to proceed in the reverse order. Despite the technical nature of terms like 'illocution' and the partly technical nature of terms such as 'statement' and 'reference' we will assume that fluent speakers of a language may know a great deal about the illocutions that can be performed in it. There may be interesting questions, then, about how to represent and organize this data, that is, how to construct a generative theory. The treatment of such questions does not necessarily await rigorous procedures for developing more data or for testing the accuracy of the theory in the way described above. In fact, it may be that such procedures can be developed in the best motivated way only if we have a well motivated and generally accurate generative theory to base them on. At a minimum, such a theory makes it clear what we need conditions of success, happiness, etc., for. Further, such a theory may be helpful in showing the sorts of terms in which such conditions must be stated.

The situation here is closely analogous to the differences in interest which separate transformationalists from traditional taxonomic linguists. Where the latter often exhibited a primary concern with devising mechanical gathering procedures for grammatical data and rigorous principles for the construction of grammars out of that data, the former were more concerned with the problems posed by finding an adequate way of describing the data already clearly at hand.

The interest of transformational grammarians is demonstrably fruitful. Whether the same sort of shift in attention will be fruitful in a study of illocutions remains to be seen, but it is the sort of thing that can only be seen by trying.

III

What would a generative theory of illocutions look like? We can get some idea by examining a partial sketch. Since our immediate concern is with the form of the theory, this sketch will be tentative. It will not be an attempt to propound truths about illocutions. A large part of it is simply to show how the theory can treat a number of received beliefs about language, most of which are due to or suggested by Austin. Where anything more ambitious is attempted, as in the treatment of reference, explicit warnings will be given.

Let us assume, first of all, that the theory contains a designated initial symbol I (for illocution). If we regard a derivation as a string of strings of symbols, then the first string in every derivation is the string consisting of I alone. The theory then contains rewriting rules, for example, 1 to 22 in the illustration [see pp. 643–44], which permit the replacement of I and every other nonterminal symbol of the theory by specified strings of symbols. If a string of strings of symbols is a derivation, then each string in it will have resulted from the immediately preceding one by the application of one rewriting rule. Further, the last string will consist of symbols drawn from a designated set of terminal symbols.

The first rewriting rule allows us to characterize the illocution in question as belonging to one of the types suggested by Austin, in Lecture Twelve of *How to Do Things With Words*.[4] The sample rules presented here concern the label EXPOSITIVE. The next rewriting rule subclassifies expositives into declarative and interrogative. The next step in a derivation is to choose a label corresponding to some particular type of illocution.[5] To avoid confusion, I have chosen ordinary English words rather than arbitrary symbols for these labels. Despite the well-known dangers of concentrating on this type of illocution, the sample rules deal with statements. This completes what we might regard as the preliminary subcategorization of illocutions.

One statement is distinguished from another by a complex variety of features. I have tentatively chosen to represent these features under four general headings: S for sentence (this is the standard designated initial symbol for generative grammars), READ for reading, INTERP for interpretation, and an assessment matrix, to be discussed shortly.[6] S is to be rewritten according to the rules of some companion syntactic theory.[7] READ is rewritten with one of a number of labels corresponding to the regular devices contained in the language for assigning meanings or senses to sentences as a function of the meanings of the words. This step gives us the means of representing the fact, for example, that

---

[4] That is, behabitives, verdictives, commissives, exercitives, and expositives.

[5] In beginning to formulate a generative theory, we might follow Austin's suggestion and choose from a long list of English performative verbs. As the theory develops, it is to be expected that some of these verbs will be shown to be superfluous or better replaced by technical terms. Labels will be superfluous if they fail to draw interesting distinctions. This may happen if, for example, every derivation containing some label A is otherwise equivalent to a derivation containing some other label B.

[6] It will thus turn out to be the case that unlike syntax, not all terminal symbols in the theory are happily regarded as formatives.

[7] There are restrictions on what sentences occur as part of a rewriting of the label 'statement'. Primarily, the sentences that may occur are declarative, nonexplicitly performative ones. Others, such as interrogative or explicitly performative ones may occur, but require special readings or interpretations. Precise statements of these restrictions are beyond the scope of the present paper.

practically any sentence can carry the sense of its negation in certain uses, that is, where it is being used ironically. These labels are then rewritten according to the rules of some companion semantic theory, such as that proposed by Katz and Fodor, where the application of these rules is suitably modified for each rewriting of READ. I have introduced the device of listing all the paths through the syntactic derivation and assigning a reading to each so as to preserve a structure to the reading of the sentence as a whole, and thus to avoid reducing the reading of the sentence to a list. Such a device may also be useful, for example, if it is necessary to distinguish ironic statements from each other by reference to the parts of the statement that are to be taken ironically. We may then reattach the symbol IRONY under each of the relevant paths.[8] However, a semantic theory with enough internal structure might render the listing of paths superfluous.

In describing the assessment matrix, I have again attempted to follow Austin's intuitions, as far as possible. This matrix is a complex symbol consisting of a list of all the pairs of terms in which particular illocutions may be assessed, except for those pairs (e.g., success-failure) which apply generally to every illocution.[9] Each pair of terms is followed by a plus or minus. If a pair of terms is followed by a plus, this is to be interpreted as saying that the illocution in question may be assessed in those terms. If it is followed by a minus, then the illocution is not to be assessed in those terms. This is to correspond to the fact, for example, that where "France is hexagonal" is to be assessed as true or false, it is a different statement than where it is merely to be assessed as rough and then good enough or not.

As a preliminary step in assigning an interpretation to an illocution, I have introduced a rule which enables us to distinguish two features of the illocution, that corresponding to the label *REF*, for reference, and that corresponding to the label *UD*, for universe of discourse. The theory assigns a reference to a statement by assigning a reference to each of the referring parts of the sentence used to make it, and to the sentence as a whole.[10] In the event that the sentence which is uttered incorporates other sentences within it, these sentences are also treated by assigning references to their referring parts and to the whole sentences. The reference of a sentence as a whole may be either null or nonnull. Since the parts have already been selected as referring parts their references are nonnull. Parts are identified as referring by considering a combination of syntactic and semantic features.

---

[8] I am endebted to John Searle and Gilbert Harman for showing me the need for this treatment of irony.

[9] As with the list of performative verbs, we can also expect that this list will be reduced as the theory becomes more refined.

[10] The device of assigning references to whole sentences is meant to capture, *inter alia*, Cook-Wilson's intuitions about logical subjects, e.g., that "John broke the window" is a different statement if it is about John than if it is about the window. Often, then, and perhaps always, the reference of the whole will be identical with that of one of its parts. The references of sentences will sometime be facts or states of affairs, as in the anaphoric reference in "That is deplorable." But the theory specifies no special sort of thing for illocutions to refer to. Incidentally, as Cook-Wilson makes clear, his intuitions are beyond the scope of any syntactic theory. The two statements in this case are not made by uttering two different sentences.

References are specified in the theory by assigning to each referring part of the illocution a set of ordered pairs consisting of a referring expression together with a reading. Referring expressions are distinguished by a configuration of syntactic and semantic features. The only restrictions on these sets, other than that concerning vacuity, is that the readings found in them do not contradict each other and do not contradict the reading assigned to the speech act as a whole by its semantic interpretation.[11] The referring expressions will generally, though not necessarily, be different from those occurring in the sentence used to make the statement. This is natural, since their purpose is to distinguish different references that may be made with the same expression.

Why represent references in this way? The first thing to note is that it is not possible to specify references simply by providing a set of referring expressions, since these will in general be ambiguous. The function of the associated readings is to disambiguate the expressions in question. The next question, then, is why include lists of referring expressions at all? There are at least two *prima facie* reasons for not doing so. First, a reading may be regarded as specifying a set of expressions, that is, those which are synonymous on that reading. This makes the inclusion of expressions seem superfluous.

Second, if referring expressions are included in a specification of references, then the theory would seem to generate two pairs of structural descriptions which, while formally distinct, are actually specifications of the same illocution. Thus, it would seem to fail to achieve even descriptive adequacy. This would come about because some specifications of reference would differ only in that there is a pair of synonymous expressions, one of which belongs to one specification, the other to the other one. But these references would then presumably pick out the same referents under the same conditions.

To see why references are specified as they are in the theory, we must first take a more global view of the problem of nonunique specifications of reference. Even if we refused to allow synonymous pairs to distinguish illocutions, there would still seem to be no guarantee that the references specified by the theory are unique. Some descriptions are, simply as a matter of fact, descriptions of the same thing. The man who wrote *Trout Fishing in America* just happens to be the man who wrote *In Watermelon Sugar*. Yet there seems to be no way of devising a generative theory of illocutions which will be able to determine when this is the case. First, since the equivalences are matter of fact, knowledge of them is not a matter of linguistic competence. Second, to determine such things, the theory would need to incorporate all matter-of-fact equivalences, which is to say virtually every fact about everything.

The question about how to represent references in the generative theory can be attacked, then, by asking whether the two problems cited above are best treated separately or along the same general lines. To see this, it may help to see how the problem about contingently equivalent references might be solved.

---

[11] Thus, the expressions may equally well be regarded as potentially referring. That is, there is obviously nothing in the generative theory which guarantees that the reference specified within a given derivation is one that was successfully made on some occasion via a particular utterance.

We can see this problem to be surmountable if we view it in a slightly different light. For every two distinct structural descriptions it generates, a generative theory can be seen as making the claim that they are descriptions of two distinct objects. Thus, in the present case, for every two distinct representations of references which are generated by the theory, the theory is committed to the claim that there correspond two distinct references to be made. What is required is an interpretation of this claim on which it is true. Such an interpretation will then help us understand what illocutionary structures tell us about utterances.

Such an interpretation is not hard to come by. We need only interpret the sets of descriptions as specifying criteria for individuating the objects referred to. That is, the theory is to be interpreted so that if a set of descriptions is a specification of a given reference, the reference will be to a particular object just in case that object (and presumably nothing else) has all the features contained in the descriptions. Suppose we then consider the case of two such sets of descriptions which differ only in that one contains one description which the other does not and consider a case where both references may be made successfully and are then references to the same thing. What is the difference in the speech acts whose structural descriptions differ only in this respect? The difference is that if the object in question were discovered not to have that further feature, then the former speech act would still contain a reference to it, whereas the latter would not. There are references to Moses which fail if the baby saved by Pharoah's daughter didn't grow up to lead the Jews out of Egypt, and references to Moses which do not. References of both sorts may occur in speech acts which share at least nearly all other relevant features in common.

Now it can be shown that a treatment of the problems posed by synonymous pairs of expressions must proceed along similar lines. Let us consider an example based on a case discussed by Leibniz in Book III of the *New Essays*. Let us suppose that at a certain time gold is defined, in terms of what seem to be the most essential of its properties, as the only substance soluble only in aqua regia. This means not only that as far as we know gold has this property, but *inter alia*, that this is regarded as decisive in critical situations.

Let us now suppose that two developments occur at about the same time. First, alchemists succeed in producing, by a cheap and simple process, large quantities of a metal which is soluble only in aqua regia. Unfortunately, this metal is always greenish and brittle. Second, scientists discover that there is an important property which is possessed by all of the old gold and none of the product of the alchemist's art. We can imagine that this property is something like having a certain atomic weight, or giving certain results under spectroscopic analysis. In view of these two events it may become necessary to revise the definition given to gold so that it includes mention of the new property discovered by the scientists. On the Leibnizian view, which I believe is correct, this means that we have come closer to discovering what the correct definition of 'gold' really is. However, this observation does not reflect on the adequacy of a previously formed semantic theory which assigned readings to 'gold' on the basis of the earlier definition.

Now let us look at some typical references to gold made before the dual discoveries and see how they might adequately be characterized. Suppose, first, that a bandit, believing Smith's safe to be full of gold, says to Smith, "Hand over all of that valuable metal in your safe." Later, an informer, believing that he knows where Smith's gold is, says to the police, "Smith's stolen metal is in the cabin on top of the hill." Are these references to be regarded as essentially references to gold, or as essentially references to something with the definition assigned to 'gold' by a currently adequate semantic theory?

To see the answer, we need only imagine the consequences if Smith, counter to expectations, presents the bandit with a pile of greenish brittle stuff, or if such a pile, formerly in Smith's safe, were found in the cabin at the tip of the hill, or perhaps under a rock at the bottom. It is quite clear that neither the bandit nor the informer would admit that that was what he was referring to.

What is crucial for determining what was referred to in these cases is that for something to be what was referred to, it must be gold. We cannot give an adequate characterization of what is crucial by listing properties which in fact we regard as essential for determining whether something is gold. So an adequate characterization of what was referred to must make use of appropriate lexical items. To say this is not to deny, for example, that one could use the word 'gold' to make a reference to something which need not in the end turn out to be gold in order to be the referent. Nor is it to deny that people could on occasion make references which were properly characterized as references to things with some set of properties, where those properties in fact are the essential ones for determining whether something is gold. It is only to say that in such cases the proper characterization of the reference would make use of lexical items which designate these properties.

Thus it becomes necessary to attach words and expressions to references to adequately distinguish the different ones that might be made. The interpretation of the theory on which its claims are true is now fairly obvious. Expressions which the semantic theory characterizes as synonymous characterize different references in that if matters of fact show the semantic theory in need of revision, the reference remains tied to one part of the lexicon rather than another. Intuitively, references may be thought of as determined by some specification of what the speaker and his audience understand, but what they understand is what may be expressed in the language they understand.

The present characterization of reference is, of course, tentative. There are at least two directions in which it might need to be revised. First, it may be that some descriptions may never be used in characterizing possible references, either because the kind of characterization they provide is not well defined or because references are never distinguished from each other by the sorts of features they contain. One might take such a position, for example, for a certain class of proper names, roughly, those not contained in dictionaries, although there seems no clear argument in favor of doing so. A better case might be made against pronouns in certain uses. Given the structure of reference specifications, rules to exclude such undesirable descriptions may refer either to lexical or to semantic features.

Second, it may be that individuating features don't operate on the all-or-nothing basis suggested by the present treatment. It may be that whether an object must possess a given feature to be the referent depends on complex considerations about what other features are present. In that case, it may be necessary to partition the set of descriptions which specifies a reference. The interpretation could assign different values to the members of each partition. It could then specify, for example, that the utterance refers to the object, if any, which has the greatest value for the difference between values of features it has and values of features it lacks, provided that value is sufficiently greater than some fixed value and the value assigned to any other object. However, it seems worthwhile to remain with the simplest possible formulation until it is demonstrated to be inadequate.

Given certain traditional treatments of statements and references, we might ask at this point whether the present theory treats references as 'intentional' or 'extensional' or, in more traditional terms, as 'subjective' or 'objective'. In the theory, references are intentional in that they do not correspond in a one-to-one way to what there is to be referred to. As reference is being construed here, there may be many distinct sorts of references to the same object. This is even the case where the same referring expression is used to make them. Some specifications of reference fail to correspond to any object at all, because nothing or too many things fit them. For some uses of "John is eating the daisies," nothing will count as John unless it is a golden unicorn. Such utterances must be so marked by the theory. Given the lack of cooperation on the part of the world, references so marked will turn out to be unsuccessful or unhappy, or something of the sort, but that is another matter. Some references are specified in this way because this is the way some possible utterances are to be understood.

On the other hand, to say that a reference is intentional is not to say that the features which correctly specify a reference are whatever the referrer intends them to be. The correct specification of a reference is not determined by what the utterer tells us about what he was referring to. There is no reason why a speaker couldn't be utterly mistaken about what features in fact determine whether an object is what was referred to. So we don't discover what references ought to look like in the theory by examining the objects referred to to determine the properties they have, or by examining what the speaker or hearer of an utterance may be actually or potentially conscious of, though both these studies may provide relevant evidence. To decide such questions we must determine the conditions under which something will count as what is referred to by a given expression in a given utterance.

Finally, we must consider what information to represent under the label *UD*. Is there information about the interpretation which is not already represented under *REF*? The following examples show that there is.

    (1) "That is a tomato."
    (2) "That is a duck."
    (3) "It's two feet long."

Let us suppose that (1) is uttered in reference to a piece of wax fruit, and that (2) is uttered in reference to a decoy duck. Let us suppose that (3) is uttered after the performance of a measurement with a ruler. We can then distinguish two cases of each utterance. There is the case where someone makes the false claim that a piece of wax fruit is a tomato and the case where he makes the true claim that a piece of wax fruit is a wax tomato and not a pear or an orange. There is the case where someone makes the false claim that a wood carving is a duck, and the case where he makes the true claim that it is a wood carving of a duck, not a brant or a goose. In utterance three, there are cases where the statement may be refuted by making a measurement with Vernier calipers and cases where it may not.

Such distinctions cannot be handled by different specifications of reference since throughout what is referred to is a piece of wax fruit, or a wood carving, or the object that was measured with a ruler. The distinctions cannot be handled by specifying different senses of words either, for if we attempted to do so, we should get an indefinite proliferation of senses for every word. It is not only a piece of wax fruit that can be characterized as a tomato, but an image on a screen, a picture in the newspaper, a Rohrschach blot, a pin cushion, a jam jar, a piece of a painting, and so forth.

In the present theory, such cases are to be handled by assigning special interpretations to terms like 'tomato', 'duck', 'hexagonal', and 'two feet long'. This may be understood either as adding additional features which are understood, but not said to apply to the object in question, or it may be understood as specifying a range of descriptions with which the stated one is to be compared. The restriction on the addition of such features is very roughly that they be compatible with the features which are explicitly stated. Unfortunately, this is much too rough to do. Ducks, for example, are animate and not wooden. I have tried to solve this problem by finding explicit formulas which serve as tests of what is permissible. Obviously, the problem is far from a complete solution. This is one area that requires much further scrutiny.

IV

Thus far, in describing a generative theory of illocutions we have exploited certain analogies that may be drawn between it and a theory of syntax. There are, of course, disanalogies as well. A number of these may cause misunderstanding about the significance of various parts of the theory.

One important disanalogy is over the significance of trees. The rewriting rules of the present theory are similar enough to the rules of the base component of a syntax for the derivations generated by either set of rules to be represented by tree structures (see the illustration [p. 645] for an idea of what such a tree structure might look like in the case of statements). Unfortunately, for present purposes, there is a natural interpretation of such trees in the case of syntax, which fails to fit in the theory of illocutions.

Roughly speaking, a tree in syntax may be regarded as representing a set of segmentations of a sentence into perceptual parts where each level of the tree represents one such segmentation. (Of course, in transformational grammar this is not strictly accurate.) The tree then provides a description of the sentence by labeling each of these perceptual segments and exhibiting its relation to each of the other segments marked by the derivation.

In contrast, a derivation in the present theory is not a segmentation of the perceptual form of anything. The features it marks in an illocution are not perceptually distinct. Some features, such as references and assessment matrices, when distinguished from other features, may fail to be perceivable at all. An attempt to find an interpretation of illocutionary trees which is at all parallel to the interpretation of trees in syntax is very likely misguided, and in any case beside the point. Trees are one way of representing certain kinds of formal relations. A theory of illocutions is no more about trees than it is about ordered n-tuples. If there is any stylistic or heuristic advantage to doing so, nothing will be lost if we think of derivations as, for example, ordered n-tuples of ordered n-tuples. The elements of these n-tuples will then correspond to the features of illocutions which the theory marks. The rules for constructing n-tuples out of these elements will correspond to the relations between these features that the theory recognizes.

It is also natural to ask whether a generative theory of illocutions must be transformational. Here again, if we regard this question as we do in syntax, then the answer will not be very significant. One reason the need for transformations is so significant in syntax is that it is a good initial working hypothesis that they are not needed. Roughly, this hypothesis amounts to the claim that one can analyze sentences adequately through a straightforward consideration of their perceptual form. On this view, the problem in describing a sentence is to find the right ways of segmenting its perceptual form, and the right hierarchical structure to impose on the various segmentations that are to be made. This hypothesis is incorporated in the formal restrictions on rules of grammar which characterize a phrase-structure grammar.[12] The reason transformations are so significant in syntax is that if they are required then the initially plausible working hypothesis is wrong. Much of the force of this claim, then, is that there are rules of grammar which violate the formal restrictions on phrase-structure rules.

In contrast, when we talk about the features that distinguish illocutions from each other, we find no obvious place for the notion of segmentation. Thus, there is not even a *prima facie* reason to believe that the theory will not contain rules which violate phrase-structure restrictions. A check of the sample rules will reveal a number that do so, but that is hardly a significant result.

On the other hand, there is a natural interpretation of the notion of a transformation on which deciding whether a theory of illocutions is transformational becomes quite interesting. It may be that certain illocutions cannot be regarded other than as combinations, or perhaps deformations of other illocutions. For

---

[12] Chomsky, "On the Notion Rule of Grammar," in J. Fodor and J. Katz, eds., *The Structure of Language* (Englewood Cliffs, N.J.: Prentice-Hall, Inc., 1964) pp. 119–36.

example, that might be the case with illocutions containing genuine truth-functional connectives.[13] The theory might then be separated into two parts, a base component, which failed to generate descriptions of some illocutions, and a set of rules which we might regard as transformations, which operate on the descriptions generated by the base component to form descriptions of the illocutions not described by it.

It would be especially significant if illocutions using certain sentences had to be derived from illocutions using others. Perhaps this would provide extra-syntactic motivation for a particular choice of syntactic transformations. Such relations between syntax and illocutions, if they exist, should be of interest to anyone interested in the study of language. But, to discover them, we must first know much more about a generative theory of illocutions.

Illustrative Fragment of Base Component

1. $I \rightarrow B, V, C, Extv, Exp$
2. $Exp \rightarrow Dec, Int$
3. $Dec \rightarrow Statement, \ldots$
4. $Statement \rightarrow S + \text{READ} + \text{INTERP} +$

opportune–inopportune	a_0
merited–unmerited	a_1
true–false	a_2
fair–unfair	a_3
accurate–inaccurate	a_4
right–wrong	a_5
precise–imprecise	a_6
fitting–unfitting	a_7
correct–incorrect	a_8
sound–unsound	a_9
good–bad	a_{10}
exaggerated–unexaggerated	a_{11}

where $a_i = +, -$

5. $S \rightarrow NP + VP$
6. $NP \rightarrow NP + S, det. + N$
7. $VP \rightarrow V + NP, V + Prep. P, V + NP + Prep. P$
8. $Prep. P \rightarrow Prep. + NP$
9. $det. \rightarrow the, \ldots$
10. $N \rightarrow Girl, Man, Lake, Park, \ldots$
11. $V \rightarrow Walk, Push, \ldots$
12. $Prep. \rightarrow through, in, \ldots$

---

[13] On this point, see Peter Geach, "Assertion," *The Philosophical Review* (1962), pp. 449–65. [See selection 3.3 above, pp. 250–61.]

13. READ → Literal, Ironic, Hyperbolic.

14. Literal → $P_o +$ ... P_n, where P_i is a path starting with S, and for all paths P starting with S, there is a $P_j = P$

15. $P_i → R_1$, Ironic, ..., where R_1 is a reading assigned by the semantic theory to the terminal symbol of P_i and P_i is dominated by READ

16. Ironic → R_1, where Ironic is dominated by P_i and R_1 is as in rule 15

17. INTERP → *REF* + *UD*

18. *REF* → $P_j +$ ... $+ P_k$ where for all $j \leq i \leq k$

    (a) P_i is a path starting with S
    (b) P_i is a path ending with S or NP
    (c) P_i contains no noninitial and nonterminal occurrence of S
    (d) if P_i terminates in NP, then there is an m such that $P_i = P_m$, P_m is dominated by READ and P_m dominates a reading beginning with the symbol (some contextually definite)

19. $P_1 → P_m +$ ... P_n (m > 1) where

    (a) P_1 is a path terminating in S
    (b) P_1 is of length greater than 1
    (c) P_1 is dominated by *REF*
    (d) for all $m \leq i \leq n$, P_i is a path beginning at the terminus of P_1 and meeting conditions 18 b, c, d.

20. $P_1 → \Sigma_1$ where

    (a) P_1 is a path dominated by *REF*
    (b) P_1 either consists of S alone or terminates in NP
    (c) Σ_1 is a set of ordered pairs, such that the first element of each pair is an expression, with NP as the dominant syntactic marker, and containing the semantic marker (some contextually definite), and the second element is a reading assigned to the expression by the semantic theory.
    (d) if R_1 is the reading attached to P_1, or the path ending in P_1 under READ, then $\Sigma_1 \cup \{R_1\}$ contains no contradiction.
    (e) $\Sigma_1 \neq \phi$ unless P_1 is a path consisting of S alone.

21. *UD* → $P_r +$ ... $+ P_s$ where for all $r \leq i \leq s$, P_i is a path beginning with S and containing VP

22. $P_i → R_i$ where

    (a) P_i is a path dominated by *UD*
    (b) Either R_i is null or R_i may be added to the reading assigned to P_i nonanomalously by (one of a number of specified means, including)
        (i) $[R_i R \text{ (and) } R(P_i)]$
        (ii) $[R_i R \text{ (of) } R(P_i)]$

SAMPLE DERIVATION

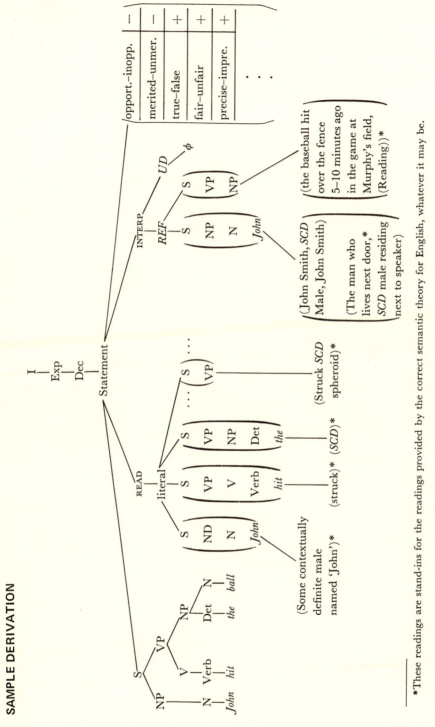

*These readings are stand-ins for the readings provided by the correct semantic theory for English, whatever it may be.

645